GOVERNING

GOVERNING

Readings and Cases in American Politics

Second Edition

Roger H. Davidson
University of Maryland

Walter J. Oleszek
Congressional Research Service

A Division of Congressional Quarterly Inc.
Washington, D.C.

Library of Congress Cataloging-in-Publication Data

Governing: readings and cases in American politics / [edited by]
    Roger H. Davidson, Walter J. Oleszek. — 2nd ed.
        p.   cm.
    Includes bibliographical references.
    ISBN 0-87187-615-9
    1. United States—Politics and Government. 2. United States—
Constitutional law—Cases. I. Davidson, Roger H. II. Oleszek,
Walter J.
JK21.G68 1991   91-30735
320.473—dc20   CIP

For Nancy
—RHD

For Janet
—WJO

Contents

PART IV: PUBLIC POLICY

12. Civil Rights and Individual Liberties   439

13. Domestic Policy   485

Preface

The second edition of this book, like its predecessor, is designed to provide the student of American government and politics with a wide range of accessible supplementary readings that illuminate contemporary and historical issues. In our selections we have sought to strike an agreeable balance between two traditional approaches taken by such collections. On the one hand are "classic" readings from estimable sources that define the field for specialists but often fail to address today's students in terms they find meaningful. On the other hand are articles gleaned from newspapers and magazines, collections of which illuminate current issues but often fail to place them in a theoretical context. We have endeavored to include the best items from both approaches.

Retained from the first volume are those items we deem indispensable to introductory courses: essays from *The Federalist Papers*, decisions from landmark Supreme Court cases, and certain enduring statements by historical figures and scholars. Selections new to this edition illuminate current political problems or address pressing issues such as low voter turnout and affirmative action.

Many of the recent selections offer practical "insiders'" observations, often from opposing points of view. Contemporary scholars represented here not only have added to the storehouse of knowledge but also have taken part in public debates on the institutions or policies they have written about. In addition, we culled the record for important statements made by figures in public life. The speeches and exchanges made by influential senators and representatives buttress our conviction that one can learn a great deal by listening systematically to what politicians say and how they say it. Finally, the selections by journalists in this volume typify the best work by leading members of the press corps; these writers go beyond careful reporting of events to illuminate and interpret trends.

In short, we took important and informative materials wherever we found them. Above all, we selected works that reveal the thinking of practitioners in government and politics and that highlight the forces and processes changing the nation's public life as it enters upon its third century. We chose readings that are contemporary but not transitory, colorful but not frivolous, and intellectually rigorous but not tedious.

The volume is divided into four parts, paralleling the structure of most introductory American government textbooks. In the essays introducing each chapter, we review the background of the chapter topic to place in context the readings that follow.

Part I covers the framework of the U.S. government, including separation of powers, checks and balances, and federalism. For insights into the founders' intentions in the Constitution, there are selections by the authors of *The Federalist Papers* as well as commentaries of modern scholars and practitioners. Readings on the theory and reality of federalism show how it has remained a central pattern in the constitutional design.

The components of the political process are treated in Part II. The first component explores the basic attributes and attitudes of the general public, which provide a backdrop for the activities of those engaged in making public policy. Important political institutions include the political parties, which have been subjected to tremendous changes and are adapting to modern technological requirements. Interest groups— such as traditional economic interests and newer forms of "citizens'" action groups—are considered as alternative channels of representation. The communications media are an equally important influence in the political process. Essays on the media examine their legal status, role in political campaigns, and place in governance. Campaigns and elections, as central animating processes of government, receive attention from many angles: legal, historical, practical, and financial.

The institutions of government—the Congress, the presidency, the bureaucracy, and the federal courts—are the subject of Part III. We contrast the intentions of the founders toward each institution with its historical evolution. The readings on Congress call attention to its dual nature: the individual legislators and the collective body for policy making. The constitutional presidency is contrasted with the modern, public presidency—with its potential for mass leadership and its dangers when the officeholder inevitably fails to meet the public's expectations of the office. The founders scarcely mentioned the bureaucracy, which today comprises 3 million civilian employees; readings on this vast government institution illuminate the political environment in which it operates. The perennial debate over the applicability of the founders' Constitution is confronted directly by the judiciary, which considers what the writers of the Constitution meant and how, or whether, their formulations can be interpreted today.

Public policy is the focus of Part IV. We give special attention to civil rights and individual liberties, for they highlight the challenges of applying broad constitutional language to contemporary realities. Selections on domestic and foreign policies reveal the distinctions between the two but also show how often they overlap. Finally, we consider current trends and reform proposals and try to convey some of the debate and ferment that characterize the study of American government on the eve of the twenty-first century.

For helping us bring this book to fruition we thank our colleagues at Congressional Quarterly. It was they who first encouraged us to consider this project, who published the first edition, and who guided us in working on this second edition. Their editors and production specialists are the best in the business. We are grateful to Kerry Kern and Jenny Philipson for the care they gave this project, and to Cyndi Smith for her technical expertise. We thank also those who commented on the first edition and encouraged us to continue with a revised edition based on our original concept. Their support is appreciated, and their comments have been taken to heart. We want also to thank our families—especially Nancy Davidson and Janet Oleszek, our wives—for their patience, good humor, and assistance during the course of this project.

PART I

THE AMERICAN SYSTEM

We the People of the United States, in Order to form a more perfect Union, establish Justice, insure domestic Tranquility, provide for the common defence, promote the general Welfare, and secure the Blessings of Liberty to ourselves and our Posterity, do ordain and establish this Constitution for the United States of America.

—Preamble, U.S. Constitution

Chapter 1

The Constitutional Framework

The American Constitution is a remarkable document. Written four years after the end of the American Revolution, it has survived for more than 200 years despite momentous domestic and international challenges and changes. Our national Constitution has even influenced and inspired constitution makers in scores of other nations. A Brazilian legal scholar observed: "The U.S. has had a tremendous influence because we have the same system of government."[1] To be sure, in the wake of the dramatic changes in Eastern Europe, constitution writers in many of those nations are contemplating the questions posed in Selection 1, "A Checklist for New Constitution Writers."

Legal realists assert that the Constitution is no more nor less than what the Supreme Court says it is. But surely it means more than the interpretations of federal judges. In large measure, the document reflects enduring principles of representative government and perspectives on political power. One commentator noted:

> [The Constitution] remains a curious document, noted for what it says and doesn't say, remarkable for its juxtaposition of powers, balancing the best and worst instincts and tendencies of the individual human beings who make up the government. Its fundamental wisdom is its understanding of human psychology and the use of and yearning for power.[2]

Although most nations have some sort of constitution, not all have written documents. The constitutions of some nations, including democratic ones such as Britain and Israel, are found in a multiplicity of written and unwritten sources. Britain's constitutional principles, for example, are contained in the Magna Carta, parliamentary statutes, judicial decisions, and informal conventions. At the same time, many authoritarian regimes boast written constitutions that articulate admirable political values. These "showcase" constitutions, however, mask the stark realities of unaccountable power and arbitrary treatment of citizens.

What Is a Constitution?

At least three responses can be offered to this question. First, constitutions are documents that outline the framework and functions of the central government. In the U.S. Constitution, for instance, the founders established three independent branches of national government, none wielding a monopoly of power. Interestingly, the Constitution does not explicitly refer to a "separation of powers." Rather, its functional equivalent is found in provisions that "all legislative Powers herein granted shall be vested in a Congress of the United States," that "the executive Power shall be vested in a President of the United States of America," and that "the judicial Power of the United States, shall be vested in one supreme Court, and in such inferior Courts as the Congress may from time to time ordain and establish."

Second, constitutions reflect the basic values, ideas, experiences, and political roots of the body politic. These in turn produce the fundamental principles for guiding political life and participation. The framers drew heavily on English law, the intellectual environment of the times, and their practical experiences with colonial governments, state constitutions, and the Articles of Confederation. Respect for personal and property rights, for example, was simply part of the civic consciousness of the time and inheres within the Constitution itself.[3] Lacking such values and experiences—which can be centuries in the making—many contemporary nations (even those with democratic constitutions) have found it exceedingly hard to establish stable governmental institutions.

Finally, constitutions are created to limit the authority of the central government so that "rulers may not arbitrarily do whatever they please, whenever and however they please."[4] With their deep and realistic understanding of human nature, the framers recognized that unbridled ambition and self-interest could undermine the constitutional system. Hence, the Constitution is filled with institutional arrangements and "auxiliary precautions," as James Madison called them, to foster the preservation of citizens' rights and diminish opportunities for tyranny. One scholar wrote: "The cause of liberty is served by the great difficulty that three separated branches would find in any effort to unite to oppress the populace. Here again, self-interest and jealous guarding of the powers of one's own office play the vital role."[5]

The Philadelphia Convention and Ratification

In the hot and humid summer of 1787, the fifty-five men assembled in Philadelphia's State House struggled with a novel responsibility: to write a new constitution. The nation was already functioning under the

Articles of Confederation, the country's first constitution. But this confederation of sovereign states was simply too weak to govern effectively. Under the Articles, for instance, the Congress lacked the authority to levy taxes or regulate interstate commerce.

Because of the weaknesses of the Articles, the Philadelphia convention was called to propose a stronger central government. Many of the delegates were under instructions from their states only to revise the Articles; instead, these men (George Washington, Alexander Hamilton, Benjamin Franklin, and James Madison among them) produced a new governing document for the nation and even declared that its authority derived from the people rather than the sovereign states.

On the convention's final day, September 17, 1787, thirty-nine delegates from twelve states signed their product. The Constitution was then submitted to the Congress with the proviso that the ratifying conventions of nine states would have to approve it before the new government would be established. Soon the country was caught up in the struggle over ratification. Those who favored the new Constitution, called Federalists, argued the merits of a strong national government. Their antagonists, dubbed the Anti-Federalists, voiced concern that an overbearing national government could jeopardize state and individual rights.

Within four months the necessary two-thirds ratified the Constitution, thereby creating the new Union. (In the end, all thirteen states ratified the document.) Part of the reason for the prompt approval might have been the writings of Alexander Hamilton, John Jay, and James Madison. Their series of eighty-five analytical newspaper essays, collectively called *The Federalist Papers,* ran in New York from October 1787 to April 1788. One objective of the articles was to sway public opinion toward ratification in that pivotal state.

The Federalist Papers were much more than campaign propaganda. Drafted by three experienced political leaders, the essays highlighted many of the considerations that had shaped the Constitution and addressed classical issues such as the nature of political power. Perhaps the most famous essay, *Federalist* No. 10 by Madison (Selection 2), explains how to control the "mischiefs of faction" so that private interests do not overwhelm public well-being.

Adaptation and Change

More than written words define a nation's fundamental law. "Living" constitutions evolve in response to changing conditions, new interpretations of the document's meaning and intent, and day-to-day developments in governing practice. The U.S. Constitution makes no reference, for example, to political parties, congressional committees, or the president's cabinet. Yet each is an important development that has contributed to the makeup of the American polity. The brevity and generality of the U.S. Constitution facilitated the adaptation of its phrases to changing times and events.

That the framers did not draft a perfect document was soon evident to all. When the Constitution was submitted to the states for ratification, opponents decried the absence of a bill of rights. James Wilson, one of the document's framers, explained that his colleagues found a bill of rights "not only unnecessary, but it was found impracticable—for who will be bold enough to enumerate all the rights of the people?—and when the attempt is made it must be remembered if the enumeration is not complete, everything not expressly mentioned will be presumed to be purposely omitted." Nonetheless, supporters of ratification quickly countered this criticism by pledging to support adoption of a bill of rights once the new government was launched. That pledge was fulfilled by the First Congress. The first ten amendments—the Bill of Rights—were quickly ratified by the states in 1791. Two hundred years later, with the nation celebrating the Bicentennial of the Bill of Rights, scholar Mark Petracca discusses "What Every Student Should Know About the Bill of Rights" in Selection 3.

The absence of a Bill of Rights was only one of the imperfections in the original Constitution. A glaring defect was its tolerance for the institution of slavery, which Supreme Court Justice Thurgood Marshall addresses in Selection 4.[7] Suffice it to say that the nation fought a bloody Civil War over this issue, and the Constitution was amended (the Thirteenth, Fourteenth, and Fifteenth Amendments) to outlaw slavery and further define citizen's rights.

Despite thousands of suggested changes, the Constitution has been amended only twenty-six times. Not only is it difficult to revise, but the flexibility of the Constitution also militates against revamping the document itself. As governing becomes more arduous and complex, however, it is not surprising that critics urge changes in the basic law. In Selection 5, "The Constitution: Thirteen Crucial Questions," James MacGregor Burns and Richard B. Morris identify thirteen issues frequently raised by those who would amend the Constitution.

Whether governance of the nation can be improved by overhauling, modifying, or junking the Constitution is an open and controversial question. On the one hand, the Constitution has withstood the test of time and continues to work, however clumsily. On the other hand, inquiry and debate about ways to improve constitutional performance are certainly appropriate—given that the founders themselves did not shrink from setting aside the Articles of Confederation for a new design. However one views the framers' intricate system of checks and balances and separation of powers, it is ultimately up to "We the People" (the opening words of the Constitution) to reflect upon the document's virtues and flaws and its capacity to meet the requirements of the fast-approaching twenty-first century.

Notes

1. *Washington Times,* December 27, 1985, 3A.
2. *Christian Science Monitor,* November 27, 1985, 33.
3. In 1913, Charles A. Beard wrote *An Economic Interpretation of the Constitution.* His study initiated a raging scholarly debate about the framers' intentions in drafting the Constitution. Beard asserted that the framers wrote the Constitution primarily to advance and protect their own economic interests. Beard's analysis came under sharp attack, and to this day his thesis stimulates efforts to understand further the nature of the Constitution. See, for example, Robert E. Brown, *Charles Beard and the Constitution* (Princeton, N.J.: Princeton University Press, 1956).
4. Martin Diamond, *The Founding of the Democratic Republic* (Itasca, Ill.: F. E. Peacock, 1981), 98.
5. Ann Stuart Diamond, "Decent, Even Though Democratic," in *How Democratic Is the Constitution?* ed. Robert A. Goldwin and William A. Schambra (Washington, D.C.: American Enterprise Institute, 1980), 32.
6. Alfred H. Kelly and Wilfred A. Harbison, *The American Constitution* (New York: Norton, 1963), 152.
7. For a comparable assessment, see the remarks of Professor John Hope Franklin, "Who Divided This House?" in the *Congressional Record,* July 30, 1990, E2539-E2540. Representative Sidney Yates (D-Ill.) included Franklin's remarks in the *Record.*

1. A Checklist for New Constitution Writers

Robert A. Goldwin

Today scores of nations around the world are engaged in drafting new constitutions. In an article for *The American Enterprise* written in 1990, Robert Goldwin, a resident scholar at the American Enterprise Institute in Washington, D.C., discusses this special political activity and offers guidance. He points out that every nation has a distinct character and history which must be taken into consideration when writing a new constitution. In Eastern Europe, for example, where many nations are now engaged in this effort, the generational conflicts and diversity of the populations make the task a particularly challenging one. Although Goldwin emphasizes that there is no universal formula for a successful constitution, he identifies a number of questions that constitution writers would be well advised to ask themselves as they undertake their work.

Americans are accustomed to thinking of constitution writing as something done hundreds of years ago by bewigged gentlemen wearing frock coats, knee breeches, and white stockings, but for the rest of the world, constitution writing is very much an activity of the present day. The Constitution of the United States is now more than 200 years old, but a majority of the other constitutions in the world are less than 15 years old. That is, of the 160 or so written national constitutions, more than 80 have been adopted since 1975. This means that in the last few decades, on average, more than five new national constitutions have come into effect every year.

Some of these new constitutions are, of course, for new nations, but the surprising fact is that most were written for very old nations, such as Spain, Portugal, Turkey, and Greece. And now, in the old nations of Eastern Europe and possibly also in the Soviet Union or newly independent parts of it, new constitutions are about to be written to replace outdated, one-party constitutions.

Those who are responsible for writing these new constitutions know they need assistance. As Professor Albert Blaustein of Rutgers University Law School recently reported, many Eastern European legal experts "haven't seen a constitutional law book for 45 years." They need not proceed without advice, though, because there are so many still-active, experienced constitution writers in scores of nations around the world that have recently adopted new constitutions. There are also experts in international constitutional law in the United States and in many other nations who would be only too glad to offer their services.

Nonetheless, except perhaps for narrow technical matters, outsiders, however expert, are limited in the help they can provide. A successful constitution must be deeply rooted in the history and traditions of the nation and its people, and its writers need a clear sense of what is central to the way the nation is constituted. For millennia, Eastern European nations have been battlegrounds for innumerable invasions, conquests, and consequent migrations. As a result, there is a great mixing of peoples who cannot be sorted out even by computer-guided drawing of borders. These peoples, who have no choice but to live side by side, are not necessarily able to love their neighbors. It seems as though everyone's grandfather was murdered by someone else's grandfather. As a result, most of these nations have diverse populations characterized by passionate hostilities. The constitutional task to make "one people"—to strengthen a sense of national unity by constitutional provisions—is a much greater concern for these nations.

Destructive Diversity

That all human beings are fundamentally equal is a central tenet of modern constitutionalism that is essential to all systems of political liberty. To assert that we are all equal means, necessarily, that we are all equally human, sharing one and the same human nature. This view is widely held and advanced, sometimes as fact, sometimes as aspiration, and denied or disputed for the most part by those who are thought to be benighted, or bigoted, or both. The universality of human nature, the oneness of humankind, is a vital element of modern democratic thought.

And yet, wherever we look in the world, we see mankind divided into tightly bound groups, set apart by racial, religious, language, or national differences. The bonds of loyalty these differences engender often override all other considerations, including even the obligations of national citizenship. Whether or not we are "all brothers and sisters under the skin," two indisputable, and indisputably linked, facts are evident everywhere: first, there is a natural, powerful fraternal bond among persons who share the same religion, or race, or language, or nationality; second, the same inclusive bond commonly has the effect of excluding those who are different, engendering hostility toward "outsiders."

In almost all countries with diverse populations—and almost all countries around the world do have significant diversity—we see, not the "domestic tranquility" spoken of in the preamble to the Constitution of the United States, but domestic hostility between fellow citizens of the same nation-states: Protestants and Catholics in Northern Ireland, Muslims and Christians in Israel, blacks and whites in the United States, Flemish and French speakers in Belgium, Armenians and Azerbaijanis in the Soviet Union, Serbs and Albanians in Yugoslavia, Greeks and Turks in Cyprus, Hausas and Ibos in Nigeria—and this list does not come close to being exhaustive. Given historic animosities in many countries of Eastern Europe, diversity presents a problem for their constitution makers.

Citizens who are members of groups significantly different from others of the population can reasonably have grave concerns: fear for their safety, concern that they will not be allowed to participate in the political, social, and economic life of the nation, and fear that they will be restricted in the practices that are characteristic of their special way of life. To address these fears, many constitutions have special provisions, usually addressed directly to groups by name, assuring them of participation in the national life and guaranteeing freedom of religion or use of language, or promising preferences in education or employment on the basis of nationality or race. The dilemma such provisions pose, however, is that they raise the differences within the population to a constitutional status and tend thereby to identify, emphasize, and perpetuate the divisions within society. Our own constitution is silent in this regard, aiming for unity by assimilation.

No Universal Formula

Years of study of constitutions confirm what common sense would suggest: that there is no universal formula for a successful constitution. A sound constitution for any nation has to be something of a reflection, although more than that, of the essence of a particular nation, and this is inescapably influenced by the character of each nation's people, or peoples, and their history.

Constitution writers may wish to make a break with their past, to make a completely fresh start, but they never have the luxury of a clean slate. They start with a population having certain characteristics (for example, homogeneous or diverse), an economy tied to its geographic characteristics (a maritime nation or landlocked), neighboring nations (peaceful or warlike) that cannot be moved or ignored, and a history that has shaped their understanding of themselves and their national aspirations. The constitution must reflect all of these elements of the nation, and the more it is in accord with these national characteristics, the better the constitution will be.

One day in Athens some years ago, while talking to a Greek judge who is also a constitutional scholar, I referred to the newness of the Greek constitution. He asked me what date I put on it, and I, somewhat surprised, said, "1975, of course." "Yes, I understand," he said, "but you could also say 1863." "But," I replied, "Greece has had nearly a dozen constitutions since then." "Yes," he said, "that's right, but they are always the same." He was exaggerating, of course, but not much. When Greece adopted its latest constitution, two issues were foremost, the roles of the armed forces and of the monarchy. However much Greek constitutions and regimes changed through the decades, these questions remained constant. There was not much leeway, not much discretion on many of the most important points. The same will be true for the nations of Eastern Europe.

Although there can be no universal formula for successful constitution writing—no canned answers that can be applied to any country in search of a new constitutional order—there are standard, universal questions that must be asked. A comprehensive list will include some questions that at first glance seem archaic or unnecessary to consider. Turkey or Portugal, for instance, did not have to dwell on the question of the role of the monarchy as Greece and Spain did, but considering how many modern nations are constitutional monarchies, it is not impossible that one or another Eastern European nation might consider some form of constitutional monarchy before the turmoil is over.

Therefore in the conviction that it is possible to develop a substantial, if not complete, list of the questions constitution writers must ask themselves in writing the constitution of any country, I offer the following enumeration for guidance.

Questions for Constitution Writers

The Preliminaries

■ How will delegates to the constitutional committee or constituent assembly be chosen? Will the new constitution be drafted by the legislative body or by a body chosen specifically for the purpose? If there is controversy about the method of selection, how and by whom will it be resolved?

■ What will be the rules and procedures of the constitution-making body, once chosen, and how and by whom will controversies on this question be resolved?

Powers and Power Relationships

■ What are the different branches of government, and what is their constitutional relationship? Are the executive and legislative branches separated or combined?

■ Is there a single chief executive, an executive cabinet, or some form of executive council? What are the executive powers, and how are they limited? Does the executive have some share in the legislative process: for instance, do laws require his signature; does he have veto power, the right to propose legislation? Does the executive have treaty-making powers, the power to declare war, command of the armed forces, law-enforcement powers, some degree of responsibility to appoint judges, power of executive pardon or clemency? Are police powers national, or is there some form of local authority? How are the executive departments established, and how and by whom are the department heads appointed and fired? How are executive salaries determined? How is the chief executive chosen, and what is the term of office?

■ Is the head of state separate from the head of government, and if so, what is the role of the head of state? How is the head of state chosen? What is the term of office? If a monarch, what is the role of the crown? Does the head of state act to dissolve the legislature, call for new elections, name a new prime minister?

■ Is the legislature unicameral or bicameral? What is the principle of representation, or is there more than one principle (for example, some legislators chosen on the basis of population, some by states or provinces)? What is the length of term for members? Under what conditions and by whom are new elections called? How are salaries of members determined and varied? Does the legislature have the power of the purse, taxing power, oversight powers, a role in executive and judicial appointments, budget-making powers, power over the monetary system, power to regulate domestic trade, foreign trade, a role in war making and treaty making, power to investigate and compel testimony, power to impeach executive and judicial officers? Do legislators have immunity from arrest? What are the conditions for dissolution of the legislature?

■ What is the system of justice and law enforcement? What is the structure of the judicial system, and how and by whom is it established? In what ways, if any, are judges subject to legislative and executive controls? How independent are judges from executive and legislative control? How are judges appointed or elected and for what terms? Are judicial salaries protected? Do the courts of law have powers of judicial review of the constitutionality of legislative and executive actions, or is there a separate constitutional court?

■ To whom are the powers assigned for the conduct of foreign policy? To what extent are they shared, and on the basis of what principle?

Where is the power assigned to declare war and to make and ratify treaties?

■ Are there powers to suspend the constitution in emergencies? If so, by whom and under what conditions? Are there protections against abuse of emergency powers?

■ Are all public officials required to take an oath of office to uphold this constitution?

■ To what extent are the executive, legislative, and judicial powers separated, and by what provisions are the separations maintained?

■ Is the national government unitary or federal, and if the latter, what form of federalism? Whether unitary or federal, is it centralized or decentralized, or some combination?

■ What are the limits of the powers of the government and of the various branches and offices, and by what means are the limits sustained?

Elections and Political Parties

■ By what methods are the various offices filled: direct popular election by universal suffrage or some indirect method; winner-take-all or some form of proportional representation? Which offices, if any, are not elective, and what is the method of appointment? Are there different methods of election or selection for different offices?

■ What is the constitutional status of political parties, or is that left undetermined?

Nonpolitical Institutions

■ What is the structure of the education system, and how is it supervised? Is the school system centralized, regional, local, or some combination? Are there provisions for ethnic, religious, or language schools? Are private schools allowed, and if so, what controls are imposed on them? Is the freedom of inquiry in university teaching and research protected?

■ What are the provisions for the media? Are there government-owned, political party-owned, or privately owned newspapers, television channels, and radio stations? Are the media regulated or licensed? What protections are there for freedom of the press, and how are abuses prevented?

■ What is the constitutional status of the military? Who is the commander in chief of the armed forces? How much and what form of civilian control is there?

■ What is the role of religion? Is there an established church, and one or more official religions? Are there church subsidies from public funds, and if so, are they on a basis of equality or are they preferential? Is there separation of church and state? Is freedom of religion protected and by what means?

Rights

■ Is there a bill of rights? What protections are there for the rights of individuals: speech, press, religion, peaceable assembly, habeas corpus,* public trial, and so on? Is there equality of all persons, or are there constitutional preferences based on race, religion, sex, nationality, or different levels of citizenship? Are the rights primarily political and legal, or are social and economic rights included? Are the rights provisions stated negatively or affirmatively? Is there a list of duties of citizens listed, and if so, are the duties linked to rights? Are there protections of rights of aliens? What are the provisions for immigration and emigration? What is the status under the constitution of international declarations of rights? Are only the rights of individuals acknowledged, or are there also protections for the rights of religious, ethnic, racial, or regional groups?

■ Are there different levels or kinds of citizenship; that is, are there qualifications or restrictions of voting rights, property rights, representation, access to education, or eligibility for public office based on race, sex, religion, language, or national origin? Do naturalized citizens have the same rights, privileges, and immunities as natural-born citizens? What are the naturalization provisions?

■ Does the constitution specify any national or official languages? Are there provisions for schools, courts, government offices, churches, and other institutions to conduct their activities in languages other than the national or official ones?

The Economic System

■ Does the constitution specify what kind of economic system shall prevail (for instance, that this nation is a socialist democracy or that the means of production shall be owned privately)? Are there provisions for managing the economy, or is a market economy of private enterprise assumed? What is the status of private property? What is the status of banks, corporations, farms, other enterprises? What are the regulatory and licensing powers? Are there government monopolies and, if so, what kind? What are the copyright and patent

---

* Protecting a citizen against illegal imprisonment.

provisions? Is there protection against impairing the obligation of contracts?

■ What is the status of international law and international organizations in relation to national laws and institutions? What is the legal status of treaties and other international obligations?

Final Questions

■ What is the amendment process? Is it designed to make amending the constitution easy or difficult? Does the amending process include the people as a whole, or is it limited to the legislature and other officials?

■ What is the process for ratifying the constitution?

A Rare Activity

The frequency of constitution writing tells us two things. First, constitutions are very important, and great investments of time and effort are needed to write them; and second, it is very difficult, and rare, to write a constitution that lasts—which is why there have been so many of them.

A complete list—and this one surely has omissions—gives no assurance of finding the right answers in writing a constitution. But an enumeration such as this provides reassurance that major issues will not be overlooked. It also reminds us what an extraordinary accomplishment our own 200-year-old Constitution is.

Making a constitution is a special political activity. It is possible only at certain extraordinary moments in a nation's history, and its success or failure can have profound and lasting consequences for a nation and its people. That is the challenge facing the constitution makers and the peoples of Eastern Europe.

2. *Federalist* No. 10

James Madison

Often called the "Father of the Constitution" because of his major role in shaping that document, James Madison was one of three who wrote *The Federalist Papers* (Alexander Hamilton and John Jay were the others). All wrote under the pseudonym Publius, but it was Madison who produced No. 10, often cited as the central essay of their collected work. One of Madison's objectives in No. 10 was to refute the argument of the French eighteenth-century political philosopher Montesquieu and others that republican government could survive only in small and homogeneous countries where there would be scant conflict among competing interests. Big and diverse nations, by contrast, would inevitably be torn asunder by divergent interests. Madison rebutted that argument by reversing its thrust. Extended republics are much better able than small countries to contain the "mischiefs of faction," because their very size and heterogeneity will inhibit the formation of private-minded coalitions that could undermine the public good. This classic of American political theory still arouses sharp intellectual debate about "pluralist democracy" (the multiplicity of factions) and how republican government can elect "proper guardians of the public weal" given the frailties of human nature.

Among the numerous advantages promised by a well-constructed Union, none deserves to be more accurately developed than its tendency to break and control the violence of faction. The friend of popular governments never finds himself so much alarmed for their character and fate, as when he contemplates their propensity to this dangerous vice. He will not fail, therefore, to set a due value on any plan which, without violating the principles to which he is attached, provides a proper cure for it. The instability, injustice, and confusion introduced into the public councils, have, in truth, been the mortal diseases under which popular governments have everywhere perished; as they continue to be the favorite and fruitful topics from which the adversaries to liberty derive their most specious declamations. The valuable improvements made by the American constitutions on the popular models, both ancient and modern, cannot certainly be too much admired; but it would be an unwarrantable partiality, to contend that they have as effectually obviated the danger on this side, as was wished and expected. Complaints are everywhere heard from our most considerate and virtuous citizens, equally the friends of public and private faith, and of public and personal liberty, that our governments are too unstable, that the public good is disregarded in the conflicts of rival parties, and that measures are too often decided, not according to the rules of justice and the rights of the minor party, but by the superior force of an interested and overbearing majority. However anxiously we may wish that these complaints had no foundation, the evidence of known facts will not permit us to deny that they are in some degree true. It will be found, indeed, on a candid review of our situation, that some of the distresses under which we labor have been erroneously charged on the operation of our governments; but it will be found, at the same time, that other causes will not alone account for many of our heaviest misfortunes; and, particularly, for that prevailing and increasing distrust of public engagements, and alarm for private rights, which are echoed from one end of the continent to the other. These must be chiefly, if not wholly, effects of the unsteadiness and injustice with which a factious spirit has tainted our public administrations.

By a faction, I understand a number of citizens, whether amounting to a majority or minority of the whole, who are united and actuated by some common impulse of passion, or of interest, adverse to the rights of other citizens, or to the permanent and aggregate interests of the community.

There are two methods of curing the mischiefs of faction: the one, by removing its causes; the other, by controlling its effects.

There are again two methods of removing the causes of faction: the one, by destroying the liberty which is essential to its existence; the other, by giving to every citizen the same opinions, the same passions, and the same interests.

It could never be more truly said than of the first remedy, that it was worse than the disease. Liberty is to faction what air is to fire, an aliment without which it instantly expires. But it could not be less folly to abolish liberty, which is essential to political life, because it nourishes faction, than it would be to wish the annihilation of air, which is essential to animal life, because it imparts to fire its destructive agency.

The second expedient is as impracticable as the first would be unwise. As long as the reason of man continues fallible, and he is at liberty to exercise it, different opinions will be formed. As long as the connection subsists between his reason and his self-love, his opinions and his passions will have a reciprocal influence on each other; and the former will be objects to which the latter will attach themselves. The diversity in the faculties of men, from which the rights of property originate, is not less an insuperable obstacle to a uniformity of interests. The protection of these faculties is the first object of government. From the protection of different and unequal faculties of acquiring property, the possession of different degrees and kinds of property immediately results; and from the influence of these on the sentiments and views of the respective proprietors, ensues a division of the society into different interests and parties.

The latent causes of faction are thus sown in the nature of man; and we see them everywhere brought into different degrees of activity, according to the different circumstances of civil society. A zeal for different opinions concerning religion, concerning government, and many other points, as well of speculation as of practice; an attachment to different leaders ambitiously contending for pre-eminence and power; or to persons of other descriptions whose fortunes have been interesting to the human passions, have, in turn, divided mankind into parties, inflamed them with mutual animosity, and rendered them much more disposed to vex and oppress each other than to cooperate for their common good. So strong is this propensity of mankind to fall into mutual animosities, that where no substantial occasion presents itself, the most frivolous and fanciful distinctions have been sufficient to kindle their unfriendly passions and excite their most violent conflicts. But the most common and durable source of factions has been the various and unequal distribution of property. Those who hold and those who are without property have ever formed distinct interests in society. Those who are creditors, and those who are debtors, fall under a like discrimination. A landed interest, a manufacturing interest, a mercantile interest, a moneyed interest, and many lesser interests, grow up of necessity in civilized nations, and divide them into different classes, actuated by different sentiments and views. The regulation of these various and interfering interests forms the principal task of modern legislation, and involves the spirit of party and faction in the necessary and ordinary operations of the government.

No man is allowed to be a judge in his own cause, because his interest would certainly bias his judgment, and, not improbably, corrupt his integrity. With equal, nay with greater reason, a body of men are unfit to be both judges and parties at the same time; yet what are many of the most important acts of legislation, but so many judicial determinations, not indeed concerning the rights of single persons, but concerning the rights of large bodies of citizens? And what are the different classes of legislators but advocates and parties to the causes which they determine? Is a law proposed concerning private debts? It is a question to which the creditors are parties on one side and the debtors on the other. Justice ought to hold the balance between them. Yet the parties are, and must be themselves the judges; and the most numerous party, or, in other words, the most powerful faction must be expected to prevail. Shall domestic manufactures be encouraged, and in what degree, by restrictions on foreign manufactures? Are questions which would be differently decided by the landed and the manufacturing classes, and probably by neither with a sole regard to justice and the public good. The apportionment of taxes on the various descriptions of property is an act which seems to require the most exact impartiality; yet there is, perhaps, no legislative act in which greater opportunity and temptation are given to a predominant party to trample on the rules of justice. Every shilling with which they overburden the inferior number, is a shilling saved to their own pockets.

It is in vain to say that enlightened statesmen will be able to adjust these clashing interests, and render them all subservient to the public good. Enlightened statesmen will not always be at the helm. Nor, in many cases, can such an adjustment be made at all without taking into view indirect and remote considerations, which will rarely prevail over the immediate interest which one party may find in disregarding the rights of another or the good of the whole.

The inference to which we are brought is, that the *causes* of faction cannot be removed, and that relief is only to be sought in the means of controlling its *effects*.

If a faction consists of less than a majority, relief is supplied by the republican principle, which enables the majority to defeat its sinister views by regular vote. It may clog the administration, it may convulse the society; but it will be unable to execute and mask its violence under the forms of the Constitution. When a majority is included in a faction, the form of popular government, on the other hand, enables it to sacrifice to its ruling passion or interest both the public good and the rights of other citizens. To secure the public good and private rights against the danger of such a faction, and at the same time to preserve the spirit and the form of popular government, is then the great object to which our inquiries are directed. Let me add that it is the great desideratum by which this form of government can be rescued from the opprobrium under which it has so long labored, and be recommended to the esteem and adoption of mankind.

By what means is this object attainable? Evidently by one of two only. Either the existence of the same passion or interest in a majority at the same time must be prevented, or the majority, having such coexistent passion or interest, must be rendered, by their number and local situation, unable to concert and carry into effect schemes of oppression. If the impulse and the opportunity be suffered to coincide, we well know that neither moral nor religious motives can be relied on as an adequate control. They are not found to be such on the injustice and violence of individuals, and lose their efficacy in proportion to the number combined together, that is, in proportion as their efficacy becomes needful.

From this view of the subject it may be concluded that a pure democracy, by which I mean a society consisting of a small number of citizens, who assemble and administer the government in person, can admit of no cure for the mischiefs of faction. A common passion or interest will, in almost every case, be felt by a majority of the whole; a communication and concert result from the form of government itself; and there is nothing to check the inducements to sacrifice the weaker party or an obnoxious individual. Hence it is that such democracies have ever been spectacles of turbulence and contention; have ever been found incompatible with personal security or the rights of property; and have in general been as short in their lives as they have been violent in their deaths. Theoretic politicians, who have patronized this species of government, have erroneously supposed that by reducing mankind to a perfect equality in their political rights, they would, at the same time, be perfectly equalized and assimilated in their possessions, their opinions, and their passions.

A republic, by which I mean a government in which the scheme of representation takes place, opens a different prospect, and promises the cure for which we are seeking. Let us examine the points in which it varies from pure democracy, and we shall comprehend both the nature of the cure and the efficacy which it must derive from the Union.

The two great points of difference between a democracy and a republic are: first, the delegation of the government, in the latter, to a small number of citizens elected by the rest; secondly, the greater number of citizens, and greater sphere of country, over which the latter may be extended.

The effect of the first difference is, on the one hand, to refine and enlarge the public views, by passing them through the medium of a chosen body of citizens, whose wisdom may best discern the true interest of their country, and whose patriotism and love of justice will be least likely to sacrifice it to temporary or partial considerations. Under such a regulation, it may well happen that the public voice, pronounced by the representatives of the people, will be more consonant to the public good than if pronounced by the people themselves, convened for the purpose. On the other hand, the effect may be inverted. Men of fractious tempers, of local prejudices, or of sinister designs, may, by intrigue, by corruption, or by other means, first obtain the suffrages, and then betray the interests, of the people. The question resulting is, whether small or extensive republics are more favorable to the election of proper guardians of the public weal; and it is clearly decided in favor of the latter by two obvious considerations:

In the first place, it is to be remarked that, however small the republic may be, the representatives must be raised to a certain number, in order to guard against the cabals of a few; and that, however large it may be, they must be limited to a certain number, in order to guard against the confusion of a multitude. Hence, the number of representatives in the two cases not being in proportion to that of the two constituents, and being proportionally greater in the small republic, it follows that, if the proportion of fit characters be not less in the large than in the small republic, the former will present a greater option, and consequently a greater probability of a fit choice.

In the next place, as each representative will be chosen by a greater number of citizens in the large than in the small republic, it will be more difficult for unworthy candidates to practise with success the vicious arts by which elections are too often carried; and the suffrages of the people being more free, will be more likely to centre in men who possess the most attractive merit and the most diffusive and established characters.

It must be confessed that in this, as in most other cases, there is a mean, on both sides of which inconveniences will be found to lie. By enlarging too much the number of electors, you render the representatives too little acquainted with all their local circumstances and lesser interests; as by reducing it too much, you render him unduly attached to these, and too little fit to comprehend and pursue great and national objects. This federal Constitution forms a happy combination in this respect; the great and aggregate interests being referred to the national, the local and particular to the State legislatures.

The other point of difference is, the greater number of citizens and extent of territory which may be brought within the compass of republican than of democratic government; and it is this circumstance principally which renders factious combinations less to be dreaded in the former than in the latter. The smaller the society, the fewer probably will be the distinct parties and interests composing it; the fewer the distinct parties and interests, the more frequently will a majority be found of the same party; and the smaller the number of individuals composing a majority, and the smaller the compass within which they are placed, the more easily will they concert and execute their plans of oppression. Extend the sphere, and you take in a greater variety of parties and interests; you make it less probable that a majority of the whole will have a common motive to invade the rights of other citizens; or if such a common motive exists, it will be more difficult for all who feel it to discover their own strength, and to act in unison with each other. Besides other impediments, it may be remarked that, where there is a consciousness of unjust or dishonorable purposes, communication is always checked by distrust in proportion to the number whose concurrence is necessary.

Hence, it clearly appears, that the same advantage which a republic has over a democracy, in controlling the effects of faction, is enjoyed by a large over a small republic,—is enjoyed by the Union over the States composing it. Does the advantage consist in the substitution of representatives whose enlightened views and virtuous sentiments render them superior to local prejudices and to schemes of injustice? It will not be denied that the representation of the Union will be most likely to possess these requisite endowments. Does it consist in the greater security afforded by a greater variety of parties, against the event of any one party being able to outnumber and oppress the rest? In an equal degree does the increased variety of parties comprised within the Union, increase this security. Does it, in fine, consist in the greater obstacles opposed to the concert and accomplishment of the secret wishes of an unjust and interested majority? Here, again, the extent of the Union gives it the most palpable advantage.

The influence of factious leaders may kindle a flame within their particular States, but will be unable to spread a general conflagration through the other States. A religious sect may degenerate into a political faction in a part of the Confederacy; but the variety of sects dispersed over the entire face of it must secure the national councils against any danger from that source. A rage for paper money, for an abolition of debts, for an equal division of property, or for any other improper or wicked project, will be less apt to pervade the whole body of the Union than a particular member of it; in the same proportion as such a malady is more likely to taint a particular country or district, than an entire State.

In the extent and proper structure of the Union, therefore, we behold a republican remedy for the disease most incident to republican government. And according to the degree of pleasure and pride we feel in being republicans, ought to be our zeal in cherishing the spirit and supporting the character of Federalists.

3. What Every Student Should Know About the Bill of Rights

Mark P. Petracca

The Bicentennial of the Bill of Rights in 1991 prompted this article in *The Political Science Teacher* by Mark P. Petracca of the University of California, Irvine. He provides a history of the formulation of this important document, discussing the political pressures and compromises that played a part in its ratification. In noting that the Bill of Rights affects numerous aspects of daily life in the United States, Petracca goes on to emphasize that we cannot always depend on the national government for its enforcement. "The 'spirit of liberty' which emanates from the Bill of Rights," he states, "needs to be kept alive by each new generation of Americans."

In June of 1789, Representative James Madison fulfilled a campaign promise to his Virginia constituents by asking colleagues in the House of Representatives to consider a group of constitutional amendments designed to secure basic individual liberties. By December of 1791, ten of these were ratified by the necessary number of states, becoming the first amendments to the new Constitution—the U.S. Bill of Rights. Despite the bicentennial "burnout" which some individuals are experiencing, the bicentennial of the Bill of Rights—which we begin in earnest [in 1991]—should be a most meaningful occasion for every American. The Declaration of Independence made the nation a possibility; the Constitution created the structure of public authority in the nation, but the Bill of Rights has done nothing less than define the very quality of public and private life in the United States. If the Constitution is a "living document," then surely the Bill of Rights is *about* daily living and the freedom we have to experience life. This makes the Bill of Rights America's most important "founding" document.

The Bill of Rights has been variously described as "a shield to every American citizen," "the one guarantee of freedom to the American people," "fetters against doing evil which no honest government should decline," and "the foundation of liberty against the encroachments of government." However, even as we celebrate its bicentennial, ignorance, indifference, intolerance, ideology, and perhaps even modernity threaten the viability of its guarantees. Historian Michael Kammen calls it a "subtle attack," while others see it as a direct frontal assault. For the past forty years, surveys have shown that Americans are uninformed about the provisions contained within the Bill of Rights, at best, and hostile to them, at worst. Of greater concern is the "gray truth," as attorney Marvin E. Frankel puts it, that "civil liberties and civil rights are not very popular in the land of the free."

The popularity of the Reagan-Meese attack on the applicability of the Bill of Rights is but one recent exemplification of this argument. During the 1980s, as Archibald Cox explains, "The President and Attorney General Meese lambaste[d] the Court for disregarding the intent of the Framers of the Constitution in order to impose on the country what they charge are social experiments flowing from the Justices' personal values." In particular, Attorney General Meese strongly advocated a reversal in the doctrine of "selective incorporation," which applied the

Bill of Rights to state and local authorities through provisions of the 14th Amendment.

The complexity of problems we face as a post-industrial society makes the application of the Bill of Rights a difficult, but not an impossible, task. We may begin a defense against these modern assaults by identifying seven items that every student (and every American for that matter) should know about the Bill of Rights.

1. *The Framers of the Constitution originally opposed the Bill of Rights.* Ironically, James Madison and most other delegates to the Constitutional Convention in 1787 opposed a proposal to establish a bill of rights and continued to oppose it during subsequent ratification debates. Late in the Convention, on September 12, George Mason introduced a motion to preface the proposed Constitution with a bill of rights. While the convention voted unanimously against the proposal, four primary arguments were advanced to sustain opposition to a bill of rights by the Federalists. (1) It was unnecessary in a constitutional republic founded upon popular sovereignty and inalienable natural rights. In addition, since many (but not all) states had bills of rights, federal guarantees were not needed. (2) A bill of rights would be dangerous for, as Alexander Hamilton put it in *Federalist Paper* No. 84: "They would contain various exceptions to powers which are not granted; and, on this very account, would afford a colorable pretext to claim more than were granted. Why declare that things shall not be done which there is no power to do?" (3) It would be impracticable to enforce since its security would inevitably depend on public opinion and on the general spirit of the people and of the government. (4) The Constitution is itself a bill of rights as is the constitution of each state making further efforts to secure these rights redundant.

2. *The Bill of Rights is the result of political pressure and compromise.* The absence of a bill of rights in the Constitution was a major obstacle to ratification and provoked some of the strongest protests by the anti-Federalists in opposition to the proposed government. George Mason of Virginia refused to sign the Constitution, saying that without a bill of rights he "would sooner chop off his right hand than put it to the Constitution as it now stands." One anti-Federalist responded to the Federalists' defense of the Constitution by insisting that in a representative government a bill of rights was absolutely necessary "to secure the minority against the usurpation and tyranny of the majority." A [Maryland] framer was even more emphatic: "The truth is, that the rights of individuals are frequently opposed to the apparent interests of the majority—For this reason the greater the portion of political freedom in a form of government the greater the necessity of a bill of rights." Indeed, for another anti-Federalist it was "astonishing, that this grand security, to the rights of the people, is not to be found in this constitution."

Since the Federalists were not completely convinced of the undesirability of a bill of rights as to prefer the defeat of the Constitution to ratification with an accompanying bill of rights, they agreed to support a bill of rights once the First Congress was assembled.

Madison's change of mind on this matter is attributable to the antifederalist composition of his congressional constituency and the considerable correspondence with Thomas Jefferson. In order to be elected to the House of Representatives, Madison had to respond to the concerns of his constituency about the absence of a bill of rights. In addition, he was strongly influenced by Jefferson's claim in December of 1787 that "a bill of rights is what the people are entitled to against every government on earth, general or particular; and what no just government should refuse, or rest on inference." Jefferson was dismayed that the new Constitution did not contain a bill of rights. By October of 1788, Madison admitted to Jefferson that he had found reason to concede that, while less essential than in other forms of government, a bill of rights might be a prudent precaution: "The political truths declared in that solemn manner acquire by degrees the character of fundamental maxims of free Government, and as they become incorporated with the national sentiment counteract the impulses of interest and passion." Thus, Madison justified the submission of a bill of rights to Congress on "declaratory grounds." Once these rights are declared and venerated by the people, as political philosopher Martin Diamond explains, they "serve as an ethical admonition to the people, teaching them to subdue dangerous impulses of passion and interest." Of course, the value of declaration followed by veneration is lost if we are not well educated about the Bill of Rights and its contemporary implications for society.

3. *The Bill of Rights is an anti-majoritarian document.* The great constitutional rights contained within the Bill of Rights are protections against majority pressures and majority power. Too often we forget that the Bill of Rights is part of the constitutional framework which protects us from the tyranny of the majority when we are weak, helpless, or just outnumbered. The Bill of Rights is an attempt to curb what Jefferson called "elective despotism"—the potential for tyrannical and perverse policies emerging from the elected branches of government. Jefferson disapproved of "the want of a bill of rights, to guard against the legislative as well as the executive branches of the government" in the Constitution. Likewise, when Madison introduced the amendments to the First Congress he noted the fear of "abuse of the executive [and] . . . the legislative power," and stressed that the purpose was to "control the majority from those acts [against the minority] to which they might otherwise be inclined." As Justice Robert Jackson observed some 150 years later: "The very purpose of the Bill of Rights was to withdraw certain subjects from the vicissitudes of political controversy, to place them beyond the reach of majorities and officials and to establish them

as legal principles to be applied by the courts." As individual liberty has been threatened in this century by the growth of the American state and the rise of presidentialism, the Bill of Rights has emerged as one of the principal defenses a citizen has against these assaults.

4. *The doctrine of "selective incorporation" has only recently applied the Bill of Rights to state and local authorities.* Once the Bill of Rights was ratified in 1791, the Congress was forbidden to abridge free speech, press, religion, and so forth. However, state legislatures *could* abridge them (unless prohibited by their state constitutions)—and they did! The individual was entitled to a fair, speedy, public jury trial, to confront accusers, and couldn't be forced to incriminate herself *if* the case was in a federal court. If the case was in a state or municipal court—and most were—the individual had no such protections. Not until the Supreme Court utilized the "due process" clause of the 14th Amendment (passed in the aftermath of the Civil War in 1868)—first in the 1930s and then again in the 1960s—were certain rights applied to state and local authorities.

This judicial doctrine is called "selective incorporation"—"incorporation" because certain rights are held to be incorporated within the due process clause of the 14th Amendment, and therefore, applicable to the states; and "selective" because the court retains the discretion of deciding which rights are in and which are not. Under this doctrine, for example, First Amendment protections of speech, press, and assembly were incorporated in 1927, 1931, and 1937 respectively; Fourth Amendment rights against illegal searches and seizure in 1949; Fifth Amendment rights against self-incrimination in 1964 and against double jeopardy in 1969; Sixth Amendment rights to counsel in 1963 and to a speedy trial in 1967; and Eighth Amendment rights to be free of cruel and unusual punishments in 1962.

This doctrine was a primary target of former Attorney General Edwin Meese. According to Meese, "The Bill of Rights was designed to apply only to the national government. Nowhere else has the principle of federalism been dealt so politically violent and constitutionally suspect a blow as by the theory of incorporation." Presumably, the Attorney General prefers that the freedoms guaranteed to us by the Bill of Rights as citizens of the United States should not apply to us as residents of individual states. Jefferson believed in the universal necessity of a bill of rights to guard against the potential excesses of government. Presumably, Mr. Meese would have a difficult time justifying his assault on incorporation to Mr. Jefferson.

5. *The Bill of Rights does not contain all of the amendments originally proposed by Madison.* Madison proposed a total of seventeen constitutional amendments to the House of Representatives. Of these, twelve were approved by the House and Senate and ten were eventually ratified by the states. The two amendments approved by Congress but not ratified included an amendment to establish the ratio of representatives to population for the House; and one requiring that no law changing the compensation of Senators and Representatives could take effect until an election of Representatives had intervened. This amendment would have made it impossible for Congress to give itself a pay increase *without* facing the electorate first—as almost occurred [in 1990]. Of the remaining five amendments not approved by Congress one stands out as significant. Madison proposed that: "No State shall infringe the equal rights of conscience, not the freedom of speech, or of the press, nor of the right of trial by jury in criminal cases." This would have applied the Bill of Rights to state authorities. The many advocates of states' rights present in the First Congress easily defeated this amendment in the Senate. As indicated above, the nation would have to wait until the mid-20th century for the Bill of Rights to be extended to state and local authorities.

6. *The Bill of Rights touches daily life in America.* The Bill of Rights is not just about court cases, landmark decisions, or judicial doctrines. It fundamentally influences the quality of public and private life in America. Under its protection, we are able to criticize elected officials and non-elected bureaucrats without retribution or punishment. We do not worry about unexpected intrusions or invasions of public authority in our private lives. We speak and write freely and, therefore, are at liberty to think freely as well. We are comforted by the many freedoms it provides and at the same time are made complacent by their normality and certainty. Conversely, all too frequently we are angered by the use of the Bill of Rights to protect those in society who appear undeserving of its benefits. This is a quintessential dilemma. However, a far greater threat to the Bill of Rights and the nation awaits us if we fail to know and recognize the rights which it guarantees and their significance for life in America. Without declaration and acknowlodgement, there can be no veneration or enforcement. The eventual evisceration of these individual liberties will be the result.

7. *There are notable rights missing from the Bill of Rights.* There are probably a great many rights which citizens assume or imagine are contained in the Bill of Rights which are just not there. For example, the right to housing, public welfare, or bankruptcy are nowhere guaranteed in the Constitution. Freedom from hunger or impoverishment is not guaranteed by the Bill of Rights. Even the right of privacy is nowhere mentioned in the Constitution, although the Court has recognized that a right of personal privacy, or at least a guarantee of certain zones of privacy, is constitutionally protected (however troublesome the source of this protection remains). Most surprisingly of all, there is no constitutional right to education. This is a great irony since education is the one capacity necessary for the enforcement of the Bill of Rights and essential to democratic governance. "I know of no safe depository of the ultimate powers of the society but the people themselves," said Thomas

Jefferson (1820), "and if we think them not enlightened enough to exercise their control with a wholesome discretion, the remedy is not to take it from them, but to inform their discretion by education. This is the true corrective of abuses of constitutional power." As we battle for the soul of the Bill of Rights, this corrective is in great demand—but is one which the document itself cannot provide.

The Bill of Rights is not self-enforcing, nor, as history has shown, can we always depend on the national government for its enforcement. Rather, enforcement depends on the vigilance and education of all Americans. As the renowned jurist Learned Hand noted: "Liberty lives in the hearts of men and women; when it dies there, no constitution, no law, no court can save it; no constitution, no court can even do much to help it." The "spirit of liberty" which emanates from the Bill of Rights needs to be kept alive by each new generation of Americans. It is a spirit which can only be effectively nurtured by education, self-reflection, appreciation, and toleration. The Bill of Rights is more than a legacy to be preserved, honored, or celebrated; it is a vision of respect, tolerance, and humanity to be experienced and embraced in the daily web of life.

4. Race and the Constitution

Thurgood Marshall

In a speech presented to the San Francisco Patent and Trademark Law Association in 1987—the year marking the 200th anniversary of the U.S. Constitution—Supreme Court Justice Thurgood Marshall demythologizes that document by focusing on its inherent defects. He addresses, in particular, the constitutional denial of liberty, equality, and justice to African-Americans. Justice Marshall, the first and most distinguished African-American to serve on the Supreme Court [Clarence Thomas, named by President Bush to succeed the retiring Justice Marshall, might be the next], states that the framers of the Constitution never reconciled the "contradiction between guaranteeing liberty and justice to all, and denying both to Negroes." According to Marshall, the "true miracle" of the Constitution was not its birth but rather its life over the course of two centuries, involving much sacrifice and struggle, which has triumphed over many of the flaws in the original document.

Nineteen eighty-seven marks the 200th anniversary of the United States Constitution.... Like many anniversary celebrations, the plan for 1987 takes particular events and holds them up as the source of all the very best that has followed. Patriotic feelings will surely swell, prompting proud proclamations of the wisdom, foresight, and sense of justice shared by the Framers and reflected in a written document now yellowed with age. This is unfortunate—not the patriotism itself, but the tendency for the celebration to oversimplify, and overlook the many other events that have been instrumental to our achievements as a nation. The focus of this celebration invites a complacent belief that the vision of those who debated and compromised in Philadelphia yielded the "more perfect Union" it is said we now enjoy.

I cannot accept this invitation, for I do not believe that the meaning of the Constitution was forever "fixed" at the Philadelphia Convention. Nor do I find the wisdom, foresight, and sense of justice exhibited by the Framers particularly profound. To the contrary, the government they devised was defective from the start, requiring several amendments, a civil war, and momentous social transformation to attain the system of constitutional government, and its respect for the individual freedoms and human rights, we hold as fundamental today. When contemporary Americans cite "The Constitution," they invoke a concept that is vastly different from what the Framers barely began to construct two centuries ago.

For a sense of the evolving nature of the Constitution we need look no further than the first three words of the document's preamble: "We the People." When the Founding Fathers used this phrase in 1787, they did not have in mind the majority of America's citizens. "We the People" included, in the words of the Framers, "the whole Number of free Persons." On a matter so basic as the right to vote, for example, Negro slaves were excluded, although they were counted for representational purposes—at three-fifths each. Women did not gain the right to vote for over a hundred and thirty years.

These omissions were intentional. The record of the Framers' debates on the slave question is especially clear: The Southern States acceded to the demands of the New England States for giving Congress broad power to regulate commerce, in exchange for the right to continue the slave trade. The economic interests of the regions coalesced: New Englanders engaged in the "carrying trade" would profit from transporting slaves from Africa as well as goods produced in America by slave labor. The perpetuation of slavery ensured the primary source of wealth in the Southern States.

Despite this clear understanding of the role slavery would play in the new republic, use of the words "slaves" and "slavery" was carefully avoided in the original document. Political representation in the lower House of Congress was to be based on the population of "free Persons"

House of Congress was to be based on the population of "free Persons" in each State, plus three-fifths of all "other Persons." Moral principles against slavery, for those who had them, were compromised, with no explanation of the conflicting principles for which the American Revolutionary War had ostensibly been fought: the self-evident truths "that all men are created equal, that they are endowed by their Creator with certain unalienable Rights, that among these are Life, Liberty and the pursuit of Happiness."

It was not the first such compromise. Even these ringing phrases from the Declaration of Independence are filled with irony, for an early draft of what became that Declaration assailed the King of England for suppressing legislative attempts to end the slave trade and for encouraging slave rebellions. The final draft adopted in 1776 did not contain this criticism. And so again at the Constitutional Convention eloquent objections to the institution of slavery went unheeded, and its opponents eventually consented to a document which laid a foundation for the tragic events that were to follow.

Pennsylvania's Gouverneur Morris provides an example. He opposed slavery and the counting of slaves in determining the basis for representation in Congress. At the Convention he objected that "the inhabitant of Georgia [or] South Carolina who goes to the coast of Africa, and in defiance of the most sacred laws of humanity tears away his fellow creatures from their dearest connections and damns them to the most cruel bondages, shall have more votes in a Government instituted for protection of the rights of mankind, than the Citizen of Pennsylvania or New Jersey who views with a laudable horror, so nefarious a practice." And yet Gouverneur Morris eventually accepted the three-fifths accommodation. In fact, he wrote the final draft of the Constitution, the very document the bicentennial will commemorate.

As a result of compromise, the right of the Southern States to continue importing slaves was extended, officially, at least until 1808. We know that it actually lasted a good deal longer, as the Framers possessed no monopoly on the ability to trade moral principles for self-interest. But they nevertheless set an unfortunate example. Slaves could be imported, if the commercial interests of the North were protected. To make the compromise even more palatable, customs duties would be imposed at up to ten dollars per slave as a means of raising public revenues.

No doubt it will be said, when the unpleasant truth of the history of slavery in America is mentioned during this bicentennial year, that the Constitution was a product of its times, and embodied a compromise which, under other circumstances, would not have been made. But the effects of the Framers' compromise have remained for generations. They arose from the contradiction between guaranteeing liberty and justice to all, and denying both to Negroes.

The original intent of the phrase, "We the People," was far too clear for any ameliorating construction. Writing for the Supreme Court in 1857, Chief Justice Taney penned the following passage in the Dred Scott case, on the issue whether, in the eyes of the Framers, slaves were "constituent members of the sovereignty," and were to be included among "We the People":

"We think that they are not, and that they are not included, and were not intended to be included. . . . They had for more than a century before been regarded as beings of an inferior order, and altogether unfit to associate with the white race . . . ; and so far inferior, that they had no rights which the white man was bound to respect; and that the negro might justly and lawfully be reduced to slavery for his benefit. . . . [A]ccordingly, a negro of the African race was regarded . . . as an article of property, and held, and bought and sold as such. . . . [N]o one seems to have doubted the correctness of the prevailing opinion of the time."

And so, nearly seven decades after the Constitutional Convention, the Supreme Court reaffirmed the prevailing opinion of the Framers regarding the rights of Negroes in America. It took a bloody civil war before the 13th Amendment could be adopted to abolish slavery, though not the consequences slavery would have for future Americans.

While the Union survived the civil war, the Constitution did not. In its place arose a new, more promising basis for justice and equality, the 14th Amendment, ensuring protection of the life, liberty, and property of all persons against deprivations without due process, and guaranteeing equal protection of the laws. And yet almost another century would pass before any significant recognition was obtained of the rights of black Americans to share equally even in such basic opportunities as education, housing, and employment, and to have their votes counted, and counted equally. In the meantime, blacks joined America's military to fight its wars and invested untold hours working in its factories and on its farms, contributing to the development of this country's magnificent wealth and waiting to share in this prosperity.

What is striking is the role legal principles have played throughout America's history in determining the condition of Negroes. They were enslaved by law, emancipated by law, disenfranchised and segregated by law; and, finally, they have begun to win equality by law. Along the way, new constitutional principles have emerged to meet the challenges of a changing society. The progress has been dramatic, and it will continue.

The men who gathered in Philadelphia in 1787 could not have envisioned these changes. They could not have imagined, nor would they have accepted, that the document they were drafting would one day be construed by a Supreme Court to which had been appointed a woman and the descendent of an African slave. "We the People" no longer enslaved, but the credit does not belong to the Framers. It belongs to those who refused to acquiesce in outdated notions of "liberty," "justice," and "equality," and who strive to better them.

And so we must be careful, when focusing on the events which took place in Philadelphia two centuries ago, that we not overlook the momentous events which followed, and thereby lose our proper sense of perspective. Otherwise, the odds are that for many Americans the bicentennial celebration will be little more than a blind pilgrimage to the shrine of the original document now stored in a vault in the National Archives. If we seek, instead, a sensitive understanding of the Constitution's inherent defects, and its promising evolution through 200 years of history, the celebration of the "Miracle at Philadelphia" will, in my view, be a far more meaningful and humbling experience. We will see that the true miracle was not the birth of the Constitution, but its life, a life nurtured through two turbulent centuries of our own making, and a life embodying much good fortune that was not.

Thus, in this bicentennial year, we may not all participate in the festivities with flag-waving fervor. Some may more quietly commemorate the suffering, struggle, and sacrifice that has triumphed over much of what was wrong with the original document, and observe the anniversary with hopes not realized and promises not fulfilled. I plan to celebrate the bicentennial of the Constitution as a living document, including the Bill of Rights and the other amendments protecting individual freedoms and human rights.

5. The Constitution: Thirteen Crucial Questions

James MacGregor Burns and Richard B. Morris

James MacGregor Burns, Woodrow Wilson Professor of Government at Williams College, is a nationally known political scientist and author. Richard B. Morris is professor emeritus of history at Columbia University. They cochaired Project '87, a scholarly group organized to celebrate the Constitution's bicentennial. In this article from *A Bicentennial Chronicle*, published by Project '87 of the American Historical Association and the American Political Science Association, the authors discuss thirteen enduring issues in the context of contemporary developments. They consider the expectations of the Framers and the provisions of the Constitution and ask numerous questions about the responsiveness of the document to contemporary issues.

1. Too much — or too little — national power? Are the limits placed on the federal government's powers by the Constitution realistic and enforceable?

The Framers wanted a national government strong enough to exercise certain general powers but not so powerful as to threaten peoples' liberties. In their reading of history and their own experience they had seen all too many republics turn into despotisms. "In framing a government which is to be administered by men over men," wrote James Madison, "the great difficulty lies in this: you must first enable the government to control the governed; and in the next place oblige it to control itself." Thus the Framers carefully enumerated the powers delegated to the national government while, in the Bill of Rights, reserving the rest to the states and the people. Congressional legislation, executive acts, and decisions by the federal judiciary have broadened national power enormously in the face of internal and external threats to our national security and economic well-being. Has this trend gone too far? Or is the national power in fact inadequate in the face of social unrest, economic instability and international turbulence? Will it be even less adequate in our Third Century—the age of continuing technological change, nuclear danger, and intense pressure on national and global resources?

2. Does federalism work? Is the Constitution maintaining an efficient and realistic balance between national and state power?

The United States did not invent federalism, but under our Constitution it has a distinctly indigenous form—equality of the states in the Senate, and a Bill of Rights which, through the Tenth Amendment, reserves to the states or the people powers not delegated to the United States by the Constitution. Nevertheless, the American union exercises its power directly on the individual, and under the Constitution's supremacy clause congressional statutes and treaties constitute the supreme law of the land. Drastic changes in the direction of centralization have taken place since the Civil War, especially during and after the New Deal,* including the nationalization of most of the Bill of Rights.

*Programs and policies introduced during the presidency of Franklin D. Roosevelt in the 1930s.

The Income Tax Amendment of 1913, which has led to the federal government's collecting an overwhelming portion of the tax revenue, has further weakened state power. To sustain state solvency, Congress promulgated a Revenue Sharing Act in 1972 [now repealed], but it is doubtful whether the ensuing limited fiscal relief to the states has restored the balance of power of the federal structure. Can federalism work without continued federal handouts? Must federal control of revenue mean federal domination of state action?

3. Is the judicial branch too powerful? Are the courts exercising their powers appropriately as interpreters of the Constitution and shapers of public policy?

A whole cluster of cases—from Dred Scott through the New Deal decisions, the recent civil libertarian cases and culminating in Brown v. Board of Education (1954-desegregation), Baker v. Carr (1962-reapportionment), and Roe v. Wade (1973-abortion)—show that where Congress fails to act, the Supreme Court has ventured into the field of policymaking, in areas ranging from human freedom to definitions of privacy. It has been asserted that "the Constitution is what the judges say it is." Is this role for the courts a proper and necessary one in a democracy? Does it bespeak a vacuum of power in Congress and a tendency of the representative body to evade making decisions in cases where public opinion is sharply divided? Could the current move to limit the jurisdiction of the federal courts endanger the Bill of Rights, among other safeguards to individual freedom? Can a federal union survive without lodging somewhere a power to declare laws unconstitutional, to ensure separation of powers, to apply to laws a strict scrutiny in instances of impaired fundamental rights, and to make explicit the avowed intent of the Preamble, "to establish justice"?

4. Balancing liberty and security: How can republican government provide for national security without endangering civil liberties? For the Framers, liberty—the protection of individual rights against governmental or religious interference—lay at the heart of a constitutional republic. The Bill of Rights is the enduring and eloquent testament to their commitment to liberty. But Americans have differed over the meaning of liberty—does it mean the right to speak, to assemble, to print, to pray, to bear arms without limit of any kind? Is the essential role of republican government simply to leave people alone in their exercise of these rights, or to take a positive role in expanding these liberties, or even to broaden some rights—such as free speech— and to narrow others—such as the right to bear arms? And are civil and political and religious liberties enough—what about economic and social rights? During World War II Franklin D. Roosevelt promulgated the Four Freedoms—freedom of speech and of worship, but also freedom from want and from fear. Does government have the right and duty under the Constitution to guarantee all these "freedoms" and at the expense of whose liberty? Finally, what is the proper role of government in resolving conflicts between individual rights and national needs—for example, the right of free speech and assembly during war? Can republican government provide for national security without endangering civil liberties?

5. Suspects' rights: How can republican government protect its citizenry and yet uphold the rights of the criminally accused?

The rise of crime in the United States has raised tensions between certain guarantees in the Bill of Rights, the capacity of the legal system, and measures intended to curb lawlessness. Article II protects the right to bear arms, but gun control measures seek to restrain gun ownership. Article IV protects citizens from governmental searches without warrants, but conflicts arise over collection of evidence in potentially criminal situations. Articles VI, VII and VIII stipulate the rights of the criminally accused to counsel, trial by jury, and protection from excessive bail and cruel punishment, but the complexity of procedures required to administer the criminal justice system, including constitutionally-mandated rights, results in practices like plea-bargaining which are often troublesome to observers. These issues are of immense concern to the public, which demands personal security and at the same time supports the basic principles of criminal justice in a democratic society. Can these conflicting interests be reconciled?

6. "All men are created equal": What kinds of equality are and should be protected by the Constitution and by what means?

A major contemporary issue is the distinction between equality before the law and equality in distribution of resources and benefits. The former deals with a limited set of governmental procedures, like voting. The latter embraces all interests and would require social policy to achieve equality. Questions are constantly arising about equality: Can a state deny welfare to a person only briefly resident? Can a state, by using property taxation as a basis for school finance, allocate less money to poor districts? Can universities use quotas to promote affirmative action? Does the Constitution guarantee equality of opportunity or equality of result, and which do we want? Finally, we must address the question of how much the government should intervene in sensitive areas like health, education and housing, in order to equalize economic and even "social" opportunity.

7. Women's rights: Does the Constitution adequately protect the rights of women?

Women are not mentioned in the original Constitution. Nonetheless, the description of the qualifications of a Representative as a "person" permitted a woman to be elected to Congress in 1916 even before they were guaranteed the right to vote by a federal Constitutional amendment. The 14th Amendment too speaks of "all persons" being entitled to citizenship, bars any state from enforcing any law which shall "abridge the privileges or immunities of Citizens of the United States," prohibits any state from depriving "any person of life, liberty or property without due process of law" and from denying "to any person within its jurisdiction the equal protection of the laws." While none of these provisions discriminates on the basis of sex, the Supreme Court to date has not interpreted them to bar sex distinctions in law outright. The Constitution, through the 19th Amendment, specifically prohibits only one form of sex-based discrimination; no state may now deny women the franchise. In a variety of other crucial areas, however, the Constitution contains no explicit guarantees of women's rights. The defeat of ERA [Equal Rights Amendment, in 1983] raises anew the question of whether the present protections of the Constitution can be interpreted as providing affirmative guarantees of sexual equality, and if not, what alternatives should be pursued?

8. Safeguarding minorities: Does the Constitution adequately protect the rights of blacks, native Americans, ethnic groups, and recent immigrants?

The Constitution historically has protected various economic and regional groups against national interference—19th-century industrial capitalists, slave holders, religious minorities, political dissenters. On the other hand, it has failed to protect American blacks, both before and after Emancipation, other racial groups, including native Americans and Japanese-Americans, and leaders and members of alleged "radical" groups suspected of "subversion." The trend in this century, as a result of congressional legislation, presidential action, judicial decisions, the efforts of organized minorities and civil liberties and civil rights groups, has been toward much stronger constitutional guarantees of minority rights. Will this trend continue? Is it imprudent to depend so heavily on federal judicial sensitivity to minority concerns? Can we strengthen majority rule *and* protect minority rights?

9. The Constitution faces outward: Does the President possess adequate power—or too much power—over war-making and foreign policy?

Except in his capacity as commander-in-chief, the President receives the bulk of his powers under delegation and authority of Congress. The experience of the Civil War, World War II, and the Vietnam War reveals that the President can exercise extraordinary powers in wartime both to subvert civil liberties and to dispatch troops into war zones without explicit direction of Congress. Are these measures necessary for the national defense? The War Powers Act [of 1983] was designed to make the commander-in-chief more responsive to the people's representatives in Congress. Whether it will do so has yet to be tested, especially in view of the recent Supreme Court decision [in 1983] invalidating the legislative veto.

In foreign affairs, the President under the Constitution is the principal actor, although treaties require the assent of the Senate to be valid. While in most instances the consent of the Senate has become a formality, there have been and continue to be occasions when the necessity for Senate ratification does produce a struggle between the President and the Senate. Such contests took place over the adherence to the Covenant of the League of Nations, the Panama Canal Treaty and the Canadian Fisheries compact. Should the two-thirds requirement for a treaty be lowered to a simple majority or a three-fifths majority in order to minimize such conflicts, or should the Senate be a more active partner than it has been?

10. Too many checks and balances? Does the constitutional separation of powers between the President, the Congress and the Judiciary create a deadlock in governance?

Determined to make government their servant and not their master, the Framers contrived a most ingenious system of pitting the legislative branch against the executive, Senate against the House, and, in effect, the judiciary against either or both the other branches. The "accumulation of all powers, legislative, executive, and judiciary, in the same hands," Madison said, was the "very definition of tyranny." The Framers not only gave different branches different powers but required their members to be chosen by—and hence responsive to—diverse and conflicting "constituencies." "Ambition," Madison summed it up, "must be made to counteract ambition." Their handiwork can still be seen on the front page of virtually any newspaper today. Is the checks-and-balance system out of date, a relic of the "horse-and-buggy" era? Does it unduly hobble the federal government as it seeks to cope with an overwhelming tide of problems? Or is governmental quarreling, inefficiency, delay and even impotence a price we must pay—are willing to pay—to keep "government off our backs."

11. "Government by the people": Does the evolving constitutional system, including political parties and interest groups, strengthen fair and effective representation of the people or undermine it?

We are used to majority rule in House and Senate, town meetings, city councils, student governments. Counting heads, and deciding in favor of the side having the votes of a majority seems an easy, practical, and fair way to settle differences. The Constitution, however, was not established solely on the basis of majority rule, but on the protection of regional and local minorities as well. By controlling one body, such as the Senate, a regional, economic or political minority could veto actions by the majority. This arrangement differs sharply from the parliamentary system, where simple majorities can and do make crucial decisions. Over the years the extension of the right to vote, the rise of a national party system that united like-minded presidents, senators and congressmen, and such changes as the direct election of United States senators, tended to make national government somewhat more majoritarian. Recent decades, however, have often seen the executive and legislative branches politically divided, inhibiting simple majoritarian decisions. Moreover, even leaders and parties winning nationwide majorities have trouble putting through their programs in the face of the strength of economic and social interest groups. Do these groups advance or threaten the goal of "government by the people?" Have we ever in our history attained this goal?

12. The Constitution and the economy: Can the Constitution be utilized more effectively to provide economic security and promote the well-being of all Americans?

The Constitution was created not in a vacuum, but largely in response to the severe depression which the Articles of Confederation were powerless to arrest. Hence, the charter granted to Congress powers over commerce and taxation and included various fiscal prohibitions on the states in the full-faith-and-credit clause, the export-import clause, and the clause against impairing the obligation of contracts. Hamilton's enunciation of implied powers, his interpretation of the taxing power, and his insistence on honoring the public credit contributed to the upward economic thrust in the first decade of our history. Thus, from the start the government was a friend of private enterprise. The degree to which the Constitution has been employed to promote business enterprise and yet discipline its abuses has varied with national administrations and the personnel of the federal courts. But the power to promote the public welfare resides in the Constitution, and its use depends finally upon the public conception of its necessary and proper function, especially in the times of economic crisis. Are we satisfied with its performance today?

13. Constitutional flexibility: Should we make changing our fundamental charter of government simpler and more democratic?

The Constitution provides two formal ways for amending it: 1) by a two-thirds vote of Congress and a three-quarters vote of the state legislatures or state conventions; 2) by a convention to be called by the legislatures of two-thirds of the states, whose amendments shall be ratified by the legislatures of three-quarters of the states. This procedure was a modification of the Articles of Confederation, which required a unanimous vote of *every* state to amend the Articles. The states have made no use of their power to initiate amendments. From the start all amendments to the Constitution have been proposed by Congress and not by the state legislatures, and only one of them, the 21st Amendment repealing prohibition, was effected through ratification by convention rather than state legislatures. The defeat of recent amendments and the prospect of a cluster of other proposals have given rise to serious questions: Do we need further amendments to the

Constitution? Is the present amendment procedure too restrictive or have judicial interpretation, legislative and executive actions proven adequate to meet most needs for Constitutional flexibility? If a constitutional convention is called by the states, can its proposals be restricted to the terms of its summons? Does the convening of a new constitutional convention threaten the very foundation of the original document?

Chapter 2

Federalism: National, State, and Local Government

The federal system established by the Constitution is, at first glance, easy to understand (although the term *federalism* is not found in the document). Federalism means a dividing and sharing of authority among different levels of government. The Constitution assigns some powers to the national government and reserves others for the states. From the first, however, the theory and the reality of federalism have been anything but simple. The Anti-Federalists came close to defeating ratification because they worried that the national government would overwhelm state sovereignty. The bloody Civil War was fought in large part over the issue of states' rights.

The Constitution provides not only an institutional division of power (among the three branches) but a geographical distribution as well (between the national government and the states). The federal principle, stated in the Tenth Amendment, provides that the "powers not delegated to the United States by the Constitution, nor prohibited by it to the States, are reserved to the States respectively, or to the people." Even with the Constitution's "supremacy clause," which makes national laws and treaties the "supreme law of the Land," it is simply impossible to make precise and permanent allocations of authority between the states and the national government. Boundary disputes between them are typically refereed by the umpire of our federal system: the Supreme Court.

The Constitution enumerates Congress's powers, but Congress is not limited solely to those responsibilities. Indeed, it possesses, in the words of constitutional scholars, "implied," "inherent," "residual," "resulting," or other deduced powers. They flow from the combination of Congress's enumerated powers and the "elastic clause" (Article I, Section 8). That clause permits Congress to make all laws "necessary and proper" to carry out its enumerated powers. And what is necessary and proper is interpreted by the Supreme Court.

The landmark *McCulloch v. Maryland* decision of 1819 (Selection 6), written by Chief Justice John Marshall, upheld Congress's power to charter a bank in Baltimore, Maryland. (McCulloch, a bank cashier, refused to pay a state tax levied against the national bank.) The Constitution, of course, makes no reference to chartering banks. Taking a broad view of national governmental authority, Justice Marshall upheld Congress's right to establish the bank. In doing so, he established the fundamental concept of "implied powers," which since has been used to buttress the growth of the central government.

> We admit, as all must admit, that the powers of the government are limited, and that its limits are not to be transcended. But we think the sound construction of the Constitution must allow to the national legislature that discretion, with respect to the means by which the powers it confers are to be carried into execution, which will enable that body to perform the high duties assigned to it, in the manner most beneficial to the people. Let the end be legitimate, let it be within the scope of the Constitution, and all means which are appropriate, which are plainly adapted to that end, which are not prohibited, but consist with the letter and spirit of the Constitution, are constitutional.

McCulloch v. Maryland also asserted the Supreme Court's right to review decisions of state legislatures, executives, and courts.

Federalism's Strength and Weaknesses

The experience of the United States with federalism reveals both advantages and disadvantages. On the one hand, federalism can foster social, economic, and political experimentation, increase avenues for political participation, and make the government more responsive to local problems. Selection 10, "Welfare Reform: The Issue That Bubbled Up From the States to Capitol Hill," discusses how the welfare initiatives of the states galvanized the national government to take comparable action. On the other hand, federalism can permit national initiatives to be frustrated by local interests and lead to political and ideological tensions among levels of government. Whatever its strengths and weaknesses, federalism has been an enduring constitutional arrangement for over two hundred years (see Selection 7, "The Enduring Features of American Federalism").

Intergovernmental trends and relationships have undergone major transformations as successive generations and political leaders have grappled with the idea of federalism. Sen. Dave Durenberger (R-Minn.) remarked:

In its first months every new administration invents a theory of federalism to reflect its philosophy in domestic policy. We've had dual federalism, cooperative federalism, creative federalism, new federalism, layer-cake federalism, marble-cake federalism, fruit cake federalism. Today, we have the worst of all federalisms—budget federalism.[1]

These diverse slogans reflect federalism's dynamism and the efforts of leaders to accommodate its meaning and application to changing circumstances. Federalism's dynamism is addressed by John Kincaid of the U.S. Advisory Commission on Intergovernmental Relations in Selection 8, "The Changing Face of Federalism."

In this century, the national government has gained enormous influence within the political system. Wars, economic calamities, attitudinal changes (such as citizens' increased expectations of federal government assistance), inefficiencies within state governments (part-time legislatures, for example), and the nationalization of scores of issues (such as air and water pollution) stimulated centralization in Washington, D.C. From the New Deal to the Great Society* to the programs of the late 1970s, federal financial assistance to states and localities increased tremendously. One scholar wrote:

The government in Washington went from spending the least, for domestic purposes, of the three levels—national, state, and local—to spending nearly twice as much as the lower levels combined. In addition, the lower levels were drawn under Washington's influence through more than 500 federal grant programs comprising more than one-fourth of state and local budgets, and a host of regulations associated with the grants as well as with national policies concerning civil rights, pollution, health, and safety.[2]

It is not surprising that scholars, journalists, and political commentators throughout that era emphasized the national government as the source of funds, programs, and ideas and its place at the "top" of the federal system. Critics of the massive federal role in intergovernmental relations dubbed it "dysfunctional federalism."[3]

Things began to change in the 1980s, however. President Ronald Reagan, like other chief executives before him, urged a fundamental reexamination of the national government's growth and scope. His traditional campaign themes—"Get government off the citizen's back" and "Government is the problem, not the solution"—adroitly tapped a public wellspring of concern about an overcommitted, underachieving federal establishment.

* Programs and policies initiated during the presidency of Lyndon B. Johnson in the 1960s.

Once in the White House, Reagan embarked on a drive to reduce the national government's domestic responsibilities. He employed his considerable talents as communicator and agenda setter to shrink the federal government's domestic role and to slow expenditures for various social programs (although military and security spending was another matter). His annual budget presentations to Congress consistently underscored his goal of cutting back and even dismantling numerous federal programs. At the same time, Reagan successfully escalated expenditures for the military and reduced tax revenue. Reducing taxes limited the amount of money available at the federal level for new program initiatives.

Part of the Reagan agenda was a New Federalism plan. He launched the proposal in his January 26, 1982, State of the Union address to Congress. The New Federalism had two major components: a "swap" and a "turn back." Under the swap, the federal government would take charge of the state-run Medicaid program for the poor, and the states would assume the costs of food stamps and welfare programs. The turn back involved returning control of more than forty federally funded programs to the states. Funds to operate these programs would come from a new federal trust fund, which would be phased out gradually over five years. Then the states would have to raise their own revenues for any of the programs they wished to continue. (As a former governor, Reagan contended that most states had quietly but gradually transformed themselves into effective and competent units of governance.)

The New Federalism proposals quickly aroused opposition, and none passed Congress. State and local officials, as well as national legislators, wondered where the money would be found to support the swap and turn-back plans—given defense increases, mushrooming interest payments on huge annual deficits, and entitlement costs (Social Security and pension payments, for example). Some scholars have found that the Reagan initiatives enhanced the role of states and encouraged localities to look to their own capitals rather than to Washington for program assistance. "The federal government is pulling away from domestic and social programs, and state governments have taken on added duties and importance," said two Princeton professors. "Because of this, Ronald Reagan's version of 'new federalism' may turn out to be the major sleeper issue of his presidency." [4]

Too Much Government?

In the 1990s several issues loom in discussions of federalism. One is public attitudes toward government itself. President Reagan, to be sure, capitalized on the public's antigovernment mood to win election twice.

By contrast, President George Bush, an advocate of public responsibility and public service, won election in 1988 emphasizing the need for "kinder and gentler" government. This theme, coming in the aftermath of the domestic program cutbacks and consolidations of the Reagan years, implied a larger national role, and President Bush did propose national initiatives in such areas as education, drug abuse, and clean air. In his version of the New Federalism, President Bush proposed in his 1991 State of the Union message that $15 to $20 billion worth of domestic programs be consolidated into block grants and turned over to the states for their management.

The public appears to be of two minds about whether there is too much government. William D. Ruckelshaus, former administrator of the Environmental Protection Agency, observed that the American people "are ideologically conservative and operationally liberal. In theory, they are against too much government until the elimination of a particular program affects their own well-being." [5] In short, the citizenry will set limits on making the public sector smaller and the private sector larger. As Harvard professor James Q. Wilson put it:

> The people want no cuts in spending in many broad policy areas, including health, education, law enforcement, and environmental protection. However much citizens may agree that there is waste in government and that the government as a whole spends too much, it is hard to find any support for a broad movement toward a minimal state. [6]

Citizens may pay lip service to Thomas Jefferson's admonition that the best government is one that governs least, but their actions frequently belie their words.

Another important issue that affects federalism is the total federal debt (over $3 trillion in 1991) and annual deficits in the range of $300 billion. Not only do such huge deficits pose long-term problems for the health of the economy, but they restrain new or expanded government initiatives (which, depending upon one's point of view, may be beneficial or not). Citizens argue for their favorite national services, but they are reluctant to pay higher taxes to support other government programs.

Based on the November 1990 gubernatorial election results, which saw the defeat of state governors who raised taxes, citizens remain opposed to higher taxes, in part because they believe that federal and state governments will spend their tax dollars wastefully and unwisely. This public attitude, combined with economic downturn, cuts in federal grants to states and localities, and continued citizen pressure for governmental services, helped trigger massive fiscal distress among states and cities. "I think you would have to go back to the Great

Depression to find similar anguish," declared Henry Aaron of the Brookings Institution in Washington, D.C.[7] Where the federal government can run deficits, all states but one (Vermont) must balance their budgets. Hence, they face twin dilemmas: cut services or raise taxes.

Causing further distress among states is the federal government's penchant (as a way to get around the huge deficit) for initiating or expanding programs but requiring the states to finance and administer them. Growing use of federal mandates has aroused the ire of many governors (see Selection 9, "Those Maddening Mandates"). Mandates, said one governor, represent "either a backdoor tax increase or pushing off on states things that Congress, if it had any guts, would do itself."[8] From Congress's point of view, mandates permit lawmakers to create programs without raising taxes or expanding the bureaucracy.

Finally, these diverse and conflicting pressures make it harder to determine which level of government can best perform what types of functions. Some governors, for instance, want the federal government to concentrate on defense, Social Security, debt management, welfare, and a few other activities and "leave to the state and local government education, as much of roads as possible, prisons, clean water, initiatives for healthy children, and economic development."[9]

Part of the dilemma in the sorting out process is the lack of clear guidelines. Divisions between public and private, domestic and international, and national and state issues frequently are murky and commonly overlap one another. As Selection 11 points out, the rise of local "shadow governments" adds to the murkiness. Schools, roads, fire and police protection, and transit issues are traditionally state and local concerns. "That does not mean," observed Rep. David Obey (D-Wis.), "that they're *exclusively* state and local responsibilities." He continued:

> We have a national Constitution that guarantees individual rights to schoolchildren, and those rights were not, in fact, guaranteed historically by all our state and local jurisdictions. The national government has a moral, legal and constitutional obligation in those cases to exercise its responsibilities.[10]

In sum, federalism is a political system midway between confederation, in which the central government acts as the agent of the states, and the unitary state, in which all governing power resides in the central government. The interplay of national and state relations is a pervasive feature of our political landscape. The inevitable clashes that occur between the levels of government are typically worked out through laws, practical accommodations, and day-to-day collaboration in resolving public problems. As one scholar explained, "The role of government in a free society must be a matter of continuous negotiation among members of its public." [11]

Notes

1. *Congressional Record,* February 8, 1984, S1111.
2. John E. Chubb, "Federalism and the Bias for Centralization," in *The New Direction in American Politics,* ed. John E. Chubb and Paul E. Peterson (Washington, D.C.: Brookings Institution, 1985), 273.
3. David B. Walker, "Intergovernmental Relations and Dysfunctional Federalism," *National Civic Review* (February 1981): 68-82.
4. *Wall Street Journal,* September 18, 1984, 30.
5. *Congressional Record,* April 25, 1984, S4766. It is ironic, indeed, that public confidence in government increased under President Reagan. "The historic irony of Reagan's presidency," wrote an analyst, "is that the most antigovernment President in 60 years has refurbished the public's tattered faith in government" (Ronald Brownstein, "The Crest of the Wave," *National Journal* [August 2, 1986], 1890).
6. James Q. Wilson, "Why Reagan Won and Stockman Lost," *Commentary* (August 1986): 20.
7. *New York Times,* December 30, 1990, 1.
8. *Wall Street Journal,* September 14, 1989, A22.
9. *USA Today,* February 20, 1986, 9A.
10. *U.S. News & World Report,* December 14, 1981, 65.
11. *New Republic* (April 9, 1984): 35.

6. *McCulloch v. Maryland* (1819)

Congress chartered the first bank of the United States in 1791 after a bitter struggle over whether the national legislature had that authority. Alexander Hamilton, a strong proponent of the bank, locked horns with Thomas Jefferson, who argued that Congress lacked the authority to charter banks. The charter of the first bank expired in 1811 but was renewed in 1816 despite the unpopularity of the national bank in many sections of the country. The Second Bank quickly came under criticism for inefficient management and for causing a financial depression.

It was in this climate that the state of Maryland passed a law imposing an annual tax of $15,000 on the national bank. McCulloch, a bank cashier in the Baltimore branch, refused to pay the state tax. The state of Maryland brought suit against McCulloch, and the case eventually reached the Supreme Court. Chief Justice John Marshall delivered the opinion and articulated a doctrine that still guides the Court today: "implied powers" for the Congress. Marshall also recognized in *McCulloch v. Maryland* limits on the right of states to interfere with a federal agency. Although Marshall's opinion aroused the ire of strict constructionists (people who believe the national government should be limited to the powers enumerated in the Constitution), many scholars consider it his most important ruling.

Mr. Chief Justice Marshall delivered the opinion of the Court, saying in part: In the case now to be determined, the defendant, a sovereign state, denies the obligation of a law enacted by the legislature of the Union, and the plaintiff, on his part, contests the validity of an act which has been passed by the legislature of that state. The Constitution of our country, in its most interesting and vital parts, is to be considered; the conflicting powers of the government of the Union and of its members, as marked in that Constitution, are to be discussed; and an opinion given, which may essentially influence the great operations of the government. No tribunal can approach such a question without a deep sense of its importance, and of the awful responsibility involved in its decision. But it must be decided peacefully, or remain a source of hostile legislation, perhaps of hostility of a still more serious nature; and if it is to be so decided, by this tribunal alone can the decision be made.

On the Supreme Court of the United States has the Constitution of our country devolved this important duty.

The first question made in the cause is, has Congress power to incorporate a bank? . . .

The government of the Union, then (whatever may be the influence of this fact on the case), is emphatically and truly a government of the people. In form and in substance it emanates from them, its powers are granted by them, and are to be exercised directly on them, and for their benefit.

This government is acknowledged by all to be one of enumerated powers. The principle, that it can exercise only the powers granted to it, would seem too apparent to have required to be enforced by all those arguments which its enlightened friends, while it was depending before the people, found it necessary to urge. That principle is now universally admitted. But the question respecting the extent of the powers actually granted, is perpetually arising, and will probably continue to arise, as long as our system shall exist.

In discussing these questions, the conflicting powers of the general and state governments must be brought into view, and the supremacy of their respective laws, when they are in opposition, must be settled.

If any one proposition could command the universal assent of mankind, we might expect that it would be this: that the government of the Union, though limited in its powers, is supreme within its sphere of the Union, is supreme within its sphere of action. This would seem to result necessarily from its nature. It is the government of all; its powers are delegated by all; it represents all, and acts for all. Though any one state may be willing to control its operations, no state is willing to allow others to control them. The nation, on those subjects on which it can act, must necessarily bind its component parts. But this question is not left to mere reason: the people have, in express terms, decided it, by saying, "this Constitution, and the laws of the United States, which shall be made in pursuance thereof," "shall be the supreme law of the land," and by requiring that the members of the state legislatures, and the officers of the executive and judicial departments of the states, shall take the oath of fidelity to it.

The government of the United States, then, though limited in its powers, is supreme; and its laws, when made in pursuance of the Constitution, form the supreme law of the land, "anything in the constitution or laws of any state, to the contrary notwithstanding."

Among the enumerated powers, we do not find that of establishing a bank or creating a corporation. But there is no phrase in the instrument, which, like the Articles of Confederation, excludes incidental or implied powers; and which requires that everything granted shall be expressly and minutely described. Even the Tenth Amendment, which was framed for the purpose of quietening the excessive jealousies which had been excited, omits the word "expressly," and declares only that the powers "not delegated to the United States, nor prohibited to the States, are reserved to the States or to the people"; thus leaving the question, whether the particular power which may become the subject of contest, has been delegated to the one government, or prohibited to the other to depend on a fair construction of the whole instrument. The men who drew and adopted this amendment, had experienced the embarrassments resulting from the insertion of this word in the Articles of Confederation, and probably omitted it to avoid those embarrassments. A constitution, to contain an accurate detail of all the subdivisions of which its great powers will admit, and of all the means by which they may be carried into execution, would partake of the prolixity of a legal code, and could scarcely be embraced by the human mind. It would probably never be understood by the public. Its nature, therefore, requires, that only its great outlines should be marked, its important objects designated, and the minor ingredients which compose those objects be deduced from the nature of the objects themselves. That this idea was entertained by the Framers of the American Constitution, is not only to be inferred from the nature of the instrument, but from the language. Why else were some of the limitations, found in the ninth section of the first article, introduced? It is also, in some degree, warranted by their having omitted to use any restrictive term which might prevent its receiving a fair and just interpretation. In considering this question, then, we must never forget, that it is a constitution we are expounding.

Although, among the enumerated powers of government, we do not find the word "bank," or "incorporation," we find the great powers to lay and collect taxes; to borrow money; to regulate commerce; to declare and conduct war; and to raise and support armies and navies. The sword and the purse, all the external relations, and no inconsiderable portion of the industry of the nation, are intrusted to its government. It can never be pretended that these vast powers draw after them others of inferior importance, merely because they are inferior. Such an idea can never be advanced. But it may, with great reason, be contended, that a government, intrusted with such ample powers, on the due execution of which the happiness and prosperity of the nation so vitally depends, must also be intrusted with ample means for their execution. The power being given, it is the interest of the nation to facilitate its execution. It can never be their interest, and cannot be presumed to have been their intention, to clog and embarrass its execution by withholding the most appropriate means. Throughout this vast republic, from the St. Croix to the Gulf of Mexico, from the Atlantic to the Pacific, revenue is to be collected and expended, armies are to be marched and supported. The exigencies of the nations may require that the treasure raised in the north should be transported to the south, that raised in the east conveyed to the west, or that this order should be reversed. Is that construction of the Constitution to be preferred which would render these operations difficult, hazardous, and expensive? Can we adopt that construction (unless the words imperiously require it) which would impute to the framers of that instrument, when granting these powers for the public good, the intention of impeding their exercise by withholding a choice of means? If, indeed, such be the mandate of the Constitution, we have only to obey; but that instrument does not profess to enumerate the means by which the powers it confers may be executed; nor does it prohibit the creation of a corporation, if the existence of such a being be essential to the beneficial exercise of those powers. It is, then, the subject of fair inquiry, how far such means may be employed.

It is not denied, that the powers given to the government imply the ordinary means of execution. That, for example, of raising revenue, and applying it to national purposes, is admitted to imply the power of conveying money from place to place, as the exigencies of the nation may require, and of employing the usual means of conveyance. But it is denied that the government has its choice of means; or, that it may employ the most convenient means, if, to employ them, it be necessary to erect a corporation.

. . . The power of creating a corporation, though appertaining to sovereignty, is not, like the power of making war, or levying taxes, or of regulating commerce, a great substantive and independent power, which cannot be implied as incidental to other powers, or used as a means of executing them. It is never the end for which other powers are exercised, but a means by which other objects are accomplished. No contributions are made to charity for the sake of an incorporation, but a corporation is created to administer the charity; no seminary of learning is instituted in order to be incorporated, but the corporate character is conferred to subserve the purposes of education. No city was ever built with the sole object of being incorporated, but is incorporated as affording the best means of being well governed. The power of creating a corporation is never used for its own sake, but for the purpose of effecting something else. No sufficient reason is, therefore, perceived, why it may not pass as incidental to those powers which are expressly given, if it be a direct mode of executing them.

But the Constitution of the United States has not left the right of Congress to employ the necessary means, for the execution of the powers conferred on the government, to general reasoning. To its enumeration of powers is added that of making "all laws which shall be necessary and proper, for carrying into execution the foregoing powers, and all other powers vested by this constitution, in the government of the United States, or in any department thereof."

The counsel for the state of Maryland have urged various arguments, to prove that this clause, though in terms a grant of power, is not so in effect; but is really restrictive of the general right, which might otherwise be implied, of selecting means for executing the enumerated powers.

In support of this proposition, they have found it necessary to contend, that this clause was inserted for the purpose of conferring on Congress the power of making laws. That, without it, doubts might be entertained, whether Congress could exercise its powers in the form of legislation.

But could this be the object for which it was inserted? ... That a legislature, endowed with legislative powers, can legislate, is a proposition too self-evident to have been questioned.

But the argument on which most reliance is placed, is drawn from the peculiar language of this clause. Congress is not empowered by it to make all laws, which may have relation to the powers conferred on the government, but such only as may be "necessary and proper" for carrying them into execution. The word "necessary" is considered as controlling the whole sentence, and as limiting the right to pass laws for the execution of the granted powers, to such as are indispensable, and without which the power would be nugatory. That it excludes the choice of means, and leaves to Congress, in each case, that only which is most direct and simple.

Is it true, that this is the sense in which the word "necessary" is always used? Does it always import an absolute physical necessity, so strong, that one thing, to which another may be termed necessary, cannot exist without that other? We think it does not. If reference be had to its use, in the common affairs of the world, or in approved authors, we find that it frequently imports no more than that one thing is convenient, or useful, or essential to another. To employ the means necessary to an end, is generally understood as employing any means calculated to produce the end, and not as being confined to those single means, without which the end would be entirely unattainable. Such is the character of human language, that no word conveys to the mind, in all situations, one single definite idea; and nothing is more common than to use words in a figurative sense. Almost all compositions contain words, which, taken in their rigorous sense, would convey a meaning different from that which is obviously intended. It is essential to just construction, that many words which import something excessive, should be understood in a more mitigated sense—in that sense which common usage justifies. The word "necessary" is of this description. It has not a fixed character peculiar to itself. It admits of all degrees of comparison; and is often connected with other words, which increase or diminish the impression the mind receives of the urgency it imports. A thing may be necessary, very necessary, absolutely or indispensably necessary. To no mind would the same idea be conveyed, by these several phrases.... This word, then, like others, is used in various senses; and, in its construction, the subject, the context, the intention of the person using them, are all to be taken into view.

Let this be done in the case under consideration. The subject is the execution of those great powers on which the welfare of a nation essentially depends. It must have been the intention of those who gave these powers, to insure, as far as human prudence could insure, their beneficial execution. This could not be done by confiding the choice of means to such narrow limits as not to leave it in the power of Congress to adopt any which might be appropriate, and which were conducive to the end. This provision is made in a constitution intended to endure for ages to come, and, consequently, to be adapted to the various crises of human affairs. To have prescribed the means by which government should, in all future time, execute its powers, would have been to change, entirely, the character of the instrument, and give it the properties of a legal code. It would have been an unwise attempt to provide, by immutable rules, for exigencies which, if foreseen at all, must have been seen dimly, and which can be best provided for as they occur. To have declared that the best means shall not be used, but those alone without which the power given would be nugatory, would have been to deprive the legislature of the capacity to avail itself of experience, to exercise its reason, and to accommodate its legislation to circumstances....

But the argument which most conclusively demonstrates the error of the construction contended for by the counsel for the state of Maryland, is founded on the intention of the convention, as manifested in the whole clause. To waste time and argument in proving that, without it Congress might carry its powers into execution, would be not much less idle than to hold a lighted taper to the sun. As little can it be required to prove that in the absence of this clause, Congress would have some choice of means. That it might employ those which, in its judgment, would most advantageously effect the object to be accomplished. That any means adapted to the end, any means which tended directly to the execution of the constitutional powers of the government, were in themselves constitutional. This clause, as construed by the state of Maryland, would abridge and almost annihilate this useful and necessary right of the legislature to select its means. That this could not be intended, is, we should think, had it not been already controverted, too apparent for controversy. We think so for the following reasons:

1. The clause is placed among the powers of Congress, not among the limitations on those powers.

2. Its terms purport to enlarge, not to diminish the powers vested in the government. It purports to be an additional power, not a restriction on those already granted. No reason has been or can be assigned, for thus concealing an intention to narrow the discretion of the national legislature, under words which purport to enlarge it. The Framers of the Constitution wished its adoption, and well knew that it would be endangered by its strength, not by its weakness. Had they been capable of using language which would convey to the eye one idea, and, after deep reflection, impress on the mind another, they would rather have disguised the grant of power, than its limitation. If, then, their intention had been, by this clause, to restrain the free use of means which might otherwise have been implied, that intention would have been inserted in another place, and would have been expressed in terms resembling these: "In carrying into execution the foregoing powers, and all others," etc., "no laws shall be passed but such as are necessary and proper." Had the intention been to make this clause restrictive, it would unquestionably have been so in form as well as in effect.

The result of the most careful and attentive consideration bestowed upon this clause is, that if it does not enlarge, it cannot be construed to restrain the powers of Congress, or to impair the right of the legislature to exercise its best judgment in the selection of measures to carry into execution the constitutional powers of the government. If no other motive for its insertion can be suggested, a sufficient one is found in the desire to remove all doubts respecting the right to legislate on that vast mass of incidental powers which must be involved in the Constitution, if that instrument be not a splendid bauble.

We admit, as all must admit, that the powers of the government are limited, and that its limits are not to be transcended. But we think the sound construction of the Constitution must allow to the national legislature that discretion, with respect to the means by which the powers it confers are to be carried into execution, which will enable that body to perform the high duties assigned to it, in the manner most beneficial to the people. Let the end be legitimate, let it be within the scope of the Constitution, and all means which are appropriate, which are plainly adapted to that end, which are not prohibited, but consist with the letter and spirit of the Constitution, are constitutional. . . .

If a corporation may be employed indiscriminately with other means to carry into execution the powers of the government, no particular reason can be assigned for excluding the use of a bank, if required for its fiscal operations. To use one, must be within the discretion of Congress, if it be an appropriate mode of executing the powers of government. That it is a convenient, a useful, and essential instrument in the prosecution of its fiscal operations, is not now a subject of controversy. All those who have been concerned in the administration of our finances, have concurred in representing its importance and necessity; and so strongly have they been felt, that statesmen of the first class, whose previous opinions against it had been confirmed by every circumstance which can fix the human judgment, have yielded those opinions to the exigencies of the nation. . . .

After the most deliberate consideration, it is the unanimous and decided opinion of the Court, that the act to incorporate the Bank of the United States is a law made in pursuance of the Constitution, and is a part of the supreme law of the land. . . .

It being the opinion of the Court that the act incorporating the bank is constitutional; and that the power of establishing a branch in the state of Maryland might be properly exercised by the bank itself, we proceed to inquire: Whether the state of Maryland may, without violating the Constitution, tax that branch?

That the power of taxation is one of vital importance; that it is retained by the states; that it is not abridged by the grant of a similar power to the government of the Union; that it is to be concurrently exercised by the two governments: are truths which have never been denied. But, such is the paramount character of the Constitution, that its capacity to withdraw any subject from the action of even this power, is admitted. The states are expressly forbidden to lay any duties on imports or exports, except what may be absolutely necessary for executing their inspection laws. If the obligation of this prohibition must be conceded—if it may restrain a state from the exercise of its taxing power on imports and exports, the same paramount character would seem to restrain, as it certainly may restrain, a state from such other exercise of this power, as is in its nature incompatible with, and repugnant to, the constitutional laws of the Union. A law, absolutely repugnant to another, as entirely repeals that other as if express terms of repeal were used.

On this ground the counsel for the bank place its claim to be exempted from the power of a state to tax its operations. There is no express provision for the case, but the claim has been sustained on a principle which so entirely pervades the Constitution, is so intermixed with the materials which compose it, so interwoven with its web, so blended with its texture, as to be incapable of being separated from it, without rending it into shreds.

This great principle is, that the Constitution and the laws made in pursuance thereof are supreme; that they control the constitution and laws of the respective states, and cannot be controlled by them. From this, which may be almost termed an axiom, other propositions are deduced as corollaries, on the truth or error of which, and on their application to this case, the cause has been supposed to depend. These are, 1. That a power to create implies a power to preserve. 2. That a power to destroy, if wielded by a different hand, is hostile to, and incompatible with, these powers to create and preserve. 3. That where this repugnancy exists, that authority which is supreme must control, not yield to that over which it is supreme. . . .

The power of Congress to create, and of course to continue, the bank, was the subject of the preceding part of this opinion; and is no longer to be considered as questionable.

That the power of taxing it by the states may be exercised so as to destroy it, is too obvious to be denied. But taxation is said to be an absolute power, which acknowledges no other limits than those expressly prescribed in the Constitution, and like sovereign power of every other description, is trusted to the discretion of those who use it ....

The argument on the part of the state of Maryland, is, not that the states may directly resist a law of Congress, but that they may exercise their acknowledged powers upon it, and that the Constitution leaves them this right in the confidence that they will not abuse it....

That the power to tax involves the power to destroy; that the power to destroy may defeat and render useless the power to create; that there is a plain repugnance, in conferring on one government a power to control the constitutional measures of another, which other, with respect to those very measures, is declared to be supreme over that which exerts the control, are propositions not to be denied. But all inconsistencies are to be reconciled by the magic of the word CONFIDENCE. Taxation, it is said, does not necessarily and unavoidably destroy. To carry it to the excess of destruction would be an abuse, to presume which, would banish that confidence which is essential to all government.

But is this a case of confidence? Would the people of any one state trust those of another with a power to control the most insignificant operations of their state government? We know they would not. Why, then, should we suppose that the people of any one state should be willing to trust those of another with a power to control the operations of a government to which they have confided their most important and most valuable interests? In the legislature of the Union alone, are all represented. The legislature of the Union alone, therefore, can be trusted by the people with the power of controlling measures which concern all, in the confidence that it will not be abused. This, then, is not a case of confidence, and we must consider it as it really is.

If we apply the principle for which the state of Maryland contends, to the Constitution generally, we shall find it capable of changing totally the character of that instrument. We shall find it capable of arresting all the measures of the government, and of prostrating it at the foot of the states. The American people have declared their Constitution, and the laws made in pursuance thereof, to be supreme; but this principle would transfer the supremacy, in fact, to the state.

If the states may tax one instrument, employed by the government in the execution of its powers, they may tax any and every other instrument. They may tax the mail; they may tax the mint; they may tax patent rights; they may tax the papers of the custom-house; they may tax judicial process; they may tax all the means employed by the government, to an excess which would defeat all the ends of government. This was not intended by the American people. They did not design to make their government dependent on the states. . . .

It has also been insisted, that, as the power of taxation in the general and state governments is acknowledged to be concurrent, every argument which would sustain the right of the general government to tax banks chartered by the states, will equally sustain the right of the states to tax banks chartered by the general government.

But the two cases are not on the same reason. The people of all the states have created the general government, and have conferred upon it the general power of taxation. The people of all the states, and the states themselves, are represented in Congress, and, by their representatives, exercise this power. When they tax the chartered institutions of the states, they tax their constituents; and these taxes must be uniform. But when a state taxes the operations of the government of the United States, it acts upon institutions created, not by their own constituents, but by people over whom they claim no control. It acts upon the measures of a government created by others as well as themselves, for the benefit of others in common with themselves. The difference is that which always exists, and always must exist, between the action of the whole on a part, and the action of a part on the whole— between the laws of a government declared to be supreme, and those of a government which, when in opposition to those laws, is not supreme.

But if the full application of this argument could be admitted, it might bring into question the right of Congress to tax the state banks, and could not prove the right of the states to tax the Bank of the United States.

The Court has bestowed on this subject its most deliberate consideration. The result is a conviction that the states have no power, by taxation or otherwise, to retard, impede, burden, or in any manner control, the operations of the constitutional laws enacted by Congress to carry into execution the powers vested in the general government. This is, we think, the unavoidable consequence of that supremacy which the Constitution declared.

We are unanimously of opinion, that the law passed by the legislature of Maryland, imposing a tax on the Bank of the United States, is unconstitutional and void.

This opinion does not deprive the states of any resources which they originally possessed. It does not extend to a tax paid by the real property of the bank, in common with the other real property within the state, nor to a tax imposed on the interest which the citizens of Maryland may hold in this institution, in common with other property of the same description throughout the state. But this is a tax on the operations of the bank, and is, consequently, a tax on the operation of an instrument employed by the government of the Union to carry its powers into execution. Such a tax must be unconstitutional. . . .

7. The Enduring Features of American Federalism

Martha Derthick

In their ongoing dialogue with the federal government, the states are increasingly asserting their role as vital units in the process of governance. In this article published in 1989 in *The Brookings Review*—a publication of the seventy-five-year-old Washington, D.C., research organization, the Brookings Institution—Martha Derthick discusses the reasons for this changing position. Derthick, a professor of government and foreign affairs at the University of Virginia, then moves on to examine some of the "elemental and enduring truths of American federalism" that account for the states' fluctuating power over the years in relation to Congress and the federal government, as well as the means by which a greater independence has been achieved.

It is a commonplace of scholarship that American federalism constantly changes. And it is a commonplace of contemporary comment that the states are enjoying a renaissance. Their historic role as laboratories of experiment is acknowledged with praise. Their executives and legislatures are increasingly active, seizing issues, such as economic development, that the federal government has failed to come to grips with. State courts are staking out positions on individual rights in advance of those defined by the U.S. Supreme Court, while state attorneys general pursue consumer protection and antitrust cases that federal agencies have ignored. The states' share of government revenue has gained slightly on that of the federal government in the 1980s, and considerably surpasses that of local governments, contrary to a pattern that prevailed until the 1960s. The states' standing with the public and with prospective employees has improved. The governors are getting their share of good press and, what may be almost as important, of presidential nominations. As a result, state governments are perceived to have improved their position in the federal system.

Yet it is worth recalling how different the impression was but a short time ago, and how little has changed in some respects. Early in 1984 the Advisory Commission on Intergovernmental Relations published a much-noticed report, *Regulatory Federalism*, detailing a wide range of new or expanded federal controls over state government. In 1985, in the case of *Garcia* v. *San Antonio Metropolitan Transit Authority*, the Supreme Court declined to protect the state governments from congressional regulation under the Constitution's commerce clause and then washed its hands of this crucial federalism question. In the spring of 1988 the court removed the constitutional prohibition on federal taxation of income from interest on state and local government bonds (*South Carolina* v. *Baker*).

Certain regulatory excesses of the federal government vis-a-vis the states have been modified in the past several years; rules regarding transportation of the disabled and bilingual education are two examples. Yet not even under Ronald Reagan did the federal government step back from the new constitutional frontiers mapped out in the last decade or two—frontiers such as the Clean Air Act of 1970, which addresses the states with the language of outright command (Each state shall . . . ''). The president's executive order of October 1987 on federalism may be interpreted as an attempt to draw back, with its rhetorical statement of federalism principles and its instructions to executive agencies to refrain from using their discretion to preempt state action. But to read it is to be reminded of how little unilateral power the president has. The drawing back can succeed only to the extent the national legislature and courts concur. Nor did the Reagan administration consistently adhere to its professed principles. Substantive policy goals often were in tension with devolution of power to the states; the Reagan administration could be counted on to opt for devolution only when that tactic was consistent with its pursuit of a freer market and lower federal spending.

American federalism is a very large elephant indeed, and it is hard for a lone observer to grasp the properties of the whole beast. One needs to be abreast of constitutional doctrines; of legislative, judicial, and administrative practices of the whole range of government activities, from taxation to protection of civil liberties to pollution control; of the development or disintegration of political parties (are they decaying at the grass roots? at the center? both? neither?); of the volume and locus of interest group activity; of trends in public opinion and public employment, and more. To understand the condition of federalism, one needs to comprehend the functioning of the whole polity.

Granting that the federal system is always in flux, it is harder than one might suppose even to detect the dominant tendencies. While most academic analysts probably would assert that centralization is the secular trend, such distinguished scholars as Princeton political scientist Richard P. Nathan and Brandeis historian Morton Keller have argued that centralization is not inexorable and that the evolution of American federalism follows a cyclical pattern, with the federal government and the states alternately dominating.

Mapping the Terrain

Fighting the customary temptation to concentrate on change, I want to try to identify some elemental and enduring truths of American federalism. I want to map the features of the terrain, a metaphor that may be in fact apt. Our federalism is much like a piece of earth that is subject to constant redevelopment. It can be bulldozed and built up, flattened and regraded, virtually beyond recognition. Yet certain elemental properties of it, the bedrock and the composition of the soil, endure. I will start with propositions that I take to be purely factual and then proceed to others that are more analytical and normative, hence debatable.

The states are governments in their own right. They have constitutions that derive from the people and guarantee specific rights. They have elected legislatures that make laws, elected executives that enforce laws, and courts that interpret them—and not incidentally interpret the laws of the United States as well. State governments levy taxes. Their territorial integrity is protected by the U.S. Constitution, which also guarantees them equal representation in the Senate and a republican form of government. These creatures that walk like ducks and squawk like ducks must be ducks.

Nevertheless, the states are inferior governments. In our pond, they are the weaker ducks. The stubbornly persistent mythology that governments in the American federal system are coordinate should not obscure that fact. The two levels of government are *not* coordinate and equal, nor did the winning side in 1787 intend them to be. One cannot deny the existence of the Constitution's supremacy clause and the prescription that state officers take an oath to uphold the Constitution of the United States, or the fact that the framers of the Constitution fully expected an instrumentality of the federal government, the Supreme Court, to settle jurisdictional issues in the "compound republic," as James Madison called it. See *Federalist* No. 39, in which Madison makes a feeble, unsuccessful attempt to deny that the court's having this function gives the federal government a crucial advantage.

Whether the federal government has always been superior in fact can certainly be debated. At various times and places its writ did not run very strong. Ours was a different system in the 19th century, and it is significant that the full impact on federalism of the post-Civil War Amendments on civil rights was long delayed. Only recently has the South ceased to have a deviant social system. But on the whole, the federal government has won the crucial conflicts. Surely its ascendancy is not currently in dispute. Not only are the states treated as its administrative agents; they accept such treatment as a fact of life. Not since *Brown* v. *Board of Education* (1954) and *Baker* v. *Carr* (1962) have truly strenuous protests been heard from the states against their palpably inferior status.

The states' status as governments, even though inferior ones, gives Congress a range of choice in dealing with them. It may choose deference, displacement, or interdependence. In domestic affairs Congress always has the option of doing nothing, knowing that the states can act whether or not it does. Sometimes Congress consciously defers to the states, judging that the subject properly "belongs" to them. Perhaps just as often, Congress today is not deliberately deferential but fails to act for lack of time or the ability to reach agreement. It defaults. The area of congressional inaction, be it through deference or default, is reliable quite large. It normally includes new issues, such as AIDS or comparable worth. States remain on the front lines of domestic policy, the first to deal with newly perceived problems. Congress tends to defer or default on particularly difficult issues, such as the amount of support to be given to needy single mothers with children.

Congress rarely employs its second option, complete displacement, although explicit invocations of it, using the term "preemption," are more frequent now than they used to be. The third option, interdependence, is very common, I would think predominant. Through some combination of inducements, sanctions, or contractual agreements, Congress enters into collaborative arrangements with the states in the pursuit of national ends. The most common techniques are conditional grants-in-aid, which are characteristic of programs for income support and infrastructure development, and qualified preemptions, which are typical of the "new" regulation, including environmental protection and occupational health and safety. Congress sets standards but tells states that if they meet or exceed the national standards, they may retain the function, including administration.

The vigor and competence with which state governments perform functions left to them does not protect them against congressional incursions. Here I mean to challenge one of the leading canards of American federalism. Whenever Congress takes domestic action, that action is rationalized as a response to the failures of the states. Congress has had to step in, it is said, because states were not doing the job. The only thing one can safely say about the origins of nationalizing acts is that they are responses to the power of nationalizing coalitions. When Congress acts, in other words, it is not necessarily because states have failed; it is because advocates of national action have succeeded in mustering enough political force to get their way. State inaction may constitute part of their case, but state actions that are offensive to their interests may do so as well. Pathbreaking states have often demonstrated what can be done.

Congress's usual choice, moreover, is to cooperate with the states, not to displace them, and in the relationships of mutual dependence that result, it is a nice question just whose deficiencies are being compensated for. The federal government typically contributes uniform standards and maybe money. The states typically do the work of carrying out the function. The more they do and the better they do it, the more they are likely to be asked or ordered by Congress to do.

In cooperating with the states, Congress again has a choice. It can emphasize their status as governments, or it can emphasize their inferiority as such. Our ambiguous constitutional system enables Congress to view the states as equals or as agents. Congress gradually has abandoned the former view in favor of the latter. It has done so with the acquiescence of the Supreme Court, which once tried to defend "dual federalism—that is, the notion that the states were sovereign, separate, and equal—but which has long since abandoned that doctrine. And Congress does not indulge its agents. Ask any federal bureau chief. Congress is very poor at balancing the ends and means of action. All major federal executive agencies—the Environmental Protection Agency, the Social Security Administration, the Immigration and Naturalization Service, to cite just a few—are laboring under a burden of excessive obligation.

Because states are governments, they may bargain with Congress. Bargaining is the usual mode of intergovernmental relations. State governments, even when treated by Congress as administrative agents, are agents with a difference. Unlike federal executive agencies, they are not Congress's creatures. Therefore they can talk back to it. They can influence the terms of cooperation.

This bargaining between levels of governments is good, depending on how the states use it. Here again I mean to challenge what I take to be a conventional view. Fragmentation of authority in the federal system is ordinarily portrayed, at least in academic literature, as a severe handicap to the federal government's pursuit of its goals. The federal government would be more effective, it is commonly said, if it did not have to rely so heavily on other governments. I believe, to the contrary, that the federal government needs a great deal of help, of a kind that can best be supplied—perhaps can only be supplied—by governments. It needs help with all aspects of governing, that is, with all the functions that legislatures, courts, and executives perform. Beyond that, it needs a great deal of help quite specifically in adjusting its goals to social and economic realities and to the capacities of administrative organizations.

Madison may be cited in support of this view—not the famous passage in *Federalist* No. 51 that one might anticipate, in which he argues that "the different governments will control each other, at the same time that each will be controlled by itself," but a passage less remarked, yet perhaps more prescient, in No. 62. In this essay on the Senate, Madison wrote: "A good government implies two things: first, fidelity to the object of government, which is the happiness of the people; secondly, a knowledge of the means by which that object can be best attained. Some governments are deficient in both these qualities; most governments are deficient in the first. I scruple not to assert, that in American governments too little attention has been paid to the last."

The deficiency in our attention to the means of government has never been more glaring. All institutions of the federal government—Congress, presidency, courts—have far more to do than they can do, but the executive agencies as the instruments of government action are arguably the most overburdened of all. Perhaps even more glaring today than the federal government's shortfall of institutional capacity is its shortfall of fiscal capacity. It has obligations far in excess of its willingness or ability to meet them. Whether that is a product of party politics or has other causes need not concern us here. The fact of the deficit is plain enough.

State governments help fill the federal government's performance gaps. They do much of the work of governing, as Madison anticipated. Even as an ardent nationalist, at the time of the Constitutional Convention, he held to the view that the national government would not be suited to the entire task of governing "so great an extent of country, and over so great a variety of objects." Just how right he was has never been clearer. But if the states help fill the federal government's implementation gaps, they also are very much at risk of being victimized by them. Congress will try to close the distance between what it wants and what the federal government is able to do independently by ordering the states to do it.

An Appeal to Talk Back

The states are entitled to talk back. As governments in their own right, they have an independent responsibility to set priorities and balance means against ends. Because they are closer to the practical realities of domestic problems and because they lack the power to respond to deficits by printing money, state governments are in a superior position to do that balancing.

This appeal to the states to talk back is not a call to defiance, but a call to engage federal officials in a policy dialogue—and, having done so, to address those officials with language suitable to governments. If states habitually present themselves as supplicants for assistance—supplicants like any other interest group—they will inevitably contribute to the erosion of their own status.

I believe that the states *are* increasingly using the language of governments, rather than supplicants, in their dialogue with the federal government. The enactment in 1988 of welfare reform legislation, which a working group of the National Governors Association helped to shape, is an example. The governors drew on the state governments' experience with welfare programs to fashion changes that would be both politically and administratively feasible, besides containing improved assurances of federal funding for welfare.

There are numerous explanations for the new, more authoritative voice of the states. One is that individually the states have heightened competence and self-confidence as governments, whatever the range among them (and the range between, say, Virginia and Louisiana is very great). Another is that the decline of federal aid under Presidents Carter and Reagan has compelled greater independence. A third is that self-consciousness and cohesion of the states as a class of governments have increased, as indicated by the development of organized, well-staffed mechanisms of cooperation. Their shared status as agents of Congress and objects of its influence has caused the states to cooperate with one another today to a degree unprecedented in history, even if they remain intensely competitive in some respects, such as the pursuit of economic development.

I have concentrated on relations between the states and Congress to keep the subject focused and relatively simple. But the federal judiciary rivals the legislature as a framer of federal-state relations. Federal courts, like Congress, can choose to emphasize the states' standing as governments or their inferiority as such. Like Congress, over time the courts have come to favor the latter choice, so that states today are routinely commanded to implement the detailed policy decisions of national courts as well as the national legislature.

For the states, it is one thing to talk back to Congress, quite another and much harder thing to talk back to the federal courts. Yet here as well, they have been trying to find ways to talk back more effectively. The National Association of Attorneys General and the State and Local Legal Center, both with offices in Washington, now offer advice and assistance to state and local governments involved in litigation before the Supreme Court. Such governments in the past have often suffered from a lack of expert counsel.

It is no use to portray these developments in federal-state relations as a transgression of the framers' intentions, at least if we take the *Federalist* as our authoritative guide to those intentions. Alexander Hamilton foresaw with evident satisfaction the federal-state relation that obtains today. In *Federalist* No. 27, he wrote that "the plan reported by the convention, by extending the authority of the federal head to the individual citizens of the several States, will enable the government to employ the ordinary magistracy of each, in the execution of its laws. . . .

Thus the legislatures, courts, and magistrates, of the respective [states], will be incorporated into the operations of the national government . . . and will be rendered auxiliary to the enforcement of its laws." This is exactly what has happened.

What Hamilton would certainly not be satisfied with, however, is the federal government's management of its own administrative and fiscal affairs. One therefore feels entitled to invoke Madison on the states' behalf. It is not enough today that the states help the national government with governing, the function that both Hamilton and Madison foresaw. It is important as well that they perform a modern version of the balancing function that Madison in particular foresaw. This requires that in their policy dialogue with the federal government they assert, as governments in their own right, the importance of balancing ends and means.

8. The Changing Face of Federalism

John Kincaid

In this 1987 article from *State Legislature*, published by the National Conference of State Legislatures, John Kincaid discusses the changing world economy and examines whether it has contributed to what he calls "competitive federalism," in which the federal government and the states are shifting roles. Kincaid is director of research at the U.S. Advisory Commission on Intergovernmental Relations, on leave from North Texas State University where he is a professor of political science. Kincaid pinpoints fiscal pressure as the major source of conflict and competition between the states and the federal government during the 1980s. He calls for a renewed emphasis on the classic idea of federalism as a partnership in order to tackle the problems facing the United States.

A sharp exchange between White House aide Gary L. Bauer and Hartford, Conn. Mayor Thirman L. Milner at the January 1987 meeting of the U.S. Conference of Mayors captured the mood of what may be a new era in American federalism. Mayor Milner had suggested that the Reagan administration cut defense spending in order to save money for domestic programs, such as drug abuse education. "I don't have any time for Pentagon-bashing," replied Bauer, "and don't sit in your cities and tell us what our budget should be."

Will such harsh exchanges vanish with a new administration? Probably not. A new administration may soften the rhetoric, but with a $2 trillion national debt and record trade deficits ($169.8 billion in 1986), the federal government can no longer ride to the rescue with a full complement of cavalry. Indeed, the states may have to rescue the federal government occasionally, as they have, to some extent, in international trade. Without state export initiatives, the trade deficit would be higher.

A number of developments have contributed to the rise of what might be called "competitive federalism" in the 1980s. One of the most significant has been the profound change in the world economy.

When the U.S. economy was dominant, it was common to speak of state and local economies as "little" economies, almost wholly dependent upon the fortunes of the national economy. "What can we do?" asked state and local officials. "We are, as in the Great Depression, powerless to act against national economic forces." Consequently, state and local officials turned to the federal government for relief from economic distress.

But now the U.S. economy is no longer able, even if willing, to bail out states and localities in every instance. The U.S. economy and its state and local economies must all compete against powerful foreign economic forces. As a result, the federal government cannot fine-tune the nation's economy the way it once thought it could when the U.S. economy drove the world. The U.S. government is no longer a nearly autonomous decision maker. Today, it too must cope with powerful external economic forces, just as state and local governments have always had to do.

This is a significant development for federalism because one of the great forces behind the expansion of federal power in this century was the assumption that the nationalization of the economy by big business and interstate commerce required an ever greater policymaking role for the federal government. Many Americans also assumed that the strength of the economy would support equally strong domestic and foreign policy initiatives by the federal government. The United States could, as President Lyndon B. Johnson believed, have an abundance of both "guns and butter." Now, however, the internationalization of the U.S. economy and the weakening of its competitive position suggest that we can no longer rely on those assumptions. All three governments—federal, state and local—must carve out new roles for themselves.

The relevant economic actors for the states today are not only other states, the federal government and big business, but also other prosperous countries like Japan and West Germany. Similarly, the nation's great cities must compete with other great cities like Hong Kong, Tokyo,

Frankfurt and London, just as American farmers must now compete with farmers in Europe, Asia and Latin America.

Change in the way America does business at home and abroad will, therefore, require changes in our understanding of the federal system. Specifically, cooperation and coordination—the classic idea of federalism as a partnership—will have to be given renewed emphasis, however adverse the circumstances. Most important, we will have to abandon the hierarchical idea that federalism is a system of "levels" of government, with the national government being the top level—a kind of command and control center—and state and local governments being lower levels. Such a view in today's economic and fiscal climate can lead to institutional paralysis and missed opportunities as "lower level" officials wait for funds or signals from "above."

Citizens who looked for competence, energy and reform in the American political system once turned to the national government. But now that the federal government has its own problems and can no longer claim superior competence in every field, citizens must look to the states for bold action on many fronts.

Fortunately, nearly all of the states have improved their ability to govern in recent years. Many states are bigger, more robust and more competent than many of the world's independent nations. Hence, most states have the ability to govern effectively, even if the will to do so lags behind occasionally.

Furthermore, one of the ironies of the new world economic competition is that it has demonstrated the potential power of "little" economies. If small countries like Japan and tiny places like Singapore can become powerful actors in the world economy, why can't states do the same? Indeed, they can, and many are trying to do so. . . . This is not to say that a state can or should go it alone, but that the normal reflex of looking to the federal government should be replaced by one that looks more to self-governance, and that may, on occasion, even ask the federal government to get out of the way of state initiatives.

For the immediate future, though, we are likely to see heightened conflict as federal, state and local officials learn how to cope with new domestic and international challenges. Several other factors will also add friction to intergovernmental relations.

For one, constitutional issues have occupied an unusually prominent place in discussions of federalism during the past several years. There are four reasons for this.

First, the bicentennial of the U.S. Constitution has stimulated interest in constitutionalism, including state constitutions. After all, state constitutions came first; Massachusetts has the oldest (1780) written constitution still in effect in the world today.

Second, the Reagan administration made it a point to raise constitutional questions about the current condition of federalism. In May 1986,

President Reagan signed a statement of federalism principles developed by his Domestic Policy Council. However, the administration [did not make] much legislative and judicial progress on its "new federalism" agenda. In a number of areas, such as the regulation of truck weights and sizes, the administration ignored its federalist objections to "big government." Furthermore, the federal government continues to impose mandates, especially mandates without money, on the states.

Third, the U.S. Supreme Court sent a shock wave through the federal system by its 1985 ruling in *Garcia vs. San Antonio Metropolitan Transit Authority*, which overturned *National League of Cities vs. Usery* (1976). In *Garcia*, the Court majority essentially said that it would not protect state interests against congressional exercise of the interstate commerce power. Instead, said the Court, the states must look to the political processes of federalism to protect their interests. Although Justice William Rehnquist, one of the dissenters, predicted that *Garcia* would be overturned in the future, for the time being the *Garcia* decision promises to inject more competition into the system as the Court diminishes its role as "umpire" and as states seek to use the political process to further their interests against the federal government, interest groups and each other.

Fourth, fiscal issues have sparked constitutional controversies as well. Thirty-two states have petitioned the Congress to call a constitutional convention to consider a balanced budget amendment. Furthermore, in what may be one of the most bizarre episodes in American constitutional history, an amendment to prohibit members of Congress from giving themselves an immediate pay raise, which was approved by the First Congress in 1789 but ratified by only six states, has been revived for ratification because the First Congress set no limit on the ratification period. The 1789 amendment has now been ratified by 18 states, and [more] are expected to consider ratification [in future years].

During the past decade, there has also emerged a "new judicial federalism," one that has seen state high courts place a greater emphasis on their state constitutions. For example, in a growing number of cases, state high courts have relied on independent interpretations of their state bill of rights to extend greater protections to citizens than those provided by U.S. Supreme Court interpretations of the U.S. Bill of Rights. Such state judicial activism is likely to introduce still greater diversity and competitive "forum shopping" in the federal system.

Another factor adding friction to the federal system is the "guns vs. butter" debate. The intensity of debates during the past several years over federal funding for defense vs. clean water, community development, roads and highways, education, welfare and other domestic programs indicates that the ancient competition between guns and butter may have caught up with the American people for the first time in their history. Americans have no prior experience with a need to make such tradeoffs in peacetime. Consequently, insofar as defense spending is less economically productive than domestic spending, and insofar as defense needs drain resources from domestic needs, continued friction is likely between federal officials who want to spend more on guns and state and local officials who want to spend more on butter.

More generally, fiscal pressure has become a major source of intergovernmental conflict and competition during the [1990s]. Federal aid to state and local governments has declined. The huge federal deficit, coupled with a still sluggish economy, has tightened the fiscal screws on policymakers. More pressure will be added if, as projected, federal tax reform results in a net loss of revenue for the federal government next year. Federal tax reform has also required governors and legislators in most states to face some difficult taxing and spending issues this year.

At the same time, a new kind of fiscal debate has emerged. This is the question of whether more government spending results in better policy. During the 1960s' era of affluence, it became common to measure policy efforts in dollar amounts, in what might be called the fiscal version of the Vietnam syndrome: namely, the more fiscal firepower you direct at a problem, the more likely you are to solve it.

After some 20 years of hefty spending on health, education and welfare, however (to say nothing about defense) many citizens are wondering why Johnny still can't read, why the poor are still with us in large numbers and why the United States ranks 17th in the world in infant mortality. While research results are mixed, considerable evidence suggests, for instance, that there is no necessary relationship between spending per se and the quality of education.

Here the states may be leading the way. Constitutional and statutory constraints on taxing and spending more or less compel state officials to think carefully about public priorities. Hence, while states have increased spending for education in recent years, they have also placed unusual emphasis on institutional and procedural reforms. Attention to such matters as merit pay, teacher competency and education, classroom discipline, parent-school cooperation and the quality of leadership provided by school principals seems to reflect a renewed understanding that a critical factor in public policy is not how much money is spent, but how it is spent. Whether the recent round of education reforms will work remains to be seen; nevertheless, many state officials recognize that, as in war, victory is not assured by superior firepower, but by such things as intelligence, planning, strategy, flexibility and morale.

Similarly, states are likely to be called upon during the next several years to design new institutional approaches to welfare services without substantial increases in funding. Most of the major national proposals for welfare reform call for greater work requirements for recipients, greater efforts to require absent fathers to provide financial support for their children, greater emphasis on alleviating the problems of teen-age pregnancy and parenthood and a greater effort to coordinate the nation's many means-tested programs into coherent packages sensitive to local conditions.

While many states have already begun to address these issues, any action by the federal government is likely to be accompanied by a call for the states to serve as experimental laboratories. State and local officials, however, are concerned about whether the federal government will provide incentives for innovation, and more funding or at least a minimum level of income support for the poor in all states. Will welfare reform be coupled with reductions in funding for other domestic programs, and will it require greater state fiscal participation? That could lead to greater differences between the states, greater migration of the poor from low-benefit to high-benefit states, and greater interstate competition.

In most states, welfare and education reforms have been linked to economic development. It is in this realm especially that we have seen increased competition between the states—competitive federalism without Washington, so to speak. The major question here is whether states will be tempted to pursue "beggar thy neighbor" policies that will, in the long run, harm all. Indeed, another great motivation for the expansion of federal power in this century was a desire to reduce disparities between the states and, in the process, reduce and moderate competition between them. Reductions in federal aid and the turning back of federal programs to states, even if accompanied by revenue sources, are therefore likely to heighten interstate competition.

In many respects, the debate over competition in the federal system boils down to questions of equity and efficiency. Those who advocate cooperative federalism, with a powerful interstate equalizing role for the federal government, maintain that equity is the litmus test of good polity. Those who advocate competitive federalism, with a relatively weak domestic role for the federal government, maintain that competition improves efficiency, thereby producing better public services at lower cost. If competition is beneficial in business, sports, courtrooms and elections, it may also be good in government. Competition, according to its advocates, will keep state and local officials on their toes and make them more attentive to citizen preferences.

State and local officials, of course, worry that competition could degenerate into mindless competition that beggars one's neighbors and leads to overly generous concessions to business that only hurt the state. Legislators seem to be especially concerned about the effects of tax rates on the location decisions of business and industry. Most of the research, however, indicates that while tax rates are important, they are often not the most important factor in location decisions. Instead, such factors as access to robust markets, efficient transportation, skilled labor, cost-effective energy, good public services and amenities are frequently more important.

Furthermore, what is often overlooked is that most businesses are small to medium in size and that these businesses create many new jobs. The location decisions of small and medium-size businesses are often affected by very personal factors, rather than tax rates alone, such as whether the owner grew up in the state, whether the owner likes a particular community, whether the owner has family and friends nearby and whether the owner feels that there is good police and fire protection.

This suggests that competition can be handled in ways that improve the quality of life in every state. Such competition will require cooperation and negotiated understandings among the states about rules and ethics. While super-competition among states for big business installations has garnered the most headlines, states have found many ways to cooperate on these matters. Even abroad, for example, members of the Council of States in Europe have developed informal rules of competition along with mechanisms of cooperation.

Indeed, increasingly, the critical problem is not so much one state raiding another state for business, but other nations raiding the United States for business. This raises the competitive stakes for the states, and calls for action by individual states as well as coordination among the governments in the federal system.

Still another basic issue in the debate over competitive federalism, one related to economic development, is who should make decisions, and in what fields—national majorities or coalitions of minorities acting through the Congress, or 50 different state majorities acting through their own legislatures? Which mechanism best expresses citizen preferences and which, therefore, is more democratic? Needless to say, these questions go to the heart of federalism. However, as state legislatures assume more policy responsibilities, greater diversity is likely to arise among the states as they pursue different goals and policy options.

Although it is dangerous to draw analogies from other fields, one of the basic principles of modern biology is that genetic diversity and biochemical individuality are essential to the survival of the species, in part because diversity promotes adaptation to change. Many observers have argued that the same principle applies to society. Social diversity promotes progress and adaptation to change. In this regard, federalism is a form of government uniquely qualified to preserve diversity within bounds of unity as well.

Although neither side is likely to win the debate decisively, the debate over competition and cooperation does help to sharpen our thinking about federalism and pubic policy. The federal system has been a remarkably resilient form of government, one that has allowed the United States to be the first continental-size polity in the history of the world to be governed in a reasonably free and democratic manner—for 200 years. Understanding federalism in light of old principles and new challenges can allow the present generation to make beneficial use of that resiliency.

9. Those Maddening Mandates

Elaine S. Knapp

With the national government strapped for money because of huge fiscal deficits, members of Congress have initiated or expanded programs by mandating that states and localities carry out their initiatives. Moreover, federal lawmakers often fail to provide any revenue for these programs. Elaine Knapp, who is managing editor of *State Government News*, where this article was published in 1990, discusses the frustration that states feel in implementing unwanted federal mandates.

When federal highway officials ordered Colerain Township to take down many of its stop signs, residents worried about safety called Ohio Sen. Stanley Aronoff, who represents the Cincinnati-area township. "It's one of the largest townships in Ohio with nearly 60,000 people and I think I heard from all of them," Aronoff says. While there were more signs than could be justified under federal uniform traffic rules, township trustees listened to public fears about speeding drivers and kept the signs up. Choosing to take a cautious rather than standard approach to road safety, trustees told the feds to take the signs down themselves. So far they are still standing.

Not all such bouts with the federal government over intrusive demands turn out so serendipitously.

"Federal mandates that require a state to take specific actions that cost a lot of money or punish the state by withholding federal funds are a major frustration for state legislatures," says Aronoff, president of the Ohio Senate. He calls federal mandates maddening and many other state officials agree.

Money is a major issue. "The feds put burdens on states without providing the funding," says Kansas Rep. Bill Reardon, assistant minority leader.

Federal social services mandates cost Kansas an estimated $100 million a year, according to Sen. Majority Leader Fred Kerr, who says the state even formed a task force to deal with the problem.

Maryland Sen. Barbara Hoffman says, "The worst mandates are the ones that come without any money, for example, Medicaid."

States are expected to shell out $2.5 billion in fiscal 1991 just for Medicaid expansions Congress passed in the last three years, according to the National Governors' Association. That's in addition to the $34.2 billion states spent on Medicaid this year.

"Medicaid funding is breaking our budget," says Colorado Sen. Bill Owens.

States are struggling to make ends meet. In an unusual move for an election year, nearly half the states raised taxes this year, including highly visible sales and income taxes.

Medicaid mandates are straining New Hampshire's bare-bones budget, says Rep. Donna Sytek. "There are few options. Medicaid is going to be a real burden."

State leaders also say the federal government takes away their power to decide how to spend taxpayer funds. "Congress is setting priorities for the states," says Ann Lichtner, director of intergovernmental relations for the North Carolina Department of Administration.

North Carolina had to pay catastrophic Medicare benefits for people at the poverty level, without the option of spending the money on poorer people on Medicaid. "We might have preferred to raise benefits for those who were poorer," Lichtner says.

Badly timed federal demands also wreak havoc on state budgets, as happened when Congress in late 1989 ordered Medicaid expansions by April 1, 1990. "States were already into their budgets and there was no time to prepare," she says.

States also resent the federal penchant for walking out on programs, leaving state and local governments to pick up the tab. "Congress is the greatest at mandating legislation and then cutting funding," says Virginia Sen. John Chichester.

Minnesota Rep. Phyllis Kahn says the feds pulled out before paying their share for a Minneapolis sewer system. That left the state and city paying for federally required separate systems for street runoff and sewage disposal.

Federal sewer mandates also keep small towns from trying innovative water treatment methods that might cost less and work better, according to Kahn. "I'm upset about mandates that don't allow flexibility or creativity. I'm a firm believer in the idea of states as laboratories of democracy," she says.

Kahn blames pressure from industry for pre-emption of state and local governments. "It's easier to get standards industry can live with at the federal level and 50 different standards."

But, federal ceilings on state environmental standards can smother progressive solutions, according to Kahn. She cites Minnesota's battle for tougher restrictions on radioactive releases as an example of how states sometimes need to be stricter than the federal government. Even though the state lost its fight in court, the federal government eventually raised its standard to Minnesota's level.

Nebraska Sen. Chris Abboud agrees that states don't need to be told what to do by a Big Brother federal government. "The closer government is to the people, the better able it is to meet their needs," Abboud says.

Abboud also views the federal increases in gasoline, alcohol and other excise taxes as an intrusion into the states' domain.

The federal government also is taking away state powers and adding to state costs by changing the tax exempt status of state and local bonds, according to Wyoming Treasurer Stan Smith. Federal regulations make it difficult for states to finance housing and other public purpose projects, Smith says.

Most state officials are not optimistic that the federal government will change its ways. Complaints to federal officials usually have little effect. "Typically we get a sympathetic ear, but it doesn't change," says Kerr of Kansas.

The state view of federal mandates also seems unlikely to change. Of mandates in general, Sytek of New Hampshire speaks for many frustrated state leaders when she says, "I don't like any of them."

10. Welfare Reform: The Issue That Bubbled Up from the States to Capitol Hill

Julie Rovner

The passage of a new welfare act in 1988 created an historic partnership between the states and the federal government. To an unprecedented degree, governors and other state officials played a major role in crafting the legislation that brought about the first major overhaul of the nation's welfare laws in half a century. In this article published in *Governing* in 1988, Julie Rovner, who covers health and welfare issues for the *Congressional Quarterly*, documents the governors' bipartisan crusade for welfare reform that eventually won support on Capitol Hill.

The rhetoric surrounding enactment of the new federal welfare law focused on how it would create a new relationship between welfare recipients and the governments that help them. But the unprecedented participation of governors and other state officials in crafting the reforms also justifies the argument that it creates a new relationship between the states and the federal government as well.

"This was a historic partnership, and I can only hope that we'll see more of it in the future," said Democratic Governor Bill Clinton of Arkansas, co-chairman of the National Governors' Association working group on welfare reform and a key player in making the new welfare law a reality.

"This is an indication of the new federalism," said Republican Governor Michael N. Castle of Delaware, Clinton's co-chairman. "It's a policy that actually began at the state level and then bubbled up to the federal level, as opposed to almost any health and social service policy in the last 50 years, which started at the federal level and went back down." Congressional sponsors of welfare reform are quick to agree. "The governors were the ones who originally conceived of these changes," said U.S. Representative Thomas J. Downey, the New York Democrat who steered the new law through the House. "What they want is paid attention to."

Democratic U.S. Senator Daniel Patrick Moynihan of New York, sponsor of the Senate version of the bill and veteran of a quarter century of failed welfare-reform attempts, was unequivocal. Without the work of the governors, he said, "there would be no legislation. The experimental mode of the states and their enthusiasm is what brought [Congress] to the debate." The experiments cited by Moynihan include a number of state welfare-to-work programs, such as California's Greater Avenues to Independence (GAIN), Massachusetts' vaunted Employment and Training Choices (ET) and New Jersey's Realizing Economic Achievement (REACH). Obeying the unwritten rule that such programs must bear a catchy acronym, the new federal law requires states, by 1990, to implement what has been formally named the Job Opportunities and Basic Skills program: JOBS, of course.

The creation of the JOBS program—the centerpiece of the welfare reform law—is the embodiment of an emerging consensus on welfare that prompted President Reagan to put welfare reform on the congressional agenda in his 1986 State of the Union message and stirred the NGA, a year later, to endorse welfare reform by a near-unanimous vote. The president was not at all specific, simply calling for legislation to help welfare recipients "escape the spider's web of dependency." Some aspects of the governors' plan, on the other hand, included considerable detail.

That was important politically.

The governors' bipartisan support for a specific blueprint for reform became a convenient shield to hide behind for members of Congress who advocated similar reforms. "For members who were on the fence and don't like voting for welfare, being able to point to the governors' involvement really helped," said Representative Downey. On the other side of the Capitol, Senator Moynihan insisted on calling his measure "the governors' bill," and delighted in telling anyone who would listen how it was approved by a 49-1 vote at the governors' association convention. That stretched the truth. Some governors had not come to this particular convention; as many as 10 others left before the welfare policy came up. Still, the proposal was adopted with only a single dissenting vote, from Wisconsin Republican Tommy G. Thompson.

The exaggeration probably did not matter much. What did matter was not just the promising record of the new welfare-to-work programs in a number of states or the success of Clinton, Castle and others in working out a reform plan and selling it to their peers. More important was the persistent work the governors put into the task of persuading Congress to enact reforms that made sense from the states' point of view—substantively, financially and administratively. The governors left their mark on each of these aspects of the welfare reform law.

The consensus that finally brought about the first major overhaul of the nation's welfare laws in half a century found congressional liberals accepting the concept that mothers of even small children should work. Conservatives, in turn, acknowledged that both the federal government and state governments have a responsibility to provide not only the education and training that will enable welfare mothers to get jobs but also the support services, such as child care and continuing medical coverage, that will enable them to keep jobs once they get them.

That consensus broke down repeatedly during the law's two-year trip to enactment, and the effort was declared dead more often than George Bush and Michael Dukakis attacked each other over the summer and early fall. The final product was a compromise of the most classic sort, with each side getting what it wanted most and swallowing what it earlier vowed never to accept.

Conservatives, led by President Reagan, got requirements that states enroll set percentages of their welfare recipients in work or training programs and a first-ever federal requirement that at least one of the unemployed parents in a two-parent welfare family work part time at community service or another job. Although the number of two-parent families currently on welfare is small—some 236,000 out of the total family caseload of 3.8 million—the administration insisted on this provision because of the symbolic importance it attaches to work.

Liberals swallowed the work requirements and, in return, got quite a lot. They got a guarantee that the federal government will pay a share of the costs of education and job training for the next seven years, without the need for Congress to pass annual appropriations. Uncertainties about federal funding from year to year had discouraged major state training efforts under the predecessor Work Incentive program, known as WIN; provision for consistent, reliable funding this time around was the governors' top priority.

Liberals also got a requirement that welfare recipients who get jobs and go off the welfare rolls will continue to be eligible for subsidized child care and health benefits for a year. The automatic termination of these benefits for those who get jobs has long been seen as one of the biggest deterrents to moving mothers off welfare.

They got a stipulation that no parent will be required to accept a job that would result in a reduction in the family's net cash income. And the liberals got their long-sought goal of requiring all states to pay some benefits to poor two-parent families. Twenty-seven do so now.

Conservatives and liberals worked together, along with the governors, to make sure the new law did not perpetuate a crucial flaw in WIN, created in 1967. WIN unrealistically required states to enroll virtually every welfare recipient in job training or work. Even though more than half the caseload was later made exempt, the goals still never became attainable and the existence of statutory work and training requirements that could not be met enhanced the conviction, in Congress and elsewhere, that WIN was a failure and welfare reform an impossibility.

In large measure because of WIN's poor record in moving large numbers of welfare families off the rolls, the percentage of welfare recipients required to work or enroll in educational or job-training programs under the new law was kept low. These "minimum participation rates" for single parents start at 7 percent of the welfare caseload in 1990 and rise in four steps to 20 percent in 1995. (There are exceptions for mothers of children under age three—or under one, at the option of the state—and for a few other categories of people, such as those who are old or unable to work.) It was the governors who insisted that the participation rates should not be too high. That would force them, they said, to spread resources too thinly, thus doing little good for large numbers of people instead of making significant progress with fewer people. "Workfare" (unpaid work) requirements for one of the parents in two-parent welfare families are higher, rising to 75 percent by 1997.

In addition to its JOBS program, what is formally known as the Family Support Act of 1988 is a law of many provisions and considerable complexity.

Some of its key elements were hardly controversial at all. Most notable among these are the sections that expand and strengthen procedures for collection of child support payments from absent parents, almost all of them fathers. Building on ground-breaking programs in Wisconsin and Texas, the law will require, in increasing numbers of cases, states to withhold court-ordered child support payments from the paycheck of an absent parent even if the parent has not fallen behind on the payments. By 1994, states will be required to institute immediate wage withholding not only for all welfare families and any non-welfare parent who asks for help in collecting child support, but also under every new child support order issued in the state.

States also will be required to strengthen efforts to establish paternity for children born out of wedlock, even those who are not on welfare. Washington will pay 90 percent of the cost of blood tests and other laboratory work to establish paternity. In the past, the general view has been that it was not worth the effort to establish paternity if the father was a 17-year-old high school dropout. But, as Moynihan pointed out repeatedly, 10 years down the road the 17-year-old will be a 27-year-old and likely to have some source of income, while his illegitimate offspring will still be in grade school and in need of support.

Additional federal assistance in locating absent parents is also provided—including a requirement, which becomes effective in 1990, that both parents must supply their Social Security numbers when birth certificates are issued for their children. And, in an effort to introduce some measure of uniformity to child support payments, the law will require states to tell judges to use guidelines based on the absent parent's income, barring good reasons for not doing so.

As is so often the case with programs that are funded by the federal government but run by the states, the new law is full of new requirements. States are required to implement a JOBS program in every political subdivision, unless they can show that it is not necessary or feasible; required to pay benefits to poor two-parent families; even required to procure only licensed child care for welfare children whose parents are participating in work or training programs. They must also install an automated system for statewide tracking and monitoring of child support payments and periodically review support orders. They must make sure that no work assignment under the JOBS program displaces any currently employed worker and establish grievance procedures to handle alleged violations of this rule. These and many other requirements are imposed with a vast range of deadlines and effective dates.

But the new law is also full of options—many of them a direct result of on-the-scene participation of governors and other state officials in the writing of the law. States will be given significant leeway in setting up their JOBS programs, and indeed the law seems to resemble a Chinese restaurant menu, allowing states to pick two from column A (work programs) and three from column B (education programs).

A letter from the NGA also helped remove from the Senate-passed version of the bill a plan requiring states to make those who have gone off the welfare rolls pay an income-related premium for part of their extra year of Medicaid coverage. Governors complained that it would be virtually impossible to determine each family's monthly income and the appropriate premium. The payments were made optional.

Some of the optional provisions were included because ideological conflicts could be resolved no other way. The most important one: States will be permitted, but not required, to deny welfare payments to parents under the age of 18 who are living on their own, with no parent or older person in the household. This has long been a conservative objective.

The governors did not get everything they wanted. Consistent, adequate funding, though better than before, is still not assured under the new law. Because the White House insisted on it, federal funding for the JOBS program is subject to a national cap, which starts at $600 million in 1989 and rises to $1.3 billion in fiscal 1995. That means that Washington will pay a fixed portion of the cost—at least 50 percent, and more for poorer states—but only until the dollar ceiling for the year is reached. Federal funding for part of the cost of such support activities as child care and Medicaid will come under no such ceilings, however.

Even with the guarantee of federal funding for the support services, attendees at a Washington workshop on administering the new law expressed concern over the ability of poorer states to pay their share of them.

Another worry was whether there would be enough jobs for those who complete training and education programs. In parts of western Alabama, said Carol Gundlach, state coordinator of the Alabama anti-hunger coalition, "real unemployment is 50 percent and the major industry is welfare. What you've got to have is job development or else you're training people for nothing." The biggest concern was the fear that miracles had been promised. "The rhetoric that has surrounded this bill is that we have an instant solution to this problem," said David L. Rickard of Arkansas Advocates for Children and Families.

Castle agreed that "every training success involves tremendous work." But he was upbeat about money. He estimates that his state will get an additional $1 million per year from Washington under the new law to help with its two-year-old welfare-to-work program. "Some people ask if there's enough funding," he noted. "It's a start. A lot of this is experimental, it's new, and you cannot expect it to arise full bloom at its first blush."

The governors began their quest for a national welfare program that would transform an income maintenance program with a minor jobs component into a jobs and training program with a minor income maintenance component soon after Reagan issued his 1986 call for welfare reform. Then-NGA Chairman Lamar Alexander, a Republican who was governor of Tennessee, asked Clinton and Castle to co-chair a governors' working group on the issue.

From the outset, said Castle, the members of the group knew the policy that they would draft had to be more than a mere statement of intent. "From the very beginning, we knew that the policy was something we wanted to enact into legislation," he said, "and that's one of the reasons we drafted it—to go to the Congress with."

By February 1987, the Clinton-Castle working group had produced a bipartisan plan that called for mandatory work and training programs for welfare recipients, with the savings that would ultimately be realized by reducing the welfare rolls plowed back into increased benefits. Originally, they had proposed concurrent benefit increases in low-benefit states, but an uprising by a number of Republican governors, led by New Hampshire's John H. Sununu, [subsequently President Bush's chief of staff] sank that idea.

Indeed, benefit increases in the law as finally passed are few. A provision of the House bill that would have provided federal incentives to low-benefit states to raise their payments was eliminated from the final package, partly because of its cost and partly because of the fears of the White House and congressional conservatives that making welfare more attractive would encourage welfare dependency.

The governors did not end their activities with approval of their plan. Clinton seemed all but a member of Congress during consideration of the measure, traveling to or phoning Washington repeatedly. What's more, he participated in a closed-door session of the House Ways and Means subcommittee when it was actually writing the bill. It was an unprecedented involvement by a governor, some say.

"I was almost stunned," said Clinton later of the invitation to join the drafting session. "I wasn't prepared for it. I was just there to give testimony and encouragement."

When the House was preparing to vote on the bill last December, it was Clinton who worked on a dozen or so recalcitrant Southern Democrats at a lunch in the Capitol. He followed up later with phone calls, and at least one member, North Carolina Democrat Tim Valentine, said the "courteous persuasion" of Clinton and others was what won his support. "I have been touched by the feelings of the governors more than anything else," Valentine said at the time.

Also pitching in was Louisiana's governor-elect, Buddy Roemer, then still a House member, who persuaded all of his state's Democrats in the House to support the measure. Said U.S. Representative Jimmy Hayes of the man then about to take over the helm of his economically troubled state, "We don't want to do anything to add to his nightmare."

The enthusiastic Clinton also was cordially received in the Reagan White House, keeping open lines of communication with, among others, domestic policy adviser Charles Hobbs and Joseph Wright of the Office of Management and Budget. New Hampshire's Sununu is also credited with keeping the White House on board at crucial moments.

Said Clinton, "This was a very unusual thing both at the level of involvement of the governors with the Congress and the level of bipartisan involvement from the states and federal government crossing together."

"Bill was willing to work hard, to talk to people," said Castle. "It certainly prompted me to make a lot of phone calls and write a lot of letters."

The governors also kept up the drumbeat when it seemed that congressional interest was flagging. Last February, after the House had passed its bill by a narrow margin and while Senate action was still uncertain, a group of governors, including Clinton, Castle and Republican Thomas H. Kean of New Jersey, trudged from office to office at the Capitol, paying personal calls on most of the principals in the welfare battle, helping set the bill back on track. Welfare proved a particularly apt issue for the governors to become so intimately involved in. "It's logical," said Democratic U.S. Senator John D. Rockefeller IV, former governor of West Virginia, "because they've got to implement it."

Said Republican U.S. Senator William L. Armstrong of Colorado, who helped craft the final compromise, "There was a general belief that [the governors] knew what they were talking about."

What remains unclear is whether the new relationship forged between the governors and federal legislators was just "a magic moment," as Clinton termed it, or a model for future endeavors.

Not surprisingly, the governors say it will be a model for the future. "I think this is what you're going to see more of in the next three or four years," said Castle. "I would suggest in drug policy you may see it; in dealing with AIDS you may see it." He noted that the welfare bill was not the first time the governors had gotten organized to shape legislation to their liking. It was a working group headed by former South Carolina Governor Richard W. Riley, a Democrat, that gave Congress the push to expand Medicaid to cover more poor women with children and women pregnant with their first child as part of the drive to reduce infant mortality.

Clinton expects to see the relationship grow and prosper on issues such as child care, parental leave and acid rain. "Whenever you've got a problem where there's a core American value that Republicans and Democrats can agree on, and which you know will have to be addressed at the federal level, and where the federal government cannot solve the problem without heavy involvement from the states, I think there is this opportunity," he said.

Even a few members of Congress agree. "Federalism is the sharing of responsibility, and we should not determine the share without the help of those who would be affected," said Downey. "The whole idea of federalism is dealt with properly when governors do this kind of work and provide this kind of help."

Still, Downey said he did not see the new relationship as a model for all problems facing both the federal government and the states. Governors are too often parochial, he said, and "they always complain they don't have enough money."

But the effort seems to have energized some for a future fight. "It took two and a half years out of my life and put a few more gray hairs in my head," said Clinton, "but it was exhilarating because I felt we were actually doing something together, where we put aside all the political rhetoric, all the smoke and mirrors and actually worked together for the common good."

11. The Shadow Governments

Joel Garreau

Joel Garreau, a *Washington Post* staff writer specializing in local government, explores the privatization of government in the United States. Today these shadow governments, including homeowners' associations and public-private partnerships, are the "largest form of local government." Many of them, according to Garreau, "have powers far beyond those ever granted governments in this country," although they are not subject to traditional legal checks on their authority. More than twenty million Americans, he states, are affected by their power to levy taxes, provide police protection and other essential services.

In Montgomery County [Maryland], there is a private 28-person police force that, in the evenings, rides Metrobuses paid for by Maryland taxpayers. If the riders appear to the police to be undesirables, the officers forbid them to leave the bus inside the Leisure World retirement community. In the morning, this force forbids the residents of nearby subdivisions to use those same stops to board Metrobuses. The officers have the right to carry guns and make arrests.

In Reston [Virginia], the Regency Square Cluster Association fines its residents $50 if they fail personally to help clean the neighborhood on the last Saturdays of April and October. If the fine is not paid, the association has the right—so far unexercised—to slap a lien on the offender's house and, if desired, sell it at auction.

The Metropolitan Washington Airports Authority has $1 billion in bonding authority and a chairman who muses about pumping water from the Shenandoah River over the Blue Ridge Mountains, down the center of I-66 and into the Occoquan Reservoir to save Northern Virginia from thirst.

These are only three of more than 2,000 shadow governments that exist in the Washington area. Nationwide, their like has become the largest form of local government in the United States.

These shadow governments levy taxes, regulate behavior, adjudicate disputes, provide police protection, plan regionally, channel development, enforce esthetic standards, build roads, fill potholes, remove snow and provide recreation, and they are the driving force behind the hottest social service in the United States today—day care.

They are central to a new American society in which office parks are in the child-rearing business, parking-lot officials run police forces, private enterprise builds public freeways, and subdivisions have a say in who may live there.

"The privatization of government in America is the most important thing that's happening, but we're not focused on it. We haven't thought of it as government yet," said Jerry Frug, professor of local government law at Harvard.

These shadow governments have powers far beyond those ever granted governments in this country. They can regulate the colors of a person's living room curtains, prohibit the organization of everything from a Rotary Club to a Boy Scout troop, and specify what, if anything, a person can park in his or her driveway. Nonetheless, the names of their leaders never appear on a public ballot, and they are frequently not subject to the checks and balances of the Constitution.

What these governments really are, say urbanologists, are highly original, locally invented, special-purpose attempts to stave off anarchy in the cities that are emerging nationwide in places that used to be suburbs. Typically, the newer the emerging city, the less likely it is to have traditional urban government. Therefore, the more common and powerful are the shadow governments that people create.

Like all solutions, critics say, these vacuum-filling shadow governments create problems. For example, how does a resident fight city hall if he or she cannot find it? How does he or she "throw the bums out" if there is no elected council?

In the Washington area alone, as many as 14 emerging cities were identified in a March 8 Washington Post survey. Emerging cities have more jobs than households, have more people commuting into them than out, and are perceived as destinations for entertainment and shopping as well as jobs. Examples of emerging cities include Tysons in Virginia, which is bigger in terms of jobs than downtown Miami, and Rockville/Gaithersburg in Maryland, which is bigger than Baltimore.

In its continuing examination of emerging cities, the Post asked urban affairs, legal and government specialists, "Who runs these new cities?"

The cities are rarely incorporated, never match political boundaries, and sometimes do not even appear on conventional maps.

"We go into these new cities and ask, 'Who's the mayor? Who's the city council?' They never have any!" said Ralph Stanley, former head of the federal Urban Mass Transportation Administration.

It turns out, nonetheless, that they are governed—in most cases by shadow governments.

The *Post* survey found three types of shadow government, each of which is examined in the accompanying articles:

■ Private-enterprise shadow governments, such as homeowners associations.

■ Public-private partnership shadow governments, such as the coalition of developers and political officials that tackled the Tysons road shortage.

■ Arms of conventional public government with highly unconventional powers, some of which have the potential to become regional governments.

Walter Scheiber, executive director of the Metropolitan Washington Council of Governments, provided a four-part definition of government, shadow or otherwise. A government:

■ Assesses fees to support itself.

■ Legislates.

■ Modifies its residents' behavior.

■ Has the power to coerce to accomplish the first three tasks.

In addition, the leaders of shadow governments are never directly accountable to the voters at large in a public election and are frequently not subject to the constraints on power that the Constitution imposes on elected governments.

For example, the Constitution prohibits governments from enacting laws abridging freedom of speech. Because shadow governments are usually not regarded legally as governments, they are generally free to make their own rules. There are about 110,000 private-enterprise shadow governments alone in the United States, deeply touching more than 20 million Americans.

"Picture an America in which you live in a condo community, private, and then work in one of these [emerging city] places," said Harvard's Frug. "You can privatize the schools, security, garbage collection. What would be the realm in which democracy would then operate? There's no reason Tysons [Virginia] has to be run by the board of directors. Democratize Tysons Corner!"

Shadow governments are usually democratic, after a fashion. But, significantly, they rarely have much use for the principle of one-person, one-vote.

For example, the shadow government that runs the 1,016-home Montebello condominium in Fairfax County [Virginia] does hold elections, but they are not subject to the Voting Rights Act. Only property owners may vote, not just any citizen over 18 as in a public election. What's more, the vote is weighted to five digits to the right of the decimal point according to how much a person owns. The owner of a one-bedroom place gets 0.06883 of a vote. The owner of a two-bedroom place with a den gets 0.12350 of a vote.

This is a one-dollar, one-vote democracy. It hearkens to the early days of the republic when the vote was reserved for white male property owners who were viewed as having the biggest stake in how the society was run, scholars said.

In fact, those interviewed for this article repeatedly volunteered how strikingly similar shadow governments are to the legal and governmental structures that served the republic in its early years.

"It's a return to the 19th century in which there was no legal distinction between a city and a private corporation. All had the same powers and restrictions. Railroads could take your land and pay you for it without your consent. You could do anything privately that you could do publicly," said Frug.

Shadow governments "move into vacuums," said Edmond F. Rovner, special assistant to Montgomery County Executive Sidney Kramer. "They get into one issue, and they've got a professional here and a technician there. And then they'll give you an opinion on what you're ordering for lunch. And before you know it, they've named two of your children. They eat up power, like the science-fiction movies. They eat living things and derive power from what they've ingested. They dump on people who appointed them and develop an independent power base. In our county, that's the Park and Planning Commission."

The members of the Montgomery County Planning Board of the Maryland-National Capital Park and Planning Commission "were the one-eyed man in the land of the blind. 'We have the numbers, the formulae, the charts, the tables," said Rovner. "What kind of county do you want? What kinds of people? That's what you're determining when you determine lot size. Those are valid decisions for a community to make. But the decisions ought to be made by people who owe their power to the consent of the governed. Park and Planning is neither elected or anointed. Park and Planning is answerable to nobody."

It is no coincidence that many of shadow governments were formed to address the problems of the automobile. "Water and sewer were the controlling things for development," says Montgomery County's Robert S. McGarry. "Transportation is the issue now."

McGarry has created shadow governments for Bethesda and Silver Spring [Maryland], called "Urban Districts," from his position as head of the Montgomery County Department of Transportation. From 1977 to 1983, he ran the sewer-building Washington Suburban Sanitary Commission.

"The Washington Suburban Sanitary Commission used to be a

shadow government," said Rovner. "But now the sewer lines are almost all in place, so they don't play the kinds of games they once did. Their act is so cleaned up, they're no longer powerful."

Many shadow governments are markedly more efficient than the public kind. "There's no question that they're faster and cheaper. The incentives of prompt performance are stronger in the private sector," said Robert C. Ellickson, a professor at Stanford University's law school.

"People can coordinate with one another to their mutual advantage more than is generally recognized," Ellickson continued. "Take the English language. The people living on the island of Great Britain came together and just created a language. Nobody was put in charge. People are now coordinating in a sophisticated way. I think it's terrific that property owners paid for these roads. The right people did it, and they did it cheaper. This is not a calamity. This is a terrific thing."

But because shadow governments are usually created specifically to produce goods and services for those who can afford them, they rarely consider the concerns of the poor. "These are governments by the wealthy for the wealthy. It is plutocracy, not democracy," Frug said.

Shadow governments also disturb some experts because of their lack of accountability to the larger society. "They're setting up internal courts. Due process is not required. The 14th Amendment [which guarantees equal protection and due process for all] does not apply," said Douglas Kleine, research director for the Community Associations Institute, a group that represents various kinds of private shadow governments.

"The application of the 14th Amendment would cause all kinds of things. It would subject the board of directors to the Voting Rights Act. In Reston and in Burke, you're elected by district [to the community association]. If the 14th Amendment applied, and you want to redraw those lines, you'd have to go to the Justice Department. You couldn't have one-dollar, one-vote, or one-house, one-vote.

"The First Amendment? The association newsletter is a house organ. It's just like a company newsletter. Editorial guidelines usually include the statement that this isn't a First Amendment vehicle. It's there for us to communicate with you, not you to communicate with each other."

Defenders point out that if the larger society finds the actions of these private governments objectionable, it is not without recourse. Covenants such as those prohibiting house sales to blacks and Jews have been readily thrown out when challenged in court. At the same time, these proponents say, as private corporations, shadow governments have as much right, for example, to print what they choose as does *The Washington Post*.

What critics find ominous is that shadow governments have a dual nature, with private freedoms and public responsibilities. In effect, critics ask, should shadow governments be so unrestrained?

"Where is the envelope for democracy?" mused CAI's Kleine. "That's a good question." Shadow governments, he said, "are the ones providing the most visible services to people. Recreation. The architectural control powers are very similar to zoning and health code kinds of powers. Providing police forces in some situations. More rarely they provide fire departments.

"They exist where local government doesn't have the capacity to provide services."

PART II

THE POLITICAL PROCESS

The American citizen is virtually one of the governors of the republic. Issues are decided and rulers selected by the direct popular vote. Elections are so frequent that to do his duty at them a citizen ought to be constantly watching public affairs with a full comprehension of the principles involved in them, and a judgment of the candidates derived from a criticism of their arguments as well as a recollection of their past careers.

—Viscount James Bryce, *The American Commonwealth,* 1888

Chapter 3

Public Opinion and Participation

What are the distinctive political attributes of Americans? Observers around the world have been asking this question for more than two centuries. "What then is the American, this new man?" wondered the French-born J. Hector St. John de Crèvecoeur (1735-1813), who lived in the New World for many years. In his *Letters from an American Farmer* (1782), he declared that freedom and prosperity quickly worked to assimilate immigrants from many nations.

In promoting the idea of the North American as "this new man," Crèvecoeur espoused the European notion that Americans are profoundly different from their forebears in other lands.

> *He* is an American who, leaving behind all his ancient prejudices and manners, receives new ones from the new mode of life he has embraced, the new government he obeys, and the new rank he holds. . . . Here individuals of all nations are melted into a new race of men, whose labours and posterity will one day cause great changes in the world.[1]

Today's foreign observers look upon the New World with more mixed emotions. Still, the magnetic field created by the United States is felt in every corner of the world. American products—food, music, and fashions—intrigue people and set international trends. The nation is also a major exporter of political and economic ideas, even in some instances of governmental institutions and constitutional provisions. More than a few nations have adopted portions of the U.S. Constitution for their own use. As the world's surviving superpower, the United States has forged political and military alliances with virtually every country in the world.

Attempts to discern the nation's political character are bound to miss many variations and nuances. Despite Crèvecoeur's assertion, America has never quite been a "melting pot" capable of absorbing all new citizens and homogenizing them into a single people. Even by the time the Frenchman Alexis de Tocqueville (1805-1859) toured the continent in the early nineteenth century, the United States was so large and diverse that what one found depended to a great extent upon where one traveled and with whom one spoke. Succeeding waves of immigrants—from eastern and southern Europe, Africa, Asia, and Latin America—both enriched our culture and ensured its increasing and sometimes bewildering diversity.

This diversity continues to unfold as a result of demographic changes. Demographer Blayne Cutler, in Selection 12, reminds us that the fictitious "average American" has changed dramatically, particularly over the last generation. Although Crèvecoeur spoke of the American as "this new man," today's average American is a woman who is likely to work outside her home and to hold distinctive political views. Other characteristics of our population—its mobility, its aging, its racial diversity—have profound consequences for political attitudes and public-policy demands.

People's Beliefs and Attitudes Do Matter

In a democratic society, what people think has a great impact on what the government does. Their deeply held values and beliefs shape political life, determining the kinds of politicians who win election, their responses to issues, and their behavior in office.

Americans adhere to a broad set of basic beliefs and values that shape the nation's politics and policies. Their attitudes also set limits on the available options for resolving public policy issues. Relying on public opinion surveys and other systematic studies, political scientist Samuel Huntington has identified certain elements as "the American creed"; for social psychologist Alex Inkeles those elements form the "American character." [2] Among these distinctive traits is the perception of the United States as a Promised Land. The belief that Providence set this nation aside for a race of righteous people appears repeatedly in literature and political rhetoric from the era of the Puritans to the present day. Whatever its shortcomings or setbacks the nation continues to command the allegiance of an overwhelming majority of its citizens, few of whom wish to emigrate to another country.

Another trait is a belief in self-reliance, autonomy, and independence. These homely virtues are continually extolled, if not always followed. Americans tend to believe that a person's own efforts, not luck or fate, account for success or failure in life. Despite their individualism, Americans are committed to voluntary communal action and cooperation with neighbors. "Americans of all conditions, minds, and ages, daily acquire a general taste for association and grow accustomed to the use of it," observed Tocqueville.[3] This habit has endured, and in recent years interest groups have proliferated at all geographic and governmental levels.

Americans' views of politics, however, are at best ambivalent. People feel politically secure and think that they need to be concerned about what the government is doing only when a crisis occurs. Americans know painfully little about political events, officials, or institutions. Their attention to political affairs is, at best, sporadic. Their natural reaction to politics and politicians is one of wariness and distrust, occasionally bordering upon cynicism.

Of more immediate concern to policymakers are people's opinions about their lives, their futures, and the problems they face. In Selection 13, survey researcher Louis Harris probes emerging public attitudes that impinge upon public policy options. The portrait Harris sketches is a far cry from the optimistic self-confidence with which Americans are traditionally associated. Citizens of the 1990s, Harris observes, are uncertain about their jobs and their future living standards; they worry about a host of problems, from crime and drugs to environmental quality. They expect activist government to address these problems, even if they balk at higher taxes to pay for the resulting services.

One Community or Many?

Even these traits and attitudes, broad as they are, may be diluted or canceled out by the tides of particularism that characterize our era. Harris discerns "a craving for community, a sense of community that draws the country together." Yet that sense of community now seems elusive. Since the Industrial Revolution, commentators have worried that technological advances, especially mass production and mass communication, would make all of us consumers of the same products, information, and ideas. True, technology has overleaped geographic localism and transformed our world into a "global village" where we are instantly touched by the actions of others who may be far distant. But technology also promotes social, cultural, and intellectual diversity that the eighteenth-century founders could hardly have imagined. Such diversity is likely to diminish the strength of community values and of the nationalism that once provided Americans with a ready identity.

Historian Daniel Boorstin coined the phrase "consumption communities" to describe people connected by what they buy rather than where they live. One observer remarked, "We are, in part, defined by the computer lists we're on; the lists for catalogs, magazines, credit cards, alumni associations, unions, and trade groups."[4] Yet these channels favor the particular over the general; they enhance individual or subgroup loyalties rather than community-wide identity. Computerized mailing lists record this increasing separateness, but it is given concrete form by specialized organizations and communications networks. If the consumption of goods reflects this diversity, the range of contemporary ideas, values, causes, and lifestyles does so even more.

For an alarming number of citizens, membership in such "consumption communities" has been accompanied by declining attention to, and identification with, the nation's common political life. Distracted and satiated by commitments and entertainments of every kind, people seem to have little time left for the responsibilities of citizenship. In Selection 14, political analyst Michael Barone raises the question of why our citizens seem to have foresaken elections and other obvious modes of political activism, apparently preferring to retreat into various private pursuits. The result, if Barone is correct, could be to isolate politics from other areas of life. Political offices may increasingly be occupied by professionals skilled at using the perquisites of office to prolong their careers. On the other hand, the great mass of citizens—lacking firm partisan loyalties, disinclined to learn about politics, and holding only the most superficial and fleeting political notions—may play an ever more passive role, marked by indifference punctuated by occasional sudden outbursts of approval or disgust. It is hardly an inspiring prospect for citizenship.

Alternatively, in Selection 15, Benjamin Barber posits the theory that citizens live in two different democracies. One consists of the cities and towns where people live and work; the other democracy is in Washington, D.C., which citizens often follow almost in the same way that spectators watch sports on television. How to encourage civic activism in both arenas is a contemporary challenge.

Notes

1. J. Hector St. John de Crèvecoeur, "What Is an American?" in *Political Thought in America: An Anthology,* ed. Michael B. Levy (Homewood, Ill.: Dorsey Press, 1982), 23.
2. Samuel P. Huntington, *American Politics: The Promise of Disharmony* (Cambridge, Mass.: Harvard University Press 1981), 14-15; Alex Inkeles, "The American Character," *The Center Magazine* (November/December 1983), 25-39.
3. Alexis de Tocqueville, *Democracy in America,* ed. Phillips Bradley (New York: Vintage Books, 1958), 2:114.
4. Robert J. Samuelson, "Computer Communities," *Newsweek* (December 15, 1986), 66.

12. Meet Jane Doe

Blayne Cutler

Who are these people called Americans? One answer lies in our basic attributes—age, gender, education, occupation, family status, and so on. The nation's demographic characteristics are of more than academic interest; they comprise the raw material of our political attitudes, preferences, and demands. What we are, in other words, helps to determine how we approach politics and what we expect government to provide for us. We therefore begin our survey of public opinion and participation by examining the attributes of that mythical creature, the "average American." In this essay, published in 1989 in *American Demographics*, Blayne Cutler reminds us that the average American has changed gradually but perceptibly from one generation to the next.

Jane Doe is in a rut. She's better educated than ever before. She's going to live longer, too. But Jane's sitting in the suburbs watching thirty-something close in on fortysomething. She can't help but notice she's shorter (5'4"), fatter (143 pounds), and older (32) than most of the people she sees on TV. Jane's got ten credit cards but little to spend on anything but food and shelter.

At about 6:30 every morning, Jane gets in her eight-year-old car, as she will do over 1,500 times a year. She has made sure her two television sets, six radios, VCR, stereo, and kitchen appliances are all turned off. She tucks $104 securely in her wallet and drives about ten miles to the office.

When she comes home to her husband and one or two children, Jane will face another three and a half hours of housework and child care. Little does she know it, but she is sure to be a victim of crime—not once, but three times in her life. Poor Jane. It wasn't always this way.

Fifty years ago, the average American—a 29-year-old man—could find a blue-collar job in the country's growing cities with no more than a ninth-grade education. One hundred years ago, single and 22 years old, he was America's farmhand.

No one really lives the average American life. But a look at the average American's characteristics reveals the most important trends in how people live. Marketers spend millions trying to determine the direction of American lifestyles, but all it really takes is a little perspective.

No Place Like Home

The home of the average American today is often temporary and costly. She lives in a 1,700-square-foot dwelling that's more than 25 years old, and she spends more than one-third of her income on housing.

Although the average American still lives in the state of her birth (as 61 percent of all Americans do), she has a one-in-five chance of picking up and moving in a year. She moves at least 11 times in her life. Although her home is worth about $60,000, the average American could sell her house for more than $84,000 if she leaves it on the market for the usual 86 days.

The odds of owning a home are no better today than they were in 1890, when the share of owner-occupied households was 66 percent. Home ownership fell to 41 percent in 1940, then rose to 65 percent by 1986. As a home-owner, the average American has a median net worth of $75,000. Her friends who rent have a median net worth of just $5,000, according to the Federal Reserve Board.

Marriage is still the lifestyle of choice for the average American, who considers herself romantic, traces her first "crush" back to age 13, and is bound to fall in love at least six times in her life, according to the book *Lover's Quotient* by Nancy Biracree. She waited until age 24 before tying the knot, but the more educated she is, the longer she waited to marry. At age 32, she has more than a 50 percent chance of becoming single again through divorce. The odds are nine out of ten that she will be widowed at some point in her life.

But single life is not new to Americans. It was more common before World War II, in fact. Thirty percent of men and 23 percent of women have never married today. But 44 percent of men and 34 percent of women had never married in 1890. In 1940, 35 percent of men and 28 percent of women had not married.

Average Americans in 1890 and 1990 both experience many years of single life, but the woman in 1990 may be lonelier than her great-grandmother was. That's because today's average American lives with fewer people. Average household size has shrunk from nearly five people in 1890 to fewer than three today. Americans have fewer children, and they rarely live with grandparents, aunts, uncles, or cousins as they more often did in the past.

Although the average American still lives in a family house-hold, many Americans do not. Just 72 percent of households are families today, compared with 92 percent in 1940. Married couples were 71 percent of households in 1940, and just 58 percent today.

Material Girls

Today, Americans own 150 million televisions, 495 million radios, 182 million telephones, 137 million cars and light trucks, 111 million bicycles and tricycles, 14 million pleasure boats, and almost 6 million motorcycles.

Homes are no longer a quiet refuge. Televisions or radios are on for 11 hours a day in the average American home—most of the time people are awake. With cable, the average household can browse among nine channels.

Thirty-seven percent of what's in the mailbox is an unsolicited sales pitch (18 pieces of direct mail per month). Moreover, the average American will make six telephone calls a day. In the future, as cordless telephones, answering machines, computers, camcorders, satellite dishes, and hand-held TV screens become part of the life of the average American, white noise will come of age.

Consumer spending began on a massive scale when John Doe first moved to the city in 1920. In that year, the census found more urban residents (51 percent) than rural for the first time. The number of cities with 100,000 or more residents has grown from 28 in 1890 to 93 in 1940 and 182 today.

Unlike the average American 50 years ago, whose factory job often was located downtown, today's average American has a white-collar job somewhere on the "urban fringe" and will spend about 20 minutes commuting the ten miles to work. Commuting alone costs over $1,300 a year.

But the sprawl of urban life also means a smaller share of Americans live in the largest cities. In 1940, 12 percent of the population lived in central cities with a population of 1 million or more, compared with only 8 percent today.

By 1980, the suburbs overshadowed Main Street. In that year, the census found more people living in the suburbs of metropolitan areas than in the cities. If current trends continue, Main Street will continue to lose customers: the suburban population is projected to reach 62 percent of the total metropolitan population by 2000.

Regionally, the average American is moving southwest. Florida, Texas, California, and other states in the South and West account for more than half the population today, up from 37 percent in 1890 and 42 percent in 1940.

More than half of all Americans live within 50 miles of a coastline. It is only a matter of time before the West Coast outgrows the East. The West has been the fastest-growing region in the country for more than a century. In 1940, 1 in 10 Americans lived in New York State. Today, 1 in 10 Americans lives in California—up from 1 in 50 a century ago.

The center of the American population, the place where an equal number of Americans live in all directions—was somewhere east of Baltimore in 1790. The population center was near Cincinnati by 1880. In 1940, it had reached the Indiana-Illinois border and was veering to the southwest. Today it is in Jefferson County, Missouri, just south of St. Louis.

"The geographic center of the U.S. is in Kansas, " says Joel Miller at the Census Bureau. "The population center is to the east, but it has been dragged west and south every decade since 1920."

Marketers who think they're targeting the "new" American working woman are shortsighted. "In the 1890s, when the population was employed in agriculture, the two-earner household was normal," says Tom Merrick, president of the Population Reference Bureau.

Industrial life forced spouses into the roles of breadwinner and bread baker. But postindustrial society is blurring the mix of home and market economies, says Merrick. The share of households in which men are the sole earners "peaked around 1940. Now it's swinging back the other way."

In large part, the return to dual-earner marriages comes from the changing job structure. In the mid-1970s, the American labor force became more white-collar than blue-collar. In 1940, the average American was a manual laborer or service worker. In 1890, nearly half of workers were farmers.

In 1970 the average American was a high school graduate. Today, she has nearly one year of college, according to the National Center for Education Statistics. In 1940, the average American had only 8.6 years of schooling under his belt. In 1890, he barely had a grammar school education.

After taxes, the average American now has $10,964 (1982 dollars) in disposable income. That's nearly three times the amount he had in 1940 ($3,700 in 1982 dollars), according to the Department of Commerce.

Food and shelter have always absorbed most of the average American's disposable income. But in recent decades, housing costs have replaced food costs as the number-one financial drain. Food cost the average household nearly half of its spending money a century ago, compared with 28 percent in 1940, and just 15 percent today. But housing costs now account for more than 30 percent of the total budget—up from 28 percent in 1940 and 15 percent in 1890.

Transportation spending as a share of the household budget has doubled since 1940. Households spent 10 percent of their income on transportation then, versus 21 percent today. Clothing expenses have fallen from 12 percent in 1940 to 5 percent today. And despite the alarm about rising medical costs, health care takes only about five cents of every household dollar now, up from four cents in 1940.

Unmelting Pot

Today, racial diversity is becoming the norm, Non-Hispanic whites are 78 percent of the population, but they will make up only 74 percent by 2000.

"In 1890 we had lots of immigrants, and in the 1980s we have lots of immigrants," explains Tom Merrick. "The country moved from great diversity to homogeneity in 1940. Now it has gotten more diverse again."

Rather than meeting German, Polish, or Italian coworkers as he did in the last century, the average American now works with Hispanics and Asians. But the challenges are the same. The important issues today, such as whether English should be the official language, and whether immigrants take jobs from native-born Americans, were also important issues a century ago, says Merrick.

The nation's racial and ethnic diversity directly affects the kinds of goods and services the average American buys. "The more homogeneous the society, the more there is a mass market" says Merrick. That's why General Motors and General Electric succeeded when they did. And it's also the reason they could fail today.

"If you look at the typical market basket in the 1890s, it was limited— a dozen items or so. With the growth of manufacturing and the mass market, consumption increased, but there was still a narrow range of choice. Segmentation is really something that has happened since 1960," says Merrick.

While the population becomes increasingly diverse, national attitudes are converging, thanks to telecommunications. "The information explosion is exposing people to ideas they couldn't get before," explains Tom Biracree, author of *The Almanac of the American People.* "From a marketer's standpoint, that means you can reach more people. But if you fail, you fail with everyone. If Ralph Nader complains about something in Washington, the news gets out faster than ever."

The average American is fictitious, but her importance is not. Using shortsighted comparisons is a common and costly business practice. "We hear people in campaigns talk about who the American people are and what they want," says Biracree. But the numbers show that some national leaders need to brush up on the average American's history.

What does a poor Hispanic woman in Queens have in common with a middle-aged Mormon in Walla Walla, anyway? "A woman from the inner city and a woman from Washington State have the same hopes and dreams for their kids, the same concerns about crime, the desire to have a home and to balance careers with raising a family," says Biracree. "There are certain areas of life in which people have almost universally average interests."

13. Issues for the 1990s: Shifting Opinions, New Ideas

Louis Harris

Public attitudes and preferences are a prime raw material for making public policies. Although policymakers do not consult citizens on every issue, they are nonetheless keenly aware of what is on the public's mind. What do people regard as the most pressing problems facing the society? What are the issues about which people care most passionately? What developments or events would trigger vocal reactions on the part of citizens? Louis Harris is a distinguished public opinion analyst. Relying on his opinion surveys, he gave the following briefing to the Congressional Clearinghouse on the Future, a special caucus composed of interested members of the House of Representatives and the Senate. His briefing was subsequently published in *What's Next?* in 1987.

The problem of the trade deficit is serious, the dependence of the United States on foreign capital to underwrite the nation's debt is a high risk. The export of jobs in basic industry is damaging, and the worry over just how competitive American industry really is in the world, all are problems that 8 out of every 10 people in the nation and 9 in 10 of the business leaders think are very serious problems.

Any public official or prominent spokesperson for business or labor or any other major institution will get in trouble by trying to minimize this problem.

But there is remarkable restraint and levelheadedness that seems to be prevailing. The basic instinct of the people and their leaders is not to blame others abroad for the plight the United States is in, but rather to search our own discipline, our own institutions, our own system, and our own management capabilities before blaming others.

By margins of 2 to 1 or better, our own surveys of public opinion have shown that the American people reject the notion of going the protectionist route. To be sure, in textile, shoes, steel, microchip and other industries, there is real pressure to take restrictive measures. Today some politicians will think they are cashing in on protectionist sentiment, but this is distinctly not the prevailing mood in the country.

Thus, virtually no one in the public buys the easy notion of quick fixes on making America more competitive with the rest of the world.

Down deep, both the public and the leadership are convinced that the United States must make radical changes in the status of its labor force. It must train a whole new generation to be superior in math and science and in problem-solving, and that means an education system that is much more effective than is today's. Americans are aware of the fact that Japanese students outscore American high school students in math, science, and other key subjects.

They want in the future to educate a work force that is so much better educated and so much more creative and capable of solving problems and knowing where to find answers to problems that it will once again be unique and capable of outproducing the rest of the world. Fundamentally, mark it well, the American people are opting against cutting living standards in order to compete with Korean mass production labor on assembly line jobs, on the one hand, and for reaching the level of productivity in new industries to heights that will add to productivity, on the other.

First, the American people have become frightened about the consequences to themselves and their families from toxic waste dumps that have not been cleaned up, drinking water that might be contaminated, products that are not safe, working conditions that are not safe, and preventive measures on health that simply are not taken in industry. Second, industry has become cynical about getting away with relatively high risks in the health, safety and environmental areas, encouraged as it has been that federal enforcement in these areas will be lax. Mark it well, this kind of mentality set by business will cost it dearly. A big 78 percent of the American people are critical of business for not respecting the law, and 68 percent are critical of business on respecting health, safety, and environmental laws. In the post-Reagan era, business had better expect a crackdown from government in these areas that could be much more severe than it has ever faced in the past.

Business and Labor Issues

Without doubt, over these past six years, the power of labor unions has been diminished rather severely. Unions have not grown as the labor force has expanded and now are down to only 18 percent who are members, compared with 33 percent back in the 1950s. This has allowed business to strip away many of the ground-rules which unions had saddled business with over the years in their collective bargaining contracts. Labor has had to take pay cuts, imposition of productivity controls, an end to featherbedding and other make-work practices, an end to strict seniority, and other changes.

However, there are distinct signs now that the honeymoon with American business is over. Business now gets negative not positive marks on providing jobs for workers, a basic and fundamental attribute. The swing in the positive feeling on this score alone since 1979 has been 34 points from positive to negative. Basically, on dimension after dimension, business simply no longer has the reservoir of goodwill it once had. And with this happening, and with a damaged president [Reagan] no longer capable of easing the defense of business, then it is fair to expect that business' ability to withstand drives by organized labor might well be diminished in the immediate years ahead.

More likely than labor making a spectacular comeback is that both business and labor will be lumped together as institutions that are viewed with suspicion by the American people and by most in political power. Mark it well, however, that the function of workers dealing with their bosses as a group will not disappear. By 3 to 2, workers who do not belong to unions and have no strong reason to join, nonetheless recently said they felt they could get better results by dealing with their employer as a group than as individuals.

Issues for the 90s

Issues of compassion, such as helping the poor, giving women a better break, helping children whom most feel have been neglected, all of these are having something of a comeback.

There is a strong return of conscience on the race issue. The number who oppose busing for racial purposes has dropped in 6 months from 78 percent down to 53 percent—25 points. The number of white parents pleased with the experience of their children in busing is up from 54 percent to 74 percent since 1982. The pendulum on race is swinging back from active neglect to caring and compassion.

Indeed, there are a host of issues moving into view. Mark them well.

The issues of teenage pregnancy and birth control, along with sex education, are settled as far as the American people are concerned. By 84 percent to 10 percent, people want sex education in the schools. By 69 percent to 29 percent, they want condoms distributed in the schools. AIDS and teen pregnancies have settled those issues.

But as the right to life movement seems to be dying, the right to die movement is aborning. By 72 to 18 percent, people favor the hopelessly ill elderly directing their physicians to put them out of their misery.

People believe in genetic engineering-gene splicing by 23 to 1, but only to avoid fatal disease later in life, not to produce a new superior breed nor to prevent some from conceiving.

Children are going to be rediscovered after a period of benign neglect. Only 8 percent of households with adults in them are in poverty. Twenty-three percent of households with children under 18 and under are in poverty. A big 73 percent feel with child abuse, missing kids, high drop-out rates, teen suicide up—children have been badly treated. They need help from you.

A hallmark of the 1980s, most agree, has been unbridled greed. Eighty-two percent think greed drives business, especially Wall Street. A marked backlash against excessive greed is not mounting across this country. People are demanding radical changes to restrict predatory takeover efforts, on the one hand, and overprotective corporate management, inured with golden parachutes, on the other. There will be hard demands upon you to write basic ground rules for corporate governance.

In the health field, we are entering a world where heart by-pass operations will be replaced with drug treatment, where you will be quadrupling funding on AIDS research so a cure will be found in the 1990s to end this modern black plague. Preventive medicine will grow three-fold with incentives on costs you likely will provide.

From what I am saying, a great return to compassion for the lot of others is about to take place in this country. It is becoming respectable again to want government back. A recent Gallup Poll shows that in 1982, 43 percent of those surveyed wanted less government. In 1986, the number who wanted less was 28 percent. In 1982, only 27 percent wanted more government, but by 1986 this had risen to 41 percent.

In turn, this raises a central question only you can solve: how to restore shattered faith in government. To be effective, government in the end must have bright, dedicated, honorable, selfless people. Government service must be converted from a sinecure for those serving out time to the place where humanity can better serve humanity. Public service must once again be seen as a higher calling. You must set the example. You must lead the way. You most provide incentives to attract the best.

Most of all there is a craving for community, a sense of community that draws the country together, that sparks the feeling of doing something good for something bigger than your own comfort or greed. . . .

14. The Age of Indifference

Michael Barone

Americans exhibit a persistent ambivalence toward government and politics. On the one hand, compared to citizens of other nations, Americans are conspicuously patriotic, pointing with pride to their Constitution and governmental system. On the other hand, they have always been acutely suspicious of politicians and government actions; they display scant personal enthusiasm for politics, either as a vocation or an avocation. Today this is especially true for the relatively affluent middle and upper classes, who provide the core of political support and potential political leadership, but whose lives are increasingly over-loaded by job pursuits, not to mention self-fulfillment and leisure-time activities. Michael Barone, a senior writer for *U.S. News & World Report*, in which this article appeared in 1989-90, co-founded the *Almanac of American Politics* some years ago.

In a world where millions are enthusiastically turning to democratic politics, Americans are increasingly turning away from it. The trend could intensify during the next decade, with most American politicians slugging it out before a mostly indifferent audience. Yet this indifference should not be taken as a sign that the political system has failed. To the contrary, Americans are mostly satisfied with the direction of the economy and foreign policy and with their leaders. Polls in the last five years have shown little anxiety over the central issues of foreign policy and the economy. (Discontent typically is registered over second-magnitude issues like drugs.) And Presidents Bush and Reagan during these years have averaged higher job ratings than any Presidents since John Kennedy and Dwight Eisenhower.

The public's indifference to national politics is actually a reverting to form. Americans historically have organized their politics around voluntary ties, rather than government rules. For the America of the 1990s in many ways resembles the America described by Alexis de Tocqueville* 150 years ago, where "political associations are only one small part of the immense number of different types of associations found there." The Reagan policies of the 1980s decentralized government at least to some

---

* French thinker and author of *Democracy in America,* published in 1835.

extent, and the forces that will shape the early part of the 1990s will strengthen the move toward decentralization. In this atomistic country, many functions undertaken by centralized governments elsewhere are performed here by what Tocqueville called "little private societies held together by similar conditions, habits, and mores"—or what George Bush dubbed "a thousand points of light."

The good news about this America is that people tend to leave others alone. The bad news is that they don't much care about them. In politics that means apathy will reign, with continued low voter turnout. It will be sound-bite politics in which candidates concentrate, as Bush did with steely discipline in 1988, on the few pivotal occasions when large numbers of voters were watching, such as during conventions and debates.

However, this does not necessarily mean voters reject government activism generally. It does mean that activism will continue to move to state and local governments. Americans are calling on mayors to stop crime and drugs, they want their state governments to improve education and build new transportation systems, and they are even sometimes willing to pay higher taxes for these services. They see government as an instrument to encourage individuals to perform better and to punish those who do bad things. Rigid, centralized federal programs will continue to inspire skepticism. But supple, custom-crafted state programs that speak to local needs and build on local pride, like the education-reform programs of many states in the South, are likely to have great appeal.

Given this ambivalent attitude toward government activism, and given the fact that in foreign policy America seems likely to be heading toward untrodden ground in the post-cold-war era, neither party is likely to have a lock on the electorate. Both parties have shown themselves capable of electing governors and senators in every state of the union, and many statehouses and Senate seats can change hands. Nor is the Presidency permanently Republican or Congress forever Democratic. A moderate Democrat like Lloyd Bentsen or Bill Bradley capable of carrying the West Coast and a few Southern states, might beat a Republican like Dan Quayle or Jack Kemp sometime in the 1990s. On Capitol Hill, the Republicans are only a few seats away from winning Senate control. If they should sprout a crop of strong challenger candidates and get a better break on redistricting, they could win the 40-odd seats they need for control of the House by the end of the decade.

But change is not likely to come from charismatic leadership. Americans can get all the chills down their spines they want from the vast array of entertainment available to them. From their politicians they seem increasingly to want a certain dull competence at dealing with the distasteful business of government. That helps to explain Bush's high job ratings, despite his lack of charisma.

The 1990s are likely to put a premium on well-known candidates—the kind of graying, middle-aged, white males who were deprecated by the political trend spotters of the 1970s and 1980s. Such candidates may never win oratory contests, but they will have every chance in the next few years to show they can govern—and lead. Much less in demand, at a time when the system seems to be performing tolerably well, will be the rebels who stirred hearts and surprised pollsters in earlier years, like George McGovern or Jimmy Carter, or temperamental outsiders, like John Anderson, Jerry Brown, Gary Hart and Jesse Jackson.

It is certain that those who succeed in politics in the 1990s will not be those who protest against America. Underneath Americans' surface indifference toward the minutiae of politics lies a much deeper vein of pride in the nation and its achievements. Cultural values are usually a stronger force in American politics than economic envy, as Bush proved in 1988. But nationalism can work for either party. Americans are looking not only for expressions of pride but for ways to tie their diverse nation together. Democrats from Franklin Roosevelt to Lyndon Johnson knew how to do that, and Democrats in the 1990s may learn again.

All bets are off, of course, in case of disaster—a major economic collapse, a return to cold war with a post-Gorbachev Soviet Union, a hot war with Islamic fundamentalists, a hostile border with a revolutionary Mexico. And there are likely to be changes in course resulting from existing tensions within America itself. The continuing surge of immigration and the entry of recent immigrants into the electoral stream are setting up a competition of Democrats and Republicans, which neither party is assured of winning. There is a tension between a trend toward greater restraint in personal lives and a greater tolerance for diversity. It is not yet clear how this will be resolved. And most Americans continue to be troubled by the homeless on their streets and the festering problems of the urban underclass. These lingering problems may well dominate the nation's agenda in the next decade.

While Americans do not feel the need for great and inspiring leaders, they might reconsider their role as followers. Tocqueville feared that if citizens had neither the instinctual patriotism inspired by an ancient monarchy nor "the reflective patriotism of a republic," they would "retreat into a narrow and unenlightened egoism." Americans' indifference to politics and disinterest in inspiring leadership may result from the system's success in producing a strong economy and a successful foreign policy. But the system does not automatically produce such results. As Americans enter the 1990s, they seem to think they can afford to be uninterested in politics. But there is no guarantee they will be in that happy position for the whole decade.

15. Two Democracies: Ours and Theirs

Benjamin R. Barber

"We live not in one, but two democracies," according to Benjamin R. Barber, Walt Whitman Professor of Political Science at Rutgers University and director of the Whitman Center for the Culture and Politics of Democracy. In this essay published in the *Kettering Review* in 1988, Barber discusses "our" democracy, composed of cities, towns, and communities where citizens live, and "their" democracy, which is represented by Washington, the seat of alien bureaucracies to most Americans. He notes that being a citizen in America today seems to mean little more than being a client of that bureaucracy, with citizens listening to politicians but not talking to one another on vital issues. The only genuine democracy, he asserts, is one in which people are actively engaged in civic life, talking to one another and thereby helping to shape public policy. Barber is the author of many books, including *Strong Democracy* (1984), *The Conquest of Politics* (1988), and with Patrick Watson the prize-winning television series "The Struggle for Democracy" (1989).

We live not in one, but two democracies. One of those democracies is out there in the towns and the communities and the cities where citizens live—people who live and think and talk and work together; block associations, PTAs, community organizations, all of the neighborhood groups of local civic space. Then there is that *other* democracy represented by Washington, DC, a conglomeration of alien bureaucracies, felt by most Americans as a distant but formidable entity, abstract but powerful. When we find ourselves in a political season the second of those two democracies, the representative politics of Washington, becomes a spectator sport for the rest of the country: not something that we Americans do, but something that we watch, mostly on television. It's a politics we don't participate very much in. We're not allowed to participate in a politics that offers little opportunity for civic engagement. We can vote once every couple of years, and if you define citizenship by voting, that means that you spend five or ten minutes every two years or four years as a citizen. We spend more time tying our shoes.

Defined that way, our citizenship is not a very exciting or enthralling prospect. Moreover, about half of us don't participate even in that elementary responsibility of citizenship; and even fewer participate in the primaries. In the last primaries the figure has hovered between 23 and 30 percent, 30 at best. For the young the statistics are still worse— less than 18 percent of those between 18 and 25 vote in national elections. Primaries are in any case not won by the number of voters but by the amount of money spent. There has been an astonishing and frightening correlation between who spends big and who wins the primaries, and that correlation teaches us something about democracy when it is understood as the election of representatives who govern us.

Do we really want to call democracy that spectator sport in which citizens sit in front of their television sets watching political salesmen spend a lot of money trying to buy the 20 or 30 percent of the electorate that participates in the primaries and the 50 percent of the electorate that participates in federal elections? Democracy was once thought to mean "self-government" rather than "electing representatives who govern us."

One of the problems with the concept of citizenship in America is that to be a citizen today seems to mean little more than to be a client of a bureaucracy, to be a consumer of political services. We think of ourselves as individuals with interests belonging to groups which have interests, and our political responsibility is to let the bureaucracy, let the politicians, let the statesmen know what we want, in fact, what each of us wants. The chief political question that every politician asks—and to this extent politicians are solicitous of us as citizens—is what do you want? You are supposed to tell them, "Here is what I want: I want a new sewer down my street; I want a tax break; I want jobs; I want something for me, my family, my particular group."

When we use the language of "I want" we're not using the language of citizenship. The language of citizenship is the language of "This would be good for us," or "*What* would be good for us?" When good citizens sit down to talk about issues they do not ask, "What do *I* think? What do I want?" but, "What would be good for our community? What would serve all of us as a public?" They move away from privatistic modes of thinking into a more public mode—a political, or civic mode of thinking—where the question is what is good for us as a community and neighborhood? Or as a city, a state, a nation, (and now more and more often) a world?

This is "we" thinking rather than "I" thinking: What do *we* need, what is good for us as a *world-in-common*? Thinking in these terms can lead to policies quite different from the policies that emerge from privatistic thinking—whose policies generally represent log rolling, mutual back-scratching, dividing up the pie into so many comparable pieces. Even the new citizen groups that are beginning to find their way into the American political process, the minority pressure groups, are mimicking the dominant majorities, saying: "Well now, here is what *we* want. Now you've got to take *us* into account. We want a wedge of the pie, too, and it better be a big wedge!" Rather than saying, "How can we play a role in a larger community? What kind of community might we all live in—that would serve all of us as neighbors, as members of a state, or a national community?

If you want people to start thinking in public rather than private terms, in civic rather than sectarian terms, in the terms of public goods rather than private interests, it requires not just talking and not just action, but certain *kinds* of action. The representative democratic system constituted by the professional politicians has its own kind of talk. We are all familiar with it. The politicians talk *at* us. The democrats (with a small "d") occasionally talk *to* us, not just at us. The ones that don't care about us at all talk at us; the ones that are interested in participatory democracy talk to us. But that's as far as it goes.

But talking *at* and talking *to* us does not begin to engage us, the public, in the kind of discourse that citizenship requires. Indeed, even under ideal conditions, when we get to talk *with* the politicians, where we talk some and they talk some, that also is not finally what democracy is about. The most important conversation in a democracy is not the one between the politician and the citizen, but the one carried on between the citizen and the citizen—lateral communication, not vertical communication—citizens talking to one another, not being talked at or talked to by politicians and not even talking with politicians who are equals. We live in a nation that is replete with democratic institutions, but most of those institutions are geared toward either allowing politicians to talk to one another, like the Congress, or the committee system, or allowing the politicians to talk to us in the way made possible by the media: we sit and listen; they talk and talk. And we are considered good citizens if we sit and allow ourselves to be talked to. The others tune into "Dynasty" or "Dallas." We're good citizens if we watch the evening news instead, or CNN or C-Span, and allow ourselves to be talked to. Where are the institutions in this country that permit citizens first of all, before they talk to or listen to the politicians, to talk to one another?

There are in fact two sets of interests that have to be reconciled; the interests of private individuals and the interests of citizens who are members of the natural community. In good marriages I know the husband and wife say: "It's funny, I don't think of myself as a single person. When I think of my interests now, I see they have grown to include your interests. And if you're hurt, if you don't have the right job, if you're unhappy, I'm unhappy. I may still be selfish but the ambit of my selfishness has grown to include you." And then you have children, and again, while there are some parents who strike bargains with their children, and say, "Well if you want to do this, then I'm going to do this," on the whole, as parents we come to say, "I now think of myself as someone who has a responsibility for a child, and what happens to that child becomes part of my interests"—not a competitor with my interests, but *part* of my interests.

Now on the whole, unfortunately, in America it stops right there, but it shouldn't stop there. Surely when we move onto a block we come to share certain things with the people who live in our neighborhood. They are our fellow citizens of the neighborhood. It's not that the neighborhood has one set of interests and we have another, and we have to make a deal with them, have to enter an adversarial proceeding with them, and need an arbitrator to straighten things out. It is rather that we go from being a parent to being a neighbor. And as neighbors, we now have selfish interest that includes the interests of other people on the block.

And of course as we continue to expand in that direction we become, in time, citizens. A citizen is not an altruist. Democratic participation does not require altruism—sacrificing your own interest for the good of the country. It requires rather the expansion of your own sense of what your interests are to include the interests of your town, your city, the state, the nation—and for those who are truly citizens, the globe, because we are all here as neighbors on the globe, and what happens in Japan and what happens in Russia and what happens on the West Bank and what happens in Argentina does finally affect our interests as well.

So citizenship is first of all an issue of self-understanding: how we understand ourselves, what we think of our interests, *how* we think of our interests. Do we conceive of ourselves as solitary, isolated, separated, sectarian, economic animals pursuing private interests? Or do we see ourselves as linked into a web of relationships that ultimately makes everyone on the globe our neighbor?

The kind of talk that needs to go on in a genuinely democratic marketplace is talk that leads us to an awareness of our membership in larger communities, that exposes invisible connections, invisible links that only talk reveals, so that we begin to understand that we necessarily are engaged in a form of membership in a larger association that makes us citizens whether we really like it or not.

We are really citizens, like it or not, but there are two kinds of citizens: those who *recognize* they are citizens and those who don't. There is really no such thing as a non-citizen, because we are all tied up in those webs of power and interdependencies that define our condition. That's always been true for human beings. Aristotle wrote, "Man is a political animal," by which he meant we are, by nature involved in a web of politics. We can't get away from it.

A lot of Americans say, "Oh, I'm not interested in politics." Maybe not, but politics is interested in them. Power touches them, affects them, and the person who says "it doesn't matter to me" is either a hypocrite or someone who is simply ignorant of the political connections in which he or she is really involved—involved simply by virtue of breathing, living, drinking water, sending kids to school, paying taxes.

There is another thing that we need to think about when we sit and talk together, and that is the question of what we talk *about* when we talk, because it is not just a matter of talking about issues laid on the table for us by someone else. Democracy and the art of politics are, first of all, about the forging of language, how you frame questions, the terms you use. If we are going to understand one another we have to discover and explore the terms used by our neighbors and to *create* understanding by finding the terms that will enable us to discover common ground.

Take the issue of abortion. Who's for infanticide? Who's for fetus murder? Anybody? If that is what it is called, if that is what we *name* it, and then we take a poll on what we have named it, take a vote on that understanding, clearly we are going to come up with one result. On the other hand, if we call it the right of women to control their own bodies, if we call it choice or women's rights, and take a vote on *that* understanding, we may come up with the opposite result. There is some truth in both of these definitions, but the real argument, the real discussion, the real talk has to be about what you get when your talk takes you to the underlying reality that both sets of terms disguise. And the real issue in citizen democracy is *who* makes the definition? Who sets the agenda? Who controls political discourse?

I said at the beginning that there are two kinds of democracy in America—or two kinds of government to which the term *democracy* is often applied. Only one of those seems to me to be genuinely democratic, and that is the kind of democracy and the kind of civic art that grow out of citizens talking to one another, deliberating, thinking, and in time influencing events, participating in and helping to make the policy decisions, and then executing those decisions by actually carrying them out in their communities. That is the democracy that seems to be at the heart of what many Americans have done all of their lives, generation after generation. The problem is that we haven't recognized that kind of democracy. We haven't called it politics. We don't call the PTA democracy, although that's what the PTA really is, a true American democracy.

Jefferson's dream: a democracy of vigorous citizens engaged in civic life locally and naturally.

Chapter 4

Political Parties

In 1972 journalist David Broder wrote a book titled *The Party's Over;* thirteen years later two political specialists wrote *The Party Goes On.*[1] Whether one thinks that parties are undergoing decline, dealignment (the demise of strong voter attachment to the parties), realignment, or resurgence, no one can deny that our two-party system has been subjected to tremendous changes. In "Can the System Be Saved?" (Selection 16) historian Arthur Schlesinger, Jr., analyzes party functions over time and contends that the parties are in trouble "because they failed to meet national needs in their season of supremacy and because they have lost one after another of their historic functions."

Evidence of the decline (some even say decay) of parties has been gleaned from numerous sources. The following statement summarizes some of the forces that have undermined the traditional roles parties played in politics.

> The last few decades comprise an era of tremendous change for American political parties. Newly enacted campaign finance laws have served as a catalyst for the growth of vast numbers of political action committees (PACs), which now compete with parties for influence over candidates and voters. Party-initiated reforms in the nomination process have restructured the roles of party organizations in candidate recruitment and selection. The emergence of a more independent and more volatile electorate has helped to bring about changes in the tactics that candidates and parties use to garner support. Finally, technological innovations developed in the field of public relations have been adapted to the electoral arena, enabling candidates and parties to use new, more sophisticated means for contesting elections. The impact of these changes has been so overwhelming that it has sparked a debate among political scientists over the efficacy of political parties and their prospects for survival.[2]

The mushrooming growth of modern political action committees (from 608 PACs in 1974 to more than 4,600 in 1991) is a new political phenomenon. Because of the importance of money in legislative elections (the average House race in 1990 cost more than $406,000, the average Senate contest $3.3 million), PACs—legal entities created to raise money—excel at generating large sums of cash for Democratic and Republican incumbents, much less for their challengers. In the November 1990 congressional elections, Senate incumbents "outraised their challengers in PAC money, 3.5 to 1, while House incumbents had an overwhelming 11.5 to 1 advantage in PAC receipts." [3] Overall, PACs contributed more than $150 million of the $445 million spent in the 1990 congressional races.

In his 1991 State of the Union message, President George Bush recommended that PACs be abolished. His proposal does not lack overtones of partisanship. Because PACs give disproportionately to incumbents—and there are more Democratic officeholders than Republican—many Republicans are sympathetic to eliminating or weakening the electoral influence of PACs. Many Democrats advocate spending limits and public financing of campaigns. These proposals are anathema to most Republicans in part because they believe GOP challengers must often spend more (just to acquire "name recognition" via television, for example) in order to oust entrenched Democratic officeholders.

Compounding the arguments over campaign expenditures are disagreements about whether the much-maligned PACs deserve such criticism. Some lawmakers and scholars argue that PACs encourage citizen participation in politics and that their spending is public and accountable. Instead of corrupting the political process, PACs "are a classic expression of American political activity, citizens banding together to pursue a common objective." [4] What might replace PACs also worries some commentators. Special interests and wealthy individuals might exert even greater influence in campaigns without any of the rules and regulations that govern public disclosure of PAC contributions. In short, whether congressional Democrats and Republicans will significantly change the current campaign financing system remains an outstanding issue.

However, partisan reform movements have "restructured" the presidential nominating process. This was particularly the case for the Democrats, who in the 1960s were in turmoil over civil rights and the Vietnam War. The stormy 1968 Democratic National Convention in Chicago, marred by violent protests outside the convention hall, ended in the nomination of Vice President Hubert Humphrey even though he had not entered a single primary. (Primary elections permit rank-and-file partisans to choose candidates or delegates rather than leaving the choice to the party organization.) Liberal Democrats were incensed with Humphrey for supporting President Lyndon Johnson's conduct of the Vietnam War. Critics of the 1968 nominating process also objected to the underrepresentation of women, blacks, and young people and to the selection of most delegates by party caucuses or conventions rather than by popular vote.

Revamping the Selection Process

One result of the bitter 1960s struggle was a series of Democratic party commissions formed to revamp the delegate-selection process. Their success was reflected in the growth of party primaries—from seventeen in 1968 to thirty-seven in 1988. Some analysts contend, however, that the reform process weakened rather than strengthened the Democrats. They argue that presidential candidates can win nomination on their own, without the aid of state and local party organizations and leaders. The party is then sometimes saddled with candidates who reflect the views of activists who won them the nomination rather than broad party sentiment or the views of the average voter.

Not surprisingly, scholars and commentators continue to debate how the presidential selection process should work. In "Point-Counterpoint: Selecting Presidential Candidates" (Selection 17), political scientist James David Barber argues that "peer review" of candidates by experienced political officeholders is the preferred method. Analyst Michael Barone disagrees with this approach, favoring the primary system. An indication that the presidential selection system remains in ferment is the proposal by California Democrats to choose about 40 percent of their 1992 national convention delegates at party caucuses to be held before the start of the presidential primary season.

Both national parties appear to have different problems as the 1990s get under way. Democrats are in charge of Congress and most other elective positions in the United States—except the White House. William Galston's article (Selection 18) outlines how a Democrat might win the presidency, on which the Republicans seem to have an "electoral lock." Needless to say, both parties are striving during the 1990s to change this electoral pattern. Intraparty feuds, common to Democrats because of their diverse coalitional base, have even erupted within Republican ranks (see Selection 19) as they struggle to define their partisan message for upcoming electoral battles.

From the voter's perspective, there has been an erosion of loyalties toward either party. Partisan identification is simply weaker today than it was during the 1950s, and straight-ticket voting has given way to ticket-splitting. Moreover, the number of voters who call themselves independents jumped from 21 percent in 1952 to more than 27 percent in 1991. The well-educated U.S. electorate, kept informed by an aggressive press and media that seem even to "recruit" candidates, is able to evaluate candidates without partisan advice or cues. (Scholar Joseph A. Schlesinger argues that the rise of a free-floating electorate increases the competition between the parties and produces stronger parties than before.[5])

Technology also has weakened the parties, say some theorists of the decline-of-party school. Candidates rely more on computer "software" than party "shoe leather" to win elections. Professional campaign consultants provide an enormous range of services, including fund raising, polling, and media advertising, which enable candidates to bypass party organizations. Some analysts assert that candidate-centered organizations are a *response* to weakened parties; others, that they are a *cause* of weakened parties. Whether cause or effect, candidate-centered campaigns are replacing party-centered politics. Officeholders elected under these conditions owe little or nothing to the formal party organization and its leaders. They are independent entrepreneurs who can push their own agendas rather than their party's.

Despite these changes, the demise of parties appears much exaggerated. Parties exhibit many vital signs and demonstrate a capacity to adapt to new and changing circumstances. A variety of developments, in addition to the rise of competitive parties noted by Schlesinger, illustrates the point.

Gains from Technology

Technology has helped revitalize both parties. Democrats and Republicans have invested heavily in computers to target potential voters, to raise money, and to distribute information. Both parties and their candidates have employed artful television campaigns to enhance their public credibility. National party committees actively recruit, train, and elect candidates to the House of Representatives and the Senate, a phenomenon that analysts refer to as the "centralization" of congressional campaigns.[6] These diverse developments have reinforced the nexus between candidates and parties.

These contrasting views—decline versus resurgence—reinforce the notion that the two-party system is in ferment. Instead of the machine politics, patronage, and voter loyalty of the past, we see both parties adjusting to new political circumstances. The parties are reassessing, for example, their basic position toward the national government. Democrats, long the advocates of an activist federal government, "acknowledge the limitations of government"; Republicans, long-time proponents of the private sector, emphasize the responsibility of government to "get certain jobs done in society."[7] Major and rapid demographic changes, such as the aging of the population, the maturing of the "baby boomers" (those born between 1946 and 1964) as a huge part of the electorate, and the addition of new immigrant groups (Asians and Latinos, for instance), are forcing both parties to reshape their message and appeal. Such adjustments can be divisive, however. "The [Democratic] party is divided over whether its constituency should be based on class, race, generation, or geography," noted one commentator. "It is also searching for policies that can adapt New Deal principles to contemporary realities."[8]

Party professionals, scholars, journalists, and legislators are equally divided over whether a major realignment of political forces is under way in America. (The dominant alignment for nearly half a century has been centered on a Democratic coalition consisting largely of urban workers, minority groups, intellectuals, southerners, and the rural poor.) Since 1980, when the GOP won the White House and the U.S. Senate for the first time in twenty-six years, extensive debate has questioned whether a new philosophic consensus has emerged to dominate national policy making. That consensus emphasizes conservative themes (regulatory reform, private enterprise, strong defense, and tax cuts) and a reduction in the growth and scope of the national government's domestic activities.

Some scholars assert that dealignment best characterizes the state of the party system. "Fewer Americans than ever before now claim enduring attachments to a political party," declared one political scientist.[9] Others wonder whether the nation is in the midst of one of its periodic realignments. Triggered by "critical elections," a realignment often results when a new majority party "must formulate policy within the context of a fundamentally changed political environment as well as in response to a sharply altered issue agenda."[10] Realignment, of course, can appear in many guises: issues, parties, public attitudes, groups, or election results can reflect the change of orientation. Some commentators maintain that the American political system has evolved into a two-tier system: Republicans usually control the White House, Democrats usually control the Congress. In "Party Time, Realignment" (Selection 20) Everett Carll Ladd disputes the contention that "we don't know how to answer this [realignment] question; in fact, we have all of the answers before us."

To say that the United States has a dynamic party system is surely an understatement. Change is ever present. The difficulty is to determine its intensity and direction: toward realignment, dealignment, reinvigoration, decomposition, or all of them simultaneously. As one scholar observed:

This modern party will continue to perform increasingly important functions in politics as services are further developed and candidates rely more and more on the party's resources. It is not possible to predict whether the parties will ever achieve a more cohesive role in developing public policy. The ultimate limits of party activity have not yet been reached, and may not be for some time. What is clear is that, despite the hard times they have suffered, the parties do, indeed, go on.[11]

No one can foresee the future of the party system. At this juncture it seems that the parties have risen to contemporary challenges by assuming new roles and responsibilities or by finding new ways to perform old functions. Certainly a rather new departure for the party system is the rise of a "congressional Democratic party" and a "Republican executive party." James L. Sundquist in Selection 21 explores the ramifications of our new era of coalition government: divided party control of Congress and the White House.

Notes

1. David Broder, *The Party's Over* (New York: Harper & Row, 1972); Xandra Kayden and Eddie Mahe, Jr., *The Party Goes On* (New York: Basic Books, 1985).
2. Paul S. Herrnson, "Do Parties Make a Difference? The Role of Party Organizations in Congressional Elections," *Journal of Politics* (August 1986): 589-590.
3. *Washington Post,* February 25, 1991, A7.
4. *Roll Call,* February 21, 1991, 12.
5. Joseph A. Schlesinger, "The New American Political Party," *American Political Science Review* (December 1985): 1152-1169.
6. *New York Times,* August 26, 1986, A14.
7. *Los Angeles Times,* September 8, 1986, 16.
8. *Village Voice,* April 8, 1986, 18.
9. Paul Allen Beck, "The Dealignment Era in America," in *Electoral Change in Advanced Industrial Democracies: Realignment or Dealignment?* ed. Russell J. Dalton, Scott C. Flanagan, and Paul Allen Beck (Princeton, N.J.: Princeton University Press, 1984), 263.
10. Edward G. Carmines and James A. Stimson, "The Dynamics of Issue Evolution: The United States," in *Electoral Change,* 134.
11. Kirk J. Nahra, "A Brave New Role: The Fall and Rise of American Political Parties," *Harvard Journal on Legislation* (Summer 1986): 666.

16. Can the System Be Saved? The Short Happy Life of American Political Parties

Arthur Schlesinger, Jr.

There is little doubt that significant changes have occurred in America's party system since the late 1960s. Schlesinger, a renowned historian and Albert Schweitzer Professor of the Humanities at City University of New York, analyzes the party system over time and concludes that it is in trouble. In this article published in the British magazine *Encounter* in 1983, he suggests two ways it may be revitalized.

As the high Soviet official said to the visiting U.S. Senator,"We have so much trouble with one single party—how do you ever manage with two?" Much has been written recently in the United States about the travail of the party system. Indeed the trouble is real enough. A century ago, in the presidential election of 1880, 79.4% of Americans eligible to vote cast their ballots. In 1980 only 52.3% did. Each figure bespoke its time. In no presidential election between the Civil War and the turn of the century did voter turnout fall below 70%. In every presidential election since 1960, turnout has been lower than in the one before.

What has happened over a hundred years to the American as political animal? It can hardly be said that those dutiful voters of a century ago flocked to the polls because of the glamour of their leaders. The 1880 choice—James A. Garfield v. Winfield Scott Hancock—was no more inspiring than the choice the republic endured in 1980. The dreary candidacies of those post-Civil War years moved Lord Bryce* to write his famous chapter on "Why Great Men Are Not Chosen President."

Of course there have been significant changes since 1880 in the composition of the American electorate. Over the last 70 years the 19th Amendment (women's suffrage), the Voting Rights Act (blacks), and the 26th Amendment (18-year-old vote) have successively enlarged the pool of eligible voters. But the newly-enfranchised tend, for an interval

---

* James Bryce, Viscount Bryce (1838–1922), English historian and author of *The American Commonwealth*.

at least, to vote less than adult white males long accustomed to the process. Each enlargement has consequently reduced the ratio of turn-out. The lowest 20th-century figures—49.2 and 48.9%—came in 1920 and 1924 after the vote went to women.

Still, the voting pool was steadily enlarged in the 19th century by an influx of immigrants even less accustomed to the process than native-born women, blacks, or 18-year-olds. Yet white male immigrants were rather promptly incorporated into the political system. The agency that seized and indoctrinated them was the political party. In the 20th century the Party has proved notably less successful in mobilising women, blacks, and the young. The conspicuous difference between 1880 and 1980 lies in the decay of the Party as the organising unit of American politics.

Parties have always represented the great anomaly of the American political system. Deplored and even feared by the Founding Fathers, unknown to the Constitution, they imperiously forced themselves into political life in the early years of the republic. Their extra-constitutional presence acquired in surprisingly short order a quasi-constitutional legitimacy. By the time the first President born-an-American-citizen took his oath of office, parties had become, it seemed, the indispensable means of American self-government. (It was fitting that this President, Martin Van Buren, was himself both the creative practitioner and the classic philosopher of the role of Party in the American democracy.)

This extra-constitutional revolution took place because parties met urgent social and political needs. In the dialect of the sociologists, parties were functional. Their existence contributed in a variety of ingenious ways to the maintenance and stability of the system.

Thus the Thirteen Colonies that joined precariously together to form the American Union were separated by local loyalties, by diverging folkways, by imperfect communications; yet they were pledged to establish a Nation. The parties, as national associations, were a force, soon a potent force, against provincialism. "The party system of Government," Franklin D. Roosevelt once said, "is one of the greatest methods of unification and of teaching people to think in common terms of our civilisation...." When by the middle of the 19th century sectional tension between North and South had split most national institutions (even the churches), party organisation was the last bond of union to give way.

Moreover, parties performed a vital function in the national government itself; for they supplied a means, it soon turned out, of overcoming one of the paradoxes of the Constitution. The Founders' doctrine of the "separation of power," literally construed, threatened to defeat the ideal of concerted action which is the essence of effective government. The need to make the new government work demanded a mechanism that would coordinate the executive and legislative branches. The Party now furnished the connective tissue essential to unity of administration.

The parties found other functions in a polity groping to give substance to the idea of democracy. As vehicles for ideas, they furthered the nation's political education, both defining a framework of national consensus and debating national issues within that framework. As instruments of compromise, they encouraged, within the parties as well as between them, the containment and mediation of national quarrels. As agencies of representation, they gave salient interests a voice in national decisions and thus a stake in the national political order. As agencies of recruitment, they brought men into national service and leadership. As agencies of mobilisation, they drew ordinary people into the political community. As agencies of social escalation, they opened paths of upward mobility to ambitious men debarred by class or ethnic prejudice from more conventional avenues to status. And parties were, as noted, a primary agency of "Americanisation," receiving, digesting and assimilating immigrants from abroad, initiating them into the rites of politics, tending, as was said, "to fuse them into one mass of citizenship, pervaded by a common order of ideas and sentiments, and actuated by the same class of motives. . . ."

On the local level, the political organisation, while organised for purposes of self-advancement and self-enrichment, prevailed because it also met social needs. Without mistaking the Party Boss for a sort of early social worker, one may still agree that city machines gave many people lost in an impersonal and demoralising economic world a rare feeling of human contact. The patronage jobs, the food baskets, the Thanksgiving turkey, the ever available precinct captain, the sense (as Martin Lomasney told Lincoln Steffens) "that there's got to be in every ward somebody that any bloke can come to—no matter what he's done—and get help"—all this led, in Herbert Croly's phrase, to "a much more human system of partisan government."

In an age lacking developed forms of mass entertainment, parties even became an essential source of diversion and fun.

> To take a hand in the regulation of society and to discuss it [Tocqueville noted] is his biggest concern and, so to speak, the only pleasure an American knows. This feeling pervades the most trifling habits of life; even the women frequently attend public meetings and listen to political harangues as a recreation from their household labors. Debating clubs are, to a certain extent, a substitute for theatrical entertainments.

In view of the manifold functions served, it is no surprise that American parties rather quickly planted their roots deep into the political culture. The immediate post-Civil War years were, I suppose, the golden age of political parties. Party regularity was higher, party loyalty deeper and party stability greater than at any other time in American history. People inherited their politics as they did their religion, and no more thought of abandoning their party than of abandoning their church. Independent voting was scorned, even when, as in 1884, it was urged by the most highminded spokesmen of the genteel tradition. "A good party," Thomas B. Reed said, "is better than the best man that ever lived." Or, in the sonorous language of Senator Ratcliffe in Henry Adams's *Democracy* (1880),

> Believing as I do that great results can only be accomplished by great parties, I have uniformly yielded my own personal opinons where they have failed to obtain general assent.

How remote this all sounds! The contrast between 1882, say, and 1982 could hardly be more spectacular. A century after the golden age, all the gauges that measure Party efficacy register trouble. By every test Party loyalty in the old style is nearing extinction. "Ticket-splitting" has become epidemic. On billboards and bumper stickers candidates minimise when they do not conceal their party affiliations. The party of those voters who designate themselves "independents" has for some years beaten the Republican Party in public opinion polls. The proportion of independents is particularly high among the young, whose habits predict the electorate of the future. The classic political machine has generally disappeared, even in Chicago. Recent presidential elections have been marked not only by the decline in turnout but by the rise of personalist political movements—George Wallace in 1968, Eugene McCarthy in 1976, John Anderson in 1980. All these developments are symptoms of a party order in a state of dissolution. The most astute of our analysts, Samuel Lubell, has written of "a war of the voters against the party system." What in the world has happened?

Living as we do amidst the ruins of the traditional party system, we see a great nostalgia arising for the "good old days" of Party supremacy. This nostalgia may well conceal some of the reasons for Party decline. For political scientists bent on the revitalisation of the Party system have an unduly romantic conception of the golden age; or so, at least, the historian is tempted to think. It was no doubt a golden age for the Party as an institution. It was hardly a golden age for Presidents or for public policy. As the testimony of Reed and Ratclife suggests, the Party, originating as a means to other ends, had become after a while the end in itself. Like all institutions, the interest in organisational survival superseded the functions that had initially called the Party into being. The religion of Party, however ennobling it may appear in sentimental retrospect, was not universally revered even in its days of glory.

For the zenith of party supremacy in the United States coincided with the nadir of politics as a profession. As party became king, the quality of men entering politics declined. Not a single notable President led the nation in the 40 years between Abraham Lincoln and the first Roosevelt; and Lincoln was a minority President and Roosevelt an accident. Lesser politicians were generally mediocrities when they were not thieves.

"I am not a politician," said Artemus Ward, "and my other habits are good."

"Reader, suppose you were an idiot," wrote Mark Twain. "And suppose you were a member of Congress. But I repeat myself".

We are admonished these days to recall the blessings of Boss rule. Contemplating the invasion of political parties by meddlesome amateurs and zealots streaming up through primaries and caucuses, some insist how much better it was in the good old time when a few bosses could retire to the smoke-filled room and come out with a strong candidate and a "balanced ticket." Yet bosses rarely propose candidates they cannot control. The great Presidents of the 20th century all won nomination over the prostrate bodies of Party Bosses. The typical candidate to emerge from a smoke-filled room is, of course, Warren G. Harding. New ideas have gained access to politics precisely through hard-to-control reformers like Theodore Roosevelt, Woodrow Wilson, Franklin Roosevelt, John Kennedy and, in his peculiar way, Ronald Reagan—all leaders who had to take their parties away from the bosses and remould them in their own images. Bosses are responsive to local interest and local boodle; reformers to national concerns and national aspirations. Let us not succumb to sentimental myths.

Moreover, as Party loyalty, regularity and discipline increased, so did the capacity of parties to evade pressing issues. In the last half of the 19th century the major parties did badly in expressing popular urgencies. The result was increasing resort to Third Parties and to non-party movements pressing issues the major parties ignored—issues the major parties grudgingly coopted only when necessary to assure their own survival.

The 19th-century cult of Party, in fact, stifled the art of politics. Walt Whitman, the old Jacksonian, retained the ante-bellum faith in politics as the method of democracy. He condemned "the fashion among dillettants and fops ... to decry the whole formulation of the active politics of America as beyond redemption, and to be carefully kept away from." He urged young men "to enter more strongly yet into politics.... Always inform yourself; always do the best you can; always vote." Then he added with emphasis,

> Disengage yourself from parties. They have been useful, and to some extent remain so.... But these savage, wolfish parties alarm me. Owning no law

but their own will ... it behooves you to convey yourself implicitly to no party, nor submit blindly to their dictators, but steadily hold yourself judge and master over all of them.

Party supremacy, in short, bred political frustration. Whitman looked for the redemption of politics to

the floating, uncommitted electors, farmers, clerks, mechanics, the masters of parties—watching aloof, inclining victory this side or that side—such are the ones most needed, present and future.

Such sentiments prophesied the steady drift of voters from parties that has characterised the evolution of American politics over the last century.

One must again ask: what happened? The parties, when they set themselves up as ends in themselves, became to a degree their own gravediggers. But they were also the victims of changes in the political environment. For the modern history of political parties has been the story of the steady loss of the functions that gave parties their classical role.

The rise of the mass media reduced the centrality of parties as the means of national unification. The rise of a civil service based on merit largely dried up the resources of patronage. The decline (until rather recently) of mass immigration deprived the city machine of its historic clientele. The professionalisation of social work and the growth of the welfare state reduced the role of parties in ministering to the poor and helpless. A more diversified society opened better avenues of upward social mobility. The development of the modern mass entertainment industry gave people more agreeable diversions than listening to political harangues. And parties in recent times have conspicuously neglected their obligation to recognize urgent popular concerns. Many of the well-known movements of our own age have developed outside the party process. Civil rights, women's liberation, the ecological movement, and most recently the anti-nuclear movement—all surged up from the grass roots to impose themselves on our politics.

The decline of parties has been under way a long time. The "Progressive period" at the start of the 20th century saw an active assault on entrenched party organisation through devices of direct democracy. This particular assault languished rather quickly. But the erosion of parties continued. The 20th century had no shrewder politician than the second Roosevelt. FDR had no 19th-century illusions about the sanctity of party. A Democrat, he cast his first presidential vote for a Republican, appointed two Republicans to his cabinet when elected President himself (and two more in the shadow of war), and a few months before his death was exploring the possibility of a political alliance with the very man the Republicans had run against him four years earlier. "People tell me that I hold to party ties less tenaciously than most of my predecessors in the Presidency," he told a Democratic Party dinner in 1940. ". . . I must admit the soft impeachment." Parties, FDR added,

> are good instruments for the purpose of presenting and explaining issues, of drumming up interest in elections, and, incidentally, of improving the breed of candidates for public office.
>
> But the future lies with those wise political leaders who realise that the great public is interested more in Government than in politics. . . . The growing independence of voters, after all, has been proven by the votes in every Presidential election since my childhood—and the tendency, frankly, is on the increase.

The tendency that FDR discerned greatly intensified in the next 40 years and has landed the parties in the condition of desuetude we gloomily acknowledge today.

It was this situation that produced the zeal of a dozen years ago for Party reform. That reform movement has been much understood. It is currently fashionable to ascribe the contemporary Party crisis to changes in Party rules. But the reform movement of the 1960s, unlike the Progressive movement at the turn of the century, represented a serious effort to hold the Party together and thereby to save the Party system. The theory of the reforms was to tame the new social energies and incorporate them into the Party process. In particular, it was to do for women, non-whites, and the young what 19th-century parties had done for immigrants. Nor can one reasonably argue that the enlargement of citizen participation is such a bad thing in a democracy.

Some of the reforms—the modernisation of procedures, for example, the new strength and autonomy conferred on the national committee, and the larger representation of women and of minorities—probably gave parties a somewhat longer life-expectancy. Other rule changes carelessly or deliberately ignored the interests of parties as institutions; but most of these mistakes have already been corrected. In any event, the idea that rule changes caused the party crisis, and that repealing those changes will cure it, is akin to the delusion of [the French poet and dramatist Edmond] Rostand's Chantecler that his cock-a-doodle made the sun rise. Political scientists should never forget Bryce's sage reminder: "The student of institutions, as well as the lawyer, is apt to overrate the effect of mechanical contrivances in politics." Party reform was not a cause of but a response to deeper maladies.

Parties are in trouble, in short, because they failed to meet national needs in their season of supremacy and because they have lost one after another of their historic functions. And today a fundamental transformation in the political environment is further undermining the already shaky structure of American politics. Two modern electronic devices—television and the computer—are having a devastating and conceivably fatal impact on the Party system.

The old Party system had three tiers: the Politician at one end, the Voter at the other, and the Party in between. The Party negotiated between the politician and the voter, interpreting each to the other and providing the links that held the political system together. The electronic revolution has substantially abolished the mediatorial function.

Information about political choices now flows from other and stronger sources. Television presents the politician directly to the voter, who judges candidates more on what the tiny screen shows him than on what party leaders tell him. Computerised public-opinion polls present the voter directly to the politician, who judges the electorate more on what the polls show him than on what Party leaders tell him. The political organisation in consequence is left to wither on the vine. The prime Party function that A. Lawrence Lowell classically described as "brokerage" has become largely obsolescent.

The Party has lost its domination of the lines of information and communication between the political world and mass opinion. It has lost most of its power to select top candidates, too. This loss is often blamed on the state-wide proliferation of presidential primaries—again the fallacy of ascribing to structure what is really the result of deeper tendencies. Presidential primaries have been around for a long time. It took television to transform them into the controlling force they are today. Television has given the ordinary citizen a new sense of entitlement in the political process. The drama of the "dark horse" magically conjured out of the smoke-filled room has gone, never to return. Presidential nominating conventions, once forums of decision, have become in the electronic age ceremonies of ratification. A person born in the last year that a convention required more than one ballot to choose the presidential candidate would be 30 years old today.

The Party, in addition, is losing its control over campaigns. Television and polling have created a new breed of electronic professionals. Assembled in election-management firms, these media specialists, often working indifferently for one party or the other, usurp the role once played by the party organisation. The most successful specialists—David Garth, for example—insist on total command of campaigns as a condition of their services.

Can the Party system be saved? I must confess scepticism about many of the popular remedies. Proposals to centralise and discipline the parties run against the grain of American politics as well as against the centrifugal impact of the electronic age. Obviously we must do what we can to avoid weakening the Party system further. Such schemes as the direct election of Presidents, a national primary, a national initiative and referendum, might well administer the *coup de grâce* and must be resisted. The provision of free television time to the national Party committees would be modestly useful in propping the parties up. But most structural remedies will have limited effect. The attempt to shore up structure in face of loss of function is artificial and futile.

The Party "is simply no longer indispensable as an agency of mass mobilisation; or as an agency of presidential selection; or as an agency of information and communication; or as an agency of brokerage; or as an agency of welfare and acculturation; or even as a manager of campaigns." If present tendencies continue, parties will soon have little more to do than collect money, certify platforms and provide labels for the organisation of elections and legislatures. The question that engages historians and political scientists today—and ought to engage practical men more than it does—is whether this decay of the Party system is irreversible.

The pessimists think it is. Analysts as different in their personal politics as Walter Dean Burnham and Kevin Phillips argue that the contradictions between capitalism and democracy have reached the point where the liberal tradition has run out of steam and has nothing more to contribute. The welfare state, it is observed, has failed; the free-market alternative is far down the road to failure; and the cumulative result of frustration on the part of citizens and impotence on the part of government will lead to a dismissal of traditional Party politics and a crisis in the foundations of the constitutional régime.

Others, more optimistic, see the present disintegration of the party as a predictable phase in the confused interlude that precedes realignment and revival—a phase in the deconstruction and reconstruction of party systems that American politics has experienced before and will experience again. I have a certain sympathy with this view; for history reminds us of a cyclical rhythm in American politics, a perennial alternation between conservatism and innovation, between the market and the state. As a nation, America goes through seasons of action, passion, idealism, reform and affirmative government, until the country is exhausted. Thereupon Americans demand respite and enter into seasons of privatisation, drift, cynicism, hedonism and negative government. For the moment, the public is in the conservative phase of the cycle. If history is a guide, it will not be in that phase forever.

One may almost speak, I think, of the inevitability of a return to affirmative government in the years ahead. This will come as a technical imperative, a functional necessity; for our major problems are problems that the market is structurally incapable of solving. Big government no doubt might take a reactionary as well as a liberal form; but the historical dialectic suggests that liberal interventionism will receive one more chance before Mr. Kevin Phillips's regressive populist authoritarianism takes over.

Attractive as this more optimistic view is, it still does not address itself directly to the startling changes in the political culture wrought by the electronic revolution.

The question remains: what functions are left to parties in the electronic age?

There are at least two ways, it seems to me, by which these decrepit organisations may acquire a new lease on life. What counts in a democracy at the end is, after all, not money nor publicity nor incumbency, but whether or not policies work. A major source of the anxiety and frustration that darken the climate of our politics today is surely the gnawing fear that all our masters are intellectually baffled by and analytically impotent before the long-term crises of our age—that they know neither the causes nor the cures and are desperately improvising on the edge of catastrophe.

The first need therefore is to revive parties as incubators of remedies. One wishes that the intellectual energy expended in recent years on saving the party by procedural reform had been devoted instead to the substance of our problems. Nor, may I add, are substantive problems going to be solved by large committees with two representatives from every state, Puerto Rico and the District of Columbia. Ideas are produced by individuals working in solitude. They are refined and extended by informal discussions with other individuals. They are disseminated when political leaders, conscious both of the world's problems and their own ignorance, reach out for counsel. The incubation of remedy depends, not on techniques of party organisation, but on the intelligence and resourcefulness of people outside the organisation and on the receptivity and seriousness of individual politicians, who will then use the parties as vehicles for ideas.

The second hope for Party restoration follows in sequence. It lies in the election of competent Presidents who will thereafter act to revitalise their party in the interest of their own more effective command of the political process. The future of the Party may well be as an instrument of Presidents who, in order to put new programmes into effect, invoke the party to overcome the separation of powers in Washington and to organise mass support in the country. The first year of President Reagan shows that this can happen, even in the electronic age. If his remedies had worked, he would not be in trouble today—and when remedies don't work, no amount of organisational legerdemain can redeem a Presidency.

I believe that we must make a stern effort to find a role for political Parties in the days ahead. We must make the effort because the alternative will be a slow, agonised, turbulent descent into an era of what Walter Dean Burnham has called "politics without parties." Of course this is the way America began. But even in those simple 18th-century days the Constitution, as we have seen, required parties for effective operation. One shudders at the consequences for the American polity of "politics without parties" in the high-technology age.

The crumbling away of the historic parties would leave political power in America concentrated in the leaders of personalist movements, in the interest groups that finance them, and in the executive bureaucracy, which will increasingly supply the major element of stability in an ever more unstable environment. The rest of the voters might not even have the limited entry into and leverage on the process that the Party system, for all its manifold defects, has made possible. Without the stabilising influence of parties, our politics would grow angrier, wilder, and more irresponsible.

We cannot reclaim the past by act of will. As Henry Adams observed:

> The sum of political life, was, or should have been, the attainment of a working political system. Society needed to reach it. If moral standards broke down, and machinery stopped working, new morals and machinery of some sort had to be invented.

This is surely the problem for American statecraft today—to come up with the morals, machinery, and ideas demanded by the harsh tasks of the remaining years of the 20th century. We will never attain a working political system by concentrating on the revision of party rules and structure. We will attain it only by remembering that politics is the art of solving problems.

17. Point-Counterpoint: Selecting Presidential Candidates

James David Barber
Michael Barone

Choosing presidential candidates is no easy task. Democrats and Republicans have evolved their own selection process. Some scholars, such as James David Barber of Duke University, argue that the current system is "seriously flawed." Barber contends, in an essay published in *The New York Times* in 1988, that what is needed to improve the system is a "peer review" screening process. Politically experienced men and women, all knowledgeable in the work of government, would convene in their respective national party caucus to assess the various presidential candidates and "find the best [candidate for] President."

Michael Barone, an experienced Washington political analyst currently with *U.S. News & World Report*, argues against presidential selection by "peer review" in his essay printed in the *Washington Post* in 1988. Instead, he contends that it is "primaries, not caucuses, that produce [presidential] candidates able to win and govern." Party caucuses, he suggests, are not forums filled with seasoned political pros; they are often dominated by the supporters of various candidates.

James David Barber:
Pick Presidential Candidates
By Peer Review

Despite all the despair voiced about the process of picking Presidents, there is hope.

Scholars are beginning to recognize that the problem is not simply how to design the institution of the Presidency but rather to find the right person for that highly personalized job. Journalists increasingly realize that reporting horse-race odds, campaign strutting and the candidates' speculations about what they might do in the job has become boring and useless for readers and reviewers, who want to know how each candidate would perform in the White House.

Still, the process is seriously flawed. It has taken enormous time, money, energy and attention just to weed the field down to a set of contenders worth serious consideration. Only about one out of three Americans cares enough to vote these days. The process needs fixing if this country is to find the leaders it needs to survive and advance in an era of extraordinary challenge.

Among the many flaws in the current system, the worst is the absence of peer review. To hire an executive or an editor or a professor, one wants a resume but also letters of recommendation. We need to bring in the judgment of persons practiced in the candidate's line of work, including those who have worked directly with him or her over the years.

For a potential President, the relevant line of work is government and the relevant peers are government officials: Senators, Representatives and governors. What each party needs is a national caucus that brings these peers together and gets them to recommend candidates—ideally, three or four—for members of the party to select in a national primary.

What good would that do? A pair of national caucuses at the start of campaign '88, in January, would have spared the necessity of checking out Hart, Haig, Biden, Kemp, Jackson, Robertson, du Pont and perhaps a few others. Newsworthy as they may be, not one is qualified to be President—as most top officials know.

A national caucus might well have drafted better nominees than we now have. Instead of poking around for months among marginal and exotic candidates, we could have been concentrating on the relative merits of real alternatives—people like Nunn or Cuomo for the Democrats and Bush or one of the Bakers for the Republicans. The result, reasonable to hope for, would be a statesman in the White House.

Back to the smoke-filled room? Back to the bosses? No healthy skeptic is going to suppose that the national caucus would congregate only the pure to plan the good. No doubt the caucus would feature self-interest, ambition, corruption and dirty dealing, along with the sunnier side of official leadership.

But unlike the olden days, when we had no primaries, whoever the caucus picked would be submitted to the party membership, who would choose the party's nominee. Call it checks and balances—the model set up 200 years ago by the Constitution-makers because they, too, were skeptics.

The Framers tried to set peer review into the selection of Presidents by inventing the Electoral College. They got the numbers roughly right (one for each Senator and Representative) but mistakenly excluded other office holders; as a result, the electors quickly became what Edward Corwin, a constitutional scholar, called "party dummies," mere carriers of popular preference.

That is basically what convention delegates have become; they are there to have a jolly time, make friends, get on TV and cast a first ballot vote as determined by a primary, an action that typically designates the nominee. Delegates are chosen not for political experience, professional judgment or commitment to Government after the next election. They are party people who get to attend an inspiriting rally to set off the campaign. Fine. But you do not let the cheerleaders pick the coach.

A national party caucus system, requiring no constitutional amendment or abolition of the present primary-and-convention system, might help us find the best President, which we had better do if we want our children to survive. In addition, it might start momentum toward the one reform most urgently needed: the development of national political organizations that would coordinate consensus and affect government results. We could call them political parties.

Michael Barone:
Curb the Caucuses

For 20 years skeptics have argued that political party reforms have taken too much of the decision-making power away from well-informed, politically experienced party bosses who have a vested stake in their parties' electoral success. The 1988 contests, however, have demonstrated that this argument applies with greater force against the party caucuses (which the critics of the reforms tend to approve) than the primaries (at which they look askance.)

This is not just because the Iowa caucuses did a much poorer job of predicting winners than the New Hampshire primary—although they did. You remember Iowa: the state which on Feb. 8 gave us Presidents Dick Gephardt and Bob Dole and vice presidential nominees Paul Simon and Pat Robertson. New Hampshire's record of voting for every presidential winner (though not every presidential nominee) since 1952 seems by early April at little risk: it backed George Bush and Michael Dukakis.

Bush and Dukakis are the kind of experienced, well-disciplined, reputedly moderate politicians whom critics of party reform felt would be picked by party pros but not by primary voters. Voters, after all, proved vulnerable to enthusiasms for fringe candidates like Eugene McCarthy and George McGovern or dangerous demagogues like George Wallace. The party pros who dominate caucuses, it was assumed, would make no such mistakes.

But in 1988 Bush and Dukakis have won their major victories in primaries. The big winners in caucuses, from Iowa to Alaska to Maine to Michigan, have been not seasoned centrists but this season's reverends, Robertson and Jesse Jackson. Both have demonstrated some appeal in primaries as well, but in their crucial tests, before favorably disposed electorates in South Carolina and Wisconsin, they proved unable to win in five or ten thousand polling places what they had gained in much smaller number of caucus sites.

Most instructive are the results in my own home state, Michigan. Michigan reverted to caucuses after George Wallace won with a big margin in 1972 (the day after he had been shot in Maryland). The result has been, for both parties, that pathetically small numbers of enthusiasts end up casting the presidential nominating votes of a state of 9 million people.

The Republicans' complicated precinct system allowed Robertson's tax-exempt Freedom Council to persuade several thousand evangelicals and others, in alliance with backers of Jack Kemp, to win control of the Republican party structure. The Bush campaign's clever maneuvers gave it control of the crucial January 1988 convention. But, for a while, Robertson, with the fervent support of perhaps 10,000 voters, could trumpet that he had won 1988's first victory.

The Michigan Democrats' "firehouse primary" caucus system allowed any eligible voter claiming to be a Democrat to cast a vote—but only between 10 and 4 on a Saturday and at only 576, rather than the usual 11,000, voting locations. In 1988 some 212,000—from a state that cast 3.8 million votes in the 1984 general election—came in and voted. About 40 percent of them—no one is sure, because no exit poll was taken—were black, and Jesse Jackson, with the 20 percent vote among whites he had been receiving in other caucus situations (much of it from Michigan's large graduate-student proletariat and Arab-American populations), beat Dukakis by 54 percent to 28 percent.

What Michigan did not show—though some observers looking only at the percentages for each candidate assumed it did—was that large numbers of white blue-collar workers were voting for Jackson. Quite a few whites did vote for Jackson in Connecticut and Wisconsin, but only enough to put him on the short end of 58-28 and 48-28 percent margins against Dukakis.

Why are caucuses now such easy pray for candidates with support from enthusiasts? Because one of the assumptions of the critics of party reform is no longer true—that there exists a group of party leaders who remain involved in party affairs and dominate the party structure from one election year to the next. Today party organizations are empty shells. The slots within them—the precinct delegate and county convention positions—mostly wait to be filled by the enthusiastic backers of any candidate who can manipulate 10,000 people in a state of millions.

At the same time, opinion has changed in ways that make primary voters more moderate and responsible, less angry or anxious to "send them a message." But the same qualities make ordinary voters more apathetic, so they can easily be outvoted or outmaneuvered in caucus systems that require any substantial commitment of time by comparative handfuls of enthusiasts and extremists who care not a fig for the views of the large majority of their fellow citizens.

Before you decry the dullness and vapidity of the choices that voters appear to have made in 1988, consider what they had to do. They had to decide between some 13 declared candidates, two of whom (Bush and Dole) they knew and liked fairly well, two of whom they knew something about but tended rather to dislike (Hart and Jackson), and the other nine of whom they knew nothing at all about. They had to choose in a country in which no single issue dominates the political landscape and in which old political labels tell very little about what a candidate believes in or would do. Despite Americans' general lack of interest in politics and government, they were able to make intellectually defensible choices—and the choices they made in primaries were certainly more defensible, by almost any criterion, than those made in caucuses.

There is an argument for having a few contests in the primary season that put a premium on organization and reward a candidate with enthusiastic support from a small segment of the electorate. But it is not the same argument that has long been made for caucuses, which are supposed to be the voice of seasoned political insiders. Nelson Polsby's definitive "Consequences of Party Reform" argues for a mixed system, with caucuses in states where parties are strong. But 1988 tells us that there are few of these states left. It is primaries, not caucuses, that produce candidates able to win and govern.

18. Putting a Democrat in the White House

William A. Galston

William A. Galston, a professor of public affairs at the University of Maryland and issues adviser to Walter Mondale in his 1984 quest for the presidency, examines why the "Democratic party has lost the ability to sustain a presidential majority based on a progressive agenda." In this 1989 article from *The Brookings Review*, he argues that Democrats have avoided their fundamental problems and practiced the "politics of evasion." Instead of facing reality, they have focused on less consequential matters such as fund-raising and technology, media and personality.

If the party doesn't change its strategy, Galston states, Democratic presidential candidates will continue to lose the White House to Republicans.

Half a century ago, Franklin Roosevelt set the Democratic party on a new, progressive course. For decades his legacy—economic opportunity, social inclusiveness, international strength—formed the foundation of the party's achievements and the basis of its support. Today this inheritance is depleted. The Democratic party has lost the ability to sustain a presidential majority based on a progressive agenda.

The causes of that decline are not obscure. Some of the party's presidential nominees have campaigned in inhospitable circumstances, and some have been inept. But the chief difficulty goes far deeper. Over the past two decades, too many Americans have come to see the Democratic party, at least at the presidential level, as inattentive to their economic interests, indifferent if not hostile to their moral sentiments, and ineffective in defense of their national security. It is these perceptions, rooted in the history of the past generation, that predisposed crucial portions of the electorate to believe the charges George Bush leveled against Michael Dukakis last year.

For too long Democrats have ignored their fundamental problem. They have focused on fund-raising and technology, media and momentum, personality and tactics—on everything except what matters most. Rather than facing reality, they have embraced the politics of evasion. The result has been repeated defeat. And if the party doesn't change, it will keep on losing.

After the reverses of the past 20 years, after the fiasco of 1988, it would be reasonable to expect a spirit of concern, even a sense of urgency within Democratic circles. Instead, complacency is pervasive. "We may lose the presidency," goes the argument, "but we will continue to control both houses of Congress and the majority of governorships and state legislatures. The elections of 1990 look promising. Besides, the presidential winds are about to shift—indeed, are already shifting—in our direction."

A more shortsighted stance is hard to imagine. To be sure, some developments in 1988 were positive, and if things go badly enough for the incumbent, the Democrats could eventually win a presidential election. On balance, though, the presidential trends are far from favorable; and if Democrats continue to be unsuccessful at the presidential level, the divided government to which the party has grown accustomed may be replaced by trickle-down Republicanism.

In 1992 reapportionment will shift 18 House seats, most of them moving from Democratic to Republican states. The last time reapportionment coincided with a presidential election, Republicans won nearly two-thirds of the open sets. It could well happen again.

The risks are even higher in the Senate. Of the 34 seats up in 1992, Democrats must defend 20, and 11 of those seats are held by senators elected for the first time in 1986. Ten of the new senators won with 55 percent or less of the popular vote, 8 with under 52 percent. Four squeaked by with only 50 percent. If the Democratic presidential ticket is weak once again, Republicans could easily gain control of the Senate in 1992.

In short, while political scientists and pundits speak of a "split-level realignment" into a congressional party and a presidential party, rising Republican strength at the presidential level could gradually spread to the Senate and House, governorships, state legislatures, courthouses, and finally to party identification. The process already well under way in states such as Texas and Florida could turn out to be a harbinger of the Democrats' national fate.

Replacing Myth with Reality

Democrats still have time to avert disaster. But to do so, they must discard comforting myths and confront the true dimensions of their decline.

Myth 1: Nonvoters are the problem, and higher turnout is the solution.

Reality: A CBS/*New York Times* post election survey indicated that if every eligible voter had cast a ballot, Bush would still have won—by a larger margin.

Myth 2: Democratic nonvoters are the problem, and selective mobilization is the solution.

Reality: Such a mobilization would help, but it isn't enough to get the job done. A recent study by voting analyst Ruy Texeira showed that if blacks and Hispanics had voted at the same rate as whites, Dukakis would still have lost the election by more than 4 million votes. If the poor had voted at the same rate as the nonpoor, Dukakis would still have lost by 5 million votes.

While a final judgment must await better data, preliminary analysis suggests that selective mobilization of Democratic core constituencies at national average voting rates would not have changed the results of the presidential election in even a single state.

Myth 3: The rise of upscale professional and white-collar voters has damaged the Democratic party's ability to compete.

Reality: Upper-income voters—those with family incomes above $50,000 in 1988 dollars—were just as likely to support the Democratic nominee in 1988 as they were in 1976, when Jimmy Carter won 38 percent of their vote. For that matter, lower-income voting behavior has not changed either; 62 percent of the voters with incomes under $12,500 (in 1988 dollars) supported Carter in 1976, 63 percent voted for Dukakis in 1988.

The most significant change has occurred in the heart of the middle class—voters with family incomes between $25,000 and $50,000—40 percent of the total electorate. Fifty-one percent of these voters supported Carter, while only 43 percent supported Dukakis.

The stark fact is that the Republican party is no longer the exclusive preserve of the rich. If only voters with family incomes of $50,000 or less had participated in the 1988 presidential election, George Bush would still have won.

Myth 4: The party's most significant losses since 1976 have come among white Protestants, for whom Jimmy Carter held a special appeal.

Reality: While the swing among southern white Protestants from the Democrats to the GOP has been large, nationally the percentage swing among Catholics has been even larger—by some measures, twice as large. Jimmy Carter won 55 percent of the Catholic vote, Dukakis only 47 percent.

Compared with the benchmark of Reagan's 1984 victory, Bush was 6 points weaker among Protestants but only 2 points weaker with Catholics. Other data suggest that Dukakis's failure to make significant headway among Catholic voters dashed his hopes in such key heartland states as Pennsylvania, Illinois, and Michigan.

Myth 5: Because the party's nominees have feared the liberal label, the centrist timidity of their general election campaigns has turned off core Democratic supporters.

Reality: Dukakis won 82 percent of the liberal vote, versus only 74 percent for Carter. Dukakis took 89 percent of the black vote, significantly higher than Carter's 83 percent. Nor is there any solid evidence to support the view that turnout decline since 1976 has been disproportionately concentrated in these two (overlapping) groups.

Myth 6: Democratic presidential nominees have been losing because the electorate has grown significantly more conservative.

Reality: At least as measured by voters' self-descriptions, remarkably little ideological change has occurred over the past four election cycles. In 1976, 20 percent of the electorate called itself liberal. In 1988 that figure had dropped only two points, to 18 percent. In 1976, 31 percent of the voters called themselves conservative. Twelve years later, that figure was up only two points, to 33 percent.

The real problem is the electorate's perception that the Democratic party's nominees have become more liberal. Carter won the support of 30 percent of the self-identified conservatives in 1976. Dukakis won only 19 percent. This drop in conservative support accounts for more than half of the five-point decline in overall national support from Carter's 50 percent to Dukakis's 45 percent.

Ideological uniformity within the political parties and ideological differentiation between them is more pronounced at the presidential level today than it was 12 years ago. Compared with 1976, liberal voters today are far more likely to vote Democratic, conservatives to vote Republican. This ideological sorting-out has worked to the advantage of Republicans for the simple reason that the number of voters who consider themselves conservative is nearly double the number who call themselves liberal.

Myth 7: The gender gap has worked increasingly in favor of Democratic presidential nominees.

Reality: Dukakis and Carter were each supported by 51 percent of women voters. (By some measures, a slightly lower percentage voted for Dukakis.) By contrast, Dukakis's support among men was nine points lower than Carter's (42 percent versus 51 percent). The gender gap is not the product of a surge of Democratic support among women, but the result of the erosion of Democratic support among men.

In short, the Democratic party has been losing ground among voters, not nonvoters; among the middle class, not the rich or the poor; among Catholics as well as Protestants; among nonliberals, not liberals; among whites, not minorities; among men, not women. Intensified mobilization of groups that still support Democrats is important, but it cannot by itself compensate for the broad erosion of support in other parts of the electorate. The Democratic party has no alternative: if it wishes to rebuild a presidential majority, it must regain competitiveness among the kinds of voters it has lost in the past generation.

The party's presidential problem is more than demographic; it is geographic as well.

Of all the myths now current, perhaps the most misguided is the California dream—the conclusion, drawn from the past election by many Democrats, that their rising strength in the West can counterbalance the collapse of southern support for Democratic presidential nominees and that the party therefore doesn't have to work hard at regaining competitiveness in the South.

This latest exercise in the politics of evasion fails the test of basic political arithmetic. Gains outside the South cannot fully compensate for a southern wipeout. If Dukakis had prevailed in all the western states where he had a chance, carried the heartland states he narrowly lost, and won all the eastern states within reach, he still would not have assembled enough electoral votes to win.

The underlying logic of the electoral college shows why. There are 155 electoral votes in the southern and border states, 41 in the Plains and Rocky Mountains states with impregnable Republican majorities, and 23 more in reliably Republican states of the Midwest and Northeast. If the South is conceded to the Republican presidential nominee, he begins with a base of 219 electoral votes and needs only 51 more. New Jersey,

138 ■ William A. Galston

Ohio, and Michigan are enough to put him over the top—and George Bush carried them handily, with margins of 8 to 14 points.

It only gets worse in 1992. According to projections from preliminary census estimates, reapportionment will net the states in the Republican base 12 additional electoral votes, for a total of 231. New Jersey and Ohio would be just about enough to give Bush the victory—even if he were to lose California and a host of other states he carried last time.

If Democrats try to win without the South in 1992, the Republicans would be able to concentrate their organization, financial resources, and candidate's schedule to win 39 electoral votes in the same pool of states from which Democrats would have to garner 267. (The Democratic nominee begins with the District of Columbia's 3 electoral votes.) The Republican nominee would start holding two pairs while his Democratic opponent would be drawing to an inside straight. If the Democrats are competitive only in states with 310 electoral votes, the odds against their nominee attaining 270 are dauntingly high. The conclusion is unavoidable: if Democrats do not compete—and compete strongly—in every region of the country, their chances of regaining the presidency are vanishingly small.

When I say "every region," I mean just that. The biggest surprise of 1988 was not that Dukakis was trounced in Dixie, but that he failed to prevail in heartland states such as Illinois, Pennsylvania, and Michigan where the costs of Reaganomics have been so high and where class and ethnic identification should have worked strongly in his favor. The Democrats have more than a southern problem, and they need more than a southern remedy.

The Road Ahead

Democrats must choose between two basic strategies. The first is to hunker down, change nothing, and wait for some catastrophe—deep recession, failed war, or a breach of the Constitution—to deliver victory. This strategy has a number of disadvantages. It places the party entirely at the mercy of events. It puts Democrats in the position of tacitly hoping for bad news—a stance the electorate can smell and doesn't like. And it is a formula for purposeless, ineffective governance.

The other strategy—active rather than passive—is to address the party's weaknesses directly. The basic formula is straightforward. The next Democratic nominee must be fully credible as commander-in-chief of the armed forces and as the prime steward of the country's foreign policy; he must squarely reflect the moral sentiments of average Americans; and he must offer a progressive economic message, based on the values of social opportunity and individual effort, that can unite the interests of those already in the middle class with those who are struggling to enter it.

There is almost certainly a powerful constituency for such a message. A wealth of data suggests that the American people are uneasy about the place of the American economy in the world; that they favor a diverse and tolerant society; and that they understand the dependence of strength abroad on economic and social progress at home. They are ready to endorse a program that invests in the future, rebuilds international competitiveness, and helps out with the increasingly unaffordable basics of middle-class life such as first-time homeownership, child care, education, and health.

Adoption of such a program would place the Democratic nominee squarely in the mainstream, on the side of average families. It would help bolster a multiracial coalition based on shared values and common interests. It would be consistent with the party's historic commitments. And it would be credible. A CBS/*New York Times* poll last year found that 64 percent of the electorate identified Republicans as the party of the rich; only 9 percent thought it favors the middle class, and 20 percent felt it treats all classes the same. By contrast, 24 percent thought Democrats favor the middle class, and 39 percent believed that they treat everyone equally.

The difficulty is that swing voters do not respond to a progressive economic message, even when one is offered, because Democratic presidential candidates have failed to win their confidence in other key areas. Credibility on defense, foreign policy, and social values is the ticket that will get Democrats in the door to make their affirmative economic case. If they don't hold that ticket, they won't even get a hearing.

Consider the figures assembled by a bipartisan consortium of respected public opinion researchers. On election day, 67 percent of the voters thought Bush would deal with the Soviets better than Dukakis would; on arms control negotiations, it was Bush 64, Dukakis 22; maintaining a strong defense, 66 to 22; fighting terrorists, 57 to 26. Even in keeping the country out of war, a traditional Democratic advantage, Bush held a 47-36 edge. More than a third of the electorate, 37 percent, had reached the conclusion that Dukakis would actually weaken national security; only 8 percent thought Bush would. Numerous surveys indicate that these issues were very important to swing voters who eventually decided to support George Bush. The message is clear: if the next Democratic nominee isn't credible to the people as a potential commander-in-chief, he won't be elected president.

On the central social issue of our time—violent crime—the situation was no brighter. Overall, Bush enjoyed a 52-35 edge. Among voters who cared intensely about the death penalty, the margin was 61-24. If the next Democratic nominee can't deal credibly with the challenge of enhancing what Rep. Bill Gray has called personal and family security, he won't be elected president. Once again, it is just that simple.

The Democratic party's vulnerability on social issues goes far beyond crime. In a CBS/*New York Times* poll last year, 73 percent thought that the United States had experienced a severe breakdown in moral standards over the past 20 years; only 22 percent disagreed. But for too many Americans whose support is essential, the Democratic party has contributed to this breakdown. In their eyes, Democrats have become the party of individual rights but not individual responsibility; the party of self-expression but not self-discipline; the party of sociological explanation but not moral accountability.

The next Democratic nominee must convey a clear understanding of, and identification with, the social values and moral sentiments of the vast majority of Americans. The firm embrace of programs, such as national service, that link rights to responsibilities and effort to reward, would be a good start. But Democrats must go further. The American people overwhelmingly believe that the central purpose of criminal punishment is to punish—that is, to express moral outrage against acts that injure the community. It would certainly help if the party's next nominee could articulate this view convincingly and back it with a tough, effective program.

The needed changes cannot come from policy commissions or mid-term conventions or party functionaries. They can only come from leaders—candidates for the presidential nomination—with the courage to challenge entrenched party orthodoxies and to articulate new visions. That means the party must give up the litmus tests that have for so long throttled debate. It will mean controversy, even conflict. But productive conflict is far better than a barren and spurious unity.

The Republican party was transformed into a governing party during the 1970s because it was willing to endure a frank internal debate on political fundamentals. Democrats must at long last set aside the politics of evasion and embark on a comparable course.

19. Why Are Republicans Fighting Like Democrats?

David S. Broder

"The Democrats have no monopoly on feuding," asserts the noted political analyst and *Washington Post* columnist David Broder in an article published in that newspaper in December 1990. Broder examines the fissures within the national Republican coalition, pointing out that as the GOP coalition approaches majority status, it is more likely to experience the splits faced by the Democrats over the past sixty years or more. The intra-party feud among Republicans, reminiscent of traditional Democratic battles, reflects divisions that are, according to Broder, "partly generational, partly institutional (White House vs. Congress) and, as always in politics, partly personal."

If it seems that you cannot pick up a newspaper these days without reading about Republicans running against other Republicans for congressional leadership and campaign committee jobs, Republicans assailing other Republicans over their policy heresies, Republicans flinging manifestos, newsletters and press releases at each other, the impression is correct.

The battling that has broken out in recent weeks inside George Bush's White House and the Republican Party is not unexpected or unnecessary. It may even turn out to be healthy. But it is mislabeled and misunderstood—even by some of the participants.

Some of the contests represent no more than conflicting ambitions, but others have the earmarks of deeper political and ideological divisions. And people who are accustomed to seeing the Democrats hurling custard pies and heavier missiles at each other seem shocked that it should be the Republicans who are involved in an uncivil civil war.

They should not be. The closer the GOP coalition comes to majority status, the more likely that splits similar to those the Democrats have faced for 60 years or more will occur. The divisions are partly generational, partly institutional (White House vs. Congress) and, as always in politics, partly personal.

The confusion arises from the effort to cram all this ferment into the convenient conservative vs. progressive dichotomy journalists and politicians alike have used to describe Republican factions since the Bull Moose-Old Guard split between Teddy Roosevelt's and William Howard Taft's forces early in this century. Whatever this is, it's not Eisenhower vs. Robert Taft or Goldwater vs. Rockefeller.

If you ask why the debate has erupted at this particular moment, the obvious answer is that it began with the autumn budget battle. The deficit summit President Bush asked for was endlessly frustrating for congressional Republicans; even those who were in on the negotiations found themselves shunted into a secondary role, as White House Chief of Staff John Sununu and budget director Richard Darman tried to strike a deal with congressional Democrats. When that bargain turned out to include tax hikes along with spending cuts, many Republicans on Capitol Hill rebelled.

Recalling vividly how useful the "no new taxes" pledge had been to Bush in his 1988 campaign for the White House they took it unkindly— to put it mildly—when he "caved in" to the Democrats and undercut similar pledges they had made in preparation for their 1990 races. White House arguments that the budget deal would improve prospects for a healthy economy in Bush's reelection year only made many congressional Republicans more convinced he was prepared to sacrifice their 1990 ambitions to help himself in 1992.

That is part of a larger complaint about Bush's leadership—or really his lack of leadership. Paul Weyrich, the head of the Free Congress Foundation, said, "This is the first time in a long time that the conservative movement has not had a clear leader; I think even Bush would agree he's not that leader today. We are back where we were after the death of Bob Taft and before the emergence of Barry Goldwater and the succession of Ronald Reagan. And when we don't have a leader, we fragment."

Former Tennessee governor Lamar Alexander, now [Secretary of Education], said, "The presidency is preoccupied with war-and-peace questions, and it's virtually a full-time job to stay one step ahead of the world." But after the Cold War, Alexander added, "Americans have to define who we are and what tasks we need to be about, and that job isn't getting done."

In less polite terms, a veteran of past Republican administrations said, "It all goes to the Oval Office. Whatever Ronald Reagan's shortcomings—and he certainly had them—he was a leader who gave the party a clear sense of direction. Bush has not done that."

As Alexander suggested, the criticism applies particularly to domestic policy—the area Bush has acknowledged takes second place in his interest to national security and foreign policy issues. And the complaints about the "vacuum" in domestic affairs are sharpened by the election just past and the election campaign soon to begin.

The reason ideological warfare has broken out now, said the Heritage Foundation's Burton Yale Pines, "is that we had the 1990 elections and they were terrible." Republican losses were not severe by historical standards, but the voters cut short the careers of several outstanding House members who were defeated in races for senator or governor. "A lot of good candidates got burned this year," pollster Linda Divall remarked, "and there's a growing frustration within the party that, the way things are going, we're not going to control the House or Senate in the foreseeable future."

Agreeing with that assessment, V. Lance Tarrance, a Houston-based GOP pollster, said, "I have not seen as much disappointment and frustration at the local level in 20 years as I've seen since this election. To the rank-and-file volunteer precinct captains, the budget agreement looked like appeasement. They're not so much angry as disappointed and confused as to what our direction and even our expectations should be. We've won five of six presidential elections, but we're barely staying even in the rest of the game; we're not developing the momentum we need."

Because the program Bush puts before Congress and the country inevitably will forecast the issues in the 1992 campaign, the forces who are vying to fill the policy vacuum have focused their efforts on what Bush will propose in January when he delivers his State of the Union address.

Junior staff people in the White House, led by presidential assistant James Pinkerton and encouraged by Secretary of Housing and Urban Development Jack Kemp, are pressing the president to seize the offensive from Capitol Hill Democrats by embracing an ambitious social agenda of his own. Their efforts to define what Pinkerton calls a "New Paradigm" for domestic policy have been publicly ridiculed by Darman and kept firmly in hand by Sununu.

The Kemp-Pinkerton caucus has strong support among younger congressional Republicans, who are frustrated by their lack of leverage on Capitol Hill. It is no accident that these same Republicans—notably House Minority Whip Newt Gingrich (R-Ga.) and a previous occupant of that post, Sen. Trent Lott (R-Miss.)—led the revolt against the budget compromise forged by Darman and Sununu. Their opposition was based in part on principle, but equally important was their belief that if party differences were blurred by compromise on an issue as fundamental as taxing-and-spending priorities, the rationale for overturning the persistent Democratic majorities in Congress would disappear.

Sununu and Darman see their intra-party adversaries as intransigent ideologues, more interested in proving a theory than in running a government. Gingrich, Lott, Kemp and Pinkerton believe, equally fervently, that their adversaries have been so captured by the Washington power game they have abandoned all principles and cannot be relied on to provide any coherent message—either for the Bush administration or the next Bush campaign.

How this will be resolved may not be clear until Bush submits his new budget in January. In a talk last week, Bush pleased the conservative activists pushing the "New Paradigm" programs by saying that present programs "are not working for the people . . . who want to pull themselves out of dependency and into a life of self-sufficiency in a safe, clean and drug-free community."

But those who know him well are nearly unanimous in guessing the president will seek to straddle the divisions rather than choosing one side over the other. In a comment that seemed to foreshadow that kind of Bush decision, Robert Teeter, the Michigan pollster and Bush confidant who will play a key role in the reelection campaign, argued that the constraints of the budget all but rule out anything very ambitious on the domestic side. "At the same time," he said, "it's healthy to have people looking for newer, better and more conservative ways to get at our domestic problems."

The "Chinese restaurant menu" approach, as some have called it— taking one proposal from Column A and another from Column B—has served Bush well in his political career. But that kind of approach also has led to charges of inconsistency, as Bush has tacked this way and then that to stay in touch with the shifting center of Republican orthodoxy and political power. And it leads some Republicans to express fears that even if the measured tactical approach gets Bush reelected, it would not provide coattails for other Republicans in what many of them had hoped would be a watershed election year.

"I think we're looking at another 1972," one Republican operative said, referring to the year in which Richard Nixon won landslide reelection but Republicans made few House gains and actually lost two Senate seats. A White House insider offered the thought that the internal debate is only partially generational but more accurately reflects the tension between what he called "the Nixon-Ford heirs and the Reaganites" who have found places in Bush's carefully balanced administration.

In this view, the Nixon-Ford wing, including Darman and most Cabinet members, "are interested in some small reforms, but basically take an approach to governing that leads them to maintain the status quo and negotiate with Congress." The Reaganites, including Kemp and many younger White House staffers, want bigger and more radical changes and are prepared to challenge the Democratic Congress—even if it makes the day-to-day work of governing more difficult. Sununu, who was originally identified as being a Reaganite, more and more has operated in alliance with Darman to keep the Nixon-Ford approach on top.

What both sides in the struggle are trying to decipher is how much the 1990 election shifted the ideological balance of power. It weakened the conservative base slightly on Capitol Hill, where most of the defeated House members and the lone senator to lose reelection came from conservative ranks. The party's southern flank was breached by the loss of governorships in Florida, Texas and Oklahoma—although all three of those states remain as cornerstones for the Bush electoral-college coalition in 1992.

What was striking was the election of Republicans to replace Democratic governors in Minnesota, Michigan, Ohio and Massachusetts—four states that virtually have to be part of a successful Democratic presidential candidate's electoral coalition. With the GOP retaining governorships in Illinois, Iowa and Wisconsin, the party's historical base in the Midwest now is in its best shape in years, and becomes a possible offset to the weakened Dixie stronghold.

Even more important is the emergence in this election of a group of moderate-progressive Republican governors who could conceivably help revive that declining and submerged spectrum of the party. They are led by Pete Wilson, shifting from the Senate to the California governorship, and they include Jim Edgar, the new governor in Illinois, George Voinovich in Ohio, Arne Carlson in Minnesota and William Weld in Massachusetts.

They are not identical in political history or outlook, but most are what former governor Alexander calls "activist populist governors," intent on using their offices to improve the economies and tackle the social problems in their states. Alexander, who served as a role model for that kind of approach in his eight years in Nashville, said that "because of their visibility, the governors are the ones who most likely will define the domestic agenda—and make that the president's national agenda.

One political reason to think that Alexander may be proved right is that candidate Bush in 1988 relied on governors like Sununu (then in New Hampshire) and his counterparts in Florida, South Carolina, Illinois, Wisconsin, Texas and California as his principal political allies. "The governors will be his key allies again," predicts Republican pollster Linda Divall.

That means he will have to listen attentively to what they say in 1991 and 1992—and their message is likely to reinforce the Kemp-Gingrich-Pinkerton approach. The Brookings Institution's A. James Reichley, an authority on the Republican Party, said, "It's ironic, but these moderate and progressive governors may make Bush look with more favor on the Kemp approach. They are activists and almost all of them have, in their constituency, urban industrial cities with serious social problems. They are going to push the federal government to move in a more activist direction."

That kind of alliance would come as no surprise to Alexander, who decided five years ago to invite Gingrich to join his informal "Blackberry Farm" effort to define—in activist terms—a "second stage of the Reagan revolution."

As Gingrich said in an interview last week, the realization that unites those prodding Bush to be more creative in his domestic policy is "the understanding that we have run out of Reagan initiatives and we're just sitting here, with half the party in despair because the White House is saying that governing means raising taxes and compromising with the Democratic Congress."

"There's no unity in talking about unity," Gingrich said. "You only get unity by moving dynamically toward a clear goal."

If the policy debate now engaging Republicans leads to that clear goal, it could provide them with the momentum they need for a sweeping 1992 party victory. Meantime, it is furnishing proof that the Democrats have no monopoly on feuding.

20. Party Time, Realignment

Everett Carll Ladd

"Has the United States been going through a realignment?" asks Everett Carll Ladd in this article published in *Campaign & Election, The Journal of Political Action.* Ladd, who is director of the Roper Center for Public Opinion Research at the University of Connecticut, analyzes several key factors that must be considered in answering this question. Among them are the changes in partisan support not only on a regional basis but also in terms of race and age groups. Discussing the extent to which a new major party has emerged on the national scene, Ladd concludes that the current situation has resulted in a different transformation than those occurring earlier in our nation's political history.

American political scientists and journalists have feasted on the idea of *partisan realignment,* writing about it endlessly. But we have handled the subject poorly, managing to make something quite simple and straightforward appear complex and full of contradictions. Has the United States been going through a realignment? The literature suggests we don't know how to answer this question; in fact, we have all of the answers before us.

The only qualification needed involves a reminder that the literature on realignment uses the term with three somewhat different meanings: (1) major social groups voting differently than in the past; (2) a significant change in the partisan balance of power; and (3) the emergence of a new majority party. Has the American polity experienced realignment? Yes, if either the first or second meanings are employed; no, if the last construction is the one intended.

Groups Voting Differently

The American party system has always been defined by the way social groups are positioned in it—by the distribution of their party loyalties and their congressional and presidential ballots. Never perfectly clear and fixed, these group alignments have shown considerable persistence historically. Major shifts in the sum-total of group alignments vis-a-vis the parties—realignments—are infrequent and momentous.

We may, of course, quibble about how big a shift in the way groups distribute their party loyalties is needed before we may call it "major" and hence truly a realignment. But this distinction is irrelevant here since everyone agrees that the many changes in partisan support of the last quarter-century are huge. Three examples are sufficient to remind us of the magnitude of these shifts. First, the *regional* alignment has changed greatly. In the 1930s and 1940s, for instance, the South was still securely the most Democratic part of the country, by all measures. Today, nothing of this historic alignment remains. Though blacks have been enfranchised all across the region since the early 1960s, and vote heavily Democratic, the shift away from the Democrats among white southerners has been so massive as to move the region into the Republican camp in national politics. As is usually the case, the shift occurred first in presidential voting: No Democratic presidential nominee since Lyndon Johnson has won majority support among white southerners.

By the time of Campaign '84, Republican presidential strategists could count on Dixie as an absolutely secure, unshakeable bastion. Republican gains in party identification have lagged behind those in presidential voting, but by 1984 polls showed, for the first time ever, clear pluralities of white southerners identifying with the GOP. We have seen nothing less than the net partisan conversion of an entire region.

The New Deal years were a time when *class* lines were fairly strong by American standards and the Democrats held a decisive edge over the Republicans in working-class support. Post-World War II affluence changed all this, however, and by 1969 George Meany could describe his AFL-CIO membership as both middle-class and conservative. Ronald Reagan outpolled his Democratic opponents in 1980 and 1984 among blue-collar voters; and despite an all-out effort for Mondale by union leadership in 1984, Reagan won half the union-member vote. Trade unionists don't form a Republican stronghold, of course, but they have moved a long way from their "reliably Democratic" status of the New Deal years.

With regard to *age*, the Republicans' best group until the latter part of the 1970s were those who began their political participation before the Great Depression. The Democrats built their secure New Deal Era majority on their success in winning disproportionate numbers of new voters across several succeeding generations. So great was this success that American election analysts came to assume an almost natural association between youth and relatively heavy Democratic support. Since about 1977, however, the GOP has been picking up strong backing among the youngest voters—so that its best generations now include both the oldest and the youngest, those over 75 years of age (the pre-New Deal cohorts) and those under 25.

When the youngest voters swing to a party, it is likely to benefit not only in the immediate election but in the long run—because the first-formed party loyalties of young people tend to persist. Beyond this, though, young people are seen as a "forecaster" group, a kind of electoral weathervane. Since they have relatively little political experience they are especially susceptible to the currents of the day. Over the last four years, as never before since the Great Depression, the youth weathervane has been showing a Republican breeze. Part of this is simply Ronald Reagan: Generally popular among his countrymen, the oldest president the United States has ever had is especially highly regarded by young people. In March and April, 1985, Gallup polls of the general public showed about 55 percent approving Reagan's handling of the presidency, while about 35 percent disapproved. The Gallup Youth Survey taken at the same time found, however, a whopping 69 percent of persons 13 to 18 years of age approving the President's handling of his office; just 23 percent disapproved.

The partisan shift of the young extends well beyond Reagan's personal popularity, though. Consider this Gallup question: "When you are old enough to vote, do you think you will be more likely to vote for candidates of the Republican party or for candidates of the Democratic party?" When the Gallup Youth Survey first asked this to young respondents in December 1982, 45 percent said the Democrats, 33 percent the Republicans, while 22 percent either had no preference or no opinion. By March/April 1985, an enormous shift had occurred: the Democrats' 12-point margin during the last recession had been supplanted by a 19-point Republican lead—52 percent for the GOP, 33 percent for the Democrats, and 15 percent no clear preference or no opinion. Almost certainly this is the best GOP showing among the young since the onset of the Depression.

A Changing Party Balance

If realignment means fundamental shifts in group attachments and voting, then it is a *fait accompli*. Not all of the shifts have been in a Republican direction; the Democrats' position today is vastly stronger among black Americans, for instance, than it was during the New Deal years. Still, the net swing has been to the Republicans, fulfilling the second meaning of realignment—that the partisan balance of power must be altered significantly. The mixture of Republican gains and Democratic weakness that constitutes this aspect of realignment first became evident in presidential voting. It took longer for the factors that shifted the presidential balance to make themselves felt in the more general assessments and images of the parties, but they have now done so.

The Republicans have made large and fairly steady gains in party identification since they touched bottom just after Watergate. According to Gallup, in 1977 self-described Democrats outnumbered Republicans 49 percent to 20 percent. The GOP had narrowed this gap appreciably by election time 1980 and, Gallup has found, over the last nine months the party has achieved essential parity with the Democrats. Other surveys show the same thing. For example, an ABC News/*Washington Post* poll completed June 22, 1985, found 48 percent identified with or leaned to the Democrats, 45 percent to the Republicans. Similarly, the CBS News/*New York Times* poll of May 29-June 2, 1985 showed the public (with leaners included) 45 percent Democratic and 44 percent Republican. In New Jersey an Eagleton Institute poll of April 29-May 8 of this year recorded 45 percent identifying as Democrats, 42 percent as Republicans. In Connecticut, a May survey by the Institute for Social Inquiry put the GOP narrowly ahead of the Democrats, the first time in 51 "CONNPOLLs" reaching back to 1979 that the GOP had ever led.

The GOP now leads the Democrats on most of the key performance assessments. For example, a Gallup poll of March 8-11, 1985, found 48 percent of the public describing the GOP as the party that will do better "keeping the country prosperous," while only 32 percent picked the Democrats. Gallup Polls in the summer and fall of 1984 got essentially the same responses—by far the largest Republican margin ever recorded. "Prior to 1981," Gallup noted in releasing these data, "the Democratic party enjoyed a near-monopoly on the prosperity issue." Thirty-nine percent of those interviewed by Gallup in the March poll identified the Republicans as the party "more likely to keep the United States out of World War III," while 33 percent named the Democrats (and the remainder, 28 percent, either saw no difference or had no opinion).

The Republicans' new-found strength as the party best able to manage the economy was well shown by a Harris survey of April 1-3, 1985. Fifty-three percent named the Republicans—just 35 percent the Democrats—as the party most likely to follow policies "that would keep the economic recovery on track." The GOP had a ten-point edge (48 percent to 38 percent) as the party more likely to "reform the tax system," and an 11-point edge (47 percent to 36 percent) as the party that would do a better job "balancing the budget." The latter is especially interesting, since the U.S. has experienced its largest peacetime deficits ever in the 1980s, under a Republican president. The main point, though, is that the proportion of Americans who find the Republicans a credible governing party, better able than the Democrats to confront key problems, is larger now than at any time since the Depression.

A New Majority Party?

Has realignment taken place in the third sense in which the term is used—the rise of a new majority party? The answer, quite simply, is no. The Democrats are no longer the majority party in the U.S., but the Republicans haven't achieved majority status in their stead. The GOP has strengthened its position enormously in presidential politics, but the Democrats still control the House of Representatives nationally and a majority of the state houses. The Republicans have made substantial gains in party identification, but these gains have only brought them to parity. Indeed, Reagan pollster Richard Wirthlin describes the GOP not as the *new majority party* but as the *new parity party*, having at last pulled even with the Democrats in the underlying mix of party support.

For long stretches in American history one party has held fairly clear majority status—as the GOP did from 1896 up to the Great Depression, and the Democrats did for the next several decades. But there is no necessary reason why one party has to have a clear, persisting edge over its rival. The U.S. really didn't have a majority party from the end of the Civil War up into the mid-1890s: for three decades the Republicans and Democrats were remarkably evenly balanced. Today, the degree of volatility in partisan fortunes dictated by a highly-educated electorate with multiple sources of political cues and information, and by television and personality-dominated electioneering, makes the very idea of a stable majority/minority party relationship less likely than in the past.

As to the future, we can all read the tea leaves, and hope or fret as the case may be. As of now, though, the realignment that has so clearly occurred in the first two understandings of the term has brought the United States to a period of partisan parity rather than one-party ascendancy. This is not at all like New Deal realignment—but then, why should it be? The social and political conditions of the 1930s were *sui generis*, and so was the partisan response they required. The social and political conditions of the 1980s are also unique, and we will not understand their party transformations by belaboring the past.

21. Needed: A Political Theory for the New Era of Coalition Government

James L. Sundquist

What James L. Sundquist calls "a momentous change" has taken place in the American governmental system since the mid-1950s. For the sixth time in nine presidential elections from 1956 to 1988, the country has experienced a divided government, with one party in the White House and the other in control of at least one house of Congress. Sundquist, a senior fellow emeritus at the Brookings Institution in Washington, D.C., and author of numerous books on American government and politics, discusses the implications of this "unique version of coalition government" in this article, published in the *Political Science Quarterly*. He urges students of government to devise a theory that will explain how the government can and should work during this new era of divided leadership.

On November 8, 1988, when the American voters decreed that Republican George Bush would succeed Ronald Reagan in the White House but the opposition Democratic Party would control both houses of the Congress, it was the sixth time in the last nine presidential elections that the electorate chose to split the government between the parties. As in 1988, so in the earlier elections of 1956, 1968, 1972, 1980, and 1984, the people placed their faith in Republican presidential leadership but voted to retain Democratic majorities in the House of Representatives and in the first three of those elections (as well as in 1988), Democratic majorities in the Senate also.

This is something new in American politics. When Dwight D. Eisenhower took his second oath of office in 1957, he was the first chief executive in seventy-two years—since Grover Cleveland in 1885—to confront on Inauguration Day a Congress of which even one house was controlled by the opposition party. Sometimes the opposition would win majorities in the House or the Senate, or both, at the midterm election, but even such occasions were relatively rare. In the fifty-eight years from 1897 through 1954, the country experienced divided government during only eight years—all in the last half of a presidential term—or 14 percent of the time. Yet in the thirty-six years from 1955 through 1990, the government will have been divided between the parties for twenty-four years—exactly two-thirds of that period.

A generation ago, then, the country passed from a long era of party government, when either the Republican or the Democratic Party controlled both the presidency and the Congress almost all of the time, to an era when the government was divided between the parties most of the time. Under these circumstances, the United States has its own unique version of coalition government—not a coalition voluntarily entered into by the parties but one forced upon them by the accidents of the electoral process.

It is the argument of this article that the advent of the new era has rendered obsolete much of the theory developed by political scientists, from the day of Woodrow Wilson to the 1950s, to explain how the United States government can and should work. That theory identified the political party as the indispensable instrument that brought cohesion and unity, and hence effectiveness, to the government as a whole by linking the executive and legislative branches in a bond of common interest. And, as a corollary, the party made it possible for the president to succeed in his indispensable role as leader and energizer of the governmental process; it accomplished that end because the congressional majorities, while they would not accept the president's leadership by virtue of his constitutional position as chief executive—institutional rivalry would bar that—would accept it in his alternate capacity as head of the political party to which the majorities adhered.

The generations of political scientists who expounded this theory paid little attention to how the government would and should function when the president and the Senate and House majorities were not all of the same party. They could in good conscience disregard that question because intervals of divided government in their experience had been infrequent and short-lived. Whenever the midterm election brought a division of the government, anyone concerned about that could take a deep breath and wait confidently for the next presidential election to put the system back into its proper alignment. As late as 1952 it had always done so in the memory of everybody writing on the subject. But since 1956, that has no longer been a certainty. It has not even been the probability. And that represents a momentous change in the American governmental system, for institutional processes and relationships are profoundly altered when the unifying bond of party disappears.

This article briefly reviews the antiparty doctrine that the Framers wrote into the Constitution but promptly abandoned. Then it presents the theory of party government and presidential leadership as it was explicated by authoritative and influential political scientists in the era that ended in the mid-1950s, and finally discusses the implications of the obsolescence of that theory since the transformation of the governmental system during the past three decades.

The Antiparty Theory
and its Abandonment

Party government was, of course, not the intent of the Framers who met in Philadelphia in 1787. Quite the opposite. Their views—which are well known and need not be set forth at length here—were, in a word, antiparty. The word "party" appears only rarely in James Madison's account of the proceedings of the 1787 convention. The preferred terms were "faction" and "cabal," and they were used only for purposes of condemnation. No more powerful diatribe against political parties has ever been penned than *The Federalist*, particularly Madison's No. 10, in which he denounced "the violence of faction" as "this dangerous vice" that introduces "the instability, injustice, and confusion" that have "been the mortal diseases under which popular governments have everywhere perished." If a majority party can win the whole of governmental power, Madison reasoned, what is to prevent it from oppressing the minority? As Madison saw it, the natural party division would be between "those who hold and those who are without property," between "those who are creditors, and those who are debtors." He feared that a majority party made up of the propertyless would exhibit "a rage for paper money, for an abolition of debts, for an equal division of property."

In *The Federalist*, particularly in No. 10 but also in Nos. 47, 48 and 62, Madison saw the whole constitutional design as a defense against the danger that any "interested and overbearing majority" or "sinister combinations" could gain control of the entire government. Raising decisions to the national level would place them in the hands of men who had risen above the factionalism of the states, and factions would be more difficult to organize on a national scale. The separation of powers among the branches—and within the legislature between two bodies—would further guard against the threat that majority rule might lead to "tyranny" and "oppression." And so would the method devised for selecting the president. Rejecting the two obvious ways of making that choice—either election by the people directly or election by the Congress—the Framers conceived that peculiar institution, the electoral college, as a nonpartisan, antiparty apparatus, a kind of search committee, not unlike those that corporations and universities and city councils set up nowadays to select a new executive. The college would be made up of men mostly unknown to each other, who would not meet as a body, who would not even be in communication across state lines. As Madison put it at the Convention, "there would be little opportunity for cabal, or corruption...."

But by the end of [President John Adams'] term [1797-1801], the spirit of party was flourishing. In the election of 1800, a fledgling two-party system—reflecting to a degree the cleavages between the propertied and the landless, between creditors and debtors, which Madison had identified as fundamental—was in operation, with two slates of candidates running nationally. The electoral college was hardly formed when it ceased to be the intended body of nonpartisan statesmen with complete discretion and independent judgment and became what it has since remained—a body of faceless partisans that merely registers the choice of the voters between or among national party candidates. "The election of a President of the United States is no longer that process which the Constitution contemplated," one of the Framers, Rufus King, told the Senate in 1816. In his retirement years, James Madison himself acknowledged that parties are "a natural offspring of Freedom." By that time of course, Madison had been elected and reelected president as a party nominee.

The Theory of Party Government and Presidential Leadership

Madison did not expound a new theory to supplant the one that he had been so instrumental in embedding in the Constitution. But without benefit of much explicit doctrine, the nation's political leaders developed in practice the system of party government—as distinct from nonpartisan government—that settled into place in the Jacksonian era and prevailed throughout the next century and a quarter. In each presidential election two national parties sought exactly what the Madisonian theory written into the Constitution was supposed to forestall: the capture of all three of the policy-making elements of the government—the presidency, Senate and House—by the same faction or party, so that the party could carry out its program.

No major party has ever said, "We want only the presidency," or only the Senate or the House. They have always said, "give us *total* responsibility." Since early in the nineteenth century, they have presented their programs formally in official party platforms. Asking for total power in the two elected branches, they have been eager to accept the total responsibility and accountability that would accompany it.

That was the theory of party government; and not only the politicians, but the people accepted it. The parties lined up naturally on opposite sides of whatever were the great issues of the day—creating a national bank, opening the West with turnpikes and railroads and canals financed by the national government, prohibiting slavery in the western territories, raising or lowering tariffs, mobilizing the national government to help the victims of the Great Depression, and so on. The people listened to the arguments of the two parties and made their choices. And when they did, the party they elected had a full opportunity to carry out its mandate, because when the voters chose a president each four years they normally entrusted control of the Congress to the president's party, thus making it fully responsible. From Andrew Jackson's time until the second election of Dwight Eisenhower in 1956, only four presidents—Zachary Taylor elected in 1848, Rutherford B. Hayes in 1876, James A. Garfield in 1880, and Grover Cleveland in 1884—had to confront immediately upon inauguration either a House of Representatives or a Senate organized by the opposition. In the nineteenth century these results may have been largely an artifact of the election process itself. The parties printed separate ballots listing their slates, and the voter selected the ballot of the party he preferred, marked it, and dropped it in the box. Yet after the government-printed, secret ballot came into universal use early in this century, straight-ticket voting and the resultant single-party control of the government continued to prevail. The voters gave the Republican Party responsibility for the entire government in the 1900s, again in the 1920s, and finally in 1952; and they chose the Democratic party in the 1910s, 1930s, and 1940s. No president in the first half of this century ever had to suffer divided government upon taking office, and few had the problem even after the normal setback to the president's party in the midterm election. . . .

A century and a half of experience had evidently convinced political scientists that the "frightful despotism" foreseen by Washington and the political "oppression" that haunted Madison were figments of an eighteenth-century imagination fevered by the struggle against George III. The preeminent instance in all that time of usurpation of power by a president—that of Abraham Lincoln at the outset of the Civil War—had turned out, after all, to be a necessary assertion of leadership in the noblest of causes. So too, it seemed, were the unilateral interventions of Franklin Roosevelt on the side of the Allies in the months before Pearl Harbor. In 1947, Louis Brownlow, of Roosevelt's Committee on Administrative Management, could exult that "during the whole history of the thirty-two presidents, not one has been recreant to his high trust—not one has used his power to aggrandize himself at the expense of our settled institutions." The [1950] Committee on Political Parties [of the American Political Science Association] even turned the argument around; it had the foresight to acknowledge the possibility of presidential excess but contended that disciplined parties would restrain an ambitious president by forcing major decisions into the context of a party's collective leadership. [Harvard Professor Richard] Neustadt's [1960] dictum that what is good for the president is good for the country would prevail until Vietnam and Watergate—the later Irangate—aroused scholars to an awareness that presidential power might be abused. . . .

By the 1960s, political science had developed a dominating theory as to how the American constitutional system should—and at its best, did—work. The political party was the institution that unified the separated branches of the government and brought coherence to the policymaking process. And because the president was the leader of his party, he was the chief policy maker of the entire government, presiding directly over the executive branch and indirectly working through and with his party's congressional leadership over the legislative branch as well.

The Old Theory in a New Era

This established theory presupposed one essential condition: there would in fact be a majority party in control of both branches of government. Rereading the literature of the midcentury, one is struck with how easily this condition was taken for granted. The writers could well do so, for in the twentieth century until 1955, the government had been divided between the parties only for four periods of two years each, and in each case in the last half of a presidential term—those of Taft, Wilson, Hoover, and Truman. A scholar who happened to be writing during or immediately after one of these intervals (or who was commenting on state governmental systems) might observe in parenthetical style that divided government could sometimes obscure responsibility, impede leadership, and thus thwart the fulfillment of the party government ideal. But the aberration was passed over quickly, without interrupting the flow of the basic argument. In the normal state of affairs, one party would have control of the policy-making branches of government; the other would be in opposition. . . .

Divided government invalidates the entire theory of party government and presidential leadership, both elements of it. Divided government requires that the United States "construct a successful government out of antagonisms," which [Woodrow] Wilson warned could not be done, and renders impossible the "close synthesis of active parts" that he found necessary. How can a party cast its web over the dispersed organs of government to bring a semblance of unity . . . if it controls but one of the branches? . . . How can the president lead the Congress if either or both houses are controlled by the party that fought to defeat him in the last election and has vowed to vanquish him, or his successor as his party's candidate, in the next one? . . .

The question at once arises: In our twenty-two years thus far of forced coalition government, have those gloomy forecasts been fulfilled? . . .

. . . My own conclusion is that the predictions of the sages of the earlier generation have been borne out in this modern era of divided or coalition government. True, in the administrations of the four Republican presidents who had to make their peace with House Democratic majorities—and usually Democratic Senate majorities as well—there were significant accomplishments. President Dwight D. Eisenhower achieved a successful bipartisan foreign policy, and President Ronald Reagan managed to carry enough Democrats with him to enact for better or worse the essentials of his economic program in 1981. In subsequent Reagan years, the Congress and the administration collaborated across party lines to enact measures to bring illegal immigration under control, rescue social security, and reform the tax code. But Eisenhower and the Democratic Congress were stalemated on domestic measures throughout his six years of coalition government; the Nixon-Ford period was one of almost unbroken conflict and deadlock on both domestic and foreign issues; and the last seven years of Reagan found the government immobilized on some of the central issues of the day, unwilling to follow the leadership of the President or anyone else and deferring those issues in hope that somehow the 1988 election would resolve matters and render the government functional again.

By common consent, the most conspicuous among the urgent but unresolved problems has been, of course, the federal budget deficit, which has been running at between $150 billion and $200 billion a year since the great tax cut of 1981 took effect. The national debt now stands at well over $2 trillion, more than doubled in seven years of divided government. The United States has suffered the shock of falling from the status of a great creditor nation to the world's largest debtor nation, living on borrowing from abroad. The huge trade deficit, the shortfall in investment, and high interest rates are all blamed on the inability of the government to get the budget deficit under control. For all these reasons, virtually all of the country's responsible leaders—the president, the congressional leaders, and members of both parties in both houses—have for nearly over half a dozen years been proclaiming loudly and in unison that the nation simply cannot go on this way. The experts from outside—in the academic world, the Federal Reserve System, on Wall Street, in foreign countries—likewise agree that these deficits are economically perilous, whether or not they can be termed morally outrageous as well.

But during all that time that the country has seen a virtual consensus on the urgency of this problem, its governmental institutions have floundered in trying to cope with it. President Reagan sent the Congress his program, but the Congress flatly rejected it. The legislators in their turn floated suggestions, but the President killed them by promising a veto if they were passed. The congressional leaders and others pleaded for a summit meeting between the executive and legislative branches to hammer out a common policy. Finally, in November 1986, the meeting took place. But it is a measure of the national predicament that it took a half-trillion-dollar collapse in the stock market—a five-hundred-billion-dollar panic—before the two branches of the U.S. government would even sit down together. It was easier for Mikhail Gorbachev to get a summit meeting with the President of the United States than it was for the Speaker of the United States House of Representatives. And even the domestic summit that was finally held essentially papered over the problem rather than solved it. . . .

But, some will argue, even if these or other instances can indeed be considered governmental failures attributable to mistrust between the unwilling partners of a forced coalition, the performance of recent unified government has been no better. The Kennedy and Carter years cannot claim overwhelming success, they will maintain, and while Lyndon Johnson proved to be a spectacular presidential leader of the Congress in the enactment of his Great Society measures in 1964 and 1965, he also led the country into the quagmire of Vietnam that in turn launched a devastating spiral of inflation. That is the difficulty of arguing from cases. . . .

Competition is the very essence of democratic politics. It gives democracy its meaning, and its vitality. The parties are the instruments of that competition. They are and should be organized for combat, not for collaboration and compromise. They live to win elections in order to advance their philosophies and programs. Therefore, each party strives and must strive to defeat the opposing party. But in a divided government, this healthy competition is translated into an unhealthy, debilitating conflict between the institutions of government themselves. Then, the president and Congress are motivated to try to discredit and defeat each other. Yet these are the institutions that, for anything constructive to happen, simply have to get together.

The average citizen reacts by simply condemning all politicians as a class. "Why don't those people in Washington stop playing politics and just get together and do what's right?" But that is not in the nature of things. Political parties, as the textbooks have always told us, are organized because people have genuine, deep disagreements about the goals and the programs of their societies. If a coalition government is to work, the leaders of committed groups have to be willing to submerge or abandon the very philosophies that caused them to organize their parties in the first place. They have to set aside the principles that are their reason for seeking governmental power. And they will do that only under compulsion of clear and grave necessity—usually, in other words, after deadlock has deteriorated into crisis.

In the American form of coalition government, if the president sends a proposal to Capitol Hill or takes a foreign policy stand, the opposition-controlled House or houses of Congress—unless they are overwhelmed by the president's popularity and standing in the country—simply *must* reject it. Otherwise they are saying the president is a wise and prudent leader. That would only strengthen him and his party for the next election, and how can the men and women of the congressional majority do that, when their whole object is to defeat him when that time arrives? By the same token, if the opposition part in control of Congress initiates a measure, the president has to veto it—or he is saying of his opponents that they are sound and statesmanlike, and so is building them up for the next election. . . .

Our struggles with coalition government have demonstrated also the truth of the established wisdom concerning presidential leadership: in the American system there is simply no substitute for it. The Congress has 535 voting members, organized in two houses and in innumerable committees and subcommittees; every member is in principle the equal of every other member, and nobody can give directions to anybody else and make them stick. Such a body is simply not well designed for making coherent, decisive, coordinated policy. As the old theory told us, the system works best when the president proposes and the Congress disposes, when the president sets the agenda and leads, as everyone expects him to.

But how can leaders lead if followers don't follow? In divided government, presidential leadership becomes all but impossible. The president is not the leader of the congressional majority. He is precisely the opposite—the leader of their opposition, the man they are most dedicated to discredit and defeat. With great fanfare and immense hope, the people elect a president each four years. But then, most of the time these days, they give him a Congress a majority of whose members tried their best to beat him in the last election and will do so again in the next. To lead in those circumstances would be beyond the capability of any mortal. No one should blame presidents when they fail in a time of coalition government. It is the system that is at fault.

Nobody planned it this way. The country in no way made a conscious decision thirty years ago to abandon the responsible-party system that had served it well for almost the whole life of the nation. It was simply an accident of the electoral system. Almost unique in the world, the United States has an electoral process that permits people to split their tickets—to vote one way for president and the other way for Congress, if they so choose. And that is what enough of them have done to produce a divided outcome most of the time of late.

Re-reconciling Theory and Practice

Today there is a disjunction between theory and practice, between the long-accepted and not-yet-abandoned ideas about how the government of the United States should work and the way in which it is now compelled to try to work. How can theory and practice once again by synchronized? . . .

Those who think that the model of party government and presidential leadership was wrong, and who would advance the post-1955 structure of coalition government as the new ideal, have an obligation to provide a new body of theory that will tell us what is the substitute for presidential leadership and congressional followership, how the partners in the American coalition government should relate to one another for that type of government to function well, and how those relationships can be brought about. What is the role of parties in such a system, and will strengthening them simply intensify the confrontation between the branches and render deadlocks more implacable? Should the agitation within the discipline for stronger parties be reversed and should weaker parties be made the goal? How would the weakening of congressional parties affect the efficiency of the Congress and its status vis-à-vis the presidency? Does the answer—or part of it, at least—lie in bipartisan mechanisms such as the one that resolved the social security issue and the National Economic Commission that was created in 1988 to grapple with the budget deficit? Can these be multiplied and regularized to anticipate and forestall crises rather than simply cope with them when they reach the desperation stage? If we are to accept coalition government as ideal, or even as satisfactory, we need a body of theory as fully developed as the one it superseded, followed by institutional innovation based on the new theory. No such body of theory has even begun to emerge.

By the same token, those who still cherish the idea of party government have an obligation of equal gravity. They must come to grips with the question of how our election system, or the composition and powers of the branches of government, should be altered to restore unified government as the normal state of affairs. And if that means—as it surely does—that the Constitution itself should be changed, how can that be brought about? That question obviously is not one for the fainthearted. But for any serious student of American government to contend that all of the issues raised by coalition government can simply be set aside, because whatever is is best, is not an answer. The times demand a more responsible political science than that.

Chapter 5

Political Interest Groups

The United States is a nation of joiners. Indeed, one of the first orders of business for the Pilgrims after coming ashore at Plymouth Rock in 1620 was to draw up an agreement about how they would organize themselves—the Mayflower Compact. Many commentators have remarked on a tendency in Americans to create groups for collective action. "In no country in the world," wrote Alexis de Tocqueville in the 1830s, "has the principle of association been more successfully used or applied to a greater multitude of objects than in America." [1] Group action remains a singular feature of U.S. politics today.

Why this propensity for group action? Certainly the traditions of association have much to do with it, underscored by legislative assemblies, congregational church government, and other voluntary activities. Constitutional guarantees nurture these private groups. The Bill of Rights protects freedom of speech, freedom of association, and freedom to petition the government. Groups—for-profit corporations and nonprofit associations alike—enjoy legal protections that make freedom of action possible.

In Selection 22, "The Mischiefs of Faction Revisited," the continuing importance of private groups is argued by John Gardner, founder of Common Cause, one of the most successful civic-action organizations of recent years. Gardner articulates the belief that the U.S. government cannot possibly solve all of the country's problems and that business, labor, and civic associations must step in to fill the gap.

Changing Patterns of Group Power

Traditionally, groups have formed to promote economic objectives. Business groups include corporations (the most typical business organization), trade associations, and small and minority-owned firms.

Organized labor embraces a multitude of local unions linked by broad craft or industrial unions that span the entire nation. Those on the receiving end of government programs or benefits—for example, veterans, government pensioners, and business people in regulated industries—organize to conduct their dealings with the government.

Today, many of the most active interest groups do not represent direct economic interests; that is, they do not manifest people's interests as producers or wage earners, but as consumers, taxpayers, pursuers of ideals, and users of goods, services, and the nation's resources. These organizations include environmental groups, civil rights groups, citizens' activist groups, religious groups, and state and local government lobbyists. The objectives of these diverse organizations reveal a middle-class society whose political goals have expanded to include more than the bread-and-butter issues of jobs and income.

These noneconomic organizations constitute the fastest-growing type of group, and represent perhaps a fifth or more of all active associations. They flourish despite the so-called free-rider problem: that is, because they seek "collective" benefits, which are received by those in a class or segment of society whether or not they are members of the formal group. In other words, individuals in such broad categories— consumers or retired people, for example—will reap benefits from the group's activities whether or not they join. "Rational" individuals, so the argument goes, need not be members or pay dues—hence, the term "free rider."

The American Association of Retired Persons (AARP) demonstrates how successful groups can overcome the free-rider problem. Professional managers are employed who use up-to-the-minute techniques such as media appeals and targeted mailing to reach and mobilize members. AARP also offers benefits available only to members: health insurance, prescription plans, travel programs, and a mass-circulation magazine, *Modern Maturity*. Finally AARP benefits from the fact that its constituency has affluence, leisure time, and political clout.

AARP's rival, the National Committee to Preserve Social Security and Medicare, illustrates the less savory aspects of contemporary interest groups. This organization recruits members through extensive mailing lists and "hot-button" tactics designed to alarm citizens, such as telling senior citizens that Social Security is endangered. This group, and thousands like it, is essentially a mass-mailing operation whose business is self-perpetuating fundraising.

Such groups figure prominently in Normal J. Ornstein and Mark Schmitt's article on "The New World of Interest Politics." (Selection 23).

Group Resources and Techniques of Influence

Each group that enters the political arena brings with it a unique mixture of resources. Money is important, but the number and geographic distribution of its members and the group's social status, political skills, and organizational efficiency also affect its success. Depending on its resources, a group can employ many techniques of influence. These include both personal contacts with decision makers (lobbying) and indirect grass-roots activities to create public pressure on officeholders. Recent studies have shown that organizations are using an ever-increasing number of techniques to advance their interests.[2]

The tactics of lobbyists hold a perennial fascination for journalists and other observers of political processes. In Selection 24, Richard Sachs reminds us that lobbying is as old as the republic and as American as apple pie. Although James Madison had convinced himself (and others) that "factions" would be so numerous as to balance out one another, aggressive lobbyists soon appeared on the scene, bending public policy in various ways. Virtually unchecked lobbying accompanied westward rail expansion, the rise of the trusts, and labor-management strife. And although lobbying regulation has been tried by a number of states, Congress did not address the problem directly until after World War II.

One flourishing form of group activity is the political action committee (PAC), which collects money and distributes it to candidates. Corporate PACs are the most prominent, but there are as many PACs representing labor unions, trade associations, membership organizations, and even individual political figures. (For further discussion of PACs, see Introduction to Chapters 4 and 7.)

One political action committee, Snack PAC (the Snack Food Association), is colorfully described by Peter Carlson in Selection 25. This PAC is representative of a large number of entities that are adjuncts to trade associations.

People commonly look upon interest-group activity with a certain amount of disdain. After all, aren't Americans opposed to shadowy special interests that bend public policy to their will? The problem with this point of view is that each of us at some time may exert pressure on our representatives on an issue we believe is important. Interest groups may be directed toward good or evil purposes, depending upon one's point of view. In the nineteenth century, vigorous lobbying helped the railroad companies to grab vast tracts of western land, but the antislavery movement forced the issue to the point of civil war and eventually emancipation. In our own day, groups are involved in every type of cause, based on private greed as well as lofty ethical goals.

Any attempts to control or limit group activity raise the issue of balancing the public's right to know about lobbying with the lobbyists' right to free speech, assembly, and petition.

Today, interest groups seem almost to have supplanted political parties as the chief channel for conveying citizen opinion to the government. In fact, groups represent people's interests and views with a variety and richness that parties cannot match. Although groups cannot produce governing coalitions as parties can, they reach farther than the parties into the drafting and implementing of vast numbers of public policies. The diversity of group life reflects the factionalism inherent in modern America.

Notes

1. Alexis de Tocqueville, *Democracy in America,* ed. Phillips Bradley (New York: Vintage Books, 1958), I:198.
2. See, for example, Kay Lehman Schlozman and John T. Tierney, *Organized Interests and American Democracy* (New York: Harper & Row, 1986).

22. The Mischiefs of Faction Revisited

John Gardner

The founders of our republic worried about what James Madison termed "the mischiefs of faction." Lacking the unified symbol of a monarch, could a nation so varied in background and scattered in geography cultivate the loyalty of citizens and unity of purpose necessary for a vigorous national government? Some people, then more than now, equated divisiveness or dissension with treason. Madison, in contrast, sensed that factionalism was rooted in human nature, and he proposed to harness that factionalism for the common good. Although in the United States pluralism often yields conflict or stalemate, Madison was correct in viewing factions as inevitable. How voluntary citizen action can produce creativity and humane services is explained in contemporary fashion by Gardner, one of the nation's most respected senior statesmen, in this article published in the *Kettering Review* in 1983. Secretary of health, education and welfare from 1965 to 1968, Gardner in 1970 founded the citizens' group Common Cause, serving as its chairman until 1977; three years later, he founded Independent Sector, a clearinghouse for voluntary groups. He is the author of numerous books and articles, many about leadership and civic action.

Observing the innumerable conflicting interests that characterize our society, one thinks of James Madison, who understood so well what he called "the mischiefs of faction."

> The instability, injustice, and confusion introduced into the public councils (by faction) have, in truth, been the mortal diseases under which popular governments have everywhere perished.
> (*Federalist Paper*, No. 10)

He saw no way of suppressing faction short of destroying liberty—a "remedy ... worse than the disease." The causes, he said, are "sown in the nature of man."

How could a newly formed nation deal with that ancient, stubborn problem? One might sum up his answer as follows: since factions there will always be, let them be numerous and conflicting, increasing the possibility that they will counteract one another; and let our representative institutions be so designed as to make it difficult for any one interest to dominate a jurisdiction or for various interests to act in concert to form an oppressive majority.

The governing institutions designed by Madison and his contemporaries met those criteria remarkably well. But the mischiefs of faction have evolved in curious and troubling ways, and today they threaten the coherence of our society. One cannot contentedly quote Madison on faction as though nothing had changed. He saw what could be seen by an observer of piercing insight two centuries ago. We owe it to his memory to ask what that sharp eye and clear mind would make of the scene today.

Some Present-Day Realities

Let us list some present-day realities that the eighteenth century could not have foreseen—realities that Madison would surely focus on were he alive.

1. The specialization of contemporary society has vastly increased the number and variety of factions. Every branch, limb, and twig of business, labor, and agriculture is organized to pursue its particular interest. Every profession and subprofession is organized. Religions and causes are organized. So are counties, hospitals, and junior colleges. The proliferation seems without limit. There is nothing inherently bad in the proliferation—but it increases the scale and intensity of the problem.

2. There have been advances in the techniques of organizing that enable each tiny sliver of special interest to discover its strength and act effectively—or to have its strength discovered and exploited by others. The traditional sequence is that a group, seeking to further some shared interest, spends years building its membership and organizing itself. More recently an alternative pattern has emerged: individuals hoping to find enough allies to form a group consult a direct mail house and arrange for a test mailing. If it succeeds, they may find themselves presiding over a nationwide group in a matter of weeks. An even newer development is that the direct mail house itself may select a "cause," form an appropriate sponsoring committee, and do a test mailing at its own expense. If the response is good, it recovers the cost and has created a new client. In sum, there now exists a remarkably effective process for generating interest groups.

3. An organized group, once it sets out to pursue the interest of its members, develops skills in lobbying and "working the media" that are far beyond anything the nineteenth century ever imagined. A relatively small interest group can bring great force to bear at its particular leverage point. Some groups employ sophisticated television techniques that would not have been conceivable to Madison and his contemporaries.

4. The interest groups have penetrated government. They effectively control some cabinet departments, many sub-cabinet bureaus and agencies, some independent regulatory agencies, much of the Congress of the United States—even, to a lesser degree, parts of the judiciary. (One of the most persistent myths in American life is that government and the private sector are two quite separate entities. In truth, not only do the searching fingers of government probe every corner of the private sector, but private interests infiltrate every corner of government.) In a flourishing symbiosis, politicians use the interest groups and are used by them. If an interest group has potential power, the politicians will seek it out. The senator has access to direct mail lists, and his computerized typewriter can automatically insert a sentence on school prayer when it is typing letters to people on the pro-school-prayer list.

5. The financial burden placed on politicians by the soaring cost of campaigns has led to a flood of campaign money from organized groups seeking access and influence. Only old-fashioned people give or take bribes any more. The preferred means of buying political outcomes is the campaign contribution. And, as in all commerce, those with the most money tend to prevail. Heaven help the group with a just cause and an empty purse.

The existence of conflicting interests is as inevitable today as it was 200 years ago. Most of the organized groups have legitimate concerns; some have concerns that are, by any standards, urgent. The existence of the groups is a manifestation of our pluralism, and the conlict is often a sign of vitality. But some of the consequences are distressing.

The intensity of the conflict today creates in each particular group a kind of siege mentality. Each group is convinced of the rightness of its aims and, believing itself to be engaged in a lonely fight for survival, feels victimized by other groups in the society.

People who think of themselves as victims are in no mood to work with others to shape a constructive future. How many times have we seen a major American city struggling to solve its problems while every possible solution is blocked by one or another powerful union or commercial or political interest? Each has achieved veto power over a piece of any possible solution, and no one has the power to solve the problem. Thus do the parts wage war against the whole.

To understand the resulting paralysis of government as the policy-maker experiences it, imagine a player of checkers confronted by a bystander who puts a thumb on the checker and says, "Go ahead and play, just don't touch this one," and another bystander who puts a thumb on another checker with the same warning and then another bystander and another. The owners of the thumbs—the organized groups—don't want to make the game unwinnable. They just don't want you to touch their particular checkers.

Madison did not appear to be particularly concerned about the possibility of chronic stalemate as an outcome of "the dangerous vice" of faction. He worried about instability, injustice, confusion—and the oppression that might result if any particular interest commanded a majority. Those are grave consequences, but today we have to consider another possible outcome: the paralysis induced by multiple conflicting interests may blunt our sense of purpose and make it impossible to act on our shared concerns.

It is a prime characteristic of our situation that we must take conscious thought and exert conscious effort to restore the integrative processes that will yield a measure of coherence. If Madison were here today, he would point out as he did two centuries ago the value of the integrative processes built into our representative institutions. No doubt in the middle years of this century we went through a period of excessive faith in big government. But we will not be helped if the pendulum swings to excessive disdain for government. A complex and swiftly changing society in a turbulent world requires a vigorous and stable government.

Madison might even be moved to remind us that when equally worthy groups want mutually incompatible things, unless we want them to shoot it out, we must expect that they will turn to the much-maligned arena of politics. The reconciling of multiple conflicting interests that cannot be reconciled in the marketplace or elsewhere is not an unfamiliar or inappropriate task for our political and governmental institutions. It is one of their central and traditional functions.

But to perform those tasks, our representative institutions must be in considerably better shape than they are today. This does not imply more or bigger government. It could mean less government—but, above all, responsive and accountable government.

The Private Sector

The task of coping with fragmentation and restoring coherence to the society is only in part a task of government. One task that must be carried through chiefly in the nongovernment sector—a task essential in coping with fragmentation—is the regeneration of shared values. A free society holds together only if the laws and governing institutions are congruent with deeply and widely held attitudes and values.

... A strategically important part of our society is the so-called voluntary or independent sector, made up of nonprofit, nongovernmental institutions. We value individual initiative, but it is not enough in itself: there has to be a natural linkage between individual and community. In the voluntary sector such linkages are easily forged. The countless organizations of this sector permit private initiative for the public good.

The role of the private sector, profit and nonprofit, is crucial in the attempt to strengthen the communities of this country. Many federal programs have addressed themselves to the task of restoring our communities. Some of the results have been good, but it is no exaggeration to say that *every* successful effort to that end has involved some measure of leadership from the private sector, profit and nonprofit. The point is important because if we succeed in reweaving the fabric of this unraveling society, it will begin at the local level.

Citizenship and Leadership

. . . Leadership of a special kind will be needed to knit our society back together again. Historically the nation has moved not in response to a single leader but to many leaders functioning at many levels and in all segments of the society—in and out of government. Given the extraordinary fragmentation of our society today, the first duty of our dispersed leaders is to reach out to one another—across the boundaries that separate the highly organized, warring segments of our society—business, labor, government, farmers, professional groups, and so on—to restore coherence.

Unfortunately, our dispersed leaders, many of them extremely able, have succumbed to the general fragmentation. A high proportion of leaders in all segments of our society—business, labor, the professions, etc.—are rewarded for singleminded pursuit of the interests of their group regardless of the damage it may do the common good. This is what is expected of them. But suppose the expectations changed. Suppose we made it customary to ask some uncomfortable questions of the men and women who have achieved prominence in the organizations and institutions that make up our society: Are they one-segment leaders, insulated from other parts of the community? Do they fatten on the deference of their own little circle without ever seeking to understand the other worlds that make up the republic they think they love? Or do they make an effort to reach out across boundaries, to communicate with other segments, and to move diverse groups toward a workable consensus?

We must develop networks of leaders who accept some measure of responsibility for the commonwealth. Call them *networks of responsibility*—leaders of disparate or conflicting interests who undertake to act together on behalf of the shared concerns of the community or nation. Such networks will not flourish in the contemporary climate if they resemble the old establishments in being exclusionary. Access and openness to participation must be their hallmark. Two examples:

1. For a dozen years now, the National Urban Coalition and local coalitions around the country have been bringing together business, labor, political, and minority leaders to collaborate on problems of urban decay.

2. When New York City was facing its severest tests—in the mid-70s—union leaders, bankers, real estate people, city officials, and many others joined hands to rescue the city.

The examples could be multiplied. But the existing responsibility networks are frail and fragmentary. One must hope that we shall see a major surge in the building of such networks. Some will be local, some national. Some will focus on economic issues, some on urban development, some on education.

If leaders in all segments of our society form such responsibility networks among diverse, striving groups, top political leaders will surely find their work greatly facilitated. The mayor will find that, in addition to all the multiple special interests pressing in on him, there is a "constituency for the whole"—so will governors, senators, representatives, and the president. It is hard to think of any other event that would so quickly restore the attractiveness of public life.

Pluralism has been a prime source of our liberty and our creative impulses. We treasure it and would not permit any turn of events that might threaten it. We can deal with the paralysis and fragmentation that affects us without sacrificing pluralism. We flourished for generations as a pluralistic society that enjoyed a strong measure of coherence and was not paralyzed by its multiple conflicts. We can do so again—but not without effort.

23. The New World of Interest Politics

Norman J. Ornstein and Mark Schmitt

Numerous interest groups have played a role in the nation's political life since its very earliest days. Even so, the veritable explosion of organized groups in the 1960s and 1970s came as something of a surprise to observers of American politics. Many of these newly powerful groups have been associated with the rise of such causes as civil rights, environmentalism, and consumerism. Many have defied conventional wisdom in that they represent not economic interests associated with jobs or earnings, but rather more diffuse social and even philosophical concerns. Norman J. Ornstein and Mark Schmitt of the American Enterprise Institute in Washington, D.C., conduct a tour of this new world of interest-group politics in their article published in *The American Enterprise* in 1990.

When Congress put together the Medicare Catastrophic Coverage Act of 1988, it trusted the endorsement of the most powerful and established of Washington lobbies for the elderly, the American Association of Retired Persons (AARP). With 31 million members from the most politically active segment of the population, and with a legion of lobbyists among a total staff of 1,300 located in a gleaming office building in the heart of the nation's capital, the AARP has everything an interest group needs—prestige, money, constituents, and a noble mission. Its imprimatur gave Congress everything it needed, too, to pass this landmark piece of legislation.

Less than a year later, when Congress frantically backpedaled on the Medicare Catastrophic Coverage Act, AARP looked less like the diligent advocate for the elderly and more like a hidebound, out-of-touch bureaucracy making its constituents' golden years more burdensome. Angry senior citizens quickly decried the higher Medicare premiums and other levies as the "AARP tax." The grass-roots reaction to the rise in Medicare premiums "was not anticipated because it had AARP's blessing," Senator Bob Packwood said in retrospect.

What is going on here? This hardly fits our textbook understanding of how interest groups and lobbies work in Washington. "The interests are always awake while the country slumbers and sleeps," warned the late British statesman William Gladstone—but here is a case of an interest in an apparent extended reverie that turned into a nightmare. For decades, we have argued about whether interests are insidious, whether they push their narrower needs over the national interest, or whether they possess unfair advantages because of their money and access. But we have always assumed that interests will represent—at the very least—their interests.

Our misgivings about their influence remain the same, but the world in which Washington interest groups operate has transformed itself in the past two decades from a closed-door marketplace of political influence by a few established interests to something like a Moroccan *Casbah*, with thousands of groups clamoring for the attention of government as well as potential members and donors. The old divisions, such as business versus labor, are there, but with many new twists—it is just as often business versus business, or business and labor versus domestic or foreign competitors.

These days, groups with similar interests compete with each other (the National Organization for Women and the National Women's Political Caucus, for example, or the Sierra Club and the Audubon

Society, or the Conservative Caucus and the National Conservative Political Action Committee), and groups with divergent interests squabble fiercely where their territories intersect. Groups now build layers of professional staff, lawyers, professional fund-raisers, and "grassroots consultants." They often employ former members and staffers of Congress, most of whom have developed their professional careers in Washington and have little direct connection with the constituencies they now represent. These well-paid staffs look for immediate results, emphasizing short-term tactics over the long-term goals of the groups' members. As a consequence, they are gradually losing touch with their own memberships and slipping out of sync with today's political climate.

Organizations as different as the National Rifle Association (NRA) and the National Organization for Women today face problems juggling the agendas of their leaders, staff, and members. We can no longer assume that an interest group has reached an understanding or a consensus on what constitutes its interest.

And that's not all. At the same time that AARP went on its walkabout, another phenomenon of modern interest politics emerged: an apparently irrational internecine warfare among groups, reflecting a strange new tension about who is responsible for what in the interest-group community. The *Washington Post*'s David Ignatius recently chronicled the plight of a consortium of environmental groups that endorsed a "Blueprint for the Environment," a wide-ranging document comprising 511 recommendations, including one that urged the United States to resume participation in global population-control efforts that had been curtailed during the Reagan administration.

Whether the environmental groups that signed the document read all 511 recommendations, much less endorsed each and every one, is open to question. Nevertheless, the anti-abortion lobby mobilized for total war. The National Right to Life Committee, for example, alerted its members that the Audubon Society "is now a pro-abortion organization" and unleashed torrents of letters to the other groups in the consortium labeling them "babykillers." The head of a group called Trout Unlimited was furious: "We don't have a position on abortion. We never will. We deal only with trout!"

The time and effort expended on these inside-the-Beltway catfights are certainly one reason these groups are drifting apart from their constituents. Groups spend more time looking over their shoulders to ensure that no other groups encroach on their well-crafted niches in the political ecosystem of Washington than they spend pursuing their stated objectives. Douglas Johnson, National Right to Life director, was particularly blunt about why his group was so exercised by the environmentalists: "Environmental groups ... should stay out of our bailiwick, and we'll stay out of theirs."

Even fiercer competition these days occurs among groups trying to fill the same niche—the same constituents, the same agenda, the same sources of funding. This is a partial explanation for the AARP's debacle: over the past few years a new and ruthless challenger began breathing down AARP's neck—James Roosevelt's National Committee to Preserve Social Security and Medicare. The Roosevelt group is first and foremost a fund-raising operation, shameless in making its direct mail look like time-sensitive official correspondence from the Social Security Administration.

With a minimal presence and a miserable reputation in the nation's capital—it didn't help to be named one of the "worst interest groups" by the *Washington Monthly*—the Roosevelt group could accomplish very little on Capitol Hill. But by tapping into AARP's funding base and encouraging the elderly to accept nothing less than a comprehensive home-care program, the Roosevelt group forced AARP to demonstrate some kind of legislative progress. In a year of sharp fiscal constraints, the result was the Medicare Catastrophic Coverage Act, a law that turned out to be catastrophic for the AARP.

Although this interest-group turmoil is recent, it represents the culmination of changes in the world of Washington interest groups since World War II. When nineteenth-century reformers gave the word "interests" a bad name, they had in mind a tiny sector of commercial enterprises that could afford a presence in Washington. To be sure, unlike Gladstone's Britain, America always had many and varied mass-based organizations—a phenomenon that particularly struck de Tocqueville—but few other than organized labor could be considered political "interest groups" engaged daily in the task of influencing policy.

In the past few decades, though, interest groups have proliferated and changed. Mass-based membership organizations have become an integral part of interest politics and lobbying. The National Organization for Women, the AARP, and the Sierra Club have obvious differences, yet all three, and scores of others, seek to represent the loose, often noneconomic interests of diverse populations, each reached by the creative use of computerized direct mail.

Unlike an earlier time, none of these organizations stands alone. For each, there is at least one group trying to do the same thing. The postwar widening of Washington interests brought our democracy very close to the sort of pluralism envisioned by James Madison in *Federalist Paper*, No. 10. Interests could pose no threat if every conceivable interest—economic or noneconomic—was adequately represented. But instead of lively pluralism, today's interest groups are remarkably bland. Each peddles the same lowest common denominator of fear, funding appeals, and minor legislative progress, trying to captivate the same core of charitably inclined or ideologically active donors. The flow of activity in interest groups is not from the bottom up—from the grass roots to the leaders—but from the top down. One prime objective for all groups is to keep other groups from encroaching on their market share; another is to keep those checks and letters coming in. It is no wonder, then, that the public sees Washington as isolated and out of touch with the country. Legislators bear most of this criticism, but as the AARP incident shows, the groups that claim to intervene on behalf of constituents may be more out of touch than the lawmakers.

The founders of most mass-based interest groups, at least until very recently, were citizens who came to Washington to make their voices heard. Those founders, though, have long since turned over the reins to a new class of professional interest-group managers with degrees in such fields as nonprofit management, experience solely in Washington, and membership in groups such as the American Society of Association Executives. The AARP was founded in 1958 by a retired school principal from California who had trouble getting insurance. When it launched its lobbying effort on the Medicare Catastrophic Coverage Act, AARP hired a new director whose resume included stints at the National Association of Realtors and the U.S. Chamber of Commerce. With lobbying for the public interest thus reduced to a set of interchangeable techniques, it's no surprise that all the groups' letters, ads, and lobbying appeals look and sound alike—and no surprise that their constituents are growing cynical and restless.

Interest groups, of course, need professional staffs because they have increasingly become commercialized. These groups are more than collections of people with the same affinities, affiliations, or interests; they are businesses with bottom lines of their own. Many are quite explicit about it: the AARP, with an estimated $10 million annual cash flow from magazines, discount pharmaceuticals, and other commercial services, would be one of the largest corporations in the Washington, D.C., area if it went public. The Roosevelt group produces millions of dollars in profits—about 70 percent of its revenues—for associated firms specializing in direct mail. The internal conflicts of interest posed here, apparent or real, are legion. The AARP, relying heavily on its pharmaceutical business, lobbied hard for a generous prescription-drug provision in the Medicare Catastrophic Coverage Act. The Roosevelt group needs to use increasingly hysterical appeals to contributors to keep its direct-mail business running—whether a real crisis exists or not.

Even less well-heeled groups are businesses in a sense, each with two sometimes conflicting clients. Each group must sell itself to its members as their most effective advocate in Washington. And each group must sell itself to legislators as the legitimate proxy for those voters. If a group succeeds at one and not the other, the result is trouble for the group and for the political system. In the case of the elderly, the Roosevelt group sold itself best to its constituents, and the AARP sold itself to the legislators. We have seen the results.

The National Rifle Association still claims the loyalty of the voters it represents through its membership, but it may have paid a steep price in its credibility in Washington and elsewhere. As the organization fought laws that would control undetectable plastic handguns, armor-piercing bullets, and assault weapons, it turned to a lavish mass-media campaign featuring Charlton Heston on television, and a full-page ad in newspapers suggesting that if the Chinese students in Tiananmen Square had had the benefit of our own Second Amendment, they would have been armed and therefore able to fight back against China's soldiers.

These ads indicate that the organization is playing a risky game of ever-increasing stakes to hold on to both its voters and its legislators, purveying ever more apocalyptic images to convince members that the NRA's legislative agenda is in their best interests—and that they need the NRA to pursue it. The organization has already lost the support of many law-enforcement officials and groups around the country and has gone through a messy internal shakeup. Still, even though observers periodically declare that the NRA has "gone too far" and predict that it will fade as a political force, the organization has so far avoided this fate, and no serious competitor has appeared to challenge them for the anti-gun-control niche.

That the disaffection of interest groups from their constituents has grave consequences for the political system should be apparent to anyone who has observed the perils of the Democratic Party in the 1980s. Ironically, the first mass-based interest group, organized labor, was also the first group to lose the unshakable political loyalty of its members. The Democratic Party, which trusted labor as the proxy for middle-class workers, paid the price. In 1984, the party went out of its way to cultivate the support of the AFL-CIO and other unions, winning the backing of all except the Teamsters, but a majority of white union voters backed Ronald Reagan. Similarly, Walter Mondale satisfied the demands of the National Organization for Women when he put a woman on his ticket. But women backed Reagan by 54 to 46 percent.

So far, the Republican Party has escaped major damage from the interest groups with which it is allied, but this may change. Before the Supreme Court's decision in the *Webster* case [a 1989 case limiting abortion rights], the GOP's alliance with the pro-life groups did not threaten the party's base among affluent, educated voters who tend to favor abortion rights, but now that the issue is less abstract, some believe the GOP will suffer. But here, too, Democrats may be hurt by the uncompromising stance of pro-choice interest groups.

After World War II, as interest groups proliferated, political party organizations began to decline. The Democrats in particular compensated for the breakdown of local political machines by relying on emerging interest groups—labor, civil rights groups, environmental coalitions—to perform some of the machine's duties and to secure the allegiance of voters. The party paid a price for this change, becoming known as the "party of special interests," but the price would have been worth paying if those interests had delivered the political loyalties of their members.

Voters need some kind of structure to mediate between their day-to-day interests and the federal government; if interest groups can't do it, perhaps political parties will have to reassemble as modern versions of their older selves. In a sense, this dilemma lies at the heart of all the Democratic Party's navel-gazing this year.

Unfortunately, this is a difficult time to ask the national parties to reclaim their role as mediators between citizens and government. Neither party is a complete national party, reaching from the grass-roots level to the White House. Republicans seem to have a lock on the upper tier of national politics, but in many states the GOP barely exists at the community level. Democrats monopolize local offices, but they have trouble bringing voters' concerns together at the national level. If revitalized parties cannot take the place of weakened interest groups, the best solution may be for interest groups to become more democratic, less dominated by staff, more sensitive to their own internal conflicts, and more willing to accept compromise even if it cuts down on direct-mail revenues.

Before we lose too much sleep over the dissension and turmoil embroiling interest groups, we should note that the problem is an inevitable result of what is best in American politics today: that we live in a time of comfortable consensus, when the vast majority of Americans agree on our goals as a society but differ only on the specific policies to achieve them. We are not going to significantly expand or contract domestic spending, taxation, civil liberties, or social services this year or the next. Nearly everyone can accept this except the staffs of interest groups, who are paid well to demonstrate short-term progress. The torpor of today's politics compels these staffs to embrace the kind of policy progress that might be worse than no action at all (*a la* catastrophic care) or to paint apocalyptic images of the clock being turned back on our freedoms (NRA, pro-choice groups). These interest groups have trouble seeing that policy is neither moving in their favor nor moving against them—it is standing still. For many such groups, the politics of consensus presents far more confusion than did the sharp divisions that nearly split American society in the 1960s. For most of the rest of us, it's fortunate that we're not asking much of Washington today, since it's not clear who would represent our interests there if we were.

24. A Short History of Lobbying

Richard Sachs

The role of interest groups and lobbyists in the making of public policy has been debated since the nation's earliest days. Balancing the selfish wishes of factional groups with the public interest was a matter of prime importance for James Madison. For better or worse, "factions" were endemic to the growth of the nation, and lobbying became an enduring feature of policymaking. In this article published in 1986 for the U.S. Senate under the title "Congress and Pressure Groups: Lobbying in a Modern Democracy," Richard Sachs, an analyst for the Congressional Research Service of the U.S. Library of Congress, reviews the history of lobbying. He discusses the principal lobbying techniques, the efforts by Congress to control lobbyists, and the debate over whether interest groups are desirable or harmful for American politics.

Arguably, lobbying, more than any other aspect of American political history, is possessed of a particular "demonology," a roster of greedy and venal people and a litany of escapades that reflect the dark side of democracy. This section recalls some of those men and events; describes Congress' early efforts to stem perceived abuses; and follows the transition of lobbying from the nineteenth century "old lobby" of "representatives of corporations, patronage-brokers [and] 'wire-pullers'" to the twentieth century "new lobby" of hundreds of associations, societies, institutes, federations, consultants and lawyers at work to influence decisions in a diverse and complex political milieu.

Madison's Theory of Faction

Popular opinion has held negative views of lobbying and lobbyists since the earliest days of the American Republic. James Madison, father of the United States Constitution, was particularly concerned with the allegedly pernicious influence of what was termed "faction" in the language of the day. In *Federalist Paper*, No. 10, Madison succinctly and unsympathetically defined faction as a number of citizens, whether amounting to a majority or a minority of the whole, who are united and actuated by some common impulse of passion, or of interest, adverse to the rights of other citizens, or to the permanent and aggregate interests of the community.

Yet despite his obvious disapproval, he recognized that the existence and activities of factions were an unavoidable part of democratic government, and that the mischiefs of the former could only be cured by constraining the latter. This Madison refused to countenance. Instead, he concluded "that the causes of faction cannot be removed, and that relief is only to be sought in the means of controlling its effect."

Madison's fears, and those of the other founders, were realized as the new Constitution was implemented: factional groups within Congress began to coalesce almost immediately, leading swiftly, perhaps inevitably, to development of the Federalist and Anti-Federalist (Democratic-Republican) parties. So, too, individuals and groups began to appear at the convening of the First and all subsequent Congresses to press their causes and interests before the legislature. . . .

Lobbying in the early days of the republic was essentially an activity carried on by individuals or ad hoc coalitions established for specific purposes and carried forward for only a limited period.

Nicholas Biddle's determined, though unsuccessful, campaign for charter renewal for his Bank of the United States,* in the face of unswerving opposition by President Andrew Jackson, has been characterized as a landmark in the development of "professional" lobbying. As his chief lobbyist, Biddle relied on the services of one of the most distinguished public figures of the day: Senator Daniel Webster was on retainer to the Bank throughout the struggle, even while leading the fight on the Senate floor to overturn Jackson's veto of the charter. This indisputable conflict of interest has been regularly cited in support of the pejorative view of lobbying, along with Webster's famous private communication with Biddle:

> I believe my retainer has not been renewed or refreshed as usual. If it be wished that my relation to the Bank should be continued, it may be well to send me the usual retainers.

By the middle of the nineteenth century, the United States had begun to make the transition from an agrarian republic to a modern industrial nation. The Civil War sped and intensified this transformation while establishing the federal government and the city of Washington as focal

---

* Biddle was president of the Bank of the United States from 1822 to 1836.

points for the efforts of various commercial interests and their increasingly numerous representatives.

Lobbying and the Development of American Railroads

In 1862 President Abraham Lincoln signed the Pacific Railway Act, in which the United States government undertook to assist in the construction of a transcontinental railroad. Support consisted of direct construction loans to the Union Pacific and Central Pacific Railroads and a program of generous land grants to other operators. The agents of various groups of financiers and promoters competed furiously in Washington for congressional approval of their particular projects, with the eventual result that three additional lines, the Sante Fe, Southern Pacific, and Northern Pacific, were given charters and large land grants in the fifteen years following the Civil War.

Rail lobbyists also secured passage of additional legislation designed to maximize the value of lands granted by the United States: under the Desert Land Act (1877) and the Timber and Stone Act (1878), grantee lines were able to exchange barren lands included in their right-of-way strips for more salable parcels elsewhere. In all cases, the proceeds from resale or resource development accrued to the railroads as profit.

The Credit Mobilier scandal of 1872 epitomized both the power of the rail lobby in Washington, and the potential for abuse of both public funds and public trust that grew out of the hectic rush to span the continent....

The extraordinary burst of industrial expansion following the Civil War marked the beginning of America's Gilded Age, a period of boom and bust, exuberant confidence, almost unfettered capital power, and great social change.

Lobbying prior to the Civil War had been largely the preserve of individual agents—"hired guns"—who had few permanent attachments and could be retained to promote almost any bill they felt appropriate. These veterans began to be replaced by the permanent representatives of various interests in the last third of the century. In addition to the rail lobby, industrialists' agents successfully lobbied for maintenance of high tariffs on imported manufactures—a basic element of Republican party platforms—and veterans' organizations sought to expand Civil War pension coverage, while on the other hand the Women's Christian Temperance Union and allied groups continued their persistent, and ultimately successful, campaign for prohibition.

Some of the lobbying techniques of the Gilded Age would be familiar to any Washington representative in the 1980s: positions were analyzed, favorable arguments arrayed, speeches prepared, personal contacts with members of key committees pursued, and appearances were made at committee proceedings. Even a grass-roots campaign was effectively employed in the interest of securing favorable legislative outcomes.

Certain other practices of late nineteenth century lobbyists reflect the unique exuberance of the period. . . . [Lobbying often took place] in the elegant parlors of certain society matrons, where members of Congress were lavishly entertained while subjected to the subtle pressures of the lobbyist. Ben Perley Poore noted:

> [T]he most adroit lobbyists belong to the gentler sex. . . . They are retained with instructions to exert their influence with designated Congressmen. . . . To enable them to do their work well, they have pleasant parlors, with works of art and bric-a-brac donated by admirers. Every evening they receive, and in the winter, their blazing wood fires are often surrounded by a distinguished circle. . . . Who can blame a Congressman for leaving the bad cooking of his hotel or boardinghouse, with the absence of all home comforts, to walk into the parlor web the cunning spider lobbyist weaves for him?

Although the hostesses in these cases were often on retainer for particular individuals, associations, or corporations, a surprising number were lobby agents in their own right, as was noted by James Bryce in *The American Commonwealth.* . . .

It was during this period, in 1876, that the House adopted a resolution requiring all lobbyists to register with the Clerk of the House. This marked the first congressional effort to regulate lobbying. This requirement was apparently in effect only for the 44th Congress.

But although Congress took little action to regulate lobbying, state legislatures were considerably active. . . .

Woodrow Wilson's Attack on "The Lobby"

Woodrow Wilson capped a career as a distinguished scholar of American government and, later, as successful reform governor of New Jersey when he was inaugurated President in 1913. But as early as 1885, Wilson had warned against "the power of corrupt lobbyists to turn legislation to their own purposes. [The citizen] hears of enormous subsidies begged and obtained; of pensions procured on commission by professional pension solicitors; of appropriations made in the interest of dishonest contractors; and he is not altogether unwarranted in the conclusion that these are evils inherent in the very nature of Congress."

Wilson, along with other commentators, had identified the autonomous structure of congressional committees at the time as a major reason for the success of lobbying efforts:

> [T]he power of the lobbyist consists in great part, if not altogether, in the facility afforded him by the Committee system. . . . It would be impracticable to work up his schemes in the broad field of the whole House, but in the membership of a Committee he finds manageable numbers. If he can gain the ear of the Committee, or if any influential portion of it, he has practically gained the ear of the House itself.

As President, Wilson first clashed with an enhanced lobby early in his term. As part of the administration's reform program, Rep. Oscar W. Underwood, House Majority Leader, had introduced a bill substantially reducing tariff rates on imported manufacturers, a historic reversal of the protectionist policies in effect since the Civil War. The "tariff lobby," representatives of numerous manufacturing interests across the country, responded with an intensive campaign on all levels, from grass-roots activities to personal lobbying of members of both houses of Congress in the Capitol. Surprised at the intensity of his opposition, President Wilson replied with a sharply worded attack on the lobby:

> Washington has seldom seen so numerous, or so insidious a body. The newspapers are being filled with advertisements calculated to mislead the judgement not only of public men, but also the public opinion of the country itself. There is every evidence that money without limit is being spent to sustain this lobby and to create an appearance of a pressure of public opinion antagonistic to some of the chief items of the tariff . . . It is thoroughly worth the while of the people of this country to take knowledge of the matter. Only public opinion can check and destroy it.

President Wilson's charges were soon given additional credence when the *New York World* published an article by Martin Mulhall, former chief Washington agent for the National Association of Manufacturers, detailing his highly questionable lobbying activities, which had included alleged bribery of sitting members of Congress. . . .

The years of the Wilson Administration also witnessed an accelerating trend toward institutionalization of interest group representation. When the United States entered the First World War in 1917, the federal government faced an unprecedented challenge of organizing the private sector for participation in the war effort. Federal coordination agencies, such as the War Industries Board, the Food Administration, and others, officially requested the establishment of trade associations in many industries which had not previously been served by such groups. Organized to promote cooperative planning and standardization of products during wartime, the new associations, established in all segments of American society, continued in existence after 1918, acquiring the peacetime mandate of promoting the interests of their members.

Over a period of 150 years, lobbying in Washington evolved from a small group of agents representing commercial interests and utilizing techniques of questionable propriety to a diverse corps of lobbyists representing agrarian, labor and social interests as well as business, and using techniques of persuasion easily recognizable by lobbyists today. During this period, Congress expressed concern both with improprieties by lobbyists and, as years went on, their growth and evolving techniques. Congress reacted with investigations and disclosure legislation but found it difficult to resolve the conflict between regulation and petition and speech safeguards. Then as now, congressional investigations focused on alleged lobbyist wrong-doing; in doing so, they helped to reinforce the perception of lobbying as a sinister force in the governmental process.

25. Leader of the Snack PAC

Peter Carlson

Presidents come and presidents go, but lobbyists are a permanent fixture in Washington, D.C. As *Washington Post* staff writer Peter Carlson notes, "representatives of the people are far outnumbered by representatives of trade associations, advocacy groups, unions and corporations that attempt to influence them." In this article published in the *Washington Post Magazine* in 1988, Carlson chronicles the life and intensive lobbying efforts of Steve Eure, who as director of government relations for the Snack Food Association is "the man paid to keep America safe for snack foods."

Steve Eure was sick and tired. Literally laid low by a flu, he was home from work and fast asleep when the phone rang. Groggy, he rolled over and answered it, only to hear a congressional aide pour bad news into his fevered ear: HR 2148, the bane of Eure's professional life, had suddenly leaped from the legislative back burner and was slated for a quick markup in a House subcommittee.

That news straightened Eure up faster than a whiff of smelling salts. He'd been fighting HR 2148 for more than a year. The bill was, he believed, another example of Big Government threatening those things Americans hold most dear. Things like popcorn and potato chips.

HR 2148 would require any foods containing palm oil, palm kernel oil or coconut oil to identify the oil, on the label, as "a saturated fat." To Steve Eure, lobbyist for the Snack Food Association, those were fighting words.

Not that they weren't accurate. These "tropical oils" are indeed saturated fats. They are also ingredients in various snack foods. Popcorn, for instance, just doesn't taste the same when cooked in anything but coconut oil, according to the snack people. And popcorn manufacturers feel that putting the phrase "a saturated fat" on their label is like putting a skull and crossbones on their label. The manufacturers of various other crunchy morsels feel the same way.

Steve Eure, 36, the man paid to keep America safe for snack foods, snapped into action. Flu or no flu, he started working the phones, rallying the troops. He called his allies at the National Food Processors Association and the National Confectioners Association and the American Frozen Food Institute. He called lobbyists for Frito-Lay and Kraft and Kellogg and General Mills and Procter & Gamble. He called a law firm and a PR firm representing the Philippines, Malaysia and Indonesia, where the tropical oils are produced. He informed them all of the imminent markup and urged them to bombard the subcommittee on health and the environment with a chorus of raspberries for HR 2148. Then he started arranging a strategy meeting and jotting down ideas for amendments designed to strew thumbtacks along the bill's path toward passing.

Eure's wife watched him sitting there in his sickbed, surrounded by papers and phone books, wheeling and dealing. "Who do you think you are?" she asked "FDR?"

Face it: The Franklin D. Roosevelt's of this town come and go, but the Stephen E. Eures are forever with us.

In Washington, representatives of the people are far outnumbered by representatives of the trade associations, advocacy groups, unions and corporations that attempt to influence them. More than 3,200 associations are headquartered in the Washington area, employing more than 80,000 workers. That makes associations the third largest industry in town, just behind government and tourism, according to the American Association of Association Executives, which is one of Washington's two associations of association honchos. The other is the Greater Washington Society of Association Executives.

"Americans of all ages, all conditions and all dispositions constantly form associations," Alexis de Tocqueville wrote in 1835. That was a prescient observation, coming more than a century before the advent of such Washington institutions as the National Association of Margarine Manufacturers, the American Hot Dip Galvanizers Association, the National Association of Governors' Highway Safety Representatives and the American Association of Sex Educators, Counselors and Therapists, among many others.

In Washington, even lobbyists have their own trade association. And why not? There are certainly enough of them. About a third of the city's associations have at least one lobbyist on staff, and many of the others hire local law firms or public relations agencies to lobby for them. All in all, the Washington area can boast—if that's the right word—of a lobbyist population somewhere between 5,500 (according to the executive director of the American League of Lobbyists) and 20,000 (according to a former executive director of the American League of Lobbyists).

Steve Eure, the Snack Food Association's director of government relations, is an infantryman in this vast gray-suited army of special interests. Like other Washington professions—politics and journalism come to mind—it is not a universally beloved field of endeavor. "I suspect," he says, "that my mother probably cringes when I tell people I'm a lobbyist."

Eure, a veteran of 11 years on the Hill, exhibits no such chagrin. Back in the late '70s, fresh out of college and working as a lowly staffer for the House Agriculture Committee, Eure looked with envy on the lobbyists who flocked around, flashing their business cards. He'd be trying to juggle 20 different issues at a time, and these guys would sashay in to give a spiel on their one pet project. "I thought, God, that'd be easy. Focus on one issue. Get some specialty going. Be responsible for covering that one issue. and there was also the social side. You know: 'Let's go out to lunch.'"

In 1981, he got his chance to make the classic Capitol Hill fence-jump: The American Meat Institute hired him to lobby his old colleagues working for the Agriculture Committee. He was not disappointed. "It was fun: strategizing, and doing lobbying behind the scenes, and PAC checks and schmoozing and boozing and golf tournaments and all that crap that you hear about. And it all goes on. I had a great time and learned a lot there."

In 1985, he moved to the Snack Food Association, then known as the Potato Chip and Snack Food Association. A trade group representing about 140 manufacturers of potato chips, nacho chips, tortilla chips, popcorn, pretzels and pork rinds, among other delicacies, SFA is housed in a spacious Alexandria office where the signs on the restroom doors read "Mr. Chips" and "Ms. Chips," and the decor runs to antique popcorn machines and a six-foot wooden statue of an ear of corn.

From this command post, Eure runs the association's government relations effort. He puts out a newsletter and writes a Washington column in the SFA's monthly magazine, *Snack World* (formerly "Chipper Snacker"). He runs the association's political action committee, which is called ... you guessed it, Snack PAC. He plays Santa Claus on Capitol Hill twice a year, distributing cans of chips to hundreds of hungry politicians. And, of course, he lobbies. In congressional offices, in committee hearing rooms, in Capitol Hill restaurants, on the fairway at Congressional Country Club, wherever he's called to defend the fragile chip from the iron heel of Big Government, that's where you'll find Steve Eure.

Two days after the fateful sick-bed phone call, Steve Eure was stalking the halls of Congress, trying to stymie HR 2148. He carried seven folders of position papers, one for each of the day's appointments with aides working for members of the subcommittee. The first, at 9 o'clock, was in the office of Bob Whittaker (R-Kan.), who was, unfortunately for Eure, a co-sponsor of the bill.

"Is he 100 percent for it?" Eure asked Whittaker's legislative aide.

She nodded her head in an emphatic yes. "He's eager to vote for it."

Undaunted, Eure launched into his pitch anyway. The bill is not really a health bill, he said, it's a trade bill. The three oils that the bill would label as saturated fats are all imported from Pacific islands. Domestically produced soybean oil—which also contains saturated fat, though not as much as the tropical oils—would be exempt. The bill, he said, is designed not to protect American arteries from fat but to give American soybean farmers an advantage over foreign competitors. "You're identifying 5 percent of the total fat with this bill," he said. "Is that fooling the public? I think it is."

The aide did not look convinced.

"Is he entertaining any amendments?" Eure asked.

"No."

The next appointment went even worse. After Eure gave his spiel about how HR 2148 was really a trade bill, not a health bill, the aide revealed that he had coronary artery disease. "I'm on a diet that specifically tells me to avoid coconut oil and palm oil," he said. "Obviously, they feel it's something to single out."

Out in the hallway, Eure shook his head. "The guy's dying of heart disease. It makes it a little difficult to make my pitch to him."

Things were not looking good for Steve Eure. It was as if he were fighting motherhood and apple pie. No, worse: He was fighting for saturated fat and against American farmers. HR 2148 already had more than 160 co-sponsors, including 12 of the 18 members of the subcommittee scheduled to mark it up. Eure's strategy was to stall the markup with "obstructionist" amendments and keep the bill off the House floor. A sympathetic conservative, Tom Bliley (R-Va.), had agreed to offer some amendments. Now Eure appeared at the office of another conservative, Jack Fields (R-Tex.), in the hope that Fields might be persuaded to do the same.

In the office foyer, Eure eyed the decor—57 plastic hard hats, each emblazoned with the name of an oil company. "I guess I should get him a hard hat with a snack-food label on it," he said.

An aide led him into the office of the congressman, who was, at the moment, back in Houston. The room was decorated with the heads of wild beasts dispatched into eternity by the congressman: a zebra, a water buffalo, a wart hog and several distant cousins of Bambi. Eure was quite relieved that he was not lobbying against big-game hunting.

Fields' aide told Eure that the congressman would probably vote against HR 2148. It was the best thing he'd heard all day. In fact, it was the only good thing he'd heard all day.

"We'll be drafting a few amendments and directing them to Mr. Bliley," he said. "If you'd entertain some, that's fine. If you'd rather not, that's fine, too. But obviously I'd like to spread them around."

The aide thought Fields was probably to busy to entertain any amendments. But she did share some information she'd heard: Mickey Leland (D-Tex.), another subcommittee member and a co-sponsor of HR 2148, was wavering, worried about the effect the bill might have on the fragile economies of the Philippine and the other nations that produced the tropical oils.

Suddenly, things looked a bit brighter for Steve Eure. Out in the hallway, he started thinking out loud: If a liberal Democrat like Leland was joining the conservative Republicans who opposed the bill, maybe there was hope. Maybe Fields could persuade fellow Texan Leland to persuade Leland's fellow Democrat, Henry Waxman (D-Calif.), who chaired the subcommittee, to postpone the markup.

Maybe, Eure thought, HR 2148 would just go away, at least until next year.

As jobs go, it's not a bad one. There's no heavy lifting, unless you consider unloading cans of snack food at the House and Senate office buildings twice a year heavy lifting. Steve Eure works in a comfortable office. He drives a company car. He makes a good salary, though he declines to reveal just how good it is. And he gets to play golf on company time.

"Golf is a great game for lobbyists," he says. "I can't think of a better way to spend a morning with somebody than riding around a golf course, letting 'em win. But I think you should always do a little bit of business. Let 'em know you're not just fluff, that you have some concerns, knock a few ideas around. And you ought to do that on the front nine."

On the back nine, he says, you should just have fun.

"You can argue the issues till you're blue in the face or you can play golf, and you can probably get further playing golf," he says. "If you don't have the competence to talk about issues and converse with politicians on a professional level, you're not going to be taken seriously. But if you've got that—and it isn't that hard—then the golf and the cocktails and the dinners and all that does go far."

Steve Eure is not a political junkie. No fires burn in his belly. He follows politics, of course, but only because it's his job. He's not an ideologue or a passionate partisan. He's not trying to save the world—or even the whales. "Some lobbyists are representing something because they have a personal interest in it" he says. "I don't. I have a professional interest in it. It's my job. But when you're up on Capitol Hill, it's just as complex and challenging when you're talking about snack foods as when you're talking about GM."

He does fantasize, he admits, about using his lobbying skills for something more gratifying to the soul than snack foods. "I dream of it," he says. "I'd like to sign up with Amnesty International or some environmental group or some worthy charity or cause and make a difference. What could be more satisfying? It would be a terrific accomplishment, personal and professional. But I don't know if I could find the right blend between cause and responsibility and salary and location and everything else."

Ten years from now, Steve Eure figures, he'll still be lobbying or maybe running his own trade association. "It's a nice little professional community, and people have a lot of fun," he says. "We're all on opposite sides or the same side, depending on what the issue is. I don't think anybody gets their nose bent personally on any of it. It's just our job."

The night before HR 2148 was scheduled for markup, Steve Eure had a dream. He was a ballplayer sitting on the bench during the late innings of a close World Series game. Suddenly, the manager sent him up to pinch-hit. The first pitch came in so fast he didn't even see it. Ball one. "Just swing at the next three pitches," he told himself. "Go down swinging." So he swung at the next invisible pitch and hit it over the left-field fence. As he scored the winning run, his teammates mobbed him, shaking his hand and pounding his back. "So this is what it's like," he thought.

Back in the real world, things didn't seem as glorious. The next afternoon, Eure sat with other food industry lobbyists in a hearing room in the Rayburn Building and handicapped his chances: slim to nil. Even with Leland on his side, he figured he had only four or five votes on the 18-member subcommittee. Worse, he'd heard rumors that the full committee might vote on the bill in a couple of days, and he figured he'd lose there, too.

As Eure sat waiting for these grim events to unfold, somebody announced that the markup had been moved to a room downstairs. As several dozen dark suits shuffled out the door, Eure turned to the lobbyist from the Confectioners Association and smiled sardonically. "The march of death," he said.

Downstairs, Eure sat and waited for the subcommittee to appear. It never did. Instead, somebody announced that the markup had been canceled. Suddenly, the other lobbyists crowded around Eure, shaking his hand, congratulating him.

It was like his World Series dream. Well, sort of.

"Champagne on me," he said.

No explanation was given for the cancellation, but Eure had his theory, which later proved true: The bill's proponents did not want to proceed until they'd satisfied Mickey Leland.

"Never in a million years would I have guessed that a liberal representative from Houston like Mickey Leland would be opposed to this bill because of his concern with the Philippines," Eure said as he strolled along Capitol Hill. "Never in a million years. That's why you never give up. You keep fighting every step of the way."

Eure figured he'd be fighting HR 2148 again, probably in January. But that didn't preclude a little celebrating now.

At the bar in Bullfeathers, he took a sip of his victory beer. Then he did something any self-respecting snack food lobbyist ought to do in those circumstances: He asked the bartender for a platter of nachos.

Chapter 6

Communications Media and Politics

Politics could not exist without channels of communication. Public officials must communicate with one another and with their electorates. As citizens, most of what we know about the action of government and the conduct of politics comes to us secondhand—for that matter, by many hands—through communications media. In modern mass society, that means through large, complex, and costly media enterprises, such as newspapers and magazines, press associations, radio and television outlets, and cable and satellite systems.

Like it or not, we are heavy consumers of the communications media. Some would say we are prisoners of the media. The average grade-school child, studies show, spends about twenty-seven hours a week watching television—nearly as much time as is spent in school. The average adult American spends nearly three hours a day watching television, two hours listening to radio, twenty minutes reading a newspaper, and ten minutes reading a magazine. (Much of this attention to the media may be casual or spent in conjunction with other activities—which suggests that many media messages are lost or ignored in the process.) Since the 1960s, television has been the chief source of news for the broadest range of citizens; today, about two-thirds of all Americans rely chiefly on TV for their news.[1]

It is axiomatic, then, that the media exert a pervasive influence on politics. But this is not new. For centuries the human voice was the chief carrier of political ideas; a gift for oratorical flourish (plus a set of leather lungs) was the mark of a gifted politician. As communications technology advanced, each new form became a carrier of political messages—letters, books, pamphlets and broadsides, newspapers, telephone and telegraph, then radio and television. Each era, defined by its distinctive mix of communications modes, manifested its own style of political discourse, its own way of expressing political ideas. Although television has by no means eliminated other forms of communication, it is by common assent the essential medium of our time. We tend to see the political world through the images it provides, and our memories of political events are, like as not, recollections of things we have seen on TV. Our political discourse—simple, direct, disjointed, short on verbal elegance but long on visual symbolism—owes much of its character to television.

Of course, politics play a secondary and even unimportant role in most media. Television is first and foremost a vehicle for entertainment. The same is true of radio, the movies, and much of what goes into print. Political science teachers may dig into their daily newspapers to find the government news, but editors and publishers know that such readers are a small minority, smaller than in times past. That is why even quality newspapers have advice columns, astrology tables, crossword puzzles, and exhaustive coverage of social events, gossip, and sports. The weekly news magazines, which once regularly put political leaders on their covers, rarely do so today; sex, drugs, entertainment, and pop culture sell better on the newsstands. The media, which affect politics so profoundly, nonetheless seek their audiences and revenues elsewhere.

The Structure of the Media

Major media outlets are large businesses. Although about 11,000 newspapers are published in the United States, the major voices are the 1,800 or so daily papers. Two-thirds of these dailies, which claim three-fourths of the circulation, are owned by large chains. Many are parts of communications conglomerates with holdings in radio, television, cable systems, and book publishing. Putting out a large metropolitan newspaper requires a sizable staff and expensive printing equipment. This is one reason why fewer and fewer newspapers compete in given communities and why those that remain often share plants and facilities.

Although there are fewer papers today than at the turn of the century, there are more alternatives for readers. More than 12,000 magazines and periodicals are published in this country. They cover a bewildering range of topics, and many treat political subjects occasionally if not regularly. There are journals of opinion, trade and professional journals, inspirational and self-help magazines, hobbyists' outlets, business and labor union "house organs," and newsletters. "Something for everyone" is the order of the day.

In recent years this diversity has dissolved the early monopolies of electronic media. More than 10,000 radio stations, 1,200 television stations, and 7,800 cable television systems now operate in the United States. For at least two generations, national political coverage was dominated by the large networks, which alone had the money and outlets to gather and market news nationwide. More recently cheaper technologies and more diverse outlets—cable and microwave systems, satellite links, and minicam recorders, for example—have democratized electronic news gathering and dissemination. Local outlets need not rely upon networks for all their news. In the 1950s, Americans who lived in a major media market enjoyed perhaps four or five television channels and ten or twelve general-purpose radio stations. Today we can choose among dozens of channels (through cable) and as many radio stations, each of which gears its programming to a given audience.

Communication is an enterprise that enjoys a special place in any political democracy. The First Amendment to the Constitution enjoins Congress to "make no law . . . abridging the freedom . . . of the press." "A responsible press is an undoubtedly desirable goal," Chief Justice Warren Burger declared in a 1974 ruling, "but press responsibility is not mandated by the Constitution and like many other virtues it cannot be legislated."

The tardiness of the press in focusing on the savings and loan (S&L) scandal is analyzed in Selection 26 by Ellen Hume of the *New York Times*. By any measure, the losses recorded by high-flying S&Ls in the 1980s must rank as one of the greatest political scandals in American history. Elements of the scandal included greedy and incompetent businessmen; complicitous accountants and lawyers; compliant politicians who profited from S&L contributions; government regulators who looked the other way; and an administration that preached a hands-off policy toward industry excesses. Yet the sordid story was slow to reach the front pages, not only because of the nature of the story and the structure of the media but also because of the stonewalling by S&L and government officials.

The Media and Elections

Campaigns and elections are made-to-order media events. And why not? After all, they are efforts to communicate and persuade. For much of our history, candidates refrained from public electioneering, leaving it in the hands of their supporters and the partisan press. Today's candidates, however, are often defined by their media campaigns, which soak up much of their time and funds.

Another side of media influence is coverage of campaigns and elections. Taking note of the extent to which candidates and their managers gear their efforts toward the media, many commentators have blamed the media for everything they do not like about election results. Some conservatives are sure they discern a liberal bias in the national media. They are not, however, the only complainers. Liberals, for their part, often regard media outlets as fronts for the huge firms that own them. Many are convinced that candidates who dedicate themselves to mastering media techniques enjoy special benefits that make it hard for the unsophisticated media-user to win at the game.

Although evidence can be found to buttress criticisms such as these, the overall verdict on media influence has to be qualified. S. Robert Lichter and his colleagues (Selection 27) examine press performance during the 1988 presidential campaign. They found little evidence of overt bias in the press; in any case, little that the press said could hide the fact that George Bush ran a far more effective campaign than his rival, Michael Dukakis.

Other commentators are less sanguine about the role of the press in reporting electoral contests. Nowadays, presidential candidates hardly ever confront reporters, much less the general public, in anything like an open forum. Surrounded by security officers and programmed by consultants, candidates and their advisers are seemingly in control of the campaign and its agenda; reporters feel they have lost the ability to influence the content and issues of the contest. David S. Broder, Pulitzer Prize-winning political correspondent for the *Washington Post,* issues a manifesto urging a more activist role for the press in campaign coverage (Selection 28). Responding to Broder's call, many reporters and newspapers have taken a more active role in questioning candidates and criticizing their advertisements.

Students of the media detect another set of biases that pervade news coverage of politics and other topics. These biases include favoring the simple over the complex, the concrete over the abstract, and the sensational over the typical. As one pundit put it, "a crisis is an event which happens in the presence of a journalist." [2] In covering campaigns, reporters tend to stress the "game" or the "horse race" rather than issues or policy positions. Reporters try to heighten the sense of conflict and climax—staples of good news stories—in several ways. They sensationalize every conceivable confrontation. Reporters also call the races and declare "winners" and "losers," even when the results are ambiguous or inconsequential, and they harp on personality or stylistic quirks. Thus the media account of a major campaign may be little more than a comic-book version of the real thing, and it may inhibit voters from getting important information about the candidates and issues from which they must choose.

The Media and Governing

The media's role hardly ends once the election returns are counted and the winning candidate takes the oath of office. Governing decisions— forming and implementing policies—are made in the context of media coverage, or lack of coverage. Certain events and personalities are magnets for media attention; disasters (the explosion of the space shuttle *Challenger,* for example), scandals (Watergate or the Iranian arms imbroglio), and personalities (presidents and media celebrities) draw coverage that is often lurid and excessive. At the same time, many pressing issues and problems are ignored because they lack the colorful elements that make "a good story."

In such a situation, government officials spend much of their time trying to make the best of the news environment they face. To push public policy in one direction or another, politicians seek publicity. Most often this is done by formal means—speeches, press conferences, press handouts, ceremonial events, and the like. Frequently, however, public officials cultivate publicity by off-the-record communications— "leaks" to friendly members of the press to serve a particular purpose. Also, diligent reporting may uncover information that the administration would rather conceal. One of the most astute students of government-press relations, Stephen Hess, describes the various types of leaks and evaluates their purposes in Selection 29, "A Guide to 'Leaks' in Government."

Because of today's specialized media coverage, students can follow political and government affairs even though they live and work far from the nation's capital. Cable television has brought a bonanza for students of politics: the Cable-Satellite Public Affairs Network, or C-SPAN, which broadcasts House and Senate floor proceedings, key congressional committee hearings, and various public affairs speeches and conferences.

Even those whose blood pressure rises at the thought of the power of the media must concede that the media are indispensable for a knowledge of the world of politics. "Were it left to me to decide whether we should have a government without newspapers, or newspapers without government," Thomas Jefferson observed, "I should not hesitate a moment to prefer the latter." [3] Yet later, when Jefferson himself was president, he declared that "the man who never looks into a newspaper is better informed than he who reads them; inasmuch as he who knows nothing is nearer to truth than he whose mind is filled with falsehood and errors." [4] What modern politician, official, or political observer has not shared Jefferson's contradictory feelings about the press?

Notes

1. Alexander Szalai et al., eds., *The Use of Time* (The Hague, Netherlands: Mouton, 1972); and John P. Robinson, *Changes in Americans' Use of*

Time, 1965-1975 (Cleveland, Ohio: Cleveland State University, August 1977).

2. *The Listener*, April 21, 1983, 11.
3. Thomas Jefferson to Col. Edward Carrington, January 16, 1787, cited in *Bartlett's Familiar Quotations* (Boston: Little, Brown, 1980).
4. Thomas Jefferson, cited in *The Politics of the Presidency*, ed. Richard A. Watson and Norman C. Thomas (New York: John Wiley & Sons, 1983), 191.

26. Why the Press Blew the Savings and Loan Scandal

Ellen Hume

Like a tree that falls in a forest where no ears can hear it, a news event that is not reported makes no noise. An unreported event might as well not have happened. Some important stories are more apt to be reported than others for reasons that stem from the nature of the stories and from the structure and assumptions of the media. The scandal of mismanaged savings and loan companies was a big story that for a long time was underreported by the press corps. *New York Times* reporter Ellen Hume explains in her 1990 article why journalists ignored the accumulating S&L problems. Part of the answer lies in the shape of the story itself: it was a "dull" topic filled with numbers and initially of minor interest to citizens. The structure of the media also played a part: it was a local story that initially escaped the notice of the national press corps. Finally, industry executives, government regulators, and politicians had every reason to adhere to "business as usual."

Every taxpayer deserves an answer to this question: Why did the well-paid, well-educated and constitutionally protected press corps miss the savings and loan scandal, which is the most expensive public finance debacle in U.S. history?

The press-bashers are having a field day, charging that journalists, who ferreted out the details of Gary Hart's dates and Vice President Dan Quayle's academic embarrassments, weren't able to deliver the goods when it really mattered. If the press had seen and reported earlier the savings and loan industry's eight-year suicidal spree, the subsequent political pressure might have saved taxpayers tens or even hundreds of billions of dollars.

Here are some of the factors that led to the press's disappointing performance on the scandal:

It was a "numbers" story, not a "people" story. While the trade press, including the National Thrift News (now renamed the National Mortgage News), reported important developments in the scandal years ago, it was all too complicated and boring to interest many mainstream journalists. Regulatory changes—such as the accounting tricks and reduced capital requirements that helped paper over the first phase of the savings and loan crisis in the early 1980's—weren't big news.

A reporter with *The Houston Post*, Pete Brewton, tried to ask candidate George Bush a question about the savings and loan scandal during a 1988 campaign trip to Texas. He says that the national press corps and Bush campaign aides showed contempt for the "boring" topic and quickly changed the subject.

The story was outside the Beltway. Along with the trade press, many local reporters aggressively covered savings and loan failures in their communities, including *The Dallas Morning News*, *The Miami Herald* and *The Los Angeles Times*.

But local reporting generally isn't read by journalists from the national news organizations that set the agenda for Washington's policy makers. And while regional reporters for the major news organizations and freelancers also had good stories, "not one paper covered it thoroughly from beginning to end," concludes Gregory Hill, The *Wall Street Journal*'s San Francisco bureau chief.

The villains were a bipartisan, politically powerful group. The credibility of Charles Keating, who now is singled out as the prototypical thrift villain in most news accounts, was actively boosted not only by five U.S. senators from both parties but also by Alan Greenspan, before Mr. Greenspan became chairman of the Federal Reserve Board, and by the Arthur Young accounting firm. While Michael Dukakis tried to raise the savings and loan problem during the Presidential campaign, both parties shied away because no one knew how to fix it without raising taxes.

The victims didn't complain. Because the deposits were insured by the Federal Government, there weren't any pictures on the evening news of anguished citizens lining up outside closed savings and loans.

Government regulators had special reasons for keeping quiet about the problem. With the exception of the former chairman of the Federal Home Loan Bank Board, Edwin J. Gray, high-level regulators were reluctant to disclose the facts, often for political reasons. They said they were afraid of triggering runs on lending institutions.

Many pertinent documents were kept secret by law. Regulators' examination reports aren't available even under the Freedom of Information Act, because lawmakers fear they might cause bank panics. Reporters also don't have access to credit reports or other crucial loan documentation that might have tipped them off to the under-capitalized loans pervasive in weak thrifts.

Some information about mortgages made by a Texas institution in California might be on file in a county in California, but not at the Texas lending institution. "If our tax dollars are going to support the deposits," says Mr. Brewton, "all the loan information should be made available from the Federal regulators."

The press simply isn't equipped to do everything the public expects it to do. Journalists have been expected to replace the regulators thrown out of business during the past decade. Journalists should be better watchdogs. But in the crush of competitive deadlines they can't do what a regulator or a Congressional oversight committee with subpoena power can do—especially since people can lie to the press without paying any price for it.

Journalists have gotten used to having their information pre-digested. "We usually depend on governmental institutions or groups like Common Cause or Ralph Nader or General Motors or somebody to make sense out of all this data for us," observes Brooks Jackson, a Cable News Network reporter who has won awards tracking money and politics for his former employer, *The Wall Street Journal*.

Serious investigative journalism has fallen on hard times. It is considered too wasteful for today's bottomline oriented journalism corporation managers. In addition, the press has become more the keeper of the status quo than the challenger from outside, partly because reporters tend to be much better paid than they used to be, and they hobnob with the policy makers they're allegedly monitoring.

"Whenever they wanted to find out what was going on, they went to the industry," says Mr. Gray, who tried in vain to interest the politicians and the press in the spreading scandal.

There is plenty of blame to go around, from the regulators to Congress to Wall Street. But there also should be embarrassment and soul searching at the highest levels of journalism.

Our inability to unravel and explain the importance of the Iran-contra abuses, the Housing and Urban Development influence-buying schemes and the savings and loan excesses is a scandal in itself. When politicians and regulators aren't doing their jobs, good journalism is more important to a democracy than even journalists would like to admit.

27. Media Coverage in Election '88

S. Robert Lichter, Daniel Amundson, and Richard E. Noyes

Dissatisfaction with media coverage of political campaigns is as widespread among commentators as is discontent with the campaigns themselves. The 1988 presidential contest between George Bush and Michael Dukakis was perhaps no worse than average (although it was certainly no better). Its vapid content and negative advertising nonetheless vexed thoughtful observers, many of whom felt that the press should have blown the whistle on the more scurrilous aspects of the campaign. However, in their examination of TV network coverage, published in *Public Opinion* in 1989, S. Robert Lichter and his colleagues at the Center for Media and Public Affairs contended that this coverage was balanced, tough, and focused on the issues. Despite this contention, their data actually substantiate the perennial charge that the press concentrates on reporting the contest itself rather than the issues and candidate attributes: of the top four story topics listed in Table 1, only one—policy issues—was outside the traditional horse-race focus. Crime was the most pressing issue with the electorate, which helps explain the potency of an infamous Bush TV spot branding Dukakis as soft on the crime; the spot cited the case of a parolee, Willie Horton, who then committed a murder. As for media treatment of the two contenders, no amount of commentary could obscure the fact that Bush ran a more effective media campaign than his Democratic rival. For a less sanguine assessment of the press's role in 1988, see journalist David S. Broder's comments in Selection 28.

If George Bush won the election, it must be the media's fault. That's the conventional wisdom that has poured forth from op-ed pieces, news talk shows, and "news analysis" articles ever since Election Day. TV news, we are told, was seduced by Bush speechwriter Peggy Noonan's sound bites, manipulated by media strategist Roger Ailes's photo-ops and attack ads, and shunted away from serious reporting by its own fascination with the horse race. Ever since the polls closed, the campaign has been depicted as a shallow and superficial process that manipulated, misinformed, and misled the electorate, an affair as nasty and brutish as life in [seventeenth-century English philosopher Thomas] Hobbes's state of nature (though not, alas, as short).

Table 1 Top Ten Story Topics

			Number of Stories
Campaign issues	339	The debates	103
Strategy and tactics	338	Vice presidential choices	23
Policy issues	282	Media coverage	22
Horse race	168	Past campaigns	20
The electorate	108	Reagan's role	18

In a *New York Times* op-ed column, former network correspondent Marvin Kalb charged that television news was "so preoccupied with photo opportunities and sound bites, so manipulated by media experts, so driven by polls that it lost sight of its journalistic responsibilities. . . ." As a result "the overall tone of the coverage was shallow and distinctly timid." The bottom line: "TV news made no sustained effort to challenge (Bush). . . ."

These postmortems seem to be dissecting a different campaign from the one monitored by the Center for Media and Public Affairs. . . . After analyzing all 735 general election stories that appeared on the ABC, CBS, and NBC evening news from August 19 through November 7, we found that the networks' coverage was notable for its balance, toughness, and focus on the issues—precisely the opposite of the critics' charges.

The charge of "horse racism" is a hardy perennial, but its bloom may finally be fading. In their study of television's 1984 general election coverage, Maura Clancey and Michael Robinson noted a shift away from the usual prevalence of horse-race stories. The new beneficiary of media attention was not policy issues ("enduring disputes about how *government* should behave") but campaign issues ("short-term concerns about how *candidates* or their *campaigns* should behave"). As Table 1 shows, 1988 coverage was cast in the same mold. Campaign issues like disputes over Dan Quayle's National Guard service, negative ads, and mudslinging barely edged out discussions of strategy and tactics as the most frequent topic of campaign news. Policy issues came in third, and horse-race news ran a distant fourth.

In fact the general election witnessed a dramatic reversal of the primary season in this regard. Throughout the primary campaign, over twice as many stories focused on the candidates' positioning for the nomination as their issue positions. [In the fall of 1988] that ratio was nearly reversed, with 282 stories on policy issues and only 168 on the horse race. As Table 2 indicates, crime, defense, and the economy were each covered in over 100 stories. Between forty and eighty stories apiece dealt with unemployment, drugs, taxes, the environment, education, and the budget deficit. (Many stories covered more than one issue.)

Table 2 Top Ten Policy Issues

			Number of Stories
Crime	142	Taxes	70
Defense	121	Environment	54
The economy	121	Education	46
Unemployment	77	Budget deficit	45
Drugs	74		

Critics of [1988's] horse-race coverage usually focus on the profusion of poll reports, many of them commissioned by the networks themselves. The real issue here is the propriety of such coverage, not its preponderance. The horse-race coverage was heavily poll driven, but the polls didn't drive the issues off the air.

A Supine Press?

The other major complaint is that the networks let Bush and his image makers make patsies out of them. This passivity in the face of Republican skills at media manipulation allegedly gave Bush free rein to get his chosen message out each day. Thus, Kalb bitingly termed Roger Ailes a "de facto producer of the evening news," and *Newsweek* called for a return to "the days when reporters and editors picked the sound bites." Once again, it is hard to square this portrayal with the data presented in Table 3. [In the fall of 1988] 1,137 judgments from all sources were aired on the personal character, public records, campaign styles, issue stands, or other attributes of George Bush and Michael Dukakis. The result was mainly bad news for both men. Negative judgments outweighed positive ones by the same two-to-one margin (66 to 34 percent) for both candidates. Even the number of evaluations was virtually identical—564 for Bush and 573 for Dukakis.

Media criticism outweighed praise by roughly the same two-to-one margin among both partisan sources (the candidates and their supporters) and nonpartisan ones (reporters, pundits, and ordinary voters) on all three networks, and on the major dimensions along which the candidates were evaluated—their issue stands, records in office, and performance on the campaign trail.

So Bush was *not* allowed to deliver his sound bites without challenge. On November 4, for example, he attacked Dukakis for financial mismanagement, while holding up a *Boston Herald* headline that read, "What a Mess!" CBS's Eric Engberg identified the *Herald* as a "pro-Bush Boston tabloid" and commented tartly, "Bush, without taking note of the fact

Table 3 Good Press

	Bush	Dukakis	Number of Sources
Source			
All sources	34	34	1,137
Partisans	32	35	795
Nonpartisan	38	31	342
Networks			
ABC	34	36	372
CBS	30	33	414
NBC	37	32	345
Topic			
Issues	31	27	221
Job performance	22	32	168
Candidate performance	34	36	418
Character	43	45	18
Networks			
Post convention (8/19-8/28)	75	26	78
Pre first debate (8/29-9/25)	23	28	288
Between debates (9/26-10/13)	28	31	216
Post second debate (10/14-11/7)	36	40	555

Note: Data based on clearly positive or negative source evaluations on ABC, CBS, and NBC nightly newscasts 8/19-11/7/88.

that the federal deficit is now $155 billion, *acted* like an outraged prosecutor." Engberg closed by noting that the Bush campaign had "trotted out" some Massachusetts Republicans who said "with straight faces" that the vice president was surprised at this state of affairs.

Bush may have gotten the sound bite he wanted that night, but the *story* was about the act he was putting on, and the tone was one of unmistakable sarcasm. Similarly, in his September 15 report about an earlier Bush attack on the "Massachusetts miracle," ABC's Brit Hume commented acidly, "Bush says he wants a kinder, gentler America, but there's nothing kind or gentle about the way he's campaigning."

CBS's reporting was even more aggressive on September 16. After Bush claimed that Massachusetts had lost thousands of jobs, Engberg stated flatly, "Wrong!" He then rebutted Bush point by point. On October 19, ABC's Richard Threlkeld performed a similar vivisection on Bush's notorious "tank" ad that painted Dukakis as dovish on defense. Such stories could hardly have done more to inoculate viewers against the candidate's intended message.

Of course Dukakis didn't fare any better. The airwaves were increasingly filled with complaints about his dullness, arrogance, and disorganized campaign techniques. For every story that protested Bush's new-found pugnacity, another ripped Dukakis's ineptitude as a counter-puncher. On November 6, NBC's Tom Pettit summed up one line of criticism: "While Bush was burning up the campaign trail, Dukakis was fiddling with state functions." After a shot of Dukakis posing with children (and looking distinctly unpresidential), Pettit noted sarcastically, "Remember, this is the Democratic candidate for president." He then ridiculed the Massachusetts governor for "displaying keen knowledge of gardening" at an agricultural event where he talked about compost piles. Pettit concluded, "This is what you call a turning point. Dukakis discussing composting, while George Bush was out being ferocious."

If the coverage was anything but fluff and puffery, why the flurry of assertions to the contrary? First, there's the frustration factor. Part of the battle for the presidency is the struggle for control of the battlefield—the media agenda. The combatants are the candidates on one side and the journalists on the other. Both sides win some and lose some, and journalists always come away licking some wounds.

Remember 1984, which saw practically none of [1988's] notorious negative campaigning? It was derided as an issueless exercise in feel-good politics. On election eve NBC correspondant Chris Wallace complained that Reagan had waged "a campaign long on glitz and short on substance . . . a cynical campaign, manipulative . . . (that) offered pomp and platitudes." Since 1972, television has set the rules for presidential politics. Journalists disdain those who play the game poorly and resent those who play it well.

The complaints, however, do have some basis in reality. Bush ran a better media campaign than Dukakis, which is not the same as fooling the media or getting good press. The issues mentioned most often on TV news—crime and defense—were Bush's key issues. And Dukakis was called a liberal on the evening news sixty-five times [in the fall of 1988], compared to only fourteen times during fourteen months of primary campaigning. The proportion of the public who found him "too liberal" nearly doubled from May to October. But it's not television's fault that the Democrats lacked a coherent media strategy or that Dukakis proved a poor pugilist.

The one time that Bush clearly benefited from good press was during and just after the Republican convention. His coverage in late August [1988] fulfilled all the conditions for the type of media breakthrough enjoyed by Jimmy Carter in 1972, Gary Hart in 1984, and Jesse Jackson earlier [in 1988]. By Exceeding expectations he briefly dominated the field as a highly visible, viable, and desirable candidate. Why the sudden shift? The traditional convention honeymoon coverage was magnified by journalistic amazement that the 97-pound weakling of American politics had turned into a muscle-bound macho man. His media image and poll ratings soared in tandem as he kicked sand into his rival's face. It was a textbook demonstration of the power of positive viewing.

So, did television give Bush an unfair boost after all? We think not, unless the canons of media fairness are interpreted to require balanced coverage during every week of the campaign. Bush's good press plummeted even before Labor Day and ran behind Dukakis's the rest of the fall. At the time, moreover, notions of a media boost for Bush seemed absurd. The question being raised in late August was whether the media had done in the Bush campaign by its aggressive coverage of the Quayle controversy.

During the twelve days after his selection on August 16, Quayle was the subject of ninety-three stories on the evening news—more coverage than any presidential candidate but Bush had received throughout the entire primary campaign. Quayle's 21 percent positive rating from non-partisan sources at the height of the controversy was nearly as low as we logged for Gary Hart during the Donna Rice scandal in May 1987. (Quayle's image never recovered. His nonpartisan good press score rose to only 31 percent, compared to an unbeatable 100 percent for Lloyd Bentsen.)

Ironically, the Quayle affair worked to Bush's advantage by keeping him on-screen every night defending his running mate in a decisive, resolute manner that reinforced his new take-charge image. In addition it moved up the kick-off of the fall campaign. Bush roared out of the gate like an Oklahoma "Sooner," while Dukakis was still awaiting the traditional Labor Day starter's gun. In fact some of Bush's edge in good press derived from criticism of his opponent on precisely this point. As ABC's Jim Wooten noted on August 29, "The governor may remember in November what he didn't do in August."

Voter Perceptions

Finally, the media's role must be understood within the broader dynamics of how voters decide. The playing field was tilted in Bush's direction ... by the combination of peace, prosperity, and a still-popular president. And voters' perceptions are formed not only by the campaign drama but by the stage on which it is played out. Bush needed only to actualize this potential advantage by convincing voters that he was not a bumbling effete snob out of touch with their concerns. He accomplished this by focusing attention on his opponent's flaws rather than his own virtues.

George Bush has always had a media problem. Previous studies found that he attracted mostly negative press during the 1980 and 1984 campaigns as well as the 1988 primary season. He didn't convert many reporters to his cause ... and his coverage showed it. Nonetheless, 1988 will be remembered as the year Bush succeeded in turning his media image from a threat into an opportunity.

28. Five Ways to Put Sanity Back Into Elections

David S. Broder

Modern political campaigns—expensive, technologically sophisticated, and professionally directed—elicit the same kind of criticism that has accompanied American campaigns since the rise of mass politics more than 150 years ago. The principal objections are that campaigns tend to shun issues for style and are apt to play fast and loose with the facts. Because modern campaigns are essentially mass-media efforts, their very elaborateness and sophistication pose a threat to the journalists who cover them. No longer do reporters document and explain campaigns to their audiences; they are now merely bystanders witnessing these electoral contests directed at the public. David S. Broder of the *Washington Post* offers a five-point plan, published in the *Post* in 1990, to wrest control of the campaign agenda from candidates and their managers.

It's the start of another political year, and the question that demands an answer is: Will the . . . campaign serve the voters or sicken them? The . . . mid-term election in 1986 and the presidential campaign of 1988 left a bad taste in people's mouths, not because of who won what but because so many of the winning candidates in both parties force-fed a garbage diet of negative TV ads down the country's throat. . . .

We need to do something about this win-at-all-costs mentality that is undermining our political process. By "we," I mean, first of all, the political reporters like me, who cover the campaigns. Too often we let the candidates and their image-makers use cheap negative attacks to drive out legitimate policy arguments. We need to re-import some of the reformist zeal that I saw energizing politicians, journalists and the public on a recent trip to Eastern Europe.

As it is, we have an increasing gap—really, a chasm now—between the campaign process and the governmental process. The late Sen. Thruston B. Morton (R-Ky.), when he was Republican national chairman, would say, time and again, "The purpose of politics is to establish a government." But today, winning seems an end in itself, by whatever means it takes. After the election, the consultants who masterminded the campaigns collect their checks and get ready for the next round of battles. Only then do the individuals who've been elected try to figure out how to govern.

American voters are not dumb. They have caught on to the fact that they are being conned, that campaigns are increasingly costly distractions, designed to stir their emotions while camouflaging the hard choices the government must make.

Americans heard a lot in 1988, for example, about George Bush's views on prison furloughs, an issue he hasn't mentioned since becoming president. But they heard nothing about how he proposed to bail out the savings and loan industry, the most expensive decision of his first year in office. Then in 1989, the president and Congress negotiated a "solution" that rescued the industry. And the voters, who were cut out of any chance to hear alternatives discussed, had the honor of picking up a bill that will probably total more than $200 billion.

And we wonder why voters are cynical!

It doesn't have to be this way. There's nothing about the temper of the times or the technology of our communications system that dictates that campaigns be negative or nauseating. Consultants and candidates complain that the TV stations make it difficult if not impossible to buy prime-time ads of more than 30 seconds. But 30-second ads can be used to communicate a clear, positive policy statement, if the candidate chooses. That's what Ronald Reagan did in 1980, looking straight into the camera and telling people he intended to cut taxes, boost defense spending and "get government off your back." He was elected on a platform so clear it constituted a policy mandate to Congress in 1981.

Some would legislate a requirement that ads like Reagan's of 1980 be the norm for campaigns. They would require any statement about an opponent be made by the candidate himself—figuring that it would inhibit some of the mud-throwing now done by actors or invisible voice-over narrators hyping inflammatory visual images.

Such measures might reduce the sludge content in TV campaigns, but they carry a high cost in government restriction on the freedom of political speech. A better alternative is for the press to step up to its responsibility in policing the political arena.

On the basis of 30 years on this political beat, I have a five-point agenda I'd suggest to my colleagues in the press. It certainly can be improved, but I hope it serves as a starting-point, not just for discussion, but for vigorous involvement and action by the press and the electronic media this year. Here's my plan:

■ *The preemption strategy.* The first step—and the most important—is to challenge the operating assumption of the candidates and consultants that the campaign agenda is theirs to determine. They absolutely believe that the issues they highlight and those they skirt are for them to determine on the basis of what their research—their polls and focus groups—tell them will "move the vote."

Well, that assumption is a lot of malarkey. The campaign really belongs to the voters. It is the only part of the political-governmental cycle when they have the right to have their questions answered, their concerns addressed.

Now, it won't improve things a bit if the press simply tries to substitute its agenda for that of the politicians and consultants. That's no more democratic or undistorted than what we have now. It's the voters who deserve to be in the driver's seat.

So how do we find out what they have on their minds? We ask them. Certainly polls can help discern the issues of greatest importance. But the old-fashioned way may be the best. There is no substitute for shoe-leather reporting, walking precincts, talking to people in their living rooms. Editors need to get their reporters out into neighborhoods early in the political year to ask people what concerns them the most.... "Issues" may be abstractions, but when you ask people what concerns them, they tell you—in clear and often passionate voices....

If we do our homework—spend enough time with the voters, early in the campaign—we can and should define that voters' agenda clearly on our pages. The candidates are, of course, free to talk and advertise about any subject in the world. But we in the press are free—and obligated—to keep calling them back to the voters' agenda in every news conference and in every public forum. Being persistent—to the point of being obnoxious—is fully justified when we know we are asking the questions the voters want answered.

It's every bit as important that when the candidates talk about those concerns, we report them fully, and do everything we can to keep the dialogue going. But if they try to change subjects, we ought to report that fact prominently too.

■ *Inoculation.* This second strategy is one our colleagues in television are particularly well positioned to apply. Early in the election cycle, it would be helpful to remind people of the way their emotions were manipulated by negative ads in the last campaign. I've looked at some of those commercials from other years. Ripped from the context of the times, they are really ugly and disturbing. Seeing them again, before the new versions go on the air, might help inoculate viewers against the effects of this political poison.

On the print side, we need to hold the consultants accountable for their past campaigns. Many of them are good sources of ours; some are good friends. But the plain fact is that they have become the new bosses of American politics, and many of them have histories that include repeated use of negative ads to undercut the opposing candidates and to distract attention from the voters' real concerns. When a consultant takes on a campaign in a state or a district, he should be asked, publicly, by the press how he justifies his past actions and whether he intends to use the same tactics in this campaign.

If these consultants feel free to rummage around in candidates' pasts, looking for ammunition for their negative ads, we in the press should feel no inhibitions about asking the consultants to justify and defend their own track records.

■ *Interrogation.* The press should establish, at the outset of the campaigns, one simple ground rule: The candidates will be available to answer questions about every ad, every piece of direct mail, that goes out of their headquarters, at the time it goes on the air or into the mail. No ducking and hiding behind campaign managers or other intermediaries. A candidate who is not prepared to take responsibility for what his campaign does with the biggest part of its budget is a candidate who has a weak claim to public trust. Let's put the issue to them early, and then hold them to their commitment when the slugging gets rough.

■ *Investigation.* We should treat every ad as if it were a speech by the candidate himself. In fact, it will be seen and heard by far more people than any speech he gives to a live audience.

We routinely flyspeck those speeches, weighing the assertions against the evidence, setting the political charge against the context of the relevant information. We need to do this, just as routinely, with political ads: Demand the supporting evidence from the candidate airing the ad, get rebuttal information from his opponent and then investigate the situation enough ourselves that we can tell the reader what is factual and what is destructive fiction.

And we ought not to be squeamish about saying in plain language when we catch a candidate lying, exaggerating or distorting the facts. The consultants have become increasingly sophisticated about insinuating—visually or verbally—charges that they avoid making in literal terms.

We have to counter that sophistication by becoming increasingly blunt when we are exposing such falsities. And we need to report the falsity more than once. Some politicians and consultants believe cynically that as long as they can drive their advertising message home by endless repetition, they needn't worry about an occasional print piece or television story questioning their statements.

■ *Denunciation.* This final strategy is not for reporters: Reporters can report, but not condemn. But columnists, commentators and editorial writers have the license—and the obligation—to apply verbal heat to those who sabotage the election process by their paid-media demagoguery. And the evidence suggests that such denunciations can have an effect.

Those in the business tell me that there's always a calculation before any candidate "goes negative" on his opponent as to the risk of a backlash. And there are obviously cases where negative ads have boomeranged against those who used them. We should do everything we can to increase boomerang supply in 1990.

Well, those are my five strategies. Cumulatively, they constitute an effort to break the vicious cycle of current campaign and coverage patterns. In recent years, as the candidates and consultants have relied more and more on negative ads to win their races, the press and television have responded by focusing on those ads, suggesting that they are manipulative but not effectively exposing and denouncing them. The result has been that even as we have decried these tactics, we have magnified their effectiveness by publicizing the very messages we deplore. And in the process, we have probably deepened pubic cynicism about politics without doing anything that might remedy the practices that make people cynical.

We have been inhibited by thinking that if we did any more, we would be thought partisan. But we need to become partisan—not on behalf of a candidate or party—but on behalf of the process.

That won't be easy or comfortable, because many of the politicians and more of the consultants are pals of people in the media. But we in the press weren't given a privileged position in this society so we could cultivate personal friendships with people in power. We have our own obligations to the people who read, listen to and watch the news. It's time we started fulfilling them.

29. A Guide to "Leaks" in Government

Stephen Hess

Most press coverage of government focuses on formal, staged events: speeches, rallies, hearings, press conferences, and the like. Such scheduled events are convenient for both news sources and news gatherers. They allow sources to control the timing and format of information; for reporters, they offer convenience of scheduling and solve the time-consuming task of tracking down sources for stories. But on many occasions, reporters and sources find it necessary to bypass these staged events in favor of off-the-record comments. These confidential asides flatter reporters and are valued because they may provide the makings of a "scoop" and may involve more accurate information than the spoon-fed contents of press conferences or news releases. For officials, off-the-record conversations offer the chance to say things that cannot be said "on the record"—to test public reaction to a proposal, to defend the source's reputation, to affect the outcome of a bureaucratic dispute, or simply to cultivate the news gatherer. Hess, a senior fellow at Washington's Brookings Institution, provides a guide to the fine art of "leaking" as practiced by officials and encouraged by reporters. A former newspaper columnist, speechwriter, and White House staffer, Hess has been studying Washington news gathering since 1977; his series of books, called "Newswork," include *The Washington Reporters* (1981), *The Government/Press Connection* (1984), from which the following selection is taken, and *The Ultimate Insiders: U.S. Senators in the National Media* (1986).

In the *New York Times* on August 8, 1983, Michael deCourcy Hinds and Warren Weaver, Jr., reported: Langhorne A. Motley, the new Assistant Secretary of State for Inter-American Affairs, told a Congressional committee last week that departmental efforts to consult with the lawmakers on Central American policy had been disrupted by "premature unauthorized partial disclosure" of plans.

"Do you mean leaks?" one member of the panel asked.

"Yes," Mr. Motley replied.

After information comes through the formal channels—press release, speech text, public document, news conference, briefing, interview, and observation of an event—reporters gather additional information through informal means that have come to be lumped together as leaks. The leak deserves a better fate than to share a common definition with rumor, gossip, and other back-channel exchanges between sources and reporters. As defined by Motley, a leak is a "premature unauthorized partial disclosure," as distinguished from a "premature authorized partial disclosure," which is a plant. Or, depending on one's vantage point, a plant is a beneficial leak.

The leak is rarely a tool of press officers, whose domain is the formal channels of information. Robert Pierpoint of CBS says that during the six presidencies he covered, a White House press secretary only once leaked information to him. The primary reason spokesmen try to stay out of the leaking business, according to former presidential press secretary George Reedy, is that "since manipulation of the press involves favoritism to some newsmen it inevitably creates antagonism among others." Nor is leaking often practiced in the lower civil service. The bureaucrats' world faces inward. They know best how to maneuver within their own agencies; journalists, except possibly for some specialized reporters are outside their ken and represent risk beyond possible gain.

The United States Constitution provides reporters with a legislative branch in which they can always find someone who will enjoy sharing the president's secrets with them. John Goshko, who reports from the State Department for the *Washington Post*, recalls that a good story came from a congressional staff member who was talking to a *Post* congressional reporter, Margot Hornblower, who then told Goshko. "When the congressional staffer read the story he could never have known that he was the source," says Goshko. According to a wise departmental press officer, "we just assume that anything given to the Hill will be leaked and act accordingly." It is a painful lesson for presidents to learn. . . .

The greatest frustration for presidents may be when they are forced to realize that most executive branch leakers are their own people—political appointees—rather than the faceless bureaucrats they campaigned against. "A government," as James Reston was first to note, "is the only known vessel that leaks from the top."

From the journalists' point of view, writes Tom Wicker in the *New York Times*, "What Presidents are apt to consider leaks . . . are often more nearly the result of good work by reporters diligent and intelligent enough to ask the right questions of the right sources at the right time." Former Secretary of State Dean Rusk, quoted in *The Foreign Service Journal*, offers a hypothetical example of how the process can work:

> A reporter is leaving the State Department at the end of the day when he sees the Soviet ambassador's car drive up. Figuring that the ambassador has brought a message, the reporter gives the machinery a chance to work, then starts calling around. After being told he's on the wrong track at several offices, he gets to the fellow on Berlin, who has been told never to lie directly to the press. The reporter says, "John, I understand that the Soviet ambassador has just come in with a message on Berlin." So the man says, "Sorry, I can't say a thing about it. Can't help you on that." Ah! He's got it. In the absence of an absolute denial, he's on the track. He figures out what the Berlin problem looks like and then calls a friend at the Soviet embassy. "By the way," he says, "what's the attitude of the Soviet Union on this particular point on Berlin?" He listens for a few moments, then he [writes] his story [for] the next morning on the message the Soviet ambassador brought in about Berlin.
>
> The chances are that the president will call the secretary of state and ask, "Who in the hell has been leaking news over at the Department of State?"

It is a "curious delusion among upper bureaucrats and high officials," Stewart Alsop concluded in 1968, "that a reporter cannot possibly reach the same rather obvious conclusions that government officials reached unless the reporter has had illicit access to secret information."

Viewed from inside government, a typology of why leakers leak would include:

■ Ego leak: giving information primarily to satisfy a sense of self-importance: in effect, "I am important because I can give you information that is important." This type of leak is popular with staff, who have fewer outlets for ego tripping. Assistants like to tell (and embellish) tales of struggle among their superiors. I believe ego is the most frequent cause of leaking, although it may not account for the major leaks. Other

Washington observers disagree. Many reporters and officials prefer to think of leaks as more manipulative and mysterious, but this also serves their egos.

■ Goodwill leak: a play for a future favor. The primary purpose is to accumulate credit with a reporter, which the leaker hopes can be spent at a later date. This type of leak is often on a subject with which the leaker has little or no personal involvement and happens because most players in governmental Washington gather a great deal of extraneous information in the course of their business and social lives.

■ Policy leak: a straightforward pitch for or against a proposal using some document or insiders' information as the lure to get more attention than might be otherwise justified. The great leaks, such as the Pentagon papers in 1971, often fit in this category.

■ Animus leak: used to settle grudges. Information is disclosed to embarrass another person.

■ Trial-balloon leak: revealing a proposal that is under consideration in order to assess its assets and liabilities. Usually proponents have too much invested in a proposal to want to leave it to the vagaries of the press and public opinion. Most likely, those who send up a trial balloon want to see it shot down, and because it is easier to generate opposition to almost anything than it is to build support, this is the most likely effect.

■ Whistle-blower leak: unlike the others, usually employed by career personnel. Going to the press may be the last resort of frustrated civil servants who feel they cannot correct a perceived wrong through regular government channels. Whistle-blowing is not synonymous with leaking; some whistle-blowers are willing to state their case in public.

Leaks can be meant to serve more than one purpose, which complicates attempts to explain the motivation behind a particular leak. An ego leak and a goodwill leak need not be mutually exclusive: a policy leak also could work as an animus leak, especially since people on each side of a grudge tend to divide along policy lines; and all leaks can have policy implications regardless of motive.

Beyond the basic leaks, experienced reporters and officials enjoy trying to identify elaborate variations, such as "the daring reverse leak, an unauthorized release of information apparently for one reason but actually accomplishing the opposite," says Hugh Heclo. . . .

At a news conference on January 19, 1982, President Reagan delcared that leaks had "reached a new high." Although the *Sporting News* does not keep administration-by-administration statistics, his claim was probably correct. This new record, some contended, resulted from the number of undisciplined ideologues that Reagan brought to Washington, the theory being that leaks rise in direct proportion to the ideological content of an administration. Others argue that it comes from the president's management style: "If every policy is constantly up for a committee decision," said a *Wall Street Journal* editorial, "you are constantly inviting contending parties to fight it out through leaks to the press." Still, all modern presidents, regardless of ideology or other distinguishing features, have complained bitterly about leaks, and it is likely that the record of the present president will fall to each successive president as government gets bigger and more complex, as more documents are necessary to produce decisions, as more duplicating machines reproduce documents, and as more reporters look over the government's shoulder. There are no countervailing forces that will realistically shrink the information glut or the access to it.

Some reported leaks have undoubtedly endangered national security, as government claims, but the number must be very small. . . .

Reporters broadcast government secrets all the time, but secrets are produced in government by people with the authority to stamp *Secret* on documents. This has the effect (not always desired in government) of making them more valuable to reporters. Given the generally held opinion that the government is wildly excessive in what it chooses to call a secret—I even saw foreign newspaper clippings that had been classified—a more realistic security classification system, including some penalty for personnel who overclassify documents, would automatically cut down on the number of secrets that get reported in the news media. Government, I contend, is quite good at keeping its real secrets.

To say that government's informal channels of communication actively promote the public good has become a fashionable position in some quar-ters. "Our particular form of government wouldn't work without it," wrote historian Bruce Catton. Political scientist Richard E. Neustadt argues that "leaks play . . . a vital role in the functioning of our democracy," and pub-lisher Katharine Graham claims they are a "funda-mental . . . even neces-sary, component of our system of government and its communications with the people." Yet a case-by-case study of leaks . . . shows that they are episodic, flaring up, then dying out; they occur for a great many reasons that do not necessarily have anything to do with the public interest; they are never placed in a historical context; and they only conform to the prior-ities of the person doing the leaking. Neither the reporter nor the gov-ernment official is thinking of democratic theory when they make their exchange.

Some leaks may promote the public good. . . . Others may injure the public good. . . . leaks qua leaks, then, are not an unalloyed good, although they are a means of protest that is justified for some types of dissenters who do need protection.

To discuss the leaking of information as if it were a rational and necessary system of communicating among Washington players is to assume that the players to whom messages are supposedly being sent via the media understand the senders' intentions. If that were so, then regular leaks would be a useful way of communicating from one agency to another, from one individual to another within an agency, and from one branch of government to another without having messy confrontations or denials or wasted time and red tape. Sometimes things do work this way. More often the senders are so clever or so inept as to be totally misunderstood, or else the messages get garbled in transmission. In other cases, there are so many different interpretations of what is being accomplished, by whom, and for what purposes as to seriously call into question the utility and rationality of leaks as an intragovernmental means of communications.

The game of giving and receiving leaks does give pleasure to the players. Washington infighting, it is said, is in direct proportion to what is at stake: the stakes are high, hence the leaks. Rather, I think that the people who are most likely to come to Washington with each political administration bring with them a high talent and tolerance for intrigue. In their previous lives—whether in universities, corporations, foundations, unions, or law firms—this talent probably was manifested privately. Who cared? But political Washington provides the opportunity for public intrigue. Reporters and readers now care or should. The public ultimately learns more than it would otherwise. Public officials may even act more honorably knowing how hard it would be to keep secret a dishonorable act.

From the point of view of the White House, leaks consistently throw off a president's timing and frame issues in a perspective that is not of his choosing. In political terms a president is fair game; in democratic terms it could be argued that a president should have the opportunity to make his case as effectively as possible, with the opposition then having the same right. In management terms, leaks or the threat of leaks may lead to hurried or conspiratorial decision making. Especially in situations in which presidents have a strong desire to maintain surprise, the lesson they seem to learn in order to avoid leaks is to turn inward: involve the absolute minimum number of advisers in the formulation stage and compartmentalize so that technicians will not know how the pieces are going to be fitted together. The problem, as Jody Powell pointed out, is that "the damage done by leaks must be carefully balanced against the damage done by excluding people who can contribute to the decision-making process."

"How do you cope with leaks?" President Reagan was asked by *U.S. News & World Report* at the end of 1981. "I've been told that you don't," he replied. "Everybody who has been around here for a while tells me it is just the nature of the place." Nearly two years later, on November 23, 1983, the headline across the front page of the *Washington Post* read, "Reagan Ordered Sweeping FBI Probe of Staff for Source of Leak." So to stop leaks, presidents resort to wiretaps and lie detectors. They always fail. In a system of such breathtaking diversity, they always will. Nor is it clear that, on balance, it is in a president's best interest to stop leaks. Is a president more leaked against or leaked for? Most experienced Washington reporters would contend that the answer is obvious. About the investigation reported on November 23, a *Post* headline concluded on December 12, "Justice Probe Fails to Disclose Source of Leak." In the article beneath the headline, reporter Lou Cannon quoted one White House official as saying, "there is no evidence that reporters were told anything we didn't want them to know."

Chapter 7

Campaigns and Elections

Elections are the central rituals of democratic systems. They celebrate the individual citizen's membership and participation in the community's decisions. They certify the legitimacy of officials chosen by the people. Elections allow the voters to signal their approval of the regime in power or to express their disapproval and set in motion an orderly transfer of power.

Accustomed to being asked frequently to cast their ballots on one public issue or another, citizens of the United States tend to treat their voting privileges casually. Denial of those privileges puts things in their proper perspective. In the 1980s the world witnessed the spectacle of newly empowered voters in many places, including the Philippines, Eastern Europe, and the Soviet Union. The passionate defense of the franchise by these citizens serves to remind us how precious the right of free elections really is.

As these examples suggest, elections must be meaningful if they are to meet democratic standards. It is not enough to grant universal suffrage, even on the principle of "one person, one vote." The election ought to offer a real choice of alternatives; and once registered, the results ought to make a difference in the conduct of government. Not all elections meet these tests all of the time, even in the most democratic systems. ("None of the above" sometimes seems the most satisfying choice, even in presidential contests.) But elections that are repeatedly judged meaningless can only dilute the sense of legitimacy accorded the governing system.

Nor is there any guarantee that electoral choices will be well informed or rational. Most citizens, after all, see politics through their peripheral vision; they devote only intermittent attention to political matters and do not want to take the time needed to inform themselves fully. Politicians, for their part, find it useful to blur certain aspects of their records and deal in generalities to alienate as few voting groups as possible. Even well-informed citizens may be puzzled at which alternatives would best serve their interests. No claim is made that democratic choices are always the wisest, only that they are more apt to encompass the community's viewpoints and more likely to command citizens' support. "Let the people think they govern," said William Penn, founder of Pennsylvania, "and they *will* be governed."

Rules of the Electoral Game

Elections are conducted in accord with laws, rules, and practices, which help determine who votes and what the election results will be. In general, everyone who is at least eighteen years old and not in prison or mentally incompetent has the right to vote. But to vote, a citizen must register—a voluntary act on the citizen's part, not automatic or mandatory as in some nations. Registration is handled locally according to state laws. Before registering, a person must be a resident of the local area; federal law limits state residency requirements to thirty days for presidential elections and fifty days for state and local elections. Registration rules are designed to prevent fraud, but they have the incidental effect of disenfranchising many voting-age people such as transients, resident aliens, and those confined to institutions.

Historically, states limited registration because of property, race, or gender or employed tests for literacy, knowledge, and even "good character." Such actions are now banned as a denial of equal protection of the laws. The broadening of the franchise to embrace more and more people is perhaps the most fundamental transformation of the Constitution over its two centuries of operation.

In view of the expanded franchise, a puzzling paradox is the overall decline in voter participation. As voting barriers have been lowered, it seems, people have decided to turn away from elections. For example, the Twenty-sixth Amendment granted eighteen-year-olds the right to vote in 1971. No doubt the amendment's authors hoped to attract voters of the baby-boom era, but citizens in the eighteen-to-twenty-five-year-old category are the group least likely to go to the polls.

Distressingly low voter turnout is a leading characteristic of American political behavior. Only about half the eligible citizens take part in quadrennial presidential elections; in midterm elections the figure ranges from 35 to 40 percent—figures that are lower than those for any of the other western democracies.

Various explanations for declining turnout have been advanced. One emphasizes the demographic diversity of today's expanded franchise. According to this argument, voting rates have fallen because of the addition of groupings with traditionally low rates of participation— young voters, blacks, and Hispanics. Although this explanation has some validity, it fails to consider the fact that voting has declined despite rising educational levels—the single strongest correlate of political participation.

Another explanation is that barriers to voting, although significantly lowered over the years, are still high enough to discourage many from voting. Registration requirements, the lack of election-day holidays, even the frequency of elections in the United States, are blamed by structuralists who believe the government should make voting easier for citizens.

Others argue that people fail to vote because they disapprove of the candidates, see little choice between the parties, or are disaffected from politics in general. If the latter is to blame, it seems to have affected elections more than other types of participation, which remain robust.

Some analysts reject all these explanations, arguing instead that voter turnout is really not as low as most figures seem to show. Unlike many other nations, the United States does not maintain wholly accurate statistics on eligible voters, nor are voting rolls promptly purged of those who have died, moved, or become ineligible. These views, and others concerning voter turnout, are aired in Selection 30, "Pro-Con: Are Americans Abandoning Elections?"

Techniques of Campaigning

Campaigns are intense efforts at mobilizing supporters, persuading the undecided, and neutralizing the opposition. At each stage of U.S. history, campaigning has reflected the prevalent technology of communications. The earliest campaigns were left in the hands of trusted supporters and fierce partisan newspapers. Candidates themselves stood demurely on the sidelines. The era of Andrew Jackson ushered in mass political activities—stump speeches, parades, costly entertainment, and huge rallies. After 1880, campaign literature—advertisements and mass mailings—became accepted as literacy rose and printing costs dropped. In the twentieth century, radio and television became the primary vehicles for reaching voters.

From the advent of mass electorates (that is, from about the 1830s) until the recent past, campaigns were conducted by cadres of dedicated and faithful partisans. Party leaders chose the candidates, planned and executed the campaigns, and mobilized loyal supporters on election day. The office-seekers' qualities and appeals differed widely, of course, but candidates were presented to, and perceived by, the voting public overwhelmingly in paritsan terms.

Faced with ever larger electorates and dwindling grass-roots party organizations, today's politicians are left to forge their own campaign organizations and arrange for financing with the help of hired firms of pollsters, fund-raisers, mass mailers, advertisers, and media consultants. Campaign styles and techniques vary with the type of election—whether it is competitive or safe, whether it is an open seat or one defended by a successful incumbent, whether the incumbent is considered vulnerable, whether it is a race for the Senate or for the House of Representatives, and so on.

Contemporary campaigns are addressed in Selections 31 and 32. In "Myths of Modern Nominating Campaigns," political scientist Everett Carll Ladd discusses the politics of nominations. It is no longer possible for candidates to be chosen by a group of political bosses "in some smoke-filled room." Rather, nominations are an open, public process. Nominees for public office must normally win a primary election, before which they are examined by the media and probed by public opinion polls. Returning to the days of party monopoly over nominations does not seem a realistic possibility.

The new breed of professional campaigners is described by journalist Paul Taylor in Selection 32, "Consultants Rise via the Low Road." Their campaigns are elaborately planned and implemented. Increasingly, such campaigns are waged on radio and television. In the hands of skillful media people, they not only highlight the candidate's strong points and portray a glowing image but attack the opponent's weak points (so-called negative campaigning). Such campaigns are waged because politicians assume that they are effective; however, such artful and expensive campaigns run the risk of falling victim to faddism and voter fatigue.

Financing Campaigns

Contemporary campaigns are very costly. Approximately a billion dollars were spent in the 1987-88 campaign cycle for national, state, and local candidates. Since the 1970s, campaign finance has been subject by law to disclosure and regulation. This issue has also been the focus of debate and reform proposals.

The existing campaign finance legislation (the Federal Election Campaign Act of 1971, as amended in 1974 and 1976) is shaped not only by congressional sentiment but also by the Supreme Court's interpretations. Because it chose to view individual contributions as akin to the exercise of free speech, the Court has refused to permit Congress to limit a candidate's overall spending (including use of personal funds), an individual's overall contributions to all political races, or an individual's political spending that is independent of candidates. Only presidential candidates are subject to limits, and only if they accept public financing. Matching public funds are available to each presidential candidate in the general election and to each candidate in the primaries who meets certain eligibility requirements. If they accept public financing, presidential candidates must agree to abide by overall spending limits.

House and Senate contests are subject to no monetary limits, however. Senate races generally cost millions of dollars; House contests, hundreds of thousands. The 1986 California senatorial race between incumbent Alan Cranston (D) and Rep. Ed Zschau (R) was a freewheeling media affair that cost $25.5 million, making it the costliest congressional election ever. Political contributors usually regard incumbents as a better investment than challengers; thus incumbents have several times as much money to spend as their opponents. Because incumbents usually have less urgent needs for money than their challengers, their favored position amounts to a "double whammy" for opponents: those who have, receive more; those who have not, receive less.

As discussed in the Introduction to Chapter 4, political action committees (PACs) have played an increasingly important role in elections since the mid-1970s. PAC money forms an ever-increasing portion of the election budgets of congressional candidates. In the 1989-90 electoral cycle, PAC contributions comprised 38 percent of total receipts in House campaigns and 22 percent in Senate races.[1]

Many observers, including reformers and so-called public interest lobbyists, argue that far too much money is poured into federal campaigns, and that groups with a stake in policy outcomes use their contributions to gain access to officeholders and favorable treatment in policy decisions. But any revisions of the law must be enacted by incumbent politicians, who have large stakes in the way the rules are written. The two parties, moreover, react differently to reform proposals because their funding sources differ. Republicans, the wealthier party, oppose overall campaign spending limits, which they believe would inhibit their efforts to counteract the Democrats' incumbency advantages. With more House and Senate incumbents and more funds derived from PACs, the Democrats are not in favor of curbing PAC contributions. In Selection 33, "A Field Guide to Election Spending Limits," *Congressional Quarterly* reporter Chuck Alston offers a probing yet irreverent review of the various combatants and their arguments.

Note

1. Federal Election Commission, "1990 Congressional Election Spending Drops to Low Point" (February 22, 1991), 1.

30. Point-Counterpoint:
Are Americans Abandoning Elections?

Juan Williams
Warren J. Mitofsky and Martin Plissner

With each new national election, the low turnout reminds us that Americans are increasingly choosing not to exercise their right to vote. Most students of voting behavior concede the problem but dispute the causes that lie behind the nonparticipation. The two articles that follow explore the range of arguments. Reviewing the reasons typically cited for nonvoting, Juan Williams, a staff writer for the *Washington Post Magazine*, concludes in his 1988 article that citizens decline to vote because they feel disconnected from the competing parties and candidates. In contrast, two officials of CBS News, Warren J. Mitofsky, director of elections and surveys, and Martin Plissner, executive political director, state in a *New York Times* article, published in 1988, that the seemingly low turnout should be blamed on poor accounting methods and antiquated voter-registration procedures.

Juan Williams:
Why America Doesn't Vote

In North Dakota, anyone can show up on election day and vote. But voter turnout has been dropping fast in recent elections. In Maine, Minnesota and Wisconsin, where same-day registration has been adopted, voter turnout is still in decline. All over the United States, regardless of the ease of registering to vote, the location of the polls, or even the pizzazz of the candidates, the results are the same: voter turnout is in a downward spiral, falling, falling, falling. . . .

The standard explanations for low voter turnout are:

- It's still too hard to register.
- The political establishment actively discourages participation because new voters might challenge its interests.
- The American people are too wrapped up in their own private lives to concern themselves with public issues.
- The candidates are too dull and the issues are too tepid.
- The media is to blame (add your favorite media villainy here). . . .

Even voting experts are no longer arguing that it is a default of civic responsibility for an American not to vote. In this emerging school of thought, itself gaining momentum as the rush away from the polls quickens, the voters are victims and the culprit is the campaign. Some experts now agree that it is a rational response for voters to shun the decaying political process. . . .

"I'm not urging anyone to vote this year given the conduct of the campaign," said Curtis Gans, director of the Committee for the Study of the American Electorate, who adds he feels personally compelled to make the effort to vote. "It's reasonable for a voter to say 'Nothing about this campaign is relevant to me.' What this campaign says quite loudly is that our essentially television-driven politics and lack of clarity about choices has reached a level we need to address."

"I've pretty well accepted that this campaign has been a turn-off and discouraged voting," said Walter Dean Burnham, professor of government at the University of Texas at Austin. "One poll I saw had 71 percent of the voters dissatisfied with the candidates they have to choose between for president. That is the highest cluster of negatives we've ever seen—by a huge margin."

An added disincentive is that voters have few state-wide races to excite them.

"Except for 1952, this election has the highest number and percentage of uncontested House seats [41 seats in non-southern states where the two-party system usually produces contested elections]," said Burnham. "And we have a 98.5 percent retention rate in the House. Something is wrong."

"Pundits have been busy trying to explain why the turnout has dropped when the more important question is why is the campaign so dull. Why are the political parties acting like this; why are there no candidates who speak to people and their needs?" said Richard A. Cloward, who with Frances Fox Piven is author of "Why Americans Don't Vote."

In that book, Cloward and Piven charge that the U.S. power structure has deliberately tried to discourage lower-income and other out-groups from voting by making it needlessly difficult for them to participate. But now Cloward is framing the issue in much less radical terms.

"The real question," Cloward asked, "is what happened to American politics that campaigns are run like this?"

Cloward's question is also being asked by venerable institutions like the National League of Women Voters. [In 1988] the league refused to go along with the prefabricated television appearances that Dukakis and Bush passed off on the public as debates. Was the league beseiged by angry voters for abdicating their traditional role as sponsors of the presidential debates? Quite the contrary.

"We've received thousands of letters congratulating us for having the strength to stand up and talk publicly about the manipulation of this campaign," said Nancy Neuman, president of the league. "The candidates are manipulated, the ads are manipulated. . . . People are hungry to have someone in national life talk about principles. There is a huge lack of credibility. I think people wonder, 'If these candidates have to be so rehearsed, so scripted, then what are the people who handle them hiding from the pubic. What's wrong with these guys?' "

"The problem the American voters face is that they can't show through the ballot box a rejection of this campaign," added Neuman. "It is going to take a citizens' movement to show that rejection.". . .

In most European democracies the voter turnout rate is about 80 percent, compared to American rates that run, at best, in the mid-fifties. According to G. Bingham Powell, chairman of the school of government at the University of Rochester, the major factor contributing to the difference between American and European voter turn-out is "attitudinal."

"Americans have been as active in their communities, contributed as much money and worked as hard for candidates," said Powell. "The real difference is the sense that politics affects life. We've lost that."

"People don't feel they can make a difference," said Curtis Gans. "We have a 20 year disinclination to register and vote coupled with a negative campaign [that] tends to confirm the dark side of the voters' inclination not to participate. There is indifference that starts in the home, in school, in civic education where people don't see the point of political activity. They don't see results. And there is alienation, a sense of lack of message from the parties and the emphasis on candidates as television actors."

"If we eliminated all the barriers to registration and voting, people still would be turning away from the polls," said Ruy Teixeira, a Washington political analyst at Abt Associates. "The real reason people are not voting is that they feel disconnected from the political system, detached from the political parties. They feel they get no response from the government, they see less and less political activism and therefore they don't see any connection or meaning in casting a vote. Everyone needs that motivation. It is not enough to make the act of voting easier. People still need to feel it is a meaningful act that expresses something and right now it does not."

This feeling of lack of connection to the political life of the country is evident in the past two presidential campaigns. In both cases the standard interpretation is that President Reagan beat President Carter and then Walter Mondale easily, earning himself a mandate for leadership. In fact, statistics show that if all eligible American voters are taken into account the true popular vote results would be these:

In 1980—Reagan 26.7 percent; Carter 21.6 percent; John Anderson 4.3 percent; and nonvoters 47.7 percent.

In 1984—Reagan 31.3 percent; Mondale 21.6 percent; 4 percent other; and—the winner—46.7 percent for nonvoters.

[In 1988] nonvoters are expected to win by even a higher margin.

Black voters are expected to show the sharpest decrease in turnout: a 25 percent drop is expected, taking black Americans back under the 50 percent turnout rate they exceeded for the first time in 1980.

Why will blacks stay home? First, the massive voter registration efforts of 1984 are gone. Second, blacks—overwhelmingly Democratic voters—are not inspired by Dukakis. Fewer blacks support him than the last Democratic candidate, Walter Mondale. But the main reason for expected low turnout among black voters is that they, just like other voters, have witnessed a general election campaign which, they feel, ignores their needs and concerns. . . .

As far as many black voters can see, the closest blacks have come to being part of this campaign is as stereotypes evoked by the Willie Horton (blacks as murderers and rapists) ads used by the Bush campaign to polarize white voters and pull them away from the Democratic ticket.

"Flowers grow when there is water on them and the sun shines," said Jesse Jackson, who attracted 90 percent of the black vote in the Democratic primaries. "In this campaign the voters are being kept in the dark. People are being fed through the TV—they are not getting light or water. They are tired of a TV diet of one-liners. The voters are anemic. . . ."

One course left now for the disaffected is to try to create some new political force, possibly a third party behind a labor or left-liberal banner. Some think that "new" party should be the Democratic party. But that would drive more fearful white voters and conservative Democrats into the Republican fold and surrender any chance of winning the presidency. More than that, such a realignment would debilitate the Democratic coalition which still competes successfully at every other level of American politics below the White House.

The American political conundrum is that while a lack of defined issues apparently breeds voter indifference, a sharpening of issues breeds political divisiveness and social polarization. Can it be that the American consensus can only be sustained by apathy?

Warren J. Mitofsky and Martin Plissner: Low Voter Turnout? Don't Believe It

About 89 million Americans voted [in 1988], several million less than in 1984. Not only was this the first time since 1944 that the number of voters declined from one Presidential election to the next, but the rate of voter participation appears to be the lowest since World War II.

These figures on so-called voter turnout are touching off a fresh wave of national self-flagellation. While such an exercise is not without merit, it has a lot less merit than the figures suggest.

For the last three elections, the figure on voter turnout has hovered around 53 percent; this year, it appears to have dropped to about 49 percent. That does not mean, however, that approximately half the people in America who could have exercised their right to vote did not.

That 49 percent is assumed to be the percentage of "eligible voters" who go to the polls. But it isn't. Rather, it is the figure that results from dividing the total vote for President by the voting age population. Both of these numbers are suspicious.

The voting age population represents the number of people in the country who are at least 18 years old. It includes aliens, legal and illegal, many people confined to institutions and discharged felons—none of whom can vote. It also includes people who have moved since the closing date for registration. Simply put, it adds up to a lot of people—as much as 10 percent—who are plainly not eligible to vote.

The other part of the equation, the recorded vote for President, is also misleading. It excludes as much as 5 percent of the people who actually go to polls but for some reason—confusion over voting procedures, spoiled ballots or a decision not to vote for President—are not tallied in the Presidential vote.

If the correct number of people going to the polls and the real number of eligible voters could be determined, we'd guess that the turnout for 1984 and other recent Presidential elections would be closer to 65 percent than 53 percent. [In 1988] it would still reach 60 percent or so.

Whatever the real figure for stay-at-homes, the usual suspects thought to generate indifference among voters are already being rounded up by the professional analysts. These analysts are telling us that a jaded electorate, turned off by a campaign devoid of issues, negative advertising and nine-second sound bites, has once again registered its resentment by staying away in droves.

The main reason people don't vote, however, has very little to do with the quality of the candidates or the campaign or the polls or the projections. Rather, it is the unique barriers to voting created by our archaic system of voter registration that keeps people from the polls.

The national election studies, conducted at the University of Michigan, show that in every Presidential election since 1964, at least 86 percent of those who are registered to vote do so. Thus, either universal registration or no registration would raise voter participation sharply.

Indeed, in countries whose high rates of voter participation are cited as models, such as Sweden, governments have active programs for seeking out and registering voters. They do not, as we do, rely on the voter to take the initiative to register well before the election takes place.

Our country, with so many different systems for providing positive identification—drivers' licenses, Social Security numbers, bank cards—could readily contrive standards for identifying persons eligible to vote without prior screening by a registration office.

Americans are already voting at a greater rate than the phony "voter turnout" figures suggest. Motivating the rest of them to go to the polls is not the real problem. No, the problem is getting voters over the hurdle imposed by the requirement of prior registration. Don't blame the American voters. They are doing the best they can.

31. Myths of Modern Nominating Campaigns

Everett Carll Ladd

Nominating campaigns, especially at the presidential level, are at least as complex and often as hard-fought as general election contests. Presidential candidates are chosen by their national party's quadrennial national conventions, but the delegates to the conventions are selected in a bewildering variety of ways: local and state caucuses and conventions and state primary elections. Some delegates (called "super-delegates" by Democrats) are chosen automatically because they are party officials or elected officeholders.

When presidential candidates turn out to be lackluster or unsuccessful, critics are quick to blame the nominating processes. Several common criticisms of these processes are misdirected, according to Everett Carll Ladd, executive director of the Roper Public Opinion Research Center and professor of political science at the University of Connecticut. In his article published in *Public Opinion* in 1988, he states that the media's role in screening candidates is unlikely to be mitigated, or even improved in quality, by innovations in the nominating process. Nor is there any alternative to today's long and arduous campaigns, which are needed to test the appeal of candidates. Altering the nominating processes, he concludes, would resolve none of these dilemmas and might even make things worse.

In every presidential campaign from 1968 to the present, the nominating system has come in for strong criticism. Reflecting this dissatisfaction, no two contests since 1968 have been held under the same basic rules.

The restless search for reform seems ill-conceived on several different grounds. First, it mistakenly assumes that there is some neat structural fix to the inadequacies of our nominating system, if only we could find it. Second, it grossly undervalues the importance of stability in the rules of the game under which all essential aspects of elections are contested. And third it misunderstands the sources of the system's deficiencies, so its search for remedies is misguided.

In 1912 the nomination system brought forth impressive final contenders: Woodrow Wilson, Theodore Roosevelt, and William Howard Taft. Eight years later basically the same institution yielded the significantly less luminous Warren G. Harding and James M. Cox. Like its predecessors, our present system is likely to display great variations in the caliber of those nominated. It isn't deterministic.

In his thoughtful book *Reforming the Reforms*, James W. Ceaser develops the case that presidential nominating rules can do relatively little to achieve desired outcomes. Reform of the nominating process has been spurred in part by the search for changes to help assure that we get great presidents. "This search, however, is somewhat like the quest for the Holy Grail—obligatory, perhaps, but unlikely to reach its goal. In the first place, 'great' statesmen are not always in ready supply. Greatness, alas, is a rare quality.... Second, there is no system the human mind can devise that can guarantee the discovery of political greatness, even when it exists." Ceaser approvingly quotes Adam Smith, who wrote in *The Wealth of Nations* [1776] that the skills of a potential statesman are "invisible ... always disputable and generally disputed."

Stephen Hess maintains that, even as the United States has made major changes in the way it selects its presidential nominees over the past century, successful candidates have continued to be drawn from the same sort of people. " ... In broad outline, then and now, and with rare exception, serious contenders for the nomination are professional politicians, people of extraordinary ambition who cannot be discouraged by changes in the rules of the game." A particular candidate will be helped more by one change in the process than will another, Hess recognizes. But for a long time and through many shifts in rules, those possessed of a very special kind of drive or ambition have come to the fore in American presidential politics.

In Defense of Stability

James Ceaser reminds us that "the success of an institution depends nearly as much on its stability as on its quality." This is so because a political institution "is a structure that channels political activity, setting the limits of permissible behavior and patterning action in predictable ways." While institutions can always be made better, "the more stable they become the more useful they are." The continuing experimentation with the presidential nomination system over the last two decades—and the steady stream of yet more plans to design it anew—has become a problem in and of itself.

I have made my own modest contributions to this problem. In offering "a better way to pick our presidents," I argued in 1980 that we would improve things if we managed to combine in the selection system large doses of two differing, even conflicting, elements: peer review by party leaders, and a strong voice for rank-and-file voters. The former would be achieved by providing that one-third of all national convention delegates be chosen outside the primaries, in their capacities as party officials and officeholders. The remaining two-thirds would be chosen in state delegation-selection primaries held in every state on a single day—the third Tuesday in June, for example. Each state's delegates would be divided among the candidates in proportion to the candidates' respective shares of the state's total vote, with perhaps a threshold of 10 percent of the vote required before one gets any delegates.

Under this system a candidate who ran strongly in the national primary and would almost surely add enough support from party leaders to be nominated on the first ballot. If he received 60 percent of the primary vote, for example, across the fifty states, he would go to the convention assured of roughly 40 percent of the first-round convention ballots—that is, 60 percent of the two-thirds of the delegates chosen through the primary. It would be surprising if the candidate couldn't pick up another 10 percent from the party officials. Otherwise, the convention would go on to further balloting, with no delegate bound but all delegates aware of voter preferences. Bargaining and negotiation would finally produce the nominee.

I still think that many of the assumptions that underlay my plan are sound. I am much less inclined to argue confidently on its behalf today, though, than I was in 1980. We all need to be careful lest our laudable enthusiasm for making things better lead us to urge the parties to tinker with their procedures constantly. This argument is something more than insisting we need to be sensitive to "the unintended consequences of purposive social action." It is also more than insisting upon the need to recognize that every system of presidential selection has its own weaknesses and biases. It involves, especially, the judgment that there is a vital national interest in achieving order, stability, and predictability in election machinery. Electoral reform should be approached from a perspective that recognizes how important it is to settle on something and stick with it.

People in a democracy need to have confidence that the basic rules governing the way they choose their leaders have a durability that reflects an underlying propriety and legitimacy. Constant change suggests that rulemaking is a shallow, cynical political game.

Changes sometimes have to be made, and interested parties and groups will inevitably differ on where their interests lie. But stability in electoral rules and procedures is in the national interest. The proper goal of reform is to remove *electoral machinery* as far as possible from partisan debate and endless tinkering. The United States's single-member district, simple majority system seems to offer the model. It certainly has its biases, but both parties have learned to live with it; and the American electorate has come to see it as involving generally fair, justifiably permanent rules of the game.

Misstating Present Problems

Many of the deficiencies that observers have detected in how we choose presidential nominees originate outside the nominating system itself. The much-criticized role played by the national media is an illustration.

The news media's immense part in picking our presidents is indeed striking. Aspiring wits remark that we now have a three-party system—CBS, NBC, and ABC. But this new, heightened electoral role is just one part of an expansion of the press's role throughout the governing process. In 1959 Douglass Cater described the press as "the fourth branch of government," which was apt if a bit premature. Today journalists are no longer outsiders reporting on the real movers and shakers of politics: they have themselves become key players in the continuously evolving American constitutional system. The enormous audience reach of the contemporary media and their lack of a serious institutional rival in political communication assure them political power and centrality.

As to its part in the nomination process, does the press focus too much on the horse race—on who's ahead, and on how the candidates are running, rather than on how they might govern? Does it impart a lack of perspective as it mercilessly hypes the early nomination contests? Does it risk even reshaping the outcome when it vastly exaggerates the meaning of certain preliminary results—such as, ... Bush's [1988] "devastating" loss in Iowa and Dukakis's "stunning" setback in Michigan? It seems to me that it does indeed do all these things and that the list of its failings is longer still. But since political parties will never again dominate communication on candidates and elections as they once did, and an independent press certainly will dominate this vital process, the only question worth pondering is how the press can be helped to do its job better. It's hard to envisage nomination rules changes that, in the present setting, would help resolve our press problems.

Peer Review

Another example of misstating the sources of our present difficulties is the common argument that we have seriously eroded "peer review" in our current nominee selection system. In this view the old party-centered selection arrangements worked better than what we now have because they provided for decisive final scrutiny of would-be nominees by those who knew them best, the party leaders and officeholders who were their natural peers. The 1952 Democratic nomination contest is frequently cited as an example of the special merit of the old order. Estes Kefauver charged through the presidential primaries like a freight train, winning 65 percent of all votes cast. Still, party leaders didn't think Kefauver had the right stuff, so it was bye-bye Estes and hello Adlai Stevenson.

It is hard to see the basis for the argument that today's system has short-circuited peer judgment. Throughout our long campaigns, candidates are examined in minute detail by many different political elites. Among them are those who give money to campaigns and those who staff them; members of the national press who follow the candidates everywhere and investigate them endlessly; and party leaders of the traditional sort, such as state and county chairmen. Candidates' peers among institutional leaders and activists may fail to examine them in sufficient depth. But peer review is alive and well. Just ask Gary Hart—who in one short week was pushed from front-runner all the way out of the race by perhaps the most ruthless application of peer judgment in American history.

One can argue that the community of peers judging candidates these days is simply too large and too diverse. Traditional party leadership—the peers of yesteryear—was interested in the long-term health of the party and how it would be affected by a particular nominee. This interest is uncommon—and some would say inappropriate—among many of the new peers, including the national press. Given the size and institutional diversity of the political community that now does the judging, peer review is bound to be exercised much more publicly than it used to be. Some of this can be profoundly annoying—when, for example, journalists vie on who can deliver the most outrageous put-downs on such television "gong shows" as "Crossfire."

It is hard to conceive any successful remedy to such conditions, though, that does not somehow shrink or restrict the community of peers. Parties may be strengthened in certain ways, but so long as the political community that judges candidates remains as large and heterogeneous as it now is, the current peer review system will persist. Apart from questions of the wisdom of trying to return the political community to something approaching its size and composition in earlier eras, I simply cannot imagine how it could be achieved.*

Scaring Off the Best and the Brightest

One also hears that today's long and arduous presidential campaigns put a daunting burden on the candidates. But do we have a satisfactory alternative? How someone who seeks the highest elective office is expected to convince his fellow citizens that he is worthy of it is a problem for every democracy. In some countries there is a ministerial ladder to be climbed. A promising politician is given a junior ministry in his party's government and then, if the confidence seems merited, he is given more demanding posts. His designation as party leader and then prime minister, if a legislative majority is conferred, are the top rungs. Of course, ministerial progression rarely works in this neat, idealized fashion, but parliamentary systems really do use it as a means of "credentialing" their top leadership. The United States has never had this option, however, given its separation of powers and the weakly organized and undisciplined political parties such a system requires.

In the United States some who would be president have previously held major national posts, of course, or otherwise achieved public recognition. Walter Mondale in his 1984 run and George Bush [in 1988] are examples. But in virtually every election in the country's history some who had not yet established themselves as national figures have sought the presidency. In the past many of them have used their leadership of a party bloc or faction as a springboard. The standing that Sen. Richard Russell long enjoyed among southern Democrats is an example. These blocs have weakened, however, in response to the nationalization of the electorate and the development of media-centered campaigns. Consequently, would-be nominees have found it harder to establish themselves and their claims.

* In Selection 17, James David Barber advocates a national caucus to consider potential candidates for president, composed of government officials who would recommend candidates for the party to put forth in a national primary.

What is left for capable politicians who have substantial accomplishments but not national stature and who want to "go national"? They can present themselves in long presidential campaigns where party activists and rank-and-file voters have ample opportunity to look them over, doing their utmost to convince this jury that they are qualified for the country's highest office. Would those who form the juries really want the campaigns to be shorter and otherwise less burdensome on these candidates? As the campaign progresses, the pubic has a chance to see presidential hopefuls not previously well known to them operate in a variety of forums. Though they don't perfectly reflect the demands of the presidency, these forums or contexts unquestionably give insight into the candidates' leadership ability, policy perspectives, personalities, and ethical judgment under pressure. The current credentialing system, based on extended campaign exposure, emerged when no satisfactory alternative could be found. It can be replaced only when and if such alternatives are put in place. I know of none.

Some may interpret the above arguments as a prescription for complacency. There are severe limits on what can be achieved through changes in nomination processes, no matter how artfully the changes are designed. Recognizing the importance of stability in such a fundamental constitutional process requires greater restraints on our insatiable appetite for rules changes. And many of the problems identified in the current nomination processes grow out of much larger developments in American society and politics. Even if it is granted that they really are problems, they can't be remedied through changes in the nomination system as such. So don't bother doing anything.

In fact, I think, the above arguments point to a different conclusion. We should increase efforts to make the prevailing system work as well as possible. Peer review can be exercised more intelligently, without changing the present community of peers. The enlarged role of the national press does not mandate absurd exaggeration of the results of the Iowa caucuses. Coupled with a receptivity to the idea of gradual state-centered, evolutionary change in the rules, a serious commitment to "making do" can work wonders.

32. Consultants Rise via the Low Road

Paul Taylor

Today's highly structured, media-oriented political campaigns have fostered the growth of a small but influential campaign consulting industry. Traditional political commentators (mainly editorial writers and political scientists) tend to regard these consultants ambivalently, suspecting them of supplanting the time-honored shapers of campaigns—party leaders and journalists. Consultants have been blamed, moreover, for a resurgence of negative political advertising, as *Washington Post* political correspondent Paul Taylor notes in his 1989 article. Even candidates have a love-hate relationship with their new handlers; while more than a few officeholders owe their jobs to shrewdly managed campaigns, they are quick to distance themselves from the more controversial tactics of their consultants.

The political campaigns of 1988 have already taken their lumps in the court of public opinion. It was a very good year only if you liked your politics petty and go-for-the-throat—so said the voters, the news media, the losing candidates, even a few of the winners.

Now come the political consultants. Like carousers on the morning after, they too are fretting over the gaudy, brawling, barren way the nation conducts its political discourse. Some are even wondering if they're a part of the problem.

"No, we're not unfairly blamed. We're at the heart of it," said Democratic pollster Alan Secrest. "It's accepted now—chop the other guy's legs out before he does it to you."

"There are times, crass as one is, you still have some ideals, and I personally feel more disgust with the process," agreed Don Sipple, a Republican media consultant.

"The problem is, you can lie on a TV commercial and voters may not know it's a lie," said Geoffrey Garin, a Democratic pollster. "With the cynicism of voters, they're inclined to believe the worst."

These reflections were prompted by an election year that featured more negative television advertising than ever before in the 36 years that televised commercials have been part of the political landscape, and by a presidential campaign in which the consultants themselves became major figures. Roger Ailes, the creator of George Bush's television ads, was the archetype of the master manipulator whose creations may have been more important than anything said by a candidate on the stump.

What Ailes and his colleagues do for a living is help candidates get elected by calibrating what sells and what doesn't in the political marketplace.

They have discovered—through decades of polling, ad-testing, focus-group interviewing, and trial and error in creating television commercials—that the traffic will bear a good deal more than they once believed: more attacks, more distortions, more contrivances, more trivia, more half-truths.

The consultants' critics contend that their ads fuel the very apathy and cynicism that make the commercials work. A vicious cycle appears to be in place. As the dialogue of democracy gets cheesier, more voters turn off, tune out and—come Election Day—stay home. The consultants react by dishing out still cheesier ads the next time around to try to appeal to these depoliticized voters.

Consultants and their clients have much in common, but one difference is fundamental. Only the clients have to govern once the campaign ends. The consultants move on to other campaigns, their professional standing and monthly retainers rising and falling with their latest batting average.

With winning their only bottom line, consultants often confront a subtle tension in their relationships with clients. Candidates typically want their ads to show off what splendid statesmen and princely human beings they are. And consultants typically tell them: "People won't pay any attention. Better to knock your opponent's head off."

More and more, the clients listen. Partly, that's because the massive increases in the cost of campaigns make them feel profligate if they don't heed the advice of the "experts." Partly it's that the consultants are now able to demonstrate, with something approaching numerical precision, which ads work and which don't. And partly it's the knowledge that the opponent has the same technology at his disposal.

"The techniques have gotten so refined, the weapons so powerful, that if you don't use them, you will lose them, because the other side will use them on you," said Democratic pollster Paul Maslin. Over the past decade, Maslin said, he has seen candidates' attitudes toward negative ads evolve from revulsion to grudging acceptance to something close to "an addiction. . . . It's like taking a shot . . . because you can see the way they move the numbers."

Still, Maslin and his colleagues take issue with the puppeteer image of their profession sometimes portrayed in the press. "I don't find candidates delivering themselves unto my hands to be their molder," said Mark Mellman, another Democratic pollster. "My clients say to me: 'Given who I am, what's the most effective issue I should use?' I would never presume to make a decision. That's not my job. I give advice."

More and more, the advice Mellman and his colleagues give is to attack. Thus, the nation was treated to a presidential campaign last year devoted in large measure to a conversation about flags and prison furloughs.

"One of the fundamental facts of psychology is that negative information is processed more deeply than positive information," Mellman said. "People say they hate the stuff, but that's not the point. The point is, they absorb the information." ...

Another Democratic pollster, Stanley Greenberg, argued that the phenomenon of negative and vacuous TV spots is more tied to the issue vacuum of the late 1980s. "There are times in our national life when there are no great historical battles being waged," he said. "In the absence of great issues, there are a lot of opportunities to use the advanced technologies of modern campaigns—people meters, focus groups, multivariate analysis—to win races that trivialize the discourse."

"You always expect the voters to rise up in anger, but in some respects, they can't—and even if they can, they don't," said Garin. ...

Similarly, Maslin said, the more that political campaigns are waged as a rat-a-tat-tat of distorted, 30-second charges and countercharges, the more cynical and disbelieving the viewing public becomes. And that raises the threshold for grabbing their attention. "Unless you jolt them, you won't get results," Maslin said.

"Jolting" apolitical voters hasn't meant engaging them in a discussion of the deficit, national defense, the savings and loan and nuclear waste crises or any of the other issues that politicians confront once in office. Increasingly, it has meant finding "hot button" issues that are more accessible to the voters' daily lives, more entertaining, more personality-oriented. ...

Not everyone in the political consulting business or in academia thinks the emphasis on negative campaigning is necessarily bad.

"I like negative ads better than positive ones," said Michael Jay Robinson, a professor of government at Georgetown University. "They tell you more, and I'm always interested in knowing what a guy is against. I think you get more honesty." ...

There are examples of attacks exploding in the face of the attacker. A vivid recent one was the effort of Cleveland Mayor George Voinovich (R) in [the 1988] Senate race to tar Sen. Howard M. Metzenbaum (D-Ohio) as soft on child pornography. Metzenbaum's consultants responded by putting popular Sen. John Glenn (D-Ohio) on the air to denounce the ads as the lowest "gutter politics" he'd ever seen, and to remind voters that Metzenbaum has four daughters and six grandchildren. The race, which had been expected to be competitive, instantly became a rout. But backlashes of this sort tend to be the exceptions that prove the rule. The rule: attacks work.

The corollary is that to launch an attack in 30-second dollops is to invite a debate that will wallow in shallowness, distortion, half-truth and false inferences. Consultants have developed a sixth sense about what the market will bear. They know full well, for example, that journalists will usually blow the whistle on outright errors of fact, and these are to be avoided at all cost.

"In terms of being able to distort or mislead people, you're never running in the clear," said Republican consultant Charlie Black, one of the few who think the standards of truthfulness have become tighter. "Back in the 1970s, you could say all kinds of outrageous things. Now, in almost any state you go into, you've got at least one, maybe four or five state newspapers that will call your hand. Some of these state capital press corps are tougher than the national guys."

Even if outright falsehoods are dangerous, there's still a broad field of half-truth into which the consultants can roam, largely free of scrutiny from a press corps that is often reluctant to strike too prosecutorial a stance in the midst of a campaign. "The tolerance for error in ads is much greater than it was 10 years ago," contended Douglas Bailey, GOP consultant and publisher of *Hotline*, a daily political trade publication that covered many of [the 1988] ads. "It used to be that one error will sink you; now, one provable fact will get you past the critics."

Even these dollops of half-truth have their defenders. "We have adapted ourselves to the voters," said Black. "They have a short attention span. They don't follow government and politics every day—they don't want to. They won't sit around the family kitchen table and read the two parties' platforms. They want things put simply." . . .

"The dialogue of politics has become so sterile because campaigns more and more are designed to repeat back to voters things they already believe," Greenberg said.

There is a more benign view of the low turnout and relatively unsubstantial campaigns of 1988: that the nation was peaceful and relatively prosperous, that the electorate was content and felt no need for a national conversation about tomorrow. "I happen to think it was a good election," said Georgetown's Robinson. "In the end, the public did what it always does—it rewarded policy successes."

"Negative ads are good medicine for the political process," said Castellanos. "It may not always taste good, but it makes us healthier. . . . Campaigns are better today than they ever were. So don't go looking for the Golden Age of Politics. This is it."

But many Democrats argue that Bush "won ugly" [in 1988], and in the process stripped some of the sheen off the office he was seeking. Never before had a campaign for the presidency featured so many negative ads.

At the same time, it is the bipartisan consensus of the consultants that Bush's campaign was a technical masterpiece—an example of brilliant exploitation of the new political technology. . . .

"In an age when voters are so fluid on matters of ideology and party, so much of getting the message right becomes a matter of tapping the right emotions and using the right language," Greenberg said. "That's what focus groups get you that polls don't. You get the texture."

Once ads have survived pre-testing and are being broadcast, pollsters have two ways to determine if they are working. One is the tracking poll, which records changes in the race nightly and which, like the focus group, has become a regular part of modern political campaigns. The other is post-testing of commercials. Pollsters arrange for targeted voters to watch the ads at home, then survey them by telephone and compile a score card on such criteria as saliency, credibility and empathy.

Ronald Reagan's White House took this kind of market research a step further. Every time the president gave a televised speech or news conference during [his second term], his pollster, Richard Wirthlin, would assemble a focus group somewhere in the country and hook them up with "people meters—little dials they could turn to register a running commentary of approval or disapproval.

The next day, Wirthlin would give the White House a chart that looked like an electrocardiogram—marking, down to the word, the gesture and split second, exactly what had and hadn't worked the night before. Phrases that drew positive responses were repeated by Reagan in speech after speech; the turnoffs were discarded.

"I helped to make a great communicator half a degree greater," Wirthlin said.

The new political technology cannot be repealed, so its impact is likely to endure. Bailey, who helped mastermind an earlier campaign that won wide admiration among his peers—Gerald R. Ford's almost-successful, come-from-behind race in 1976—is one of the practitioners of this trade who is dismayed at the direction it has taken the nation's politics. "The biggest problem," Bailey observed in an interview [in 1988], "is that it's no longer necessary for a political candidate to guess what an audience thinks. He can do it with a nightly tracking poll. So it's no longer likely that political leaders are going to lead. Instead, they're going to follow."

33. A Field Guide to Election Spending Limits

Chuck Alston

Modern political campaigns are costly; finding the money to run them is a major preoccupation of public officeholders, their party organizations and campaign aides. Campaign finance is also a federally regulated activity whose rules and requirements are hotly debated by politicians and scholars alike. As with so many public issues, "where you stand depends on where you sit." Agreement on new rules has been stalled because those who write the laws are themselves incumbent politicians with a stake in the outcome. Academic experts inconveniently remind everyone that seemingly attractive "reforms" may not succeed, and indeed may spawn unintended or undesirable consequences. Chuck Alston, a *Congressional Quarterly Weekly Report* reporter specializing in campaign finance, conducts a hard-eyed but whimsical review of reform options and their proponents in his 1990 article for that publication.

Step into a Republican nightmare. It is 1992, and control of the Senate is on the line. Of the 34 seats up for grabs, 20 belong to Democrats, which makes 1992 the GOP's best shot at majority status since losing it in 1986. But Republican challengers can't fully exploit what they consider their deadliest weapon —money— because a new law, written by Democrats, limits campaign spending.

This is Republican hell: Every incumbent wins re-election, there's no place to spend a huge war chest and minority status takes on the stench of permanence. The vision frightens Republicans, who for the second time in three years are fighting in the Senate to make sure it remains just a bad dream.

State Democrats have made state-by-state spending limits the central feature of their proposed election finance overhaul.... They consider it the only sure way to curtail the incessant fundraising that diverts senators' attention and influences their actions. David L. Boren of Oklahoma, the Democratic floor manager, said limits represent "real reform." Without a cap, spending will merely pop up elsewhere under a new guise, he said.

The Republican leader, Bob Dole of Kansas, complained about the Democrats' almost "clinical fixation on arbitrarily determined spending limits." It is a "form of incumbency protection," he said. The Republican proposal (S 2595) centers on how money is raised—for instance, it would

eliminate political action committees and promote in-state fundraising—
not how much is spent. It would limit spending only to the extent that
candidates raise less. .... Sen. Bob Packwood, R-Ore., calls spending limits
the "touchstone difference" between the parties. "I would hope that reform would not get hung upon the sole issue of spending limits," he said.
His hopes could be dashed easily. .... [A] tour of the two camps they represent and the ground in between makes it clear that they will not easily
abandon their positions. What follows is a guided tour of the battleground.

The Democrats use a formula based on a state's voting-age population
to set limits varying from $1.8 million to $9.6 million. This includes
spending for primaries and 25 percent in additional spending allowed
for money raised through small in-state contributions.

Participation would be voluntary; candidates who enlisted would
spend their own money in a primary but receive substantial public
funds for the general election. Other incentives include subsidized mail,
free television time and low-cost television rates.

Had every 1988 candidate abided by the limits, challengers would
have gained $21.7 million and incumbents would have lost $23.6
million, according to Common Cause, the public interest lobby that
favors limits. Incumbents spent $101.3 million in 1988; challengers spent
$49.2 million.

Whack-a-Mole

Support for spending limits originates in the theory that campaign
finance operates like an arcade game called Whack-a-Mole. The mole
pops up in one hole, and you whack him down. But then he pops up
somewhere else. Similarly, campaign spending, whenever it is suppressed in one form, always pops up elsewhere.

Thus, the Democrats contend that the only sure-fire way to curb
spending is to say, "This much and no more." Once a limit is set, the
campaign equivalent of an arms control agreement, the spending race
comes to an end. The Senate schedule becomes less beholden to the
fundraising demands of members; incumbents bow and scrape less to
special interests. Challengers aren't scared away by an incumbent's huge
war chest, and incumbents can go back to legislating.

The Scope of the Problem

Democrat Robert C. Byrd of West Virginia found a simile for Senate
campaign spending in the GOP's mascot.

"Campaigns have become like bloated rogue elephants rampaging across the American landscape. . . . It is time we put this overweight, fat, clumsy beast on a diet. His cash intake must be drastically reduced."

Byrd is right that, over the long term, spending has exploded. Candidates who made it to the general election spent $26 million on their Senate campaigns in 1972. Spending reached $185 million in 1988. . . . The escalation is also not as bad as it first seems if inflation is discounted, as measured by the Consumer Price Index (CPI). The 1988 campaigns cost $65 million in 1972 dollars. That is a 147 percent increase over 1972 spending, a substantial leap to be sure, but far less dramatic than the 600 percent increase that includes inflation.

Campaigns pay staff and rent and buy postage, buttons, bumper stickers, newspaper ads and television—lots of television. TV ads accounted for 43.5 percent of 1988 Senate campaign budgets, according to a study commissioned by the National Association of Broadcasters. This includes incumbents who ran with virtually no opposition. So it's probably unfair to compare campaign costs with a marketbasket of consumer goods such as fuel, food, housing and health care.

A look at the cost of buying television time shows how campaign costs have risen considerably faster than inflation overall. The cost of a 30-second prime-time ad, calculated on a cost per audience rating point, from 1982 to 1988 advanced 61 percent in Albuquerque, N.M.; 95 percent in Miami; 106 percent in Phoenix; 138 percent in Gainesville, Fla.; 141 percent in Cleveland; and 204 percent in El Paso, Texas, according to 1987 testimony to the House Administration Committee by campaign consultant Frank Greer. The CPI, compounded annually, rose less than 25 percent during this period. . . .

Eggheads v. Goo-Goos

Government reformers usually cover their flanks with academic angels. In this debate, the "good government" crowd, led by Common Cause, is largely on its own.

The reason is orthodox political science. Most academics have concluded that rigid spending limits and competitive congressional elections are mutually exclusive concepts.

The academic heavy lifting was done by political scientist Gary Jacobson for his 1980 book, *Money in Congressional Elections*. Studying elections in the 1970s, Jacobson demonstrated empirically that in contests between incumbents and challengers, challengers get the most value out of every dollar they spend. This is because a challenger is generally not as well-known as the incumbent, who benefits from free mail, from good will engendered by helping constituents and from easy access to the media.

Jacobson's rule led to an obvious corollary: Limiting a challenger's spending can limit his chance of winning. This, of course, has become orthodox Republicanism as well. . . .

Of course, not every challenger who wins needs to outspend an incumbent. Consider the six Democrats who ousted incumbent Republicans in 1986 without outspending them.

All six were established politicians: . . . They did not need to spend as much as most challengers just to achieve name recognition.

"The 1986 Democratic experience indicates that attractive candidates with sufficient funds can beat incumbents spending more money," University of Southern California political scientist Herbert E. Alexander wrote in 1989. "Five challengers won despite being outspent by $1 million or more; four of the five were outspent by a ratio of nearly 2-1. This suggests a doctrine of sufficiency."

To put it another way, challengers need not spend more than an incumbent. They must, however, be able to spend a *sufficient* amount of money to get their message across.

A report by the Committee for the Study of the American Electorate, a Washington-based nonpartisan research group, noted that only nine of 32 winning challengers from 1978 to 1988 outspent the incumbent. But only seven of the challengers stayed within the proposed Democratic limits—suggesting that the sufficient level is somewhat higher than the Democrats would set.

How Much Is Enough?

This is the $64,000 question of spending limits. The trick is to set limits high enough for challengers to win but not so high as to keep spending at obscene levels.

A panel of advisers named by Dole and Majority Leader George J. Mitchell of Maine recommended "flexible spending limits": firm spending limits for money raised from political action committees or out-of-state individuals, and unlimited spending for any money raised from in-state individuals.

But they didn't set limits. "We had no figures in mind," said Alexander, a panel member. "All we agreed on were the words 'reasonably high.' "

Adding to the difficulty of setting limits is the unique case every state presents: The cost of ads in its television markets, the strength of its labor unions, the two-party tradition, etc.

Consider what it took two Democrats to win in 1986. Florida's Graham spent 80 cents per eligible voter; South Dakota's Daschle spent $8.02, according to the Committee for Study of the American Electorate.

If 80 cents per eligible voter became the basis for all spending caps, the California limit would be slightly more than $17 million. If $8 were the limit, it would be $170 million. . . .

This is an issue Congress isn't about to turn over to a commission. As University of Virginia political scientist Larry J. Sabato said: "The frequent call for spending ceilings in congressional races is a bad reform idea that sounds good. On the surface, it is an undeniably attractive proposition. . . . But who would determine the ceilings? The Congress would, of course—a body composed of 535 incumbents who are fervently convinced of the worthiness of their own re-elections."

Free Spending Equals Free Speech

The Supreme Court, among others, has equated campaign spending with free speech protected by the First Amendment. Thus, the government cannot impose mandatory spending limits. Conservative Republicans, in particular, often argue against spending limits on these grounds.

This is why spending-limit proposals usually offer candidates incentives to participate voluntarily. It is also why Sen. Ernest F. Hollings, D-S.C., contends that the only way to limit spending is with a constitutional amendment.

One way to attack the cost of campaigns is to attack the rates charged for television ads. Candidates now pay the highest rate to ensure that they get the exact time and audience they want. No point in making your pitch about Social Security on Saturday morning, or answering an opponent's attack ad two days late.

The most popular proposal to address TV costs would allow candidates to purchase the most expensive time—time that cannot be bumped from the broadcaster's schedule—at the cheapest possible rate. This could in effect reduce spending capping it, unless candidates just purchase more ads.

The savings would vary from market to market. Beth Clark, a time buyer at FGI, a North Carolina marketing and advertising agency, estimated that the proposal would trim TV costs 5 percent to 25 percent.

Republicans argue that it is the money that passes unseen through the system that does them in. So they are arguing fiercely for limits on what is known as "non-party soft money," chiefly unregulated money spent by labor unions on politics. Most of this accrues to the benefit of Democrats. Republicans see little point in going along with spending limits on campaigns if the Democrats' allies can continue to spend unlimited amounts outside the campaign.

You can't spend what you don't have. Republicans propose eliminating all political action committees, a major source of campaign money, and cutting the amount candidates can take from out-of-state contributors in half, to $500 per election. "The effect will be to drive campaign spending down," Packwood said. . . .

A New Paradigm

Frank J. Sorauf, a University of Minnesota political scientist and author of *Money in American Elections*, like most of his colleagues has hewed to the doctrine that spending limits favor incumbents. But now, he said, he wonders whether a system of spending limits and public financing might alter politics so dramatically that it would change the nature of candidates themselves. "It raises the possibility that you might get better challengers," he said.

Maybe the academics and government reformers have something in common after all, for Sorauf's argument is also used by Common Cause President Fred Wertheimer. He contends that the case against spending limits generally focuses on the races in which a challenger exceeded the limit to win.

"To take a system that is not producing competitive races and defend it on the basis of a few races misses the larger focus," Wertheimer said.

The one certainty, most political scientists agree, is that any change in spending will produce unintended consequences. What's in store if spending limits become law?

Sorauf's paradigm is one vision. Another is political scientist Alexander's new pecking order. He theorizes that the formula for spending limits would create competitive races in some states but not others. This would eventually influence seniority in Congress because states without competitive races would constantly return their incumbents. The Senate would begin to look like it did in the days of the Solid South, when the Democratic Party rose to dominance.

PART III

THE INSTITUTIONS
OF GOVERNMENT

The actual art of governing under our Constitution does not and cannot conform to juridical definitions of the power of any of its branches based on isolated clauses or even single Articles torn from context. While the Constitution diffuses power the better to secure liberty, it also contemplates that practice will integrate the dispersed powers into a workable government. It enjoins upon its branches separateness but interdependence, autonomy but reciprocity.

—Justice Robert Jackson, *Youngstown v. Sawyer*, 1952

Chapter 8

Congress

Constitutionally, Congress is the "first branch of government." The founders strongly favored lawmaking by representative assemblies and thus viewed Congress as the prime national policymaker. Article I of the Constitution assigns Congress broad enumerated powers and includes an "elastic clause" to implement those specific provisions. By contrast, the presidency and the courts are outlined in broad-brush fashion in Articles II and III, respectively.

During the 1787 Constitutional Convention, the framers devoted more than half their time to debating the role of Congress. Some, for example, wanted a unicameral rather than a bicameral legislature. Three years and one year were proposed as terms of office for House members; two years was the compromise. James Madison's *Federalist Paper* No. 51 (Selection 34) illuminates the framers' intentions concerning checks and balances and their applicability to Congress. "In republican government," said Madison, "the legislative authority necessarily predominates."

> The remedy for this inconveniency is to divide the legislature into different branches; and to render them, by different modes of election and different principles of action, as little connected with each other as the nature of their common functions and their common dependence on the society will admit.

Bicameralism is perhaps Congress's most conspicuous organizational feature. Each chamber has a distinct process for considering legislation, and each determines its own rules of procedure. Their relative size explains much about why the two chambers differ. Because it is much larger, the House is a more structured body than the Senate. The restraints imposed on representatives by rules and precedents are far more severe than those affecting senators. The House's rules limit extended debate and permit determined majorities to achieve their policy objectives; the Senate ensures freedom of expression and minority rights—whether those of the minority party, a small group, or even one senator. In brief, the Senate emphasizes individualism in decision making; the House works through voting blocs.

Decisions in Congress are shaped by a vast number and variety of people: the members and their staff aides, the White House, the departments and agencies, and the courts. And these are just the "official" decision makers. The legions of informal decision makers include the lobbying groups, law firms, and consulting organizations that seek to influence policies and the journalists who report and interpret those decisions.

It is no secret that today's legislators operate in a pressure-cooker environment. In this century, the business of Congress has expanded both quantitatively (overseeing a massive and sophisticated federal establishment, for example) and qualitatively (addressing new and complex problems, such as genetic engineering); Heavy legislative and constituency demands are made on all legislators. Selection 35 focuses on the constituent work of Rep. John Lewis, D-Ga., a key civil rights leader.

No matter how busy they may be, legislators must vote on a wide range of issues. On any given day, members may be required to vote on bills affecting foreign aid, Medicare, mass transit, taxes, arms control, or marine fisheries. How members should vote on such issues—whether they rely upon constituency, conscience, party, or other sources—is a classic question of representative government. In Selection 36, "How a Member Decides," Rep. Lee H. Hamilton (D-Ind.), a senior House member, offers thoughtful observations on the major influences on voting behavior. Some votes even affect the institutional image of Congress, such as those involving legislative ethics. In Selection 37, former representative Otis Pike (D-N.Y.) examines some of the ethical challenges facing lawmakers.

A Dramatic Upheaval

Since the 1970s, Congress has undergone a dramatic upheaval in its organization and operation. Once known for its rigid adherence to seniority (the custom by which the longest continuously serving members of the majority party chair the committees, regardless of ability), the institution has relaxed the system, creating what some call "juniority," so that more members may hold leadership positions. Power in both chambers was diffused to scores of members, staff aides, informal groups, and subcommittees. With gavel-to-gavel television reporting of floor proceedings, Congress opened its doors further to public observation; coverage of the House began in 1979, of the Senate in 1986. On some occasions, legislators complain that the "sunshine" (openness to public scrutiny) is so intense they are in danger of suffering from sunstroke. That lament points toward another modern development—the increase in the number, diversity, and sophistication of interest groups and their ability to generate political heat and create instant constituencies in support of issues.

Scores of other developments accentuate the notion of "participatory democracy" in Congress. Because of such changes, whose effects are evident in the 1990s, Congress has become more democratic, more responsive, more accountable, and more open to the public. Innovations in the legislative process have reinforced Congress's important representative responsibilities (giving voice and visibility to the numerous concerns of the body politic) and emphasized its oversight duties (reviewing the administration of laws). However, the disadvantage of having so many participants in decision making is that Congress now often takes much longer to write and pass legislation.

Congress's untidy and decentralized policymaking procedures open it to sharp criticism from many quarters. Scholars, journalists, and even its own members lament Congress's inefficiency, slowness, and piecemeal approach to legislating. These aspects of congressional decision making seem inherently unattractive and have prompted some commentators to recommend wholesale changes (typically, the adoption of features of European parliaments) in our national political system.[1]

There is little question that Congress, like any institution, can improve its methods of operation. Yet there is value, often overlooked, in Congress's slowness and messiness. Alexander Hamilton in *Federalist Paper* No. 70 observed that "promptitude of decision is oftener an evil than a benefit. The difference of opinion, and the jarrings of parties in [Congress], though they may sometimes obstruct salutary plans, yet often promote deliberation and circumspection, and serve to check excesses in the majority."[2] In Selection 38, "In Defense of a Messy Congress," journalist Albert R. Hunt cautions that although Congress often appears inept, it "isn't *supposed* to operate neatly, efficiently, or expeditiously." Its "rough edges" result from our system of checks and balances, and its conflicts mirror those of the voting public.

The changes in Congress emanate both from internal circumstances and pressures from the larger, external environment of social, economic, and political forces. To cope with these pressures and forces, the contemporary Congress has improvised new policymaking procedures and strategies. In Selection 39, "Crumbling Committees," analyst Richard Cohen highlights recent internal changes that "have quietly revolutionized the sources of legislative power on Capitol Hill, eroding the influence of once all-powerful committees and their bosses." Party leaders such as Senate Majority Leader George J. Mitchell, D-Me., regularly establish ad hoc task forces that may assume policymaking responsibilities previously exercised by committees. Senator Mitchell, for example, has appointed a party task force to review President George Bush's national energy program.

Some of these innovations reflect the difficulty of getting things done in the House and Senate. This has been a source of recurrent public irritation. Criticism of Congress seemed to reach new heights as this decade got underway (see Selection 40, "Congress-Bashing for Beginners"). The profound public dismay even prompted a nationwide effort to limit the terms of lawmakers. Two political scientists, in a point-counterpoint analysis, examine this issue in Selection 41. It is quite likely that Congress-bashing will remain a popular pastime for many—perhaps because the legislative branch represents and responds so well to the interests, foibles, and contradictions of the citizenry. As Representative Bill Gradison (R-Ohio) observed:

> I think the frustration . . . might be from folks who have an agenda of things they want laws passed on, and they're having difficulty doing it. But I read that as a strength of the system, not a weakness. The Congress is working about as the Founding Fathers intended, which is not very well. Or to put it more positively, they wanted to make it hard to pass laws.[3]

Notes

1. See, for example, James L. Sundquist, *Constitutional Reform and Effective Government* (Washington, D.C.: Brookings Institution, 1986).
2. Paul L. Ford, ed., *The Federalist* (New York: H. Holt and Co., 1898), 470.
3. Christopher Madison, "A Class Apart," *National Journal* (March 9, 1991): 567.

34. *Federalist* No. 51

James Madison

Federalist No. 51 is a classic in political science. It addresses an age-old issue of democratic governance: how to strike the right balance between a government strong enough to be effective yet not so strong that it threatens the rights and liberties of the people. In an oft-quoted statement, Madison put it this way: "In framing a government which is to be administered by men over men, the great difficulty lies in this: you must first enable the government to control the governed; and in the next place oblige it to control itself." Madison's answer, in the main, is found in the Constitution's elaborate system of checks and balances.

To what expedient, then, shall we finally resort, for maintaining in practice the necessary partition of power among the several departments, as laid down in the Constitution? The only answer that can be given is, that as all these exterior provisions are found to be inadequate, the defect must be supplied, by so contriving the interior structure of the government as that its several constituent parts may, by their mutual relations, be the means of keeping each other in their proper places. Without presuming to undertake a full development of this important idea, I will hazard a few general observations, which may perhaps place it in a clearer light, and enable us to form a more correct judgment of the principles and structure of the government planned by the convention.

In order to lay a due foundation for that separate and distinct exercise of the different powers of government, which to a certain extent is admitted on all hands to be essential to the preservation of liberty, it is evident that each department should have a will of its own; and consequently should be so constituted that the members of each should have as little agency as possible in the appointment of the members of the others. Were this principle rigorously adhered to, it would require that all the appointments for the supreme executive, legislative, and judiciary magistracies should be drawn from the same fountain of authority, the people, through channels having no communication whatever with one another. Perhaps such a plan of constructing the several departments would be less difficult in practice than it may in contemplation appear. Some difficulties, however, and some additional expense would attend the execution of it. Some deviations, therefore, from the principle must be admitted. In the constitution of the judiciary department in particular, it might be inexpedient to insist rigorously on the principle: first, because peculiar qualifications being essential in the members, the primary consideration ought to be to select that mode of choice which best secures these qualifications; secondly, because the permanent tenure by which the appointments are held in that department, must soon destroy all sense of dependence on the authority conferring them.

It is equally evident, that the members of each department should be as little dependent as possible on those of the others, for the emoluments annexed to their offices. Were the executive magistrate, or the judges, not independent of the legislature in this particular, their independence in every other would be merely nominal.

But the great security against a gradual concentration of the several powers in the same department, consists in giving to those who administer each department the necessary constitutional means and personal motives to resist encroachments of the others. The provision for defence must in this, as in all other cases, be made commensurate to the danger of attack. Ambition must be made to counteract ambition. The interest of the man must be connected with the constitutional rights of the place. It may be a reflection on human nature, that such devices should be necessary to control the abuses of government. But what is government itself, but the greatest of all reflections on human nature? If men were angels, no government would be necessary. If angels were to govern men, neither external nor internal controls on government would be necessary. In framing a government which is to be administered by men over men, the great difficulty lies in this: you must first enable the government to control the governed; and in the next place oblige it to control itself. A dependence on the people is, no doubt, the primary control on the government; but experience has taught mankind the necessity of auxiliary precautions.

This policy of supplying, by opposite and rival interests, the defect of better motives, might be traced through the whole system of human affairs, private as well as public. We see it particularly displayed in all the subordinate distributions of power, where the constant aim is to divide and arrange the several offices in such a manner as that each may be a check on the other—that the private interest of every individual may be a sentinel over the public rights. These inventions of prudence cannot be less requisite in the distribution of the supreme powers of the State.

But it is not possible to give to each department an equal power of self-defence. In republican government, the legislative authority necessarily predominates. The remedy for this inconveniency is to divide the legislature into different branches; and to render them, by different modes of election and different principles of action, as little connected with each other as the nature of their common functions and their common dependence on the society will admit. It may even be necessary to guard against dangerous encroachments by still further precautions. As the weight of the legislative authority requires that it should be thus divided, the weakness of the executive may require, on the other hand, that it should be fortified. An absolute negative on the legislature appears, at first view, to be the natural defence with which the executive magistrate should be armed. But perhaps it would be neither altogether safe nor alone sufficient. On ordinary occasions it might not be exerted with the requisite firmness, and on extraordinary occasions it might be perfidiously abused. May not this defect of an absolute negative be supplied by some qualified connection between this weaker department and the weaker branch of the stronger department, by which the latter may be led to support the constitutional rights of the former, without being too much detached from the rights of its own department?

If the principles on which these observations are founded be just, as I persuade myself they are, and they be applied as a criterion to the several State constitutions, and to the federal Constitution, it will be found that if the latter does not perfectly correspond with them, the former are infinitely less able to bear such a test.

There are, moreover, two considerations particularly applicable to the federal system of America, which place that system in a very interesting point of view.

First. In a single republic, all the power surrendered by the people is submitted to the administration of a single government; and the usurpations are guarded against by a division of the government into distinct and separate departments. In the compound republic of America, the power surrendered by the people is first divided between two distinct governments, and then the portion allotted to each subdivided among distinct and separate departments. Hence a double security arises to the rights of the people. The different governments will control each other, at the same time that each will be controlled by itself.

Second. It is of great importance in a republic not only to guard the society against the oppression of its rulers, but to guard one part of the society against the injustice of the other part. Different interests necessarily exist in different classes of citizens. If a majority be united by a common interest, the rights of the minority will be insecure. There are but two methods of providing against this evil: the one by creating a will in the community independent of the majority—that is, of the society itself; the other, by comprehending in the society so many separate descriptions of citizens as will render an unjust combination of a majority of the whole very improbable, if not impracticable. The first method prevails in all governments possessing an hereditary or self-appointed authority. This, at best, is but a precarious security; because a power independent of the society may as well espouse the unjust views of the major, as the rightful interests of the minor party, and may possibly be turned against both parties. The second method will be exemplified in the federal republic of the United States. Whilst all authority in it will be derived from and dependent on the society, the society itself will be broken into so many parts, interests and classes of citizens, that the rights of individuals, or of the minority, will be in little danger from interested combinations of the majority. In a free government the security for civil rights must be the same as that for religious rights. It consists in the one case in the multiplicity of interests, and in the other in the multiplicity of sects. The degree of security in both cases will depend on the number of interests and sects; and this may be presumed to depend on the extent of country and number of people comprehended under the same government. This view of the subject must particularly recommend a proper federal system to all the sincere and considerate friends of republican government, since it shows that in exact proportion as the territory of the Union may be formed into more circumscribed Confederacies, or States, oppressive combinations of a majority will be facilitated; the best security, under the republican forms, for the rights of every class of citizens, will be diminished; and consequently the stability and independence of some member of the government, the only other security, must be proportionally increased. Justice is the end of government. It is the end of civil society. It ever has been and ever will be pursued until it be obtained, or until liberty be lost in the pursuit. In a society under the forms of which the stronger faction can readily unite and oppress the weaker, anarchy may as truly be said to reign as in a state of nature, where the weaker individual is not secured against the violence of the stronger; and as, in the latter state, even the stronger individuals are prompted, by the uncertainty of their condition, to submit to a government which may protect the weak as well as themselves; so, in the former state, will the more powerful factions or parties be gradually induced, by a like motive, to wish for a government which will protect all parties, the weaker as well as the more powerful. It can be little doubted that if the State of Rhode Island was separated from the Confederacy and left to itself, the insecurity of rights under the popular form of government within such narrow limits would be displayed by such reiterated oppressions of factious majorities that some power altogether independent of the people would soon be called for by the voice of the very factions whose misrule had proved the necessity of it. In the extended republic of the United States, and among the great variety of interests, parties, and sects which it embraces, a coalition of a majority of the whole society could seldom take place on any other principles than those of justice and the general good; whilst there being thus less danger to a minor from the will of a major party, there must be less pretext, also, to provide for the security of the former, by introducing into the government a will not dependent on the latter, or, in other words, a will independent of the society itself. It is no less certain than it is important, notwithstanding the contrary opinions which have been entertained, that the larger the society, provided it lie within a practical sphere, the more duly capable it will be of self-government. And happily for the *republican cause,* the practicable sphere may be carried to a very great extent, by a judicious modification and mixture of the *federal principle.*

35. Rep. John Lewis: Scarred Survivor Brings Home Lessons of the 1960s

Laura Parker

Laura Parker, a staff writer for the *Washington Post,* highlights the legislative career and constituent activities of John Lewis, D-Ga., a black civil rights leader of the 1960s. Parker's article, published in the *Post* in 1990, recounts Congressman Lewis's meeting with Atlanta students and his continuing effort "to build in America a truly interracial democracy."

The school is in an unused wing of Rich's department store, a few floors from the Magnolia Room where the Rev. Martin Luther King, Jr. was arrested in 1960 for trying to buy lunch in the white's-only tea room. The local congressman arrives late, having lingered too long signing autographs for children at an Arbor Day ceremony. He strides up a flight of stairs and moves through the mattress department to the long hallway leading to Rich's Academy, a high school of last resort for troubled teens.

For John Lewis, a Democrat in his second term, this is part of a weekly ritual, making the rounds in his Atlanta congressional district. For the students, a living legend has walked into the room.

The great battles of the civil rights movement of the 1970s were fought before these students were born. To them, the familiar battle-grounds—Montgomery, Greensboro, Birmingham—are merely places in history books. Lewis was there. He was in the streets of Selma, Ala., on the "Bloody Sunday" 25 years ago that led to passage of the Voting Rights Act of 1965. He was a foot soldier in a movement that changed the American landscape, jailed 40 times and beaten so often that he speaks with a slight impediment.

"Forty times," he repeats softly. "Not for stealing, not for beating anybody up, not for using drugs." He pauses and looks out over this new generation of young black southerners and says, "You, too, have a contribution to make."

In an era of politics by television soundbites and convictions inspired by opinion polls, Lewis, 49, has a clarity of purpose not often seen in Congress today. A quietly pugnacious man, his very life, 25 years in the trenches, represents a dedication that has won him the kind of praise and stature rarely bestowed on junior members.

His advice is sought on issues involving the homeless, poverty and drug abuse. He has worked to establish a national African-American museum affiliated with the Smithsonian Institution. House leaders have made him part of the leadership by appointing him at-large whip.

"When someone walks out of the history book and takes the oath of office, that person carries a certain cachet and respect that the used-car salesman and the insurance salesman and the entrepreneurs don't command when they raise their right hands and take the oath of office for the first time," a House leadership aide said.

Lewis spends nearly every weekend with constituents, tending to the bread and butter of politics—the hospital fund-raiser, the Rotary speech—and goes about it with dignity and grace. He feels compelled to teach the lesson of the 1960s to the next generation of constituents because he says the mission now is the same as 25 years ago: "to build in America a truly interracial democracy."

Lewis has begun his day at another school, whose white students knew nothing of life in the 1950s, with "whites-only" drinking fountains and segregated movie houses, where blacks sat in the balcony while whites took seats on the main floor.

But the students at Rich's Academy have heard about the lunch-counter sit-ins and Freedom Rides. They are intent, watching curiously, listening carefully as Lewis describes a life that has spanned an era, traveling a long and rocky road.

Lewis speaks plainly and simply about his early life on a farm in rural Alabama. "My father was a very poor sharecropper, a tenant farmer," he says. "If someone had told me 30 years ago that I would be in the Congress, I would have said, 'You're crazy. You're out of your mind.'"

In the 1940s, a place in Congress was far out of reach for a poor black boy whose father could not even register to vote. Lewis wanted to be a preacher. On the farm, he was in charge of tending the family's chickens. The $18.95 incubator advertised in the Sears Roebuck catalogue was too expensive, so he marked the eggs with a pencil, pulling out those ready to hatch a little early so the hen would stay on the nest with the rest.

"I preached my first sermons to the chickens," Lewis says. With his bothers and sisters, he presided over baptisms of chicks, funerals of chickens. During that period of his life, he held his first nonviolent protest. He refused to eat when one of his charges showed up on the family dinner table.

This talk about saving the souls of little chicks is designed to bring a chuckle from the audience, and it does with these city-bred teenagers. It is a poignant tale, Lewis's way of setting the scene for the struggles to come.

Lewis is short and stocky. The scars from his beatings are visible on his balding pate. He has neither the good looks nor the great oratorical skills of fellow civil rights activist Julian Bond, whom he defeated in 1986. But he is outgoing and warm and carries himself with the quiet dignity of a Nelson Mandela.

For the students, Lewis recounts his first meeting with King, his education at American Baptist Theological Seminary in Nashville—Troy State College in Alabama, his first choice, did not admit blacks—and his rise to chairman of the Student Nonviolent Coordinating Committee, which worked around the South registering blacks to vote.

"We would dress up in a coat and tie," Lewis said of sit-ins in which he participated in Nashville and Greensboro. "We would sit there all day. Someone would spit on you. Someone would pour drinks on you. They would call the white demonstrators 'nigger lovers.' But no one would strike back."

The students sit transfixed, brows furrowed. They have heard about Selma, too, but not from Lewis, who led 600 civil rights marchers across the Edmund Pettus Bridge and into the history books.

The march was organized to draw attention to the murder of activist Jimmie Lee Jackson, shot during a voting-rights demonstration. But as the marchers crossed the bridge, they faced a sea of blue, Alabama's finest. The troopers used tear gas, nightsticks and electric cattle prods to end the march. Lewis was beaten and left unconscious.

"To this day I do not know how I got back to the church," he said. "I thought I would die. I was gasping for my last ounce of breath."

One of the remarkable things about Lewis is that he is not bitter about his experiences. He is patient and tenacious, but not bitter.

In Congress, Lewis has yet to establish himself as a major player. His committee assignments—Interior and Insular Affairs, and Public Works and Transportation—are not high profile. Moving up, he said, is a matter of time and seniority.

"I used to say to my colleagues in the movement: You must pace yourself, take the long view," he said.

Although a member of the Congressional Black Caucus, Lewis has maintained his independence from it and said he hopes that there will be no need for such an organization someday. "The Democratic Party has been divided and splintered into so many pieces," he said. "Somehow, we have to get to the point so we can forget about race and color."

That point does not seem as near as Lewis, ever the optimist, would like. As the original marchers return to Selma this week to note the 25th anniversary of the voting rights march, Selma again is alive with racial divisiveness, this time about education, an issue that Lewis said is as critical as voting rights was in 1965.

At Rich's Academy, Lewis also tells students that there still is distance to cover on that long and rocky road. He admonishes them to become involved and help with the causes of the 1990s—education, housing, health care. The students express uncertainty about what they can do.

"Register and vote," Lewis tells them quietly. "People died to give you the right to vote."

36. How a Member Decides

Rep. Lee Hamilton

Lee Hamilton was first elected to the House from Indiana in 1964 and has been there ever since. One of the most respected and thoughtful of House Democrats, Hamilton is the ranking Democrat on the Foreign Affairs Committee and chairs the Permanent Select Intelligence Committee. The *Almanac of American Politics*, a highly regarded reference book on national politics and the Congress, notes that Hamilton "is one of those relatively rare members who can sway a vote in committee or on the floor just because members, of both parties, respect his judgment and fairness." In this report to his constituents, which was reprinted in the *Congressional Record*, Hamilton identifies several factors that affect the vote of a member of Congress.

A question that has intrigued me is how various Members of Congress decide how to vote. Members cast about 400 votes a year on the most difficult and controversial issues on the national agenda. My impression is that in deciding how to vote, Members weigh three goals: they want to make good policy, gain respect inside Congress, and get re-elected. It is impossible to name all the factors that influence the vote of individual Members. They must balance many changing pressures, expectations and demands every day. In the end, of course, they must rely on their own judgment about the merits of a particular bill or amendment, but that judgment is influenced by many factors. Among the most important are these:

Constituents

Constituents are the most important influence on a Member's voting decision. Whether Members are agents of their constituents' wishes or free to exercise their own judgment is a classic question in a representative democracy. Members have a duty to listen carefully to their constituents and to consider their views. After all, Members are not representatives if their actions bear little or no relationship to the views of constituents. Members may not always vote with the views of a majority of their constituents because in the absence of a referendum they cannot be certain what they think. But all Members ask themselves on each vote where their constituents stand on the issue. On those issues where the constituency expressed strong preferences, the Member is almost certain to favor them. Representatives who fail to reflect generally the views of their constituents will soon need other work. If they vote in a way their constituents may not approve, they will explain their votes in terms their constituents will respect, even if they do not agree.

Colleagues

Members learn to identify certain colleagues whose judgment they respect on particular issues. Other Members are important sources of information because, as professional politicians, they will tailor their advice to a Member's needs; they are often well-informed on the issue; and they are available at the time of the vote. Members do not seek advice from just any colleague. Instead they seek out those who over time have earned the respect and attention of their colleagues. Members also pay special attention to the other Members of their state delegation—as well as to state and local officials—because they share common interests and problems.

Lobbies

Interest groups are neither the most nor least important influence on Congress. Lobbyists can help or hinder a Member's work. They can provide members with easily digested information and innovative proposals.

They can identify allies, help round up votes, and aid election campaigns. They can provide or withhold campaign contributions, support or oppose a Member's reelection. Members ignore lobbyists at their peril.

The Executive

The President is, in many respects, the chief legislator. He and his Vice President are the only officials elected by all the people. Although the President's lobbying activities do not differ significantly from those of other groups, the President's prestige, or standing in the polls, is often persuasive to Members. At the same time, partisan distrust may create opposition to the President's position. With his excellent sources of information, his ability to initiate legislation, to appeal to all Americans, and to set the legislative agenda, the President has formidable power in the legislative process. But that power no longer yields the unique advantage it once did, as other sources of information—the Congressional Budget Office, the Congressional Research Service, the Office of Technology Assessment, for example—have grown in respect and influence.

Party Leadership

Political party leadership has much less effect on Members' decisions. Members of Congress do not hear often from their party leaders about specific votes on legislation. They do hear often from the leadership of their party in the Congress, i.e. the Speaker and the Majority and Minority leaders. The leadership does have resources besides gentle persuasion. It controls the scheduling of bills, parliamentary rulings, choice committee assignments and prerogatives, and it can choose, within limits, who is recognized to speak on the floor. The effects of these tools are not unimportant, and on close votes are often decisive.

Media

News media may have their greatest effect on Congress as agenda setters. By focusing attention on a particular issue, they can get the American people and the Congress to deal with it. The stories the media emphasize, and how those stories are treated, have a real effect on which issues Congress considers and which it puts off. In considering a vote, Members must anticipate how that vote will be played by the media.

Staff

It is a mistake to underestimate the importance of congressional staff in the legislative process. Because of Members' hectic schedules, they rely on staff to help them evaluate legislation. Today's staffers usually have a good appreciation of political processes, but their main strength is substantive technical knowledge. As a result, staffers have become important actors in the legislative arena. The greater their expertise, the more Members rely on them, and the more they shape the legislative product.

Members of Congress vote several times every legislative day on diverse and complex issues. Usually they have more information than they can assimilate, so they need and seek help. They cannot be experts on every bill that comes before the Congress. If all of the factors on which a Member ordinarily relies agree, the decision is easy. If these factors point to opposite conclusions, the decision becomes difficult. It is then that decision-making becomes a very personal matter. When the voting clock is running down the Member must make a decision. The Member knows that in our democracy he or she alone will be held accountable for it.

37. Congressional Ethics

Otis Pike

In recent years public approval of Congress has steadily deteriorated, according to polls that indicate little faith in the integrity of our nation's elected representatives. Otis Pike, a former Representative of New York (1961 to 1979) and a sometime journalist since his voluntary retirement from the House, discusses the public's low regard for Congress, especially its legislative ethics. In this article, which was first presented as his testimony before the Special House Task Force on Ethics in 1989 and reprinted that year in the *Congressional Record*, Pike contends that Congress faces a much greater problem than ethics; it lacks the courage to tackle the serious problems facing the nation. Only when it musters the political will to do so will it truly "be held in high regard or deemed ethical."

Ethics has replaced mom, the flag and apple pie as something one must not only be for these days, but appear to be doing something about. We may not be able to define it: we aren't sure whether the word is singular or plural, but we know it when we see it. Ethics is, or are, "in" and must have their, or its, day. So did the pursuit of witches in New England and heretics in Spain, both embraced by gentlemen so positive that they were uniquely qualified to oversee the morals of others that they had no qualms about inflicting excruciating pain on those others. Always, of course, in order to make them better people and the world a better place.

In the book *Congress and the Nation* vol. 1, published by Congressional Quarterly and covering the years 1945-64, the word "ethics" cannot be found in the index. It is not in the Constitution. That is not to say that the Government does not constitutionally regulate morals. It requires businesses to close on Sunday, then changes its mind. It decrees that booze is unlawful, then changes its mind. It establishes red light districts, moves them, then closes them. It makes gambling illegal—and conducts lotteries.

When you legislate ethics, then, you are shooting at a moving target. Anybody that can spend 10 or 20 years pondering what to do about easy issues like acid rain or where to dump nuclear waste may not be able to give enough lead to targets that have puzzled all the religions of the world for millenia.

Take a concept like "conflict of interest." At one end of the spectrum it is easy. Pure black. You don't take bribes. You go to jail if you do. It has been a crime since before there was a Congress. It gets grayer. You don't take a political contribution in exchange for a promise to do something. The old "quid pro quo" test. How about a promise to consider something? To keep the door open? To answer the phone? Do you take political contributions from PACs that want something? They wouldn't exist if they didn't want something. At the other end of the spectrum it is almost pure white. Your job is conflicts of interest. Do you consider, first, on any given issue your conscience, your country, your district, your party, or the next election? The easy answer is that you never let self-interest interfere with the common good. Easy answers are best couched in elegant words that mean whatever you want them to.

If you have an account in a savings and loan, is it in your self-interest to bail them out? Yes. Should you vote on it? Yes. If you own stock in a savings and loan, should you vote for their bailout? I say "no," but I'm not sure. I would be surer if it were a 1,000 shares than if it were 10. If you had to paint a portrait of ethics, you would need many shades of gray.

So, to mix a couple of metaphors, you take this fast moving gray target and try to write rules that will hit it. That is the easy part.

Then, you ask an institution that was wholly designed to accommodate partisans to enforce those rules without being partisan. You are asking pigs to fly. On July 30, 1979, there was a recorded vote on a motion to table a resolution calling for the expulsion of Representative Charles C. Diggs Jr. (D-Mich.). The vote was 205 to 197. The resolution to expel was partisan, the motion to table was partisan, the vote was partisan. In essence, Republicans voted 10 to 1 to expel, Democrats voted 3 to 1 not to. That's partisan.

In their proceedings against Jim Wright,* I believe the ethics committee did the very best they could; did their darndest to be judicious. No one, however, can look at the pattern of votes on the various allegations without seeing some partisanship. If the matter even reaches the floor of the House, anyone who believes that Democrats and Republicans will vote the same way believes that donkeys and elephants, at least, can fly.

I believe that the morals and ethics of Congress are high. Democratic ethics are no higher than Republican ethics and Republican ethics are not higher than Democratic ethics. A wholly political institution, however, will never make wholly non-political decisions in tough cases.

That is by no means the worst part. You were not sent here to peek through the windows of each other's private lives. You weren't even sent here to appear ethical. You were sent here to write laws and resolve problems. Your preoccupation with each other's ethics is preventing you from doing your jobs. It is taking too much of your time and worse, it is creating an atmosphere and an institution in which suspicion, bitterness, personal dislikes and private vendettas make cooperative efforts in writing laws increasingly difficult. That is serious.

The founding fathers didn't write into the Constitution any requirement that legislators, presidents or judges be ethical, they had enough faith in the people to elect good officials. They did write in provisions for removing bad ones. We have less faith in the people now, which is fair, for after a generation of legislating ethics they have a lot less faith in us. In 1965 a Lou Harris poll found that the public approved of Congress 64 to 25. In 1987 a poll by U.S. News and World Report showed that a majority of those polled believed that many or most Government officials took bribes.

Unhappy with our 64 to 25 favorable rating, we went to work. In 1968 the Congress broke with the system that had worked fairly well for 179 years and wrote its first financial disclosure law. We hoped the public would hold us in higher esteem if we stripped, financially, in public. We were rewarded by being held in the same lofty regard as other strippers and instead of applause heard only the ancient and endless cry of the voyeurs, "Take it all off."

1976 was a terrible year. Congressman Wayne Hayes (D-Ohio) put a girl friend of minimal secretarial skill on the payroll, married someone else, and the girl friend blew him away in the *Washington Post*. It was

* Wright resigned from the House in June 1989 in part because of ethical issues.

juicy. Andrew J. Hinshaw (R-Cal.) was convicted on two counts of bribery. Henry Helstoski (D-N.J.) was indicated for taking bribes to introduce immigration bills. Allan T. Howe (D-Utah) was found guilty of soliciting sex from two undercover policewomen posing as prostitutes. A steady dribble of leaks from the Justice Department named seven Congressmen as having gotten large gifts from a South Korean businessman named Tongsun Park. Former Representative Jim Hastings (R-N.Y.) was indicated for having taken kickbacks from his staff. The law enforcement authorities had acted in every one of those cases, but the outcry was loud. We had to get in the act too.

The Congress has passed a code of conduct for Federal employees in 1958. Charley Bennett wrote it and it was just grand. Eleven sentences. In 1977 a committee headed by David Obey (D-Wisc.) wrote infinitely more comprehensive rules of behavior that had only one salutary effect of which I am aware. They drove me out of Congress and enabled me to earn a refreshing amount of money. The key word is earn. Charley Bennett's 11 lines turned into a code so tangled that Mr. Obey recently referred to it as a "thicket" and so confusing that he recently accused the Ethics Committee of not understanding their own rules.

Have they made the House a more ethical place? They have not. In the 10 years before 1977, 12 Members of Congress were indicted and convicted or pleaded guilty to serious crimes. Three pleaded guilty to misdemeanors. In the 10 years after 1977, 17 Members of Congress pleaded guilty to or were convicted of serious crimes and two were allowed to take counseling on sex offenses. The charges against the 19 post-ethics transgressors ran the gamut from driving offenses through sex offenses to very serious charges of accepting bribes. They included members of both political parties. They had one thing in common. With one exception, every convicted criminal who had been here in 1977 had voted for the ethics code. The one exception was on the committee that wrote it. All of the charges were prosecuted by Federal or local prosecutors who are always delighted to bring charges against Republicans or Democrats alike with even-handed non-partisan fervor.

Are the rules ethical? Well, yes, but they are largely political in heritage. They were created because of public revulsion at the Watergate, Wayne Hays, and other congressional scandals. The concept that unearned income is ethical but earned income must be limited reverses the ethics of Horatio Alger and at least the Democratic Party. It was a political decision, made necessary by the fact that there were already so many millionaires in Congress that they couldn't have passed the bill if they had limited unearned income. They treated rich people better than poorer people, which is a peculiar ethical fixation.

For political reasons, proper loopholes were created for important people. The majority leader of the House and the chairman of the Rules Committee and some other mavens had written books, so book royalties were exempt. Since leaving Congress, undefeated and unindicted, I have made some money writing a syndicated column. Earned money, thus unethical. If I had taken the identical columns, bound them into a book and collected royalties on them I could have rendered the same words ethical. Nonsense.

Members of Congress should be able to write books or teach or farm or practice law or medicine or engage in any lawful activity in which they engaged before coming to Congress. They should disclose where their money comes from and trust the people to judge their behavior. You are not going to get, or deserve, the esteem of the public by treating yourselves as second-class citizens or by treating wealthy Members better than non-wealthy Members.

There are very fundamental reasons for this. Your rules are not bad because they are political rules, politically enforced or because they are incomprehensible or because you are so preoccupied with them that you can't get around to doing your jobs. It is worse than that. All over America thousands of good and honorable people look at the environment you have created here and decide they would never be interested in entering that environment. They take pride in their own morals and ethics; they value their privacy; they do not undress in public.

There is a gentle book that has been on the best seller list for a long time. It is *All I Really Need To Know I Learned in Kindergarten,* by Robert Fulgham. The title story reminds us that we learn the rules by which we conduct our lives very early. We bring them with us to Congress. We tell the truth about our allies and our opponents. We don't cheat or steal or take bribes or tolerate people who do. We serve our country when our country needs us and carry our ideals and loyalties and ethics in our hearts and not on our sleeves.

No one learns his ethics in Congress. No one needs to be told by his colleagues what is right and fair and honorable. There are more than enough criminal statutes by which to prosecute those who violate the standards of our society.

Ethics is not as great a problem with Congress as is courage. Your ethics rules have emasculated you. Not all of you: a few are still willing to stand up and say you deserve a pay raise or vote against a defense bill or for a tax increase or vote against Israel when you are convinced she is wrong or say "no" to any powerful lobby. . . . When you cut a Member off from the honorable work he did before he came here, made him burn his bridges, made him have to keep his job to feed his family you sapped his courage. He has to get re-elected. This makes him less courageous—and less ethical.

This Nation was built by men who couldn't, and wouldn't have lived by your rules. They were terrible men who drank, caroused and gambled. Some kept mistresses; some were worse. They connived and made deals and some grew rich in office. Robert Morris of Pennsylvania, who the old text books called the financier of the Revolution was asked to get ammunition for Washington's Army. He did, through his own trading company and wrote, "There has never been so fair an opportunity for making a large fortune since I have been conversant in the world." Daniel Webster said the birthplace of the Revolution was a tavern in Boston. The marines were born in a tavern.

You can talk about ethics forever and pass more rules and reveal yourselves until all of your and your spouse's finances, food, drink, sex, religion, clothing, vacations and the hours and minutes and place of your arising and retiring are public records. You will never be held in high regard or deemed ethical while you say you can't balance a budget unless a constitutional amendment makes you; while you accept gloriously optimistic economic projections rather than deal with real ones; while you write a Gramm-Rudman bill to require a balanced federal budget and then spend days finding ways to get around it; while you let one man make $550 million a year while thousands sleep in the streets.

Former Ways and Means Committee Chairman Wilbur Mills (D-Ark.) could have been booted out of Congress. He was an alcoholic and he fell for a stripper named Fanne Foxe; he chased her right up on the stage. His ethics might have been deemed a trifle too shabby for a Member of this institution, but he would never have tolerated the fun and games and smoke and mirrors and moving costs off-budget and from year to year and annual deficits and growing debt that have transferred us from the biggest creditor to the biggest debtor nation in the world.

I will close with the words of Abigail Adams, who at the birth of our Nation said, "We have too many high sounding words, and too few actions that correspond with them."

38. In Defense of a Messy Congress

Albert R. Hunt

Although Congress often looks inept, argues Albert R. Hunt, it does reflect the country; that is, national divisions and conflicts on the fundamental issues of the day are typically mirrored in Congress. In this article published in *The Washingtonian* magazine in 1982, Hunt concedes that some reforms may be needed, but that sweeping changes in

Congress would do more harm than good. This viewpoint, although not shared by all analysts, underscores the theme that Congress's purported vices are often its virtues. Hunt is national political and congressional correspondent for the *Wall Street Journal*.

In early 1975 a group of newly elected House Democrats struck up a conversation with [Rep.] Jimmy Burke of Massachusetts. The contrast was stark: the young, ambitious Watergate babies, eager to reform or even replace the political system they so successfully ran against, and Jimmy Burke, the cynical, cigar-chomping old party warhorse.

Jimmy Burke offered some unsolicited advice to the fresh-faced newcomers. There is a simple formula for longevity in the House of Representatives, he explained: "Vote for every tax cut and every spending program and then vote against any increase in the debt ceiling."

One of the freshmen was incredulous. "Why, if everyone did that," he righteously declared, "the whole system would break down."

"What?" replied Jimmy Burke, removing the cigar from his mouth. "You think this place is on the level?"

Jimmy Burke is gone, but his conviction that Congress isn't on the level remains. Editorial writers lament the shortcomings of our national legislature; it is, they tell us, cowardly, chaotic, and crooked. Presidents enjoy railing against Congress, too. With [the 1984] election approaching, Ronald Reagan, that great communicator, may coin some of the more memorable pejorative phrases. Curiously, he'll have allies on Capitol Hill. Increasingly, members of Congress, who run against the institution to get elected, manage the neat trick of continuing to run against it while serving there.

The failings of Congress even bridge the usual gap between the so-called experts and the man on the street. "Professional critics maintain that it [Congress] is too obese, arthritic, parochial, nonresponsive, overresponsive," writes Republican Senator William Cohen of Maine in a forthcoming book. "Even the average citizen, who does not possess a doctorate in political science, is frustrated or disappointed in the workings of Congress."

Public-opinion surveys are devastating. On the issue of honesty and ethics, last September's Gallup poll rated the lawmakers below stockbrokers, newspaper reporters, and funeral directors.

The bill of particulars:

■ Congress is inept. It took years after the 1973 Arab oil embargo for the House and Senate to enact any energy legislation, and then it pleased almost nobody. Speed isn't Congress's forte. When the legislators a few years ago were given a month to pass an important measure, television commentator David Brinkley observed: "It is widely believed in Washington that it would take Congress 30 days to make instant coffee work."

■ Congress is bulky and bureaucratic. Today there are almost 31,000 people working for Congress, about the size of the regular Argentine Navy—and some would say about as competent. Since 1946, the annual appropriations for Congress have soared 2,278 percent, or six times faster than the rate of inflation.

■ Congress is avaricious. Almost any powerful special-interest group with lots of campaign cash seems to find a receptive audience in the current Congress, which some call "the best money can buy." Representative David Obey, a Wisconsin Democrat, warns: "We're beginning to look a lot like the state legislatures in the days of the railroads' and mining companies' domination—bought and intimidated." Not to mention the "criminal class" publicized in Abscam.

■ Congress is shallow, more preoccupied with publicity than policy. Representative Barber Conable, a New York Republican and one of the more thoughtful members of the House, cringes at the political clichés he frequently hears around the Hill: "Never adopt a political philosophy that won't go on a bumper sticker," or "If you have to explain anything, you're in trouble." Conversely, a lot of attention is paid to image-making. The 535 senators and representatives churn out about 15,000 press releases a year.

■ Congress is craven. In the House, many of the newer, supposedly brighter members are called "bed-wetters" by their more senior colleagues because of their perpetual nervousness over tough issues. "There seems to be a terminal timidity in Congress these days," worries Richard Fenno of Rochester University, one of the knowledgeable political scientists studying Congress.

■ Congress has lousy priorities. "We spend more time discussing pay raises than we do nuclear war," laments Senator Patrick Leahy, the Vermont Democrat.

■ Congress lacks the legislative giants of yesteryear, some people suggest. Dean Rusk [former secretary of state] has spoken nostalgically of the congressional "whales" of the past: Sam Rayburn, Robert Taft, Lyndon Johnson, Richard Russell, Wilbur Mills, and Everett Dirksen. These men exercised power and made the system work—in sharp contrast to the little fish of today, it is said.

With all these problems, serious people suggest the need for wide-ranging changes on Capitol Hill. Bold moves, they argue, are necessary if an important institution is to function effectively in this complex world. The underlying premise here is that as the problems have gotten greater, the performance of Congress has gotten worse.

Few are better qualified to assess this premise than Bryce Harlow, who directed congressional relations for Presidents Eisenhower and Nixon and was a close confidant of [the late Speaker of the House] Sam Rayburn. He also is a very wise man.

"This Congress isn't performing more poorly ... or much better ... than most in the past," Bryce Harlow says. "Congress meanders when the American people are indecisive. It dawdles when the American people don't care. It gets nervous and frightened when the people are riled up. And it acts when the people demand action." He concludes: "Congress almost magically mirrors what the American people want."

Congress, or most any legislative body, is reactive by nature; it tends to respond most forcefully when there is strong executive leadership. But with a more complex society and more vocal interest groups, the demands are greater. "We are asking so much more of Congress now," notes Republican Representative [now Defense Secretary] Dick Cheney of Wyoming. "That makes comparisons very misleading."

Still, some of the current criticism is tame by historical standards. After Congress enacted its first pay raise in 1816—from $6 per diem to $1,500 a year—the voters threw out two-thirds of the members of the House in the next election. Fifteen years later, Alexis de Tocqueville, the fabled Frenchman, was anything but awed by the U.S. House of Representatives. The people's body, he charged, had a "vulgar demeanor.... The eye frequently does not discover a man of celebrity within its walls."

As for the lack-of-whales theory, Charles Ferris, who as chief aide to Mike Mansfield played a prominent role in the Senate throughout much of the 1960s and '70s, says: "A lot of them looked like giants when they were surrounded by pygmies; overall, there are more talented people around today." Similarly, Robert Peabody, a Johns Hopkins political scientist specializing in congressional leadership, says: "These legends get bigger and bigger with every passing year. My guess is if you look at the current Congress, there are several whales sprouting. In a decade, we'll be talking about the Howard Bakers or the Tip O'Neills or the Bob Doles or the Sam Nunns, among others, as whales. Or at least as extremely big fish."

Before judging how well the old whales ran affairs of state, a few facts are helpful. In the 86th Congress, with almost a two-to-one majority, the vaunted Sam Rayburn still was able to override only two of President Eisenhower's 24 vetoes. It was under the leadership of Everett Dirksen, Richard Russell, and Wilbur Mills that the Vietnam War started and the seeds of economic catastrophe were planted by trying to finance both the war and the Great Society without raising revenues to pay for them.

So are the earlier-mentioned criticisms not valid? They are, though most are exaggerated. The simple fact is that Congress isn't *supposed* to operate neatly, efficiently, or expeditiously. Any system of checks and balances has built-in tensions and rough edges. Bismarck * said the two

* Otto von Bismarck (1815-1898), first chancellor of the German Empire.

things one never should watch being made are sausage and legislation. And he was talking about a legislative process much tidier than ours.

Yet somehow Congress not only muddles through, but usually responds pretty well to clear-cut crises. Witness the Depression, World War II, the civil-rights battles of the 1960s, Watergate, and perhaps the Reagan economic revolution of the 1980s.

There are ways to improve Congress, to create needed oversight, to reduce the role of money in politics, to curb the deficiencies of staff and a crazy-quilt committee system, and to make the process more thoughtful. These all are and should be discussed and debated. But the greatest threat lies in responding to the particular passions of the moment with sweeping changes that almost surely will produce an inferior institution. Accordingly, the more prominent reforms that should be avoided are:

1. *Don't turn to a European-style parliamentary system.* Two years ago in *Foreign Affairs* magazine, Lloyd Cutler, the Washington lawyer and counselor to President Carter, wrote a provocative article entitled "To Form a Government." Mr. Cutler argued it is almost impossible to govern in America today; the choices are more difficult than in earlier times, there is more interdependence on the rest of the world, and power is too diffused on Capitol Hill. "In Parliamentary terms, one might say, under the U.S. Constitution, it is now not feasible to 'form a government,' " he wrote.

Without endorsing any, Cutler offered several constitutional changes that he suggested might make governing more feasible. All have their roots in European models. For instance, House terms would be extended to four years and members would run on a ticket with the President and Vice President. (Logically, this should include the Senate, too, but as Cutler admitted, "No one has challenged the Gods of the Olympian Senate by proposing to reduce their six-year terms.") Other possibilities would allow the President to select half his Cabinet from Congress and provide mechanisms for calling new federal elections.

On closer examination, most of these suggestions would lead to more, not less, instability. The European models don't cry out to be imitated. "Italy's parliamentary system, of course, has had great success in forming governments—several dozen, at least, in the post-war era," political scientists Thomas Mann and Norman Ornstein wrote in rebuttal to Cutler. And the strife and strain in our system, they noted, still "in many ways compares favorably with Britain, where dramatic policy reversals often follow a change in government: Witness the Conservative and Labour governments' struggle over nationalizing, denationalizing, and renationalizing the same industries."

Most worrisome is that, with our diverse population, a parliamentary-type system almost surely would result in a proliferation of parties. "I don't think there is any way we could keep our existing party arrangement in a parliamentary system," says Representative Thomas Foley, a Washington state Democrat and [now] House [Speaker]. "The Democratic party would break up into three or four parties and the Republicans into at least two." There is nothing in the Constitution about the need for two, and only two, political parties. But this system has created order and stability. If Congress, racked by regional factions and special-interest caucuses, is splintered today, just imagine trying to form a coalition with five or six parties.

2. *Don't change the length of House terms.* The arguments that Cutler and others advance for a longer House term are essentially twofold: First, House members spend considerably more time running for office than legislating once they get there. And a representative barely takes his or her seat before every issue is weighed with an eye to the next election. "You can't deal with an issue like Social Security until we have longer terms," says Representative Obey. When one sees lawmakers start gearing up for re-election in the summer of odd-numbered years or hears thoughtful men like David Obey or Tom Foley advocate longer terms, it causes a sympathetic reaction.

But the drawbacks are more striking. "The problems of this country aren't going to be resolved by having fewer elections; the American people are changing their minds about three times a week now," says Barber Conable. Bryce Harlow has argued against changing the two-year term for 25 years, first against his old boss, President Eisenhower. "What I said then is even more true today," he says. "These are times we should get the government closer to the people, not further away."

Former Democratic representative Abner Mikva of Illinois, now a federal judge, had more reason than most to hate two-year terms: He won reelection in a Republican-oriented district by fewer than 700 votes in each of his last two elections. Yet he was a great defender of biennial congressional campaigns, insisting that they were among "the great educative experiences" of his political life because they "forced constructive dialogue on very important issues."

Further, if the people hadn't had the opportunity to vent their feelings about Vietnam and Watergate in the elections of 1966 or 1974, we might have suffered a political nervous breakdown. Finally, however, there is one clear refutation of the premise that longer terms produce a more thoughtful, far-sighted legislative body—the United States Senate.

3. *Don't limit terms or legislative assignments.* A decade ago, it was argued that the most important corrective for Congress's ills was mandatory retirement—either a limit of twelve years in Congress or forced retirement at age 70. At the time, Congress did resemble a geriatric ward. Of the 21 committee chairmen in the House, three were over 80, five others were over 70, and four more were in their late sixties; the average age was 67. In the Senate, six of the seventeen regular committee chairmen were septuagenarians.

It is hard to remember what a burning issue this was in 1972; in 1982 one of the hottest political properties in the Democratic party is 82-year-old Claude Pepper, the Florida congressman. In the House today there are as many chairmen in their forties as in their seventies (three each); in the Senate only two chairmen are over 70 and five are under 50. Like many other problems, this one corrected itself.

A thornier issue is whether to limit service on particular committees. The argument has its attractions. Members often become enamored of the agencies and programs they are supposed to be checking and balancing—Armed Services, Agriculture, Ways and Means, and Finance are good examples. Forced turnovers might jolt some of the cozy arrangements among the "unholy trinity" of lawmakers, bureaucrats, and lobbyists.

Along with the fact that lawmakers will never buy this reform, there are substantive problems, too. As government becomes more complex, there is a strong argument for having more experienced hands dealing with difficult issues. "Revolving terms is an attractive concept, a little more like the citizen legislator," acknowledges Professor Fenno. "But the problem is that most new guys then just wouldn't be any match for the executive-branch bureaucracy."

4. *Don't repeal most of the congressional reforms of the past decade.* A widely held myth is that Congress, in an overreaction to Watergate, went on an orgy of reform that has crippled the legislative process. Several years ago *Los Angeles Times* columnist Ernest Conine penned a typical complaint: "Much of what is wrong with Congress results from well-intended but disastrous attempts at reform." He suggested eliminating many of these "goody two-shoes" reforms.

But most of the important institutional changes, which primarily affected the House, were not a reaction to Watergate; they predated that scandal by several years. With one or two exceptions, there is little evidence that these reforms have incapacitated the legislative process.

In 1973, both houses moved to end the practice of writing legislation behind closed doors. The result of these "sunshine" actions has not been to produce better—or worse—legislation. But it does quiet public cynicism that something sinister is going on behind closed doors and perhaps even permits a slightly better understanding of the political process.

Another important reform ended the practice of secret votes on amendments in the House. No doubt that makes it easier to pass some mischievous and misguided amendments that appeal to zealous interests and are therefore difficult to vote against publicly. But in the [1990s] does anyone seriously think it feasible to go back to secret voting?

One of the most fundamental reforms in the House subjected all committee chairmen and top subcommittee chairmen to ratification by the Democratic caucus. This single change has practically ended arrogant abuses of power by unaccountable chairmen; they know a majority of their party colleagues could unseat them. A prime example is Mississippi's Jamie Whitten, for almost 30 years an autocratic chairman of the Agriculture Appropriations subcommittee. In 1979, he became chairman of the full Appropriations Committee, and it is widely agreed that these days he is a model of fairness and responsiveness to his fellow Democrats. Actually, it would be a good idea to have Senate committee chairmen subject to private-ballot approval in a party caucus. This is a reform that works better than anyone dreamed.

"The old days were marked by most members being shut out of meaningful participation in the legislative process," notes Richard Conlon, director of the liberal House Democratic Study Group. "We have created a more open, a fairer, and a better legislative process."

5. *Don't look for brighter or better members of Congress.* Frustrated analysts and citizens invariably decide that Congress would work better if only we could get smarter, more dedicated public servants. What's called for, they say, is the best and brightest. But judging by academic pedigree, intelligence, or knowledge of issues, the recent Congresses are among the brightest since the early days of the republic. And that may be a problem.

"The newer bright and able members care about *everything*," Angus S. King Jr., a former Senate staffer, wrote in *Newsweek*. "They seem congenitally incapable of specializing in the old sense; they might still get especially involved in particular issues, but they also reserve the right to study, debate, submit amendments to, and make independent judgments on every bill that comes across their desks. In short, too many dedicated public servants gum up the works."

What Congress needs is not better leaders but more followers. With a few more followers—call them hacks—not only might the place work a little better, but it would also be more fun. Competence may be up, but the color quotient in Congress is down considerably from a decade ago.

There are some modest changes that might improve Congress. None is a panacea, and the legislative results on most major issues would be unaffected. Still, here are half a dozen improvements that would make the institution better:

1. *Publicly finance congressional campaigns and curb political-action committees.* No single move would do more to improve the perception, and perhaps the performance, of Congress than an overhaul of the campaign-financing system. Sweeping changes are called for only in rare moments.

"The special interests, with their PACs, dominate the legislative process as never before," charges Fred Wertheimer, president of Common Cause. From the other side, Robert McCandless, a leading Washington lawyer and lobbyist, admits: "I won't even take a client now unless he's willing to set up a political-action committee and participate in the [campaign contribution] process."

The power of political-action committees must be checked; Democratic Senators Sam Nunn of Georgia and [now Governor] Lawton Chiles of Florida, two moderate lawmakers, propose outlawing PACs altogether. Short of that, several reins are possible: One is to lower the maximum amount any political committee can give in one election from $5,000 to $2,500, while boosting the maximum amount for individual contributions from $1,000 to $5,000. An overall limit also ought to be imposed on the amount any congressional candidate can take from all PACs, perhaps $75,000 for House members and a sliding scale for senators based on the number of voters in their states.

Then, some system of public financing is essential for general elections. The government could match private contributions of $100 or less and set a reasonable spending ceiling. If a rich candidate refused to take the monies, and thus abide by the spending ceiling, the opponent would still get the public funds but also would be freed of the ceiling. And the government-licensed television stations should be required to offer some free advertising time to candidates with proven support.

Numerous arguments are raised against public financing and a campaign spending ceiling. Such a system would amount to an incumbent-protection act, critics say, because challengers need more money to overcome the advantages of incumbency. It would further erode the power of political parties, they add. And better-heeled Republicans argue that their interests are better served by the current system.

A few facts are worth noting, however. In the last three House elections, [98] percent of incumbents have won general-election contests. In the last election, 305 incumbents outspent their opponents, while only 30 challengers outspent incumbents. If public financing were an incumbent-protection act, it would have been enacted years ago by incumbents; instead, they keep the current system, which truly is an incumbent's delight. (Two presidential campaigns have been financed with public monies; both times the incumbent lost.)

As for harming political parties, how can any system be more detrimental than the current one? With the advent of polling and television, political parties never will be what they once were. But the only way they can offer any protection or political umbrella is by reducing the influence of special interests.

2. *Restructure congressional committees.* "Congress in its committee rooms is Congress at work," Woodrow Wilson wrote almost 100 years ago. Today, Congress in its committee rooms is also Congress in confusion. The committees and subcommittees—184 in the House, 136 in the Senate—are inefficient and duplicative. In almost every major area—energy, health, transportation, welfare—there are dozens of overlapping jurisdictions crippling efforts to reach consensus legislation.

In the 95th Congress, a computer study found there were 11,000 separate occasions on which House members were expected to be in two or more committee meetings simultaneously. During the same period, a House study found that with all these responsibilities, the typical House member had an average of eleven minutes a day to read. This affects downtown Washington, too. During a five-week period early this year, Federal Reserve Board Chairman Paul Volcker had to testify before seven congressional committees.

This system is crazy, but changing it is almost impossible. A poll of House members in 1979 found that 70 percent felt the committee system needed "major repair" but that Congress lacked the will to do it. Serious efforts at reform—led by the knowledgeable Missouri Democrat Richard Bolling in the House and by former Democratic senator Adlai Stevenson in the Senate—were gutted. An overhaul still is needed in both bodies. But if that proves politically impossible, piecemeal reform is the only recourse. "It may make more sense to use a retail strategy than a wholesale strategy anyway," says political scientist Richard Fenno. If so, the most propitious starting places are the House Ways and Means Committee and the Senate Finance Committee. Their jurisdictions include not only all the tax laws, but also national health insurance, welfare, Social Security, unemployment compensation, and international trade. This legislative menu should be chopped in half.

3. *Reduce congressional staff by one fifth.* "Senators, I fear, are becoming annoying constitutional impediments to the staff," cracks Senator Patrick Leahy. "Someday, we may just allow the staff to vote and skip the middle man."

Aggressive staff members have dominated much of the legislative process, especially in the Senate, in recent years. Much of the initial growth was a justifiable reaction to the Nixon administration's cavalier treatment of Congress in the late 1960s and early '70s. "Congress really was deficient in expertise and too reliant on the executive branch," recalls political scientist Robert Peabody. "But they overcompensated."

Two caveats are in order here. There are hundreds of first-rate staffers on Capitol Hill. The staff of the Joint Committee on Taxation, serving the House Ways and Means and Senate Finance panels, is unsurpassed in its substantive knowledge of the tax system. The top leadership aides, from both parties and on both sides of the Capitol, are easily a match for the top executive-branch staff.

Further, the Senate Republicans deserve credit for actually reducing the size of personal staff by 3 percent and the size of committee staff by more than 14 percent since taking control last year. That's the first time in years that an actual reduction took place. Still, most of the cuts were concentrated in two or three obviously bloated staffs. (Strom Thurmond cut his Judiciary Committee staff to less than two thirds what it had been under Edward Kennedy.) And despite the cuts, the cost of running the Senate still climbed 10 percent this year.

But it's the nature of staff activity, even more than sheer size, that creates problems. As the American Enterprise Institute's Michael Malbin has convincingly argued, "staff entrepreneurialism" flourishes these days. All the pressures are for staffers to come up with new measures to make the boss (and the staffer) look good. The mushrooming staff, Malbin laments, has turned into a "mechanism for generating more work instead of helping Congress manage its existing work load better." Capitol Hill is full of specialists in narrow fields who devise schemes in absolute isolation from how they fit into the broader picture. Malbin also worries that the reliance on staff prevents members from communicating with one another, a depersonalization of the legislative process.

4. *Reduce the amount of legislation and encourage more oversight.* Even if staff entrepreneurs are cut, Congress still must find a way to legislate less. Last year 8,719 measures were introduced in the House and Senate, and 921 were passed. Together, the two bodies were in session for 1,732 hours.

At the same time, Congress does a miserable job of checking on the effectiveness of the programs it passes and the agencies it appropriates monies for. The tendency is to go for splashy headlines or quick political dividends. "There's no payoff for oversight," notes Representative Conable. "People like to build legislative monuments, they like to have their names on things. But oversight is an exhausting, detailed, thankless requirement."

It isn't easy to make oversight more rewarding. But it is possible to reduce the possibilities for legislative monuments. A modest way is to go to multi-year appropriations and authorization cycles. One such proposal, by Republican Senator William Roth of Delaware, would put the government on a two-year fiscal cycle, starting in January, of even-numbered years. The thirteen appropriations bills would be combined into a single two-year bill; the spending levels could be changed later by a two-thirds vote of both houses.

If authorizing and appropriating legislation were approved only every other year, it is legitimately feared, Congress would lose even more leverage to the executive branch. But that's where thorough, hard-nosed oversight—especially outside of Washington, examining how major programs actually affect people—would be a little more encouraged. The bonus would be that, with somewhat fewer legislative vehicles, lawmakers and their staffs would be dreaming up slightly less mischief.

5. *Sunset all entitlement . . . provisions.* . . . [S]unset laws—under which agencies or programs automatically expire unless positively renewed— are a promising approach if handled properly. Sunset provisions already have been applied to some new departments and agencies approved by

Congress. The next step should be to those areas not subject to ordinary review, namely the politically sensitive entitlement ... provisions.

Thus, all major entitlement programs, including Social Security, food stamps, Medicare, and guaranteed student loans, would have to be reauthorized periodically or expire. As it is, these measures, like old-man river, just keep rolling along unless Congress specifically moves to alter them. More often than not, they receive almost no scrutiny and become the "uncontrollables" that cause many of our budget woes.

6. *Devise a new way to set congressional pay.* In the relative scheme of inflation, jobs, war, and peace, how much money politicians are paid seems pretty insignificant. But few issues arouse more public passion or cause Congress to make a bigger fool of itself than pay and perquisites. Politically afraid of direct pay boosts, the members turn to surreptitious back-door methods such as last year's secretive move to give members an automatic tax write-off of up to $19,000 a year. The predictable public outcry ensued and this latest outrage was repealed.

The issue of congressional pay always has been a problem. Only [thirteen] times in its 193-year history has Congress voted itself a pay raise, and on almost every one of those occasions it drew fire. But—and this will infuriate otherwise rational people—the fact is that lawmakers today [require an adequate compensation.]

If some action isn't taken, there are two possible results: Either Congress will be populated mainly by millionaires with no sense of how the ordinary citizen copes, or the lawmakers will continue to hustle fees of up to $2,000 for speaking before every interest group around. [In 1990 and 1991, the House and Senate raised Member salaries to $125,100 and prohibited the acceptance of speaking fees as personal income.]

While few of the freshman lawmakers measure up to Henry Clay, who became Speaker his first year in the House (indeed, the new Senate Republican class is one of the most mediocre in years), there haven't been many more gifted newcomers recently than Representative Barney Frank, a Massachusetts Democrat, or Senator Slade Gorton, a Washington state Republican. And there's something inherently interesting about an institution where two of the most innovative economic thinkers—Jack Kemp and Bill Bradley—are exjocks.

The press has a duty to cover all the inadequacies of Congress. The place is inefficient and slow. But for those who argue for efficiency and speed, there is a simple test: for conservatives, were they pleased with the salad days of Great Society legislation in 1965 and 1966, and, for liberals, were they delighted with the Reagan budget and tax-cut blitzkrieg of 1981?

There have been times when Congress moved swiftly: the Gulf of Tonkin Resolution, later interpreted as a blank check for the Vietnam War; most of the Great Society programs; and [in 1981] the Senate Finance Committee approval, in four days, of a massive tax cut that reduced taxes over seven years by more than $1 trillion. A slow, measured pace may have its frustrations; it also has its rewards.

Finally, it's important not to lose sight of where the American people are. They want a tougher defense posture and a nuclear freeze. They want to cut government spending but retain higher benefits for Social Security or student loans. They are against federal regulation, but they want the government to make the air cleaner than ever. They are for economic growth, but they don't want to give most of the tax breaks to fat cats. Yet we are surprised, even dismayed, when Congress displays some of this same schizophrenia.

39. Crumbling Committees

Richard E. Cohen

Significant changes have taken place in the way Congress handles legislation. Until recently congressional committees and their leaders were all-powerful. Nowadays, according to Richard E. Cohen, the committees no longer exert as much influence and indeed may even be obstacles to getting things done. The new less formal procedures have altered power relationships, opening up many opportunities for rank-and-file members of Congress, but at the same time have led to some shortcomings in the legislative work product, concludes Cohen. A longtime reporter covering Congress for the Washington-based *National Journal*, where this article was published in 1990, Cohen was the recipient that year of the Everett McKinley Dirksen Congressional Leadership Research Center award for the best reporting on Congress.

Woodrow Wilson would hardly recognize Congress these days. "Congress in its committee rooms is Congress at work," the 32nd President, while a graduate student in 1885, wrote in *Congressional Government*. Wilson's book, still a political science classic a century later, talked of how Congress handled most legislation through a hierarchical system dominated by committee chairmen.

In recent years, however, internal changes have quietly revolutionized the sources of legislative power on Capitol Hill, eroding the influence of once all-powerful committees and of their bosses. Today, committees are often irrelevant or, worse yet, obstacles.

Congress has turned to these new arrangements, in part, to ease the lawmakers' burden. "The erosion of the committee process has made life more difficult in the Senate," said a former top Senate aide who is now a corporate lobbyist. But the informal, closed-door sessions that have resulted from this erosion "may be an attribute for Senators working in a fishbowl, where every lobbyist knows what is happening before he does."

There are other reasons for the new procedures, including the reforms of the 1970s that some blame for exacerbating committee turf battles and producing too many subcommittee chairmen. The move away from committee dominance is also driven by nonlegislative concerns: On some politically volatile issues, party leaders have simply concluded that the committee process doesn't work.

Here's how Congress, especially the Senate, has gone outside the committee system to handle key legislation during [1990]:

■ Efforts by White House and congressional budget summiteers to force deep cuts in the deficit have largely preempted the jurisdiction of congressional committees, notably the tax-writing panels. Although the members of the House Ways and Means and Senate Finance Committees would probably have a major voice in writing the details of any tax bill that emerges from a summit deal, they have already largely relinquished their authority to make the broad decisions. Their chairmen—Rep. Dan Rostenkowski, D-Ill., and Sen. Lloyd Bentsen, D-Texas—have consented to arrangements that allow a wider group of Members to craft tax policy. "All Members see [raising taxes] as a tar baby, and they want to get rid of it," a close observer said.

■ The Senate version of the clean air bill was drafted [in 1990] during a monthlong series of meetings convened and masterminded by Senate Majority Leader George J. Mitchell, D-Maine. The meetings were held in Mitchell's office, with key Senators and Bush Administration officials attending. This extraordinary step was taken after it had become clear that the Senate would never approve the legislation written by the Environment and Public Works Committee because of the opposition of the Administration and powerful private interests. Even in the House, where the bill was handled largely by the Energy and Commerce Committee, most of the major issues were resolved privately by the committee's leaders, sparing the full committee and the House from the potentially painful task of choosing sides.

■ The Senate version of a comprehensive anticrime bill, which was approved in July [1990], came to the floor despite the almost total absence of debate or formal action by the Judiciary Committee and with most of the important decisions made off the floor by party leaders. In the House where the rules give the majority party added leverage,

Judiciary Committee Democrats worked with party leaders on their own version of the bill, which has been sent to the floor.

■ The internal debate over campaign finance legislation began after Democrats and Republicans developed separate positions and sought—with little success—to bridge the differences in bipartisan negotiations. The House and Senate committees with jurisdiction over the issue have been largely bypassed.

■ The pay raise-ethics package Congress approved [in late 1989] was developed outside the formal committee structure by special leadership-controlled panels in each chamber.

A common feature of these informal arrangements is that all of them have taken shape behind closed doors, with party leaders controlling the process. In at least one aspect, therefore, Wilson's portrayal of Congress remains valid. "One very noteworthy result of this system," he wrote, "is to shift the theater of debate upon legislation from the floor of Congress to the privacy of the committee rooms."

Shifting Power

This topsy-turvy handling of major issues reflects some broader internal changes. They include the breakdown of the seniority system, an erosion of party discipline, the paralysis resulting from divided party control of the White House and Congress, increased partisan sloganeering and the growing influence of 30-second campaign spot commercials.

The new, less formal procedures have led to other shortcomings in the legislative work product. "The committee process is designed to weed out problems," J. Thomas Sliter, a former top Senate Democratic aide, said. "But when bills are put together on an ad hoc basis, the trouble can be that there are no hearings and more staff control, which increases the risk of unintended consequences."

Members of Congress have complained that they have little idea what they are voting on when they are presented on the floor with an anticrime or an environmental bill, for example, that runs several hundred pages. Although tax bills are typically written inside the Ways and Means and Finance Committees, even those panels assign the task of writing the details to the committee staffs. The committees have been embarrassed occasionally when they have learned about the impact of the bills that have emerged.

The crumbling of the committee system has not affected all major bills. In addition to tax measures, appropriations and defense policy legislation are still mostly committee-produced products that generally receive rubber-stamp approval on the House and Senate floors. Nevertheless, the chairmen of these committees have been forced to be mindful of the wishes of their party leaders and of the full chamber. As the budget negotiations have demonstrated, even influential chairmen can find that their maneuverability is severely limited, often to the benefit of party leaders.

"Budget realities have had an enormous impact on the way tax legislation is written," David H. Brockway, former chief of staff of the congressional Joint Committee on Taxation, said.

"In the not-distant past, the hallmark of the Senate was weak leaders and strong chairmen," said Robert G. Liberatore, who was staff director of the Senate Democratic Policy Committee from 1981-84. "The loss of power by committee chairmen and the increased chaos in the use of Senate rules to promote a Senator's views have required leadership to be more involved in keeping things going."

The altered power relationships have come in response to the often-tumultuous political changes of the 1980s—notably, the division of political power between the White House and Congress and the shifts in control of the Senate in 1980 and again in 1986.

"The institution is groping to find ways to get things done when it's difficult to do anything," said Norman J. Ornstein, a congressional scholar at the American Enterprise Institute for Public Policy Research.

Congress is resorting more frequently to the informal procedures in part because the Bush Administration has been "more aggressive in arguing its views," Sen. Wendell H. Ford, D-Ky., said. "With the Administration leading the [Senate] Republicans almost in lockstep, that means that even if a bill is reported by a committee, the bill often won't move" without further negotiations. The President's effective use of the veto, which he has exercised 13 times without an override, has enhanced his influence at Congress's expense.

In the Senate more than in the House, Democrats have been forced to improvise because of turnover in the ranks of committee chairmen and party leaders. "Prior to 1980, there was an entrenched senior Member-staff structure in the Senate that had been there for more than a decade," said Leon G. Billings, a lobbyist who was a top aide to then-Sen. Edmund S. Muskie, D-Maine. "That was seriously disrupted for Democrats in the six-year hiatus [of 1981-87, when the GOP controlled the Senate]. More-junior senators, who were less well versed on specific issues, took over."

Two key examples are the Senate Budget Committee and the Environment and Public Works Subcommittee on Environmental Protection, both of which Muskie chaired until he resigned in 1980 to become Secretary of State. [In 1989], those panels were taken over by new chairmen with little leadership experience on the issues at hand; in each case, control of these issues has been moving toward the leadership.

Mitchell, who also took office as Majority Leader [in 1989], has denied any significant loss of committee influence. But a process that puts the budget and clean air and other issues in the leadership's hands seems tailor-made for him because he is more issue-oriented than recent Senate leaders.

The Senate Budget Committee has become virtually a nonparticipant in budget policy, as evidenced by the decision [in 1990] of chairman Jim Sasser, D-Tenn., not to bring to the Senate floor the committee's annual resolution setting spending and revenue targets for the next fiscal year.

At the Senate Appropriations Committee, chairman Robert C. Byrd, D-W. Va., in effect set his own spending ceiling to guide his panel's work.

Though the Senate Environment Committee ultimately lost control of the clean air bill to the Mitchell-sponsored negotiations, the chairman of its Environmental Protection Subcommittee, Max Baucus, D-Mont., has been a central figure in moving the bill; he has worked closely with Mitchell, who preceded him as subcommittee chairman. "The committee could have met the Administration's objections earlier if they had been fully stated," Baucus said. He rejected the view of some observers that his own inexperience was a factor.

Lawmakers also have made many issues more difficult to handle because they want to use legislation to make political statements—for themselves or for their party, as Senate Democrats sought to do on the crime bill. And legislative procedures, never models of efficiency, have become more cumbersome as they are subjected to greater demands.

"The problems we face are becoming more complex, and the solutions don't fit neatly into the baskets represented by the committee system," said David E. Johnson, a former top aide to Mitchell who is now a Washington lobbyist and an informal advisor to the Majority Leader. "When I started working for Muskie in 1973, the Senate was a much different place. There was more respect for seniority and learning your committee assignment. Now, it seems that there is more of an entrepreneurial spirit in the Senate and in politics, generally."

Wilson's observation in 1885 that committees predominate because "the House is conscious that time presses" remains apt.

Congress functions most smoothly when bills are written in committee with bipartisan support. On most committees, the members generally seek that approach, if only because what they produce is more likely to win support on the House or Senate floor if a consensus has developed.

"Task forces usually are created only after a committee has run into a problem moving a bill," said Thomas A. Daschle of South Dakota, the co-chairman with Mitchell of the Senate Democratic Policy Committee. "They may enhance the influence of a chairman if they can improve his ability to move a bill through the floor."

Members often seek assignments to committees that deal with the issues in which they and their constituents are most interested. And that means that the committees can become captives of the interest groups most affected by their work. Seats on the Agriculture Committees tend to be filled by lawmakers representing farmers, for example, and western and southern Senators gravitate toward the Energy and Natural Resources Committee.

"On the key committees that Senators want to be on—Finance, Appropriations, Armed Services—there tend to be more-balanced views," said Liberatore, who is a lobbyist for Chrysler Corp. "Many of the others are constituent committees, which generally have more staff control, and there is less interest by members in the details of programs."

Trouble can arise if committees ignore the views of other Members—for example, industrial state lawmakers who object to environmental controls on power plants—or if they fail to find common ground on politically polarizing issues.

"There is no concerted effort to bypass committees," said Sen. Wyche Fowler Jr., D-Ga., whom Mitchell tapped as assistant floor leader. "That's much more difficult for leadership to manage." The need for informal mechanisms, in part, "has to do with the personalities and effectiveness" of chairmen, Fowler added.

Even seemingly routine action on bills can often become snarled. When the Senate in June 1989 acted on the child care bill—one of the Democrats' top domestic priorities—it was initially written by Labor and Human Resources Committee Democrats, who are mostly sympathetic to organized labor and child care groups. Before the measure could win Senate passage, however, Mitchell was forced to file a floor substitute that substantially watered down the original version and added provisions that the Finance Committee had prepared. Because most Republicans opposed the measure, the support of Orrin G. Hatch of Utah, the Labor Committee's senior Republican, was vital to Senate passage.

Hatch took a more traditional minority role when his strong opposition triggered an angry debate on the pending Civil Rights Act, which the Labor Committee drafted. As a result, committee chairman Edward M. Kennedy, D-Mass., sought but ultimately failed to work out differences directly with White House chief of staff John H. Sununu. Kennedy and Sununu had conducted similar negotiations a year ago to expedite Senate passage of landmark legislation expanding the rights of disabled persons.

In the House, the two committees with child care jurisdiction—Education and Labor and Ways and Means—were badly split over the financing mechanism. Their differences stemmed, in part, from a jurisdictional fight.

House Speaker Thomas S. Foley, D-Wash., and Majority Leader Richard A. Gephardt, D-Mo., worked for months to resolve those differences but ultimately failed; in March [1990], the House passed a bill that included the two conflicting approaches. Republicans hope that the threat of a presidential veto will give them leverage in a House-Senate conference committee, where they favor the Ways and Means approach of greater tax credits and fewer strings on federal grants.

Some committees and committee chairmen have been ill-equipped to deal with hot-button issues—controversial topics requiring quick action and a sensitivity to partisan implications.

Pay raise and campaign finance bills, for example, have become known as "leadership issues." They require party leaders' extensive participation because "they involve the Members themselves and need bipartisan support," said Rep. Martin Frost, D-Texas, who has served on informal leadership panels dealing with both issues.

The committees with nominal legislative jurisdiction over these issues—chiefly, the House Administration Committee and the Senate Rules and Administration Committee—have become house-keeping panels to which most members devote little time. That represents a change from the early 1970s, when those committees were central in drafting campaign finance laws. But House and Senate party leaders have included members of those committees on the informal pay raise and campaign finance panels.

"These are issues that require the leadership to play a critical role to overcome the parochial interests of individual Members," Common Cause president Fred Wertheimer said. "After 15 years of the parties' battling each other and incumbents benefiting from the current system, that makes it harder to resolve. . . . On these issues, accountability is not with the committee system, it's with the party leaders."

It's not only the majority leadership that can preempt a committee. According to Ford, who chairs the Rules Committee, he and other Senators from each party [in 1990] were working on major parts of the campaign finance bill when Minority Leader Robert Dole, R-Kan., forced an end to the negotiations. "We were making progress, and then some other Republicans got their noses out of joint," Ford said. "I understood that it was because of Dole." Dole, who has opposed Democratic efforts to impose strict spending limits, eventually joined Mitchell in creating an informal group that tried but failed to reach a bipartisan agreement.

Sometimes, overlapping committee jurisdictions are obstacles to moving legislation to the floor. Issues such as education, trade and drug control may be in the jurisdiction principally of a single committee of the House or Senate. But several other committees can and often do argue for a share of the jurisidiction so that their members can get a piece of the action.

"There are so many overlapping jurisdictions, which create difficulties in working out problems," Daschle said. "And many more Members desire to be involved, even though they are not on the committee with jurisdiction." That helps to explain, for example, why eight Senate committees and nine House committees worked on parts of the 1988 Trade Act.

Reformers made several efforts in the 1970s to overhaul committee jurisdiction but failed, for the most part, because of opposition from Members who feared a loss of influence. The most far-reaching plan was prepared in 1973-74 by the House Select Committee on Committees, which was chaired by Richard Bolling, D-Mo., who retired in 1982 after serving 34 years as an influential Member.

"It's not possible for many bills to go through the committee system until Congress redoes itself," said Bolling, who has become an adviser to Gephardt. "It's nutty now. But this is not the time to reform, either strategically or politically." [Bolling died in 1991.]

Other major changes in the mid-1970s, which were the culmination of lengthy efforts by Bolling and other Democratic reformers, served to weaken the roles of the once-autocratic committee chairmen. They included the adoption of the new congressional budget process; the election in 1974 of the "Watergate babies," nationally oriented House Democrats with little respect for their elders or for House traditions; and the strengthening of the House Democratic Caucus, which demonstrated its new muscle in 1975 by ousting three senior committee chairmen. Intentionally or not, these changes contributed to Congress's internal gridlock.

Ford said that a study of Senate committee jurisdictions would be timely. "I don't preclude it in the next session," he said.

"Congress prefers strong chairmen," Fowler said. "But the proliferation of chairmen has weakened the committee system. You no longer have the whales on any complex issues. You usually have two to three committee chairmen and eight or nine subcommittee chairmen, all jealous of their turf."

Assertive Members

Reduced committee influence can open up many opportunities for rank-and-file Members. Sen. Phil Gramm, R-Texas, may be the best example. In 1985, as a first-year Senator, he prepared and cosponsored a floor amendment that resulted in radical changes in the federal budget process. Four years earlier, while a second-term House Democrat, Gramm pulled off a similar coup when he successfully sponsored a floor amendment that made major cuts in domestic spending programs. Those moves did not endear Gramm to the many lawmakers in both parties who take a more traditional view of the legislative process. But they have made him one of Congress's most influential Members.

Many Senators prefer the relative stability of the committee process—when it is working well. "Politicians generally don't like grandstanding and how it affects their colleagues," Billings said. "Most of them want to accomplish the best legislation that they can. That requires a normalized process."

Informal mechanisms that substitute for the more structured committee process often strengthen the hands of individual Members. "A Senator can have more leverage in an extra-committee context," Sliter said. "It's more likely to be free-form because you are not going against the chairman. . . . Task forces can be more democratic in their operation and can prod a chairman not to be autocratic."

In the closed-door negotiations on the clean air bill, for example, individual negotiators—including those from the Administration—could stymie an agreement more easily than they could have done in a standing committee, which is ruled by majority vote.

Baucus justified the informal approach, noting that "it's such a complex bill with so many titles that it was more appropriate to address it on a cohesive basis within the core group. The proof of our success is in the pudding. We met the objective of passing a bill that is a major improvement over current law."

Supporters of more-stringent clean air requirements contend that the cost and complexity of the provisions and the growing number of Members with an interest in the legislation made a battle royal unavoidable, especially in the Senate, where opponents can more easily put up roadblocks. "We knew that there were people in the weeds waiting to make a big fight and that some parts of the committee bill would be whittled away," said Robert Hurley, the Environment Committee's minority staff director. "Had we known the intensity of the opposition, we might have made some adjustments in committee."

In other cases, so many Members want a piece of the action that a chairman willing to work outside the formal structure can turn the chaos to his advantage. When the Senate took up the broad crime bill [in 1990], for example, Senators offered more than 300 floor amendments. Judiciary Committee chairman Joseph R. Biden Jr., D-Del., worked for days with Strom Thurmond of South Carolina and Hatch, the committee's senior Republicans, to narrow the list to a more manageable 18, half from each party. These private negotiations became, in effect, a makeshift bill-drafting session involving 100 Senators and their aides, not the 14 Judiciary Committee members.

A host of political factors shaped the back-room dickering off the Senate floor. Democrats wanted to place their imprint on a crime bill but also wanted to limit votes on controversial issues that might prove embarrassing to Democratic Senators seeking reelection in the fall. Republicans wanted to help President Bush get a crime bill, but many of them were unhappy about efforts to expand the bill to include gun control measures. Members of both parties who are up for reelection wanted an opportunity to offer amendments that would display their "law and order" credentials.

"Many Members wanted to offer an amendment so that they could be on C-SPAN or have a 30-second campaign spot," a Democratic aide working on the bill said. "The reality is that this is a big part of the legislative process."

Earlier, Biden had decided to make the fight on the Senate floor rather than in his committee, which never formally acted on the omnibus measure. Still stung by the 1988 presidential campaign, in which Bush scored points by attacking Democratic nominee Michael S. Dukakis on crime issues, Senate Democrats sought to use the bill to make a partisan statement.

"The Biden bill does more to combat crime then the Administration's proposal, while at the same time remaining more sensitive to constitutional concerns," a July 10 handout prepared by Biden's staff declared.

New procedures intended to supplement the work of the committees may also enhance the power of congressional leaders, especially those in the Senate. "By picking who is on the team and putting a spin on the outcome, leadership can exert more control," a Senate Democratic source said.

At the same time, the added responsibilities can complicate the lives of party leaders, who already have to balance a range of legislative and political demands. Increasingly, however, Members are selecting leaders—such as Mitchell, Gephardt, Dole and House Minority Whip Newt Gingrich, R-Ga.—who have demonstrated that they can not only speak to national constituencies but can also deal with internal pressures.

In addition, Bush and top White House officials have been more interested in resolving legislative details with congressional leaders than their recent predecessors have—in part, congressional sources suggest, because Bush spends less time than other Presidents did developing a White House legislative agenda.

Until recent years, active Presidents did not have to contend with strong congressional leaders seeking their own podiums. Sam Rayburn of Texas, who was House Speaker in 17 of the years from 1940-61 and was probably the century's most skillful lawmaker, prided himself on his ability to work closely with Presidents and committee chairmen. But to the public at large, he was not very well known.

"Rayburn had half the power" of later Speakers, said Bolling, whom many regarded as Rayburn's protégé. "But he had enormous prestige from the ability to understand what could be done and how to tell a President."

Mitchell may be setting a new model for Senate leaders as he tries to combine the roles of legislative agenda-setter and national party spokesman. [In 1989], for example, he engaged in public and private lobbying to kill, virtually single-handedly, Bush's proposed cut in the capital gains tax rate, which was backed by a majority of Senators, including members of the Finance Committee.

"George Mitchell takes a much more flexible approach to leadership," Ornstein said. "This is an era when leaders use whatever tools work and seek new ones, where necessary. . . . They have to be more creative and improvisational."

Byrd, who was Mitchell's predecessor as Majority Leader, used task forces and other ad hoc arrangements chiefly to help establish a party position on issues. But on legislative procedures, Byrd was more inclined to be deferential to committee chairmen. Dole, for his part, has been a more assertive leader than his predecessors and seeks to wield influence from the top.

Mitchell, in effect, has taken elements of each approach. "Sen. Mitchell uses task forces as an opportunity to be more directly involved in negotiations," Daschle said.

Mitchell, in an interview, denied that Senate operations or leadership responsibilities have been overhauled. "The issues are more complex, and individuals are more involved," he said. "But there is not a change in the way the Senate does its business."

For Mitchell and the other party leaders, the budget summit has been an important test. With the deficit remaining at high levels and tax and spending issues increasingly difficult to resolve, both the White House and congressional leaders have, in effect, given up on the committee process. They view the summit talks as the best opportunity to break the stalemate.

"I do think that it's a way of highlighting the importance of the issue," said Fowler, whom Mitchell tapped as his budget summit representative. "The President is trying to head off a crisis of budget sequestration," or across-the-board spending cuts.

Many factors have complicated the process of seeking a budget agreement, not the least of which is the relationship between party leaders and committee chairmen. On the one hand, the summiteers have wanted to present Congress and the public with a fait accompli that would require a single up-or-down vote in the House and Senate. But they also have sought to develop the framework for an agreement that is politically supportable, while relying on several committees to write the details—chiefly, Appropriations, Armed Services and the tax-writing panels.

A budget accord would make "academic" the money bills that have been working their way through Congress, House Minority Leader Robert H. Michel, R-Ill., said. The Appropriations and tax-writing committees would be working under tight deadlines and following a detailed outline prepared by the summiteers as they wrote the legislation.

Whether it is the budget or other issues, party leaders have often said that they do not want to put their own "stamp" on issues. In an increasing number of cases, however, they have found that if they don't, no one else can.

40. Congress-Bashing for Beginners

Nelson W. Polsby

Disparaging remarks about Congress and complaints about the congressional role as it relates to the constitutional separation of powers have long been voiced. This "ancient but now slightly shopworn American custom of Congress-bashing," as Nelson W. Polsby observes, has over the years led to structural reforms that have considerably strengthened the presidency. In this article, published in *The Public Interest* in 1990, Polsby, a noted political scientist and director of the Institute of Governmental Studies at the University of California at Berkeley, critically examines some issues and proposals that come under the category of Congress-bashing. These include opposition to an increase in congressional salaries and the proposal for a presidential item veto. If presidents had the line-item veto, they could single out parts of a bill for veto while signing the remainder into law. Congress could still exercise its authority to override the President's veto of the line items. (Polsby's arguments on limiting the terms of members of Congress is presented in Selection 41 as part of a "Point-Counterpoint" discussion.)

On a shelf not far from where I am writing these words sit a half a dozen or so books disparaging Congress and complaining about the congressional role in the constitutional separation of powers. These books date mostly from the late 1940s and the early 1960s, and typically their authors are liberal Democrats. In those years, Congress was unresponsive to liberal Democrats and, naturally enough, aggrieved members of that articulate tribe sought solutions in structural reform.

In fact, instead of reforms weakening Congress what they—and we—got was a considerably strengthened presidency. This was mostly a product of World War II and not the result of liberal complaints. Before World War II Congress would not enact even the modest recommendations of the Brownlow Commission * to give the president a handful of assistants with "a passion for anonymity," and it killed the National Resources Planning Board outright. After World War II everything changed: Congress gave the president responsibility for smoothing the effects of the business cycle, created a Defense Department and two presidential agencies—the NSC [National Security Council] and the CIA [Central Intelligence Agency]—that enhanced the potential for presidential dominance of national security affairs, and laid the groundwork for the growth of a presidential branch, politically responsive to both Democratic and Republican presidents.

Congress and the Goring of Oxen

Though it took time for the presidential branch to grow into its potential, the growth of this branch, separate and at arm's length from the executive branch that it runs in the president's behalf, is the big news of the postwar era—indeed, of the last half-century in American government. It is customary today to acknowledge that Harry Truman's primary agenda, in the field of foreign affairs, was quite successfully enacted even though Congress was dominated by a conservative coalition, and what Truman wanted in the way of peacetime international involvement was for the United States quite unprecedented. Dwight Eisenhower's agenda was also largely international in its impact. Looking back, it seems that almost all Eisenhower really cared about was protecting the international position of the United States from diminution by Republican isolationists. Everything else was expendable.

Congress responded sluggishly and in its customary piecemeal fashion. It was right around John Kennedy's first year in office that liberals rediscovered that old roadblock in Congress, a "dead-lock of democracy," as one of them put it. It was Congress that had thwarted the second New Deal after 1937, the packing of the Supreme Court, and Harry Truman's domestic program; it was Congress that had stalled civil rights and buried Medicare; it was Congress that had sponsored the Bricker Amendment to limit the president's power to make treaties. Are memories so short that we do not recall these dear, departed days when

---

* The 1937 Brownlow Commission—named after its chairman, Louis Brownlow, and appointed by President Franklin Roosevelt—examined the issue of managing the executive branch and recommended that the president's supervisory role be strengthened by expanding the White House staff.

Congress was the graveyard of the forward-looking proposals of liberal presidents? Then, Congress was a creaky eighteenth-century machine unsuited to the modern age, and Congress-bashers were liberal Democrats.

To be sure, Congress had a few defenders, mostly Republicans and Dixiecrats, who found in its musty cloakrooms and windy debates a citadel (as one of them said) of old-time legislative virtues, where the historic functions of oversight and scrutiny were performed, where the run-away proposals of the presidency could be subjected to the sober second thoughts of the people's own elected representatives, and so on.

Why rehash all this? In part, it is to try to make the perfectly obvious point that Congress-bashing then was what people did when they controlled the presidency but didn't control Congress. And that, in part, is what Congress-bashing is about now. Today, Republicans and conservatives are doing most (although not all) of the complaining. It is worth a small bet that a fair number of editorial pages claimed that the separation of powers made a lot of sense during the Kennedy-Johnson years—but no longer say the same today. On the other side, backers of FDR's scheme to pack the Court have turned into vigorous defenders of the judicial status quo since [Supreme Court Chief Justice] Earl Warren's time.

There is nothing wrong with letting the goring of oxen determine what side we take in a political argument. In a civilized country, however, it makes sense to keep political arguments civil, and not to let push come to shove too often. There is something uncivil, in my view, about insisting upon constitutional reforms to cure political ailments. What liberal critics of Congress needed was not constitutional reform. What they needed was the 89th Congress, which, in due course, enacted much of the agenda that the Democratic party had built up over the previous two decades. History didn't stop with the rise of the presidential branch and the enactment of the second New Deal/New Frontier/ Great Society. President Johnson overreached. He concealed from Congress the costs of the Vietnam War. He created a credibility gap.

This, among other things, began to change Congress. The legislative branch no longer was altogether comfortable relying on the massaged numbers and other unreliable information coming over from the presidential branch. They began to create a legislative bureaucracy to cope with this challenge. They beefed up the General Accounting Office and the Congressional Research Service. They created an Office of Technology Assessment and a Congressional Budget Office. They doubled and redoubled their personal staffs and committee staffs.

Sentiments supporting this expansion began, oddly enough, after a landslide election in which the Democratic party swept the presidency and both houses of Congress. So mistrust between the branches in recent history and has by no means been entirely a partisan matter.

Nevertheless, Richard Nixon's presidency, conducted entirely in unhappy harness with a Democratic Congress, did not improve relations between the two branches of government. Johnson may have been deceitful, but Nixon, especially after his reelection in 1972, was positively confrontational.

It was Nixon's policy to disregard comity between the branches. This, and not merely his commission of impeachable offenses, fueled the impeachment effort in Congress. That effort was never wholly partisan. Republicans as well as Democrats voted articles of impeachment that included complaints specifically related to obstruction of the discharge of congressional responsibilities.

It is necessary to understand this recent history of the relations between Congress and the president in order to understand the provenance of the War Powers Act, the Boland Amendment, numerous other instances of congressional micromanagement, the unprecedented involvement of the National Security Council in the Iran-contra affair, and like manifestations of tension and mistrust between Congress and the president. * These tensions are, to a certain degree, now embedded in law and in the routines of responsible public officials; they cannot be made to disappear with a wave of a magic wand. They are, for the most part, regrettable in the consequences they have had for congressional-presidential relations, but they reflect real responses to real problems in these relations. Congressional responses, so far as I can see, have been completely legal, constitutional, and—in the light of historical circumstances—understandable. The best way to turn the relations between the legislative and the presidential branches around would be for the presidential side to take vigorous initiatives to restore comity. As head of the branch far more capable of taking initiatives, and the branch far more responsible for the underlying problem, this effort at restoration is in the first instance up to the President.

President Bush and the Item Veto

In this respect, President Bush is doing a decent job, giving evidence of reaching out constructively. It is not my impression that the Bush

---

* The War Powers Resolution of 1973, enacted over President Richard Nixon's veto, sought to limit any president's ability to unilaterally commit U.S. troops abroad without Congress's approval. The Boland Amendment, named after retired Representative Edward Boland, D-Mass., was enacted into law during the 1980s in several different forms. Its fundamental purpose was to restrict financial support to the Contras, a para-military group that sought to oust the Nicaraguan government, then headed by Daniel Ortega. The Iran-contra affair of 1985-86 refers to the effort by some executive officials to funnel money to the Contras, despite the Boland Amendment restrictions, from the profits made by selling arms to Iran in exchange for the release of American hostages.

administration has done a lot of Congress-bashing. After all, what Bush needs isn't a weakened Congress so much as a Republican Congress. Over the long run (though probably not in time to do Bush much good) Republicans are bound to regret despairing of the latter and therefore seeking the former. We have seen enough turns of the wheel over the last half-century to be reasonably confident that sooner or later Republicans will start to do better in congressional elections. The presidential item veto, the Administration's main Congress-bashing proposal, won't help Republicans in Congress deal with a Democratic president when the time comes, as sooner or later it will, for a Democrat to be elected president.

The item veto would effectively take congressional politics out of the legislative process and would weaken Congress a lot. It would encourage members of Congress, majority and minority alike, to be irresponsible and to stick the president with embarrassing public choices. It would reduce the incentives for members to acquire knowledge about public policy or indeed to serve.

By allocating legislative responsibilities to Congress, the Constitution as originally (and currently) designed forces representatives of diverse interests to cooperate. Because what Congress does as a collectivity matters, legislative work elicits the committed participation of members. The item veto would greatly trivialize the work product of Congress by requiring the president's acquiescence on each detail of legislation. Members would lose their independent capacity to craft legislation. Their individual views and knowledge would dwindle in importance; only the marshalling of a herd capable of overturning a veto would matter in Congress.

The item veto is, in short, a truly radical idea. It is also almost certainly unconstitutional. To espouse it requires a readiness to give up entirely on the separation of powers and on the constitutional design of the American government. There are plenty of people, some of them well-meaning, who are ready to do that. I am not, nor should people who identify themselves as conservatives or liberals or anywhere in the political mainstream.

The separation of powers is actually a good idea. It gives a necessary weight to the great heterogeneity of our nation—by far the largest and most heterogeneous nation unequivocally to have succeeded at democratic self-government in world history. It would take a medium-sized book to make all the qualifications and all the connections that would do justice to this argument. The conclusion is worth restating anyway: the item veto is a root-and-branch attack on the separation of powers; it is a very radical and a very bad idea. . . .

Congressional Salaries

[It] is certainly appropriate to pay our disrespects to [Ralph Nader's] completely off-the-wall effort, temporarily successful [in early 1989], at the head of a crazed phalanx of self-righteous disk jockeys and radio talk-show hosts, to deprive members of Congress of a salary increase. The issue of congressional salaries is a straightforward one. Many members, being well-to-do, don't need one. But some do. The expenses of maintaining two places of residence—in Washington and at home—make membership in Congress nearly unique and singularly expensive among upper-middle-class American jobs. Here is the point once more: it is a job, requiring skill and dedication to be done properly.

Moreover, membership in Congress brings responsibilities. National policy of the scope and scale now encompassed by acts of the federal government requires responsible, dedicated legislators. People with far less serious responsibilities in the private sector are ordinarily paid considerably better than members of Congress. Think, for example, how far down the organizational chart at General Motors or at CBS or at some other large corporation one would have to go before reaching executives making what members of Congress do, and compare their responsibilities with those of Congress and its members. Actually, most corporations won't say what their compensation packages are like. But at a major auto company, people who make around $100,000 a year are no higher than upper middle management, and certainly don't have responsibilities remotely comparable to those of members of Congress.

There is a case for decent congressional salaries to be made on at least two grounds: one is the rough equity or opportunity-cost ground that we ought not financially to penalize people who serve, and the second is the ground of need for those members who have the expense of families or college educations to think of, and who have no extraordinary private means. The long-run national disadvantage of failing to recognize the justice of these claims is of course a Congress deprived of people for whom these claims are exigent, normal middle-class people with family responsibilities and without money of their own. These are not the sorts of people a sane electorate should wish to prevent from serving.

Members of Congress, knowing very well of the irrational hostilities that the proposal of a congressional pay raise can stir up, have taken the unfortunate precaution of holding hostage the salaries of federal judges, who are now ludicrously underpaid by the admittedly opulent standards of the legal profession, and senior civil servants. An unhealthy impassive has been created, owing, at bottom, to Congress-bashing of the most unattractive kind, which exploits the ignorance of ordinary citizens of the dimensions of the members' working lives and incites citizens to a mindless social envy, in which it is assumed that paying a decent professional salary to professional officeholders is automatically some sort of rip-off.

Members of the House now make $125,100 a year; members of the Senate receive $101,900 but may accept up to $27,500 a year in honoraria, which representatives are prohibited from accepting. [In 1991, as noted earlier, the Senate raised its salary to the House's level and prohibited the acceptance of honoraria for personal income.] The bottom salary for major-league baseball players is $100,000. Some law firms in New York start new graduates of good law schools at $90,000 or more. How can we argue that members of Congress and others at the top of the federal government should not be paid at least a modest premium above these beginners' wages? There is, evidently, no talking sense to the American people on this subject.

I believe we can dismiss out of hand the charge that large numbers of members individually, or Congress collectively, live in a world all their own, divorced from realities of everyday life. The sophomores who have written attacks of this sort in recent years in the *Atlantic, Newsweek,* and elsewhere simply don't know what they are talking about. They abuse their access to large audiences by neglecting to explain the real conditions that govern the lives of members, conditions that provide ample doses of everyday life.

No doubt scandals involving various members have in recent times made Congress as an institution vulnerable to criticism. But much of this criticism is irresponsible and irrelevant. Suppose we were to discover instances of cupidity, unusual sexual activity, and abuses of power among the rather sizable staff of an important daily newspaper? Or a symphony orchestra? Or, God forbid, a university? I suppose that would shake our confidence in at least part of the collective output, but one would hope for relevant discriminations. One might distrust the ticket office, perhaps, but not the symphony's performance of Mozart; the stock tips, perhaps, but not the Washington page; the basketball program, but not the classics department. I do not think that the existence of scandal excuses us from attempting to draw sensible conclusions about institutions and their performance.

This sort of balanced and discriminating analysis isn't what proposals for item vetoes, limitations on terms of service, or depressed rates of pay are all about. They are about the ancient but now slightly shopworn American custom of Congress-bashing.

41. Point-Counterpoint: Term Limits for Lawmakers

Mark P. Petracca
Nelson W. Polsby

Mark P. Petracca and Nelson W. Polsby, both political scientists at the University of California at Berkeley, take opposing sides on the issue of limiting the terms of congressmen. As published in the Institute of Governmental Studies' *Public Affairs Report* in 1990, Petracca argues that limiting terms will put an end to "permanent government by incumbents"; Polsby counters that limiting terms won't curb special interests, improve the legislature, or enhance democracy. Nationally opposing groups have been organized to push for term limits or to derail the proposal. In general, current term-limitation proposals recommend that federal lawmakers serve no more than twelve consecutive years.

Mark P. Petracca:
Term Limits Will Put an End to Permanent Government by Incumbents

Oklahoma has become the first state in the nation to impose term limits on state legislators. In November [1990], California [became] the largest state in the nation to do the same. While more than half of the states already limit the number of terms a governor may serve, only Oklahoma now limits the terms of its legislators. [P]assage of [the] California [term limit] . . . is likely to stimulate similar movements in other large, industrial states. . . .

Americans have grown increasingly weary of the "permanent government" that dominates the U.S. Congress and most state legislatures. A successful movement in California to limit the terms of state office-holders will show that Americans are finally prepared to abolish the contemporary norm of government by incumbents.

Opponents of both propositions, including Assembly Speaker Willie Brown and other powerful incumbents (many of whom just happen to be Democrats), argue that term limitations are un-American and undemocratic. In addition, opponents claim that term limits would enhance the power of special interests and squander much needed legislative expertise. None of these arguments stand up to historical or empirical scrutiny.

In the "new world" of the 18th century, limits on the terms of officeholders or required rotation in office were viewed as a tenet of *radical democracy*. During the revolutionary and federal periods in American history, examples of this view are abundant. The Pennsylvania Constitution of 1776, considered to be the most radical constitution of the revolutionary era, had strict limits on officeholders and required rotation in office. Likewise, the Articles of Confederation (1781), which preceded the U.S. Constitution as the foundation of American national government, required rotation in office for all delegates in Article V, stating that an individual could serve as a delegate in only three out of every six years. This tradition made its way to the Constitutional Convention of 1787 through the "Virginia Plan," which called for restrictions on the eligibility of all national officeholders. While mandatory rotation did not make it to the final draft of the Constitution, many of the convention delegates assumed that voluntary rotation after brief periods of service would be the norm. Thus, there is a strong *American* precedent for term limits that emerges from radical democratic theory in contrast to the more constrained and elitist tradition of classical republicanism.

The political principle supporting term limitations is deeply rooted in ancient and post-Enlightenment theories of democratic citizenship and representation. For Aristotle, democratic citizenship was possible only where there was reciprocity of "ruling and being ruled by turn." Thus, in order for democracy to flourish there must be significant rotation in office. The power of incumbency and the desire of many politicians to pursue lifelong careers as professional legislators make significant turnover in office impossible. The Aristotelian position is consistent with the expectations of the American framers, such as James Madison and Alexander Hamilton, that most elected officials would serve for brief periods of time and then return home to resume their previous occupations. Indeed, throughout the late 18th and most of the 19th centuries, this expectation was fulfilled. Prior to the 1890s, for example, most members of the House of Representatives did not make a career out of service in the House. Rather, they served for a term or two and then voluntarily retired to take local judgeships, to run for a different office, or to pursue some other endeavor. Indeed, the framers would be distressed to discover that permanent legislatures have become a prominent feature of American politics in the late 20th century.

The antifederalists, who criticized the U.S. Constitution for its undemocratic character, also appreciated the political advantages of term limits in a political system striving to maintain a limited government.

Fearing that the Constitution was an insufficient check on government encroachments, the antifederalists called for more frequent elections, rotation in office, and a bill of rights, among other changes. Antifederalists such as New York's Brutus advocated required rotation in office to prevent the abuse of public power by entrenched incumbents. Brutus also extolled the advantages of required rotation of officeholders: "[I]t would give opportunity to bring forward a greater number of men to serve their country, and would return those, who had served, to their state, and afford them the advantage of becoming better acquainted with the condition and politics of their constituents." These advantages remain relevant to the plight of modern American politics where few individuals have the opportunity to serve due to the power of incumbency and where so many career legislators have lost touch with their constituents and the commonweal.

Opponents allege that term limits will enhance the power of special interests. To the contrary, term limits will sever the stranglehold special interests have on career politicians who seek financial support to stay in office. Empirically, as legislative turnover has declined during the last two decades, the influence of special interests at the state and national levels of government has increased. Term limitations will reduce the incentive that an officeholder has to develop long-term relationships with a specific set of interests, and special interests will have less of an incentive to develop close bonds with legislators who may only hold office for a few terms. Thus, in addition to the democratic advantage of term limits previously mentioned, they also have the effect of reducing the power of special interests in legislative assemblies.

Finally, it is often erroneously asserted that effective government requires individuals with political experience and expertise. To the contrary, professionalism and careerism in politics are the bane of democratic governance. On the one hand, democratic theory has historically privileged the role of the amateur over that of the professional in the art of self-governance. On the other hand, there is no empirical evidence that professional politicians do a better job of governing than amateurs at any level of government. Regrettably, extensive experience in government tends to produce legislators who are more interested in defending government than they are in solving serious public problems (solutions that sometimes require less, not more, government).

Limits on legislative terms may appear to be motivated by the desire of one political party to displace the dominance of another; however, this is not a partisan issue. While many legislators who are or aspire to be career legislators will be hesitant to embrace this reform, politicians from both parties must face up to the deep dissatisfaction and disenchantment that Americans feel towards legislatures. Term limits seek to restore the virtues of democratic self-rule to representative government and to stimulate effective governance by bringing new individuals into the governing process. What was once accomplished voluntarily in legislatures throughout America during the 19th century must now be accomplished by the authority of law. [Many citizens] seem determined to replace "permanent government" with democratic government by imposing term limits. . . .

Nelson W. Polsby:
Limiting Terms Won't Curb
Special Interests, Improve the
Legislature, or Enhance Democracy

It looks like the American political system is building toward another one of its periodic spasms in which the demands of political extremists are taken seriously and for the time being incorporated into the calculations and the routines of mainstream American politicians. We had such a spasm in the 1950s, when [Senator] Joseph McCarthy was accorded considerable leeway by American politicians who surely knew better, and another in the 1960s, when American political institutions— notably the presidential nominating process—came under siege from activists on the left.

There is nothing unusual or un-American about political extremism; far from it. Feelings that the political system ought to be radically changed and advocates of these feelings exist all the time in the American body politic. Extremists have rights of political expression, as we all do, and exercise them. What ebbs and flows in our political life is the willingness of the mainstream politicians who run our political institutions to defend themselves and the credence and the publicity that the news media give to complaints about the functioning of the system.

One contemporary example of such complaints is the charge currently being made that there is something radically wrong with state legislatures and Congress, that there are too many career legislators, and that state and federal constitutions need to be changed so as to put limits on the terms of service of members.

In fact, turnover in the House of Representatives today is roughly what it has been for over 30 years. Yet unlike a few years ago, when mean terms of service were more or less the same as they are today, the institutional integrity of the Congress is now held to be faulty. State legislatures are targeted with many of the same complaints.

The merits of these complaints need not detain us long. Proponents of term limitations are in some cases openly hostile to the idea of strong and effective legislative bodies. A few argue that legislative bodies made up of inexperienced citizen-legislators will be more representative of citizens at large, but do not say how these inexperienced legislators can make their power to represent felt in policy environments where both technical knowledge and political knowledge are monopolized by bureaucrats, legislative staff, and lobbyists.

Term limitations are, in fact, a recipe for depriving legislatures, and elected legislators, of power. This is alleged somehow to be good for the system. Presumably it is better to be governed by the unelected, unrepresentative actors who will gain from this radical constitutional change.

Term limitations will certainly not decrease the influence of interest groups and their money on elections. Quite to the contrary. Forcing senior members of a legislature to retire means that the new candidates who try to take their place will have to invest heavily in achieving the name recognition the veterans already have. This will require large new infusions of money and electoral alliances with interest groups who can supply it. Veteran members, proven vote getters, are much more powerful in relation to special interests than candidates who have to prove themselves in an uncertain and expensive campaign environment.

Term limitations won't improve the functioning of the legislature either. New people need time to learn their jobs. Term limitations throw away the benefits of learning from experience. Inexperienced legislators are less powerful in relation to legislative staff, executive branch bureaucrats, and interest group lobbyists, from whom they must learn the customs and routines of legislative operations and the stories behind public policy proposals.

New people in any complex institution are highly dependent on the people around them. Term limitations just shift power from elected officials to the relatively inaccessible officials, bureaucrats, and influence peddlers who surround them.

Why do we assume that new blood is automatically better than old? Of course we should pay attention to the quality of our legislators and vote against the ones whose performance we find wanting. Term limitations merely guarantee that the good ones will disappear along with the bad.

Finally, term limitations won't enhance representative democracy. Just the opposite, since they recreate an artificial barrier preventing voters from returning to office legislators they might otherwise favor. Why are we so certain that the voting public has such terrible judgment that they need a constitutional restriction to keep them from voting for incumbents they know and like? It is hard to see how restricting voters' alternatives in this arbitrary way can be proposed in the name of representative government or of democracy.

One must conclude that other forces are at work. More likely groups and interests that have a hard time winning elections from current incumbents are seeking term limitations so as to improve their chances of winning office. They are undoubtedly calculating that nonincumbents are easier to beat, or buy.

Why should ordinary citizens give credence to these sorts of constitution-wrecking proposals? The short answer is that they shouldn't. The fact that many voters express more generalized dissatisfactions by seeking to maim their political institutions is something of a triumph for the political propagandists who target legislatures as the all-purpose source of trouble.

Chapter 9

The Presidency

In the eyes of many people in this country and abroad, presidents *are* the U.S. government. They are the "best-known Americans," whether in Keokuk or Katmandu. Not even the most popular celebrities, entertainers, or athletes achieve this level of visibility. Presidents' words and deeds are chronicled exhaustively, and often fawningly, by the world's press. We are apt to think of our past in terms of the presidents who served at certain times—the Roosevelt era, the Eisenhower period, the Reagan years. In short, no other element of our government institutions or our political life remotely approaches the presidency in its ability to capture the public's attention or imagination.

It was not always thus. The framers of the Constitution had little inkling of what they had created when they put together Article II, which deals with the selection and powers of the president. In drafting Article I, on the national legislature, they were guided by hundreds of years of parliamentary development, not to mention their own experience with colonial assemblies. Legislative powers are thus enumerated in considerable detail. When they turned to describing the executive power, however, they had little to guide them. On the one hand, an "energetic executive" would be an essential element in the new governmental charter, for the lack of an executive was widely regarded as one of the greatest flaws in the Articles of Confederation. Yet a monarchy was out of the question: the recent troubles with George III could hardly be put out of their minds. Somehow a powerful but restrained executive—James Wilson of Pennsylvania wanted one of "energy, dispatch, and responsibility"—had to be fashioned.

The Presidency in the Constitution

What emerged in the Constitution was an utterly novel creation. Perhaps the framers held less a vision of the *office* than a sense of the *person* they visualized holding it. It was widely assumed that George Washington—austere, dignified, prudent—would first occupy the office, whatever its title or prerogatives. Washington's character, and the unique place he held in his colleagues' esteem, no doubt exerted as much influence over the final product as all the theoretical writings about constitutional limits on monarchs.

At a more mundane level, the specific provisions of Article II were the outcome of a series of debates among the Philadelphia delegates. Nearly every aspect of the subject brought out conflicting opinions, and the result was a hybrid of these views. The most powerful and influential minds of the convention, however—especially James Madison, James Wilson, Alexander Hamilton, and Gouverneur Morris—pushed the delegates toward a more powerful, independent executive. The presidency is to a large degree their creation.

The hopes and aspirations of the champions of strong executive power are eloquently expressed in Hamilton's celebrated *Federalist Paper* No. 70 (Selection 42). Hamilton was no friend of democratic selection (fortunately, he was countered by the more populist sentiments of Morris and others), but his statement is a vigorous argument for a powerful, independent presidency.

The president is one person, not a council or commission, and is unfettered by any prescribed advisory body. (The Constitution makes no mention of a cabinet.) The president is not chosen by Congress but is elected independently, a feature that irrevocably steered the nation away from a parliamentary form of government. The indirect election process, featuring selection by an electoral college, was an awkward compromise between those who favored popular elections and those who wanted selection by Congress or the state legislatures. Within a few years, the whole process was democratized, as states provided that electors be chosen by popular vote. Today nearly everyone regards the president as a popularly elected official, even though the electoral college remains part of the process. (This is probably the outstanding instance in which the "living Constitution" deviates from the written document.)

As for the president's duties, only a few are stated with any precision. Article II opens with the *vesting clause:* "Executive power shall be vested in a president." There is also the *take-care clause:* "The president shall take care that the laws be faithfully executed." Are such phrases simply instructions to execute the law, or do they embody special grants of authority?

Most presidential powers are exercised in conjunction with Congress. Although presidents do not pass laws, they usually must approve legislation (or two-thirds of both houses must override a presidential veto). The president is "commander in chief" (though the framers did not define the term), but Congress has the power to declare war and to raise and equip armies and navies. The president has the power to appoint ambassadors and other officers, but with the "advice and consent" of the Senate. The same goes for treaties with foreign nations, which the president negotiates but which do not take effect until the Senate ratifies them.

Strong and Public Presidents

Because of the strict system of checks and balances, presidents in the first 100 or so years only rarely lived up to Hamilton's description. Washington was, of course, unique; Thomas Jefferson led by force of his incandescent personality, as did Andrew Jackson—the most popular figure after Washington. Otherwise, so-called strong presidents were called forth by crises: James K. Polk by the Mexican War, Abraham Lincoln by the crisis of the Union, William McKinley by the Spanish-American War of 1898. The accession of the flamboyant Theodore Roosevelt after McKinley's assassination in 1901 signaled a change in the office. Woodrow Wilson, who in his 1885 doctoral dissertation had detailed the horrors of "congressional government," saw in the Roosevelt presidency the animating force that he felt the government needed. The stately cadences of Wilson's prose have seldom been equaled in commentary on the presidency (Selection 43, "The Only National Voice in Affairs").

Today's presidents are at the center of an elaborate apparatus designed to capture extensive and favorable media coverage. All occupants of the office use speeches, personal appearances, and ceremonial events to promote themselves and their programs. Nowadays, presidents are obliged to master the electronic media; and the ability to communicate directly and naturally before microphones and cameras is a prerequisite to effective leadership of the mass public. It is hardly an accident that the most successful public president of recent years, Ronald Reagan, entered politics after a career as an actor. Strategies of the so-called public presidency are explained in Michael B. Grossman's essay, "The Media and the White House" (Selection 44).

The American people expect and applaud such vigorous leadership. They harbor high expectations of incumbents, and judge harshly those who fail to live up to their hopes. Johnson, Nixon, Ford, and Carter seemed to fall short of public expectations, but the expectations themselves, though dashed temporarily, survive undiminished.

When Reagan entered office in 1981, and seemed to fulfill the public's view of what a president should be, the concept of the office revived. By the midpoint in his second term, Reagan seemed to have broken the disappointing pattern of his predecessors. He won reelection by a landslide (capturing forty-nine of the fifty states); his standing in the polls was as high as it had ever been. Yet even Reagan was destined for a fall. Startling revelations—White House operatives had sold arms to Iran in exchange for U.S. hostages and channeled profits from the sales to insurgent forces in Nicaragua—damaged Reagan's image as a forceful, credible leader who stood firm against terrorists.

Looking back, one could give numerous reasons for the reversal of the president's fortunes: lax managerial style, refusal to grapple with substantive issues, encouragement of swashbuckling adventurism on the international front, and deterioration of the White House staff in his second term. Still, the pattern reveals the fragility of the public presidency, with its triumph of style over substance.

The paradox of Ronald Reagan—his popularity with the public contrasted with his lax administrative style—was explained in various ways. One theory held that he was a master of "hidden-hand" leadership of the type that marked Dwight D. Eisenhower's presidency. That is, he used his vague but pleasant public manner to conceal shrewd and purposeful management. Fred I. Greenstein considers this explanation in Selection 45 ("Ronald Reagan—Another Hidden-Hand Ike?") and rejects it. In the process, however, he illuminates the challenges and resources of presidential leadership.

The President as Manager

The presidency is no longer solely an individual; it is a small bureaucracy. The White House has grown by leaps and bounds since the 1930s and today numbers some 3,000 employees. About 350 of them report directly or indirectly to the president. White House policymaker Robert B. Porter outlines the task of organizing this bureaucracy in Selection 46, "Managing the White House."

Organizing the White House bureaucracy is only the beginning of the managerial presidency. Presidents must seize the legislative agenda if possible, exert leadership over the sprawling executive establishment, and try to capture the support of the general public. If these tasks are daunting in the early months of a new administration—when the president is riding the crest of a wave of public support—they become even more difficult as the administration ages. This is the subject of Charles O. Jones's "Governing When It's Over: The Limits of Presidential Power" (Selection 47).

Thomas E. Cronin has observed that "the ultimate paradox of the modern presidency is that it is always too powerful and yet it is always inadequate."[1] That is, if the president exerts forceful leadership, some observers will resent it and charge that such actions stretch the

Constitution's provisions beyond their limits. At the same time, presidents are almost always inadequate because they fall short of our highest goals for them and for the country. The American public, for its part, continues to exhibit faith in presidential leadership. Many commentators are convinced that vigorous presidential leadership is needed to overcome the potential stalemate inherent in the Constitution's scheme of checks and balances.

Note

1. Thomas E. Cronin, *The State of the Presidency,* 2d ed. (Boston: Little, Brown, 1980), 22.

42. *Federalist* No. 70

Alexander Hamilton

Of all the founders, Hamilton was the firmest advocate of vigorous executive leadership of the national government. He pronounced "energy in the executive" a primary quality of good government, as opposed to the deliberation and delay typical of legislative assemblies. In the Philadelphia convention of 1787, Hamilton fought tenaciously for this concept of the executive, a feature totally absent from the Articles of Confederation. With James Wilson of Pennsylvania, he created the potentially powerful presidency contained in Article II of the Constitution.

Hamilton was thirty years old in 1787 when he wrote fifty-one of the eighty-five essays of *The Federalist Papers*. These essays, originally published as newspaper articles, were intended to persuade legislators to ratify the Constitution. *Federalist* No. 70 is the boldest statement of the need for a powerful executive that would not raise fears of monarchical rule. In the New York convention of 1788, Hamilton pressed for ratification of the new Constitution. After five and a half weeks of seemingly hopeless fighting, he won ratification by three votes.

There is an idea, which is not without its advocates, that a vigorous Executive is inconsistent with the genius of republican government.... Energy in the Executive is a leading character in the definition of good government. It is essential to the protection of the community against foreign attacks; it is not less essential to the steady administration of the laws; to the protection of property against those irregular and high-handed combinations which sometimes interrupt the ordinary course of justice; to the security of liberty against the enterprises and assaults of ambition, of faction, and of anarchy.

There can be no need, however, to multiply arguments or examples on this head. A feeble Executive implies a feeble execution of the government. A feeble execution is but another phrase for a bad execution; and a government ill executed, whatever it may be in theory, must be, in practice, a bad government....

The ingredients which constitute energy in the Executive are, first, unity; secondly, duration; thirdly, an adequate provision for its support; fourthly, competent powers.

The ingredients which constitute safety in the republican sense are first, a due dependence on the people; secondly, a due responsibility.

Those politicians and statesmen who have been the most celebrated for the soundness of their principles and for the justice of their views, have declared in favor of a single Executive and a numerous legislature. They have, with great propriety, considered energy as the most necessary qualification of the former, and have regarded this as most applicable to power in a single hand; while they have, with equal propriety, considered the latter as best adapted to deliberation and wisdom, and best calculated to conciliate the confidence of the people and to secure their privileges and interests.

That unity is conducive to energy will not be disputed. Decision, activity, secrecy, and despatch will generally characterize the proceedings of one man in a much more eminent degree than the proceedings of any greater number; and in proportion as the number is increased, these qualities will be diminished.

This unity may be destroyed in two ways: either by vesting the power in two or more magistrates of equal dignity and authority; or by vesting it ostensibly in one man, subject, in whole or in part, to the control and cooperation of others, in the capacity of counsellors to him. Of the first, the two Consuls of Rome may serve as an example; of the last, we shall find examples in the constitutions of several of the States. New York and New Jersey, if I recollect right, are the only States which have intrusted the executive authority wholly to single men. Both these methods of destroying the unity of the Executive have their partisans; but the votaries of an executive council are the most numerous. They are both liable, if not to equal, to similar objections, and may in most lights be examined in conjunction. . . .

Wherever two or more persons are engaged in any common enterprise or pursuit, there is always danger of difference of opinion. If it be a public trust or office, in which they are clothed with equal dignity and authority, there is peculiar danger of personal emulation and even animosity. From either, and especially from all these causes, the most bitter dissentions are apt to spring. Whenever these happen, they lessen the respectability, weaken the authority, and distract the plans and operations of those whom they divide. If they should unfortunately assail the supreme executive magistracy of a country, consisting of a plurality of persons, they might impede or frustrate the most important measures of the government, in the most critical emergencies of the state. And what is still worse, they might split the community into the most violent and irreconcilable factions, adhering differently to the different individuals who composed the magistracy.

Men often oppose a thing, merely because they have had no agency in planning it, or because it may have been planned by those whom they dislike. But if they have been consulted, and have happened to disapprove, opposition then becomes, in their estimation, an indispensable duty of self-love. They seem to think themselves bound in honor, and by all the motives of personal infallibility, to defeat the success of what has been resolved upon contrary to their sentiments. . . .

In the legislature, promptitude of decision is oftener an evil than a benefit. The differences of opinion, and the jarrings of parties in that department of the government, though they may sometimes obstruct salutary plans, yet often promote deliberation and circumspection, and serve to check excesses in the majority. When a resolution too is once taken, the opposition must be at an end. That resolution is a law, and resistance to it punishable. But no favorable circumstances palliate or atone for the disadvantages of dissension in the executive department. Here, they are pure and unmixed. There is no point at which they cease to operate. They serve to embarrass and weaken the execution of the plan or measure to which they relate, from the first step to the final conclusion of it. They constantly counteract those qualities in the Executive which are the most necessary ingredients in its composition,—vigor and expedition, and this without any counterbalancing good. In the conduct of war, in which the energy of the Executive is the bulwark of the national security, every thing would be apprehended from its plurality. . . .

It is evident from these considerations, that the plurality of the Executive tends to deprive the people of the two greatest securities they can have for the faithful exercise of any delegated power, *first*, the restraints of public opinion, which lose their efficacy, as well on account of the division of the censure attendant on bad measures among a number, as on account of the uncertainty on whom it ought to fall: and, *secondly*, the opportunity of discovering with facility and clearness the misconduct of the persons they trust, in order either to their removal from office, or to their actual punishment in cases which admit of it.

In England, the king is a perpetual magistrate; and it is a maxim which has obtained for the sake of the public peace, that he is unaccountable for his administration, and his person sacred. Nothing, therefore, can be wiser in that kindgom, than to annex to the king a constitutional council, who may be responsible to the nation for the advice they give. Without this, there would be no responsibility whatever in the executive department—an idea inadmissible in a free government. But even there the king is not bound by the resolutions of his council, though they are answerable for the advice they give. He is the absolute master of his own conduct in the exercise of his office, and may observe or disregard the counsel given to him at his sole discretion.

But in a republic, where every magistrate ought to be personally responsible for his behavior in office, the reason which in the British Constitution dictates the propriety of a council, not only ceases to apply, but turns against the institution. In the monarchy of Great Britain, it furnishes a substitute for the prohibited responsibility of the chief magistrate, which serves in some degree as a hostage to the national justice for his good behavior. In the American republic, it would serve to destroy, or would greatly diminish, the intended and necessary responsibility of the Chief Magistrate himself.

The idea of a council to the Executive, which has so generally obtained in the State constitutions, has been derived from that maxim of republican jealousy which considers power as safer in the hands of a number of men than of a single man. If the maxim should be admitted to be applicable to the case, I should contend that the advantage on that side would not counterbalance the numerous disadvantages on the opposite side. But I do not think the rule at all applicable to the executive power. I clearly concur in opinion, in this particular, with a writer whom the celebrated Junius pronounces to be "deep, solid, and ingenious," that "the executive power is more easily confined when it is ONE"; that it is far more safe there should be a single object for the jealousy and watchfulness of the people; and, in a word, that all multiplication of the Executive is rather dangerous than friendly to liberty. . . .

I will only add that, prior to the appearance of the Constitution, I rarely met with an intelligent man from any of the States, who did not admit, as the result of experience, that the UNITY of the executive of this State was one of the best of the distinguishing features of our constitution.

43. The Only National Voice in Affairs

Woodrow Wilson

Woodrow Wilson was among the first Americans to earn a doctorate in political science. He received his degree from the Johns Hopkins University, and his doctoral dissertation, *Congressional Government* (1885), is still in print today. Wilson was not only a leader in the infant discipline of political science; he was also professor at and president of Princeton University, governor of New Jersey, and president of the United States (1913–1921). In his dissertation, he had examined critically the rampant power of the legislative branch—"government by the chairmen of the standing committees of Congress." By 1907 he had come to believe that a vigorous presidency could overcome the defects of the Constitution of 1787 and provide the leadership and focus for the national debate he desired. In Wilson's view, the intricate checks and balances had prevented development of the "energetic" executive Hamilton had envisioned, despite the appearance in times of crisis of strong presidents such as Jackson and Lincoln. If the presidency of constitutional design was unreliable, the presidency of national leadership was more promising. Wilson's eloquent description of the "national voice" remains the blueprint for the twentieth-century "public" or "rhetorical" presidency.

The makers of our federal Constitution followed the scheme as they found it expounded in Montesquieu, followed it with genuine scientific enthusiasm. The admirable expositions of the *Federalist* read like thoughtful applications of Montesquieu to the political needs and circumstances of America. They are full of the theory of checks and balances. The President is balanced off against Congress, Congress against the President, and each against the courts. . . .

. . . The presidency has been one thing at one time, another at another, varying with the man who occupied the office and with the circumstances that surrounded him. One account must be given of the office during the period 1789 to 1825, when the government was getting its footing both at home and abroad, struggling for its place among the nations and its full credit among its own people; when English precedents and traditions were strongest; and when the men chosen for the office were men bred to leadership in a way that attracted to them the attention and confidence of the whole country. Another account must be given of it during Jackson's time, when an imperious man, bred not in deliberative assemblies or quiet councils, but in the field and upon a rough frontier, worked his own will upon affairs, with or without formal sanction of law, sustained by a clear undoubting conscience and the love of a people who had grown deeply impatient of the regime he had supplanted. Still another account must be given of it during the years 1836 to 1861, when domestic affairs of many debatable kinds absorbed the country, when Congress necessarily exercised the chief choices of policy, and when the Presidents who followed one another in office lacked the personal force and initiative to make for themselves a leading place in counsel. After that came the Civil War and Mr. Lincoln's unique task and achievement, when the executive seemed for a little while to become by sheer stress of circumstances the whole government, Congress merely voting supplies and assenting to necessary laws, as Parliament did in the time of the Tudors. From 1865 to 1898 domestic questions, legislative matters in respect of which Congress had naturally to make the initial choice, legislative leaders the chief decisions of policy, came once more to the front, and no President except Mr. Cleveland played a leading and decisive part in the quiet drama of our national life. Even Mr. Cleveland may be said to have owed his great rôle in affairs rather to his own native force and the confused politics of the time, than to any opportunity of leadership naturally afforded him by a system which had subordinated so many Presidents before him to Congress. The war with Spain again changed the balance of parts. Foreign questions became leading questions again, as they had been in the first days of the government, and in them the President was of necessity leader. Our new place in the affairs of the world has since that year of transformation kept him at the front of our government, where our own thoughts and the attention of men everywhere is centered upon him. . . .

The makers of the Constitution seem to have thought of the President as what the stricter Whig theorists wished the king to be: only the legal executive, the presiding and guiding authority in the application of law and the execution of policy. His veto upon legislation was only his 'check' on Congress,—was a power of restraint, not of guidance. He was empowered to prevent bad laws, but he was not to be given an opportunity to make good ones. As a matter of fact he has become very much more. He has become the leader of his party and the guide of the nation in political purpose, and therefore in legal action. The constitutional structure of the government has hampered and limited his action in these significant rôles, but it has not prevented it. . . . Greatly as the practice and influence of Presidents has varied, there can be no mistaking the fact that we have grown more and more inclined from generation to generation to look to the President as the unifying force in our complex system, the leader both of his party and of the nation.

As legal executive, his constitutional aspect, the President cannot be thought of alone. He cannot execute laws. Their actual daily execution must be taken care of by the several executive departments and by the now innumerable body of federal officials throughout the country. In respect of the strictly executive duties of his office the President may be said to administer the presidency in conjunction with the members of his cabinet, like the chairman of a commission. He is even of necessity much less active in the actual carrying out of the law than are his colleagues and advisers. It is therefore becoming more and more true, as the business of the government becomes more complex and extended, that the President is becoming more and more a political and less and less an executive officer. His executive powers are in commission, while his political powers more and more centre and accumulate upon him and are in their very nature personal and inalienable. . . .

He cannot escape being the leader of his party except by incapacity and lack of personal force, because he is at once the choice of the party and of the nation. He is the party nominee, and the only party nominee for whom the whole nation votes. Members of the House and Senate are representatives of localities, are voted for only by sections of voters, or by local bodies of electors like the members of the state legislatures. There is no national party choice except that of President. No one else represents the people as a whole, exercising a national choice; and inasmuch as his strictly executive duties are in fact subordinated, so far at any rate as all detail is concerned, the President represents not so much the party's governing efficiency as its controlling ideals and principles. He is not so much part of its organization as its vital link of connection with the thinking nation. He can dominate his party by being spokesman for the real sentiment and purpose of the country, by giving direction to opinion, by giving the country at once the information and the statement of policy which will enable it to form its judgments alike of parties and of men.

For he is also the political leader of the nation, or has it in his choice to be. The nation as a whole has chosen him, and is conscious that it has no other political spokesman. His is the only national voice in affairs. Let him once win the admiration and confidence of the country, and no other single force can withstand him, no combination of forces will easily overpower him. His position takes the imagination of the country. He is the representative of no constituency, but of the whole people. When he speaks in his true character, he speaks for no special interest. If he rightly interpret the national thought and boldly insist upon it, he is irresistible; and the country never feels the zest of action so much as when its President is of such insight and calibre. Its instinct is for unified action, and it craves a single leader. It is for this reason that it will often prefer to choose a man rather than a party. A President whom it trusts can not only lead it, but form it to his own views.

... If he lead the nation, his party can hardly resist him. His office is anything he has the sagacity and force to make it.

... [We] can safely predict that as the multitude of the President's duties increases, as it must with the growth and widening activities of the nation itself, the incumbents of the great office will more and more come to feel that they are administering it in its truest purpose and with greatest effect by regarding themselves as less and less executive officers and more and more directors of affairs and leaders of the nation,—men of counsel and of the sort of action that makes for enlightenment.

44. The Media and the White House

Michael B. Grossman

As Woodrow Wilson understood, the president is "the only national voice in affairs." In Wilson's day the White House press corps was a small informal group of male reporters who worked for newspapers and magazines. Today's press corps is huge, representing news organizations of diverse types from all over the world. The revival of aggressive investigative reporting in the 1960s and 1970s, in the aftermath of the Vietnam War and the Watergate affair, led to the belief that the press has taken an adversarial stance toward the White House, emphasizing negative news and impeding presidential leadership. Lyndon Johnson, Richard Nixon, Gerald Ford, and Jimmy Carter all ran into tough, critical reporting from a skeptical press corps. Commentators worried that "the press has made it impossible to govern." Yet Ronald Reagan proved the critics wrong. Reporters repeatedly pointed out his lack of information and lax managerial habits, but the public seemed not to care. Even in the shakiest moments of his administration, the public seemed to like and trust him. An expert on White House-media relations, Michael B. Grossman teaches political science at Towson State University in Maryland. His article first appeared in *Public Affairs Report,* published in 1989 by the Institute of Governmental Affairs at the University of California, Berkeley.

At the end of the Carter Administration and during the first half of Reagan's term, many leading political analysts suggested that the enervation of presidential power stemmed in good part from the manner in which he was covered by the media. "The press has made it impossible to govern or oppose the government," [Johns Hopkins University political scientist] Francis Rourke commented. Media coverage, especially television coverage, would emphasize the negative. "Intense television coverage," Austin Ranney [a University of California, Berkeley, scholar] wrote, "deprives him [the president] of some policy options and reduces the time he has to put his programs in place and get the results." Almost as though following this script, news organizations moved quickly to unfavorable judgment. "The stench of failure hangs over the Reagan White House," the *New York Times* editorialized two years after the President's inauguration.

Whether Reagan failed during 1981-82, the "pre-teflon" era, depends on the measurement. Numerous critical stories appeared on the network news, about which the administration complained bitterly, depicting his economic and social policies as having wrought hardship for the working class and misery for the poor. His standing in the polls was the lowest of any modern president during a similar period.

In this regard, his experience was similar to that of Carter, who experienced increasingly negative press coverage and assessments during his last two years in office. His standing in the polls plummeted, and Carter suffered the ultimate humiliation of being the first elected incumbent president to lose a reelection attempt since the Great Depression.

The Reagan experience during this period, however, suggests that theories of the press's ability to undermine a presidency need further exploration and reconsideration. The "Reagan revolution," including the tax cut, defense build-up, and budget reorganization occurred during this period when his public standing was low. His standing in the Washington community obviously was very different.

The Post-Neustadtian World

The dynamics of presidential power described by Richard Neustadt [political scientist, whose classic work, *Presidential Power*, was published in 1960] suggest that presidents must convince the public while impressing the professionals of the Washington community. Presidents who earned a high level of public prestige could expect that professionals would regard them as people to be reckoned with. Similarly, a president might presume that as segments of the public became aware of his positive reputation among professionals, they would pass on the word.

Prior to Reagan, presidential approval ratings dropped from the beginning to the end of their incumbency. The aging of an administration results in the weakening of the coalitions mobilized behind a president.

[Political scientist] Robert De Clerico suggested that this was an inevitable process. The ephemeral coalitions put together to get a candidate elected are torn apart by the decisions a president must make that inevitably create enemies or at least disgruntled allies.

Reagan's experience was different. After an unusually low approval rating during his first two years, Reagan received high levels of public approval as indicated in the polls for the remainder of his term except for the early months of the Iran-contra revelations.

President as Communicator

Policies that shape a president's image involve the construction of a level of political support that will enable a president to retain public confidence, minimize the potential impact of attacks from the organized political opposition, and prevent dissension among the politically powerful in Washington from undermining his effectiveness. The main building blocks of what is referred to as political communications consist of elements that create trust in the president.

Presidents need to understand the importance of media relations for political communications. Presidents who rank high on the spectrum of success as political communicators use media relations as part of their techniques for informing the public of their goals and rallying the support needed if they are to reach them. The transition from Carter to Reagan displayed both ends of the spectrum within a short period. Their experience brings into sharp focus the importance of a president's personal skills as a communicator and the need to have a staff with the organizational skills to plan and integrate all forms of political communications. What counts for an administration is the manner in which the president presents himself, the clarity with which the administration's priorities are presented, and the staff's ability to integrate his messages to the public with the flow of more direct political communications to Congress, the bureaucracy, interest groups, and other major political actors.

More specifically, a president needs to know how his administration's relations with the media fit into this larger picture. Further, he needs to know which elements of the relationship are within his influence and which are not. The following five factors are of particular importance in determining whether a president will be a successful communicator and how he will stand on this spectrum.

1. The transition to power—the nature of the relations the president and his staff establish with the press and public during his pursuit of the nomination as well as the general election campaign, the relations established in the 10 weeks prior to the inauguration, and the first months in office.

2. The development of themes—the president's ability to develop themes that the public finds acceptable and compatible with their expectations. Closely related to this is the president's ability to appear to the media and the public in a manner that suits their expectations of what a president should be, what we refer to as "the anthropomorphic presidency." The personal skills of a president as a communicator that are specifically important to this role relate to his comfort with reporters, his facility with particular forms of media such as television, his speaking ability, and his "likeability."

3. The organizational structure and expertise for political communications within the White House—particularly the manner in which press operations are connected to other communications and liaison operations.

4. His constituency (i.e., the following he has with members of the press and with the public)—this includes the portion of the media that will be inclined to portray his version of his activities and the portion of the public that is strongly inclined to accept it.

5. The responses of news organizations to the president's efforts, their abilities to independently alter the relationship, and their desire to do so.

Party Differences

Republican communications policies seem to have a higher cash value for their presidents than those of the Democrats. Republicans bring an organized hierarchical staff when they arrive at the White House. Because they bring their managerial baggage with them when they arrive in Washington, Republicans are more likely to establish a structure capable of monitoring the flow of communications during the early months of an administration when they still have considerable flexibility. Their tighter control helps them maintain public attention on the president's agenda. Thus they increase the chance of developing and maintaining momentum for the administration's programs and acquiring political support for the president.

A striking contrast between the Reagan and Carter Administrations was the large number of prominent staff appointments by Reagan to individuals with prior experience at the presidential level. For example, David Gergen, Reagan's Director of Communications, had served in important communications positions during both the Nixon and Ford Administrations. Unlike most White House assistants, he did not need a lot of on-the-job training.

Republicans in the White House view the president's relations with the media as part of an overall strategy involving the effective use of political communications. This means that they are more concerned about the relationship between his image and his powers than with his relations with the Washington press corps. Since James Hagerty served Eisenhower, Republican press secretaries have exercised little power. On the other hand, Republican presidents beginning with Richard Nixon appointed strong communications directors who became members of the inner circle of the senior staff and were influential in formulating policies concerning the president's activities.

In contrast, Democratic presidents and their aides have focused on the problems of dealing with and responding to the Washington press corps. John Kennedy, Lyndon Johnson, and Jimmy Carter reacted to or attempted to lead the "press," referring to those reporters and columnists who reported on the presidency. Their press secretaries served as spokesmen or alter egos for them more often than did their Republican counterparts.

The Public

Among the post-Eisenhower presidents, Ronald Reagan had the largest and strongest constituency, while Jimmy Carter was elected with only soft support. Once again the two presidents are located at opposite poles of the spectrum. Presidents who bring a considerable public following when they enter office have an important ingredient for effective political communications. They begin their terms with a segment of the population that is inclined to take their sides in descriptions of some of their more controversial policies and activities. Reagan's following was built up during more than 16 years of national political activism for conservative and Republican causes. When he became president, he could call upon many groups to work for his programs and against his adversaries without reading the fine print explaining what he was doing. In the months following his election, he and his staff worked to maintain and deepen this support. Thus the administration had a very large block of supporters whom they could count on. They worked with them to make certain they would continue to be supporters. David Gergen estimated that because of them, it was unlikely that even a serious crisis would result in the kind of public failures experienced by Harry Truman and Jimmy Carter at the end of their terms. He guessed that Reagan had a bottom of 40 percent.

What affects a president's success is the way he combines his core constituency with the potential constituencies available to him once he becomes president. All presidents have an enlarged constituency of soft supporters when they begin their term. Like the media, the public is interested in learning about him. Since he has no record, he is given the benefit of public admiration for the office of the presidency. Just as presidents often misinterpret the favorable response they get in the news media during the early months of their administration, they may misread their high standing in the polls. Like the favorable stories, their standing in the polls will fade at the arrival of the first crisis unless the president has found ways to turn soft supporters into followers.

Reagan broadened his support by communicating a strong sense of being in command, having clear priorities to deal with the sluggishness of the economy, and identifying himself with the symbols of the presidency. He also showed a keen instinct for turning frustration into triumph. After the disaster at the marine barracks in Lebanon [1983], he led the national anger at those who attacked the marines. In his comments sharing sorrow at the plight of those killed in Beirut, he was careful to portray them as fallen heroes rather than as victims, and thus avoided the picture of Carter-like helplessness of the Iran hostage crisis. He also showed himself to be a president of action in his public remarks explaining the Grenada assault that took place at almost the same time. His role in this action, which gathered tremendous popular support, alleviated much of the public frustration that polls indicated had been building up as the Beirut bombing followed a series of terrorist attacks on Americans.

He also expanded his constituency among traditional Republicans of the professional and managerial class who were unenthusiastic about him in 1980. His message to them was substantive. He proposed that the way to change the country for the better was to give this class what it wanted in the way of lower taxes and less government regulation. This group stayed with him in 1984 and continued to back him as long as he maintained these policies.

The president and the White House were in constant communication with his core supporters. The White House was open to them when they got worried. Most important of all, they got the president either in person, on closed circuit television, or (least desirable) on tape. No administration in recent decades was less inclined to forget who brought them to Washington. The network they established worked as well for them as the commercial broadcasts. It was the Reagan Broadcasting System.

45. Ronald Reagan—
Another Hidden-Hand Ike?

Fred I. Greenstein

Although constitutional and popular demands upon modern presidents are unremittingly high, they differ widely in their performance styles. Dwight Eisenhower (1953-1961) and Ronald Reagan (1981-1989) were probably the most popular chief executives since World War II; both left office nearly as popular with the public as when they first took the oath of office. However, both were criticized by many commentators for practicing "hands-off" management, choosing to distance themselves from divisive controversies during their administrations. Fred I. Greenstein, professor of politics at Princeton University, has been a leading figure in the reassessment of Eisenhower's presidency. Whereas Eisenhower's critics condemned his public style as bumbling and directionless, Greenstein and other revisionist scholars claim to discern an underlying "hidden-hand" shrewdness and a firm sense of direction. Did Ronald Reagan exhibit the same hidden virtues? In his article published in *P.S.* in 1980, Greenstein explains the subtler aspects of presidential leadership and weighs the evidence regarding Eisenhower and Reagan.

Name the president. He was enormously popular during his eight years in the White House. In contrast to Truman, Johnson, Nixon, Ford and Carter, he not only entered but also *left* office riding high in the polls. Yet when he stepped down, the experts who make it their business to observe presidents closely did not join in the public adulation. The verdict of the Washington watchers was that he had been a passive participant in his own presidency, remaining disconnected from day-to-day politics and policy.

For the young this can have been only one president—Ronald Reagan. But those whose political memories reach back to the 1950s may recognize that he could also have been the only other two-term president in the post-New Deal era—Dwight D. Eisenhower.

The description of Ike as out of the loop in his own presidency was unquestioned at the time that Eisenhower left office. When Arthur Schlesinger asked a panel of distinguished students of the presidency to rank 31 American presidents in terms of greatness, they placed Eisenhower 21st—a tie with Chester A. Arthur.

Today, whether or not presidency scholars approve of Eisenhower's politics, they no longer hold that he was out to lunch. Instead, their view is that he was a shrewd, informed leader, if not one whose leadership was flawless. Eisenhower is now recognized to have been, in his own way, very much an activist president.

If an Eisenhower's reputation can be reversed in a few decades, what are we to expect of Ronald Reagan? Will Reagan too come to be viewed as a president who ran his own show?

Three steps bring me to my answer. The first is a report of what the bulk of Washington observers perceived Eisenhower's leadership style to have been during and just after he was in office; the second an explanation of why those views changed; the third an account of presidency watchers' current perceptions of Reagan's leadership style.

Until the late 1970s the very notion of an Eisenhower leadership style had been viewed by many to be an oxymoron. He appeared to be a quintessential non-leader. He was notorious for the vagueness of his replies to journalists' questions—often he even acknowledged that he had not *heard* of matters currently in the headlines. He never engaged in visible exercises of political clout. Even his rhetoric lacked the feisty determination to have his own way of a Truman or Roosevelt.

Perhaps the most striking sign of what seemed to be a politically detached president was the presence in the Eisenhower administration of visible, assertive subordinates whose activism contrasted with Eisenhower's apparent remoteness from day-to-day events. The most notable of them were the hard-bitten White House Chief of Staff Sherman Adams and the even more formidable Secretary of State John Foster Dulles. It was a plausible inference that aides such as Adams and Dulles—not Ike himself—were the true decision makers of the Eisenhower years. . . .

The change in Eisenhower's reputation was spurred by the declassification in the 1970s of many of the most sensitive records of his presidency, including his confidential letters and memoranda, his private diary, transcripts and summaries of his official meetings and telephone conversations, as well as a number of transcripts of recordings that were secretly made of his one-to-one conversations in the Oval Office. . . . Above all, the finding that leaps from the documents released in the 1970s is that Eisenhower himself was the engine of his administration's politics and policy making.

Eisenhower gave *the appearance* of reigning rather than ruling for reasons stemming directly from the distinctive way he dealt with a dilemma the Founding Fathers inadvertently built into the president's job. In most democracies, executive power is shared by two individuals with fundamentally different responsibilities: those of head of state and political leader of the government. In Great Britain, for example, the Queen represents the nation and commands broad respect. The prime minister is responsible for the intrinsically divisive political responsibilities of leading the government. In the United States we ask a single chief executive to do both.

The two responsibilities are potentially contradictory. As national leader the president is expected to walk on water, but as governmental leader he must wade through the swamps of politics. If he acts the part of chief of state and fails to lead, the country suffers and he gets the blame. If he engages in the rough and tumble of politics, his capacity to stand for the nation is diminished.

Eisenhower resolved this dilemma by playing up his status as chief of state and working hard at political leadership, *but largely without publicity.* Because he didn't take the credit for his private politicking, political scientists and Washington professionals thought he was inept. They failed to observe that his extraordinary popularity derived in part from not taking sides in political controversies.

One of Eisenhower's operating rules for being a private prime minister and public chief of state was hidden-hand leadership. When there were messy political jobs, he farmed them out. Thus during the period of the 1954 Senate hearings that led to the censure of Joseph McCarthy, he made extensive use of intermediaries in order to undermine the Wisconsin senator. He opposed McCarthy largely from behind the scenes out of the conviction that he would lose and McCarthy would gain, if he tangled directly with a political gutter fighter.

Another of Eisenhower's rules was instrumental use of language. His usages varied strikingly with the purposes he was seeking to achieve. In private memos to aides he expressed himself crisply, with elegant, almost formal statements of what they should seek to accomplish and how; in speeches his language was inspirational though never grandiose; in press conferences he was notorious for his mangled syntax and digressive answers to reporters' questions. . . .

Eisenhower's off-the-record prime ministerial leadership was also marked by a highly contingent mode of delegating authority—one in which he gave some aides extensive independent authority to work within a broad presidential mandate and kept others on short leashes. He also sometimes delegated the responsibility of announcing controversial policies to subordinates, leaving it to them to take the heat. . . .

What of the other side of Eisenhower's leadership? How did he maintain his popularity as an uncontroversial head of state? He did this in part by preventing political catastrophes, while not showing himself as the active agent in the controversial politics of keeping them from occurring. But the filmed footage of Eisenhower's public appearances is a reminder that he also remained popular by conveying a buoyant image of confidence and optimism.

The beaming, exultant Ike was so genuinely appealing we take it for granted that he aroused public enthusiasm effortlessly. That was not the case. Eisenhower revealed how hard he worked at being an exuberantly inspirational leader in a document he did not mean to see the light of day—a draft first chapter of his World War II memoir *Crusade in Europe* that reveals more of his hopes and feelings than he chose to present in the published book. Recollecting the tense days he spent in November 1942 in a damp, ill-lit headquarters deep within the fortress of Gibraltar, anxiously awaiting the intelligence on which to base his decision about whether to order the invasion of North Africa, he wrote, "During those anxious hours I first realized . . . how inexorably and inescapably strain and tension wear away at the leader's endurance, his judgment and his confidence. The pressure becomes more acute because of the duty of a staff constantly to present to the commander the worst side of an eventuality."

Realizing that the commander has the double burden of "preserving optimism in himself and his command" and that "optimism and pessimism are infectious and they spread more rapidly from the head downward than in any other direction," Eisenhower reports that he made a personal resolution: "I firmly determined that my mannerism and speech in public would always reflect the cheerful certainty of victory—that any pessimism and discouragement I might ever feel would be reserved for my pillow. . . . To translate this conviction into tangible results . . . I adopted a policy of circulating through the whole force to the full limit posed by physical considerations. I did my best to meet everyone from general to private with a smile, a pat on the back and a definite interest in his problems."

President Eisenhower was just as committed in inspiring morale as *General* Eisenhower had been. He insisted on appearing in motorcades, even though he found them bruising and exhausting. His commitment to the inspirational side of political leadership was so strong that he commended his practices to other leaders. . . .

It is understandable that the experts misjudged Eisenhower. Presidents who hide their hands conceal their leadership. Indeed only a few of Eisenhower's aides were fully aware of his *modus operandi*, and none of them published their memoirs while he was in office. . . .

If it was not possible to arrive at our present understanding of Eisenhower's leadership until the archives were open, does it follow that we are likely some day to find evidence documenting the existence of a Ronald Reagan whose political style was drastically different from what it now appears to have been? An answer requires that we review what is presently known about Reagan's leadership style.

More so than most presidents, Reagan appears to have had a leadership style that was not all of a piece. Rather, it seems to have differed between two areas of presidential responsibility that cut across the president's roles as head of state and national political leader— public and private leadership. By the former I mean the president's efforts as his administration's chief spokesman and salesman. By the latter I refer to his participation in hatching and making policies, riding herd on their implementation and determining the administration's political strategies.

We do not have to await revelations from the archives to assess President Reagan's public performance; it is sufficient to have viewed him through the television screen while he was in office to know that as chief administration spokesman he was anything but passive. Whether he was speaking as transcendent leader of the nation at the site of the Normandy beachhead or selling the administration's program to Congress and the public, Reagan was indefatigable. In this century, only the two Roosevelts, Wilson, and Kennedy were his match as presidential communicators.

Reagan appears also to have been tireless in an area of presidential leadership that overlaps the public and the private—face-to-face political persuasion. His telephone calls to members of Congress at critical times in the legislative process were well publicized. Moreover, there were many reports of his unpublicized sales pitches to American and foreign leaders. . . .

The most thorough account of Reagan's leadership style is in one of the less-well-known memoirs, that of domestic adviser Martin Anderson. Anderson's analysis, which shows that Reagan's private leadership had a distinct pattern, helps explain how he was able to have a great historical impact in spite of his extraordinary remoteness from the specifics of politics and policy.

First, because he had strong general beliefs Reagan set the administration's priorities. Everyone knew that he placed the defense build-up and the economic program ahead of everything else. Second, he was tactically flexible. He showed absolutely no remorse when he had to adjust to political opposition or to changed economic forecasts. Third, he was a good negotiator, setting his demands higher than the minimum he would accept, and accepting what he could get. Fourth, he made decisions easily and promptly. Finally, Anderson notes, Reagan delegated authority readily.

Anderson's observations do not negate the conclusions of the less analytic memoir writers. Delegation, Anderson goes on to observe, was Reagan's Achilles heel. Reagan's practice was to make decisions on the basis of the options his aides presented to him. He did not question those options or seek to refine and shape them himself. Therefore, when he had competent aides, as in his first term, things tended to go well. When his aides were deficient, as in the case of the truimvirate of Donald Regan, John Poindexter, and Oliver North, the results could be catastrophic.

This brings us to the evidence yielded by the Iran-Contra affair, an episode in which Reagan's relationship to his aides was crucial. As bad as the Iran-Contra affair was for the country, it was a bonanza for students of national affairs, yielding information that otherwise would have been classified for two or more decades. Each successive inquiry the Tower Commission (U.S. President, 1987), the Iran-Contra hearings (U.S. Congress, 1987), and the Oliver North trial (U.S. District Court for the District of Columbia, 1989)—led to new testimony and triggered the release of new documents.

After carefully reviewing White House records and hearing extensive testimony, the Tower Commission characterized Reagan's "management style" as one that "put the burden of policy review and implementation on the shoulders of his advisers." It observed that he appeared not to have been informed at all about the diversion of arms profits to the Contras and that, in the case of the sale to Iran, Reagan had "proceeded with a concept of the [arms] initiative that was not accurately reflected in the reality of the operation."

The Tower Commission's claim was not that Reagan had been inattentive to minutiae, but rather that he had failed to inform himself about the broad outlines of the operation and its relationship to his administration's other efforts, and had therefore allowed members of the White House staff to pursue policies that were internally inconsistent and contrary to his administration's objectives.

The Congressional hearings did not alter this impression of an uninformed, inattentive president who had allowed his staff to engage in seriously flawed political actions, although the executive summary of the report of the hearings stated that the evidence on what Reagan knew and when he knew it was "inconclusive." The Oliver North trial, which led to the release of several hundred pages of previously classified documents, provided evidence that at a minimum adds important nuances to what is known of Reagan's participation in administration decision making, but that at least one observer has construed as changing considerably more than nuances. . . .

Reagan's performance in national security meetings (or at least those that were declassified in connection with the North trial) can readily be compared with Eisenhower's performance in national security meetings. The contrast is stark. Far from simply beating the drums for a broad policy tendency, Eisenhower put a highly specific stamp on policy, intervening authoritatively in debates, identifying underlying issues, defining substantive and strategic options, pulling together discussions and guiding (but not intimidating) his aides. Moreover, when his aides did present him with options, he frequently reshaped them and rarely accepted them without providing his aides with guidance about how to proceed.

The documents declassified for the North trial are a reminder that in spite of the extensive existing information on the inner workings of the Reagan presidency, there is much more to come—Edmund Morris' biography of Reagan (based on the author's personal access to White House councils), the memoirs of George Shultz, Edwin Meese, Jeane Kirkpatrick, and Ronald Reagan himself, not to speak of the still-classified files of the Reagan White House.

All of this acknowledged, the evidence already in suggests that there will be no fundamental revision of present impressions of the Reagan leadership style at whatever future time a Ronald Reagan Presidential Library makes its holdings available to scholars. Rather than showing that Ronald Reagan was a hands-on chief executive, with or without a hidden-hand mode of exercising influence, the Reagan White House records are likely to show that he came closer to being a *no-hands* president.

46. Managing the White House

Roger B. Porter

The president, in the eyes of Woodrow Wilson as well as Alexander Hamilton, is an individual who provides direction and leadership to the executive branch, a political party, and even the citizenry as a whole. The years following Franklin Roosevelt's New Deal, however, brought a new dimension to the office: the presidency as an institution. Increasingly presidents have been surrounded by a sizable bureaucracy: domestic and foreign policy advisers, economists, speechwriters, public relations specialists, lawyers, and schedulers. Many of these White House operatives have vague assignments and little in common except loyalty to the chief executive. Organizing them to formulate and coordinate the president's program, especially in the early months of an administration, is a daunting challenge. Roger B. Porter, a political scientist, prepared these White House management plans before the 1988 election and later was able to help implement them as President Bush's Assistant for Economic and Domestic Policy. His plans were originally printed in the *Report to the Forty-first President*, 1988, prepared by a citizens' group called American Agenda.

A newly elected president faces a host of crucial decisions during the weeks before his inauguration. Among them is how he will organize his White House. Organizational arrangements once established are difficult and sometimes costly to change. It is a set of issues worth thinking about hard at the outset.

I. Organizational Challenges

Managing policy development in the White House involves several persistent challenges:

The Problem of Sifting and Sorting. The overwhelming and unyielding tendency in virtually every Administration is to push problems upward. No White House can solve every problem, cure every ill, nor should the President embrace every issue that gravitates to the White House. Determining what issues the President should get involved in and when is an important role of a well functioning White House policy development process.

The Problem of Accurate Map Drawing. Informed decision making by the President on those issues that merit his personal attention requires that he have drawn for him accurate assessments of substantive and political reality.

He needs to know the consequences in terms of inflation, unemployment, and real growth of the alternative choices he has on economic policy issues. In mobilizing this information and analysis, the process should engage the reservoirs of expertise and knowledge from across the executive branch and beyond.

He also needs to have an accurate understanding of the political consequences associated with his alternative choices—the likely reaction of the Congress, affected constituency groups, and the public. Both parts of the map are essential.

Policy and political assessments are likely to come from different sets of advisers. It is extraordinarily helpful to the President if these streams of advice reach him at the same time and are integrated. Indeed, the coordination of political and policy counsel in a timely way is imperative to informed, successful decision making.

The Problem of Coordination. The White House is more like a holding company than a unified staff. It is composed of individual offices each with a focus to its activities. Communicating well and keeping one another informed are important. A well coordinated White House staff also minimizes duplication of effort.

Part of the challenge of coordination involves sorting out jurisdictional responsibilities between various policy entities (the National Security Council staff, the economic policy machinery, and the domestic policy machinery).

Part of successful coordination also involves making certain that the implementing offices—legislative affairs public liaison, political and intergovernmental affairs, and press and communication—are all pulling in the same direction.

Simply stated, the White House staff has two major coordinating tasks: First, to insure that the President has a full range of high quality advice in making his decisions. Second, to make certain the President's decisions, once made, are supported and implemented.

The Problem of Integration. Not only is it important to have a recognized division of labor, it is also crucial that the various parts of the White House identify the interrelationships between the issues they have responsibility for developing and those being developed by others.

When the machinery under him does not identify these interrelationships, the burden falls on the President to do it for himself. Sometimes this works well; in other instances it does not. It is a task that a well organized White House staff should explicitly undertake.

The Problem of Building a Unified Administration. It is commonplace to observe that senior political appointees in departments and agencies face a variety of conflicting pressures—from Congressional committees exercising oversight, from constituency groups whose support they want and need, from career civil servants anxious to enhance the quality of the department's programs. Yet, they also view themselves as a part of an Administration and want to be considered loyal members of it.

From the President's standpoint he has an interest in ensuring that senior political appointees are sensitive to Administration-wide concerns and interests. Moreover, he needs not only the expertise found in departments and agencies to assist him in making informed decisions, but he needs the confidence that a united Administration will actively support his decisions during the often lengthy process of securing their implementation.

The Problem of Initiative and Control. The President is looked to in the U.S. political system to serve, as Alexander Hamilton described it, as the "energizing element." In the post-World War II period, the President has traditionally submitted not only a unified Federal budget, but also a comprehensive legislative program. More than any other official or institution, the President is in a position to shape the national agenda.

Thus, presidents not only need policy development arrangements that will generate policy initiative, they also need institutional mechanisms that will help them manage the agenda in the major policy arenas—national security, economic policy, and domestic policy.

In thinking about how to meet these challenges there are two overriding concerns:

1. The kinds of people whom presidents select for their White House staff; and

2. The way in which they are organized.

II. Personnel

Organizational arrangements are important; process matters. But in the end, structure and procedures are unlikely to overwhelm the importance of people. Both sound organizational arrangements and officials well suited to their tasks are crucial in meeting the multiple challenges facing the White House.

Recent Trends. The White House Staff has grown in size during the post-World War II period, though far less than many popular accounts suggest. What is more striking than the size of the White House Staff, however, is the visibility and public attention focused on many White House staffers.

The Brownlow Committee recommendation [in 1937] of six presidential assistants "with a passion for anonymity" seems a far distance from the behavior of some recent White House staff members. In part, this development is the result of much greater press scrutiny of the Presidency in general and White House operations in particular. Yet, the high public profile of some White House staff members raises an important question for a new president: How much visibility does he want White House staff members to seek or accept? What qualities does he consider most important for his staffers to possess?

The answers to these questions, of course, depend heavily on the roles that the President envisions for his staff and the relationship he wants between his immediate staff and his department and agency officials.

A second trend, in addition to greater visibility, is the proliferation of titles. The number of White House staff with titles that include the phrase "to the President" has grown dramatically. Insiders are sensitive to the nuances associated with the "real" pecking order within any organization. But from the outside, the proliferation of titles has greatly multiplied the number of those who may claim to speak for the President.

It is always easier to expand titles and positions than to reduce them. One consideration the new president should weigh in determining staffing structures and titles is what this conveys with respect to the number of people who are perceived as having authority to speak for him.

Personal Qualities. Some personal qualities, such as integrity and intelligence, should obviously loom large in the selection of White House staff. There is also a strong attraction to placing considerable reliance on loyalty, particularly loyalty that has been demonstrated in the past.

This emphasis on already demonstrated loyalty is reinforced by the claim that campaign aides have "earned" a place in a new Administration. There are some individuals who have developed considerable ability in the management of campaigns and in the tasks of governing, but the transferability of skills is not automatic.

Strong analytical skills, substantive knowledge, and the capacity for strategic thinking are not enough. A major function of those responsible for White House policy development is working with others throughout the Administration, mobilizing the best information and analysis from across the executive branch, and ensuring that those responsible for implementing a policy have had a role in its formulation.

Those with whom they work in departments and agencies must view them as fair, as "honest brokers," but they must also have sufficient stature so that they are viewed as peers. Part of this depends on the signals the President sends with respect to his confidence in those on his immediate staff. Part of it depends on the experience and abilities the White House staffer brings with him to his office.

One of the greatest dangers to Administration unity is when jurisdictional battles veer out of control. There will always be some struggles in any Administration over turf, but the potential for minimizing these struggles is greatly enhanced by having White House staffers with their egos well under control. The Brownlow Committee's aspiration of assistants "with a passion for anonymity" is a worthy one, even if the reality of the visibility of certain White House positions makes such anonymity difficult to maintain.

Temperamentally there is much to be said for White House staffers who are prepared to play an inside rather than an outside role. It is not necessary, and is usually unwise, for White House staff members to assume a major role as spokesmen for Administration programs.

Similarly, those who are temperamentally instinctive advocates, or who have strong policy agendas of their own, are better suited for roles in departments and agencies than in the White House.

III. Organizational Issues

There are a number of organizational issues that flow from the policy development challenges outlined above. How many channels of advice should the President rely on? Who should have control of these channels? What are the roles of the President's immediate staff and of executive department and agency officials? Should the White House have a Chief of Staff and, if so, what should be his role?

Issue 1: The Number of Policy Channels Reporting to the President

Two general principles can help in weighing how many policy channels or entities should report to the President.

The Need for Policy Integration. The first is the need to integrate policy. Several considerations argue for limiting the number of policy channels reporting directly to the President. The more entities, the more specialized and narrow their outlook and mandates are likely to be, and the more likely that some issues will fall through the proverbial crack since it will be difficult to pinpoint responsibility.

Creating several specialized committees of councils invites jurisdictional battles, inevitably duplicates effort, and can contribute to a feeling and the reality of uncertainty regarding who is responsible for what.

The more interrelated the problems facing the President, the more compelling the case to reduce the number of entities reporting independently to him. Likewise, the more groups reporting to him, the more the President must assume responsibility for fitting the pieces together. A president interested in identifying the interrelationships among issues will want those advising him to share his concern for integration and coherence. If a group reporting to him has responsibility for a broad range of related issues, they have an incentive to draw his attention to the interrelationships between the issues.

In the interest of coherence, the fewer decision making channels to the President, the better. Carried to its logical extreme, the quest for integration would result in a single entity.

The Need for Efficiency. A second series of factors also merits consideration. How much work can a single entity efficiently handle? How broad an area of public policy can it assume responsibility for and still function effectively? Any single group can consider only a finite number of issues. There are limits, even if the group is prepared to meet daily at the cabinet level. . . .

There are other good reasons for questioning the wisdom of a single channel to the President. The broader the policy area, the fewer officials who will have a genuine interest in most of the issues under consideration. It is much easier to develop a group sense of responsibility when the members attending are engaged in considering issues genuinely affecting their department.

Thus, the quest for policy integration suggests merit in limiting the number of groups reporting directly to the President, while the desire to use interdepartmental entities effectively suggests the need for more than one.

The Number of Councils and Their Specific Responsibilities. There are many possible ways of slicing the public policy pie. In thinking about specific policy areas, two additional objectives merit consideration. First, one should avoid divisions that are likely to produce consistent overlaps and jurisdictional battles. Second, the more closely a policy council's work is tied to a regular work flow, the more easily its members will develop a sense of collective responsibility. To the extent that existing institutions have worked well, they should be used.

Four principal channels of advice to the President—the budget process and three cabinet-level interdepartmental councils responsible for national security, economic policy, and domestic policy—is a reasonable division of labor, given the objectives of keeping the number of entities with direct reporting relationships to the President to a minimum while not placing excessive burdens of any single institution. . . .

This proposed division would provide direct, regular access to the President for each department. Every cabinet member should have membership on at least one of the three policy councils. A cabinet member, such as the Secretary of State whose department has strong interests in both national security and economic matters, could have membership on two councils. To prevent unnecessary jurisdictional conflicts and to insure that budgetary interests are considered throughout the policy formulation process, the Director of OMB should be a regular member of the councils dealing with economic and domestic policy, and meet with the National Security Council when issues involving major budgetary considerations are under discussion.

This four-fold division of labor—the budget, national security, economic policy, and domestic policy—leaves open the question of responsibility for the coordination of international economic policy. Such issues have grown in importance as the U.S. economy has become increasingly interrelated with the global economy. Some have suggested creating a separate council to address foreign economic policy issues. The Eisenhower and Nixon Administrations did so. But both these efforts failed to persist across administrations or to acquire a significant role in the policy making world. . . .

Issue 2: Management of the Policy Councils

The history of cabinet-level councils suggests that how well they are managed crucially influences their success. An appropriate structure, sensible procedures, and skillful management are essential.

Past efforts to manage such councils by giving lead responsibility to a department or agency have not been encouraging. The most successful ones have been White House based in terms of managing their day-to-day activities, although they have generally either been chaired by the President or a cabinet secretary.

In Washington, symbols are important. The individual with responsibility for managing policy development in one of these broad policy areas needs to have, and to be perceived as having, a close relationship with the President.

If he is to deal with cabinet secretaries as a peer, he must be viewed as being the person in the White House responsible for managing the development of national security or economic or domestic policy. For these and other reasons he should be at the Assistant to the President level.

Issue 3: Size and Roles of White House Policy Staffs

Skillfully managing the flow of information and options to the President on national security or economic or domestic policy requires both good working relationships with key departments and agencies and sufficient independent capability to undertake analysis and structure issues.

Building a united Administration entails fully involving departments and agencies in the White House decision making process. But one wants sufficient internal resources so that the President is not wholly dependent on his departments and agencies. The staff needs to be large enough to be able to exercise quality control, while not becoming so large that it is tempted to attempt to displace department and agency resources. . . .

Too small a staff renders it unable to effectively exercise quality control over the work produced by the Council. The staffs must have the capacity to do more than skillfully move papers and set meetings. Too large a staff is likely to soon be filled with advocates anxious to press for particular policy outcomes rather than focusing their efforts on managing a process. Optimally, the staffs would consist of able generalists who think and write clearly and who are good at managing people and processes. Departments and agencies are unlikely to view such a staff as a threat or a competitor.

Issue 4: Roles of a White House Chief of Staff

Some presidents have entertained the notion and even experimented with serving as their own Chief of Staff. Such arrangements have rarely worked well. Coordinating the activities of the White House staff, including the offices dealing with scheduling, personnel, speech-writing, etc., the offices dealing with the major outside constituencies (Congress, the press, interest groups, and state and local governments), and the various policy offices is a major task, a task wisely delegated by a president.

Accurate map drawing for the President requires bringing together political and substantive advice. This does not happen automatically. Someone must take responsibility for seeing that it happens. The most appropriate person is the Chief of Staff.

Assignment of responsibility for particular issues among the major policy entities dealing with the budget, national security, economic, and domestic policy is another task for the Chief of Staff. When jurisdictional matters need sorting out, a White House Chief of Staff is the logical person to see that responsibility is clearly assigned. . . .

47. Governing When It's Over: The Limits of Presidential Power

Charles O. Jones

Presidents are counseled to strike quickly after their election, to formulate plans and push them through Congress as soon as possible. The reasoning is that newly elected presidents enjoy an all-too-brief "honeymoon" of public support that is dissipated as soon as White House initiatives stir controversy and make enemies. Yet the president serves for four or even eight years; leadership must be exerted long after the election (or reelection) euphoria has faded, when critics of the president are in full cry. In his article published in *The Brookings Review* in 1989, Charles O. Jones, Hawkins Professor of Political Science at the University of Wisconsin, Madison, considers the problem of developing strategies for holding onto the reins of leadership after the election in the face of serious challenges to the president's leadership. In view of the fragile mandates granted modern presidents, such strategies are essential if they are to remain effective while in office.

A post-election cartoon in 1988 showed movers carrying a large trophy marked "mandate" out of the White House. As George Bush looks on, an aide explains: "That goes back with the Reagans, George." No one doubted that Bush had won the right to occupy the White House for the next four years. But the common observation was that he lacked a mandate.

Soon after this judgment was rendered, the new president was criticized for failing to produce large-scale proposals to deal with the issues of our time. He moved too slowly to suit the professional White House watchers. "President-elect Bush has hit the ground limping" is the way Tom Wicker of *The New York Times* saw it. "Five weeks after the election he is still hedging on major program decisions. . . ." Failure to receive a mandate was not mentioned.

Ronald Reagan was said to have received a mandate in 1980. His impressive victory over an incumbent president, combined with significant gains for congressional Republicans, surely meant that Americans wanted the kind of changes "Reaganism" represented. Yet the 1984 election was described as a "landslide without a mandate," and early talk of lame-duck status for Reagan grew louder following the 1986 mid-term elections. Mandates aren't forever.

"Governing when it's over" means figuring out not only how to govern when the election is over but also how to govern in the face of serious challenges to the president's right or power to do so. Presidents must be prepared to take advantage of opportunities; they must restore confidence and legitimacy when damaged by events like the Great Depression, Vietnam, Watergate, Americans held hostage in Iran, the Iran-contra scandal. That has always been so. But it is of special interest for the post-World War II period in which the majority party has won but four of eleven presidential elections.

Under what conditions is it said to be over for a president? And how do these conditions help us to understand the startup of the Bush presidency? Those are the questions to be treated here.

The Lame Duck

The most obvious case of governing when it's over is the lame duck. As originally applied to the president, the phrase referred to one who was not reelected—Grover Cleveland, Benjamin Harrison, William Howard Taft—and who then served during the long period from the election until the inauguration of the new president. For most of our history, that period lasted for four months, from the election in November until March 4 of the following year. In 1933 the 20th Amendment shortened the period by setting the inauguration date on January 20. However, the concept is still applicable. Jimmy Carter is the most recent case of the classic lame duck.

The 22nd Amendment, ratified in 1951, introduced a new version of the lame duck. Since "no person shall be elected to the office of the President more than twice . . . ," a *reelected* president may be labeled a lame duck for his entire second term. This perversion of the original usage is defined less in terms of legitimacy, as is the case with a defeated president, than of effectiveness. A second-term president is presumed to have lost influence precisely because he is ineligible for a third term. He is thus faced with having to govern as other politicians plot their elevation to his office.

The size of the reelection margin does not appear to compensate. Consider the 1984 election. Ronald Reagan won every state but his opponent's home state of Minnesota, which he lost by fewer than 4,000 votes in more than 2 million cast. Reagan garnered 59 percent of the popular vote—54.5 million votes, the most ever—and 98 percent of the electoral vote. Yet, as Karen S. Johnson has noted, "in the network coverage of the 1984 Presidential Election, news anchors Tom Brokaw,

Dan Rather, and special news correspondent Roger Mudd suggested that the entire second term of Ronald Reagan would be a lame-duck presidency." Theirs was a commonly accepted characterization.

When the Democrats recaptured control of the Senate in 1986, talk of Reagan's lame-duck status was renewed. The strengthening of congressional Democrats, the preoccupation of the White House with the Iran-contra scandal, and the approaching 1988 presidential election led to widespread predictions of legislative stalemate. The last two years of Reagan's presidency were expected to produce little. In fact, the 100th Congress was one of the most productive in recent decades. At the very least, that experience should encourage analysts to reconsider the lame-duck scenario, based as it is on questionable assumptions about the nature and dynamics of national policymaking in the modern age.

The Mandate

Many years ago the eminent political scientist Robert A. Dahl urged caution in deriving policy messages from political elections. "We can rarely interpret a majority of first choices among candidates in a national election as being equivalent to a majority of first choices for a specific policy," he wrote in *A Preface to Democratic Theory*. From the very start, the design for creating a government through elections made it unlikely that votes for national offices with staggered terms—House, Senate, president—could be integrated in a policy sense. Exactly the opposite was the intention; the election system was meant to reflect the perspectives of the differing groups empowered to elect (originally, eligible voters for the House, state legislatures for the Senate, and designated electors for the president).

Still the concept of the mandate is attractive, partially as a means around, or through, the complexities and ambiguities built into the election system, and the term arises frequently in post-election analysis. Some presidents are declared to have received a mandate—Franklin Roosevelt in 1932, Lyndon Johnson in 1964, Reagan in 1980; other presidents are said to have no mandate—Richard Nixon in 1968, Carter in 1976, Reagan in 1984, Bush in 1988. The phrase "landslide without a mandate" has come into favor in recent elections where Republicans have overwhelmingly defeated Democrats.

Raymond Wolfinger confronts the mandate and, like Dahl, declares that "election returns are almost always useless as measures of public opinion on particular measures." He argues persuasively that "mandates are inherently implausible." Beyond the problem of interpreting votes for officials with different electors and length of terms is simply the contrary behavior of the American voters. These passages from his essay in *The American Elections of 1984* illustrate Wolfinger's point: "For one thing, many people vote for their party's candidate almost reflexively; a cataclysm would be necessary for some faithful Democrats and Republicans to cross party lines. Others base their votes on the candidates' apparent personal qualities. . . . People who believe in mandates usually say that those who voted for a candidate did so because they favored the policies he advocated. The search for the mandate becomes a textual analysis of the winner's campaign utterances. The problem here, of course, is that candidates say a great many things. . . . As Chairman Mao might have said, 'Many issues, one vote.' "

There are cases nonetheless when one vote does seem to provide instructions on many issues. Johnson's election in 1964 and Reagan's in 1980 are such cases. Often subsequent analysis casts doubt on the validity of the mandate. It is discovered that voters were rejecting Barry Goldwater and Carter rather than endorsing the policy proposals of Johnson and Reagan. . . . But in the short term, the notion that a landslide election constitutes endorsement of a president's proposed program is a persuasive idea and can have profound political and policy effects.

Under what circumstances are the pundits likely to declare the existence of a mandate? Taking 1964 and 1980 as the recent cases, it seems to require the following five components:

■ A landslide victory as a demonstration of public support.

■ Publicly visible issues debated during the campaign.

■ Clear differences between the candidates on the issues, preferably deriving from ideology.

■ A party win as well as the personal victory for the president, notably for congressional seats.

■ A surprise. The president did better than expected, for example; or his party won more seats in Congress than had been predicted.

Put together, these conditions are taken as evidence for a mandate, for a policy message from the voters to their government. Dahl and Wolfinger argue that the evidence is circumstantial, at best, but regrettable as it may be, official Washington is more likely to listen to the post-election analysts than to two of the nation's most distinguished political scientists.

In fact, the declared mandate has a self-enforcing quality that makes it difficult to deny even should elected officials choose to do so. The expectation is: "You won it all, now do what you promised to do." Adversaries may even be willing to cooperate, as Democratic Speaker of the House Thomas P. O'Neill did following the 1980 elections. "Despite my strong opposition to the President's program," O'Neill wrote in *Man of the House*, "I decided to give it a chance to be voted on by the nation's elected representatives. For one thing, that's how our democracy is supposed to work." Given this support, a significant strategic problem for the president is how to meet expectations without setting too high a standard. For he will be measured by that standard—and most likely be judged as having fallen short—once the mandate is declared to be exhausted.

The 1964 and 1980 cases are exceptional. *Most of the time presidents must govern when it's over because it never really begins.* In one sense, I suppose, that is not saying much. It asks us to analyze the strengths and weaknesses of each individual presidency in creating standards for evaluating success. It questions the existence of a systemic executive leadership capability emanating from elections and constitutional authority. In another sense, though, failure to recognize that each president must fashion his own means of exercising power leads to distorted judgments about presidential effectiveness.

Presidents are expected to lead as though they had been granted full power to do so, even by those who earlier questioned the legitimacy of their claim to leadership for lack of a mandate. Jimmy Carter had this experience—often being measured against the early months of the Johnson administration. And George Bush may be held accountable to standards for exercising power that were established by and for Reagan during his early months in office, when he was declared to have a mandate. It is not easy for presidents to score well under these conditions. What I propose here is that we begin to pay more attention to how they try.

When It's Over from the Start

The 1988 presidential election had many special features. George Bush was the first sitting vice president since Martin Van Buren in 1836 to be elected. (It should be noted that few have tried. Nixon in 1960 and Hubert Humphrey in 1968 were the only other cases in this century.) Bush also was the first elected president since Herbert Hoover in 1928 to follow a president of his own party. These precedents, and the fact that the Democrats had regained the White House after the previous two-term winners, Dwight Eisenhower and Nixon, led many to expect a Democratic win in 1988.

Indeed, Bush won a 40-state victory that met few of the conditions for a declared mandate. While a sizable win, Bush's share of the electoral college vote (79 percent) actually ranked 13th among the 23 presidential elections in this century, and his share of the popular vote (54 percent) ranked 12th. Though there were any number of national problems, there were few the candidates chose to debate. Ideological lines were drawn on certain symbolic issues, such as furlough policy for criminals and saluting the flag, but were left murky on the major domestic and foreign policy problems. Bush could not claim a coattail effect since only two House Democratic incumbents and one Senate Democratic incumbent were defeated. In fact, the new Congress was very much like the old Congress—nearly 99 percent of House incumbents and 85 percent of Senate incumbents seeking reelection were returned. And finally there were no surprises; the election went more or less as expected. Indeed, it bored most analysts and, possibly, many voters as well. Turnout barely exceeded 50 percent—the lowest percentage in 64 years.

Thus George Bush entered the White House "in search of a mandate," as most accounts had it. He succeeded a president with whom he had served and who had left office with exceptionally high public approval. Comparisons were bound to be made—typically with Reagan's first year, not his last. Bush faced a Democratic Congress emboldened by recent policy successes and energized by new leadership in the Senate.

The case can be made, therefore, that Bush had to build his presidency from the start. He had few advantages beyond his electoral right to occupy the White House. It is unlikely that congressional Democrats viewed Bush's victory over Michael Dukakis as challenging their right to govern. After all, like Carter, Dukakis was a politician from out of town. House and Senate Democrats separated their campaigns from that of the national ticket. And, indeed, their representative in the presidential race, Lloyd Bentsen, returned, losing in his home state for the office of vice president but winning reelection to the Senate.

If the election did not automatically convey the right of leadership to George Bush, can it be said to have endorsed the Democrats' right to lead? Surely not. Their presidential candidate was overwhelmingly defeated. And the high return of congressional Democrats carried with it limited policy implications. Mandates are even more implausible for congressional elections. In 1988, as in the two previous presidential elections, the Democrats emerged from the election with neither a message nor a messenger. Further, Speaker Jim Wright was being investigated by the Committee on Standards of Official Conduct (and later resigned), Majority Whip Tony Coelho was about to be investigated (and later resigned), a new majority leader was elected in the Senate, and an early congressional battle was fought over a pay raise—a matter bound to damage the public image of Congress.

Thus the president's first advantage was simply that he was the only leader in town, and so George Bush sought to establish a government. His strategy in the early months appears to be bipartisan, consultative, inclusive, continuous, incremental, and nonideological. Accepting the limitations of a low-turnout, issueless election that returned a Democratic Congress (as well as confirmed Democratic strength in the states), Bush emphasized the need for a bipartisan approach to major issues. He sent signals before the inauguration, then confirmed his intentions in his inaugural address: "I put out my hand. I am putting out my hand to you, Mr. Speaker. I am putting out my hand to you, Mr. Majority Leader. For this is the thing: This is the age of the offered hand." The bipartisan approach soon proved successful in the development of a budget agreement and a plan for aiding the contra guerrillas in Nicaragua.

A corollary strategy to that of bipartisanship is consultation. It may be expected to be employed on any issue requiring joint action by the White House and Congress. But it is particularly effective as a governing strategy if the president uses it when he has the prerogative to act alone. The Bush White House has consulted with members of Congress in both cases. His clean-air proposals, which require congressional support, and the actions following the Panamanian elections, which don't, are two of the more important examples.

An administration that must establish its right to govern is well advised to reach out, to be inclusive. Though criticized for not doing more, the Bush administration did use cabinet and subcabinet appointments for this purpose. The president and his political advisers also sent signals to various minority groups that the White House would consult them much more frequently than the Reagan White House did.

Continuity was also part of the transition strategy. Certain appointments were made in the latter months of the Reagan administration that could be carried over—Attorney General Dick Thornburgh, Education Secretary Louis Cavazos, Treasury Secretary Nicholas Brady. Other Reagan cabinet members, or former members, were reassigned—Elizabeth Dole, from Transportation to Labor; Clayton Yeutter, from trade representative to Agriculture; William Bennett, from Education to drug czar. Many subcabinet positions were also holdovers. The Bush administration was criticized for not moving more quickly to replace Reagan appointees or to fill vacancies. Yet deliberateness is a feature associated with all the strategic moves mentioned here. Establishing a governing strategy following a no-mandate election typically requires patience, at least in the absence of a major crisis.

Finally, and consequently, new directions for a no-mandate president are likely to be incrementally pursued. Bold policy plans are bound to be criticized as lacking public support. Because he was vice president in the administration of his extremely popular predecessor, Bush's new policy directions will be taken in oblique rather than sharp angular moves. An incrementalist is likely to be less ideological and therefore, perhaps, less predictable and less able, or motivated, to propose an integrated program.

Meanwhile the role of the congressional Democrats in the early months of the Bush presidency has been confined primarily to cooperation. With the exception of the rejection of John Tower's nomination to be Secretary of Defense, the Democrats are finding it difficult to establish a consistent policy posture that will permit them to win when President Bush loses. It would not be popular to turn away from a president willing to "put out my hand." And so Democrats must make an effort to cooperate where called upon to do so. Yet agreements with the Republican president make it harder for the House and Senate Democrats to delineate their policy record. Democratic policy initiatives are diffused by agreements reached in advance. And independent actions, as with the minimum wage increase, are subject to veto.

The Nature of Contemporary Power

Presidents must find, understand, and protect their power. That is not a new observation, to be sure. It is the very essence of Richard E. Neustadt's *Presidential Power*. What is new since the publication of that influential book in 1960 is that American voters have frequently separated the presidency from the rest of the political system. Five times they have elected Republican presidents and returned Democratic majorities in one or both houses of Congress. In four of the five elections, the Republican candidates won by huge margins. And in the 1976 election, the Democrats won by the barest of margins with a candidate who separated himself from his party.

However fragile presidential power was before 1960, it has become more so. Presidents have to construct and reconstruct their presidencies, evaluating their advantages and commitments. Few are awarded mandates—only Lyndon Johnson and Ronald Reagan since 1960. Some, like Nixon in 1972 and Carter in 1976, proceeded as though they had received one, suffering the consequences of their miscalculation. All are affected by events—foreign and domestic crises, scandal, elections and reelections—that subtract from, or occasionally add to, their decision-making advantages. There are no pat formulas. Coalitions gathered for one issue are seldom available for the next. And reelection even by a 49-state sweep may still require a president to create additional advantages.

"Governing when it's over" is a perspective for our time. All presidents must recognize and interpret developments as a first step for determining how they will manage. Our understanding of the office in contemporary politics will be improved if we, too, comprehend the changing political and policy conditions that make this perspective credible.

When the Time Has Come

Five different conditions may require a president to "govern when it's over." These are (with recent examples):

1. The classic lame duck: a president who was defeated in his reelection bid and must continue to govern for another two and one-half months (Carter).

2. The declared lame duck: a president who wins reelection, even by a landslide, and now faces having to govern without the benefit of a third-term option (Eisenhower, Nixon, Reagan).

3. The passé lame duck: a president who cannot or does not seek reelection and must govern for two and one-half months after the election of a new president (Johnson, Reagan).

4. The unmandated president: a president originally declared to have a mandate but who experiences a loss of public and congressional support (Johnson by 1966, Reagan by 1982).

5. The no-mandate president: a president who clearly does not have a mandate, who must fashion coalitions of support for his programs (most post-World War II presidents).

Chapter 10

The Bureaucracy

One of the characteristics of the modern world is the dominance of large organizations. When marked by hierarchy, complexity, and specialization, these organizations are properly called *bureaucracies*. We encounter bureaucracies in most aspects of community life—schools, churches, membership organizations, and, of course, governments.

It is a popular myth that bureaucracies run by themselves, according to their own standards and rules. All of us have had experiences that seem to verify this view: utterly indecipherable agency forms, offices open only at times inconvenient to the clients they serve, and inconsistent or pointless regulations. "Catch-22"—a rule that is impossible to follow because another rule contradicts it—symbolizes the human cost of vast, ponderous organizations.[1]

Bureaucratic agencies do not, however, run under their own power; they must ultimately satisfy key clienteles to survive and to prosper. A federal agency may not throw out a welcome mat for every citizen who walks in the door to conduct business, but it must conform to presidential directives and respond to pressures from Capitol Hill—especially from the agency's funding and oversight committees. In addition, the agency must cultivate the key organizations with which it deals—the relevant industries, labor unions, professional societies, and other organized interests. The political environment of federal bureaucracy is the focus of this chapter.

The Bureaucracy's Political Managers

The founders devoted little attention to the bureaucratic apparatus of the executive branch. Articles I and II of the Constitution mention executive departments and department heads, but the word *cabinet* never appears in the document. The president is enjoined to "take care that the laws be faithfully executed," and agencies are clearly contemplated for such implementation. Congress is empowered to create agencies and to delegate the appointment of officials to the president, the department heads, or the courts.

The First Congress established three departments—Treasury, War (Defense), and Foreign Affairs (State). By the 1990s there were fourteen departments in the cabinet, more than sixty independent agencies and government corporations, and hundreds of bureaus. Some of the independent agencies are larger than many cabinet departments; among these are the Small Business Administration and the Central Intelligence Agency. Even within established departments there are strong agencies with distinctive missions and longstanding traditions of independence; these include the Forest Service within the Department of Agriculture, the Public Health Service within the Department of Health and Human Services, and the National Oceanic and Atmospheric Administration within the Department of Commerce.

Needless to say, the development of our national bureaucracy "has been a truly remarkable phenomenon," says Francis Rourke in Selection 48. The size and scope of the executive branch affects virtually every citizen. Concomitantly, the growth of bureaucracy has often generated public resentment and produced legislative and managerial directives that, in the judgment of some analysts, have hampered its ability to perform effectively. In "Hollow Government" (Selection 49), Ronald Moe discusses the need to develop competent government, not big government.

The bureaucracy draws strength from its size, its expertise, and its control of vital governmental functions. But who controls the bureaucracy? The president, of course, is vested with "the executive power of the United States." In reality, policy management of executive agencies is in the hands of a corps of some three thousand presidential appointees—cabinet secretaries, subcabinet officers, commissioners, and bureau chiefs. Although appointed with the "advice and consent" of the Senate, these officers serve at the president's pleasure and are responsible for infusing White House viewpoints into agency programs.

Presidential management of the bureaucracy is, however, a weak link in the federal establishment. One reason is that the president's appointees typically remain at their posts only a short while—about two years, on average. Hugh Heclo calls these political managers "a government of strangers." [2] As outsiders, they find it nearly impossible to master their jobs in such a short time, much less counter the collective knowledge and experience of the civil servants who nominally work for them. Many end up "going native": rather than serving as the president's emissaries to the agency, they become champions of the agency's work and traditions. Moreover, the use of the cabinet to advocate presidential aims and to provide collective advice appears to have fallen on hard times (Selection 50, "Creating a *Real* Cabinet").

Because they draw their missions and their funds from Congress, agencies often respond more speedily to pressures from Capitol Hill than to those from the White House. Shrewd department heads or bureau chiefs know that their agencies will fare better if they accommodate the authorizing committees, which create and oversee them, and the appropriations committees, which provide their funding. When agencies seem to be out of control—resisting presidential direction and following their own course—they often are trying simply to follow directions, implicit as well as explicit, from Capitol Hill panels.

Agencies are tied to Congress also by the statutory device known as the *legislative veto,* whereby Congress allows agency administrators to make specific decisions but retains the power to review the actions through votes of approval or disapproval by both houses of Congress, by one house of Congress (called a one-house veto), or, in some cases, by committees of one or both houses. For agency executives, the practice confers powers that Congress may not otherwise give them; for members of Congress, it preserves a right to give final approval to the executive's actions. Since 1932, when the first such provision found its way into law, several hundred statutes have been enacted (and signed by the president) containing legislative approval or disapproval features.

In 1983, however, the Supreme Court found the legislative veto to be unconstitutional. In *Immigration and Naturalization Service v. Chadha* a 7 to 2 Court majority declared the legislative veto a violation of separation of powers, of the bicameral principle, and of the Constitution's "presentation" clause, whereby legislation passed by the two chambers must be "presented" to presidents for their signature or veto.

Regardless of the constitutionality of the legislative veto, the device has the virtue of convenience for both branches. It will come as no surprise, therefore, that forms of the legislative veto remain a feature of congressional decision making. New statutes embody legislative veto provisions that are constitutional, for they require approval of the president as well as of Congress. Other provisions may be unenforceable in a court of law, but bureaucrats who prize good relations with congressional committees continue to honor them in practice.

This review of the legislative veto illuminates the key role federal courts play in determining the extent of legislative or presidential control over the agencies of government. Morton Rosenberg, a legislative attorney for the Congressional Research Service, examines several recent Supreme Court decisions that address the long-standing dispute over which national elective branch controls the administrative bureaucracy. His analysis (Selection 51) reveals that judicial principles for assessing congressional or presidential managerial control have been sharpened in recent years.

Bureaucratic Agencies and Their Publics

Operating in a political environment, executive agencies are subject to the vagaries of publicity and obscurity, popularity and opprobrium, success and failure. Some agencies perform glamorous feats and are lionized by the press and the public. The Federal Bureau of Investigation, for example, has been popular throughout most of its history. Not only has it cultivated close ties with local law enforcement agencies, but it has been romanticized in movies and television programs. The National Aeronautics and Space Administration (NASA) is another "glamour agency" that, until the explosion of the space shuttle *Challenger* in early 1986, was buoyed by laudatory media coverage. Even in the face of scandals and failures, agencies such as these can quickly regain public support, because they perform tasks that most citizens favor or admire.

In contrast, people tend to scorn agencies that do unpleasant jobs, such as the Bureau of Prisons, or that interfere with their lives, such as the Internal Revenue Service (IRS). The better IRS does its job, the more taxpayers are likely to complain. Other agencies are naturally scandal-prone; those that administer aid programs for the poor, for example, are vulnerable to investigative reporting, because their clients are perceived as straying from middle-class standards of behavior.

Whatever their record, few agencies actually die. In Selection 52, "Anatomy of an Agency That Failed," David G. Savage tells the story of the National Institute of Education (NIE), which after thirteen stormy years went out of business in 1985. NIE was plagued with uncertain leadership and encountered a host of problems in fulfilling its vague and controversial mandate. Perhaps most important, NIE failed to adjust its mission when the climate of opinion changed.

In spite of its many problems, NIE was unusual in being phased out. Most agencies, even when they have outlived their usefulness, manage to stay in business by mobilizing their supporters (including the clientele groups of users or beneficiaries that are described in Chapter 5). Faced with changing clientele, the agency may alter its mission. The Department of Agriculture, for example, has added consumer services to its traditional farm programs now that a dwindling portion of the work force is engaged in farming.

The Bureaucrats

The worker bees of the bureaucracy are the civil servants—the millions of employees who carry out the government's diverse and complex tasks. At one time it was considered proper to staff the bureaucracy with political cronies, allies of the party or candidate who won the previous election. This kind of patronage proved ineffective when, in the later nineteenth century, the federal government began to take on more complicated and important functions. Moreover, the scramble for patronage jobs was an unseemly corrupt process. When President James Garfield was assassinated by a would-be officeholder, the time for reform was at hand. The Pendleton Act of 1883, a landmark federal enactment, created a professional civil service in which workers would be chosen and promoted on merit rather than through political connections.

The fate of the federal civil service remains a matter of acute concern. In the 1980s, underfunding of most domestic agencies, coupled with relentless antigovernment rhetoric, downgraded the position of government workers and damaged their morale and effectiveness. Because civil servants' pay, benefits, and prestige lag behind that of their counterparts in private industry, it is pertinent to ask whether a first-rate staff of public employees can long be maintained. Addressing this theme in Selection 53, Paul Volcker urges elective officials and opinion leaders to strive for the restoration of public confidence in the career civil service.

Americans have reason to take substantial pride in the quality of the federal establishment. True, it is large, impersonal, and often hampered by rules and traditions; but the U.S. civil service is among the most honest in the world. Although bribery and corruption are not unknown, they are rare compared with bureaucracies in many nations. Moreover, federal agencies have had some spectacular successes; NASA's lunar space mission in the 1960s is one notable example; another is the Pentagon's "Operation Desert Storm" during the 1991 war in the Persian Gulf. The quality of life for most citizens, however, is enhanced more by the mundane successes of agencies that enforce food and drug safety, manage air flight patterns, ensure minimum retirement income, and conduct research on chronic diseases. Only vast, highly complex organizations, employing large cadres of specialists and support staffs, can perform these tasks—bureaucracies, in other words.

Notes

1. From the novel by Joseph Heller, *Catch-22* (New York: Simon and Schuster, 1961).
2. Hugh Heclo, *A Government of Strangers: Executive Politics in Washington* (Washington, D.C.: Brookings Institution, 1977).

48. Bureaucracy in the American Constitutional Order

Francis E. Rourke

The phenomenal growth of a national bureaucracy in the United States since the 1930s has generated considerable public hostility against bureaucrats and the agencies in which they work. Underlying this hostility is the fear that bigness leads to too much power. Francis E. Rourke, professor of political science at Johns Hopkins University, argues that some of these fears have proved to be unfounded. In his article published in the *Political Science Quarterly* in 1987, Rourke observes that the burgeoning bureaucracy has led to "changes in the character and operation" of the federal government, which have served to limit the power of this bureaucracy. Among these changes, he notes in particular the growing power of the White House staff, whose interaction with the president has reduced bureaucratic influence over national policy decisions.

The development of national bureaucracy in the United States since the 1930s in what can be called its modern era has been a truly remarkable phenomenon. Many more people now work for the government than did then. Bureaucratic organizations in Washington spend far more money today than was the case fifty years ago. They provide more services and their rules and regulations affect a much wider range of human activities. The impact of the decisions made by government agencies upon the lives of ordinary citizens covers not only the familiar trip from the cradle to the grave, but extends even beyond those traditional limits of the human experience, as survivors of the deceased struggle with the Veterans Administration or the Social Security system over death benefits or as government officials begin to concern themselves with what happens to the fetus before he or she even becomes a citizen.

This growth in the size of bureaucracy and the simultaneous expansion in the scope of its involvement in human affairs have generated a very strong resentment against bureaucrats and the agencies in which they work. There has been a general assumption that what is very big must also be very powerful, the lesson of the dinosaurs to the contrary notwithstanding, and the myth of an all-powerful bureaucracy has become firmly fixed in the American political imagination since World War II. . . . After being nominated as presidential candidates, Richard Nixon and George Wallace in 1968, Jimmy Carter in 1976, and Ronald Reagan in 1980 all ran against the bureaucracy, or, in Wallace's phrase, "pointy-headed" bureaucrats. . . . In short, opposition to bureaucracy and its power has been a winning strategy in recent national elections in the United States. . . .

But what is commonly overlooked in these hostile reactions to the growth of bureaucracy in the American constitutional order is that this development has triggered other changes in the character and operation of the national government, and that many of these changes have worked to limit the extent to which the expanding scope of bureaucratic activity has actually brought about a commensurate increase in the power of bureaucrats themselves. Indeed, it can be argued that the growth of national bureaucracy in the United States since the 1930s has been a far less important phenomenon than the simultaneous emergence of new ways by which the traditional institutions of American national government—the presidency, Congress, and the courts—have been able to meet and contain the challenge of a bureaucracy that many people prior to World War II anticipated would actually become a fourth branch of government in the postwar period.

Hence, the real story of contemporary American bureaucracy is not, as widely expected to be the case, about the emergence of an imperial government of career officials threatening constitutional norms. It is rather the story of how a traditional political system modified itself to cope with the arrival of a new competitor for power—a set of bureaucratic organizations that was created to carry out the directives of the president and Congress but which had the promise of becoming a power in its own right. . . . The change most often predicted in the aftermath of World War II—that the arrival of a large-scale bureaucracy would derange the American constitutional order in fundamental ways—has not occurred at all.

Reshaping the Presidency

Consider, for example, the case of the presidency. During recent decades there has been constant apprehension in the White House that the bureaucracy will obstruct presidential plans and programs and substitute its own preferences for those of a president chosen in a free election to put into effect the policies and programs for which the people have just voted. Fear of bureaucratic usurpation of power was most pronounced at the White House during the Nixon years, but in one form or another it has been a conspicuous feature of all administrations since World War II.

This fear has endured in spite of the fact that genuine cases of bureaucratic challenge to presidential authority since the war have been rare occurrences—so much so as to command widespread attention when they become public knowledge. Such cases have commonly been regarded as deviating from the norm—justified, if at all, only by the exceptional circumstances in which they occurred. Witness, for example, General Douglas MacArthur's defiance of President Harry Truman during the Korean War or the unauthorized bombing runs conducted by the air force in Vietnam during the Johnson administration. These cases of bureaucrats acting independently or in opposition to presidential orders only drew what limited justification they possessed from the fact that they occurred during controversial wars, when the legitimacy of presidential authority itself came into question in American society.

But regardless of whether the record supports these White House fears of bureaucratic sabotage, what cannot be denied is the fact that many of the ways in which the presidency has changed in recent years represent adaptations designed to cope with the growing presence of bureaucracy within the governmental structure in the United States. Not the least of these changes has been the shift toward a collegial or collective presidency—a White House in which the chief executive's power to decide and to act is exercised not only by the president, but also by a host of other White House aides and assistants lodged within the White House staff or the executive office of the president. Thus, a power that the framers of the constitution thought they were placing in the hands of a single person has now been parcelled out among a varied set of individuals who serve on the White House staff.

The principal factor forcing this pluralization of the presidency—its transformation into a collegial office—has been the desire of the White House to maintain the hegemony of the president within the executive branch in the face of what it perceives as a bureaucracy threatening constantly to spin out of control. Hence, a major task of the White House staff, and of the many offices into which this staff is now clustered, is to provide the president with information and advice about how to deal with the wide range of problems that executive institutions now confront. Otherwise the president would be entirely at the mercy of whatever data or policy suggestions the administrative agency most directly involved in a policy operation might choose to supply. . . .

So while it may narrow the circle of his advisers in disadvantageous ways, the White House staff can protect the president from becoming the prisoner of any bureaucratic information system in shaping his policy initiatives. The pluralized presidency also provides the chief executive with a cadre of aides whose policy suggestions are sensitive to his own interests rather than simply reflecting the goals and needs of some administrative agency or of the outside groups in whose behalf that agency generally acts. On occasion—as was true in both the Nixon and Reagan presidencies—his staff may even serve the chief executive as an instrument for taking actions that he does not want the rest of the government or the public to know about. History suggests that this use of the staff may lead a president to glory—as in Nixon's opening to China—or to catastrophe—as in Nixon's Watergate caper.

In addition to the assistance it provides in policy development, the White House entourage also plays a major role for the presidency today in monitoring the actions of bureaucratic organizations and officials within the executive branch charged with carrying out policy decisions. This monitoring is designed to insure that the policies that agency bureaucrats are pursuing on a daily basis are those of the president, and that they have not been altered to conform to the preferences of the bureaucracy or its clients. It also enables the White House to identify emerging issues with which they may have to deal in the future, or "big-ticket" items that are being handled in a dilatory way by the bureaucracy when they should be receiving priority attention from the White House.

Changing Presidential Styles

Over the course of recent history, individual presidents have varied a great deal in the way in which they have tried to use the collegial presidency. But they have all shared a common purpose—to create in their staffs an effective counterweight to the power of the departmental bureaucracies. John F. Kennedy, for example, in a strategy that was later to be imitated by Lyndon B. Johnson, tried to bring what he regarded as highly talented people into the White House, a group that David Halberstam was later to describe somewhat sardonically as "the best and the brightest."

But behind Kennedy's strategy of bringing talented people to the White House lay the belief that the permanent government was stodgy and unimaginative and that new ideas would have to come from outside the bureaucracy. If the White House staff could not by itself generate such innovative approaches to the social and economic problems that beset American society, then experts in the private sector would also have to be recruited to help the president cope with these problems. The institution that was created to forge cooperation between the White House staff and outside experts was the presidentially appointed task force. During the Kennedy and to an even greater extent the Johnson administrations, presidential task forces wrestled with issues that under prior presidents the bureaucracy itself would have handled. This novel approach to the task of making public policy was described by Henry

Fairlie as "guerrilla government"—a kind of "hit-and-run" warfare by outsiders upon the permanent government.

This strategy of trying to develop public policy with a minimal reliance on the bureaucracy was adopted and refined by the Nixon administration. While the Kennedy White House had looked upon the bureaucracy as being far too timid in its approach to tough public policy issues, too reluctant to strike out in the bold new directions that Kennedy's New Frontier philosophy demanded, the Nixon administration saw the problem from a quite different perspective. In its eye the permanent bureaucracy was a wily and aggressive champion of policies and programs that the voters had repudiated in the 1968 election. Bureaucracy was forever trying to nullify White House initiatives by dragging its feet in implementing presidential directives, or, even worse, by leaking information to the outside world in an effort to rally public opposition to plans or policy changes that the administration was considering. . . .

From Nixon's perspective, it made sense to concentrate control over policy development in the White House whenever possible. This strategy was most prominent in the field of foreign affairs, where the White House National Security staff achieved an ascendancy over foreign policy decision-making that no NSC staff has attained before or since the Nixon days. . . .

The Nixon administration made several attempts to achieve a similar kind of domination over domestic policymaking, but without any notable success. . . . Unfortunately for Nixon, however, domestic policy proved highly resistant to such operation by remote control from the White House. The opposition came not only from the bureaucracy, which the Nixon people had anticipated, but also from the very executives they had chosen to run these domestic agencies. These political appointees tended to see the involvement of White House aides in their agency's activities as an infringement upon their own executive prerogatives.

In addition, these agencies were closely tied to the congressional committees under whose jurisdiction they fell, as well as to a variety of domestic constituencies for whom they provided services or whose interests were affected by their decisions. They were thus locked into "iron triangles"—the coalition of executive agencies, interest groups, and congressional committees that have historically dominated major sectors of domestic policymaking. It was not easy for a White House institution like the Domestic Council to move into an area of policy already occupied by these formidable political coalitions. It was especially difficult when, as was true under Nixon, Congress was controlled by the Democrats and the iron triangles were centers of power in which the opposition party was strongly entrenched. . . .

When the Carter administration took office in 1977, it tried in many ways to distance its own governing style from that of the Nixon White

House. As part of this strategy, Carter went out of his way to underline the fact that in his presidency Cabinet members rather than the White House staff would be at the center of policymaking. However, as time wore on in his administration, Carter—like his predecessors—discovered that many problems could not be dealt with by a single department and the even more painful fact that many departments did not approach policy issues with his own political priorities in mind. . . .

The Reagan administration followed the lead of the Carter presidency in accenting the role of the Cabinet in policy development and downplaying that of the White House staff. Except in the case of the arms deal with Iran in 1986, the NSC staff never reached the heights of power under Reagan that it enjoyed in previous administrations. The fact that Reagan had so much more success than Carter in diminishing the role of the White House staff can be traced in good part to the much shorter length of his policy agenda as president. He had many fewer promises to keep than Carter. The constituency from which Reagan drew his support by and large wanted the government to do less rather than more. However, it should be noted that it was a presidential agency, the Office of Management and Budget (OMB), that led the way in the achievement of Reagan's chief policy goal when he took office—a drastic cutback in the growth of the national government's domestic expenditures.

What the experience of the White House in modern times strongly suggests is that a president's ability to practice as well as preach Cabinet government largely depends on how active a role he intends to play in the development and implementation of national policy. The more a president wishes to shape the character of his administration's policy goals, the more likely he is to accept the role of the White House staff rather than the Cabinet in the governing process, however pious may be his protestations about the virtues of Cabinet government when he first takes office. This ascendancy by the White House staff has the inevitable effect of reducing bureaucratic influence over national policy decisions, since bureaucrats have much better access to Cabinet officials and much more opportunity to shape their views on policy issues than they do with respect to the president's own staff aides, who are usually isolated in the remote precincts of the White House. The lesson of the last half-century of American politics has thus been unmistakable—as the power of the White House staff grows, the power of departmental bureaucrats recedes.

Bureaucracy as Change Agent

The central conclusion that emerges from this analysis of the operation of the presidency in modern times is that bureaucracy's unsung role in the evolution of modern American government has been that of an unwitting change agent. As we have seen, the expansion in the number and activities of bureaucratic organizations within the executive branch has been a major factor underlying the ascending power of the presidency in the contemporary constitutional order. A variety of efforts have been made during this period to help the president cope with an ever-expanding bureaucracy, and each of these efforts has added another increment of power to the presidential office. This is true of all the reorganizations the executive branch has experienced since the late 1930s, the changes that have been made in the budgetary system, and the reforms that have taken place in executive personnel procedures. The position of the imperial presidency today is in no small measure a product of a widely perceived need to prevent the emergence of an imperial bureaucracy. Moreover, presidents themselves have been quite willing to play on fears of bureaucracy to justify expanding the power of their own office. The real power of bureaucracies today thus lies not with bureaucrats but with the members of the new "political class"—the policy entrepreneurs the president has appointed to run these organizations and to shape their programs in his behalf.

The influence that bureaucracy has exerted as a change agent has been very visible in the development of the legislative and judicial as well as the executive branches of government in modern times. In the case of Congress, one of the most significant changes that a proliferating bureaucracy has triggered is an expansion in the size and proficiency of the legislative staff. This expansion has taken a variety of forms—in the size of the staffs that now serve individual members of Congress, in the number of professional experts presently attached to legislative committees in both the House and the Senate, and, finally, in the establishment or strengthening of four staff agencies that currently serve Congress as a collective body: the General Accounting Office, the Congressional Research Service, the Congressional Budget Office, and the Office of Technology Assessment.

The chief purpose, as well as the most important result, of this development has been to enable Congress to close the "expertise" gap that had opened up between itself and the presidency in the years immediately preceding and following World War II, when presidents began to benefit enormously from the bureaucratic apparatus that emerged at the White House during that period of time. . . .

The impact that the growth of bureaucracy has had upon the judicial system has been no less striking. In a variety of areas, but particularly in the field of social regulation, judges have now become major actors in the policy process, largely as a result of statutes that provide broader opportunities for private parties to challenge the decisions of executive agencies in the courts in such areas as environmental and civil rights policy. Thus agencies like the Environmental Protection Agency (EPA) or the Equal Employment Opportunity Commission (EEOC) frequently find themselves being either prodded into action or having their decisions reversed by the courts. . . .

In any case, there are clearly areas of policy today in which the old-fashioned iron-triangle paradigm no longer serves to explain the way in which policy is made. Hugh Heclo makes a very compelling argument that in many highly technical policy areas—arms control, for example, or the field of monetary policy—the iron triangle has been supplanted by an "issue network," where expertise rather than economic interest determines who participates in decision-making. It can also be argued that even in fields where the old-fashioned iron-triangle structure still stands, it has been greatly altered by the arrival of the courts as major actors in the policy process. Martin Shapiro suggests that this development has created a new iron-triangle system made up of "agency, court, and interest groups" in areas of policy where statutes have created rights or entitlements to governmental assistance for groups like the aged or physically handicapped. Alternatively, in fields of social regulation like civil rights and environmental protection, the iron triangle appears to have broadened into a quadrilateral, as the courts join pressure groups, Congressional committees, and executive agencies as partners in these highly autonomous subgovernment compartments within which public policy is so frequently made in the United States. . . .

But there is perhaps nowhere in American political life where the rise of bureaucracy has been accompanied by more changes than in the operation of the federal system. Since the 1930s state, local, and national agencies have been laced together by intricate bureaucratic networks carrying on domestic programs that are federally financed and locally administered. Some observers see this development as centralizing in its effect—transferring power from state and local to national agencies. Others argue that it has opened up authentic opportunities for decentralization, as opposed to the illusory opportunities that had previously existed, by providing states and localities with the resources to undertake many activities they could not otherwise afford. But both sides would certainly agree that the bureaucratization of intergovernmental relationships within the political system represents a fundamental change in the character of American federalism.

Legitimizing American Bureaucracy

. . . In light of these developments, what is the constitutional status of bureaucracy today? How, if at all, does it fit into the tripartite scheme of government that the framers of the Constitution devised? Is the power that bureaucracies wield legitimate power, in the sense that it is accepted by those subject to it as being rightfully exercised? In our day, bureaucracy has become an indispensable instrument of government in action. Virtually all government policies depend upon some bureaucratic organization for their enforcement. . . .

Certainly the written Constitution does not assume the presence of a bureaucratic apparatus in government sufficient to carry out the varied tasks it assigns to the president, Congress, and the courts.

Nevertheless, there is a certain aura of illegitimacy about bureaucracy—a suspicion that its presence and activities in the governmental structure are not altogether in accord with the American constitutional order. Partly, this has been a procedural concern—focused on the way bureaucracies do things. Prior to the enactment of the Administrative Procedure Act of 1946 and to a lesser extent since then, a great deal of criticism has been directed at bureaucracy on the grounds that the administrative role in both adjudication and rule-making frequently violates the constitutional rights of individuals affected by the agency decisions that flow from these processes. While passage of the Procedure Act and the growing role of administrative law judges in agency adjudication have done much to dispel that fear, it has never been completely dispelled.

But quite apart from these long-standing doubts about the constitutional propriety of the procedures that bureaucratic organizations follow in enforcing government policies, there has also been strong criticism of bureaucracy on the grounds that the policies it carries out are unconstitutional in their very nature. Critics on the right who regard the free-enterprise system as part of the American constitutional covenant have questioned the legitimacy of a wide range of government policies regulating the affairs of business organizations or distributing financial or other benefits to a variety of domestic groups.

Critics on the left are equally vehement in their objections to many bureaucratic activities in the national security sector that in their view are carried on by executive agencies like the CIA in violation of constitutional norms. Bureaucracies can thus be attacked on both the right and left as lacking in constitutional legitimacy in the United States because they perform governmental functions that are themselves regarded as inappropriate for the government to undertake. At the root of bureaucracy's problem in this regard is the fact that an expansive role for the national government in the affairs of society still lacks a certain constitutional credibility in American political culture.

Efforts have been made in modern times to relieve bureaucracy of this burden of illegitimacy. James O. Freedman has written "that governmental power in a constitutional democracy can be legitimated in only two ways: Either it must be created by the Constitution or it must be exercised by officials directly accountable to the people through the political process." It is a little late in the day for any effort to be made to repair bureaucracy's omission from the written Constitution and highly questionable whether it would succeed. So that particular door to legitimation can be regarded as permanently closed as far as bureaucracy is concerned.

The other door, however, remains at least half open. Bureaucracy can be said to make a significant contribution to the process of self-government in the United States by providing opportunities for groups of citizens to be more intimately involved in government decision-making than the traditional election system permits. Norton Long, for example, makes the argument that "important and vital interests in the United States are unrepresented, under-represented, or mal-represented in Congress. These interests receive more effective and more responsible representation through administrative channels than through the legislature." Long comes to this conclusion because the bureaucracy more closely mirrors the country from a purely demographic perspective. . . .

In a recent and very comprehensive analysis of the legitimate place of bureaucracy in the American constitutional order, John Rohr makes a similar and very persuasive argument. In his view "the administrative state heals a defect in the constitution"—the fact that it does not make adequate provision for public participation in government decision-making. The growing role of bureaucracy in government opens an opportunity for many more people to become actively involved in the work of government. They may do so as civil servants, as citizens attending public hearings, or by taking advantage of other opportunities to participate in the everyday activities of administrative agencies.

The weight of this argument was greatly reinforced when citizen participation in government became the order of the day in the 1960s during President Lyndon Johnson's administration as part of the overall design of Great Society programs. When citizen participation democratized bureaucracies by allowing ordinary people to have more influence over their decisions, it also served to legitimate the role of these organizations in the governmental process. Equally important in this regard was the tendency of Great Society programs to be decentralized—directly administered by state and local rather than national agencies.

Since then, even longer steps in this direction have been taken by handing programs over to private organizations or groups for their administration. This is the "third-party" or "private-federalism" approach to the implementation of government policies that has become increasingly fashionable. Of course, as it develops, this democratization movement not only legitimizes bureaucracy but also diminishes its power. It thus represents another of the "countervailing forces," which, as previously indicated, have helped American democracy weather the challenge posed by the rise of bureaucracy.

But in any case, what all these varied efforts to involve the pubic more directly in the administration of government programs reflect is a deep-seated belief on the part of legislative and executive officials that bureaucratic power can best be legitimized by being democratized, by bringing the decisions of public bureaucrats much more closely under the control of private citizens. . . . But there can be no disputing the fact that the knowledge and skills that bureaucrats bring to the policy process have given them an indispensable place, if not a legitimate role, in the American constitutional order. The central paradox of modern American bureaucracy thus lies in the fact that it is at one and the same time altogether indispensable and, at least in the eyes of many citizens, somewhat legitimate.

49. Hollow Government: The President's Biggest Challenge

Ronald C. Moe

"It's no secret; the federal government is in trouble." So begins Ronald Moe's analysis of the decline in managerial capacity within the executive branch of government. Moe, a nationally recognized authority on federal administrative activities at the Congressional Research Service of the Library of Congress, examines the policies that have created this situation. No progress will be made in correcting the problem, he asserts, until presidents take their managerial responsibilities more seriously. What is needed, Moe concludes, is "competent government, not big government."

It's no secret; the federal government is in trouble. The fact that many state and local governments are also in trouble may provide some perspective on the problem, but little solace. The trouble in question is more than the chronic budgetary crunch, although this surely is important. What is at risk today is the very capacity of the government to perform the tasks normally associated with government. We are not talking about the frills; we are talking about the basics.

Departments and agencies, regulated to the hilt by congressionally drawn statutes and central managerial agency directives, denied adequate personnel and resources, and often managed by marginally competent political appointees, are no longer able to assure the public that fundamental services will be provided. Unpleasant consequences have flowed from these policies now followed by successive administrations and Congresses.

The first consequence is the escalating disaggregation of the executive branch. Second, there is an increasing reliance on third parties to perform governmental functions. A final consequence of these policies is reflected in the declining capacity of the federal government to provide infrastructure support to the private sector in its bid to become a competitive player in the newly emergent one-world economy. In short, we are trying to run a country with what some have referred to as a "hollow government," and this is proving to be a costly mistake.

Disaggregating Government

For most of our history, the executive branch was fairly unified. Most of the governmental functions were assigned to agencies within departments. There were some exceptions, of course, but these were exceptions that proved the rule.

This reasonably unified, comprehensible system began to unravel during the early 1970s in part because it was associated with certain perceived presidential excesses of the preceding decade. Presidents themselves, however, began to shy away from active involvement in managerial issues, thereby creating a political vacuum soon to be filled by others, notably Congress. . . .

The implicit message today is that every agency is on its own to make the best deal possible with Congress and its interest group constituency. And the best deal generally means seeking maximum policy and financial autonomy from central executive branch oversight. Disaggregation (some might prefer the term "disintegration") is the order of the day, with agencies seeking, and often receiving, "independent" status, government corporations being created to avoid budgetary constraints, and "twilight zone" agencies, such as the National Endowment for Democracy, being brought to life to placate special interest groups. All in all, the present organizational condition of the executive branch is pretty grim.

Third-Party Government

Closely related to the organizational disaggregation of the executive branch is its growing reliance upon others to administer and deliver programs. These may be state and local governments, non-profit organizations, quasi-governmental bodies of indeterminate legal status, for-profit private corporations, or consultants. Collectively, these diverse entities are often referred to as "third-party government."

Paradoxically, while the core government and its capacity to perform are declining, the demands upon government are increasing. The demand-side pressures are reflected not only in more functions being thrust upon government (e.g., AIDS research), but also in the growing complexity of existing functions such as environmental regulation.

Although government contracting for services is as old as the republic, in recent years this has assumed a qualitative difference. Today basic policy analysis and management functions are just as likely to be contracted for as office space and supplies. And the push is on for even more contracting of federal activities. . . .

A recent Senate report on the Department of Energy concluded that the "DOE relies on private workforce to perform virtually all basic government functions. It relies on contractors in the preparation of most important plans and policies, the development of budgets and budget documents, and the drafting of reports to Congress and Congressional testimony. It relies on contractors to monitor arms control negotiations, help prepare decisions on the export of nuclear technology, and conduct hearings and initial appeals in challenges to security clearance disputes."

The situation in the Department of Energy is replicated throughout the federal government. In agency after agency, key governmental functions are being transferred, in fact if not in law, to third parties. Often the contracting, particularly for intangibles such as policy analysis and management services, is arranged without effective competition so that the federal government finds itself becoming dependent upon the contractor rather than the reverse. As Harold Seidman observed in recent Congressional testimony: "Success or failure of the many companies whose principal—and sometimes only—customer is the U.S. Government depends more on their skill in manipulating the political system than in competing in the market place."

Retreat from Presidential Management

Who is to blame for the decline in managerial capacity within the executive branch? Like most complex social problems, the blame can be widely shared. Even average citizens can be assigned some blame since it is clear that they still harbor Jacksonian beliefs that government work is simple and of little consequence. But if the subject is studied carefully, it becomes evident that the ultimate source of the decline can be traced to recent presidents, particularly those following Dwight Eisenhower. It is also clear that no real progress will be made toward reversing this national decline until presidents take their managerial responsibilities more seriously.

If you ask presidents or [Office of Management and Budget] officials, they will claim that they have been managing, and managing well all along. It is difficult to find evidence, however, that either presidents or OMB directors have sought augmented resources for agency management or have appreciated the subtler elements of public management, properly understood. They may issue perfunctory statements on the subject, but none has expended major political capital to enhance the managerial capacity of the executive branch. Instead, recent presidents have relied on the budgetary process as a substitute for management.

Presidents, like so many others, are not clear as to what is meant by the term and concept of management. They see scant political and policy payoff in addressing the issue directly. Management is generally conceived in one of two ways: as an exercise in control or as an exercise in capacity building. Economists and lawyers tend to favor the first perspective, managers the latter. Since the early 1970s, presidents have generally bought into the idea of management as control and have appointed OMB directors with a similar viewpoint.

Competent Government, Not Big Government

What is needed today is competent government, not big government. The two terms are not synonymous. Measured in terms of monies spent, our government is already big and growing. Measured in terms of personnel and management capacity, our government has been getting smaller and weaker. It is ludicrous to think, for example, that the Federal National Mortgage Association ("Fannie Mae"), with its over $300 billion unfunded liability call upon the U.S. Treasury, is being "regulated" when only one person at HUD [Department of Housing and Urban Development] is charged with that responsibility. To become competent may mean more people in certain positions. But this is hardly the thrust of what is meant by competent government.

There is no more complex social organization than the federal government. Its responsibilities are enormous and the demands it faces insatiable. In some circles it is fashionable to say that the government is unmanageable and that the president should stay clear of management problems as much as possible. This facile reasoning, particularly popular with political gurus, is wrong. Presidents do not have a choice. They are "hired" by the people of the United States to manage the government.

Their only choice is whether to be an effective or an ineffective manager. Unfortunately, most recent presidents have chosen to be ineffective managers.

The irony is that good management is also good politics. From a practical political perspective, there is little that harms a president more than the perception that somehow "he isn't managing the store." People forgive much in presidents, including strong policy differences, but they don't forgive managerial incompetence. Jimmy Carter was perceived by many as managerially incompetent, and once this perception took hold, he could never recover politically.

A commitment to building competent government requires that the president work to maintain the distinctive legal character and mission of the federal government. Public service must be restored to high standing with the people if it is to receive its share of the nation's best talent. There is nothing romantic about the desire for competent government. Competent government is, quite simply, a necessity if the United States is to be a serious player in the international arena of the 21st century. Our present "hollow government" may well be the president's biggest challenge.

50. Creating a *Real* Cabinet

Elliot Richardson and James P. Pfiffner

Although the Cabinet has become a fixture of the presidency over the years, its deliberations have generally tended to be less than productive, according to Elliot Richardson and James Pfiffner. In their article published in *USA Today* in 1990, Richardson, a member of the Cabinets of three presidents, and Pfiffner, a professor of government and politics at George Mason University, pinpoint several of the problems with the current system. They offer suggestions for restructuring the Cabinet in order to move it closer to its original purpose: providing advice on important issues for presidential decision-making.

With the [possible] elevation of the Environmental Protection Agency (EPA) to Cabinet status, bringing to 15 the number of chairs around the Cabinet table, it may be useful to reexamine the purpose of the Cabinet concept. We argue that the original function of collective advice to the President is no longer being achieved by our present Cabinet structure, and we propose an alternative.

The use of department heads as the primary advisers to the President began as a historical accident. In 1790, George Washington went to the Senate to seek its advice regarding a treaty with the Indians. However, the Senate, possibly sensitive to the separation of powers, dithered, and it soon became apparent that it did not want to play that role. Washington resolved not to return to the Senate for consultation and, by 1793, he had begun to seek regular advice from his department heads: the Secretaries of State, War, and Treasury and his Attorney General. (The Department of Justice was not created until 1870.) Since the first use of the term in 1794, the Cabinet has become a fixture of the presidency, though our Chief Executives have used the institution in different ways in varying degrees.

The idea of a "cabinet" to advise the monarch arose in England during the 16th century, and, as power began to shift from the monarch to Parliament, its role became more important. Although, in the late 20th century, the Prime Minister in Great Britain has gathered more power than in earlier decades, the PM essentially is a first among equals who are all members of Parliament. In the U.S. separation of powers system, however, the executive power of the government rests in the President, and department heads serve at his pleasure. As Abraham Lincoln declared at one Cabinet meeting: "Seven nays and one aye, the ayes have it."

The term "cabinet" in the U.S. originally was used to denote those from whom the President chose to seek advice in the carrying out of his duties. With Washington's precedent, this group customarily comprised the heads of the executive branch departments. Andrew Jackson, however, did not meet with the traditional Cabinet for his first two years in office, preferring to rely for advice on his informal "kitchen cabinet" of old friends and newspaper publishers. James Polk, on the other hand, convened his department heads 350 times during his one term.

If we return to the original function of the Cabinet to provide useful and timely advice to the President, we find that the crosscutting perspectives that he needs are less likely to come from the collected department heads than from his aides. This may explain why, over the years, power has tended to gravitate from department heads to White House advisers.

Presidents have no choice but to rely on their senior White House advisers because of the increased size and complexity of government and the interrelatedness of modern public policy. The toughest problems invariably are those that cut across the artificial boundaries between administrative jurisdictions.

Despite the rhetoric of many American presidents about "Cabinet government," collective meetings of the Cabinet do not have a history of productive deliberation. Franklin Delano Roosevelt's Secretary of the Interior, Harold L. Ickes, stated: "The cold fact is that on important matters we are seldom called upon for advice.... Our Cabinet meetings are pleasant affairs, but we only skim the surface of routine affairs." His Secretary of Labor, Frances Perkins, explained: " ... as the years went on, Roosevelt's Cabinet administration came to be like most previous ones—a direct relationship between a particular Cabinet officer and the President in regard to his special field, with little or no participation or even information from other Cabinet members. Certainly almost no 'Cabinet agreements' were reached."

Dwight D. Eisenhower established a secretariat to prepare agendas for Cabinet meetings and follow through on presidential decisions, and his administration has been cited as a model of "Cabinet government," American style. Yet, even Eisenhower was not able to use his Cabinet fully as a deliberative body. In the personal experience of the senior author [Richardson], very seldom was an issue of importance put before the collective body for deliberation and decision by the President. Another participant, Richard Nixon, remembered that most Cabinet meetings were "unnecessary and boring."

The Cabinet meetings of most recent presidents, it generally is agreed, have not been more effective than Eisenhower's. They tend to focus on bland common denominators and often degenerate into show-and-tell sessions dealing with budget breakdowns, reviews of pending legislation, or a vice-presidential travelogue. Presidents in the late 20th century need the kind of advice that is not likely to come from a collection of department heads.

Problems with the Current System

Cabinet secretaries are selected with different criteria—ideological, geographical, racial, religious, and sexual balance—than a president would use to choose close advisers. Once in office, they are subject to strong centrifugal forces. They immediately assume responsibilities toward their departments that lead them to put their own programmatic interests first.

In addition, the Cabinet is too big. With the elevation of the Veterans Administration to Cabinet status, there are 14 members, in addition to the three or four other officials that presidents may designate to sit in at meetings. This is too large a number for meaningful deliberation.... Politically, it is extremely difficult to resist pressures to elevate large agencies with powerful constituencies to Cabinet status. Ronald Reagan came to office promising to abolish two departments and ended up creating a new one.

However, size is not the most important impediment to true Cabinet deliberations. The real problem is that no department head wants to expose his or her special interests to the crossfire of fellow Cabinet officers who may be battling for the same turf or resources. Jesse Jones, Secretary of Commerce for Franklin Roosevelt, put it this way: "My principal reason for not having a great deal to say at Cabinet meetings was that there was no one at the table who could be of help to me except the President, and when I needed to consult him, I did not choose a Cabinet meeting to do so."

This departmental focus is understandable and legitimate. Department heads cannot be expected to judge impartially the merit or priority of their own programs. The Secretary of Health and Human Services is obliged to make the best case for the claims of medical research. The Secretary of Transportation equally is obliged to assert those of civil aviation. As Calvin Coolidge's Vice President and first Director of the Budget Bureau, Charles G. Dawes, noted, "Cabinet secretaries are vice presidents in charge of spending, and as such are the natural enemies of the President."

If a department head is to be effective in implementing programs and advocating presidential priorities, he or she must provide effective leadership for the department. This requires loyalty to his or her staff as well as to the President. The irony here is that a Cabinet secretary occasionally may be more effective in pressing the President's long-run interests by sticking up for his or her own people and programs in the short run.

In the Cabinet as a group, there is little common knowledge and few shared responsibilities, but the President needs to call upon people who can be counted on to share a broad perspective. Few issues worthy of his time can be delimited by the jurisdiction of one department. Most high-level policy issues cut across the jurisdictions of several departments or agencies. Decisions about selling U.S. wheat abroad may have important ramifications for the Agriculture, Commerce, State, and Defense Departments. Federal policies to address the coming shortage of scientists will involve the Education, Energy, Defense, and Labor Departments, as well as the National Aeronautics and Space Administration and the Office of Personnel Management.

These systematic interconnections demand the development and execution of coherent strategies to address complex problems. However, the perspective of any one department head is necessarily narrower than the President's. Yet, he needs advice from a perspective that is as wide as his own and not wedded to the interests of any one department. The people best able to help the President meet this challenge are those whose responsibilities transcend departmental boundaries and who can advise him on the tough calls.

Structuring a Well-Balanced Cabinet

Widespread awareness of this fact goes a long way toward explaining why the Chief of Staff, the Director of the Office of Management and Budget, the Assistant for National Security Affairs, and the U.S. Trade Representative are recognized as having more clout than most department heads. In 1985, when Treasury Secretary Donald Regan and Chief of Staff James Baker switched jobs, there was no doubt about who was increasing his power and who was ready for a less demanding position.

Others whose positions transcend departmental boundaries include the Chairman of the Council of Economic Advisers, the Assistant for Domestic Policy, and the President's Science Adviser. This inner circle, augmented by the three original department heads whose spheres of responsibility are the most inclusive—the Secretaries of State, Defense, and Treasury—would constitute a well-balanced Cabinet.

This type of Cabinet structure would move us closer to its original function—to provide timely advice on pressing issues for presidential decision. It would eliminate the fiction that the collected department heads are, in fact, the President's main advisers on major, crosscutting issues and create a group whose primary perspective is presidential, rather than departmental. Having made this change, the President then could delegate to his Cabinet the authority to resolve interdepartmental disagreements on matters that do not require his personal attention—an impossibility so long as department heads have co-equal rank. The change should not lead, however, to a requirement of Senate confirmation of any presidential adviser not now subject to it. The selection of his personal staff is a uniquely presidential prerogative.

If the Cabinet were reconstituted along these lines, the ability of the President to receive crosscutting advice and formulate coherent policy would be enhanced greatly. By no means would it eliminate the necessity for the President to seek advice and counsel from his department heads individually or in groups. Department heads have an appropriate and necessary role in advising the President on matters within their jurisdictions.

As the principal line officers of the executive branch, the President needs the personally stated and unvarnished views of those heading major departments. Their advice on policy often raises political, institutional, and implementation perspectives that are not likely to be appreciated fully by White House staffers. It is only in group meetings with the rest of the Cabinet that those perspectives get watered down or reduced to turf battles. This new arrangement would not be an excuse to insulate the President from his department heads. It would encourage him to seek their advice individually or in the most appropriate combinations. . . .

It may seem that this proposed restructuring of the Cabinet would reduce the status of department heads, but the reality of the presidency is that very little serious work gets done at Cabinet meetings. The real power of department heads rests on the confidence the President places in them and on their administrative responsibilities under the law. Sitting at the Cabinet table does not confer that power, and our proposal will not take it away.

The intended effect of our proposal is to drop the pretense that the present Cabinet has a substantive collective role. In addition, this new arrangement would recognize where the power to advise the President really lies, and thus make that power more accountable to the people.

51. Congress, the Agencies, and Separation of Powers

Morton Rosenberg

The doctrine of the separation of powers has been intensely scrutinized by the Supreme Court over the past decade, leading to several important decisions. As a result, it is now possible to give a more definitive answer to the question of who controls the agencies of government, Congress or the president. Morton Rosenberg, a specialist in American public law at the Congressional Research Service of the Library of Congress, provides historical background on this issue and discusses court rulings in this article, published in *CRS Review* in 1989. He concludes that "Congress' prerogative over the administrative bureaucracy, while not unlimited, is broad and far-reaching."

The past decade has witnessed the most intense period of Supreme Court scrutiny of the doctrine of separation of powers in history. . . . The result has been an important refinement and reconciliation of the Court's past pronouncements on separation principles that appear now to allow a more definitive answer to the critical question: Who controls the agencies of government, the Congress or the President?

The source of the dispute over control of the administrative bureaucracy can be traced back to the virtual silence of the Constitution on the matter and the manner in which the First Congress dealt with it. The mention of "departments" three times in the constitutional text makes it clear that the Framers anticipated the establishment of a governmental infrastructure, and the necessary and proper clause indicates that the creation of those departments, and the nature of the duties and powers of the officers who would run them, was left exclusively to the Congress. Left unstated, however, was the degree of ongoing control over the agencies (beyond the power to abolish them), that could be maintained by the Congress after their creation.

Article II also fails to clearly dispose of the issue. While specifically assigning national defense and foreign affairs responsibilities to the President, the vesting in him of an undefined "executive power" and the curious empowerment to require his principal executive officers to report to him in writing, coupled with the limited duty that he "take care" that others carry out Congress' directives, leave doubt as to the scope of the President's managerial authority.

The First Congress, taking its cue from the ambiguities of Article II, established patterns of structural dependence and independence of the executive branch agencies from the President that have endured to this day. Thus Congress bowed to the Constitution's textual commitment of national security and diplomatic responsibilities to the President when it established the Departments of Foreign Affairs and War, charging each department's Secretary to "perform and execute such duties as shall from time to time be enjoined on, or entrusted to him by the President" and to "conduct the business of the said department in such manner, as the President ... shall from time to time order or instruct."

But the First Congress' decisions regarding the organization of other executive duties with respect to domestic affairs reflected a far different view of the President's relation to the officers who performed them. When Congress contemporaneously created the Treasury Department, it assigned the Secretary specific statutory duties and omitted the open-ended requirement that the Treasury Secretary perform duties at the direction of the President. The Treasury statute did not even mention the President: it required the Secretary to report directly to Congress. Such direction, the context makes clear, was to come from the Congress, not the President. Indeed, for a significant period in our early history, the President did not see departmental budget estimates before the Treasury Department submitted them to the Congress, and the Secretary recommended tax policy directly to the Congress. . . . It was not until the passage of the Budget and Accounting Act of 1921 that agencies ceased the practice of negotiating their annual appropriations directly with the Congress.

This pattern of congressional control of agency structural arrangements took a new turn in the late nineteenth century with the establishment of the Interstate Commerce Commission in 1887, an agency whose members were insulated from presidential removal except for specific cause. The independent agency model was followed, without constitutional challenge, with the creation of the Federal Reserve Board (1913), the Federal Trade Commission (1914), the United States Shipping Board (1916), the Federal Radio Commission (1927), and the Federal Power Commission (1930).

Early Court Rulings

The first legal doubt case on Congress' ability to insulate executive officials from presidential control came in *Meyers* v. *United States* [1926], which struck down a congressional requirement that the President seek Senate approval for the discharge of postmasters. There the Court held that the executive had a virtually illimitable power to remove executive officials. The decision was short-lived. Nine years later, in *Humphrey's Executor* v. *United States*, a case involving the summary removal of an FTC commissioner by the President, the Court unanimously repudiated the *Meyers* broad dictum. The Court held that where an officer is performing "purely executive" duties he serves at the pleasure of the President. But where an officer performs "quasi-legislative" or "quasi-judicial" functions, the Congress may limit the executive's power to discharge only for cause.

This somewhat opaque formulation went essentially unchallenged until the early 1980s when the Reagan administration, buoyed by several Supreme Court rulings propounding a narrow, compartmentalized view of the separation doctrine, began to question aggressively the continued efficacy of *Humphrey's Executor*. It was argued that *INS* v. *Chadha* (1983), by rejecting the legislative veto as an unconstitutional exercise of lawmaking power, and *Bowsher* v. *Synar* (1986), by declaring that the role of the Comptroller General—an officer subject to removal only by the Congress—in the execution of the Balanced Budget and Emergency Deficit Control Act of 1985 impermissibly intruded into the executive function, signaled a return to the expansive, hierarchical view of executive power contained in the *Meyers* opinion. In such a "unitary executive," it was contended, the focus of constitutional removal power with respect to all executive officials must return to the President and the legitimacy of agency independence withdrawn.

The Independent Counsel Case

This expansive view of the executive's prerogative with respect to the administrative bureaucracy was, again, short-lived. In *Morrison* v. *Olson*

(1988), the government argued that since an independent counsel is removable under the provisions of the Ethics in Government Act by the executive, through the Attorney General, only for "good cause," such a statutory limitation on the President's "at will" removal authority of an officer who is exercising purely executive functions unduly interferes with the President's constitutional duties and prerogatives and thereby violates separation-of-powers principles. The Court rejected this contention and, in the process, confirmed Congress' broad power over the structuring of agency arrangements.

The Court held that the validity of insulating an inferior officer from at-will removal by the President will no longer turn on whether such an officer is performing "purely executive" or "quasi legislative" or "quasi judicial" functions. The issue raised by a for-cause removal limitation, the majority opinion explained, is whether it interferes with the President's ability to perform this constitutional duty. In the case before it the Court noted that the independent counsel's prosecutorial powers are executive because they have "typically" been performed by executive branch officials. But, the Court held, the exercise of prosecutorial discretion is in no way "central" to the functioning of the executive branch. Further, since the independent counsel could be removed by the Attorney General, this is sufficient to ensure that she is performing her statutory duties, which is all that is required by the "take care" clause. Finally, the limited ability of the President to remove the independent counsel, through the Attorney General, was also seen as leaving enough control in his hands to reject the argument that the scheme of the statute impermissibly undermines executive powers or disrupts the proper constitutional balance by preventing the executive from performing his functions.

The Sentencing Commission Case

Additional confirmation of the Court's support of a broad congressional authority over agency structure, and the flexible standard by which it will test such exercises of power, is apparent in its 8 to 1 ruling in *Mistretta* v. *United States* (1989), in which a broad-ranging separation-of-powers challenge to the United States Sentencing Commission was rejected. Petitioners argued that the commission, an independent agency in the judicial branch vested with power to promulgate binding sentencing guidelines, violated the separation doctrine by its placement in the judicial branch, by requiring federal judges to serve on the commission and to share their authority with nonjudges, and by empowering the President to appoint commission members but limiting his power to remove them only for cause.

At the outset the Court reiterated its understanding that the separation principle does not require a rigid compartmentalization of the branches but rather recognizes "that our constitutional system imposes upon the Branches a degree of overlapping responsibility, a duty of interdependence as well as independence the absence of which 'would preclude the establishment of a Nation capable of governing itself effectively.'" The function of the separation principle is to preserve this flexibility while guarding against "the accumulation of excessive authority in a single branch" through encroachment and aggrandizement by one branch against another.

Applying these principles, the Court found no constitutional infirmities in the sentencing commission. It underlined the Congress' broad authority to create and fashion the responsibilities and functions of agencies. Brushing aside an argument that the Congress could not locate an agency with no judicial powers in the judicial branch, the majority held that our "constitutional principles of separated powers are not violated, however, by mere anomaly or innovation.... Congress' decision to create an independent rulemaking body to promulgate sentencing guidelines and to locate that body within the Judicial Branch is not unconstitutional unless Congress has vested in the Commission powers that are more appropriately performed by the other Branches or that undermine the integrity of the Judiciary." The Court found none.

Congress' prerogative over the administrative bureaucracy, while not unlimited, is broad and far-reaching, encompassing the power to create, abolish, and locate agencies and to define the powers, duties, tenure, compensation and other incidents of the offices within them. The Supreme Court's most recent pronouncements in the *Morrison* and *Mistretta* cases have indicated that in separation-of-powers cases, where aggrandizement is not an issue, it will weigh the justifications for the congressional scheme in question, including the necessity to maintain Congress' "ability to take needed and innovative action pursuant to its Article I powers," against the degree of intrusion on the ability of the President to perform his assigned functions. "De minimis" disruptions are insufficient to block an otherwise legitimate congressional objective. The emphatic nature of these decisions, as well as the long history of consistent congressional practice of controlling the ordering and arrangements of administrative agencies, makes it unlikely that future proposals to insulate officials from presidential supervision and control—with the important exception of officials charged with assisting the President in his foreign affairs and national security responsibilities—will be subject to successful constitutional attack.

52. Anatomy of an Agency That Failed

David G. Savage

One of the myths about bureaucracy is that bureaucrats always get their way and that agencies never die. In reality, however, agencies, like other elements in our political system, rise and fall with political moods and opinions in the larger society. A new agency often is created in the aftermath of a crisis; public indifference may allow the agency to proceed over the years in league with those it serves; scandals may erode the agency's base of support.

The organization described in this article, the National Institute of Education, was created in 1972 to conduct research on educational problems. By the 1980s, the political climate had changed, and NIE seemed to be an inefficient and unneeded survivor of a bygone era. Moreover, the agency suffered from organizational problems and from its own clumsiness in cultivating political support. David G. Savage, education writer for the *Los Angeles Times,* where this article was published in 1985, recounts the history of NIE and why and how the agency was disbanded.

In 1970, a young White House aide who recently graduated from Harvard University worked up a long policy memo seeking to convince President Richard M. Nixon that what the nation needed was a research agency that would do for education what the National Institutes of Health had done for medicine.

Not only did the Republican President like the idea, so did the Democratic-controlled Congress, which in 1972 created the National Institute of Education.

The law spoke of the new agency bringing about "the reform and renewal" of American education through research and development. It would, said one of its backers, "bring to education the same degree of intellect, intensity and direction that we have grown to expect in health through NIH, in aerospace through NASA and even in agriculture."

But, rather than gaining new respect for education research, the institute in its early years gained a reputation for political bumbling, constantly shifting priorities and incomprehensible project descriptions.

"We get all this soft, mushy education jargon from them that doesn't tell us a thing," Rep. David Obey (D-Wis.) said in 1975.

A decade later, even Chester Finn Jr., the former Nixon aide, concluded that the agency was a "hopeless disappointment." Its "political, intellectual and organizational ailments are incurable," he wrote. Named a top adviser to Secretary of Education William Bennett, Finn in his first days on the job moved to reorganize the National Institute of Education out of existence.

Today [October 1, 1985], the agency officially goes out of business.

What went wrong? Its sponsors and critics say now that the National Institute of Education was to some degree a victim of the Watergate era, since it lacked crucial political backing during its start-up time from the Nixon White House. Its first directors also made the mistake, they say, of believing that they could ignore Capitol Hill.

But the institute's main problem may have been education research itself. Unlike research in medicine, science or agriculture, research in education rarely yields clear and useful conclusions.

"In the public mind, education research is equated with wasting money," said Finn, who makes clear that he does not entirely disagree with that assessment.

"There is a lot of lousy research in education. Some of the journals are so dull that you couldn't light a fire with them," said Gray Garwood, staff director for the House education subcommittee that oversees the National Institute of Education. "Research in education just doesn't have the glamour and status of biomedical research or research in the other hard sciences."

Disenchanted by the lack of clear results, Congress steadily whittled away the institute's budget, from a high of more than $140 million in 1973 to $53 million [in 1985], a tiny sum when compared to the $4.4 billion-a-year federal health research institute.

What is worse, many of the institute's research projects yielded conclusions that appear obvious. For example, one major project that analyzed learning in elementary schools confirmed what educators call the "time on task" notion. That is, children tend to learn more about a subject if they study it longer.

"The reaction we always got was, 'It cost you $6 million to discover that!' " one institute staff member said ruefully.

However, even the National Institute of Education's sharpest critics usually note that some of the research studies had a worthwhile effect on the schools.

For example, studies of unusually effective schools, whether in affluent or poor neighborhoods, found that their success turned on an active principal who closely monitored what the children were learning. Although it is an unsurprising conclusion, school systems throughout the nation have used it either to redirect or replace principals who saw themselves primarily as building managers or office-bound bureaucrats.

"Even if our work had an effect, we didn't get much credit for it," said the same institute official, who asked not to be identified.

Others blamed the National Institute of Education itself for failing to get credit on Capitol Hill for the good projects it had financed.

"The NIE was a case study of how not to be effective in Washington," said Michael Kirst, professor of education at Stanford University. "In fact, I use it with my students as a work-case example of how to operate in Washington."

"They never built any political bridges to the key people in Congress or to the teachers unions, the school administrators or state officials. They had no political coalition to support them," Kirst said.

The first institute officials "thought they could create an isolated, elite agency that would do purely academic research. That's just not very pragmatic, since Congress expects to see some results in the schools," said Joseph Schneider, a Washington lobbyist for 17 education research centers that depend on the education institute for funds.

By stressing practical improvements in the schools, Schneider has succeeded for more than a decade in gaining money for the education research centers, including ones at UCLA and Stanford. Congress has ordered that the centers continue to be financed after the National Institute of Education's demise.

Kirst said the institute not only ignored political lobbying but failed to set any dramatic goals for itself.

"You don't see NIH going to Capitol Hill to say they're going to work in the area of biology and chemistry. They say 'we're attacking heart disease and cancer,' " Kirst said. Rather than saying it was working on a problem such as "illiteracy," the National Institute of Education told Congress it was studying the "learning process," he said.

Sen. Paul Simon (D-Ill.), who chaired a subcommittee overseeing the National Institute of Education, said he strongly supports research in education but added, "There seemed to be a lack of focus in what they were doing. It didn't seem that they always used the money very constructively."

In 1975, after an institute official had bumbled through a budget hearing, the Senate took the unusual step of voting the National Institute of Education a zero budget. However, its supporters in the House were able to restore its budget to $70 million for the year.

But, at the start of the Reagan Administration, even the institute's own officials turned against the agency. In 1981, its director, Edward Curran, and the chairman of its policy-making council, George Roche, the president of Hillsdale College in Michigan, urged President Reagan to abolish the agency. Conservatives then took up the cause, charging that the institute was using research to inject liberal social views into the public schools.

The agency's one steadfast supporter was former House Majority Whip John Brademas, [former] president of New York University. In 1972, he sponsored the law creating the agency and helped keep up its budget throughout the 1970s. "If you look at the Defense Department, or agriculture or health, we always set aside a huge percentage for research and development. But we don't do that in education," Brademas said in a telephone interview. "That was my concern then and I would defend the same view today. In education, just as in those other areas, we need to get the same kind of thoughtful analysis and evidence about what works and what doesn't work."

Brademas said that many of the most controversial questions in education don't benefit from impartial research. Bennett said in a highly publicized speech [in 1985] that "we have no evidence" that bilingual education has helped non-English-speaking students succeed in school.

But education officials also have no evidence that other approaches would work better. Despite 17 years of controversy over bilingual education, the government has not financed studies that compare bilingual education to other methods of teaching English. The Education Department estimated recently that the nation will spend $261 billion this year on education at all age levels. But this year, National Institute of Education officials said they had virtually no money to finance new research projects.

Finn, the Bennett adviser who has reorganized the National Institute of Education into a smaller research unit within the department, said he still believes that education research can shed new light on important questions.

"As an example, there are schools attended by underclass kids that are working well. We need to find out what's going on there and how can we create more of those exceptional schools," said Finn, who over the last decade has been a prolific writer and commentator on education issues.

"In another very different area, we need to learn more about what is character, how is it acquired and what influence if any that schools can have on building character," he said. This time, however, Finn's optimism for education research efforts has been scaled back.

"Education research is a rather precarious enterprise," he said in an interview. "I think with some new priorities and new directions, we can make it work. But it's probably no better than a 60/40 chance that we'll succeed."

53. Reflections on the Effective Operation of the Federal Government

Paul A. Volcker

Paul Volcker, former chairman of the Federal Reserve Board, went on to serve as chairman of the National Commission on the Public Service. The Volcker Commission, which was composed of prominent citizens concerned about the "quiet crisis" in the federal civil service—the "erosion of morale among civil servants, the apparent lack of public respect, the inadequate pay, the inability to recruit and retain needed talent"—issued a report in 1989 that urged major changes in the government's personnel system. In an address to the Council for Excellence in Government, reprinted in the *Congressional Record* in 1990, Volcker discusses the need to restore public confidence in government and in those who serve in its administrative ranks. He reminds us of the dignity of public service and the challenge of strengthening governmental effectiveness.

Every day we are bombarded with news from at home or abroad that demands an effective response from government. Peace and prosperity; fair opportunities for our people to make a good living and to live in reasonable safety and health; prospects for clean air and water while enhancing economic efficiency—these things and more hang in the balance.

Yet, at the same time, respect for Government and those who serve it has, beyond any doubt, declined significantly in recent decades. In those circumstances it's no wonder that it seems tougher and tougher to attract a fair share of our country's talent to the work of the nation.

What a paradox it is!

How ironic that, at a time when basic American values and ideals are a source of inspiration in so many parts of the world, we seem to be more and more frustrated with our own inability to satisfy urgent collective needs here at home—to fight crime and drugs, to better educate, to rebuild our cities, and all the rest.

Like most central bankers, I have a certain reputation for worrying too much. But never, in my most sleepless nights, did I ever think that in one single year we would see so much evidence to support the thesis of the Commission on the Public Service that reform has become a matter of high national priority.

Two years ago, we used the phrase "quiet crisis" to describe the erosion of morale among civil servants, the apparent lack of public respect, the inadequate pay, the inability to recruit and retain needed talent.

Now, the noise seems almost deafening.

[The year 1989] started with stories of outright corruption in Pentagon procurement. Then, the political scandals at HUD competed for headlines with influence peddling in Congress. We even read of bribery at the Food and Drug Administration, one of those agencies we once looked upon with considerable confidence and pride, satisfied that our medicines were the best and our food the safest in the world. In this particular season, we are reminded again of the inability of the Internal Revenue Service to collect the money it is owed or even to promptly, courteously, and consistently answer the questions of honest tax payers. One hardly knows how to characterize the mixture of shortsighted public policy, political influence peddling, and maladministration that will cost hundreds of billions of dollars to make good the guaranty of savings and loan deposits.

And yet, with all this, it's still an uphill battle to get the Congress, the press, or the American people to look at, and deal with, some of the root causes of these problems in the public service. Sporadic cries of alarm about the apparent paucity of experienced candidates for key regulatory or scientific agencies; about threats to the once unquestioned professional standards of our scientific agencies; about the high dropout rates of good young government lawyers or economists—all that sounds a little hollow, when so little time and effort is devoted to changing the situation in a basic way.

Sometimes it seems that the only response we can find to the ethical lapses, or perceptions of ethical lapses, of Federal executives is to pile more and more detailed—often incomprehensible—reporting requirements and conflict of interest prohibitions onto existing law. The questions might more reasonably be asked as to why political appointees only stay two years or so, on the average, on the way to another job; why even so-called "careerists" find it harder and harder to think of public service as their career; and why those circumstances may enlarge the risks of conflict of interest.

Well, members of our Commission never thought that our Report, however eloquent and persuasive to us, would by itself ignite reform. For that reason we didn't pack up our bags and quietly slip out of town after we gave the Report to the President and leaders of Congress [in 1989]. Instead we decided to stick around for a while to lend a hand where we thought we could be helpful in stimulating discussion, in advancing our proposals, and in encouraging other groups with a continuing professional or public interest in reform. In other words, we have tried to be realists—we thought our Report could be a useful beginning, if only a "step in the process." . . .

Actually getting things done—getting legislation and Executive Orders, better education, and not least some money—is the acid test. No one ever said it would be easy. But, I think we have had a couple of significant breakthroughs . . . and some promising stirrings on a much broader front.

Most significantly, after enormous pulling and hauling, Congress with Presidential support finally enacted pay and ethics legislation for the top levels of government. Though it might not have accomplished all that we wanted, especially on the Senate side, its significance extends well beyond those immediately affected. Much of the media attention focused on the most sensitive point—Congressional salaries. Little noticed was the fact that the measure also applied to senior Federal executives and members of the judiciary. Those increases were hardly generous by some standards. But to take one important illustration, they did at least get the salaries of senior Federal judges to something visibly above what the major law firms are paying new law graduates!

While that pay legislation only directly affects a relative handful in the Executive Branch—less than a thousand of the more than 2 million—it has opened the way for the President to raise salaries for thousands more senior officials and for more comprehensive review of lower level pay scales by the Congress. And there are some hopeful indications that, with top level pay for a time resolved, Congress is ready to take on other proposals of our Commission. Indeed Senator Glenn has written me that he hopes to introduce extensive legislation soon.

Meanwhile, a new President has taken office who proudly calls himself a Federal employee—indeed most of his career has been spent in Federal service.

President Bush once said he had trouble with "the vision thing." But you and I know there is nothing the matter with his vision of the crucial importance of public service and the respect due those who do the work with competence and integrity. His spontaneous meetings with government workers involved in critical recovery operations following Hurricane Hugo and the San Francisco earthquake only reflect what he had already made plain in more formal meetings with career Federal executives when he first took office.

The President has also declared his interest in another, and in a more difficult, way. His budget proposals take encouraging first steps toward improving General Schedule pay, establishing a pilot public service scholarship program, and providing for a permanent advisory commission to oversee the public service. . . .

To sum up where we stand today, you could say that we have had a great deal of *glasnost*—or open discussion—on the kind of actions that are needed. But as yet, there has been little *perestroika*—or actual restructuring.

Right at the top of that list of unfinished business is the critical problem of General Schedule pay. Without substantial changes here, efforts to improve the overall quality and competence of the Federal workforce will falter. Senator Mikulski recently warned that the Federal government was becoming the "farm team for the private sector." The larger threat, I fear, is that it might simply descend to bush league status, *without* a capital B.

Fortunately, as I suggested earlier, there are some signs that relevant Congressional Committees are finally beginning to look at the problem seriously. There is still a large question about whether long overdue changes can be accomplished this year, but the whole idea of pay reform—including the idea of locality pay, as the Commission proposed—is on the agenda.

It will not be without its budget impact. But as we said in our report, the President and Congress have got to give a higher budget priority to Civil Service pay. And I have no doubt that a major part of that cost could be balanced—should be balanced—by higher performance and productivity within the civil service.

Strengthening the Presidential Management Intern program is another priority. For a long time, that program was a single "point of light" in a rather dismal Federal recruiting program for talented, career-minded students.

However, years of relative neglect had seen applications and interest among students falling to a point where many schools and government agencies no longer considered it worthwhile. With Connie Newman's encouragement, the program appears to be reviving. But legislative action is necessary to provide a solid foundation for the program, and there is room for significant increases in the number of interns hired each year.

A related item on our unfinished agenda—and a clear favorite of Commission members—is a proposal to establish a Public Service Scholarship Program.

We all know about the job the military has done through the years both in attracting potential leaders to the service academies and in rebuilding young people's perception of the armed forces. We believe that the availability, on a strictly competitive basis, of "Congressional" or "Presidential" Scholarships for talented young men and women, pledging in return several years of public service, would do much to enhance both the quality of key civil servants over time and perceptions of public service among students and the public at large. The Commission suggested that the program, following the precedent of the military academies, might combine nomination by a member of Congress with a selection process based on merit. Full payment of tuition, room and board to a group of, say, 1000 college juniors and seniors could prove to be an enormous bargain for the American public over a period of years.

At a more advanced level, the Commission also feels career employees should be provided greater educational opportunities, including fellowships for advanced degrees.

My personal candidate for potentially the most important reform lies in the area with which you are most familiar—Presidential and political appointees.

No one doubts that, in our system, a new administration will want its own people in key jobs. Moreover, significant flows of experienced people, back and forth, between the private and public sectors are a good way to get fresh ideas, new momentum, and needed technical expertise into the bureaucracy.

We have a tradition of political appointees and career executives working together. What we need to do is make sure that it is an effective partnership.

We are not the U.K., or Germany or France, where only a few dozen go into the Executive with a new government. Much less do we want to be a Japan, where there sometimes seems to me a question whether the bureaucratic consensus isn't more powerful than any government.

Nonetheless, there is a serious question when a good and necessary thing becomes too much. Roosevelt was accused of politicizing the executive branch when (exclusive of Ambassadors) he had fewer than 100 Presidential appointees when he took office. A quarter century ago there were 150. Now there are over 500 positions subject to Presidential appointment with Senate confirmation and another 2500 "political" appointees in the Senior Executive Service and Schedule C.

Instead of these larger numbers assuring performance and effectiveness in executing a President's program, I'm afraid the opposite is true. Inevitably, the quality of appointments is diluted as one has to find thousands of people below the relatively prestigious Under and Assistant Secretary level. As you know better than anyone, too often available candidates for secondary positions are those whose qualifications are almost entirely political, those who see government as a way station to another job, or those who in fact have difficulty in the private sector.

Looked at from the other direction, the most active, energetic, experienced young foreign service officers, or budget analysts, or Park Service rangers, or lawyers or economists—would-be careerists all—simply aren't going to stay when important and influential positions to which they might reasonably aspire are denied to them. I can tell you from my own experience with students that is the way they see life in the Federal Government—and many of the best with a natural bent toward the public service are simply "turned off" by the prospect.

There are already limits on political appointees. Our point is simply that they have been relaxed too far over the years. The Commission was so radical as to suggest that the total might be cut back by a third—all the way to the average levels of the early 1970's.

Conversely, there is evidence that we have gone too far in discouraging good political appointees by the nature of the conflict of interest and reporting requirements. The hassle—and that's really too weak a word—simply leads many honorable and qualified people to stay away. The work done by your Council and others in drawing attention to this area is important indeed.

That all adds up to an ambitious program. Obviously, given consideration and debate, the Commission's proposals will be modified, dropped, or supplemented. Needs will change.

All of that emphasizes the need for some mechanism to keep the state of the public service under active review. To that end, we believe there is a clear need for an advisory body in government which would work with OPM and OMB and the White House, assessing needs and reporting to the President and Congress on what needs to be done.

At this point, I regretfully think we have to admit the Quadrennial Commission on Pay has been a failure; not in *one* instance after its maiden effort have its pay proposals been enacted. However, it seemed to us the basic concept of a tripartite body, recast into a broader "National Advisory Council on the Public Service," may indeed be appropriate. It would bring together members of Congress, the Executive, and the public at large. The group would meet as it deemed necessary, and should be required to issue a formal report with recommendations every second year. The President and relevant Congressional Committees would then be called upon to respond to such a report and its recommendations.

There are, of course, a lot of areas we did not cover, or of which we hardly scratched the surface. One is the question of "contracting out"—the extent to which increasing privatization of functions previously carried out by government will in fact serve the public and the public purse.

The Commission, as it considered political appointments in the Executive, stepped back from examining the related question of the number of the staff on Capitol Hill. That now numbers over 25,000, and it has more than doubled in size since the early 1970's. No doubt, many extremely able people are included, but the question remains as to whether the net effect is to encourage micro-management of government programs from the Hill.

The Commission was highly conscious of the fact that State and local government officials often confront challenges as serious as those at the Federal level. Those problems are compounded as more and more responsibility is shifted to them from Washington, and they often have few management resources to fall back upon.

At the same time, it is at the State and local level where much of the "action" is these days. Some of those same young people, turned off by what they see as the labyrinth and stultification of the Federal bureaucracy, think they can, as their favorite expression goes, "make a difference" in State and local government. Certainly, with the right leadership in a State House or Mayor's office, experience shows there can be indeed innovation and excitement and satisfaction.

We have, in a small way, been trying to spread that gospel, as well as the need for Federal reform, through a series of regional dialogues. In some places, leaders of business, government and education are talking together and thinking about launching commissions or studies of their own.

[In 1990] I participated in one of these sessions in Chicago. I was impressed by the turnout—which included both candidates for governor and a host of other local leaders.

One local official involved in the Illinois program put the issue succinctly when he said "our operating assumptions are that doing government work well is important, it's hard, and not enough people give a damn." Well, in many areas, we can respond to him by saying that we can point to instances in which leaders of the local community, once galvanized, do give a damn. I hope that effort will be multiplied.

One particular area where State and local initiative is indispensable is in better educating our young people about the importance of good citizenship and community service. Our report recommended that parents and educators work to elevate the importance of civic education as a part of social studies and history curricula in primary and secondary schools. No doubt, there is a special need—and opportunity—for business to support non-profit organizations and civic groups to help in that grass roots area, among other things providing students with opportunities to practice citizenship skills right in their own communities, close to home.

No doubt, we also need to involve the private sector more systematically in efforts to improve the public service. They can bring resources to bear on the problem—and more important they can stimulate the creative thinking we need. That's one reason that this Council is in such a strategic position, bringing together people from both sectors through its Campus Public Service Weeks and other initiatives.

In that connection, I must also emphasize that both business and Government face a challenge of productively employing a larger proportion of minorities. For society, that is a moral imperative, and it will soon be a practical necessity as well.

Blacks and Hispanics will make up a far larger percentage of new entrants to the workforce in the next decade; in fact, it has been estimated that almost 50 percent of the increase in the workforce in the 1990's will be minorities. Government should be a model for the private sector in this area. It clearly needs to do better.

Well, what does it all add up to? We think we've laid out a sensible agenda and some practical and needed goals. We're encouraged that most knowledgeable observers see it that way.

A start has been made. However sluggishly, the political process is beginning to respond. But clearly that flame will need nurturing.

Those here in this room—and the thousands out there that share your experience and concern—need to tell the story that Government service can for some provide a high like no other.

The public needs to be reminded that Government is crucial; that there are some things it has to do, that it's critically important that it does those things well, and that in the end it is people—civil servants or bureaucrats, call them what you will—that have to do the job.

We all know there's a lot of cynicism out there. But there is also a deep reservoir of interest and enthusiasm for public service—most particularly among the young.

What an exciting and challenging time for young people and our government this should be!

We do need to clean up our air and rivers—and do it without breaking the back of business.

There is space that needs exploring and new energy resources that need to be found.

We need to defeat drugs and make our cities safe. We need to make good health care both available and affordable.

On and on—and all of it involves Government.

Here we are on the brink of an enormous triumph of American ideals and values around the world. Nation after nation wants to emulate our democracy, our freedoms, and our economic success.

How tragic—how totally unnecessary—it would be if at this time of unparalleled challenge and potential success, we let the ordinary processes of democratic government erode and corrode—and put the whole enterprise at risk....

Chapter 11

The Federal Courts

Presidents, members of Congress, and federal judges all interpret the Constitution. Each defines permissible action according to the meaning and terms of that basic document. The ballot box, too, as one scholar explained, "provides an institutional means for direct popular interpretation of the Constitution."

> One can look at the election of 1936 as a constitutional referendum in which the people of the 46 of the then 48 states voted for Franklin Roosevelt and his New Deal program despite the Supreme Court's decisions that most of his efforts to regulate the economy were unconstitutional. Certainly it had that effect on the Court, for, six weeks after the election, the justices began to yield to the president's [and Congress's] constitutional views.[1]

Although the Constitution is silent on which branch should prevail in a conflict, judicial guardianship of constitutional principles was not a novel idea to the founders. Former Supreme Court Chief Justice Warren E. Burger traces the antecedents of judicial review as far back as the Magna Carta, more than 500 years before American independence (Selection 54, "The Judiciary: The Origins of Judicial Review").

That the founders contemplated the Supreme Court's judicial review function is evident in Article III, which states that the "judicial power shall extend to all Cases . . . arising under this Constitution." In arguing for the document's ratification in *Federalist Paper* No. 78 (Selection 55), Alexander Hamilton emphasized the federal judges' distinctive responsibility: "A constitution is, in fact, and must be regarded by the judges, as a fundamental law. It therefore belongs to them to ascertain its meaning, as well as the meaning of any particular act proceeding from the legislative body."

Yet the authority of federal judges to declare acts of Congress or the president unconstitutional (as well as actions of state legislatures, executives, or courts) is a power fraught with controversy. A traditional question is why unelected federal judges, acting like a superlegislature, should have the right to sit as a kind of continuing constitutional convention and decide whether congressional and presidential actions are constitutional. No wonder that the Supreme Court is often a storm center of controversy and that its decisions sometimes provoke controversy or noncompliance.

In 1803 the Supreme Court decided the landmark case of *Marbury v. Madison* (Selection 56). *Marbury* is of historic significance because it explicitly established the Supreme Court's prerogative of passing on the constitutionality of acts of Congress. "The Constitution is superior to any ordinary act of the legislature," wrote Chief Justice John Marshall, and "a law repugnant to the Constitution is void." The Supreme Court can also, of course, *uphold* the constitutionality of challenged acts of Congress and the president.

Because so many political issues are transformed into legal suits, federal courts are continually involved in "heated political controversies, with attacks coming from the total range of the political spectrum."[2] A question running through these controversies is whether the Court's exercise of judicial review embroils it too deeply and directly in social, economic, and political issues that ought to be resolved by the popularly elected branches of government. This debate is often described as judicial activism versus judicial self-restraint. Archibald Cox, former U.S. solicitor general, put the question this way: "Should the court play an active, creative role in shaping our destiny, equally with the executive and legislative branches? Or should it be characterized by self-restraint, deferring to the legislative branch whenever there is room for policy judgment and leaving new departures to the initiative of others?"[3]

No doubt the views and values of the framers are important in constitutional jurisprudence, but uncovering the framers' original intent can be an elusive quest. Relatively few records reveal the intentions of the delegates who deliberated in secret at the Constitutional Convention. On many matters the delegates were bitterly divided. Scores of ambiguous terms and phrases fill the document itself, which defy agreement on their "plain meaning." There is also the question of how an eighteenth-century document should be applied to unforeseen contemporary problems.

Judges ultimately determine how the framers' values apply to today's circumstances. This does not mean that "there is no alternative between constitutional fundamentalism and judicial libertinism," wrote historian Arthur Schlesinger, Jr. Indeed, the Constitution prescribes values and principles (federalism, the freedoms of speech, press, and religion) that establish the "framework within which the task of adjudication must take place."[4] Recruitment of federal judges is crucial to effective governance, because these public officials serve for life (though they are subject to the unwieldy impeachment process) and their decisions influence the course of American history.

The framers understood the awesome importance of lifetime appointments to the bench and gave the responsibility for making them jointly to the president and the Senate. That the Senate's "advice and consent" responsibility is not merely ceremonial could be attested to by judges Clement F. Haynsworth, Jr., and G. Harrold Carswell, both of whom were nominated to the Supreme Court by President Richard Nixon but formally rejected by the Senate. Concern about these judges' competence and integrity were two of the factors that led to their rejection. The question of what qualifications are required for federal judges is addressed in Selection 57.

For at least the past two decades, sharp political and partisan debate has often characterized the advice and consent process. With the White House controlled by Republicans for this entire period and the Senate controlled by Democrats (except from 1981 to 1987), the consideration of Supreme Court nominations often became mired in intense partisan struggles. Many Democratic senators (and others, too) became concerned that GOP Presidents Reagan and Bush were nominating an overwhelming number of relatively young, ardent conservatives to the federal bench. Many Democrats feared that the new Reagan-Bush judges, who constituted more than half of all justices by the early 1990s, would reshape the courts to reflect conservative economic and social views on abortion, church-state relationships, affirmative action, and other issues. The confirmation hearings in 1987 on the nomination of Robert H. Bork (a federal appeals court justice) to the Supreme Court provided an example of a highly charged institutional and partisan clash between the GOP White House and Democratic Senate over the direction of the Supreme Court. The Bork nomination even spawned a massive outside public relations campaign that contributed to Bork's rejection by the Senate.

History contains abundant evidence that other presidents considered the philosophy of their judicial nominees. What troubled many senators, however, was the Republican administrations' apparent emphasis on ideological conformity for its judicial nominees. The question for the Senate then became whether ideology was a legitimate criterion for appraising nominees or whether intellect, legal excellence, temperament, and character constitute the proper standards for evaluation. In Selection 58, "Judging Judges: The Senate's Role in Judicial Appointments," Sen. Paul Simon (D-Ill.) grapples with this question by identifying several criteria for nominees to the federal bench.

The Senate's ability to evaluate candidates for the bench is difficult because there are few standards to guide the inquiry process. Senators often become frustrated when the nominees refuse to discuss their constitutional views or opinions on the ground that they do not want to prejudice their action in future cases. Nominees, for their part, shy away from rendering "advisory opinions" on pending issues or losing their intellectual independence by prejudging future cases. As U.S. Court of Appeals Judge Abner J. Mikva put it:

> What the Senate ought not do is determine, through questioning, a nominee's views on emerging constitutional doctrine, on issues likely to face courts in the near future. Why? Because these questions are really a signal to a nominee that he will become a judge only if he promises to be obsequious, to be a yes man to the powers that be.[5]

Members of the Senate Judiciary Committee were especially interested in probing David H. Souter's views and "judicial philosophy" when President Bush in 1990 nominated him to fill a vacancy on the Supreme Court. Called the "Stealth nominee" by some because of his limited public record and visibility, Senate Judiciary members thoroughly reviewed Souter's record as a New Hampshire judge and attorney general, his qualifications, and his approach to interpreting the Constitution. In the end, Souter's nomination was cleared for Senate action by a 13 to 1 vote of the Judiciary Committee. Judiciary members Orrin Hatch, R-Utah, and Edward Kennedy, D-Mass., explain their opposing views toward judge-designate Souter in Selection 59. Subsequently, the Senate, by a 90 to 9 vote, approved Souter's nomination to the Supreme Court.

Although many commentators speculate about the ways the constitutional philosophy of jurists affects Supreme Court rulings, observers have devoted considerably less attention to how justices actually go about their work. In Selection 60, "The Work of the Supreme Court: A Nuts and Bolts Description," Supreme Court Justice Byron R. White describes the substance and procedures of the justices' work, "a bird's-eye view . . . of what we do and how we do it."[6]

Notes

1. Walter Murphy, "Who Shall Interpret the Constitution?" *News for Teachers of Political Science,* Spring 1986, 11. See Louis Fisher, *Constitutional Dialogues* (Princeton, N.J.: Princeton University Press, 1988).
2. Howard E. Dean, *Judicial Review and Democracy* (New York: Random House, 1966), 9. See also Christopher Wolfe, *The Rise of Modern Judicial Review* (New York: Basic Books, 1986).

3. Archibald Cox, *The Warren Court* (Cambridge, Mass.: Harvard University Press, 1968), 2.
4. *Wall Street Journal,* January 17, 1986, 18.
5. Abner J. Mikva, "Judge Picking," *District Lawyer* (Sept.-Oct. 1985): 39.
6. For other examinations of the workings of the Court, see Nina Totenberg, "Behind the Marble, Beneath the Robes," *New York Times Magazine,* March 16, 1975, 66; David M. O'Brien, *Storm Center: The Supreme Court in American Politics* (New York: W.W. Norton, 1986); and Earl Warren, "Inside the Supreme Court, the Momentous School Desegregation Decision," *Atlantic,* April 1977, 35-40.

54. The Judiciary:
The Origins of Judicial Review

Warren E. Burger

In this essay published in *National Forum* in 1984, Chief Justice Warren Burger analyzes an important and recurring question of American politics: should judges appointed for life have the authority to strike down laws made by the popularly elected branches of the national government? Appointed to the U.S. Supreme Court as chief justice in 1969, Burger served until September 1986, when he resigned to devote full time to directing the U.S. Bicentennial Commission.

Lord Bryce, the noted English political thinker, once said:

> No feature of the government of the United States has awakened so much curiosity ... caused so much discussion, received so much admiration, and been more frequently misunderstood, than the duties assigned to the Supreme Court and the functions which it discharged in guarding the Ark of the Constitution.

In some quarters the Supreme Court's guardianship of that Ark probably has received more guarded praise than in distant places. Lord Bryce, of course, had reference to the doctrine of judicial review, sometimes described as the doctrine of judicial supremacy, in the interpretation of constitutional terms and principles. It is helpful to an understanding of the issues surrounding the unique role of the judiciary in the American constitutional system to examine one particular aspect. The setting in which *Marbury v. Madison* was decided in 1803, with all its momentous consequences for our country, is important. That great case had its antecedents in our colonial experience and its taproots in the declaration of fundamental rights of Englishmen dating back to the Magna Carta almost 500 years before our independence.

The colonial experience of living under a distant parliamentary system with no check on the legislative or executive, except that of popular will in a very limited way, led our Founding Fathers to feel strongly the need for limitations on all branches of government. They were skeptical if not suspicious of power. The intellectual spadework for the system ultimately adopted for our federal government had been done by such seventeenth- and eighteenth-century political theorists as Thomas Hobbes and John Locke. The great rationalist Montesquieu contributed the idea of a separation of powers within the government itself, with each branch acting as a kind of brake upon the others.

As the system worked, one of the functions exercised by the Supreme Court involves measuring executive or legislative action—or that of the states—against the Constitution whenever a challenge to such action is properly brought within the framework of a "case" or "controversy." The Supreme Court does not "reach out" for cases as the popular media occasionally imply; it can select cases for review, but a significant portion of the cases argued are appeals that the Court is required to review.

Some commentators on the development of the Constitution in the United States have suggested from time to time that the subject of judicial review of legislative action was not in the minds of the delegates to the Constitutional Convention in 1787. However, such an obviously important question could not have entirely eluded their attention. Some of the delegates, without doubt, looked to an independent judiciary with fixed tenure as a means of protecting the states and the people against the powers of the new national government, whose scope was as yet unseen and unknown and was therefore feared. Others, particularly the propertied classes, probably regarded a Supreme Court and an independent federal judiciary as a source of protection against the egalitarian, popular government that attracted considerable support as the French upheavals of the eighteenth century unfolded; Thomas Jefferson gave support to this trend. The delegates could not have failed to be aware that the exercise of such powers by the judiciary must in some way involve limitations on legislative and executive action that was contrary to fundamental law as expressed in the Constitution.

Some residual controversy remains as to the exercise of judicial review today but it is largely as to scope, not as to authority. It is now accepted that the first significant exercise of the power by the Supreme Court in 1803 was not judicial usurpation as Jefferson charged. But when a case or controversy is properly brought before the Court on a claim that some governmental action is contrary to the Constitution, someone must decide the issue: the Court must decide. Needless to say, the major challenges to the Court's power have occurred during those periods when, for whatever reason, the Supreme Court has been under attack for its role in contemporary affairs. As an example, many polemics as well as some of the most thoughtful and scholarly challenges were written during the 1930s when, to many of its critics, the Supreme Court represented the dead hand of the past, impeding legitimate experimentation and innovation while the legislature and the executive were trying to cope with a national economic crisis.

It is often assumed that the doctrine of "judicial review" was the invention of Chief Justice John Marshall in the most famous of all his opinions. It is true that Chief Justice Marshall first applied this keystone doctrine of our constitutional law in the *Marbury* case. But Marshall did not originate, and never claimed to have originated, a novel doctrine: he was well aware of the general acceptance of the idea that constitutional adjudication was inherent in the very nature of the separation of powers under our written Constitution. This is not to disparage Marshall, for he was the one who recognized the need to enunciate the doctrine as part of federal jurisprudence, and he seized—some have said he strained—to take the first opportunity to assert the power of the Court to measure an act of Congress by the yardstick of the Constitution.

In 1776, the very year of the Declaration of Independence, and a quarter of a century before Marshall became chief justice, the people of the town of Concord, Massachusetts, held a town meeting and adopted a resolution that "a Constitution alterable by the Supreme Legislative is no security at all to the subject, against encroachment of the Governing Part on any or on all their rights and privileges." Earlier, when the colony of Massachusetts Bay was under British colonial rule, the sturdy farm people of Berkshire County refused to let the colonial courts sit from 1775 to 1780 until the people of Massachusetts adopted a constitution with a bill of rights enforceable by judges. These episodes were well known to the delegates who labored in Philadelphia.

The premise in these events, twenty-five years before *Marbury*, was that by its very nature as an organic document defining and delegating powers to three separate coequal branches of government, a written constitution would be a limit on the acts of the legislature and executive so as to protect fundamental liberties. Where else but in the judicial branch was the appropriate vehicle for providing that protection.

In 1793, Chief Justice Spencer Roane of Virginia's highest court, and an intimate of Thomas Jefferson, wrote in *Kamper v. Hawkins*:

> If the legislature may infringe this Constitution [of Virginia], it is no longer fixed; . . . and the liberties of the people are wholly at the mercy of the legislature.

To be sure, Chief Justice Roane was speaking about the power of the state courts to strike down legislative acts contrary to the state constitution, but conceptually his view agrees with Marshall's in *Marbury*.

The English Magna Carta, of course, was intended primarily by the barons as a limitation on King John, but it has come to stand for a limitation on princes and parliaments alike. In one of the very early opinions of the Supreme Court of the United States, one of many containing references to the Magna Carta, it was said:

... after volumes spoken and written [about the guarantees of Magna Carta], the good sense of mankind has at length settled down to this: *that they were intended to secure the individual from the arbitrary exercise of the powers of government....* [Emphasis added.]

If the judiciary could not "secure the individual from the arbitrary exercise" of a power that in reality the Constitution did not grant, then truly the Constitution, as the Concord Town Meeting Resolution declared, was "no security at all."

Another thread of influence originates with the struggle between Lord Coke and the Stuart kings. Coke's writings and reports were well known to the American colonists; and even though the dictum in *Dr. Bonham's Case* is not precisely followed in England, it has been seminal in our law. In that case Coke asserted that:

... in many cases, the common law will controul Acts of Parliament, and sometimes adjudge them to be utterly void: for when an Act of Parliament is against common right and reason, or repugnant, or impossible to be performed, the common law will controul it, and adjudge such Act to be void.

And even the super authoritarian Oliver Cromwell, 150 years before *Marbury v. Madison,* said: "In every government, there must be something fundamental, somewhat like a Magna Carta which would be unalterable...." Whether the stern, dictatorial Mr. Cromwell intended to propound the idea that a judicial body like our Supreme Court, independent of and coequal with the executive and legislative branches, should be empowered to act as a sort of umpire is doubtful, but plainly he was asserting that "there must be something" to make sure fundamental rights would be "unalterable."

More than a decade before *Marbury,* justices of the Supreme Court sitting on circuit held that state laws contrary to the federal Constitution were invalid, and this was confirmed in *Van Horne Lessee v. Dorrance.* In his opinion in that case, Justice William Paterson, sitting on circuit, asserted flatly:

I take it to be a clear position; that if a legislative act oppugns a constitutional principle, the former must give way, and ... it will be the duty of the Court to adhere to the Constitution, and to declare the act null and void.

We see, therefore, that long before *Marbury,* American political leaders, including many of the most distinguished lawyers and judges, accepted as fundamental that a written constitution was a restraint on every part of the federal government. It does not disparage John Marshall's greatness as a judge or a statesman to say that when he wrote the opinion in *Marbury*, he was doing little more than declaring what was widely accepted by so many of the best legal minds of his day—at least when they could divorce politics from reason! Had it not come in *Marbury*, it would have come later, but John Marshall was not a man to wait for perfect opportunities if a plausible one offered itself. It had to be said, and *Marbury* was the fortuitous circumstance that made it possible to establish this great principle early in our history.

Although the American doctrine of judicial review, as formally articulated in *Marbury v. Madison*, is the great formal pronouncement, it is equally clear that the very words of Article III of the Constitution permit no other conclusion.

The setting in which this great case developed is familiar and important. The incumbent president John Adams was defeated by Thomas Jefferson in November 1800. Beween the time of the election and the following March when Jefferson actually took office, Adams remained in office and his Federalist party controlled the "lame duck" Congress. Soon after his defeat, Adams encouraged the ailing Chief Justice Oliver Ellsworth to resign. Adams was deeply concerned about the future and undoubtedly about what Jefferson and his party might do to the independence of the Supreme Court.

Jefferson's choice for chief justice, had Marshall not been appointed, would almost certainly have been Chief Justice Roane, who was described by Professor Charles Warren as "an ardent strict construction- ist on the Constitution." Roane had shown his basic agreement with Marshall on the subject of judicial review in an opinion for Virginia's highest court in 1793, stating:

> It is the province of the judiciary to expound the laws . . . it may say too, that an act of assembly has not changed the Constitution [of Virginia], though its words are expressly to that effect. . . . [I]t is conceived, for the reasons above mentioned, that the legislature have not power to change the fundamental laws. . . .

Underlying Jefferson's hostility to judicial power was the very fundamental difference between the Federalist belief that a strong national government was the key to the future of the new nation and the opposing belief of the Jeffersonians, who sincerely feared central- ized power and wanted to keep the states the strong and indeed the dominant political power.

Whatever his earlier beliefs, by 1803 Jefferson's distrust of and opposition to the federal judiciary had crystallized. From then onward,

Jefferson did not waver in his attitude. In a letter to a friend dated August 18, 1821, Jefferson wrote, some would say prophetically:

> It has long ... been my opinion, and I have never shrunk from its expression ... that the germ of dissolution of our federal government is in the Constitution of the federal judiciary; an irresponsible body (for impeachment is scarcely a scare-crow), working like gravity by night and by day, gaining a little today and a little tomorrow, and advancing its noiseless step like a thief, over the field of jurisdiction, until all shall be usurped from the States, and the government of all be consolidated into one. To this I am opposed. ... Like a thief!

Adams, as I have noted, was a "lame duck" president after November 1800, with a "lame duck," Federalist-controlled Congress on hand for four months after the election. Naturally, he made as many appointments as possible—persuading Ellsworth to resign to make way for Marshall was but one step. The appointment of a goodly number of federal judges was another. But the far-lesser post of a local justice of the peace was the grist of Marbury's case.

The story is too well known to be chronicled in detail. Marbury was one of those whose commission as justice of the peace was signed by President Adams and attested to by Marshall, who was still acting as President Adams's Secretary of State even after being appointed chief justice and confirmed by the Senate. But Marbury's commission was not delivered.

Marbury then sought a writ of mandamus in the Supreme Court against Madison, Jefferson's Secretary of State, to compel what Marbury claimed was the purely ministerial act of delivering the commission. In the Supreme Court the first reaction may well have been, "of course," since the Judiciary Act provided that precise remedy.

But if, as no one had even remotely suspected up to that time, Congress could not constitutionally grant original jurisdiction to the Supreme Court in any cases except those specifically recited in Article III, then the Court could say, "Yes, Marbury was duly confirmed"; and "Yes, the Commission was duly signed and sealed"; and "Yes, this Court may examine the manner in which the executive conducts its affairs"; and "Yes, delivery is a purely ministerial act"; and "Yes, it is improper that the new administration will not perform the simple ministerial act of delivery"; but the Court could also say, "However, this Court has no power under the Constitution to entertain any original action except those specified in Article III, and this case is not one of them. That being so, Section 13 of the Judiciary Act of 1789 purporting to give the Supreme Court such authority would be invalid and any action to compel the executive to deliver the commission to Marbury could not be entertained as an original action." This, in essence, is what Marshall wrote.

Jefferson and Madison had won the lawsuit—the battle; Marbury, the Federalist, had lost; but the real war, the great "war" over the supremacy of the Supreme Court in constitutional adjudication, had been won by the Court—and by the country. Not for fifty-four years after *Marbury* did the Court hold another act of Congress unconstitutional, although in *Martin v. Hunter's Lessee* (1816), Justice Joseph Story for the Court firmly asserted the power of the Supreme Court to invalidate a state statute contrary to the federal Constitution.

As with so many great conceptions, the idea of judicial review of legislation now seems simple and inevitable in the perspective of history. The people of the states delegated certain powers to the national government and placed limits on those powers by specific and general reservations. After having flatly stated certain guarantees relating to religious freedom, to speech, to searches, seizures, and arrests, would it be reasonable to think that Congress and the executive could alter those rights? Standing alone, the explicit procedures carefully providing for constitutional amendments negate the idea that a written constitution could be altered by legislative or executive action. The language of Article III vesting judicial power "in one Supreme Court" for "all Cases, in Law and Equity, *arising under this Constitution,* the *Laws* of the United States, and Treaties . . ." would be sterile indeed if the Supreme Court could not exercise that judicial power by deciding cases involving conflicts between the Constitution, federal laws, and treaties on the one hand, and acts of Congress, the executive or states on the other.

Given the extraordinary power that judicial review vests in the judiciary, the question may be raised: Who will watch the watchmen? This was a concern to some of those who opposed ratification of the Constitution. Anti-Federalist commentator "Brutus" argued that "this power in the judicial, will enable them to move the government into almost any shape they please." Another Anti-Federalist, "A Columbia Patriot," similarly wrote: "There are no well-defined limits of the Judicial Powers, they seem to be left as a boundless ocean."

It is clear that when Congress disagrees with the judicial interpretation of a statute, Congress can enact a new statute that supersedes that judicial interpretation. Congress has done this many times in our history. Similarly, in four instances Congress and the state legislatures have overridden a Supreme Court opinion through constitutional amendment. Furthermore, when appointments are made to the Supreme Court, it is surely not unnatural that presidents try to appoint, subject to Senate confirmation, justices who they hope will interpret the Constitution "properly." President Franklin D. Roosevelt failed in his effort to control the Supreme Court by seeking to increase it to fifteen justices; yet in his four terms, he appointed eight justices.

It is true that in the tenure of office of all federal judges, so essential to their independence, there is risk that power can be abused, but three tiers of federal courts have mitigated that risk, although not always to every person's satisfaction. The Draftsmen were aware of those risks, but the risks were unavoidable, since "someone must decide."

Chief Justice Harlan Fiske Stone reminded all federal judges that "the only check upon our own exercise of power is our own sense of self-restraint."

55. *Federalist* No. 78

Alexander Hamilton

In No. 78 Hamilton laid out some of the arguments for judicial review that Chief Justice Marshall later used in *Marbury v. Madison* (Selection 56). Hamilton viewed the courts as the "bulwarks of a limited Constitution" and argued for the "permanent tenure of judicial offices" to ensure the judges' "independent spirit" in the "faithful performance of so arduous a duty." Hamilton's observations, when combined with those of the previous selection, provide valuable commentary on the framers' Intent on judicial review (which they supported) and on the important role of the courts in preserving and protecting fundamental liberties.

We proceed now to an examination of the judiciary department of the proposed government.

In unfolding the defects of the existing Confederation, the utility and necessity of a federal judicature have been clearly pointed out. It is the less necessary to recapitulate the considerations there urged, as the propriety of the institution in the abstract is not disputed; the only questions which have been raised being relative to the manner of constituting it, and to its extent. To these points, therefore, our observations shall be confined.

The manner of constituting it seems to embrace these several objects: 1st. The mode of appointing the judges. 2nd. The tenure by which they are to hold their places. 3rd. The partition of the judiciary authority between different courts, and their relations to each other.

First. As to the mode of appointing the judges; this is the same with that of appointing the officers of the Union in general, and has been so fully discussed in the two last numbers, that nothing can be said here which would not be useless repetition.

Second. As to the tenure by which the judges are to hold their places: this chiefly concerns their duration in office; the provisions for their support; the precautions for their responsibility.

According to the plan of the convention, all judges who may be appointed by the United States are to hold their offices *during good behavior*; which is conformable to the most approved of the State constitutions, and among the rest, to that of this State. Its propriety having been drawn into question by the adversaries of that plan, is no light symptom of the rage for objection, which disorders their imaginations and judgments. The standard of good behavior for the continuance in office of the judicial magistracy, is certainly one of the most valuable of the modern improvements in the practice of government. In a monarchy it is an excellent barrier to the despotism of the prince; in a republic it is a no less excellent barrier to the encroachments and oppressions of the representative body. And it is the best expedient which can be devised in any government, to secure a steady, upright, and impartial administration of the laws.

Whoever attentively considers the different departments of power must perceive, that, in a government in which they are separated from each other, the judiciary, from the nature of its functions, will always be the least dangerous to the political rights of the Constitution; because it will be least in a capacity to annoy or injure them. The Executive not only dispenses the honors, but holds the sword of the community. The legislature not only commands the purse, but prescribes the rules by which the duties and rights of every citizen are to be regulated. The judiciary, on the contrary, has no influence over either the sword or the purse; no direction either of the strength or of the wealth of the society; and can take no active resolution whatever. It may truly be said to have neither FORCE nor WILL, but merely judgment; and must ultimately depend upon the aid of the executive arm even for the efficacy of its judgments.

This simple view of the matter suggests several important consequences. It proves incontestably, that the judiciary is beyond comparison the weakest of the three departments of power; that it can never attack with success either of the other two; and that all possible care is requisite to enable it to defend itself against their attacks. It equally proves, that though individual oppression may now and then proceed from the courts of justice, the general liberty of the people can never be endangered from that quarter; I mean so long as the judiciary remains truly distinct from both the legislature and the Executive. For I agree, that "there is no liberty, if the power of judging be not separated from the legislative and executive powers." And it proves, in the last place, that as liberty can have nothing to fear from the judiciary alone, but would have every thing to fear from its union with either of the other departments; that as all the effects of such a union must ensue from a dependence of the former on the latter, notwithstanding a nominal and apparent separation; that as, from the natural feebleness of the judiciary, it is in continual jeopardy of being overpowered, awed, or influenced by its coordinate branches; and that as nothing can contribute so much to its firmness and independence as permanency in office, this quality may therefore be justly regarded as an indispensable ingredient in its constitution, and, in a great measure, as the citadel of the public justice and the public security.

The complete independence of the courts of justice is peculiarly essential in a limited Constitution. By a limited Constitution, I understand one which contains certain specified exceptions to the legislative authority; such, for instance, as that it shall pass no bills at attainder, no *ex-post-facto* laws, and the like. Limitations of this kind can be preserved in practice no other way than through the medium of courts of justice, whose duty it must be to declare all acts contrary to the manifest tenor of the Constitution void. Without this, all the reservations of particular rights or privileges would amount to nothing.

Some perplexity respecting the rights of the courts to pronounce legislative acts void, because contrary to the constitution, has arisen from an imagination that the doctrine would imply a superiority of the judiciary to the legislative power. It is urged that the authority which can declare the acts of another void, must necessarily be superior to the one whose acts may be declared void. As this doctrine is of great importance in all the American constitutions, a brief discussion of the ground on which it rests cannot be unacceptable.

There is no position which depends on clearer principles, than that every act of a delegated authority, contrary to the tenor of the commission under which it is exercised, is void. No legislative act, therefore, contrary to the Constitution, can be valid. To deny this, would be to affirm, that the deputy is greater than his principal; that the servant is above his master; that the representatives of the people are superior to the people themselves; that men acting by virtue of powers, may do not only what their powers do not authorize, but what they forbid.

If it be said that the legislative body are themselves the constitutional judges of their own powers, and that the construction they put upon them is conclusive upon the other departments, it may be answered, that this cannot be the natural presumption, where it is not to be collected from any particular provisions in the Constitution. It is not otherwise to be supposed, that the Constitution could intend to enable the representatives of the people to substitute their *will* to that of their constituents. It is far more rational to suppose, that the courts were designed to be an intermediate body between the people and the legislature, in order, among other things, to keep the latter within the limits assigned to their authority. The interpretation of the laws is the proper and peculiar province of the courts. A constitution is, in fact, and must be regarded by the judges, as a fundamental law. It therefore belongs to them to ascertain its meaning, as well as the meaning of any particular act proceeding from the legislative body. If there should happen to be an irreconcilable variance between the two, that which has the superior obligation and validity ought, of course, to be preferred; or, in other words, the Constitution ought to be preferred to the statute, the intention of the people to the intention of their agents.

Nor does this conclusion by any means suppose a superiority of the judicial to the legislative power. It only supposes that the power of the people is superior to both; and that where the will of the legislature, declared in its statutes, stands in opposition to that of the people, declared in the Constitution, the judges ought to be governed by the latter rather than the former. They ought to regulate their decisions by the fundamental laws, rather than by those which are not fundamental.

This exercise of judicial discretion, in determining between two contradictory laws, is exemplified in a familiar instance. It not uncommonly happens, that there are two statutes existing at one time, clashing in whole or in part with each other, and neither of them containing any repealing clause or expression. In such a case, it is the province of the courts to liquidate and fix their meaning and operation. So far as they can, by any fair construction, be reconciled to each other, reason and law conspire to dictate that this should be done; where this is impracticable, it becomes a matter of necessity to give effect to one, in exclusion of the other. The rule which has obtained in the courts for determining their relative validity is, that the last in order of time shall be preferred to the first. But there is a mere rule of construction, not derived from any positive law, but from the nature and reason of the thing. It is a rule not enjoined upon the courts by legislative provision, but adopted by themselves, as consonant to truth and propriety, for the direction of their conduct as interpreters of the law. They thought it reasonable, that between the interfering acts of an *equal* authority, that which was the last indication of its will should have the preference.

But in regard to the interfering acts of a superior and subordinate authority, of an original and derivative power, the nature and reason of the thing indicate the converse of that rule as proper to be followed. They teach us that the prior act of a superior ought to be preferred to the subsequent act of an inferior and subordinate authority; and that accordingly, whenever a particular statute contravenes the Constitution, it will be the duty of the judicial tribunals to adhere to the latter and disregard the former.

It can be of no weight to say that the courts, on the pretense of a repugnancy, may substitute their own pleasure to the constitutional intentions of the legislature. This might as well happen in the case of two contradictory statutes; or it might as well happen in every adjudication upon any single statute. The courts must declare the sense of the law; and if they should be disposed to exercise WILL instead of JUDGMENT, the consequence would equally be the substitution of their pleasure to that of the legislative body. The observation, if it proves any thing, would prove that there ought to be no judges distinct from that body.

If, then, the courts of justice are to be considered as the bulwarks of a limited Constitution against legislative encroachments, this consideration will afford a strong argument for the permanent tenure of judicial offices, since nothing will contribute so much as this to that independent spirit in the judges which must be essential to the faithful performance of so arduous a duty.

This independence of the judges is equally requisite to guard the Constitution and the rights of individuals from the effects of those ill humors, which the arts of designing men, or the influence of particular conjunctures, sometimes disseminate among the people themselves, and which, though they speedily give place to better information, and more deliberate reflection, have a tendency, in the meantime, to occasion dangerous innovations in the government, and serious oppressions of the minor party in the community. Though I trust the friends of the proposed Constitution will never concur with its enemies, in questioning that fundamental principle of republican government, which admits the right of the people to alter or abolish the established Constitution, whenever they find it inconsistent with their happiness, yet it is not to be inferred from this principle, that the representatives of the people, whenever a momentary inclination happens to lay hold of a majority of their constituents, incompatible with the provisions in the existing Constitution, would, on that account, be justifiable in a violation of those provisions; or that the courts would be under a greater obligation to connive at infractions in this shape, than when they had proceeded wholly from the cabals of the representative body. Until the people have, by some solemn and authoritative act, annulled or changed the established form, it is binding upon themselves collectively, as well as individually; and no presumption, or even knowledge, of their sentiments, can warrant their representatives in a departure from it, prior to such an act. But it is easy to see, that it would require an uncommon portion of fortitude in the judges to do their duty as faithful guardians of the Constitution, where legislative invasions of it had been instigated by the major voice of the community.

But it is not with a view to infractions of the Constitution only, that the independence of the judges may be an essential safeguard against the effects of occasional ill humors in the society. These sometimes extend no farther than to the injury of the private rights of particular classes of citizens, by unjust and partial laws. Here also the firmness of the judicial magistracy is of vast importance in mitigating the severity and confining the operation of such laws. It not only serves to moderate immediate mischiefs of those which may have been passed, but it operates as a check upon the legislative body in passing them; who, perceiving that obstacles to the success of iniquitous intention are to be expected from the scruples of the courts, are in a manner compelled, by the very motives of the injustice they meditate, to qualify their attempts. This is circumstance calculated to have more influence upon the character of our governments, than but few may be aware of. The benefits of the integrity and moderation of the judiciary have already been felt in more States than one; and though they may have displeased those whose sinister expectations they may have disappointed, they must have commanded the esteem and applause of all the virtuous and disinterested. Considerate men, of every description, ought to prize whatever will tend to beget or fortify that temper in the courts; as no man can be sure that he may not be tomorrow the victim of a spirit of injustice, by which he may be a gainer today. And every man must now feel, that the inevitable tendency of such a spirit is to sap the foundations of public and private confidence, and to introduce in its stead universal distrust and distress.

That inflexible and uniform adherence to the rights of the Constitution, and of individuals, which we perceive to be indispensable in the courts of justice, can certainly not be expected from judges who hold their offices by a temporary commission. Periodical appointments, however regulated, or by whomsoever made, would, in some way or other, be fatal to their necessary independence. If the power of making them was committed either to the Executive or legislature, there would be danger of an improper complaisance to the branch which possessed it; if to both, there would be an unwillingness to hazard the displeasure of either; if to the people, or to persons chosen by them for the special purpose, there would be too great a disposition to consult popularity, to justify a reliance that nothing would be consulted but the Constitution and the laws.

There is yet a further and a weightier reason for the permanency of the judicial offices, which is deducible from the nature of the qualifications they require. It has been frequently remarked, with great propriety, that a voluminous code of laws is one of the inconveniences necessarily connected with the advantages of a free government. To avoid an arbitrary discretion in the courts, it is indispensable that they should be bound down by strict rules and precedents, which serve to define and point out their duty in every particular case that comes before them; and it will readily be conceived from the variety of controversies which grow out of the folly and wickedness of mankind, that the records of those precedents must unavoidably swell to a very considerable bulk, and must demand long and laborious study to acquire a competent knowledge of them. Hence it is, that there can be but few men in the society who will have sufficient skill in the laws to qualify them for the stations of judges. And making the proper deductions for the ordinary depravity of human nature, the number must be still smaller of those who unite the requisite integrity with the requisite knowledge. These considerations apprise us, that the government can have no great option between fit character; and that a temporary duration in office, which would naturally discourage such characters from quitting a lucrative line of practice to accept a seat on the bench, would have a tendency to throw the administration of justice into hands less able, and less well qualified, to conduct it with utility and dignity. In the present circumstances of this country, and in those in which it is likely to be for a long time to come, the disadvantages on this score would be greater than they may at first appear; but it must be confessed that they are far inferior to those which present themselves under the other aspects of the subject.

Upon the whole, there can be no room to doubt that the convention acted wisely in copying from the models of those constitutions which have established *good behavior* as the tenure of their judicial offices, in point of duration; and that so far from being blamable on this account, their plan would have been inexcusably defective, if it had wanted this important feature of good government. The experience of Great Britain affords an illustrious comment on the excellence of the institution.

56. *Marbury v. Madison* (1803)

In this landmark case, the Supreme Court declared in a clear-cut decision that part of a major congressional act was unconstitutional. The controversy grew out of President John Adams's appointments of District of Columbia justices of the peace in the waning hours of his Federalist administration. Some of the Federalist justices never received their official commissions because the term of the acting secretary of state, John Marshall (whom Adams had appointed chief justice) expired before the commissions could be delivered. When Thomas Jefferson took office as president, he directed his secretary of state, James Madison, not to deliver the leftover commissions. William Marbury, one of the Federalist appointees, took the case to the Supreme Court and asked for a judicial order (a writ of mandamus) to require Madison to deliver his commission; the Judiciary Act of 1789 had authorized the Court to issue such writs. The stage was thus set for a clash between the Federalist chief justice and the Republican administration. In a politically adroit decision, Chief Justice Marshall said Marbury was entitled to his appointment but that the provision of the Judiciary Act, under which the Court was to require Madison to deliver Marbury's commission, was unconstitutional.

Mr. Chief Justice Marshall delivered the opinion of the Court. [First he observed that Marbury had a vested right to the office in question, and that a writ of mandamus was the proper remedy for securing such a right. Then he turned to the problem of whether that remedy "can issue from this Court."]

The act to establish the judicial courts of the United States authorizes the Supreme Court "to issue writs of mandamus, in cases warranted by the principles and usages of law, to any courts appointed, or persons holding office, under the authority of the United States." ... The Constitution vests the whole judicial power of the United States in one Supreme Court, and such inferior courts as Congress shall, from time to time, ordain and establish. ... In the distribution of this power, it is declared, that "the Supreme Court shall have original Jurisdiction, in all Cases affecting Ambassadors, other public Ministers and Consuls, and those in which a State shall be a Party. In all other cases, the Supreme Court shall have appellate jurisdiction."

... If it had been intended to leave it in the discretion of the legislature, to apportion the judicial power between the Supreme and inferior courts, according to the will of that body, it would certainly have been useless to have proceeded further than to have defined the judicial power, and the tribunals in which it should be vested. The subsequent part of the section is mere surplusage—is entirely without meaning if such is to be the construction. ... To enable this Court, then, to issue a mandamus, it must be shown to be an exercise of appellate jurisdiction, or to be necessary to enable them to exercise appellate jurisdiction. ... It is the essential criterion of appellate jurisdiction, that it revises and corrects the proceedings in a cause already instituted, and does not create that cause. Although, therefore, a mandamus may be directed to courts, yet to issue such a writ to an officer, for the delivery of a paper is, in effect, the same as to sustain an original action for that paper, and therefore, seems not to belong to appellate, but to original jurisdiction. Neither is it necessary in such a case as this, to enable the

Court to exercise its appellate jurisdiction. The authority, therefore, given to the Supreme Court, by the act establishing the judicial courts of the United States, to issue writs of mandamus to public officers, appears not to be warranted by the Constitution; and it becomes necessary to inquire whether a jurisdiction so conferred can be exercised.

The question whether an act repugnant to the Constitution can become the law of the land, is a question deeply interesting to the United States; but, happily, not of an intricacy proportioned to its interest. It seems only necessary to recognize certain principles, supposed to have been long and well established, to decide it.

That the people have an original right to establish, for their future government, such principles as, in their opinion, shall most conduce to their own happiness, is the basis on which the whole American fabric has been erected. The exercise of this original right is a very great exertion; nor can it nor ought it to be frequently repeated. The principles, therefore, so established, are deemed fundamental. And as the authority from which they proceed is supreme, and can seldom act, they are designed to be permanent.

This original and supreme will organizes the government, and assigns to different departments their respective powers. It may either stop here, or establish certain limits not to be transcended by those departments.

The government of the United States is of the latter description. The powers of the legislature are defined and limited; and that those limits may not be mistaken, or forgotten, the Constitution is written. To what purpose are powers limited, and to what purpose is that limitation committed to writing, if these limits may, at any time, be passed by those intended to be restrained? The distinction between a government with limited and unlimited powers is abolished, if those limits do not confine the persons on whom they are imposed, and if acts prohibited and acts allowed are of equal obligation. It is a proposition too plain to be contested, that the Constitution controls any legislative act repugnant to it; or, that the legislation may alter the Constitution by an ordinary act.

Between these alternatives there is no middle ground. The Constitution is either a superior paramount law, unchangeable by ordinary means, or it is on a level with ordinary legislative acts, and, like other acts, is alterable when the legislature shall please to alter it.

If the former part of the alternative be true, then a legislative act contrary to the Constitution is not law; if the latter part be true, then written constitutions are absurd attempts, on the part of the people, to limit a power in its own nature illimitable.

Certainly all those who have framed written constitutions contemplate them as forming the fundamental and paramount law of the nation, and, consequently, the theory of every such government must be, that an act of the legislature, repugnant to the constitution, is void.

This theory is essentially attached to a written constitution, and is consequently to be considered, by this Court, as one of the fundamental principles of our society. It is not, therefore, to be lost sight of in the further consideration of this subject.

If an act of the legislature, repugnant to the Constitution, is void, does it, notwithstanding its invalidity, bind the courts, and oblige them to give it effect? Or, in other words, though it be not law, does it constitute a rule as operative as if it was a law? This would be to overthrow in fact what was established in theory; and would see, at first view, an absurdity too gross to be insisted on. It shall, however, receive a more attentive consideration.

It is emphatically the province and duty of the judicial department to say what the law is. Those who apply the rule to particular cases, must of necessity expound and interpret that rule. If two laws conflict with each other, the courts must decide on the operation of each.

So if a law be in opposition to the Constitution; if both the law and the Constitution apply to a particular case, so that the court must either decide that case conformably to the law, disregarding the Constitution, or conformably to the Constitution, disregarding the law, the court must determine which of these conflicting rules governs the case. This is of the very essence of judicial duty.

If, then, the courts are to regard the Constitution, and the Constitution is superior to any ordinary act of the legislature, the Constitution, and not such ordinary act, must govern the case to which they both apply.

Those, then, who controvert the principle that the Constitution is to be considered, in court, as a paramount law, are reduced to the necessity of maintaining that court must close their eyes on the Constitution, and see only the law.

This doctrine would subvert the very foundation of all written constitutions. It would declare that an act which, according to the principle and theory of our government, is entirely void, is yet, in practice, completely obligatory. It would declare that if the legislature shall do what is expressly forbidden, such act, notwithstanding the express prohibition, is in reality effectual. It would be giving to the legislature a practical and real omnipotence, with the same breath which professes to restrict their powers within narrow limits. It is prescribing limits, and declaring that those limits may be passed at pleasure.

That it thus reduces to nothing what we have deemed the greatest improvement on political institutions, a written constitution, would of itself be sufficient, in America, where written constitutions have been viewed with so much reverence, for rejecting the construction. But the peculiar expressions of the Constitution of the United States furnish additional arguments in favor of its rejection.

The judicial power of the United States is extended to all cases arising under the Constitution.

Could it be the intention of those who gave this power, to say that in using it the Constitution should not be looked into? That a case arising under the Constitution should be decided without examining the instrument under which it arises?

This is too extravagant to be maintained.

In some cases, then, the Constitution must be looked into by the judges. And if they can open it at all, what part of it are they forbidden to read or obey?

There are many other parts of the Constitution which serve to illustrate this subject.

It is declared that "No Tax or Duty shall be laid on Articles exported from any State." Suppose a duty on the export of cotton, of tobacco, or of flour; and a suit instituted to recover it. Ought judgment to be rendered in such a case?

Ought the judges to close their eyes on the Constitution, and only see the law?

The Constitution declares that "No Bill of Attainder or ex post facto Law shall be passed."

If, however, such a bill should be passed, and a person should be prosecuted under it, must the court condemn to death those victims whom the Constitution endeavors to preserve?

"No Person," says the Constitution, "shall be convicted of Treason unless on the Testimony of two Witnesses to the same overt Act, or on Confession in open Court."

Here the language of the Constitution is addressed especially to the courts. It prescribes directly for them, a rule of evidence not to be departed from. If the legislature should change that rule, and declare one witness, or a confession out of court, sufficient for conviction, must the constitutional principle yield to the legislative act?

From these, and many other selections which might be made, it is apparent that the framers of the Constitution contemplated that instrument as a rule for the government of courts, as well as of the legislature.

Why otherwise does it direct the judges to take an oath to support it? This oath certainly applies in an especial manner to their conduct in their official character. How immoral to impose it on them, if they were to be used as the instruments, and the knowing instruments, for violating what they swear to support!

The oath of office, too, imposed by the legislative opinion on this subject. It is in these words: "I do solemnly swear that I will administer justice without respect to persons, and do equal right to the poor and to the rich; and that I will faithfully and impartially discharge all the duties incumbent on me as _____, according to the best of my abilities and understanding, agreeably to the Constitution and laws of the United States."

Why does a judge swear to discharge his duties agreeably to the

Constitution of the United States, if that Constitution forms no rule for his government? If it closed upon him, and cannot be inspected by him?

If such be the real state of things, this is worse than solemn mockery. To prescribe, or to take this oath, becomes equally a crime.

It is also not entirely unworthy of observation, that in declaring what shall be the supreme law of the land, the Constitution itself is first mentioned; and not the laws of the United States generally, but those only which shall be made in pursuance of the Constitution, have that rank.

Thus, the particular phraseology of the Constitution of the United States confirms and strengthens the principle, supposed to be essential to all written constitutions, that a law repugnant to the Constitution is void; and that courts, as well as other departments, are bound by that instrument.

57. Qualifications for Federal Judgeships

Robert A. Carp and Ronald Stidham

Candidates for most professional positions must meet a number of formal requirements. In the case of appointments to the Supreme Court or the lower federal courts, however, Robert A. Carp and Ronald Stidham point out that there are "no constitutional or statutory qualifications." It is not even stipulated that appointees must have a law degree. Yet despite the lack of formal qualifications, there are many significant informal requirements. Carp and Stidham, professors of political science at the University of Houston and Lamar University respectively, discuss these requirements in their book, *Judicial Process in America,* from which this excerpt is taken.

Students often torture one another with horror stories of the hurdles to be overcome in order to achieve success in a particular profession. Would-be medical students are awed by the high grade-point averages and aptitude scores required for admission to medical schools; potential university professors shrink at the many years of work necessary to obtain a Ph.D., only to face the publish-or-perish requirements for a tenured position. It would be logical, then, to assume that the formal requirements for becoming a federal judge—and surely a Supreme Court justice—must be formidable indeed. Not so. There are in fact no constitutional or statutory qualifications for serving on the Supreme Court or the lower federal courts. The Constitution merely indicates that "the judicial Power of the United States, shall be vested in one supreme Court" as well as in any lower federal courts that Congress may establish (Article III, Section 1) and that the president "by and with the Advice and Consent of the Senate, shall appoint . . . Judges of the supreme Court" (Article II, Section 2). Congress has applied the same selection procedure to the appeals and the trial courts. There are no exams to pass, no minimum age requirement, no stipulation that judges be native-born citizens or legal residents, nor is there even a requirement that judges have a law degree. Despite the absence of formal qualifications for a federal judgeship, there are nevertheless some rather well-defined informal requirements.

It is possible to identify at least four vital although informal factors that determine who sits on the federal bench in America: professional competence, political qualifications, self-selection, and the element of pure luck.

Professional Competence. Although candidates for U.S. judicial posts do not have to be attorneys—let alone prominent ones—it has been the custom to appoint lawyers who have distinguished themselves professionally—or at least not to appoint those obviously without merit. *Merit* may mean no more than an association with a prestigious law firm, publication of a few law review articles, or respect among fellow attorneys; a potential judge need not necessarily be an outstanding legal scholar. Nevertheless, one of the unwritten codes is that a judicial appointment is different from run-of-the-mill patronage. Thus while the political rules may allow a president to reward an old ally with a seat on the bench, even here tradition has created an expectation that the would-be judge have some reputation for professional competence, the more so as the judgeship in question goes from the trial to the appeals to the Supreme Court level.

A modern-day example of the unwritten rule that potential judges be more than just warm bodies with a law degree is found in President Nixon's nomination of G. Harrold Carswell to the Supreme Court in 1970. After investigations by the press and the Senate Judiciary Committee revealed that Carswell's record was unimpressive at best, his nomination began to stall on the floor of the Senate. To his aid came the well-meaning senator Roman Hruska of Nebraska, who stated in part: "Even if Carswell were mediocre, there are a lot of mediocre judges and people and lawyers. They are entitled to a little representation, aren't they, and a little chance? We can't have all Brandeises, and Frankfurters, and Cardozos and stuff like that there." With such support Carswell must have wondered why he needed any detractors. In any case the acknowledgment by a friendly senator that the Supreme Court nominee was "mediocrc" probably did more than anything else to prompt the Senate to reject Carswell. Although tradition may allow judgeships to be political payoffs and may not require eminence in the nominee, candidates for federal judicial posts are expected to meet a reasonable level of professional competence.

Political Qualifications. When at least 90 percent of all federal judicial nominees are of the same political party as the appointing president, it must strike even the most casual observer that there are certain political requirements for a seat on the bench. The fact that well over half of all federal judges were "politically active" before their appointments—in comparison with a 10 percent figure for the overall population—is further evidence of this phenomenon. What are the political criteria? In some cases a judgeship may be a reward for major service to the party in power or to the president or a senator. For example, when federal judge Pierson Hall (of the Central District of California) was asked how important politics was to his appointment, he gave this candid reply:

> I worked hard for Franklin Roosevelt in the days when California had no Democratic Party to speak of. In 1939 I began running for the Senate, and the party convinced me it would be best if there wasn't a contest for the Democratic nomination. So I withdrew and campaigned for Martin Downey. They gave me this judgeship as sort of a consolation prize—and one, I might add, that I have enjoyed.

While examples like this are not uncommon, it would be a mistake to think of federal judgeships merely as political plums handed out to the party faithful. As often as not, a seat on the bench goes to a reasonably active or visible member of the party in power but not necessarily to someone who has made party service the central focus of a lifetime.

Political activity that might lead to a judgeship includes service as chair of a state or local party organization, an unsuccessful race for public office, or financial backing for partisan causes.

The reason why most nominees for judicial office must have some record of political activity is twofold. First, to some degree judgeships are still considered part of the political patronage system; those who have served the party are more likely to be rewarded with a federal post than those who have not paid their dues. Second, even if a judgeship is not given as a direct political payoff, some political activity on the part of a would-be judge is often necessary, because otherwise the candidate would simply not be visible to the president or senator(s) or local party leaders who send forth the names of candidates. If the judicial power brokers have never heard of a particular lawyer because that attorney has no political profile, his or her name will not come to mind when a vacancy occurs on the bench.

Self-Selection. For those seeking the presidency or running for Congress, shyness doesn't pay. One needs to declare one's candidacy, meet a formal filing deadline, and spend considerable time and money to advertise one's qualifications. While Americans profess to admire modesty and humility in their leaders, *successful* candidates for elected office do well not to overindulge these virtues. With the judiciary, however, the informal rules of the game are a bit different. Many would consider it undignified and "lacking in judicial temperament" for someone to announce publicly a desire for a federal judgeship—much less to campaign openly for such an appointment.

We know, however, that some would-be jurists orchestrate discreet campaigns on their own behalf or at least pass the word that they are available for judicial service. While few will admit to seeking an appointment actively, credible anecdotes suggest that attorneys often position themselves in such a way that their names will come up when the powers-that-be have a vacant seat to fill. At judicial swearing-in ceremonies it is often said that "the judgeship sought the man (or woman) rather than vice versa," and surely this does happen. But sometimes the judgeship does its seeking with a little nudge from the would-be jurist.

The Element of Luck. If all that were involved in the picking of a Supreme Court justice or a lower-court judge were professional and political criteria, the appointment process would be much easier to explain and predict. If, for instance, one wanted to know who was going to be appointed to a vacancy on the Sixth Circuit bench, one would need only to identify the person in the Sixth Circuit to whom the party was most indebted and who had a reputation for legal competence. The problem is that there would be hundreds of capable attorneys in the Sixth Circuit to whom the prevailing party owed much. Why should one of them be selected and several hundred not? Until judicial scholarship becomes more of a science and less of an art, we cannot make accurate predictions about who will wear the black robe; there are just too many variables and too many participants in the selection process. Let us look at the example of President Truman's appointment of Carroll O. Switzer to fill a vacant judgeship in 1949.

The story began in 1948 when Truman was seeking a full term as president. The campaign had not gone well from the start. Even the party faithful could barely muster a faint cheer when Truman proclaimed to sparse crowds, "We're gonna win this election and we're gonna make those Republicans like it. Just you wait 'n' see." Almost everyone predicted Truman would lose, and lose badly. Then one morning his campaign train stopped in the little town of Dexter, Iowa. An unexpectedly large number of farmers had put aside their milking chores and the fall corn harvest to see the feisty little man from Missouri "give those Republicans hell." Truman picked up a real sense of enthusiasm among the cheering crowd, and for the first time in the campaign he smelled victory.

On the campaign platform with Truman that morning was Carroll Switzer, a bright young Des Moines attorney who was the (unsuccessful) Democratic candidate for Iowa governor that year. No evidence exists that Truman met Switzer before or after that one propitious day. But when a vacancy occurred on the U.S. bench a year later, Truman's mind jumped like a spring to the name of his lucky horseshoe, Carroll Switzer. A longtime administrative assistant to an Iowa senator related the story as follows:

> I am sure that this day at Dexter was the first time President Truman and his staff were sure he could win—later proved right. I am sure that he recalled that day favorably when an appointment . . . came up in the Iowa judgeship. . . . Every time the Iowa judgeship came up, Truman would hear of no one but Switzer. Truman would say "That guy Switzer backed me when everyone else was running away, and, by God, I'm going to see that he gets a judgeship."

That morning in Dexter was Switzer's lucky day. While he had the professional and political credentials for a judicial post, no one could have foreseen that he would happen to appear with Truman the day the national winds of political fortune began to blow in the president's favor. Had it been any other day, Switzer might never have been more than just a bright attorney from Des Moines.

This account illustrates the point that there is a good measure of happenstance involved in virtually all judicial appointments. Being a member of the right party at the right time or being visible to the power brokers at a lucky moment often has as much to do with becoming a judge as the length and sparkle of one's professional résumé.

58. Judging Judges:
The Senate's Role in Judicial Appointments

Sen. Paul Simon

The author of seven books and formerly a teacher, Illinois state legislator, and lieutenant governor, Paul Simon was elected to the Senate in 1984 and reelected in 1990 and is a member of the Judiciary Committee—one of the few members not a lawyer. Because Democrats on Judiciary were concerned that many judicial nominees were only minimally qualified and too ideological, Senator Simon was assigned the responsibility by the Democrats for developing principles of judicial selection to aid members in evaluating the qualifications of nominees for the federal bench. In an address to the Senate that received praise from both liberals and conservatives (published in the *Congressional Record* in 1986), Senator Simon outlined standards for assessing judicial nominations. This selection is noteworthy, too, as an example of the thoughtful deliberations that can take place in the Senate and in Congress as a whole.

The Senate's role in the appointment of Federal judges is receiving more attention. Since the Senate has been involved in these appointments from the beginning of the Republic, this is obviously not a new question, but it presses today with special urgency. We are witnessing an enormous turnover on the Federal bench, frankly, too much of a turnover. A majority of the Federal judiciary will have changed membership during President Reagan's service in office—and on our most important court, the U.S. Supreme Court, a substantial turnover in membership is possible. Since Federal judges are lifetime appointments, what is at stake in all these changes is the character of our judicial branch for a generation, and the real-world meaning of our Constitution and Federal law.

I have concerns about the judicial nominations that have been made since I joined the Senate: I am concerned about their quality and I am concerned about their ideological bent, and we in the Senate must think harder about how we can try to assure that judicial appointments are the best possible. I am specially concerned that we lay the groundwork now for considering future nominees to the Supreme Court—that we think about our standards and processes before people are nominated and before the debate turns to specific personalities. I hope that these remarks will begin to lay that groundwork.

I start with the general view that the Senate should play an active role in the appointment of Federal judges. In contrast to Presidential nominations to executive departments, there should be no automatic presumption that the President gets the judges he wants.

The Constitution provides that the President shall "nominate" people for the Federal courts, but it also provides that the Senate must give its "advice and consent" to any appointment. I have recently reread the relevant records surrounding the adoption of this provision at the Constitutional Convention, and they are instructive. Far from supporting any idea that the President essentially controls judicial appointments, they clearly establish that the framers expected the Senate to be an active partner in the appointment process. The Convention records establish that the current provision was a compromise between those who wanted judicial appointments solely in the hands of the Senate—the prevailing position, as I said, until the end of the Convention—and those who thought the President should have a greater role. By tradition the Senate has played a prominent role in the district court nominations when the Senator or Senators are of the same political party as the President. But nominees for the circuit court of appeals have by recent tradition had significantly less Senate input.

There is a reason judicial nominees should receive the special scrutiny of the Senate. In contrast to the President's nominations to positions within his own executive branch, appointments to the judiciary are to a branch of government that is supposed to be independent of the President and for a duration exceeding his own term of office. For the President to control such appointments unilaterally would be inappropriate, especially in a political system where checks and balances are so important. The Senate is an institution in some ways not as broadly representative as it should be; we have only two women; there are no blacks, no Hispanics.

Taken as a whole, the Federal courts are another institution that is not as broadly representative as it should be. In my first year on the Judiciary committee, we reviewed 92 nominees; 70 for district courts and 22 for the appellate level. Of the 70 district nominees, 5 were women, 2 were black, 3 were Hispanic and none were Asian. Among the 22 circuit nominees, 3 were women. Not a single circuit judge nominee was either black, Hispanic, or Asian.

But the Senate is broadly representative of the country's political diversity. It does not defer to the President when it thinks his proposed budget or legislation will be bad for the country, and the same should be true with respect to his judicial nominees. While the law is more likely to have national impact than most judicial nominees, the law usually can be changed with greater ease than you can change judges.

The impact of Federal judges is so enduring that we cannot view approval of these appointees as a clerical or routine duty of the Senate.

Given that basic perspective, what criteria should the Senate use in evaluating judicial nominees as part of its advise and consent rule? A central feature of the Senate's role must be to evaluate the nominee's experience—a factor which bears on the nominee's practical wisdom about people and the world as well as more narrow professional skills. Second, we must be concerned about the nominee's integrity and moral character. Third, we must be concerned about the nominee's temperament: His or her open mindedness, judgment, evenhanded consistency, and sense of fair play.

Few if any of my Senate colleagues would disagree in the abstract with the notion that the Senate should evaluate quality factors. But we need to be more demanding than we have been in insisting that nominees be of high quality. The American Bar Association's Standing Committee on the Federal Judiciary uses four categories to rate nominees: exceptionally well qualified, well qualified, qualified, and not qualified. The next-to-the-bottom rating, qualified, in fact applies to nominees with only minimal acceptable qualifications. Since I have been on the Senate Judiciary Committee, a full 50 percent of U.S. Court of Appeals nominees—controlled entirely by the administration—have received only this qualified rating. About three-fourths of these were found not qualified by a minority of the ABA committee. During this same period, 48.6 percent of the District Court nominees—for which Senators often play a key role—also received only a qualified rating, of whom approximately 20 percent were found not qualified by a minority of the ABA committee.

These numbers are disturbing. For years, my image of Federal judges was of those who are really stellar members of the bar. That image, unfortunately, is changing, for me and many others. Those appointed to our Federal bench for life should be the best the legal profession has to offer. Too many clearly are not. Federal judges resolve matters that are of extraordinary importance not only to individual litigants but to the country as a whole. Their work is complex, and, as we are so often reminded, court dockets are extremely heavy. Competence and efficiency, along with wisdom, are essential job requirements.

I know the contending political forces that can surround judicial nominations, but the plain fact is that the job of a Federal judge is so important today that our country cannot afford nominees of borderline qualifications; we need the best. When we lower standards, we lower the prestige of the bench, and when that is lowered, the desirability to serve for the really fine minds and experienced barristers wanes. It is a downward spiral we are on and we must inaugurate an upward spiral.

Having said that, it is still true that Federal judgeships remain among the most honored and sought-after positions in American life. We need not settle for borderline qualifications. We can have the best, if only we have the will to insist upon it. This we have not done.

A more difficult question is whether Senators should limit themselves to these matters of professional quality or should also consider nominees' substantive legal views, particularly their views about the meaning of the Constitution and the role of Federal courts. This may be the most significant issue about the confirmation process facing a Senator today—and it has broad implications for the Judiciary and for the country. President Reagan, [for example,] candidly stated his intention to try to shape the substantive direction of our constitutional law by nominating judges who share his constitutional views, and who seem likely to decide cases in accordance with them. Like many others, I have become troubled by the ideological bent of [Reagan's] nominees; so it becomes important to know in what situations, if any, a Senator should withhold "consent" to a judicial nomination because of disagreement with the nominee's legal views.

My thoughts on this difficult issue, I acknowledge, are still evolving, and I am not here today to announce definitive answers. What I want to do instead is offer some comments and raise some questions, with the goal of inviting the broader debate on this subject that is needed.

I see three separate aspects to this issue that should be kept somewhat distinct.

1. Are a nominee's substantive legal views altogether irrelevant to the Senate's confirmation decision?

2. If not, what standard should a Senator use in evaluating a nominee's views?

3. In light of the standard, how should a Senator go about finding out what a nominee's views are—in particular, what can a Senator properly ask a nominee?

We often see reference to the supposedly conventional wisdom that a nominee's legal views should be altogether irrelevant to the Senate's confirmation decision. In actuality, though, it is hard to believe that many people really believe this as an absolute, since most Senators would probably vote against a nominee who believes that racial apartheid would be constitutional or who held similarly outlandish views. In fact, the so-called conventional wisdom has not actually been the convention. Time and again over the past two centuries, Senators have voted against judicial nominees whose views they deemed unacceptable. Examples of this span as far back as the Senate's rejection of John Rutledge's nomination by George Washington as Chief Justice in 1795, and include such recent examples as the Senate's rejection of G. Harrold Carswell's nomination to the Supreme Court in 1969, a rejection based on "quality" grounds and on the fact that his segregationist views on civil rights matters were deemed unacceptable.

But there are two fundamental reasons that nominees' legal views should not be altogether off-limits to the Senate. One is that just as we know that a nominee's competence and integrity will affect his views as a judge, we know that the nominee's individual views about legal matters will in some measure affect decisions the nominee makes as a judge. The reason is that judges inevitably have leeway. They must fill in gaps in the law and must resolve ambiguities about what the law is, and in doing so, a judge inevitably draws upon his or her starting point views and outlook. This is true of all judges and it is especially true of Supreme Court justices, whose leeway in giving meaning to the majestic general commands of the Constitution is particularly great, and who must resolve conflicts among lower courts on a daily basis. A Senator who considers only whether a judicial nominee will "follow the law" is ignoring the fact that the law to be followed is often not clear, and that judicial decisions are often affected by a judge's individual legal views. To contend that a Senator may not properly consider those views amounts to a contention that things highly relevant to the job—things that make a good or bad judge—may not be considered. Here we must remind ourselves that the constitutional mandate for the Senate is to "advise and consent," not merely to consent. How should we fulfill that advising role in the case of Federal judicial nominees?

A second reason a nominee's views may be relevant to the current Senate is that they were relevant to the President's own decision to nominate. As an active partner in the judicial appointment process, as the authority that must "advise and consent" to nominations in our system of checks and balances, should not the Senate evaluate any factor the President does? And if the President is trying to shape future judicial decisions by self-consciously nominating people with particular legal views, should the Senate—at least to some extent consider whether those views are appropriate ones and good for the country?

If a nominee's legal views should not be altogether irrelevant to the Senate, what standard should a Senator use in evaluating a nominee's views? This, for me, is the harder question. The choice, as I see it, is between two basic possibilities.

One is for a Senator only to determine whether the nominee's views are within the outer boundaries of reasonableness. Under this standard, a Senator would disapprove only those nominees holding unreasonably extreme views—for example, nominees who think Brown versus Board of Education was wrongly decided. Different Senators, of course, would place the boundary of reasonableness at different places. But, under this standard, the Senator would be willing to approve any nominee holding views within some broadly defined "reasonable" range, even if the Senator thought those views to be wrong and bad for the country. And this suggests a problem with this standard: It allows this President or any President, to systematically appoint people whose views fall at one end within the broadly tolerable range, even though that unilateral Presidential action could have serious consequences for the country. Why should the Senate acquiesce in this deliberate skewing of our judges and our fundamental law?

An alternative standard is more comprehensive and demanding: Are the nominee's views about the meaning of the Constitution and the role of federal courts views which, at least in their broad outlines, the Senator believes are correct ones? What are the nominee's views on key elements: Majority and minority rights, Presidential and congressional authority, Federal power and State and local authority and the meaning of the first amendment? This is a difficult area.

These standards, of course, should not mean that a Senator would vote against every nominee with whom the Senator disagrees. If a President tries to appoint too many judges whose ideological slant a Senator opposes, political compromise on both sides would be necessary to avoid deadlock. Moreover, a Senator might choose to apply this standard only in limited situations—for example, where the nominee's other qualifications are borderline. The danger in applying a more ideological standard is that the Senate should not be the abuser of ideological rigidities any more than the President should be. Some of those who criticize the rigidities of right-wing ideology would impose rigidities of the left. Both rigidities should be rejected.

Whatever standard is used, each Senator has to decide for himself or herself which particular matters are most relevant in deciding whether the nominee's views are acceptable. The question of what is relevant to each Senator is related to the final issue: How should a Senator go about learning what the nominee's relevant views really are?

The easiest sources are those in the public record: The nominee's prior judicial opinions, articles, speeches and statements. The more difficult issue is the question a Senator may properly ask nominees about their views.

Asking a nominee's general views about the Constitution and constitutional interpretation is clearly appropriate. Judicial nominees should all demonstrate their understanding that our constitutional system not only gives scope to majority rule but also guarantees minority and individual rights; that Federal courts have traditionally played a critical role in protecting those rights. Middle range questions—for example, asking the nominee "how do you assess the legacy of the Warren court?"—can also uncover relevant information without being objectionable. And the same is true of general questions concerning particular provisions of the Constitution—for example, asking the nominee "what do you think the establishment clause means?"

The problem with these relatively general questions is that they can easily generate responses that are unhelpfully fuzzy or cliched. To get answers that provide more useful information, a Senator may be inclined to ask more specific questions. But specific questions can pose more sensitive problems. For example, asking how a nominee would decide some pending or future issue improperly puts the nominee in a compromised position, even though it may well seek relevant information. These future-oriented questions ask the nominee to prejudge a matter that might come before him or her as a judge and to give an "advisory opinion" abstracted from concrete facts. These questions also create the unseemly appearance that a binding commitment about certain future cases is a quid pro quo for Senate confirmation. Such questions should be avoided.

Specific questions about prior cases or about specific issues already decided by the courts do not necessarily pose these problems, but they suggest difficulties of their own. For example, to use a nominee's views on any other single issue as a "litmus test" ordinarily would be unfair and inappropriate, and is an unreliable way to predict the nominee's overall future performance. Specifics should be probed to provide illustrations of the nominee's views about the enduring great themes of American law—federalism, free speech, equal protection, separation of powers—but not as a checklist for special interest groups. It does not seem inappropriate to question a nominee as to his or her understanding and commitment to the first amendment. Or what does the phrase "cruel and unusual punishment" mean to the nominee. Or what is there in the nominee's background to suggest that there is some sensitivity to minorities so that the equal protection clause will have real meaning to that person.

There is much to be said for a rather comprehensive Senate consideration of nominee's views when the President is considering them, particularly the views of nominees to the Supreme Court and the U.S. Circuit Court of Appeals. But we should have a fuller public debate, addressing the full range of possible objections and concerns, including those that I can mention here only briefly. I hope these remarks will help inaugurate this fuller public discussion.

Some have already objected to questioning nominees about issues, because, they say, this path would be a new one for the Senate, and they are uneasy for that reason. Even if that objection were factually true, it needs to be evaluated in light of the way the President is systemically making ideological nominations, more so than any President since Franklin D. Roosevelt.

Another concern is that a more active Senate role will produce confrontation and deadlock. But this body, which is accustomed to working out practical compromises, can work out compromises with the President in such a way that the quality of the Federal judiciary will not be reduced.

Another possible objection, this one from members of my own party, is that Democrats will be hurt by an active Senate role when we recapture the White House. It is true a Senate that restrains a Republican President from making appointments that are too ideological or lacking in quality will also restrain a Democratic President from doing that. But we should welcome that restraint. It will improve the quality of the judiciary and keep the law from being some huge pendulum, swinging whichever way the current political winds blow. There should be a stability and certitude in the law, and ideological swings erode that. In the Federalist Papers, Alexander Hamilton describes the Senate's role as being "an efficacious source of stability." A President will be thwarted only when he holds significantly more extreme views than the Senate, and seeks to use judicial appointments to impose those views.

Finally, we need to consider whether an active Senate role will make the appointments process more political and ideological, thereby undercutting the courts' authority and stature. The Senate's willingness to play a more active role may, in fact, be the best strategy for ultimately reducing the role of ideology in the process. Again, that is particularly needed for nominees to the circuit court and the Supreme Court. Senate passivity itself can allow the law to become that pendulum swinging back and forth, simply following ideological changes at the White House. The Senate's willingness to counter the President's nominations that are too ideological could well induce the President to propose fewer such nominees. The Senate's failure to play that role leaves today's appointments process ideological, but solely on the President's terms. I have spoken mostly of the Senate's role in the appointment process, but the Senate is only the final step. Excellence in judicial appointments requires that every institution involved in the process play its role as well as possible. So before closing, I want to comment on two other institutions in particular.

The first is the American Bar Association. The standing committee on the Federal judiciary of the American Bar Association has been consulted with respect to most Federal judicial appointments since 1952. All who have worked with the committee are appreciative of the service it performs in evaluating the qualifications of potential appointees, frequently on relatively short notice. I recognize the concerns that some have expressed about a private entity playing a consulting role in the appointments process, but long experience has shown the ABA committee to be a valuable and constructive force. But, the ABA's screening should be strengthened and the standards raised. The ABA committee should take pains to consult a broad range of groups, reflecting the full diversity of outlook within the legal profession, but that will be a less than completely useful gesture if something else does not happen.

Politicians are not known for their courage, and unfortunately neither are lawyers. When asked their opinions of Joe Smith, a nominee for a district judgeship, I am told the prevailing practice is to be generous, not to a fault, but to all faults. The lawyer thinks, "Joe may sit on one of my cases. I'll play it safe." What the lawyer should be thinking is, "Joe may sit on one of my cases. I ought to make sure that the presiding judge in that case is a really superior legal mind with a great sense of balance and perspective." It has often been said but it bears repeating: Lawyers owe more to the law than simply using it as a tool to make a living. The ABA committee is approving too many judges it should not be approving. The bar needs more backbone and higher standards.

Screening by the bar association should apply to the question of quality, ordinarily not to the views of the nominee. Leave that judgment to an administration and the Senate. Modifications in the ABA committee's rating system would be helpful. For a nominee to carry the ABA committee with two more votes as "qualified" than "not qualified," and then come with a favorable rating to the Judiciary Committee is for the bar association to participate in creating more and more mediocre judges. That is neither desirable nor necessary. But it is happening. A gradual lowering of the quality of the Federal judiciary is in no one's interest.

The ABA also should give us a specific recommendation that a judge should be approved or not approved. It could be argued that when the ABA tells us that a person received a "qualified" rating but that there were votes for "not qualified," that is what we are being told. Those of us who are Senators need more than oblique hints about what we should do. The ABA should tell us bluntly. That removes partisan taint from actions of the committee. And I should add that other organizations, such as the American Civil Liberties Union and Common Cause that express great interest and concern in the quality of the judiciary might soil their hands a little by taking the most simple, fundamental step of telling Members of the Senate whether they believe a nominee should be approved or not approved. But the ABA should lead the way on this.

The other institution I am concerned about is the Department of Justice, which plays such a major role in recommending nominations to the President. There is an old saying at the Department of Justice that the Department wins a case whenever justice is done. That wonderful saying reminds us that the cause of justice requires a commitment to values that transcend mere partisan advantage. I wish that a similar attitude always governed the Department's approach to judicial nominations. When Edward Levi was Attorney General under President Gerald Ford, we saw an approach worth emulating: A Department of Justice that recommended judicial nominees based primarily on professional excellence rather than ideological purity or partisan advantage. That is the best route for the Justice Department and President to follow. And if they follow this "advice," at least one Senator would "consent" to their nominations enthusiastically.

59. Point-Counterpoint:
The Souter Nomination to the Supreme Court

Sen. Orrin Hatch
Sen. Edward Kennedy

When Supreme Court Justice William J. Brennan, Jr., retired from the bench, President George Bush on July 23, 1990, named as his replacement a little-known New Hampshire federal appeals court judge, David H. Souter. "I have selected a person who will interpret the Constitution and, in my view, not legislate from the federal bench," said President Bush. Immediately, lawmakers and political activists wanted to know about Souter's background and record as well as his judicial philosophy and position on controversial issues such as a woman's right to abortion.

These and other questions were considered during Souter's confirmation hearings before the Senate Judiciary Committee. Questioning Souter for nearly twenty hours during nationally televised hearings held in September 1990, Judiciary Committee members tried to learn as much as possible about the nominee. By most accounts, his demonstrated reasonableness, competence, and good humor during several days of testimony led to the committee's favorable recommendation and then to the Senate's overwhelming vote of approval for Souter's nomination. However, in committee and on the Senate floor, Senators Orrin Hatch, R-Utah, and Edward Kennedy, D-Mass., differed significantly in their assessment of the Souter nomination. Their views are extracted here from Senate Executive Report 101-32, 101st Congress, 1990.

Sen. Orrin Hatch:
Support the Souter Nomination

Judge Souter's excellent educational and legal background and his demonstrated knowledge of the law at the hearing all attest to his competence and ability. I believe he will join the Supreme Court with an independent mind, willing to consider different points of view on the cases which will come before him.

I also believe that he will seek to interpret and apply the law according to its original meaning. I do not believe that he will impose his own policy preferences on the American people in the guise of judging. The role of the judicial branch is to enforce the provisions of the Constitution and the laws we enact in Congress as their meaning was originally intended by their framers. That meaning must then be applied to the facts and circumstances before the judge—facts and circumstances perhaps never contemplated by the framers of the legal provision being applied. But the meaning—the underlying principle of the provision—does not change.

In my view, Judge Souter's judicial philosophy is best expressed in his dissenting opinion in the 1986 New Hampshire Supreme Court case of In re Estate of Dionne and his 1990 remarks to a Massachusetts law journal. In the Dionne case, he wrote "that 'the language of the [state] constitution is to be understood in the sense in which it was used at the time of its adoption . . .' The Court's interpretive task is therefore to determine the meaning of the [Constitutional provision] as it was understood when the framers proposed it and the people ratified it as part of the original constitutional text that took effect in June of 1784." In the May 28, 1990, Massachusetts Lawyers Weekly, Judge Souter was quoted as saying: "On constitutional matters, I am of the interpretist school. We're not looking for the original application, we're looking for meaning here. That's a very different thing."

Judge Souter never departed from this view in his testimony.

I note that I don't know whether I will always agree with Judge Souter's conclusion about the original meaning of a particular statute or constitutional provision or with his application of the provision in a given case.

I have read that some people are drawing some rather firm conclusions as to how Judge Souter might have ruled or will rule in the future on some kinds of cases—whether religious liberty cases or cases involving Congressionally mandated racial preferences. The record is clear, however, that Judge Souter did not commit as to how he would rule in those areas or almost any other area. And where he may have been more forthcoming, he is entitled to change his mind after reading the briefs and hearing oral arguments, as he has done in his judicial career thus far.

I mention this to record my view that if, in a case, Judge Souter's opinion seems to be at variance with how one of us anticipated he would rule, no one should claim he misled us. Moreover, I would hope no one would then claim we ought to probe the next nominee even further than the committee probed Judge Souter. While I have often said a senator has the right to ask a nominee any questions he wishes, a nominee is not obligated to answer all questions. I believe in some circumstances he was pressed too far and said more than a nominee should have to say at a confirmation hearing. While some may claim that so long as the nominee is not asked how he will rule in a specific case, he should answer all questions. But asking a nominee whether he endorses a very specific legal or constitutional principle, where respectable arguments can be made both for and against that principle, can in many instances be tantamount to asking how he would rule in particular cases. It clearly asks a nominee, in effect, to prejudge many specific issues. Some questions were even case-specific. As one random example, the nominee was asked whether he believed *Roe* v. *Wade** was settled law. He declined to answer. There is no practical difference between asking that question and asking how he will rule in a specific case, when the issue addressed in *Roe* so clearly remains an issue which can come before the Supreme Court. Judges should feel free to rule as they see fit on the bench and not as others anticipated they would rule.

The trend begun in this committee in the mid-1950s of probing the nominee's views on controversial issues seems to have accelerated in recent years. If the trend continues, that is something I will have to bear in mind if I am here when a member of the other party sends us a Supreme Court nominee.

Finally, I want to address this issue of litmus tests that some groups are seeking to have the Senate impose on nominees, for example, on the issue of abortion.

Some urge us to reject Judge Souter because he did not commit himself to uphold *Roe* v. *Wade*. But what would happen if different senators impose litmus tests on a variety of issues—could any nominee ever be confirmed?

Some people would make a very strong case that religious liberty issues, discrimination issues, federalism issues and other issues are so crucial that we must demand to know in advance how a nominee will rule.

Ben Wattenberg, a Democrat who is a senior fellow at the American Enterprise Institute, says that quotas should be the litmus test. He criticized a 5-4 decision from June permitting racial set-asides in the FCC's award of television and radio licenses. Suppose 20 senators apply that litmus test, and 15 other senators apply a church/state litmus test seeking to reverse the school prayer decisions, and 15 other Senators impose a litmus test on reversing the *Miranda* decision** and *Mapp* v. *Ohio* [1961] imposing the exclusionary rule [illegally obtained evidence cannot be used in trials] on the states.

How can any nominee be confirmed if we viewed our role this way?

---

* A 1973 Supreme Court decision upholding a woman's right to have an abortion.

** In *Miranda* v. *Arizona* (1966), the Supreme Court established certain rights available to an accused person during police interrogation, such as apprising him or her of the constitutional privilege against self-incrimination and the right to a lawyer.

A President may one day send us a nominee supported by proabortion groups. How would they feel if other senators and I took up Ben Wattenberg's cue on imposing a litmus test on reverse discrimination, another group imposed a litmus test on overturning *Miranda* and the exclusionary rule, and a third group of prolife senators, totalling 51 senators, imposed a litmus test on reversing *Roe* v. *Wade*?

Sen. Edward Kennedy:
Oppose the Souter Nomination

I oppose the confirmation of Judge David H. Souter to the Supreme Court.

The Constitution itself is silent on the standard the Senate should apply in considering a Supreme Court nomination. The role of the Senate in the confirmation of judicial nominees selected by the President was a last-minute compromise reached by the Framers at the Constitutional Convention in 1787. Those who drafted the Constitution had originally proposed that the Senate alone should appoint federal judges. The final compromise, which assigns shared responsibility to the President and the Senate, was adopted as one of the key checks and balances to assure that neither the President nor the Senate would have excessive influence over the Supreme Court and other federal courts.

The genius of the Constitution and Bill of Rights is apparent in the establishment of an independent federal judiciary, sworn to protect the fundamental rights and liberties of individuals against the excesses of government and majority rule. The Supreme Court has the last word on the meaning of the Constitution, and its decisions have a profound impact on all of our lives.

In the past half century, the Supreme Court has played a central role in the effort to make America a better and fairer land. The Court outlawed school segregation in the 1950s, removed barriers to the right to vote in the 1960s, and established a far-reaching right to privacy, including the right to abortion in the 1970s. In other ways as well, the Supreme Court strengthened the basic rights of minorities and took steps to end the second-class status of women in our society. But in the decade of the 1980s, as a result of a strategy of ideological appointments in the Reagan years, the Court has seemed to pause in carrying out this important role, and in many cases has actually turned back the clock. On many of these issues, the current Court seems to be divided 4-4, so that the Senate's decision on this nomination is likely to tip the balance in one direction or the other.

In considering a Supreme Court nomination, the Senate must make two inquiries. The first is the threshold issue: Does the nominee have the intelligence, integrity, and temperament to meet the responsibilities of a Supreme Court Justice?

But that is only the beginning, not the end of the inquiry. The Senate also must determine whether the nominee possesses a clear commitment to the fundamental values at the core of our constitutional democracy.

In this second inquiry, the burden of proof rests with the nominee. Our constitutional freedoms are the historic legacy of every American. They are too important, and the past sacrifices made to protect those freedoms have been too great, to be entrusted to judges who lack this clear commitment. If a Senator is left with substantial doubts about a nominee's dedication to these core values, our own constitutional responsibility requires us to oppose the nomination.

This is not to suggest any single-issue litmus test. Nominees should be judged on their overall approach to the Constitution. I have frequently supported nominees whose views on particular constitutional issues are very different from my own. But the Senate should not confirm a Supreme Court nomination unless we are persuaded that the nominee is committed to upholding the essential values at the heart of our constitutional tradition.

Recent developments at the Supreme Court have increased the importance of this inquiry by the Senate. Over the past few years, the Court has retreated from its historic role in protecting civil rights and civil liberties. In case after case, the Court has also adopted narrow and restrictive interpretations of important civil rights laws enacted by Congress. The Senate is entitled to ensure that nominees to the nation's highest court share Congress's view that these laws must be interpreted generously, to eliminate discrimination in all its forms.

Judge Souter has a distinguished intellectual background. He has spent the great majority of his legal career in public service. But aspects of his record on the bench and while serving in the New Hampshire Attorney General's Office have raised troubling questions about the depth of his commitment to the indispensable role of the Supreme Court in protecting individual rights and liberties under the Constitution.

Far from dispelling these concerns, Judge Souter's testimony before this committee reinforced them. In particular, my concerns center on the fundamental constitutional issues of civil rights, the right to privacy, and the power of Congress and the courts to protect these basic rights.

If Judge Souter joins the current closely divided Supreme Court, he may well solidify a 5-4 anti-civil rights, anti-privacy majority inclined to turn back the clock on the historic progress of recent decades. If so, literally millions of Americans will be denied their rights as Americans to equal opportunity and equal justice under law.

I hope I am wrong. But I fear I am right. To a large extent, in spite of the hearings we have held, the Senate is still in the dark about this nomination, and all of us are voting in the dark. The lesson of the past decade of the Senate's experience in confirming justices to the Supreme Court is that we must vote our fears, not our hopes.

The fate of millions of men and women directly affected by the Supreme Court's decisions is too important to leave to chance. If nominees do not meet the test of demonstrating a good-faith, in-depth, abiding commitment to the basic constitutional values of the kind so obviously at stake at this turning point in our history, they can—and should—be rejected by the Senate. To apply a lesser standard is to fail our own constitutional responsibility in the confirmation process. In my view, Judge Souter does not meet that test. In good conscience, I cannot support this nomination.

60. The Work of the Supreme Court: A Nuts and Bolts Description

Justice Byron R. White

In this article, originally delivered as a lecture and subsequently published in the *New York State Bar Journal* in 1982, Justice Byron R. White pulls back the "curtain of secrecy" of the least visible branch of our tripartite system to discuss aspects of judicial decision making. A former all-American football player and Rhodes Scholar, Justice White has been a member of the Supreme Court since his appointment by President John F. Kennedy in 1962.

This lecture will be devoted to giving you a bird's-eye view of the work of the Supreme Court, the nuts-and-bolts description of what we do and how we do it.

I shall first generally describe the substance of the work we do; second, the procedures involved; and, third, some aspects of our work and of the Federal law that bear particularly on the state court systems.

1. The Substance of the Court's Work

It should be emphasized at the outset that the Supreme Court is an appellate court dealing exclusively in the Federal law.

There is, it is true, a narrow, but important, slice of our docket that arises under the head of our original jurisdiction.

These cases start and stop in our court and consist principally of cases between states that have but one forum in which to litigate with each other, namely, the Supreme Court of the United States.

These cases focus on boundary disputes, the division of interstate streams, interstate pollution and matters such as that. Important as they are, however, they may make up only a tiny fraction of our work.

Under the Constitution and the relevant statutes, our jurisdiction to review judgments of state courts extends only to cases involving Federal questions, that is, questions arising under a federal statute or the Federal Constitution. Unless such a question is involved in a state case, we have no jurisdiction to review it at all. It is also quite plain that most of the litigation in this country goes on in the state courts, and that only a very small portion of all state cases involve any Federal question.

Such questions do appear, however, with some regularity, especially in state criminal cases, the result being that we have some 1,500 petitions per term to review state cases.

Some of these petitions are granted for plenary consideration, enough to make up about one-third of the cases that are argued orally and given plenary consideration.

We have authority to review any kind of a case from a Federal court, including a diversity case that involves only state law issues. But it is rare that we accept review of a case that turns only on state or local law. The reason is that the district courts and the courts of appeal very likely know much more about state law than we do, or at least we give them credit for it.

In the event, for all intents and purposes, our work is confined to the area of the Federal law.

It is also the case that we deal primarily with legal questions, rather than issues of fact. We are not fact-finders. The historical facts have been settled by the time the case gets to us. Our questions are pure questions of law—what does a statute or the Constitution mean—or mixed questions of fact and law—do the facts that have been found add up to violation of a statute, or is there substantial evidence to support a particular legal conclusion?

About half of the cases on our argument docket present only Federal statutory issues and do not directly involve the Constitution in any way. In these cases, our mission is to discover and to enforce the will of Congress, even if to the judicial mind the result may appear quite unwise.

We take extreme pains to discover what Congress really intended or meant by the words that it used. We scour the legislative history, committee reports and debates, even prior efforts to enact similar legislation. This is often a confusing and fruitless fret.

The remaining half of our docket involves the construction and application of the Constitution of the United States.

These cases arise, as you well know, because of the decision of the founders to describe the government of the United States in a written instrument; to form a national government with limited powers, leaving all other powers with the sovereign states; to divide powers at the national level; to superimpose a series of proscriptions, prescriptions and admonitions on national and state government; and, finally, to leave the judiciary, both state and federal, the task of enforcing this pattern of government.

Although cases arising from the division of powers among the three branches at the national level are not infrequent, down through the years the most recurring issues have involved the boundaries between state and national power and the ground rules for government and governors contained in the Bill of Rights and the Civil War Amendments.

This is neither the time nor the place to go into the substance of any of the past or present interpretations of the Constitution contained in the judgments of the Supreme Court. I'm sure you've had enough of that in the last few weeks, but two observations are appropriate for present purposes.

First, as everyone knows, the language of the Constitution is indeed majestic, and in many respects its meaning has never been immediately obvious, even to the most able and well-trained men. The result is that judges, state and federal, often differ among themselves, or even with themselves from time to time, as to the meaning of this august document.

Given the difficulty of amending the Constitution and given the organization of the judiciary and the role of stare decisis in this country, what all this means is that the framers did indeed assign a novel, difficult and extremely important role to the judiciary when they anticipated that the constitutional design should be enforceable in the courts.

It is also a role that to some seems difficult to justify in a country whose government is in the hands of the elected representatives of the people.

But that has been, and it is, our way; and it is very likely that it has been better for us than it has been bad. Otherwise, it long since would have been abolished or substantially modified.

Secondly, let me remind you that all judges and other officials, both state and federal, are bound by the Constitution of the United States, which, by its terms, is the supreme law of the land.

State judges, as well as federal, must decide federal constitutional issues in the first instance when they are properly before them. Hence, they are important parts of the entire process of judicial review. What is more, every state has its own constitution that its own judiciary is expected to enforce.

Thus, the making and unmaking and remaking of constitutional law in this country is a familiar process to all judges all across the country, whether trial or appellate, and whether state or federal.

Federal constitutional issues press much harder on state judges than they once did. The main body of the Constitution no doubt contained important restrictions on state governments, but *Barron v. Baltimore* made it clear that the Bill of Rights bound only federal officials and not state authorities.

Then came the Civil War Amendments, the Thirteenth, Fourteenth and Fifteenth, which were aimed directly at states and which in the long run have been the principal basis for a vastly expanded body of constitutional law, much of it originating in state courts that were called upon to adjudicate the federal constitutional challenges to state authority.

Among other things, around the turn of the Century and continuing from time to time to this day, various provisions of the Bill of Rights, or the principles thereof, have been held applicable to the states by virtue of the due process clause of the Fourteenth Amendment.

The First, Fourth, Fifth, Sixth and Eighth Amendments must now be observed by state officials. Taken together, these were almost revolutionary developments; and they are the source of many issues that recurringly must be adjudicated in the state courts, subject to review in the Supreme Court.

II. The Procedures Involved

Let me now touch on important aspects of our organization and procedure. There are nine of us, and we always sit as a nine-man court unless someone is disqualified. We do not break up into panels; nor do we purport to have experts in various fields to whom opinions in those areas are repeatedly assigned. All of us, like most judges in the appellate courts in this country, are generalists, hearing and writing opinions in the various kinds of cases that come before us.

Until 1925, the court was required to hear almost all of the cases that disappointed litigants requested it to hear. But the court had fallen far behind, as it had before the courts of appeals were created in 1893. No one tribunal in a growing and litigious country could handle such an obligatory case load.

The court consequently went to Congress, the Chief Justice suggesting that the court should cease sitting as a court of error and confine its attention to those cases that were important to the development and coherence of the federal law.

Congress agreed and enacted the so-called Judges' Bill, which approached the problem of making almost all of the court's jurisdiction discretionary and leaving to the Justices themselves the task of selecting cases that deserved the kind of institutional attention that cases in the Supreme Court command.

There were various exceptions to this scheme. One of them, which still exists, but which may not survive for long, is the obligation to rule on the merits of the case in which a state statute has been sustained in state courts against federal constitutional attack.

These cases come to us by appeal rather than by certiorari, and we must decide their merits, either summarily or after plenary consideration.

The legislative history of the 1925 Act also indicates that Congress was assured that a case would be given plenary consideration and decided on the merits if as many as four Justices voted to do so.

The expectation was that this rule would go far to insure that all or most of the cases deserving review would be heard. There are now between 4,000 and 4,500 petitions for certiorari and statements of jurisdiction or appeal filed in the court each term. Their flow, like the Mississippi, is unceasing. Each week adds another eighty or ninety or one hundred to our docket, and they must be disposed of with regularity.

There will be over 1,000 items on the first conference list when we reconvene in the fall. The task of processing this flow and deciding which cases to hear is a substantial one, indeed, but it is not as hard as it might sound. No case will be discussed in conference and hence will be automatically denied unless at least one Justice requests that it be discussed, in which event it will come before the conference and will be voted on.

Chief Justice Taft told Congress in 1925 that about 60 percent of the cases filed were obviously without merit and should not have been filed at all. It is not much different today. About 70 percent of the cases filed do not make the discuss list and are unanimously denied. Most of these cases take very little time. Of the 20 to 25 percent that are discussed, only a relatively few command the necessary four votes. We now take and decide only about 150 cases a year.

As for the criteria for the selection of cases that are to be heard, generally it is the importance of the case that is determinative.

More specifically, if an act of Congress has been declared unconstitutional, that case is very apt to be given plenary consideration.

It is also more likely that a case will be granted if a state statute has been declared unconstitutional.

The most recurring fact indicating review, however, is the existence of a conflict on the same federal question between courts of appeals, between the federal system and the state system, or among the state courts themselves. It is in these cases that one of the principal tasks of the court is to be carried out, namely, attempting to provide some degree of coherence and uniformity in federal law throughout the land.

The judgments in all of those cases that are not reviewed remain undisturbed. They are neither affirmed, reversed, nor vacated, and the denial of the petition has no precedential value. It is not infrequent that one or more Justices will dissent from denial of certiorari, sometimes writing an opinion to this effect.

Although not all of the present Justices do so, it is an old practice and will not soon be abandoned, as I see it.

Cases that are granted are briefly, orally argued, discussed in conference, and decided most often by full opinion. Until a case is decided in conference, all Justices have the same duties with respect to that case and independently vote on its resolution. Upon decision, one Justice is assigned the task of writing an opinion supporting the judgment preferred by at least five Justices. That Justice hopes to satisfy all those on his side, and he normally tries to do so, even though the resulting opinion may include or omit something at the request of another Justice. Usually, the opinion writer succeeds in producing an opinion in which at least four others join.

Of course, often there is dissent. Last term twenty out of 125 opinions in argued cases were unanimous, eighteen were 5-to-4, and in fifty-nine others there was dissent by one or more Justices. The practice of expressing disagreement on the merits, even though a Justice is bound by the result preferred by the majority, is one of long standing. And as I see it, that practice is not likely to be abandoned in the near future.

Sometimes an opinion for the court cannot be had. That happened seven times last term. In such a case, more than one opinion supports the judgment, and it is somewhat harder to arrive at the rationale of the case. People make much of cases where there is no court opinion, but it should be remembered that the court initially followed what is still the English practice of seriatim opinions, with no attempt being made to express a majority view in one piece of writing.

Cases with only plurality opinions, after all, do involve a majority judgment and a majority holding, but they are narrower ones and perhaps harder to come by.

The writing of majority opinions is assigned by the senior Justice on that side of the case; and since every Justice is in the majority more than in dissent, the Chief Justice assigns most of the writing. Last term, for example, he was in the majority in over 85 percent of the cases. Five other Justices were in the majority in more than eight out of ten times, and every Justice was in the majority at least 65 percent of the time. In any event, as I suspect is true in appellate courts countrywide, the writing of opinions is the judge's most timeconsuming and most important task. It is here that most of the meat is cut.

In some cases in our court, it is many months before an opinion is agreed upon. Occasionally, but only occasionally, a case is set for reargument. A bit more often a case is affirmed without opinion by an equally divided court when one Justice has been disqualified. As for oral argument in our court, it is much more than a ritual extension of due process to the parties. Although we now hear most cases for only one-half hour on a side, oral argument remains an important step in the decision-making process.

It is then that all of the Justices are working on the case together, having read the briefs and anticipating that they will have to vote very soon, and attempting to clarify their own thinking and perhaps that of their colleagues. Consequently, we treat lawyers as a resource rather than as orators who should be heard out according to their own desires.

As you may suspect, however, only a fraction of our time is spent on the bench. We start on the first Monday in October and hear cases four hours a day, three days a week for two weeks. We then are off the bench for two weeks, back on for two weeks, and so on; but we're off a little longer at Christmas and after the January session.

There are seven, two-week argument sessions each term, plus every now and then a special sitting, as there was [in 1981] in the Iran litigation.

The periods off the bench are our busiest since that is when opinions should be and usually are written.

We try to adjourn by July 1 to lick our wounds and prepare for the next session.

Our conference procedures are straightforward affairs. We meet alone, without clerks or stenographers, and keep our own records. Whether we are discussing certioraris * or argued cases, each Justice in the order of seniority thereafter having an opportunity to say his piece. There is a good deal of give and take in the process, and by the time that everyone has had his say, the vote is usually quite clear; but, if not, it will be formally taken.

It is not unusual that a Justice will vote tentatively or with a question mark; and it is not rare for a Justice, however he may have voted in conference, to change his mind later, even though his changed vote produces a different result than was voted on in conference.

Of course, the opinion-writer is never happy when this happens, but as I have said, it is not exactly rare.

During an argument week, we usually have two conferences, one on Wednesday to decide Monday's cases, and one on Friday to do the

* Writs to call up the records of a lower court.

weekly certiorari list and decide the cases argued on the previous Tuesday and Wednesday. We also have a certiorari conference at the end of a two-week recess. At the Friday conferences we also decide what decisions, if any, will be announced on the following Monday or other designated day in that week. On Mondays following the Friday conference that has processed a certiorari list, we go on the bench for the purpose of distributing the order list, disposing of past weeks certiorari and motions docket, even if oral argument is not scheduled for that day.

PART IV

PUBLIC POLICY

When we are dealing with words that also are a constituent act, like the Constitution of the United States, we must realize that they have called into life a being the development of which could not have been foreseen completely by the most gifted of its begetters. It was enough for them to realize or to hope that they had created an organism; it has taken a century and has cost their successors much sweat and blood to prove that they created a nation. The case before us must be considered in the light of our whole experience and not merely in that of what was said a hundred years ago.
—Justice Oliver Wendell Holmes, Jr., *Missouri v. Holland*, 1920

Chapter 12

Civil Rights and Individual Liberties

Civil rights and individual liberties are hallmarks of a free, democratic society. In the United States the Bill of Rights rather than the original Constitution specifies most of the basic individual liberties. The First Amendment sets forth the fundamental freedoms of speech, press, religion, assembly, and petition for redress of grievances. Many jurists and scholars believe that the rights stipulated in the First Amendment constitute the fundamental conditions for self-government.

As written, however, the First Amendment limits the federal government—"Congress shall make no law..."—and not the states. Chief Justice John Marshall even ruled in *Barron v. Baltimore* (1833) that the Bill of Rights did not apply to the states. By contrast, the Fourteenth Amendment—ratified in the aftermath of the Civil War—is directed against state actions that "deprive any person of life, liberty, or property without due process of law." No one knows for certain whether Congress intended to have the Bill of Rights "incorporated" into the Fourteenth Amendment. That has been the practical result, however, as the Court gradually has applied the guarantees of the Bill of Rights to the states.[1] Selection 61, "Citizen's Guide to Individual Rights under the Constitution," explains the rights accorded U.S. citizens, especially the guarantees of the First and Fourteenth Amendments.[2] In Selection 62, "The Evolution of Our Civil Liberties," Sen. Robert Packwood (R-Ore.) traces the English heritage of many of our basic civil liberties.

A vast number of issues are associated with civil rights and civil liberties—religion, libel, privacy, pornography, civil disobedience, and so on. Many contemporary issues that are difficult to resolve may be characterized as issues of "right versus right," such as funding programs for the young versus those for the elderly, rather than issues of "right versus wrong," such as equality of opportunity for all races versus racial segregation. In discussing the 1986 election of John Lewis (D-Ga.) to the House of Representatives, then Atlanta mayor Andrew Young spoke of this distinction. Recounting Lewis's civil rights leadership during the 1960s, Young said, "He's a representative of that glorious moment in history when things were very clear. There were good guys and bad guys, and he was one of the good guys." [3]

Affirmative action is intended to correct past discrimination by giving racial minorities and other groups preference over the dominant racial majority. Many governments and private entities in the United States use various affirmative-action plans to achieve this objective. Some employers, for example, observe minority hiring goals in choosing their personnel; some schools incorporate racial ratios into their admissions policies. Such affirmative-action plans came into wide use following the 1960s civil rights struggles and the passage of the Civil Rights Act of 1964. Their remedies benefit the racial minority as a class, not only identifiable victims of bias.

For years affirmative-action programs have aroused passions because they involve race-conscious remedies. Proponents hold that special steps are needed to overcome generations of past discrimination that have inevitably masked the natural abilities of the disadvantaged minorities. Critics counter that our Constitution and laws should be color-blind and that the remedy for discrimination is not to bend standards of selection or evaluation but to remove the discrimination and encourage compensatory training. Authors of the two readings in Selection 63, "Point-Counterpoint: Affirmative Action," articulate the controversy. Benjamin L. Hooks, executive director of the National Association for the Advancement of Colored People, presents the case for affirmative action, while Professor Shelby Steele outlines its high price.

Numerous court decisions have dealt with affirmative action, raising hard questions such as these:[4]

■ While obviously repugnant, does past racial discrimination justify race-conscious action in reverse?

■ May a race-conscious plan be ordered or adopted without judicial findings or admissions of past discrimination by one of the parties?

■ May persons in the racial majority, themselves innocent of any proven discrimination, become no longer preferred in favor of individuals in the racial minority, due solely to past discrimination by others?

■ May race-conscious relief be extended to people not proved to have been victims of discrimination in the past?

The limits of free speech are another controversial area, especially when a repugnant message for many is conveyed through written, oral, or symbolic expressions. Pornography, racist speech, or sexually explicit musical lyrics are recent examples of "free speech" disputes and differences of opinion as to what kinds of expression are, or should be, protected by the First Amendment. Burning the American flag is another recent free-speech controversy.

In 1989 the Supreme Court decided (*Texas* v. *Johnson*) that a state law making flag burning a crime contravened the First Amendment's guarantee of free speech. The Court decision, presented in Selection

64, states that the flag burning represented the communication of a political message. Many in Congress were outraged by the decision and succeeded in passing the Flag Protection Act of 1989. That statute, too, was struck down (*United States* v. *Eichman*, 1990) because it violated the free-speech guarantees of the First Amendment.

Numerous lawmakers then sought to add a Twenty-seventh Amendment to the Constitution, which would permit Congress and the states to pass laws imposing sanctions for physically desecrating the flag. Debate raged back and forth over the merits of amending the Bill of Rights. In our point-counterpoint (Selection 65), two House members debate the issue of protecting the flag versus making an exception to the First Amendment's free-speech guarantees. When the House voted in June 1990 on the proposed constitutional amendment, it went down to defeat. Many lawmakers were concerned about undermining free speech. As one commentator wrote:

> The First Amendment, it is no exaggeration to say, is the world's most envied and effective charter of free utterance. Amending it merely to reverse the court on flag burning might not do fatal injury. But it would set a risky precedent. Everyone has his pet dislike among the more unusual and exotic forms of expression that pass for free speech. Once the barrier is broken and the parade of exceptions begins, where does it stop? When the First Amendment, like a weird Swiss cheese . . . becomes all holes and no cheese?[5]

In short, all nations have flags, but relatively few have a Bill of Rights.

Notes

1. See also Robert G. McCloskey, *The American Supreme Court* (Chicago: University of Chicago Press, 1960), and Howard N. Meyer, "Honor Its Promises, The Fall and Rise of the 14th Amendment," *Civil Rights Digest,* Summer 1976, 4-13.
2. The Constitution and Bill of Rights also accord procedural protections to individuals, such as protection from arbitrary arrest, searches, and imprisonment. "The history of liberty," wrote Justice Felix Frankfurter in *McNabb* v. *United States* (1943), "has largely been the history of observance of procedural safeguards."
3. *New York Times,* December 12, 1986, B6.
4. The questions are from Rory K. Little, "Race-Conscious Remedies? Affirmative!" *National Law Journal* (July 28, 1986): 13.
5. *Washington Post,* June 14, 1990, A23.

61. Citizen's Guide to Individual Rights Under the Constitution

Senate Judiciary Committee

This guide was prepared by the Senate Judiciary Committee in 1976 in response to many inquiries about the constitutional rights of citizens. Its objective is to provide citizens with a brief and understandable explanation of their individual liberties. This selection focuses particularly on the guarantees specified in the First and Fourteenth Amendments.

Each branch of the government—the legislative, judicial, and executive—is charged by the Constitution with the protection of individual liberties. In this framework, the judiciary has assumed a leading role. Chief Justice John Marshall, speaking for the Supreme Court in the early case of *Marbury* v. *Madison* (1803), declared that it was the duty of the judiciary to say what the law is, including expounding and interpreting that law. The law contained in the Constitution, he declared, was paramount and other laws which were repugnant to its provisions must fall. He concluded that it was the province of the court to decide when other law was in violation of the basic law of the Constitution and, where this was found to occur, to declare that law null and void. This is the doctrine known as "judicial review" which has become the basis for the courts' application of constitutional guarantees in cases brought before them.

The Congress also has played an important role in the protection of constitutional rights by enacting legislation designed to guarantee and apply these rights in specific contexts. Laws which guarantee the rights of Indians, afford due process to military servicemen, and give effective right to counsel to poor defendants and to the poor in a wide variety of civil cases are but recent examples of the congressional role.

Finally, the executive branch, which is charged with implementing the laws enacted by Congress, also contributes to the protection of individual rights by devising its own regulations and procedures for administering the law without intruding upon constitutional guarantees.

Before anyone can properly understand the scope of our constitutional rights, he must realize that as a function of our federal system, we

Americans live under two governments rather than one—that of the Federal Government itself and that of the State in which we live. The authority of the Federal Government is limited by the Constitution to those powers specified in it; the remainder of governmental powers are reserved to the States. The Federal Government is authorized, for example, to settle disputes between States, to conduct relations with foreign governments, and to act in certain matters of common national concern. States, on the other hand, retain the remainder of governmental power to be exercised within their respective boundaries.

Only a few individual rights were specified in the Constitution when it was ratified in 1788. Shortly after its adoption, however, ten Amendments—called the Bill of Rights—were added to the Constitution to guarantee basic individual liberties. These liberties include freedom of speech, freedom of press, freedom of religion, and freedom to assemble and petition the Government.

The guarantees of the Bill of Rights originally applied only to actions of the Federal Government and did not prevent State and local governments from taking action which might threaten an individual's civil liberty. As a practical matter, States had their own constitutions, some of which contained their own bills of rights guaranteeing the same or similar rights guaranteed by the Bill of Rights against Federal intrusion. These rights, however, were not guaranteed by all the States; and where they did exist, they were subject to varying interpretations. In short, citizens were protected only to the extent that the States themselves recognized their basic rights.

In 1868, the Fourteenth Amendment was added to the Constitution. In part, it provides that no State shall "deprive any person of life, liberty, or property without due process of law." It was not until 1925 in the case of *Gitlow* v. *New York*, that the Supreme Court interpreted the phrase "due process of law" to mean in effect "without abridgement of certain of the rights guaranteed by the Bill of Rights." Since that decision, the Supreme Court has ruled that a denial by a State of certain of the rights contained in the Bill of Rights actually represents a denial of due process of law. While the Court has not ruled that all rights in the Bill of Rights are contained in the notion of "due process," neither has it limited that notion to the rights enumerated in the Bill of Rights. It simply has found that there are concepts in the Bill of Rights so basic to a democratic society that they must be recognized as part of "due process of law" and made applicable to the States as well as the Federal Government.

To place these rights in a broader perspective, one should realize that they make up only the core of what are considered to be our civil rights—those privileges and freedoms that are accorded all Americans by virtue of their citizenship. There are many other "civil" rights which are not specifically mentioned in the Constitution but which nonetheless have been recognized by the courts, guaranteed by statute, and now are embedded in our democratic traditions. The right to buy, sell, own, and bequeath property; the right to enter into contracts; the right to marry and have children; the right to live and work where one desires; and the right to participate in the political, social, and cultural processes of the society in which one lives are a few of those rights that are considered as fundamental to a democratic society as those specified by the Constitution.

Despite the inherent nature of the rights of American citizenship, it should be emphasized that the rights guaranteed by the Constitution or otherwise are not absolute rights in the sense that they entitle a citizen to act in any way he pleases. Rather, he must exercise his rights in such a way that the rights of others are not denied in the process. Thus, as Mr. Justice Holmes has pointed out, "Protection of free speech would not protect a man falsely shouting 'Fire' in a theater and causing a panic." Nor does freedom of speech and press sanction the publication of libel and obscenity. Similarly, rights of free speech and free assembly do not permit one knowingly to engage in conspiracies to overthrow by force the Government of the United States. It is clear, then, that civil liberties carry with them an obligation on the part of all Americans to exercise their rights within a framework of law and mutual respect for the rights of one's fellow citizens.

This obligation implies not only a restraint on the part of those exercising these rights but a tolerance on the part of those who are affected. Citizens may on occasion be subjected to annoying political tirades, or strange dress, or disagreeable entertainment, or noisy demonstrations of protest. They may feel annoyed when a defendant refuses to testify or when they see a seemingly guilty defendant go free because certain evidence was inadmissible in court. But these annoyances or inconveniences are a small price to pay for the freedom we all enjoy. For, indeed, if the rights of one are suppressed, the freedom of all is jeopardized.

Ultimately, a free society is a dynamic society, where thoughts and ideas are forever challenging and being challenged. It is not without the risk that the "wrong" voice will be listened to or the "wrong" plan pursued. But, in the final analysis, a free interplay of ideas in a society produces both a clearer perception and livelier impression of truth.

The First Amendment

Congress shall make no law respecting an establishment of religion, or prohibiting the free exercise thereof; or abridging the freedom of speech, or of the press; or the right of the people peaceably to assemble, and to petition the Government for a redress of grievances.

Freedom of Religion

Two express guarantees are given to the individual with respect to his religious freedom. First, neither Congress nor a State legislature may "make any law respecting an establishment of religion." This means that no law may be passed that favors one church over another, establishes an official church to which all Americans must subscribe or support, or requires religious belief or religious nonbelief. Second, no law may validly interfere with the "free exercise" of one's religion. This clause assures that each citizen is guaranteed freedom to worship by individual choice.

The Court's modern interpretation of the Establishment Clause has supplied the notions of voluntarism and neutrality as constituting the mortar of this "wall of separation between Church and State." Governmental activity that has the purpose or primary effect of advancing or inhibiting religion or that results in excessive governmental entanglement with religion is proscribed. Moreover, the Establishment Clause guards against measures that would foster political divisiveness on religious grounds in the general community.

While Court decisions in this area are not easily categorized, we have learned that, pursuant to the notion of voluntarism, the Court has been extremely reluctant to permit any governmental involvement with private elementary and secondary schools: it has determined that students there are more impressionable, and thus more liable to be coerced than university level students.

The Establishment Clause, therefore, has been held to prohibit: (1) mandatory religious exercises such as Bible readings, or even nondenominational prayers, in the public elementary and secondary schools; (2) promoting religious creeds through the manipulation of curricula in State-supported schools; and (3) providing financial support through such measures as grants, loans, and tax credits to nonpublic elementary and secondary schools affiliated with religious institutions, even for nonreligious courses of study or for the maintenance of facilities. On the other hand, the clause has been held not to prohibit: (1) providing a neutral service such as bus transportation on an equal basis to children in both religious schools and public schools; (2) loaning secular textbooks to children attending religious schools; (3) making direct general grants to religious-affiliated colleges and universities, depending on the "character" of the college and its ability to separate secular and religious functions; and (4) releasing public school students to attend a religious period of instruction at sites off school premises. Furthermore, the Court has refused to hold that the tax-exempt status accorded church property used exclusively for worship purposes contravenes the Establishment Clause.

In interpreting the Free Exercise Clause, the Court has held that if the purpose or effect of a statute is to impede the observance of religion(s), or to discriminate invidiously among them, then the free exercise of religion is abridged. Indeed, the Court has recently established that only a compelling governmental interest can legitimize a statute restrictive of the free exercise of religion.

In this regard, it is clear that *no* statute can validly impinge upon religious thoughts, that is, religious *belief* devoid of conduct. Moreover, by applying the compelling interest test, the Court has assured that forms of conduct based on religious belief are to receive increasing protection. Thus, when a Seventh-day Adventist was fired for refusing to work on Saturdays (her holyday), the Court ruled that she was fully entitled to unemployment benefits. Similarly, Amish parents were held to be protected in their refusal to send their children beyond the eighth grade to public schools, the State interest in requiring the two years of additional mandatory schooling having failed to outweigh the legitimate devotion of the Amish to their tenets. These forms of conduct based upon religious belief have been held to be protected by the Free Exercise Clause.

Nonetheless, all activity cannot be protected by claims of religious belief. Religious conduct such as polygamy, snake handling, or the ceremonial use of drugs is not protected by the Free Exercise Clause, the Supreme Court having held that the strong societal interests in safety and morality justify the prohibition of such conduct.

Freedom of Speech

Freedom of speech is explicitly established in the First Amendment. While the English common law concept of freedom of speech meant freedom from prior restraint only, the present American theory of freedom of speech generally establishes both freedom from prior restraint and freedom from subsequent punishment for the exercise of these rights. Some justices, in fact, have suggested that freedom of speech is absolute, but a majority of the Court always has maintained that it must be balanced against other legitimate interests: in short, the Court has attempted to preserve the greatest degree of expression consistent with the protection of overriding and compelling governmental interests.

Central to the concept of freedom of speech is the freedom of individual belief. In recognition of this the Court has held that the right to associate with those who hold beliefs compatible to one's own in order to further those beliefs, whether in a political or social context, must receive basic protection from the First Amendment. The State, for example, may procure general membership lists of an organization only where there is a substantial relation between the information sought and a subject of compelling State interest.

The principal way of conveying one's beliefs is through actual expression. Generally, a citizen may speak out freely on any subject. He may exercise this right verbally, by parading, by wearing buttons, by flying flags and banners, and in a variety of other ways. He may, in short, advocate any idea he desires, no matter how unpopular or alien. Even advocacy of the use of force or violation of law may be punished only where it is directed to inciting or producing imminent lawless action and is likely to incite or produce such action. Abusive or profane language also is protected unless it is directed to a specific individual and tends to incite that person to violence.

Engaging in "symbolic speech," such as wearing black armbands or using a flag in certain ways, receives similar First Amendment protection. On the other hand conduct such as burning draft cards may be banned or punished. It is the nature of a particular activity, combined with the factual context and environment in which it is undertaken, that will determine whether it really is "symbolic speech" deserving First Amendment protection. In this determination, the Court will examine whether the conduct is effective enough to constitute "symbolic speech"; is there an intention to communicate, is there an audience, and is the symbolism capable of being understood by the audience? The gravity of the State interest also must be weighed; is the State trying to regulate content (requiring a compelling justification)? Or is it merely attempting to regulate time, place, or manner of speech? These factors will determine whether the activity is protected "speech" or unprotected "conduct."

Parading or picketing in public places is generally protected, although in locations such as military camps or courthouses, restraints may be justified. Permit systems preceding the exercise of such rights are permissible only when official discretion is narrowly bounded and rapid review of denials is assured. Once expression is permitted in a forum, the government may generally regulate only time, place, or manner of that expression. Furthermore, there is an equalitarian guarantee supporting such expression. The First Amendment requires that the arbitrary exclusion of a person or a class of persons from a public forum be subjected to the strictest of scrutiny.

Although at one time the Court required private property dedicated to public use—such as shopping centers—to be treated as public and thus open to expressive activity, it has since overruled these cases, sharply reducing access to private property for purposes of First Amendment expression.

Spending one's own money or contributed money to further one's own candidacy for public office, or to promote one's political and social views, is another protected activity. However, limitations upon how much one may contribute to a candidate for office have been sustained. The Court also has sustained governmental restraints upon the political activities of public employees. Similarly, it has recognized that in cases involving disruption of public business, the government may restrict expression by its employees, though such limitations are subject to careful judicial scrutiny.

Organized institutions, like individuals, are guaranteed freedom of expression, not so much for their own benefit but for their contribution to furthering a free interchange of ideas in our democratic society. That a profit may be derived from, for example, managing a newspaper, does not lessen the guarantee. Furthermore, this protection extends not only to political expression, but to discourse on practically any subject of some serious social value.

However, certain forms of expression—such as obscenity or hardcore pornography—are deemed without "serious" social importance and thus may go unprotected by the First Amendment. Because not all expression dealing with sex is obscene, the Court has held that the First Amendment must determine the procedural and substantive law by which speech may be adjudged obscene. Only that expression which, by the standards of the local community and taken as a whole, appeals to a prurient interest in sex, portrays sexual conduct in a patently offensive way, and does not have serious literary, artistic, political, or scientific value, may be classified as obscene. Even where there has been no official determination as to whether a particular form of expression is actually obscene, ordinances restricting the locations of theaters specializing in films exhibiting "specified sexual activities" or "specified anatomical areas" are permissible. The Court has justified this restriction of expression by claiming that the State's interest in protecting "borderline pornography" is not so great as its interest in planning the use of its property and preventing the clustering of establishments merchandising pornography.

Generally, defamation is another class of expression that has been deemed devoid of any serious social value. There is one basic exception to this classification: because of the importance of comment upon issues affecting government, the Court has carefully restrained State remedies for allegedly defamatory speech in regard to public officials, candidates for public office, and some public figures. In order to recover damages for defamatory comment, public figures must prove that it was uttered with actual malice. Practically all other citizens may recover actual damages for defamatory falsehoods so long as State law establishes a standard higher than strict liability; however, punitive damages are recoverable only upon proof of actual malice.

Freedom of the Press

Freedom of the press and freedom of speech have frequently been treated synonymously by the Court. Nevertheless, it is clear that the press does have a special place in America's heritage. Our own revolution, for example, was ignited by press pamphlets such as Thomas Paine's "Common Sense." Realizing the value of an unrestrained press to American society, the Court has been very reluctant to sanction governmental censorship of the press or management of the news. In fact, prior restraints upon press publications have come to the Court with such a heavy presumption of invalidity that the Supreme Court has *never* upheld them. Even in the Pentagon Papers case, where there was an alleged threat to national security posed by the exposure of secret governmental documents, the Court struck down any form of prior restraint. Only a "grave and irreparable" harm might justify such drastic action.

It must be noted that the recent Court trend indicates a weakening of the guarantee of freedom of the press. Publications' liability for defamation has been broadened. Furthermore, the Court has refused to strike down all prior restraints upon the press in the fair trial context, having admitted the possibility of such circumstances that would justify restraint.

Finally, it should be mentioned that freedom of the press does not insulate the press, as corporations, from those economic regulations applied to all business—such as taxation, equal employment opportunity, labor management, or antitrust laws.

All of the foregoing must be considered within the context of the printed press in the United States, for the broadcast media operate within a different Constitutional framework. Because television and radio station owners are licensees of scarce frequencies, they have been held subject to governmental regulation in a number of areas: they must, for example, guarantee equal time to reply to editorial attacks as well as provide fairness in treatment of issues. Governmental regulation cannot go so far, however, as to require broadcasters to accept paid political or public issues advertising—so long as issues are presented fairly by that station.

Freedom of Assembly and Petition

Freedom of assembly is as fundamental as the freedoms of speech and press, all three freedoms being inseparable parts of freedom of expression. While the assembly clause adds little to the protection of the rights to assemble, picket, or parade that would not already be protected by the speech clause, it does reaffirm the breadth of the rights that are guaranteed.

The right to petition is designed to enable the citizen to communicate with his government without hindrance. It assures his right to present his views both orally and in writing, and also embraces his right to travel to the seat of government.

The Fourteenth Amendment

Section 1. All persons born or naturalized in the United States, and subject to the jurisdiction thereof, are citizens of the United States and of the State wherein they reside. No State shall make or enforce any law which shall abridge the privileges or immunities of citizens of the United States; nor shall any State deprive any person of life, liberty or property, without due process of law; nor deny to any person within its jurisdiction the equal protection of the laws.

Section 5. The Congress shall have power to enforce, by appropriate legislation, the provisions of this article.

Citizenship

The purpose of the first sentence of the Amendment was to overrule the *Dred Scott* decision, which had held that blacks could not be citizens of the United States. The Amendment's ratification clearly established a national rule with regard to citizenship.

Privileges and Immunities

Alexander Hamilton proposed in Federalist Paper #80 that "the citizens of each State shall be entitled to all the privileges and immunities of citizens of the several states." In 1873, however, the Supreme Court confined the protection of the Privileges and Immunities Clause to those privileges "which owe their existence to the Federal Government, its National character, its Constitution, or its laws," which the Court deemed to be very few in number. This decision, in effect, severely limited the scope of the Privileges and Immunities Clause.

Due Process of Law

Most of the specific provisions of the Bill of Rights have been applied to the States through this clause. Its real importance, however, goes far beyond this application. For the due process clause also serves as a procedural guarantee in both civil and criminal cases, where it requires government to observe a host of restraints. Before action may be taken to deprive one of a basic liberty, his property or to restrain his exercise of rights over his property, he must be afforded notice and an opportunity to be heard before an impartial tribunal under conditions that enforce fairness. For example, public school teachers who have a reasonable expectation of tenure must be given the opportunity to have a hearing before they are dismissed. The same requirement applies before a public school student may be dismissed or suspended. Also, criminal defendants are protected from prosecution under vague statutes, and every element necessary to establish their culpability must be proved beyond a reasonable doubt. Due process also insures that prosecutors may not conceal evidence favorable to the defendant and material to his case, at least where the defendant has requested a review of the evidence in the prosecution's possession. It protects the rights of convicted persons, requiring fair treatment of them in prison. Revocation of parole and probation also must be carried out with regard to due process. In addition, the Court has begun to apply the notion of due process to those persons committed to or confined in mental institutions. Finally, as a function of due process, juvenile defendants are now afforded procedures tailored both to protect them and to preserve the uniqueness of the system of juvenile justice. Nonetheless, due process does not require a hearing in all cases where it appears that vested rights of property or liberty are affected. For example, in some contexts public employees may be dismissed without any constitutionally-required opportunity for a hearing to protest that move.

This clause has a substantive aspect as well, protecting individuals against deprivation of important property and liberty interests. Substantive due process for a significant period of our history was held to preclude government from regulating many forms of economic activity. While these restraints were abandoned in the 1930s, the Court now accords the protection of substantive due process to certain fundamental personal rights. Foremost among these is the concept of the right to privacy, which to date has been limited largely to matters involving marriage, procreation, and the parental care of children. For example, it appears that at least in the heterosexual context a sexual relationship between consenting adults in private is considered a generally protected privacy interest.

Equal Protection of the Laws

The Equal Protection Clause prohibits the State from making unreasonable or arbitrary distinctions among persons as to their rights and privileges. The Court's primary concern here is avoiding deprivation by the State of a minority group's rights, no matter how small or unpopular that group may be. Like Hamilton and Madison in the Federalist Papers, the Court under the Equal Protection Clause seeks to prevent tyranny rule by the majority. It does so by striking down almost without exception two categories of distinctions. First is the "suspect" classification in which the State distinguishes along lines that traditionally have been used as a basis for deprivation. Classifying citizens by race in order to preserve segregated schools would be one example. Any such classification is automatically considered "suspect" by the Court and is doomed to fall under its strict scrutiny. Second is where, rather than looking at the two groups being distinguished, the Court examines the interest being affected by the classification. If it is deemed a fundamental interest then this form of classification also is subject to the rigors of the Court's strict scrutiny. For example, making the fundamental right to vote contingent upon the payment of a poll tax has been ruled to be a violation of the Equal Protection Clause.

The Court has held that State regulation of commerce or other activity will be sustained if the regulatory distinction or classification does not affect a fundamental interest or represent a suspect classification.

But, as we have seen, active review—and not deference—is the posture of the Supreme Court in two major areas. First, we have observed that distinctions among certain classes are inherently suspect. Race is rarely, if ever, a proper basis for distinguishing among persons. Nationality and alienage also are improper bases of classification. It also seems settled that illegitimacy is an improper basis of classification by the State. While the sex classification is not yet considered suspect by the Court, gender distinctions do require a greater justification for validity than do ordinary classifications. Wealth or indigency also are not suspect classifications, but when combined with denials of a fundamental interest, such classifications will often be invalidated.

Second, as aforementioned, when official classification affects a fundamental interest, it can be justified only by a compelling showing that the State's interest is legitimate and cannot be served by another device. Because the right to vote has been deemed fundamental, numerous suffrage restrictions have fallen. The right to travel being fundamental, many durational residency requirements also have fallen under the Court's strict scrutiny. The right to be free of wealth distinctions in the criminal process is another interest deemed fundamental by the Court. Education, however, has not been held to be a fundamental right. The Court has sustained a State system of supporting education based on a taxing scheme permitting great disparities in financing among school districts.

Only official denials of due process and equal protection are subject to the Fourteenth Amendment, since the Amendment refers to "State." Purely private acts, however discriminatory, do not raise constitutional issues in most instances. However, if such acts implicate the government, whether through State enforcement, contrivance, or encouragement, the Amendment is applicable. This is also true where conduct is so "governmental" in character that it is tantamount to State action, such as in the nomination and election of public officials or the maintenance of public order.

Section 5 furnishes Congress with a plenary power to enforce the Amendment's provisions, but no power to restrict, abrogate, or dilute these guarantees. A number of significant pieces of legislation have been passed under this positive grant of authority. Among other guarantees, such legislation has established:

- The right to be free from racial discrimination in public dining facilities;
- The right to be free from segregation by race or color in transportation facilities;
- The right to be free from segregation in the operation of public recreational facilities;
- The right of equality of opportunity to hold public employment;
- The right to be free from racial discrimination in government housing; and
- The right to be free from purposeful discrimination by city authorities in their official relations.

It also should be noted that certain Titles of the comprehensive Civil Rights Act of 1964 (such as Titles III and IV, dealing with desegregation of schools and other public facilities) were rooted in the post-Civil War Amendments, particularly Section 5 of the Fourteenth Amendment.

62. The Evolution of Our Civil Liberties

Sen. Robert Packwood

Sen. Robert Packwood was first elected to the Senate in 1968. During the Ninety-ninth Congress (1985-1987), he chaired the Finance Committee and was one of the major architects of the historic revamping of the federal tax code. In this speech to students at Oregon's Willamette University, subsequently published in the *Congressional Record* in 1986, Sen. Packwood perceptively outlines the English origins of many of our civil liberties. Further, he describes the struggle to win basic rights and underscores the necessity of constant vigilance to preserve them for future generations.

The year was 1956. The place was Oregon. The document was the general election ballot of November of that year. The issue was fishing. The ballot description read, "prohibiting certain fishing in coastal streams."

Now go back almost 800 years. The year was 1215. The place was Runnymede, England. The document was the Magna Carta. This issue was fishing. Article 33 of the Magna Carta reads, "All fish weirs shall be removed from the Thames, the Medway and throughout the whole of England except on the sea coast." I was struck by the fact of how many issues that we deal with today seem to be eternal.

When you look at the history of government—ours for 200 years—England's for almost 600 years prior to that—it is a continual struggle of men and women to secure for themselves certain liberties that governments wish to take away.

The battle is not usually fought against those who are intent upon doing evil. It is usually fought against those who are intent on doing good—as they see it.

This country is full of good men and women intent upon helping us. Some would prevent us from driving cars in national parks. Others would require us to wear helmets while riding motorcycles. Some would insist upon protecting us against smoking—for our own good, of course. Some would muzzle the press. These people are well-intentioned.

These well-intentioned people are convinced they are right. They sincerely believe they are so right, that if you disagree with them, they are sure you are wrong. Then it's only a short step to "the end justifies the means," because they believe the end is so "right." When these people gain control of government, they become dangerous. The more I read history, and the longer I watch government operate, the more convinced I am that almost anyone can withstand adversity. If you want to test a person's character, give that person power.

If we are going to protect our civil liberties against those who are in power, we must do battle in the first trench. We don't wait until we have been shoved and pushed to a hilltop where we are surrounded and circumscribed by a government run by men and women of good intent trying to help us.

Often, when we have to battle in that first trench to protect our liberties, it is not against somebody who wants to prevent driving in national parks or to stop us from smoking. The first trench is usually a battle to defend some radical or bomb thrower or political dissident, or someone whose life style differs from those in power. We must make sure that the procedures for their defense are kept secure. A government that can put that person in prison or abuse that person's rights, without what all of us would regard as due process, can easily turn that procedure against us. Government will try just that if we choose to do something that the government, in its wisdom, thinks is not proper.

I want you to go back with me a bit through the history of England and the United States to see what England did over a period of almost 600 years, why they did it, and why we copied it almost verbatim into our Constitution and into our Bill of Rights.

England's experience was substantially different from ours. To begin with, they don't have a written constitution. All of the civil liberties of England are simply a series of parliamentary acts, or in some cases, decisions of common law courts. The English experience with government, through the centuries, was that government, be it a government of the king, or a parliamentary government—will try to take away certain liberties from the citizenry.

Initially in English history, it was presumed the monarch would try to abuse civil liberties and the parliament would protect them. Therefore, many of England's early civil liberty battles were struggles pitting the king against the parliament.

What's the first thing the king would try to do in those early days when parliament was still a fledgling institution? Of course, he would try to rule without a parliament. Parliament was a hindrance. Parliament wanted to restrict his right to imprison people and arrest people and start wars. So the easiest thing to do was to have no parliament meet. In 1330, parliament passed a statute that said, "It is accorded that parliament shall be holden once every year or more often if need be." How did we phrase it 450 years later in our Constitution? "The Congress shall assemble at least once every year." This would insure that a President would not try to set aside Congress' right to gather and assemble.

When parliament was secure in its right to meet, the next avenue that the king would use would be to imprison members for what they said on the floor of parliament. If we can't keep them from meeting, at least we can put them in prison if they say anything adverse. So the English Bill of Rights—the English Bill of Rights in 1689—simply said that, "The freedom of speech and debates on proceedings in parliament ought not to be impeached or questioned in any court or place out of parliament." How did we say it in Article I, Section V, of the Constitution? "Senators and Representatives . . . for any speech or debate in either House shall not be questioned in any other place."

Well, all right, if parliament must meet, and the members of parliament are entitled to say what they want, the king would next try to keep the citizens and parliament apart. Therefore, he would not allow citizens to petition parliament for grievances they might have against the king, and if they did so petition, try to imprison them for it.

So again, the English Bill of Rights says simply, "It is the right of the subjects to petition the king and all commitments and prosecutions for such petitioning are illegal." And how did we say it in our Bill of Rights? "Congress shall make no law . . . abridging the right of the people . . . to petition the government for a redress of grievances."

The battle continued to secure, and secure once again, more strongly, our liberties. It was a continual struggle to prevent government from taking away our right to dissent, our right to assemble, our right to a different life style, our right to appear and ask that the government change, in short—from taking away our basic political liberties.

The king found that the parliament was becoming more and more obdurate. They wouldn't give him the money for the wars that he wanted. In fact, to get any money at all to sustain his army, he found that he had to turn to parliament more often than he liked. However, one avenue to save money in the military budget was simply to quarter the soldiers and the sailors in the homes of the citizens, and make the citizens pay for their room and board. And so the English Petition of Right in 1628, says, "Your majesty will be pleased to remove the said soldiers and mariners, and that your people may not be so burdened in time to come." What did we say in our Bill of Rights? "No soldier shall, in time of peace be quartered in any house, without the consent of the owner, nor in time of war, but in a manner prescribed by law."

In addition to securing parliamentary rights vis-a-vis the king, Englishmen also continually strengthened individual liberties. The Magna Carta says: "No free man shall be seized or imprisoned or stripped of his rights or possessions, or outlawed or exiled or deprived of his standing in any other way . . . except by the lawful judgment of his equals or by the law of the land." We said it more simply in our Bill of Rights. "No person shall be deprived of life, liberty or property without due process of law."

The king, thus thwarted in his effort to prohibit fair trials, next turned to the concept of setting bail so high that a person could not afford it, or threatening punishment so cruel that a person would confess, rather than face the punishment. So in the English Bill of Rights, it simply says, "Excessive bail ought not to be required, nor excessive fines imposed, nor cruel or unusual punishments inflicted." A hundred years later in our Bill of Rights we said, "Excessive bail shall not be required, nor excessive fines imposed, nor cruel and unusual punishments inflicted."

All right, said the king, if I can't hold the man without bail, or threaten him with cruel and inhumane punishment, I'll simply let the cloud of guilt hang over his head and delay his trial for years. No you won't, said the Magna Carta, and they phrased it as follows: "To no one will . . . we deny or delay right or justice." Our Bill of Rights says, "in all criminal prosecutions, the accused shall enjoy the right to speedy and public trial by an impartial jury."

I'll try the man over and over, and over again, until I finally get a conviction, said the king. Parliament didn't even have to address itself to that. The courts of law themselves in the pleas of acquit and convict said, "a man shall not be brought into danger . . . for one and the same offense more than once." We said it in our Bill of Rights as follows: "No person shall be subject for the same offense to be twice put into jeopardy of life or limb."

Finally, when all else would fail, the king would extract confessions by torture, and use the confession in court for conviction. So the Magna Carta put it this way. "In future, no official shall place a man on trial upon his own unsupported statement." Almost 600 years later, we said it in the 5th amendment as follows: "No person shall be compelled in any criminal case to be a witness against himself."

There are many more examples from English history that we have adopted and incorporated in our Constitution and Bill of Rights. As a matter of fact, we added two protections England didn't have—freedom of the press and freedom of religion. These both grew out of our colonial experience. One of the basic tenets of our colonial history was religious diversity. We wanted that protected and, therefore, prohibited the establishment of a national church. In addition, because of the efforts of England to throttle the colonial press, we added the protection in our Bill of Rights of freedom of the press.

A key fact to remember is that our civil liberties may be as easily abused by a President, as by a Congress. England even learned that long before we became a nation. As I said earlier, from the time of the Magna Carta to the English civil war in the 1640s, the feeling in England was that the king was likely to abuse liberties, and the parliament was likely to protect them. The common citizen never paused to think that a parliament might abuse their liberties until the English civil war. In the 1640s the King and the parliament divided and fought. The parliament was full of diverse factions, but they united against the King. Parliament finally won. They beheaded the King. Then the parliamentary factions fell to fighting among themselves. One of the parliamentary factions, the Puritans—whose religious kin had left England 20 to 30 years before to come to this country—gained control of parliament. They gained it completely when a Puritan army man named Colonel Pride stood at the door of parliament in 1648. In what has come to be known as "Pride's Purge," he turned away all members of parliament who did not agree with the Puritan party then headed by Oliver Cromwell. Fifty-three members of parliament—the Puritan faction—were left to govern England. They proceeded to abuse the rights of all Englishmen. Finally, Oliver Cromwell, and his instrument of tyranny, the New Model Army, could not stand even the fifty-three. They were dismissed, and parliament dissolved. The second civil war started. Winston Churchill, in his *History of the English-speaking Peoples* phrases it so eloquently when he says, "The story of the second civil war is short and simple. The king, the lords and commons, landlords and merchants, the city and the countryside, the church, the Scottish army, the Welsh people, and the English fleet all now turn against the New Model Army. The army beat the lot. And at their head was Cromwell. . . . It was a triumph of some 20,000 resolute, ruthless, disciplined military fanatics over all that England even wished or ever willed."

From that day onward, the documents of English liberty make it obvious that neither the king nor parliament were to abuse Englishmen.

American history reveals the same sorry examples. Congress or the President can violate our liberties. It was Congress which first passed the Alien and Sedition Acts, clearly violating our First Amendment liberties. It was President Jackson who approved efforts in southern states to prohibit the receipt through the mail of abolitionist tracts mailed from the north. It was Woodrow Wilson's attorney general who lent his name to the infamous "Palmer red raids" in which efforts were made to round up alleged "red" sympathizers in 1920. It was President Franklin Roosevelt, with the immediate concurrence of Congress, who authorized the internment of native born American citizens of Japanese ancestry in World War II. It was a Congress that abused our liberties during the McCarthy era of the 1950s. It was the President who abused our liberties during the Watergate era.

If history has taught us anything, it is that there is no foolproof, safe haven which can serve as the repository of our liberties. On occasion, Congress, the President and even the courts can be swept away by the passion of the moment.

From the perspective of one who is a practicing politician, I hope we always will remember that passion can obscure judgment. We should remember that governing officials, in dictatorships and democracies, find it easy and convenient to bend to transitory, popular prejudices which would subjugate individual liberties. Those of us in public office should always remember that we can never err enough on the side of protecting individual liberty and freedom. We who have been elected to a position of public trust should be willing at all costs to withstand the buffets of a temporary storm that would trammel, or even extinguish, our freedom for the alleged common good.

[In 1976] we celebrated our 200th anniversary as a nation. We should remember that we celebrated not just 200 years of American liberty. In addition, we celebrated almost 800 years of Anglo-Saxon history during which men and women have been tortured and imprisoned, have fought and died so that we today can say what we want, do what we want and be what we want. In short, they have given us the blessings of political liberty. It is the greatest blessing anyone could ever give to us. All I ask is that you cherish it, preserve it, and protect it and pass it on to our children a bit more secure than we received it.

63. Point-Counterpoint: Affirmative Action

Shelby Steele
Benjamin L. Hooks

There seems no disputing the legacy of racism in American society. Affirmative action is a government program designed to correct decades of discrimination against disadvantaged groups. Shelby Steele, a black professor of English at San Jose State University in California, spotlights the liabilities of affirmative action. Affirmative action, he states, "tells us that racial preferences can do for us what we cannot do for ourselves." Benjamin L. Hooks, executive director of the National Association for the Advancement of Colored People (NAACP), argues that self-responsibility and self-help alone cannot ensure equal opportunity. Government must do its part through affirmative-action programs to end racism and discrimination. Both articles were originally published in 1990 in the *Los Angeles Times*.

Shelby Steele:
The High Price of Preference

In theory, affirmative action certainly has all the moral symmetry that fairness requires—the injustice of historical and even contemporary white advantage is offset with black advantage, preference replaces prejudice, inclusion answers exclusion. It is reformist and corrective, even repentant and redemptive.

Affirmative action is, among other things, a testament to white goodwill and to black power, and in the midst of these heavy investments, its effects can be hard to see. But after 20 years of implementation, affirmative action has shown itself to be more bad than good and blacks now stand to lose more from it than they gain.

In the crucible of the '60s, whites were confronted with their racial guilt and blacks tasted their first real power. In this stormy time, white absolution and black power coalesced into virtual mandates for society. Affirmative action became a meeting ground for these mandates in the law, and in the late '60s and early '70s it underwent a remarkable escalation of its mission from simple anti-discrimination enforcement to social engineering by means of quotas, goals, timetables, set-asides and other forms of preferential treatment.

What accounted for this shift, I believe, was the white mandate to achieve a new racial innocence and the black mandate to gain power. Even though blacks had made great advances without quotas during the '60s, these mandates, which came to a head in the late '60s, could no longer be satisfied by anything less than racial preferences. These mandates in themselves were not wrong, since whites clearly needed to do better by blacks, and blacks needed more real power in society. But, as they came together in affirmative action, their effect was to distort our understanding of racial discrimination in a way that allowed us to offer the remediation of preference on the basis of mere color rather than actual injury. By making black the color of preference, these mandates have reburdened society with the very marriage of color and preference (in reverse) that we set out to eradicate. The old sin is reaffirmed in a new guise.

But the essential problem with this form of affirmative action is the way it leaps over the hard business of developing a formerly oppressed people to the point where they can achieve proportionate representation on their own—given equal opportunity—and goes straight for the proportionate representation. This may satisfy some whites of their innocence and some blacks of their power, but it does very little to truly uplift blacks.

When affirmative action escalated into social engineering, diversity became a golden word. It grants whites an egalitarian fairness (innocence) and blacks an entitlement to proportionate representation (power). *Diversity* is a term that applies democratic principles to races and cultures rather than to citizens, despite the fact that there is nothing to indicate that real diversity is the same thing as proportionate representation.

Racial representation is not the same thing as racial development. Yet affirmative action fosters a confusion of these very different needs. Representation can be manufactured; development is always hard-earned. However, it is the music of innocence and power that we hear in affirmative action that causes us to cling to it and to its distracting emphasis on representation. The fact is that after 20 years of racial preferences, the gap between white and black median income is greater than in the '70s. None of this is to say that blacks don't need policies that ensure our right to equal opportunity, but what we need more is the development that will let us take advantage of society's efforts to include us.

I think one of the most troubling effects of racial preferences for blacks is a kind of demoralization or, put another way, an enlargement of self-doubt. Under affirmative action, the quality that earns us preferential treatment is an implied inferiority. However this inferiority is explained—and it is easily enough explained by the myriad deprivations that grew out of our oppression—it is still inferiority. There are explanations, and then there is the fact. And the fact must be borne by the individual as a condition apart from the explanation, apart even from the fact that others like himself also bear this condition. In integrated situations, where blacks must compete with whites who may be better prepared, these explanations may quickly wear thin and expose the individual to racial as well as personal self-doubt.

All this is compounded by the cultural myth of black inferiority that blacks have always lived with. What this means in practical terms is that when blacks deliver themselves into integrated situations, they encounter a nasty little reflex in whites, a mindless, atavistic reflex that responds to the color black with alarm. Attributions may follow this alarm if the white cares to indulge them, and if they do, they will most likely be negative—one such attribution is intellectual ineptness. I think this reflex and the attributions that may follow it embarrass most whites today, therefore, it is usually quickly repressed.

Nonetheless, on an equally atavistic level, the black will be aware of the reflex his color triggers and will feel a stab of horror at seeing himself reflected in this way. He, too, will do a quick repression, but a lifetime of such stabbings is what constitutes his inner realm of racial doubt.

The implication of inferiority that racial preferences engender in both the white and black mind expands rather than contracts this doubt. Even when the black sees no implication of inferiority in racial preferences, he knows that whites do, so that—consciously or unconsciously—the result is virtually the same. The effect of preferential treatment—the lowering of normal standards to increase black representation—puts blacks at war with an expanded realm of debilitating doubt, so the doubt itself becomes an unrecognized preoccupation that undermines their ability to perform—especially in integrated situations. Preferential treatment, no matter how it is justified in the light of day, subjects blacks to a midnight of self-doubt, and so often transforms their advantage into a revolving door.

Another liability of affirmative action comes from the fact that it indirectly encourages blacks to exploit their own past victimization as a source of power and privilege. Victimization, like implied inferiority, is what justifies preference, so that to receive the benefits of preferential treatment one must, to some extent, become invested in the view of one's self as a victim. In this way, affirmative action nurtures a victim-focused identity in blacks. The obvious irony here is that we become inadvertently invested in the condition we are trying to overcome. Racial preferences send us the message that there is more power in our past suffering than our present achievements—none of which could bring us a preference over others.

But one of the worst prices that blacks pay for preference has to do with an illusion. I saw this illusion at work recently in the mother of a middle-class black student who was going off to his first semester of college. "They owe us this, so don't think for a minute that you don't belong there." This is the logic by which many blacks, and some whites, justify affirmative action—it is something "owed," a form of reparation.

But this logic overlooks a much harder and less digestible reality, that it is impossible to repay blacks living today for the historic suffering of the race. If all blacks were given a million dollars tomorrow morning, it would not amount to a dime on the dollar of three centuries of oppression, nor would it obviate the residues of that oppression that we still carry. The concept of historic reparation grows out of man's need to impose a degree of justice on the world that does not exist. Suffering can be endured and overcome, it cannot be repaid. Blacks cannot be repaid for the injustice done to the race, but we can be corrupted by society's guilty gestures of repayment.

Affirmative action is such a gesture. It tells us that racial preferences can do for us what we cannot do for ourselves. The corruption here is in the hidden incentive *not* to do what we believe preferences will do. This is an incentive to be reliant on others just as we are struggling for self-reliance. It keeps alive the illusion that we can find some deliverance in repayment. The hardest thing for any sufferer to accept is that his suffering excuses him from little and never has enough currency to restore him. To think otherwise is to prolong the suffering.

Benjamin L. Hooks:
''Self-Help'' Just Won't Do It All

Weary of colonial rule, the angry activists stood on the banks of Boston Harbor on a cold December evening, lugged about 340 crates to the river's edge and pitched more than $10,000 worth of tea into the brisk, bustling waters.

The action of American patriots at the Boston Tea Party—which helped launch the American Revolution—was, incredibly, a pitch for affirmative action.

America's 18th-Century revolutionaries were affirming their right to self-determination and equal opportunity. Surely, we have not forgotten their rallying call, "No taxation without representation." Or Patrick Henry's impassioned, noble cry, "Give me liberty or give me death."

This is why we bristle at the current "controversy" over the value and benefits of modern-day affirmative action.

Affirmative-action critics suggest that such policies have not bene-fited poor blacks, have impeded the development of coalitions for social programs and have inhibited black Americans through a deep sense of inferiority.

These notions would be comical if they weren't so dangerous.

The irony is that these well-trained—if misguided—academicians have the opportunity to espouse such nonsense is itself due to affirmative action.

Would they have been trained at some of the nation's leading colleges without it? Would they be professors at predominantly white universities? Would they not feel the racist sting of Jim Crow's piercing whip? Would they be published in some of America's most influential periodicals?

They fail to realize that affirmative action is simply any action taken to ensure, or affirm, equal opportunity for oppressed or previously disadvantaged groups.

What's wrong with that? If a society discriminates against a people for centuries—enslaves them, lynches them, oppresses them, denies them access to jobs, homes, a good education, the political process, etc.—the just way to offer remedy is to give that people an equal opportunity.

The affirmative-action debate often gets mired in the issue of numerical goals and timetables, which are often disparagingly called quotas by critics and opponents.

The NAACP has never promoted the concept of so-called quotas. In fact, goals and timetables would never have been necessary if corporate and municipal leaders had been willing to follow the letter and spirit of the law.

Goals and timetables came about because of the failure of parties to be sincere in their efforts to provide equal opportunity. They were built in by judges who tired of the stances of interposition and nullification. The "we can't find any" argument was most often an attempt by corporate and municipal leaders to skirt the law. So judges had to construct goals and timetables to keep parties from making a mockery of the federal court. Critics who negate or ignore white America's duty to help solve black America's problems misrepresent the issue, mislead the public and subvert the struggle.

While we recognize that heightened "self-help" efforts among blacks will lessen our plight—and we at the NAACP promote such efforts—we believe what the Kerner Commission said more than 20 years ago still rings true:

"What white Americans have never fully understood—but what the Negro can never forget—is that white society is deeply implicated in the ghetto. White institutions created it, white institutions maintain it and white society condones it."

In their near-exclusive focus on what blacks should do, critics largely overlook the responsibility of government, big business and the courts in what is purported to be a fair and democratic society.

When blacks have done all they can to save themselves, white society must still do the right thing. If racism, discrimination and unequal opportunity pervade, lone efforts by blacks will remain virtually ineffective.

Certainly, critics who suggest that black Americans need to develop their individual skills and must not eternally regard themselves as victims are not totally wrong. Neither are they wrong when they urge young blacks to study, be disciplined and conscientious, and to reject the notion that achievement somehow diminishes blackness.

But they are totally wrong when they suggest, implicitly or otherwise that acknowledged black leaders are not pushing these concepts as well. We are. So, at best, these critics are doing no more than parroting our views.

I make hundreds of speeches a year in which I preach the gospel of hard work, discipline and achievement. Other leaders do the same. To suggest otherwise is a gross distortion and disservice.

While self-responsibility and self-determination must play heightened roles in our communities, we believe government cannot shirk its role.

I hasten to add that I am curious as to how this issue evolved as a controversy in the first place. Goals and timetables are as American as apple pie.

You must pay your taxes by April 15. You must not drive more than the posted speed limit. You must register to vote or apply for a passport by certain dates. Car manufacturers must ensure their cars meet certain emissions standards by certain times.

America operates by goals and timetables—and we all acknowledge and accept that. It is only when it comes to human resources that we bristle at this concept.

Naturally, we at the NAACP promote the concept of self-help. And the fact is that blacks have committed to self-help since the slave ships first docked on America's shores.

In 1990 America, we see the benefits of that self-help concept and affirmative action efforts. We have black mayors, elected officials, police officers, firefighters, journalists, judges, doctors, lawyers, captains of industry and thousands of other professionals.

More importantly, we have office clerks, secretaries, laborers, court employees and literally millions of everyday working people whose jobs are indirectly and directly linked to affirmative action and self-help.

These would have been the people mired inextricably in poverty and despair were it not for coalition-building and affirmative action.

The critics who benefited from but oppose affirmative action obscure the legacy of exclusion and discrimination that prompted such remedial efforts. They should be ashamed.

As the U.S. Commission on Civil Rights once noted, just as medical treatment is based on the diagnosis of an illness, affirmative action stems from diagnosis of a social sickness.

The remedy cannot be divorced from the illness. Critics write much about some "corrosive effect" of affirmative action but very little about the racism, oppression and discrimination that necessitates it—and which is much more corrosive and destructive.

We shall at the NAACP always promote self-help, but will never waver in our push to insist that government play its role and do its part. For how long? For as long as necessary.

64. *Texas v. Johnson* (1989)

On June 21, 1989, the U.S. Supreme Court decided by a 5 to 4 vote that Gregory Johnson's conviction for flag burning under a Texas statute was an unconstitutional infringement on his First Amendment rights. Justice William Brennan wrote the majority opinion, concluding that Johnson's conduct was designed to convey a particular message and was therefore constitutionally protected speech.

I

While the Republican National Convention was taking place in Dallas in 1984, respondent Johnson participated in a political demonstration dubbed the "Republican War Chest Tour." As explained in literature distributed by the demonstrators and in speeches made by them, the purpose of this event was to protest the policies of the Reagan administration and of certain Dallas-based corporations. The demonstrators marched through the Dallas streets, chanting political slogans and stopping at several corporate locations to stage "die-ins" intended to dramatize the consequences of nuclear war. On several occasions they spray-painted the walls of buildings and overturned potted plants, but Johnson himself took no part in such activities. He did, however, accept an American flag handed to him by a fellow protestor who had taken it from a flag pole outside one of the targeted buildings.

The demonstration ended in front of Dallas City Hall, where Johnson unfurled the American flag, doused it with kerosene, and set it on fire. While the flag burned, the protestors chanted, "America, the red, white, and blue, we spit on you." After the demonstrators dispersed, a witness to the flag-burning collected the flag's remains and buried them in his backyard. No one was physically injured or threatened with injury, though several witnesses testified they had been seriously offended by the flag-burning.

Of the approximately 100 demonstrators, Johnson alone was charged with a crime. The only criminal offense with which he was charged was the desecration of a venerated object in violation of the Texas Penal Code. After a trial, he was convicted, sentenced to one year in prison, and fined $2,000. The Court of Appeals for the Fifth District of Texas at Dallas affirmed Johnson's conviction, but the Texas Court of Criminal Appeals reversed, holding that the State could not, consistent with the First Amendment, punish Johnson for burning the flag in these circumstances.

The Court of Criminal Appeals began by recognizing that Johnson's conduct was symbolic speech protected by the First Amendment: "Given the context of an organized demonstration, speeches, slogans, and the distribution of literature, anyone who observed appellant's act would have understood the message that appellant intended to convey. The act for which appellant was convicted was clearly 'speech' contemplated by the First Amendment." To justify Johnson's conviction for engaging in symbolic speech, the State asserted two interests: preserving the flag as a symbol of national unity and preventing breaches of the peace. The Court of Criminal Appeals held that neither interest supported his conviction....

Because it reversed Johnson's conviction on the ground that [the Texas statute] was unconstitutional as applied to him, the state court did not address Johnson's argument that the statute was, on its face, unconstitutionally vague and overbroad. We granted certiorari, and now affirm.

II

Johnson was convicted of flag desecration for burning the flag rather than for uttering insulting words. This fact somewhat complicates our consideration of his conviction under the First Amendment. We must first determine whether Johnson's burning of the flag constituted expressive conduct, permitting him to invoke the First Amendment in challenging his conviction....

The First Amendment literally forbids the abridgement only of "speech," but we have long recognized that its protection does not end at the spoken or written word. While we have rejected "the view that an apparently limitless variety of conduct can be labeled 'speech' whenever the person engaging in the conduct intends thereby to express an idea," we have acknowledged that conduct may be "sufficiently imbued with elements of communication to fall within the scope of the First and Fourteenth Amendments."

In deciding whether particular conduct possesses sufficient communicative elements to bring the First Amendment into play, we have asked whether "[a]n intent to convey a particularized message was present, and [whether] the likelihood was great that the message would be understood by those who viewed it." Hence, we have recognized the expressive nature of students' wearing of black armbands to protest American military involvement in Vietnam; of a sit-in by blacks in a "whites only" area to protest segregation; of the wearing of American military uniforms in a dramatic presentation criticizing American involvement in Vietnam; and of picketing about a wide variety of causes.

Especially pertinent to this case are our decisions recognizing the communicative nature of conduct relating to flags. Attaching a peace sign to the flag, saluting the flag, and displaying a red flag, we have held, all may find shelter under the First Amendment. That we have had little difficulty identifying an expressive element in conduct relating to flags should not be surprising. The very purpose of a national flag is to serve as a symbol of our country; it is, one might say, "the one visible manifestation of two hundred years of nationhood." Thus, we have observed:

> "[T]he flag salute is a form of utterance. Symbolism is a primitive but effective way of communicating ideas. The use of an emblem or flag to symbolize some system idea, institution, or personality, is a short cut from mind to mind. Causes and nations, political parties, lodges and ecclesiastical groups seek to knit the loyalty of their followings to a flag or banner, a color or design."

Pregnant with expressive content, the flag as readily signifies this Nation as does the combination of letters found in "America."

We have not automatically concluded, however, that any action taken with respect to our flag is expressive. Instead, in characterizing such action for First Amendment purposes, we have considered the context in which it occurred. In *Spence*, for example, we emphasized that Spence's taping of a peace sign to his flag was "roughly simultaneous with and concededly triggered by the Cambodian incursion and the Kent State tragedy." The State of Washington had conceded, in fact, that Spence's conduct was a form of communication, and we stated that "the State's concession is inevitable on this record."

The State of Texas conceded for purposes of its oral argument in this case that Johnson's conduct was expressive conduct, and this concession seems to us as prudent as was Washington's in *Spence*. Johnson burned an American flag as part—indeed, as the culmination—of a political demonstration that coincided with the convening of the Republican Party and its renomination of Ronald Reagan for President. The expressive, overtly political nature of this conduct was both intentional and overwhelmingly apparent. At his trial, Johnson explained his reasons for burning the flag as follows: "The American Flag was burned as Ronald Reagan was being renominated as President. And a more powerful statement of symbolic speech, whether you agree with it or not, couldn't have been made at that time. It's quite a just position [juxtaposition]. We had new patriotism and no patriotism." In these circumstances, Johnson's burning of the flag was conduct "sufficiently imbued with elements of communication," to implicate the First Amendment.

III

The Government generally has a freer hand in restricting expressive conduct than it has in restricting the written or spoken word. It may not, however, proscribe particular conduct *because* it has expressive elements. "[W]hat might be termed the more generalized guarantee of freedom of expression makes the communicative nature of conduct an inadequate *basis* for singling out that conduct for proscription. A law *directed at* the communicative nature of conduct must, like a law directed at speech itself, be justified by the substantial showing of need that the First Amendment requires." It is, in short, not simply the verbal or nonverbal nature of the expression, but the governmental interest at stake, that helps to determine whether a restriction on that expression is valid.

Thus, although we have recognized that where "'speech' and 'non-speech' elements are combined in the same course of conduct, a sufficiently important governmental interest in regulating the non-speech element can justify incidental limitations on First Amendment freedoms," we have limited the applicability of *O'Brien's* relatively lenient standard to those cases in which "the governmental interest is unrelated to the suppression of free expression." In stating, moreover, that *O'Brien's* test "in the last analysis is little, if any, different from the standard applied to time, place, or manner restrictions," we have highlighted the requirement that the governmental interest in question be unconnected to expression in order to come under *O'Brien's* less demanding rule.

In order to decide whether *O'Brien's* test applies here, therefore, we must decide whether Texas has asserted an interest in support of

Johnson's conviction that is unrelated to the suppression of expression. If we find that an interest asserted by the State is simply not implicated on the facts before us, we need not ask whether *O'Brien's* test applies. The State offers two separate interests to justify this conviction: preventing breaches of the peace, and preserving the flag as a symbol of nationhood and national unity. We hold that the first interest is not implicated on this record and that the second is related to the suppression of expression.

A

Texas claims that its interest in preventing breaches of the peace justifies Johnson's conviction for flag desecration. However, no disturbance of the peace actually occurred or threatened to occur because of Johnson's burning of the flag. Although the State stresses the disruptive behavior of the protestors during their march toward City Hall, it admits that "no actual breach of the peace occurred at the time of the flagburning or in response to the flagburning." The State's emphasis on the protestors' disorderly actions prior to arriving at City Hall is not only somewhat surprising given that no charges were brought on the basis of this conduct, but it also fails to show that a disturbance of the peace was a likely reaction to *Johnson's* conduct. The only evidence offered by the State at trial to show the reaction to Johnson's actions was the testimony of several persons who had been seriously offended by the flag-burning.

The State's position, therefore, amounts to a claim that an audience that takes serious offense at particular expression is necessarily likely to disturb the peace and that the expression may be prohibited on this basis. Our precedents do not countenance such a presumption. On the contrary, they recognize that a principal "function of free speech under our system of government is to invite dispute. It may indeed best serve its high purpose when it induces a condition of unrest, creates dissatisfaction with conditions as they are, or even stirs people to anger." It would be odd indeed to conclude *both* that "if it is the speaker's opinion that gives offense, that consequence is a reason for according it constitutional protection," *and* that the Government may ban the expression of certain disagreeable ideas on the unsupported presumption that their very disagreeableness will provoke violence.

Thus, we have not permitted the Government to assume that every expression of a provocative idea will incite a riot, but have instead required careful consideration of the actual circumstances surrounding such expression, asking whether the expression "is directed to inciting or producing imminent lawless action and is likely to incite or produce such action." To accept Texas' arguments that it need only demonstrate "the potential for a breach of the peace," and that every flag-burning necessarily possesses that potential, would be to eviscerate our holding in [another case, *Brandenburg* v. *Ohio,* 1969]. This we decline to do.

Nor does Johnson's expressive conduct fall within that small class of "fighting words" that are "likely to provoke the average person to retaliation, and thereby cause a breach of the peace." No reasonable onlooker would have regarded Johnson's generalized expression of dissatisfaction with the policies of the Federal Government as a direct personal insult or an invitation to exchange fisticuffs.

We thus conclude that the State's interest in maintaining order is not implicated on these facts. The State need not worry that our holding will disable it from preserving the peace. We do not suggest that the First Amendment forbids a State to prevent "imminent lawless action." And, in fact, Texas already has a statute specifically prohibiting breaches of the peace, which tends to confirm that Texas need not punish this flag desecration in order to keep the peace.

B

The State also asserts an interest in preserving the flag as a symbol of nationhood and national unity. In *Spence,* we acknowledged that the Government's interest in preserving the flag's special symbolic value "is directly related to expression in the context of activity" such as affixing a peace symbol to a flag. We are equally persuaded that this interest is related to expression in the case of Johnson's burning of the flag. The State, apparently, is concerned that such conduct will lead people to believe either that the flag does not stand for nationhood and national unity, but instead reflects other, less positive concepts, or that the concepts reflected in the flag do not in fact exist, that is, we do not enjoy unity as a Nation. These concerns blossom only when a person's treatment of the flag communicates some message, and thus are related "to the suppression of free expression" within the meaning of *O'Brien.* We are thus outside of *O'Brien*'s test altogether.

IV

It remains to consider whether the State's interest in preserving the flag as a symbol of nationhood and national unity justifies Johnson's conviction.

As in *Spence,* "[w]e are confronted with a case of prosecution for the expression of an idea through activity," and "[a]ccordingly, we must examine with particular care the interests advanced by [petitioner] to support its prosecution." Johnson was not, we add, prosecuted for the expression of just any idea; he was prosecuted for his expression of dissatisfaction with the policies of this country, expression situated at the core of our First Amendment values.

Moreover, Johnson was prosecuted because he knew that his politically charged expression would cause "serious offense." If he had burned the flag as a means of disposing of it because it was dirty or torn, he would not have been convicted of flag desecration under this Texas law: federal law designates burning as the preferred means of disposing of a flag "when it is in such condition that it is no longer a fitting emblem for display," and Texas has no quarrel with this means of disposal. The Texas law is thus not aimed at protecting the physical integrity of the flag in all circumstances, but is designed instead to protect it only against impairments that would cause serious offense to others. Texas concedes as much: "Section 42.09(b) reaches only those severe acts of physical abuse of the flag carried out in a way likely to be offensive. The statute mandates intentional or knowing abuse, that is, the kind of mistreatment that is not innocent, but rather is intentionally designed to seriously offend other individuals."

Whether Johnson's treatment of the flag violated Texas law thus depended on the likely communicative impact of his expressive conduct. Our decision in *Boos* v. *Barry* tells us that this restriction on Johnson's expression is content-based. In *Boos*, we considered the constitutionality of a law prohibiting "the display of any sign within 500 feet of a foreign embassy if that sign tends to bring that foreign government into 'public odium' or 'public disrepute.' " Rejecting the argument that the law was content-neutral because it was justified by "our international law obligation to shield diplomats from speech that offends their dignity," we held that "[t]he emotive impact of speech on its audience is not a 'secondary effect' " unrelated to the content of the expression itself.

According to the principles announced in *Boos*, Johnson's political expression was restricted because of the content of the message he conveyed. We must therefore subject the State's asserted interest in preserving the special symbolic character of the flag to "the most exacting scrutiny."

Texas argues that its interest in preserving the flag as a symbol of nationhood and national unity survives this close analysis. Quoting extensively from the writings of this Court chronicling the flag's historic and symbolic role in our society, the State emphasizes the "'special place'" reserved for the flag in our Nation. The State's argument is not that it has an interest simply in maintaining the flag as a symbol of *something*, no matter what it symbolizes; indeed, if that were the State's position, it would be difficult to see how that interest is endangered by highly symbolic conduct such as Johnson's. Rather, the State's claim is that it has an interest in preserving the flag as a symbol of *nationhood* and *national unity*, a symbol with a determinate range of meanings. According to Texas, if one physically treats the flag in a way that would tend to cast doubt on either the idea that nationhood and national unity are the flag's referents or that national unity actually exists, the message conveyed thereby is a harmful one and therefore may be prohibited.

If there is a bedrock principle underlying the First Amendment, it is that the Government may not prohibit the expression of an idea simply because society finds the idea itself offensive or disagreeable.

We have not recognized an exception to this principle even where our flag has been involved. In *Street* v. *New York* (1969), we held that a State may not criminally punish a person for uttering words critical of the flag. Rejecting the argument that the conviction could be sustained on the ground that Street had "failed to show the respect for our national symbol which may properly be demanded of every citizen," we concluded that "the constitutionally guaranteed 'freedom to be intellectually . . . diverse or even contrary,' and the 'right to differ as to things that touch the heart of the existing order,' encompass the freedom to express publicly one's opinions about our flag, including those opinions which are defiant or contemptuous." Nor may the Government, we have held, compel conduct that would evince respect for the flag. "To sustain the compulsory flag salute we are required to say that a Bill of Rights which guards the individual's right to speak his own mind, left it open to public authorities to compel him to utter what is not in his mind."

In holding in *Barnette* that the Constitution did not leave this course open to the Government, Justice Jackson described one of our society's defining principles in words deserving of their frequent repetition: "If there is any fixed star in our constitutional constellation, it is that no official, high or petty, can prescribe what shall be orthodox in politics, nationalism, religion, or other matters of opinion or force citizens to confess by word or act their faith therein." In *Spence*, we held that the same interest asserted by Texas here was insufficient to support a criminal conviction under a flag-misuse statute for the taping of a peace sign to an American flag. "Given the protected character of [Spence's] expression and in light of the fact that no interest the State may have in preserving the physical integrity of a privately owned flag was significantly impaired on these facts," we held, "the conviction must be invalidated."

In short, nothing in our precedents suggests that a State may foster its own view of the flag by prohibiting expressive conduct relating to it. To bring its argument outside our precedents, Texas attempts to convince us that even if its interest in preserving the flag's symbolic role does not allow it to prohibit words or some expressive conduct critical of the flag, it does permit it to forbid the outright destruction of the flag. The State's argument cannot depend here on the distinction between written or spoken words and nonverbal conduct. That distinction, we have shown, is of no moment where the nonverbal conduct is expressive, as it is here, and where the regulation of that conduct is related to expression, as it is here. In addition, both *Barnette* and *Spence* involved expressive conduct, not only verbal communication, and both found that conduct protected.

Texas' focus on the precise nature of Johnson's expression, moreover, misses the point of our prior decisions: their enduring lesson, that the Government may not prohibit expression simply because it disagrees with its message, is not dependent on the particular mode in which one chooses to express an idea. If we were to hold that a State may forbid flag-burning wherever it is likely to endanger the flag's symbolic role, but allow it wherever burning a flag promotes that role—as where, for example, a person ceremoniously burns a dirty flag—we would be saying that when it comes to impairing the flag's physical integrity, the flag itself may be used as a symbol—as a substitute for the written or spoken word or a "short cut from mind to mind"—only in one direction. We would be permitting a State to "prescribe what shall be orthodox" by saying that one may burn the flag to convey one's attitude toward it and its referents only if one does not endanger the flag's representation of nationhood and national unity.

We never before have held that the Government may ensure that a symbol be used to express only one view of that symbol or its referents. Indeed, in *Schacht v. United States*, we invalidated a federal statute permitting an actor portraying a member of one of our armed forces to " 'wear the uniform of that armed force if the portrayal does not tend to discredit that armed force.' " This proviso, we held, "which leaves Americans free to praise the war in Vietnam but can send persons like Schacht to prison for opposing it, cannot survive in a country which has the First Amendment."

We perceive no basis on which to hold that the principle underlying our decision in *Schacht* does not apply to this case. To conclude that the Government may permit designated symbols to be used to communicate only a limited set of messages would be to enter territory having no discernible or defensible boundaries. Could the Government, on this theory, prohibit the burning of state flags? Of copies of the Presidential seal? Of the Constitution? In evaluating these choices under the First Amendment, how would we decide which symbols were sufficiently special to warrant this unique status? To do so, we would be forced to consult our own political preferences, and impose them on the citizenry, in the very way that the First Amendment forbids us to do.

There is, moreover, no indication—either in the text of the Constitution or in our cases interpreting it—that a separate juridical category exists for the American flag alone. Indeed, we would not be surprised to learn that the persons who framed our Constitution and wrote the Amendment that we now construe were not known for their reverence for the Union Jack. The First Amendment does not guarantee that other concepts virtually sacred to our Nation as a whole—such as the principle that discrimination on the basis of race is odious and destructive—will go unquestioned in the marketplace of ideas. We decline, therefore, to create for the flag an exception to the joust of principles protected by the First Amendment.

It is not the State's ends, but its means, to which we object. It cannot be gainsaid that there is a special place reserved for the flag in this Nation, and thus we do not doubt that the Government has a legitimate interest in making efforts to "preserv[e] the national flag as an unalloyed symbol of our country." We reject the suggestion, urged at oral argument by counsel for Johnson, that the Government lacks "any state interest whatsoever" in regulating the manner in which the flag may be displayed. Congress has, for example, enacted precatory regulations describing the proper treatment of the flag, and we cast no doubt on the legitimacy of its interest in making such recommendations. To say that the Government has an interest in encouraging proper treatment of the flag, however, is not to say that it may criminally punish a person for burning a flag as a means of political protest. "National unity as an end which officials may foster by persuasion and example is not in question. The problem is whether under our Constitution compulsion as here employed is a permissible means for its achievement."

We are fortified in today's conclusion by our conviction that forbidding criminal punishment for conduct such as Johnson's will not endanger the special role played by our flag or the feelings it inspires. To paraphrase Justice Holmes, we submit that nobody can suppose that this one gesture of an unknown man will change our Nation's attitude towards its flag. Indeed, Texas' argument that the burning of an American flag " 'is an act having a high likelihood to cause a breach of the peace,' " and its statute's implicit assumption that physical mistreatment of the flag will lead to "serious offense," tend to confirm that the flag's special role is not in danger; if it were, no one would riot or take offense because a flag had been burned.

We are tempted to say, in fact, that the flag's deservedly cherished place in our community will be strengthened, not weakened, by our holding today. Our decision is a reaffirmation of the principles of freedom and inclusiveness that the flag best reflects, and of the conviction that our toleration of criticism such as Johnson's is a sign and source of our strength. Indeed, one of the proudest images of our flag, the one immortalized in our national anthem, is of the bombardment it survived at Fort McHenry. It is the Nation's resilience, not its rigidity, that Texas sees reflected in the flag—and it is that resilience that we reassert today.

The way to preserve the flag's special role is not to punish those who feel differently about these matters. It is to persuade them that they are wrong. "To courageous, self-reliant men, with confidence in the power of free and fearless reasoning applied through the processes of popular government, no danger flowing from speech can be deemed clear and present, unless the incidence of the evil apprehended is so imminent that it may befall before there is opportunity for full discussion. If there be time to expose through discussion the falsehood and fallacies, to avert the evil by the processes of education, the remedy to be applied is more speech, not enforced silence." And, precisely because it is our flag that is involved, one's response to the flag-burner may exploit the uniquely persuasive power of the flag itself. We can imagine no more appropriate response to burning a flag than waving one's own, no better way to counter a flag-burner's message than by saluting the flag that burns, no surer means of preserving the dignity even of the flag that burned than by—as one witness here did—according its remains a respectful burial. We do not consecrate the flag by punishing its desecration, for in doing so we dilute the freedom that this cherished emblem represents.

V

Johnson was convicted for engaging in expressive conduct. The State's interest in preventing breaches of the peace does not support his conviction because Johnson's conduct did not threaten to disturb the peace. Nor does the State's interest in preserving the flag as a symbol of nationhood and national unity justify his criminal conviction for engaging in political expression. The judgment of the Texas Court of Criminal Appeals is therefore
Affirmed.

65. Point-Counterpoint: Flag Burning and the First Amendment

Rep. Charles Stenholm
Rep. Henry Hyde

In 1989 when the Supreme Court ruled in a 5 to 4 decision (*Texas v. Johnson*) that flag burning represented a constitutionally protected expression of free speech, the decision set off a "fire storm" of protest in Congress and the country. For example, George Will, a nationally syndicated journalist, wrote an article titled: "Obnoxious Acts Are Not Protected 'Speech.' "

Congress moved quickly to pass the Flag Protection Act of 1989, which was subsequently overturned by the Supreme Court in 1990. Spurred by this decision, President Bush and scores of House and Senate members backed a proposed Twenty-seventh Amendment to the Constitution. ("The Congress and the States shall have power to prohibit the physical desecration of the Flag of the United States.") A vigorous and emotional debate ensued about whether such action was in the public interest. Representatives Charles Stenholm, D-Tex., and Henry Hyde, R-Ill., capture the intensity of this debate in a point-counterpoint reprinted from the *Congressional Record*. In the end, the House on June 21, 1990, rejected the proposed amendment.

Rep. Henry Hyde: Amend the Constitution to Prevent Flag Burning

This vote today [on flag-burning] is an aspect of the cultural war, a kulturkampf that has been going on since the Vietnam war. President Carter referred to the mood of America as one of malaise. We are guilt-ridden. We have lost pride in our history, and we lack confidence in the future. The terms "respect" and "reverence" and a sense of the sacred, are now archaic, old-fashioned notions.

We who support the amendment to protect the flag have been driven to it by two decisions of the Supreme Court, not that we seek to do this lightly, but we who support that are called too much Norman Rockwell, and not enough John Lennon. However, I suggest to my friends who really want to think about this, we are never going to solve the problems of our society unless we can recapture a sense of reverence, a sense of respect toward ourselves and toward the American flag, one which symbolizes what we stand for.

Now, it is true this has been exploited shamelessly for political reasons. I regret that. Do not collectivize the guilt and blame all for the sins of a few. But by the same token, demagoguery is not the exclusive preserve of either side of this issue. The media has engaged in a fearful intimidation of those Members who support an amendment as the last resort for protecting the flag. We are called yahoos, cowards, cheap political creatures.

Last evening I watched a TV ad paid for by People for the American Way, with an actor from central casting wearing a hard hat over his coiffure, and telling Members there are more important problems than this constitutional amendment. "Leave the Constitution alone," he advised us. We have the budget, we have the homeless, and we have the S&L problem to solve.

Let me suggest something. There are some issues that transcend the marketplace. Man does not live by bread alone, the Bible tells us. As for free speech being in danger, do not worry about it, folks, watch HBO sometime, watch Andrew Dice Clay come into your living room and shout the most obscene things imaginable. It is on your television every night. Never worry, free speech is safe. Go to a porno movie in your town and ask yourself, is obscenity—has the term any content at all? Do not worry about free speech.

Many Americans cannot buy TV ads like People for the American Way. However, they are angry at the vulgarization of their country. They view this vote as an opportunity, a rare opportunity to take their country back from the streets. That is in danger, my friends. The gentleman from Colorado says flag-burning is not a danger to this country. Let me tell Members what the danger is: It is in the culture war, and we are losing it.

In Detroit, eight people were killed because the Pistons won the national basketball title, so some people rioted, to celebrate and eight people got killed. We barely noticed. We have the mayor of [Washington, D.C.] accused of smoking crack and more. A tidal wave of drugs, a tidal wave of murders, a tidal wave of muggings. There are more abortions than live births in the Capital City, in many cities. Does that bother Members? There is an AIDS epidemic sweeping the country. We have taxpayers funding filth and bigotry of the worst sort through the National Endowment of the Arts due to our loss of our sense of respect for the sacred. The success of the deliberate efforts to degrade and destroy the Judeo-Christian community standards that once defined our Nation, that is the danger that we face.

There are those who are very angry that the American Revolution was not the French Revolution. I suggest to my friends who worship at the altar of the first amendment, and I join them, but in the back of the church, because the right of free speech is not the most important right in that Bill of Rights. I suggest to Members the right to vote, the right to life itself are more important, and if we do not think the right to vote is more important than the right of free speech, remember Nicaragua or visit the Senate and watch them filibuster to keep other Members from voting.

Now, I suggest America is not the sole property of the professors and the columnists and the editorial writers. The veterans and their widows and their children own a piece of this country, too. This amendment does not change a word in the first amendment, not a word. It reverses a 5-to-4 decision, just as the thirteenth amendment in 1865, and the fourteenth amendment in 1867, reversed the 1857 case of Dred Scott versus Sanford, which had shredded the fifth amendment and denied to a black human being his rights as a citizen. This is not the first time. That was a good effort in the 1850's and this is a good effort today.

Freedom of speech is not absolute. It never has been in this country. There are laws against perjury, laws against slander and libel, laws against obscenity. There are copyright laws. This amendment says burning our flag joins those exceptions. Justice Rehnquist, a scholarly lawyer, said burning the flag is not a statement designed to communicate so much as it is a grunt designed to antagonize. Those Members who support an amendment have some distinguished company. Justice White, Justice Stevens, Justice Sandra Day O'Connor, Earl Warren, Hugo Black, a purist on the first amendment, Abe Fortas, have all expressed themselves that Congress has the power and Americans have the power to protect their flag. The Cross and Star of David deserve respect, of course, but not all Members march under the banner of the Cross or the Star of David. The flag is our national symbol of unity and our symbol of community, and it is unique in all of America. That symbol is transcendent.

Can we agree on that? Can we not get a symbol and elevate it and say that it unites us as a country, one Nation, indivisible with liberty and justice for all? I think so, and that is why it is different. That is why the VFW's and the American Legion, and the kids who pledge allegiance, look to us to preserve and protect the flag. Yes, you swear to defend the Constitution once every 2 years, but every day you pledge allegiance. So the two are not incompatible, but that is why it is important, and that is why the flag is different.

Now the ghost of Jefferson and the ghost of Madison have been summoned here to oppose this amendment, but I wish whoever has the power to summon ghosts would summon them from Flanders Field and have them come here and tell Members what they mean when they say, "We will not sleep if you don't keep faith with us." I do not know what that means, but I will tell Members something, I am one who despised the Vietnam Memorial. I thought it was a funereal ditch to go and be depressed in. I thought it lacked inspiration, a recognition of the nobility of the sacrifice made, and I really disliked it. However, I have been absolutely wrong. I go there and stand there and those names overwhelm me. Every one of them, a human being who loved this country as much as others do, and as much as you and I do. Then, imagine above that, another monument with the names of those who lost their lives in Korea, and in World War II, World War I, go on back, all the way to the War of 1812 and the Revolutionary War. All of those names are people we owe so much to. We owe them keeping faith with their sacrifice.

It is little enough to have the symbol of what they died for, the values they died for, special and protected. Let Members take the flag out of the gutter where the counterculture has dragged it. This is an opportunity not to get even with some creeps, but to say there are transcendent values that are important to every American, that unify Americans, that bring Americans together as a community, one Nation under God, indivisible. Is that not important? It is important, and we have to watch a falling flag and pick it up. That does not interfere or demean or shoot a hole in the Bill of Rights. It exalts the Bill of Rights.

That is what I am asking for. When everything is permitted and nothing is forbidden, I suggest to Members, Robespierre would be much more comfortable than Thomas Jefferson or James Madison.

No, we do not understand freedom if we do not understand responsibility. For every right there is a correlative duty, but we have a Bill of Rights, we do not have a bill of duties. We have 10 amendments that guarantee citizens all kinds of rights. How about one amendment that says we have a duty not to respect the flag or love the flag but just not to destroy it, not to demean it, not to defile it? Is that too much to ask, on duty? I think we need some duties and understand the responsibilities that go with the responsible exercise of freedom. The law is a teacher, and it can be a teacher here.

Well, Henry Adams, when he looked at the cathedral at Chartres, said it embodied the noblest aspirations of mankind, the reaching up to infinity. I do not say that the flag is a sacred symbol in the spiritual or religious sense, but I say it is a unique symbol, and too many people have paid for it with their blood. Too many have marched behind it, too many have slept in a box under it, too many kids and parents and widows have accepted this triangle as the last remembrance of their most precious son, father and husband. Too many to have this ever demeaned. That is not punching a hole in the first amendment. We are amending a decision of the Court that distorted the meaning of free speech and said expressive conduct of a particularly demeaning sort is protected, but if obscenity is not protected, if perjury is not protected, if copyright laws protect certain language and punish others, if we cannot burn a $10 bill, can we not protect the transcendent symbol of all that is good in our country?

Listen, the flag is falling. I ask Members to catch the falling flag and raise it up. In my judgment that does not demean the Constitution. It elevates us all to being worthy of the great country we live in.

Rep. Charles Stenholm:
The Flag or the Constitution

To say that I find flag burning vile or abhorrent is inadequate to express my disgust toward those who would commit such an act.

None of the adjectives which are being used today capture the temperature-raising, blood-pounding rage I would feel if some foul miscreant would have the nerve to stand antagonistically in front of me and ignite our beloved flag. If ever "fightin' words" were spoken, destroying the American flag would shout those words to me.

I am a firm believer in the potency of symbols. In the act of placing a wedding ring on the finger of my bride 29 years ago, I sensed the significance this symbol would have on the rest of my life. When I go to church on Sunday, I am moved by the symbols surrounding me in the sanctuary. When I first saw the Statue of Liberty, I imagined the overwhelming symbol this Lady has been to the millions of tired and poor who have fled to our land.

Likewise, our flag is a marvelous symbol of the United States of America and the ideals born and nurtured on this soil. But beyond being a national, shared symbol, the flag's symbolism can be intensely personal, in both aching and exhilarating ways. As an editorial in my district expressed, we have all seen the American flag draping the casket of a brave soldier who gave his life for his country. We have also all seen the flag waving for a victorious American athlete at the Olympics. This precious symbol can move us to tears of joy and to tears of agony.

I believe that our flag is a meaningful expression of the transcendent values which make our country the envy of the world. But if we begin chipping away at those values, if we reduce the freedom of expression, what then will that same flag symbolize?

I do love the flag because it symbolizes the United States, but I love the ideals put into words by the U.S. Constitution even more than the flag.

I agree with the Supreme Court majority which said, "Punishing desecration of the flag dilutes the very freedom that makes the emblem so revered, and worth revering." Conservative Justice Anthony Kennedy stated it best when he wrote, "It is poignant but fundamental that the flag protects those who hold it in contempt."

In the ideal world everyone would share a healthy respect for our flag and our country. But respect cannot be legislated or compulsory. We have personal freedom in America because we reject government-dictated patriotism. It's up to each American to discover a personal love of country and pride in our Nation. We Americans do not try to silence those who are wrong or who disagree with us, as we have just seen done in other parts of the world this month. We try to challenge those who disagree with our understanding of the truth. And if they refuse that challenge, then we let them continue to be wrong, or at least, to differ.

The question before all of us today is this: Which is more important, creating a new amendment for the Constitution to help protect the symbolic flag, or not infringing on the Constitution's first amendment guarantee of free speech?

Some have argued that burning a flag is not speech per se. A quick review of constitutional law shows that for generations the Supreme Court has held that not just spoken or printed words, but also songs, pictures, dances, performances, and even flags are forms of expression protected by the first amendment.

As we get into this legalistic debate over what constitutes speech it occurs to me that defining speech is about as controversial and elusive as defining the beginning of human life. In both cases, if I am to err, I would rather err towards an inclusive definition which extends protections to individuals, rather than excluding them from those protections.

It is true that the passage of this amendment would not be the first restriction of the first amendment. However, the limitations to free speech we have allowed before never involved speech which simply offends without doing further harm. Creating public hazards, precipitating material financial harm, injuring others through emperically provable falsehoods—these are forms of speech which do not deserve and do not have protection. However, speech which is offensive but which does no concrete harm otherwise should not be restricted by the same Constitution which guarantees free speech to start with.

I understand that in the Texas versus Johnson case which went to the Supreme Court [in 1989], the individuals who were burning the flag were also chanting the words, "Red, White and Blue, we spit on you." I have not heard anyone argue today that we should also enact a constitutional amendment to prohibit this offensive chant. But it is clear that the flag-burning actions of these individuals were simply an extension of that protected speech, offensive though it was.

More than 60 years ago, Justice Holmes wrote that it was the most imperative principle of our Constitution that it protect not just freedom for the thought and expression with which we agree, but "freedom for the thought we hate." I do hate the expression of those flag burners in Texas, but I am unwilling to mar the Constitution because of them. To do so only publicizes and elevates the symbolic importance of such puerile acts and individuals.

Our colleague Henry Hyde rebuts certain arguments by saying that there have been previous amendments which alter the Bill of Rights—that this, in fact, is not the first time we have amended those precious first 10 amendments. I will concede that point to my colleague, but I would also like to point out that when we have impacted the Bill of Rights in the past, it has more often been to expand the rights of the individual over the State, not to restrict the individual.

Let's look at some of those amendments. The 13th and 14th amendments protect the individual from slavery. The 15th amendment provided black individuals the right to vote. The 19th amendment gave female individuals the right to vote. The 24th amendment protected individuals wanting to vote from having to pay a poll tax. In fact, one example where an amendment sought to prohibit the individual from purchasing liquor was a dismal, unenforceable failure and required the Nation to act again to err on the side of individual rights through the 21st amendment.

That last bit of history shows us what happens when we attempt to deal with a narrow issue in this great, broad document. Actually we don't even need history for that lesson. Simply look at some of our current State constitutions and you will see documents which are no more than a collection of hundreds of statutes reflecting the concerns of the moment. The significance of these overloaded constitutions is diminished by narrow issues.

Our Nation has seen far more trying times than the current ones. We have experienced our soldiers having to fight wars on foreign soil, our own domestic war in which brother fought brother, economic depressions, political witch hunts, and much more. We have faced each of these troubled times without permanently amending the Constitution so as to restrict the rights of the individual.

Because of its broad concepts, our Constitution is as applicable today as it was 200 years ago. It is our job to see that it will still be a guiding force 200 years from now.

It is especially our job to see to the protection of the Bill of Rights, the greatest statement of individual rights anywhere. As Senator Mitchell has emphasized, every Nation has a government. Every Nation has a flag. Only the United States of America has a Bill of Rights.

How about just a little, harmless infringement of the freedom of such offensive speech, some people ask? I do not believe we can write a constitutional amendment that will be narrow enough just to fix the problem presented in the Johnson case without doing harm to the principle of free expression of the first amendment.

Is it so bad to make just one exception, this one time, just for the flag? The answer is yes; it is very bad. Principles are not things you can safely violate "just this once."

I have been told that if you drop a frog into a boiling pot of water, he will do everything in his power to escape that death-trap immediately. However, if the frog is first placed in cool water, and then the temperature is very gradually increased, bit by bit over a long period of time, the frog will simply keep adjusting. In fact, he will adjust so well, unaware of the danger surrounding him, that he will ultimately die in boiling water without seeking to escape.

Such is the danger of chipping away, bit by bit, at our principles. What comes next after the individual is restricted from burning the flag? In Revolutionary France, people were sent to the guillotine for speaking disrespectfully of the Nation, or chopping down a liberty tree. In Germany today, it is a crime to insult the words of the national anthem. Just a few weeks ago, the Soviet Union made it a crime to insult the

President. Is this the path on which we would like to embark by adjusting our principles?

Some folks have been surprised to find me on this side of this issue. Last year when the issue first arose, I cosponsored legislation to provide constitutional protection to the flag.

What hasn't changed for me over the past year is my disgust with flag burners. Like my constituents last year, I felt the immediate need to respond in some way, to express in some way how appalled I was by this unpatriotic, disrespectful activity.

What has changed for me is how I feel I should react to this flag burning. Again like many of my constituents, further reflection showed me that this issue was a complex one with competing values. I began to recognize that I was allowing myself to be manipulated by people—flag burners—who do not even deserve the time of day, much less a constitutional amendment.

In his dissent to the Johnson decision, Justice Rehnquist wrote that flag burning is designed not to communicate so much as to antagonize. I agree. But antagonizing works only if people allow themselves to react.

People who burn the flag do so to provoke those who love the flag. The San Angelo Standard Times recently made the excellent point that if a constitutional amendment passed, those same people would either continue to burn the flag—which might become even more appealing because punishment would transform them into martyrs—or they would find other ways to accomplish their task. How about getting copies of the Constitution and burning them? Or maybe replacing the words of our national anthem with foul language and singing that in public. Or perhaps submerging pictures of George Washington in a jar of urine. Their ideas will be creative, I am sure. Shall we amend the Constitution each time in response and keep the process going?

The Gregory Johnsons of the world are trying to get under the skin of decent Americans and make them betray the ideals of decency and fairness and tolerance. Most parents and teachers of children who occasionally misbehave learn early on that one of the most effective means to eliminate undesirable behavior is to ignore the child when he or she is doing it. If throwing a tantrum doesn't achieve anything for the child, there's not much point in continuing to throw it.

If, instead, we respond to the Gregory Johnsons by changing the charter of our liberties framed by Jefferson and Madison and some of the greatest thinkers of our history, then we will have allowed those ill-behaved children to change our national life.

The antics of a few shabby flag burners are of no significance, unless we give them significance. What they do does not matter; it will be forgotten. How we treat the Constitution will endure as part of our history, as part of the living text of our national charter forever.

Many have criticized us in the U.S. Congress for wasting our time on such a trivial, nonissue as this amendment. I, too, at times have thought it would be much more important to be spending our time on the budget, straightening up the savings and loan mess, passing a farm bill, enacting Davis-Bacon reform and all of the other business at hand.

As I have reflected on this vote over the past few days, however, I have come to believe that this issue has been very good for us, not only here in the House of Representatives, but all across the country. I believe that it is healthy for us occasionally to be forced to put ordinary, daily things aside and think seriously about our most fundamental national principles which have been guiding us for 200 years and which must continue to guide us into the next century.

I hope there is not a single Member today who will cast his or her vote nonchalantly, thinking this is simply a trivial exercise which may be politicized in any way useful. As I said at the beginning of my remarks, I know there are serious, thoughtful Members on both sides of this issue. But for any Member on either side who is evaluating this vote on anything other than what's best for our country's future, I say "shame on you."

I would like to close with the eloquent words of Charles Fried, former Solicitor General of the United States, who visited with me yesterday about this vote:

> There are many votes you have taken and will take in your political lives, and they will reflect deals and strategies and compromises, and they will all more or less be forgotten. But the vote you take on this, the vote you cast on amending the Bill of Rights, will stand as your monument for as long as this Country endures. Is any political advantage, is winning any election, really worth being known to your children and grandchildren and great grandchildren as one of the Congressman who drew a moustache on the Mona Lisa of our liberties? What Eichman and Johnson do will be forgotten tomorrow, if you will let it; if you add your text to Madison's and Jefferson's sacred text, that is a piece of vandalism whose mark will be with us forever.

Chapter 13

Domestic Policy

The shaping of public policies is often a mazelike process that requires many steps and involves many participants. The procedure typically has five major stages: (1) setting the agenda or identifying the problem; (2) formulating a plan to deal with the perceived problem; (3) adopting the plan; (4) implementing the policy; and (5) evaluating the policy's performance in meeting its objectives. Some policies follow closely these stages of decision-making; others gestate quickly and move through almost all the steps simultaneously. In other words, there is no fixed or single pattern of policymaking.

Similarly, no sharp lines divide domestic and international issues. In many areas the two are so interrelated that a scholar coined a new word, "*intermestic*" (from *inter*national and d*omestic*), to emphasize that many international problems affect domestic constituencies, just as many state and local concerns have international components.[1] Economic sanctions against South Africa, immigration reform, and drug trafficking are contemporary examples of issues that straddle the domestic and international arenas.

Notwithstanding their linkage, it is still helpful and convenient to distinguish between the two. This volume, therefore, contains separate chapters on domestic policy and on foreign and defense policies. Chapter 13 surveys several broad domestic issues, including budget and fiscal matters, the environment, health, our changing population, and the legalization of certain drugs. All appear destined to remain compelling contemporary issues well into the twenty-first century.

Taxes and Expenditures

Debates on taxes and expenditures are never-ending because they arise from differing perceptions of a nation's political objectives. The priorities reflected in national budgets (guns versus butter, guns versus guns, mandatory versus discretionary spending, domestic versus international activities) signify where the country has been, where it is now, and where it is heading. Disagreement among institutions and individuals over these questions is inevitable; it is part of the pulling and pushing among diverse interests to determine the mix of policies that best serves the common good.

The 1980s turned out to be the "economic decade," for issues of money dominated the national and international scene. Four unusual and troublesome developments shaped our economic discussions: (1) the huge national debt of more than $3 trillion; (2) massive annual deficits in the range of $200 billion, even during a period of economic growth; (3) the nation's transformation into the world's largest debtor (that is, the United States owes more to foreign investors than foreign investors owe to it); and (4) America's deteriorating competitive position in some areas of international trade.

The consequences of these trends are sharply disputed among elected officials and scholars. It is also unclear what can be done—immediately or in the long term—about these complex issues. There is, however, no shortage of theories about the nation's economic and fiscal situation. Analyst Jeff Faux, in Selection 66, surveys several major economic issues likely to dominate political and fiscal discourse throughout the 1990s. He suggests that when "it is the unanimous view of the experts that the economy is going in a certain path, take a look in the other direction."

National budget-making is a function of both Congress and the president. Because of today's shrinking "fiscal pie," these two branches of government have struggled in recent years to fund competing priorities and to find ways to curb the large annual financial deficits. High-level budget summit negotiations among White House staff, congressional leaders, and Office of Management and Budget (OMB) officials characterized national budget-making during the 1980s and early 1990s. For example, after five months of negotiations in 1990, Congress and the White House finally agreed to new deficit-reduction procedures and changes in the budget process. Scholar Louis Fisher, in Selection 67, argues that budgetary matters have gotten so complex and confusing that neither branch can be held publicly accountable for fiscal decisions. He urges that the president again assume full responsibility for national budget preparation.

Taxes and expenditures will remain at the top of the national agenda for the foreseeable future; the enormous federal deficit guarantees it. Interestingly, the solution to the deficit seems plain: increase revenue, cut spending, or devise some combination of the two. Part of the problem is that the voters appear to want to keep all their favorite programs but are unwilling to pay for them in taxes.

Legislators, to be sure, strive to protect programs that benefit their constituencies. "People shouldn't be critical of that," explained one House member. "We're expected to do it." [2] Getting reelected often depends on members' ability to "bring home the bacon." In Selection 68, "A Strong Arm on Spending," Dan Morgan describes how legislators' constituency interests influence decisions even in an era of retrenchment.

Environment and Health

Once perceived as largely a local or regional concern, the environment is now viewed by many as an urgent global challenge. The contemporary media are filled with stories about oil spills, ozone-layer depletion, the greenhouse effect, acid rain, toxic wastes, and deforestation, as well as related topics such as population growth, energy consumption, and economic development. It is clearly evident that the relationship between business interests and conservationists is not always easy. Their interaction covers the gamut from confrontation to cooperation. In Selection 69, "Wildlife Act: Shield or Sword?" the focus is on the clash between ecological and economic interests as Congress gets ready to consider amending the 1973 Endangered Species Act. The clash, simply put, is how to reconcile a community's economic needs, such as cutting down trees for the lumber industry, with the habitat requirements of an endangered species.

Another major contemporary concern is the escalating cost of health care. The demand for quality health care commonly exceeds citizens' willingness to pay for it. One reason for the soaring costs is discussed by Edwin Chen in Selection 70, "Doctoring, Dollars and Sense." Chen's thesis is that the advances of medical technology are the driving force behind runaway health costs. Given our society's aging population, it seems evident that this issue will remain a major item in the 1990s national agenda.

Population Trends

Demographers predict that America's population will be different fifty years from now, just as the population of today is unlike that of fifty years ago. Our society will experience even greater racial and ethnic diversity in the future than is now the case. California, for instance, is expected by the year 2010 to have a majority of non-whites (Hispanic-Americans, Afro-Americans, and Asian-Americans). The implications of a more diverse population are immense. For example, local, state, and national governments must strive even harder to absorb immigrant groups into the school system and workforce and to devise policies that will be increasingly sensitive to the broader cultural characteristics of our society. Nathan Glazer, in Selection 71 ("A Changing American Population: With What Effect?"), poses some important questions about the challenge of absorbing so many new Americans. Needless to say, numerous analysts are focusing on how the new racial and ethnic composition of America may shape, or reshape, the fundamental character of our society.

Drug Use

American society is also undergoing changes in the use of illegal drugs. More people are believed to be using mind-altering substances (between 35 and 40 million, with 6.5 million severely dependent); the illegal drug trade is estimated to total $150 billion annually.[3] Hundreds of thousands of people are arrested annually on drug-related charges. Given the size and scope of the drug problem, some public officials and analysts have suggested a different approach to its resolution: decriminalizing the use of some illegal drugs. Others are vehement in their opposition to this. In a point-counterpoint presentation (Selection 72), two professors of government take opposite sides on the legalization issue. In short, the problem of illegal drug use raises a panoply of issues, ranging from medical and legal to economic and political.

Notes

1. Bayless Manning, "The Congress, the Executive and Intermestic Affairs: Three Proposals," *Foreign Affairs* (January 1977): 306-324.
2. *New York Times,* December 31, 1983, 26.
3. *Los Angeles Times,* March 12, 1990, B7.

66. Covering the Economy in the Nervous 1990s

Jeff Faux

From the decline of the cold war to the rise of the global marketplace, the American economy is being buffeted by major forces that will affect its well-being into the foreseeable future. In this article for the *Columbia Journalism Review*, Jeff Faux reviews some of the major economic movements that are likely to affect the business front in the 1990s. Faux, president of the Economic Policy Institute in Washington, D.C. (a think tank funded by foundations, businesses, and labor unions), points out that the opening up of the American economy to international competition and the fallout from market deregulation during the 1980s will undoubtedly generate the major economic news of the 1990s.

Business and economics reporting was journalism's growth industry in the 1980s. It's a good bet that the trend will continue. With the cold war winding down, the marketplace is gradually replacing the arms race as the focus of international competition. And the widespread anxiety among Americans (including journalists) about their financial future can be counted on to maintain interest in topics—corporate profits, trade deficits, and the like—once considered too arcane for the morning edition or the nightly news.

No one can predict the big stories of the 1990s, but the underlying forces that drove the economic dramas of the 1980s—the savings and loan debacle, stock market booms and busts, leveraged buy-outs, corporate bankruptcies, regional recessions—are still in motion, and they will keep generating major news.

The most important of these forces are (1) the opening up of the U.S. economy to international competition, and (2) the fallout from the last decade of market deregulation. These fundamental trends are like geological shifts that eventually blow out into earthquakes and tidal waves. What follows are some seismic readings of economic movements that may rumble into the headlines of the 1990s.

The Squeeze on Incomes

This was the most underplayed story of the 1980s. The news media were quick to highlight the symbols of the "greed decade"—Ivan Boesky,

Leona Helmsley, and Nancy Reagan's wardrobe on the one hand, homeless people wandering the streets on the other. But fundamental shifts in living standards among the much larger middle class went relatively unnoticed. After several decades of stability, the share of income going to the middle 60 percent of American families shrank dramatically during the 1980s. Indeed, for *all* families, average combined income (adjusted for inflation) in 1989 was at roughly the same level as in 1979; after ten years this most basic measure of economic progress has scarcely moved. Real *wages* in 1989, meanwhile, were 7 percent lower than wages a decade earlier. A male high-school graduate with one to five years of work experience earned 20 percent less than his counterpart in 1979.

The reason that incomes have only stagnated while individual wages have declined, of course, is that more family members have been sent out to work. The two-earner family has not been overlooked by the press, but to a large extent it has been treated as a cultural phenomenon related to women's liberation and overachieving "yuppies." Indeed, the last five years have seen widespread press references to a "consumption binge," reinforcing the pop-Calvinist idea that the source of America's economic problems is mass hedonism. (In fact, the acceleration of consumer spending during the last decade has been almost exclusively concentrated among the richest 10 percent of the population, who benefited from the Reagan tax cuts and the speculative bubbles on Wall Street and in real estate.) At the same time, the growing need for a second earner elevated the search for decent child care into a national anxiety in the 1980s; it was also reflected in reports on alleged child abuse in day care centers and in the feature-story phenomenon of "latch-key" children.

The decline in real wages reflects the decline of U.S. competitiveness in the world. Lower productivity growth, an overvalued dollar, and aggressive targeting of U.S. markets by other nations led to the shrinkage of manufacturing industries and of the tens of thousands of services and suppliers that depend on them. While the press has covered the effect of decreasing competitiveness in industry reasonably well, it has by and large neglected the story of income stagnation. One reason is that business writers tend to spend time with corporate managers and economists who see wages as costs to cut, not as incomes to raise. Many major newspapers no longer even have a labor beat.

Another reason has to do with how the press reports newly released statistics; reporters take their cue for which numbers are important from the source—in most cases the U.S. government. Traditionally, the government gives prominence to its monthly release of the unemployment index as the basic measure of the welfare of those who work for a living. So the unemployment rate routinely gets a headline or a mention on the evening news. Meanwhile, the statistics on real wages, released without fanfare, rarely get highlighted, even though it is likely that the roughly 95 percent of the work force who are employed would be more interested in the behavior of their salaries than in the number of people who are out of work.

A continued squeeze on incomes could generate some of the big stories of the 1990s. One good bet is that there will be an increasing demand for the government to provide services that more and more families cannot afford by themselves—child care, housing, health care, and education.

And the curtain is about to drop on the Washington theater of smoke-and-mirror budgets. Rising demands for services and the cost of S&L bailouts are real and cannot be paid for with stage money. The squeeze on average incomes is also real, and resistance to taxes is still strong. With Republicans in the White House and Democrats increasingly beholden to business for financing their campaigns, there is not much political will to tax the rich at high enough rates to make a serious dent in the fiscal problem. So the only remaining significant source of income, an economic *deus ex machina*, is the potential savings from large cuts in military spending. The tug of war over the peace dividend—how much it should be, where to spend it, what to do with the unemployed defense workers and idle weapons laboratories—will be a continuing drama. Given that Pentagon largess has been scattered in congressional districts all over the country, there is the potential here for big battles within both parties.

A surprise story in the 1990s could be a revival of labor militancy. The breaking of the air traffic controllers union in 1981 shattered several decades of relative labor-management peace and ushered in an era of union retreat. Emboldened by the White House and pressured by import competition, employers forced wage-and-benefit concessions on workers throughout the decade. But financial stress on the family is building up. Increased militancy doesn't necessarily mean that unions will be successful in regaining lost negotiating power, but the much more aggressive and occasionally violent strikes by miners, telephone workers, and bus drivers in recent months may be straws indicating a more turbulent labor wind in the 1990s.

As two-earner families turn into three-earner families, another sleeper story could be the return of sweatshops and the growing use of child labor. This is the dark underside of the world of the small entrepreneur whose praises have been sung in the media throughout the 1980s. Reported federal violations of child labor laws rose from 9,000 in 1983 to 22,500 in 1989, even though the government cut the number of inspectors. As a result of a sweep of work sites in March 1990, the U.S. Department of Labor found some 11,000 violations, 1,450 of which were for minors operating dangerous machinery.

Trade Wars

Economic rivalry with the European Community and Japan will grow. Both are competitively stronger vis-a-vis the U.S. than they were at the start of the last decade and both are better positioned for the next one. Even without East Germany, the European Community is larger than the U.S. market and it will grow in strength and vitality. And recent gloating in the U.S. over the drop in the Japanese stock market notwithstanding, the fundamental position of the Japanese economy is awesome.

Japan, with a GNP only 60 percent of ours, is investing 50 percent more than the U.S. in new plants and equipment. Moreover, American children who have been posting poor test scores for twenty years are now entering prime working age. The combination of less-educated workers using inferior tools is a recipe for long-term trade problems.

Except in communities with industries hit hard by imports, the media tended to view early expressions of concern over trade as anti-Japanese racism by know-nothing workers and politicians. The term "protectionism" was used as if it were the name for a disease that needed no explanation. But as the loss of markets to imports has spread from textiles, steel, and other mature industries to computers and semi-conductors, the post-World War II support for free trade has faded, even among some prominent economists who were hard-core free-traders just a short time ago.

The 1990s will see new clashes between U.S. economic interests and traditional foreign-policy goals. For forty years, successive presidents have used access to the U.S. market to buy other nations' friendship in the cold war, even when their markets were closed to us. In the days when the U.S. dominated the world economy, the cost to domestic producers was small. Today, however, with imports threatening the survival of many U.S. companies, and with the threat of international communism fading, domestic producers will be freer to press for protection on the one hand, or for the right to export to old "enemies" on the other. One such early battle—over Pentagon restraints on the export of hi-tech machinery and equipment to Eastern Europe—has already begun.

The auto industry, hit by import competition and by foreign-owned factories producing in the U.S., will also be an early battleground. We can expect a revival of "domestic content" legislation (modeled after European laws, requiring that a certain share of the components of autos sold in the U.S. be produced in this country). The Chrysler Corporation, steadily losing market share, will probably return to the brink of bankruptcy, and that will revive demands for more systematic government assistance to industry. Phrases like "managed trade" and "industrial policy," which George Bush used as epithets in the 1988 campaign, could become economic buzzwords in the 1990s. Look for the Democrats to make common cause with alienated Republican industrialists.

A more inward-looking European Community will make it more difficult to penetrate that continent with U.S. goods, and the spreading power of Japan and the newly industrialized nations of Korea, Taiwan, Hong Kong, and Singapore will limit our exports into Asia. That leaves Latin America, whose economy will therefore become a source of important stories in the 1990s. Unfortunately, the Brady Plan, like the Baker Plan before it, has proven inadequate to remove the burden of debt from the Latin American economies—a necessary condition for the recreation of a market for U.S. goods.* Efforts to develop a U.S.-Mexico Free Trade agreement will also gather strength—and generate resistance from North American workers and smaller businesses threatened by cheap labor and Mexican nationalists.

Reregulation

A good place to look for future economic stories is any sector of the economy where regulation has been dismantled or cut back. Most regulations were put in place for a purpose—to balance interests or to curb socially destructive behavior. While lifting regulations may release new entrepreneurial energies, it also widens the scope for abuse.

The big deregulation story of the 1980s—the savings and loan crisis— should be with us for a while. If ever there was a predictable economic debacle, this was it: high interest rates inevitably put a squeeze on institutions like S&Ls, most of whose assets were locked up in long-term low-interest-rate mortgages. Deregulating the industry turned loose inexperienced managers who attempted to get higher returns by making high-risk loans. Raising the deposit guarantees only guaranteed that the U.S. taxpayer would pay the bill for the ensuing losses—$300 to $500 billion at the most recent tally.

But the lesson has only been dimly learned. Most of the press coverage of the S&L debate has focused on charges of fraud, influence-peddling, and bureaucratic incompetence. The scandals have obscured the *policy* failure. Since both Republicans and Democrats are implicated, since no one will get rich from placing more controls over the banking industry, and since depositors are insured, there is *still* no effective political pressure for reregulation.

* The Brady Plan and the Baker Plan—named after Treasury Secretary Nicholas Brady and Secretary of State James Baker respectively—are variations on the same theme: how best to alleviate the burdens of huge debts owed to foreign banks and other entities by many countries.

As a result, the combination of financial stress, federal permissiveness, and private greed that created the S&L disaster remains in the system. For example, the bailout created the huge public Resolution Trust Corporation (with deposits more than twice those of Citibank), whose job is to dispose of insolvent savings and loan institutions and their assets. The RTC is under great pressure to sell off these properties quickly—partly because of the agency's short (five-year) life span. Therefore, it is hiring private contractors to package deals. The potential for conflicts of interest in these fire sales is enormous, suggesting that we haven't seen the last of the headlines.

The insurance industry may produce the 1990s equivalent of the S&L fiasco. Many of the same conditions are present: risky junk-bond and real estate investments supported by low capital reserves, along with weak management, opportunities for fraud, and slack regulation. Unlike savings and loan depositors, insurance buyers are protected only by state guarantee funds, whose safety nets have not been tested.

A prime candidate for reregulation in the 1990s is the airline industry. Rising fares, deteriorating service, and the creation of airline monopolies around major city "hubs" have soured many businesses and political movers and shakers on airline deregulation. Another few years could see the demise of [other carriers besides] Eastern Airlines, [such as] Pan Am, and possibly several other independent carriers, strengthening the case for either more regulation or for breaking up the monopoly power of airlines over regional hubs.

Similarly, the breakup of AT&T will reverberate into the 1990s. There is a growing consensus that in order to accommodate the computer-based telecommunications systems of the future, America must rewire its homes and businesses with fiber-optic cables that can carry visual and digital electronic impulses, as well as sound. Japan and Europe are already ahead of us. This will mean titanic battles in Washington and in state capitals between the various industrial interests competing for shares of this business—AT&T, the "Baby Bells," cable companies, television networks, and computer manufacturers. The mixture of big money and politics could result in big headlines.

Cracks in the Federal Reserve Board

There are lessons in economic stories that are supposed to happen and don't, like the dog in the Sherlock Holmes mystery that failed to bark. Throughout the first part of the decade, the most respected economists around warned us that deficits were a major cause of inflation and that they would "crowd out" private investment and produce recession. . . .

The U.S. budget deficit was clearly the most overplayed economic story of the eighties. It still is. Despite the failure of the deficit to bring either economic or political disaster (Americans twice have re-elected administrations that gave them record deficits), both the business sections and the editorial pages of the nation's newspapers remain obsessed with the evils of government red ink. With some exception—on the right, *The Wall Street Journal* editorials; on the left, Tom Wicker of *The New York Times*—the substantial body of dissent from the conventional wisdom, that the budget deficit is the source of all our problems, is rarely covered.

One result of the national focus on the deficit has been to insulate the high-interest-rate policies of the Federal Reserve Board from criticism. Traditionally, political attacks on the Fed have come from populist Democrats reflecting the interest of small borrowers. But the Democrats find it more fun to blame interest rates on a Republican deficit than on the bankers at the Fed—particularly since a growing share of Democratic campaign money comes from the fiscally conservative business community. So in the press, Volcker and Greenspan have been getting a free ride.

This may change. There is a good chance that the 1990s will see rising interest rates. The opening up of Eastern Europe will increase the demand for capital from North America and Japan, as well as from Western Europe. When worldwide demand for capital increases, so does its price—interest rates. Secondly, if the Latin American debt crisis is to be resolved and lending is to be resumed, banks are going to require higher interest rates to compensate for past losses and additional risks. Add to this mix a possible inflationary rise in world oil prices, along with the increased dependence on foreign oil, and it looks as though some of the same circumstances that drove interest rates up dramatically in the late 1970s may be reforming. Rising interest rates could mean a return to old fashioned banker-bashing and the erosion of the press protection the Fed has enjoyed over the past decade.

If we've learned anything from the 1980s, it is that the financial markets have become increasingly divorced from the world of production, employment, and trade that they are supposed to serve. Predictions of disaster to the contrary, the U.S. stock market crash in 1987 and the [1990] bust in the Tokyo exchange represented the poppings of speculative bubbles, and had little effect on the underlying economic currents. And while the press tends to denounce the "short-term" horizons of American business, it makes its own substantial contribution to the notion that the purpose of business is not to invest and manage an enterprise that produces goods and employs people, but to buy a stock option at 10:00 a.m. and sell it at 10:30. The evolutionary nature of economic growth gets little attention. For example, when American companies stopped manufacturing color television sets, the story was treated as a series of isolated company decisions, explored mainly for their effect on profits and stock prices. Meanwhile, the Japanese were building up that same industry as a way to gain technical skills and generate capital for the next product innovation, VCRs; and the next, compact disks; and the next, High Definition TV; and the next . . .

Business journalism, often focused as a sort of extended investors' service, tends to miss the big picture. It is particularly myopic when it comes to the connection between economic growth and the quality and amount of social investment in such things as education, job training, highways, bridges, and public-supported basic research.

And as financial markets are increasingly divorced from production, financial journalism can be disconnected from the real worlds of readers and viewers. For one thing, the fundamental movements of the "real" economy are hard to spot, given the blizzard of information released daily by governments, companies, think-tanks, etc. For another, much of the data lags considerably behind reality. Economists will not agree that we are in a recession, for example, until the Department of Commerce's final estimate of Gross National Product has declined for two consecutive quarters (six months in a row). The practical effect is that a recession is not news until long after many readers have already experienced layoffs, plant closings, and general hard times. Also, the key statistics come out in the form of national averages, muting the shifting fortunes of individual regions and industries—where people live and work.

Faced with the bewildering array of numbers, the journalist on the economics beat inevitably must turn to "credible" sources to interpret the patterns. Herein lies another trap: because economic issues are perceived as chiefly of concern to owners and managers of business, the interpretation is often proffered by someone with something to sell.

Some self-interest is easy to spot—e.g., the stockbroker telling us that it is a good time to buy stocks, or the economist with the pharmaceutical company complaining about food-and-drug regulations. But the opinions of the university professor can be just as biased in the direction of an obsolete world view upon which his claim to expertise has been built. The solution, of course, is to widen the sources—the union shop steward as well as the company public relations representative, customers as well as sellers, the maverick as well as the much-quoted economist whose opinions regularly reflect the conventional wisdom.

The economic journalist might also take a leaf from the old business principle that the way to make money in any market is to buy while others are selling and sell while others are buying. When it is the unanimous view of the experts that the economy is going in a certain path, take a look in the other direction.

67. Federal Budget Doldrums: The Vacuum in Presidential Leadership

Louis Fisher

Major legislative budget reforms of the 1970s and 1980s have succeeded only in making the budget process more confusing and subject to deception, according to Louis Fisher, who expressed his views in an article published in *Public Administration Review* in 1990. Fisher, a senior specialist in separation of powers at the Congressional Research Service and a noted scholar on legislative-executive relations, argues that instead of appealing to institutional strengths these legislative reforms have bolstered institutional weaknesses. As a result, there is no clear perception of who is in charge of the national budget, so that the public is unable to hold either Congress or the president responsible and accountable for budget preparation and control. To remedy this situation, Fisher proposes that the full responsibility of budget preparation be shifted to the president.

The current budget process followed by Congress and the President is embarrassing both in operation and results. The Budget Act of 1974, which was supposed to correct procedural deficiencies, performed so poorly that Congress passed the Gramm-Rudman-Hollings Act in 1985 as the next-stage remedy. That statute, however, has been far more effective in sowing confusion and deception than in controlling budget deficits. The Bush Administration operates much like the Reagan Administration: the President offers little leadership for the budget crisis. For its part, Congress is reluctant to fill the vacuum for fear that it will be labeled "big spender."

Although it is fashionable to say that "the process is not the problem, the problem is the problem," the existing process is fundamentally defective because it fails to take advantage of the institutional strengths of Congress and the President. Instead, it feeds on institutional weaknesses. Make no mistake: process matters. A good process may not guarantee success, but it is a prerequisite for acceptable results. A bad process, which is what the United States government has, provides the wrong incentives for political institutions and virtually guarantees failure.

This analysis builds on the following premises and judgments: (1) the political process requires the President to play a central role in taking *personal* responsibility for submitting a budget; (2) presidential account-ability has been eroded by the Budget Act of 1974 and the Gramm-Rudman-Hollings Acts of 1985 and 1987; (3) the process since 1974 has encouraged the phenomenal budget deficits of the past decade and discourages efforts to deal with them; (4) the political process works best when Congress receives from the President a budget which presents responsible totals for aggregates (especially total spending and the level of the deficit), with the understanding that Congress will generally live within those aggregates while rearranging the priorities; (5) the current process is at war with those objectives.

No doubt there are other factors that drive federal deficits: a public that wants more services than it is willing to pay for, the growth of entitlement programs that add to uncontrollable spending, and perhaps the rise of "divided government," with one political party controlling the Presidency and the other controlling Congress. However, little can be done about those factors, while something *can* be done to make the process work with, rather than against, the institutional capacities of Congress and the President.

The Lost World of Presidential Responsibility

Throughout the nineteenth century there was little need for an elaborate budget process or explicit responsibility from the President. Customs revenues usually covered modest federal expenditures. Decades of budget surpluses allowed the federal government to liquidate the national debt inherited from the states and, after that burden was discharged, to distribute surplus funds to the states.

Under the pressure of mounting deficits at the end of the nineteenth century and the early twentieth century, Congress established committees and commissions to recommend more efficient practices by executive agencies. A commission established by President Taft recommended that the President be made responsible for reviewing departmental estimates and organizing them to form a coherent document to be presented to Congress. Nothing came of this reform during Taft's administration, but it set the stage for the Budget and Accounting Act of 1921.

The heavy costs of financing World War One precipitated the move to a modern budget system by the national government. Federal spending climbed from about $700 million before the war to $12.7 billion in 1918 and to $18.5 billion the next year. The national debt, which stood at about $1 billion in 1916, leaped to over $25 billion by 1919. To manage debts of that magnitude, members of Congress realized that new powers would have to be delegated to the President.

It is impressive to recall the attitudes within Congress at that time. The clear objective was to create a budget process to fit institutional and constitutional needs. The House Select Committee on the Budget explained its assignment: to determine "not what was theoretically desirable, but rather to determine what was practically feasible, keeping in mind at all times that to it had been committed the problem of recommending a system that would be in complete harmony with our constitutional form of government."

To accomplish that task, the Committee examined the institutional strengths of both branches and carefully thought about the methods that might make the branches coordinate their efforts more effectively. It condemned the lack of accountability in the executive branch:

> Practically everyone familiar with its workings agrees that its failure lies in the fact that no one is made responsible for the extravagance. The estimates are a patchwork and not a structure. As a result, a great deal of the time of the committees of Congress is taken up in exploding the visionary schemes of bureau chiefs for which no administration would be willing to stand responsible.

The Committee concluded that responsibility would have to be concentrated in the President. The only way to secure economy and efficiency in the expenditure of funds would be by placing "definite responsibility upon some officer of the Government to receive the requests for funds as originally formulated by bureau and departmental chiefs and subjecting them to that scrutiny, revision, and correlation that has been described." Here the Committee reached a judgment that was soundly based on constitutional and institutional considerations:

> In the National Government there can be no question but that the officer upon whom should be placed this responsibility is the President of the United States. He is the only officer who is superior to the heads of departments and independent establishments. He is the only officer of the administrative branch who is interested in the Government as a whole rather than in one particular part. He is the only administrative officer who is elected by the people and thus can be held politically responsible for his actions. Furthermore, as head of the administration it is to him that Congress and the people should look for a clear and definite statement of what provision in his opinion should be made for the revenue and expenditure needs of the Government. The requirement that the President shall prepare and submit to Congress annually upon its convening in regular session a budget will thus definitely locate upon him responsibility for the formulation and recommendation of a financial and work program for the year to ensue.

In fixing responsibility on the President, the Committee did not intend to subordinate Congress to the executive branch. Some of the budget reformers of that time wanted to copy the British parliamentary model in two ways: by concentrating power in the executive, and by prohibiting legislators from adding funds to the President's budget. It was proposed that members of Congress could add to the President's budget only by securing a two-thirds majority in each House or by obtaining the permission of the Secretary of the Treasury.

This model of parliamentary government was decisively rejected by the House Select Committee on the Budget. The budget was to be executive only in the sense that the President was responsible for the estimates submitted. From that point on it was legislative, with Congress retaining full power to increase or reduce the President's estimates. The Budget and Accounting Act was not meant to "impair either the authority or the responsibility of Congress."

The principle of presidential responsibility for submitting a budget is reflected in the statutory language. The Budget and Accounting Act directs the President to transmit to Congress a budget which shall set forth, in summary and in detail, estimates of expenditures and appropriations necessary "in his judgment" for the support of government. This notion of personal judgment is integral to an executive budget. Later I shall argue that it has been undermined significantly by congressional statutes, particularly Gramm-Rudman-Hollings, but also indirectly by the Budget Act of 1974.

The Decline of Presidential Responsibility after 1974

The institutional assignments to Congress and the President under the 1921 statute worked fairly well. Even during the Nixon Administration, when executive officials accused Congress of being "spendthrift" and operating on a national credit card, the record does not support the charge of legislative irresponsibility. From fiscal 1969 through fiscal 1973, appropriations bills passed by Congress were $30.9 billion below Nixon's requests. Over that same five-year period, backdoor spending and mandatory entitlements exceeded his budgets by $30.4 billion. In terms of budget aggregates, the figures were pretty much even.

Through its own informal and decentralized system, including the "scorekeeping reports" prepared by legislative staff, Congress stayed within the totals proposed by Nixon. Congress was able to adhere to the President's totals while significantly altering his priorities. Recent years, such as from fiscal year 1981 to fiscal year 1989, illustrate the same pattern. Congress rarely appropriates more than what the President requests. It usually appropriates less, while reserving for itself the right to shift program priorities. Rudolph G. Penner, former Director of the Congressional Budget Office, recently commented on the special capacity of Congress to do better under a decentralized, informal system than under a system that appears to be more coherent and responsible:

> I have always been struck by the fact in looking at the history of the [budget] process that it appeared chaotic in the late 19th century and early 20th century, but the results were very good in terms of budget discipline, yielding balanced budgets or surpluses most of the time, unless there was really a good reason to run a deficit.
>
> Now we have a process that looks very elegant on paper, but it is leading to very dishonest and disorderly results.

Penner identifies a crucial fact: the capacity of the President and Congress to decide budget issues reasonably well through the regular political process, disorderly as it is. The two branches perform less well when encumbered by the statutory disincentives found in the Budget Act of 1974 and the Gramm-Rudman Acts.

If the regular political system works so well, why did Congress bother to pass the Budget Act of 1974? Obviously some parts of the budgetary process did not function satisfactorily. There were serious concerns about the growth of backdoor spending (contract authority and borrowing authority) and the growth in mandatory entitlements. The unprecedented use of impoundment authority by the Nixon Administration triggered a monumental confrontation between the two branches. Deficits were growing, although their levels at that time (about $20 billion a year) seem insignificant when compared with contemporary magnitudes. The appearance of inflation (supposedly caused in part by those deficits) also convinced policy makers that the budget process needed fundamental reform.

I understand the reasons that provoked the demand for budget reform in 1974. As a staff member of the Congressional Research Service (CRS), I gave considerable assistance to various titles of the Budget Act of 1974. The issue that should be of interest now is quite different: did the statute of 1974 do as good a job as the Budget and Accounting Act of 1921 in reconciling the institutional and constitutional responsibilities of Congress and the President? If it fails that test, the fault is of overwhelming importance, no matter how sophisticated, fascinating, and impressive the technical operation of the 1974 statute might be. Recall that in 1919 the House Select Committee on the Budget wanted to propose a budgetary system "in complete harmony with our constitutional form of government." The 1974 statute and its amendments fail that basic test.

Probably no one in the 1973-1974 period anticipated the complex dynamics of budget reform. If Congress strengthened its role in the budget process, would that weaken the performance of the executive branch, particularly the leadership required of the President? There is no necessary cause and effect. Nothing in the 1974 statute prevents the President from discharging his duties, and yet the legislation has had the general effect of obscuring and weakening presidential responsibility.

The principal reason behind the undermining of executive responsibility is that the nation now has not one budget (executive) but two: a presidential budget and a congressional budget. Furthermore, the congressional budget is not one but many: the first budget resolution, the second budget resolution (now repealed), and various House and Senate versions. Under these conditions the phrases "below budget" and "above budget" no longer have meaning. The country lost a visible benchmark (the President's budget) to provide a definite reference point and political check for measuring executive leadership and congressional actions.

As a result, the public and the press now have a more difficult time keeping the two branches accountable. Consider the debate in the House of Representatives in 1983, when members asked whether a pending bill was below budget or above budget. Congressman Jim Wright, as House Majority Leader, gave this response:

> This bill is not over the budget; the amounts proposed in this amendment are well within the budgeted figures. The amounts that we have agreed to and have discussed are not in excess of the congressional budget resolution. That, of course, is the budget.
>
> Now they may be in excess of certain amounts requested by the President in his budget request of last January. But that, of course, is not the budget. Congress makes the budget; the President does not.

Wright's interpretation of the 1974 statute obviously parts company with the principles embodied in the Budget and Accounting Act. Although the framers of the 1921 statute jealously guarded congressional prerogatives, in the sense of giving Congress full freedom to increase or decrease presidential estimates, they wanted to fix personal responsibility on the President. They believed that presidential leadership and accountability were prerequisites for effective action by Congress.

The confusion of multiple budgets creates substantial costs for democratic government. Neither the President nor Congress can be held publicly accountable for the national budget. Both branches and both parties practice the "politics of blamesmanship" by attacking each other's fiscal record. Witnessing this crossfire, voters cannot fix responsibility. Instead of staying within the President's aggregates, members of Congress can raise the ceilings in a budget resolution and tell their constituents that they have "stayed within the budget." Even Presidents find this convention attractive. In 1985, President Reagan announced that he "would accept appropriations bills, even if above my budget, that were within the limits set by Congress' own budget resolution."

A stiff price is paid when a legislative process becomes overly complicated and confusing. Public accountability suffers. Congressman John Dingell voiced this objection in 1984: "What we have done over the past decade is to create a budget process that is so complex as to be incomprehensible to almost everyone. Most of the Members do not understand it beyond a superficial level. The press does not understand it. The business community does not understand it. The financial community does not understand it. And most important of all, the public does not understand it.

Members of both branches understand that not only is the budget process confusing but that confusion has a purpose: it deceives the public. Congressman David Obey, a member of the House Appropriations Committee, offered this assessment in 1982: "under the existing conditions the only kind of budget resolution you can pass today is one that lies. We did it under Carter, we have done it under Reagan, and we are going to do it under every President for as long as any of us are here, unless we change the system, because you cannot get Members under the existing system to face up to what the real numbers do. You always end up having phony economic assumptions and all kinds of phony numbers on estimating." After 1974, budgets submitted by Presidents and budget resolutions passed by Congress were chronically unreliable, regularly underestimating outlays and overestimating revenues. The result, year after year, are deficits far in excess of presidential and congressional projections.

The decline in presidential responsibility for submitting budget estimates has been dramatic. After forcing major changes in tax rates, defense spending, and domestic programs in 1981, President Reagan's subsequent budgets were largely ignored by both Houses. He remained a player by opposing tax increases and defense cutbacks, but he was unwilling to present a budget and defend it personally. Instead, he shifted the responsibility for budget preparation and deficit control to the legislative branch. Congress (including the Republican Senate) accepted this assignment and did what it could to bring deficits under control, but voters cannot hold accountable an inherently decentralized legislative body in the same way they can fix responsibility on a single President. Although Congress reasserted its control somewhat, it could never rectify the massive fiscal mistakes of 1981.

The absence of presidential leadership for the national budget continues in the Bush Administration. Instead of President Bush taking personal responsibility for the budget, U.S. Office of Management and Budget (OMB) Director Richard Darman tried to negotiate a bipartisan strategy with Congress in 1989. When that strategy failed, the blame fell on Darman, not Bush. No doubt such tactics spare the President, but that was not the purpose of the 1921 statute. Quite the contrary. It was to make the President, not the budget director, legally and personally responsible for dealing with the budget. The President's budget for fiscal 1991 magnifies the director's role even more. President Bush receives one page for his message to Congress. Darman uses 15 pages to promote his views. The framers of the 1921 legislation would be amazed. They expected the budget director to operate under the President's shadow, not vice versa. Of all the twentieth century duties expected of the President, elected by all the people and accountable to them, the budget is one of his most fundamental responsibilities.

Budget Action in 1981 and Resulting Deficits

The budget resolution required by the 1974 statute was praised because it represented a vehicle for centralized, systematic, and coherent legislative action. The authors of the 1974 statute assumed that Members of Congress would behave more responsibly if they had to vote explicitly on budget aggregates and face up to totals, rather than vote piecemeal on a series of appropriations and legislative bills. In 1974, as now, it was difficult to defend fragmentation, splintering, and decentralization, especially when reformers pressed eagerly for "coordination" and a "unified budget process."

The model of the executive budget looked appealing. The Budget and Accounting Act correctly assumed that presidential control and responsibility are enhanced by centralizing the budget process in the executive branch. Does it follow that the same benefits will flow to Congress when it centralizes its budget process?

There are substantial risks when Congress, possessing different institutional qualities, tries to emulate the executive branch. The President heads the executive branch, fortified by a central budget officer. There is no head in Congress, which is inherently decentralized between two Houses, two political parties, and a variety of committees and subcommittees. Congress created the Congressional Budget Office (CBO), but it could never have the same institutional power as the Office of Management and Budget (OMB). The executive branch is largely hierarchical. No such quality applies to Congress, which is essentially collegial in its operations.

Although the 1974 Act has generally weakened the President's budget, under special conditions it can strengthen it. Those conditions materialized in 1981. With the right President at the right time, the budget resolution can advance not congressional goals but rather the President's agenda. President Reagan attracted the necessary votes to gain control over the budget resolution in both Houses. The budget resolution became the blueprint for enforcing the President's priorities for a tax cut, defense buildup, and retrenchment of domestic programs. Once the White House seized control of the budget resolution, which embodied its overall budget strategy, subsequent action on the tax bill, appropriations bills, and the reconciliation bill became the necessary steps to implement White House policy. When the theory of supply-side economics failed to generate predicted revenues, the nation faced budget deficits of $150 billion to $200 billion a year. President Reagan entered office with the national debt at approximately $1 trillion. It now exceeds $3 trillion.

Would the actions in 1981 have happened without a budget resolution? Possibly, but President Reagan would have faced almost insurmountable hurdles in trying to enact his radical, supply-side economics with the pre-1974 budgetary process. Most likely his program would have been chopped to bits by successive committee and subcommittee action. The budget resolution gave him the centralizing vehicle he needed.

Budget analysts have agreed with that assessment. Rudolph Penner, as Director of CBO in 1985, asked: "Would the dramatic actions of 1981 have been possible without the process? It is a question that no one will ever be able to answer with certainty. I believe, however, that it would have been difficult to achieve these results using the old, muddled way of formulating budgets." Penner concluded that Reagan's objectives would have been much harder to achieve had he been forced to negotiate with the decentralized power structure that existed in Congress before 1974. Allen Schick makes a similar point:

Historically, the president has been at a disadvantage vis-a-vis Congress in their periodic budget conflicts. Congress excels as an institution that fragments issues and avoids decisions on overall objectives. Before installation of the congressional budget process, this fragmented behavior characterized legislative consideration of the president's budget. Appropriations were splintered into more than a dozen bills, tax legislation was walled off from spending decisions, and Congress did not have to vote on the totals. Members were able to profess support for the president's objectives while "nickel and diming" the budget in their action on appropriations and other spending measures.

The radical change in budgetary policy in 1981 sparked an explosion of budget deficits. It is highly unlikely that an error of that magnitude could have occurred with the decentralized process that existed before 1974. The incrementalism of that process functioned as an effective brake on extreme proposals.

The Budget Act of 1974 strengthened Reagan's hand by forcing Congress to vote on an overall budget strategy. David Stockman, Reagan's OMB Director from 1981 to 1985, explained how the centralized congressional process became a convenient instrument for implementing the Administration's goals. The constitutional prerogatives of Congress "would have to be, in effect, suspended. Enacting the Reagan Administration's economic program meant rubber stamp approval, nothing less. The world's so-called greatest deliberative body would have to be reduced to the status of a ministerial arm of the White House."

The danger of permitting a President, or the executive branch, this much control over Congress is reflected in Stockman's own assessment of the expertise available in the White House and OMB. After leaving office he admitted: "a plan for radical and abrupt changes required deep comprehension—and we had none of it."

The record of 1981 exposed serious weaknesses within Congress. Instead of following CBO's projections or substituting an economic forecast of its own, Congress accepted the Administration's assumptions. Although the Budget Act of 1974 offered Congress an independent technical capability by creating CBO, in 1981 Congress embraced the Administration's flawed and false premises. After passage of the Gramm-Rudman-Hollings Act in 1985, that congressional practice became habitual.

Gramm-Rudman-Hollings

The growth of the budget deficits after 1981, combined with President Reagan's refusal to offer constructive solutions, paved the way for the Gramm-Rudman-Hollings (GRH) Act of 1985. The statute symbolizes many things: an admission that the congressional budget process created in 1974 could not deal with deficits of that size; a conclusion that the political stalemate between President Reagan and Congress required a statutory framework to force action; and an unwillingness in Congress to delegate any additional authorities or powers to the executive branch.

When I testified before the House Government Operations Committee in October 1985, I raised a number of constitutional questions about GRH. I was particularly concerned about the congressional decision to dictate certain numbers (anticipated deficit) in the President's budget. It was my position that an executive budget, by its very nature, must reflect the numbers chosen by the President. To the extent that Congress determines ahead of time the numbers that go into the President's budget, as with GRH, it undermines the integrity and responsibility of the President's submission. I said at that time: "While it is true that the U.S. Code contains numerous directives regarding the President's budget with regard to format, deadlines, and other matter, I do not believe that Congress can tell the President what deficit to include. An executive budget expresses what the President wants, not what the Congress wants." The statute was held unconstitutional a year later, but the U.S. Supreme Court focused on the power of Congress by joint resolution to remove the Comptroller General, who was made responsible for the sequestration procedure.

Presidents have not raised a constitutional objection to the statutory deficit targets required by GRH. Executive compliance (or acquiescence) with the statute represents a political decision and does not settle the constitutional issue. The executive budget is a proposal and Congress cannot tell the President what numbers to propose. Under Article II, Section 3 of the U.S. Constitution, the President is empowered to give Congress "Information of the State of the Union, and recommend to their Consideration such Measures as he shall judge necessary and expedient." I do not see how Congress can interfere with the President's constitutional duty to present legislative proposals that *he* "shall judge necessary and expedient."

Nor am I favorably impressed that the executive branch raises no constitutional objections to the GRH deficit targets. The White House evidently finds it in its interest to relieve the President of the personal responsibility for submitting a national budget, given the magnitude of current deficits. GRH is a convenient way for the President to duck responsibility.

My testimony in 1985 also expressed concern about the provision in GRH that allowed the Comptroller General to draft a presidential sequestration order that the President himself could not alter. Under the terms of the original GRH, the President had to issue an order under his own name but without the slightest ability to control the content. I thought that procedure was repugnant both to separation of powers and to the principle of presidential responsibility. Again, executive branch accommodation in this case may be little more than an effort to sidestep responsibility for the budget crisis.

There are many objections to GRH. Its one-year focus encourages both branches to make short-run decisions that complicate long-run problems. The one-year preoccupation encourages both branches to play tricks, such as shifting costs from the current year to a previous year, or raising revenue in the current year at the cost of losing much larger amounts of revenue in future years.

The deficit targets also fairly well ensure that appropriations bills will be held to the last minute, awaiting the most recent projections. GRH thus provides an incentive for delays in the annual appropriations bills with subsequent reliance on continuing resolutions. These delays make it more likely that crucial decisions will be left to budget "summits," which "exclude most members [of Congress] and prevent the normal give and take of congressional deliberations." Most observers conclude that both branches regularly practice deceit in order to hide the size of budget deficits. Moreover, GRH relies only on outlay reductions to meet the deficit targets; it does not address the revenue side of the budget.

Equally important is the effect that GRH has on the political responsibilities of the President and Congress. With a statute operating like a "crutch," they can avoid difficult decisions needed to remedy budgetary problems. By claiming to comply with deficit targets in a statute, which may be out-of-date or irrelevant for a particular year, they fail to address reality as it exists. Because the public believes that the budget problem is being dealt with by GRH, there is less public pressure on the political branches to take meaningful steps. Senator Jim Sasser, chairman of the Senate Committee on the Budget, has explained:

> we have ended up with two sets of books.... First, we keep a set for the Gramm-Rudman game—and this is a useful fiction manipulated to give the illusion of progress—and second, we keep a set of books that are the real books. That is the real deficit. And we neglect getting around to doing something about the real deficit because of the Gramm-Rudman set of books we keep.

Congressman Marty Russo, chairman of the Task Force on Budget Process of the House Committee on Budget, made a similar point during hearings in 1990: "The President submits a budget that relies on very optimistic economic and technical assumptions and questionable savings proposals to meet the Gramm-Rudman deficit target. Congress attacks the assumptions and proposals as phony, but uses them in the budget resolution anyway." Congress uses the President's phony figures because honest figures (which are available) would increase the size of the projected deficit and make it appear that Congress is the "big spender." Once the President ducks responsibility by submitting a dishonest budget, Congress is politically bound to adopt the same mistaken assumptions.

Because of the inability of both branches to comply with GRH I, Congress has already found it necessary to enact GRH II. Unable to comply with GRH II, Congress might have to pass GRH III, pushing the problem of deficits further into the future. The drawbacks of GRH are so severe that both branches would be strengthened, not weakened, by removing the crutch. They would then have to rely on the dynamics of the political process, including political accountability, which is what the constitutional system expects.

The Need to Restore
Presidential Leadership

Repealing GRH would be one way to place greater responsibility on both branches. There is also a need to revive the President's personal responsibility for confronting budget problems and offering solutions. The system works best when the President provides leadership, including frank talks with the nation to educate voters on the problems that exist and the steps to be taken. That has not been done for many years.

The record strongly suggests that when Presidents take responsibility for budget aggregates (total outlays, total receipts, and the level of the deficit or surplus), Congress generally lives within those aggregates while imposing its own system of budget priorities. Congress can always alter those aggregates, and has frequently done so, but the institutional strengths seem to be these: the President takes responsibility for the aggregates, and Congress changes his priorities by shifting funds from one program to another. Each branch can discharge those duties very well.

How else can presidential responsibility for the budget be revived? Here I come to a suggestion that may disturb some participants in the budget process: repeal the requirement for a budget resolution. I do not see how the President can be made personally responsible for the budget so long as two budgets are proposed: one by the President, one by Congress. With one budget, the nation can fix a spotlight on the President and restore some accountability and personal responsibility. With multiple budgets, the roles and contributions of the two branches are obscured.

Much of the Budget Act of 1974 has served the government well. The Budget Committees are in a position to monitor the actions of the appropriations, authorization, and tax committees. The Budget Committees can direct the efforts of those committees in passing reconciliation bills. They can also play a central role in conducting scorekeeping operations (comparing the President's budget with congressional actions), monitoring the credit budget, eliminating some permanent appropriations to increase the controllability of the budget, and addressing other needs that require cross-cutting efforts. CBO has demonstrated its professional competence in assisting Congress in these endeavors.

But why pass budget resolutions? Do their benefits, however one might measure them, offset the substantial and inevitable weakening of the President's budget? Do the benefits outweigh the substantial and inevitable confusion that erodes public understanding and accountability? These questions are intended to push both branches in the direction of better fulfilling their constitutional and institutional responsibilities. The absence of a budget resolution should restore the importance of the President's budget, which would go a long way in helping Congress do its job and in permitting both branches to work together more effectively. If a budget process were constructed to exploit institutional assets inherent in the President and Congress, no need would exist for statutory mandates (as with GRH) or the extraordinary procedural innovations proposed in recent years (sequestration, capital budgeting, biennial budgeting, balanced budget amendments, line-item veto, and other proposals).

For the last decade, reforms have appealed to institutional weaknesses rather than to institutional strengths. By looking to Congress for comprehensive action, the unity and leadership that must come from the President have been unwittingly weakened. Creation of multiple budgets opened the door to escapism, confusion, and a loss of political accountability. Process is important. Changes in the process can encourage better discharge by both branches of their unique institutional responsibilities to the public. It is counterproductive to rely on complex statutory formulas and procedures that attempt to tell the political branches how to do their jobs. Instead, the political process and political leaders should be depended upon to confront the budget problem and deal effectively with it. It is a question of how much faith people have in the political system. Why not give it a chance?

68. A Strong Arm on Spending

Dan Morgan

Even in an era of fiscal scarcity, the appropriations committees on Capitol Hill remain important forums for influencing the flow of federal money to states and congressional districts. Needless to say, lawmakers are sometimes cross-pressured between advocating cuts in the federal deficit to highlight their "fiscal responsibility" and urging money and projects for their own constituents. Dan Morgan, a staff writer for the

Washington Post, where this article appeared in 1990, highlights how the appropriations committees employ a mix of "carrots and sticks" to mobilize votes for their domestic spending measures.

As deficit-reduction talks between the White House and Congress drag on inconclusively, the powerful appropriations committees that control the flow of federal money to home states and districts have been using a mixture of carrots and sticks to push through a package of record-size fiscal 1991 domestic spending bills.

In the Senate, Democratic and Republican leaders who helped the Appropriations Committee out of a budgetary jam several weeks ago were speedily rewarded with grants for their states in a new energy and water bill that is 13 percent larger than this year's.

But on Friday, committee Chairman Robert C. Byrd (D-W.Va.) applied a stick. He blocked language sought in another spending bill by Sen. Don Nickles (R-Okla.), who wanted the Transportation Department to resume Amtrak service on the "Lone Star Route" across Oklahoma, between Kansas City and Dallas.

"I would suggest it not be put in the committee report," Byrd declared abruptly. He then noted that Nickles, a member of the Budget Committee, had favored a sharp reduction in fiscal 1991 funds for government programs under the committee's jurisdiction. That was the end of the Nickles proposal, though Nickles can try to revive it when the measure reaches the Senate floor.

In the House, seven major domestic spending bills that add about $13.6 billion to Bush administration budget proposals passed with only minor changes, and with majorities ranging from 79.6 percent (rural development and agriculture) to 92.5 percent (transportation).

Republicans joined Democrats to defeat easily all 17 amendments to pare the bills by amounts ranging from 2 to 15.2 percent. The sole item deleted on the floor was $6 million for a tiny federal program that uses a network of radio telescopes to search the heavens for signs of extraterrestrial intelligence.

That record testifies to the popularity of appropriations bills, stuffed with programs benefiting home states. But [in 1990], said some Republicans, appropriators also have been using strong-arm tactics to discourage the critics of domestic spending.

One example is the behind-the-scenes maneuvering over a request by five Orange County, Calif., Republicans for $1 million in the 1991 transportation appropriations bill to fund design work on an 18-mile monorail system connecting Santa Ana, Anaheim, Costa Mesa, Orange and Irvine.

The earmarked funds—requested by Reps. Robert K. Dornan, William E. Dannemeyer, Christopher Cox, Dana Rohrabacher and Ron Packard—were included in the bill that passed the House July 12 on a vote of 385 to 31. All five voted for an amendment to cut the bill across the board by 2 percent. But with the exception of Dannemeyer, each departed from his usual practice and voted for the bill when it came up for final passage.

Dornan said that was no coincidence. He said he and the three others made an "exception" in agreeing to back the measure after Dornan talked with Rep. William Lehman (D-Fla.), chairman of the Appropriations transportation subcommittee.

Dornan also said he persuaded Dannemeyer to drop his plan to introduce an amendment on the floor to cut the bill by 5 percent.

"Bill Lehman is a gentleman and he just said to me, 'Can't you please ask Dannemeyer, if the bill's going to benefit Orange County, couldn't he drop the idea?'" said Dornan. Dannemeyer remembers receiving a blunter warning. "If I put in my amendment, the project was going to be deleted in the conference [that reconciles the House and Senate bills]," he said.

A congressional source confirmed the Orange County project had been discussed in the Appropriations Committee, where members from both parties agreed it was "inconsistent" to seek projects but regularly oppose appropriations bills.

A Packard spokesman said the congressman hadn't known about any deal between Dornan and the Appropriations Committee and had voted for the bill for other reasons. "A million-dollar appropriation wouldn't buy his vote," the aide said.

Rep. Harris W. Fawell (R-Ill.), whose rural and suburban district west of Chicago includes Argonne National Laboratory, said his criticism of appropriations bills has caused him problems with the Appropriations Committee.

On May 24, Fawell, speaking on the House floor, criticized several projects funded in the 1990 "dire emergency" supplemental appropriations bill. He said that speech resulted in his being "punished" when the 1991 energy and water appropriations bill began moving through Congress in June.

Fawell and two influential Illinois Democrats—Reps. Dan Rostenkowski and Richard J. Durbin—supported an additional $17 million for the Argonne Laboratory's work on advanced nuclear reactor research, to be conducted in its Idaho Falls branch. But when the bill emerged from a closed subcommittee markup on June 8, the extra funds were not included.

Fawell says he was assured by Rep. Tom Bevill (D-Ala.), chairman of the Appropriations energy and water subcommittee, that the extra funds were not included solely because the budget situation was tight and Argonne was already to be funded at the level requested by the president. But Fawell said he later was told otherwise by Rostenkowski and Durbin.

Fawell says he was "lectured" by Durbin on two occasions and told that "I was expected to bring home the bacon and couldn't get these 'watchdogs of the treasury awards.' "

Durbin, an Appropriations Committee member who specializes in improving Illinois' share of federal programs and projects, said: "Argonne has a great bunch of people who do very fine work, but this is a very tough budget year. Unfortunately, somewhere along the line Fawell made a statement that attracted the attention of the Appropriations Committee. It came back to me secondhand that this wasn't funded partly because of Mr. Fawell's approach. To have his hand out and beg for money beyond what the president asked for when he's slapping the committee with the other hand baffles me."

A Senate Appropriations panel later added the $17 million, but the item could still face difficulties at a House-Senate conference.

Fawell has continued to vote for across-the-board cuts in the spending bills. When the Treasury and Postal Service appropriations bill came to the floor he questioned a number of university and hospital grants that had been added to the General Services Administration account on behalf of members.

"A number of colleagues came over and made me feel like a skunk at the picnic," he said. "Even a friend said this is going to hurt you at Argonne." He said that persuaded him to forgo a recorded vote on his amendment to cut the unauthorized GSA projects. "I was shook up," he admitted.

Fawell said fear of the appropriators suffocates real debate on spending bills, despite the nation's "calamitous" financial condition. He has complained of a "sacred aura in regard to the Appropriations Committee."

During a July 18 floor debate on a proposal by Rep. Bill Frenzel (R-Minn.) to cut the agriculture spending bill by 7.7 percent, only a handful of House Republicans rose in support. As they did, one Appropriations subcommittee chairman after another drifted into the chamber to sit alongside committee Chairman Jamie L. Whitten (D-Miss.).

Soon six chairmen, including 6-foot-4 Marine combat veteran John P. Murtha (D-Pa.), chairman of the Appropriations defense subcommittee, were lined up like a football front line. The agriculture bill brings something to almost every county in America. Frenzel's amendment was defeated 305 to 115.

Later Frenzel said it may be harder to persuade Republicans to accept spending cuts than tax increases if both are included in a future deficit-reduction agreement.

"If you are for competitiveness, if you are for the future of this country, if you are for increasing a growing economy, then you have got to be for infrastructure, and infrastructure is not pork," said conservative

Rep. Tom DeLay (R-Tex.), extolling the transportation appropriations bill. The measure includes $30 million for Houston Metro, which is in DeLay's home city.

Sen. Frank R. Lautenberg (D-N.J.), chairman of the Appropriations transportation subcommittee, noted [in July 1990] that 77 senators had put in 486 requests for projects in their states. If all had been funded, the cost would have been $3.8 billion.

69. Wildlife Act: Shield or Sword?

Rudy Abramson

Federal protection of endangered species often pits conservationists against business interests. The former want the national government to do more to protect endangered species and to extend protection to other threatened wildlife. Business interests, on the other hand, emphasize the economic consequences of preserving endangered species, especially when such action jeopardizes a community's financial health. Rudy Abramson, a staff writer for the *Los Angeles Times*, where this article was published in 1990, examines one of the "crown jewels" of the environmental movement—the Endangered Species Act—and the impending battle between business and conservation interests over changes to the statute.

L ouiurus americanus luteolus, the inspiration and model of every American kid's favorite bed-buddy, the Teddy Bear, is about to be granted the protection of the United States government. Barring a reversal by the U.S. Fish and Wildlife Service, the Louisiana black bear—enshrined in folklore as the Teddy Bear after President Theodore Roosevelt passed up an offer to shoot a defenseless, tethered bear 85 years ago—will join the list of threatened species sometime next year. That will mean federal protection not only from hunters, but also from loggers, soybean farmers and developers who have been taking over the bear's habitat in hardwood forests of the bottomland.

So far, the reclusive black bear hasn't achieved the notoriety of the northern spotted owl, but the effort to save it from extinction is almost certain to symbolize a brewing confrontation between environmentalists and business interests over amending the Endangered Species Act in 1991 and 1992.

Indeed, the battle lines already are forming.

Conservationists contend that the government is failing to devote sufficient resources to protect officially threatened and endangered critters adequately and to extend coverage to thousands of others on a long waiting list.

But with human and wildlife populations coming into inexorably increasing conflict, business interests are preparing to demand consideration of the economic impact of saving creatures such as the spotted owl and the Teddy Bear.

"It's going to be the fight of the century," says Robert Irwin, a lawyer for the National Wildlife Federation, "and it's not going to be one-sided."

Interior Secretary Manuel Lujan Jr. concedes that Congress is in no mood to weaken the act, but he and some staunch supporters of the law are unhappy with the kind of crisis management exemplified by the spotted owl case in which Pacific Northwest timber exporting was restricted by federal law, in part to save the owl's habitat.

"Instead of being the protection that it should be for endangered species, the act has become a tool for people who want to stop some particular thing," Lujan says. "It was intended as a shield and not as a sword," he complains.

Although battles over the spotted owl and the celebrated case of the Tennessee minnow, which delayed a TVA dam in the late 1970s, have made the law controversial at times, its supporters contend that it has served well in thousands of tests over its 17 years.

The issue is an important one.

Approximately 600 domestic species are now listed as threatened or endangered, with 3,000 more plants and animals on a waiting list. Of that 3,000, about 600 are known to be at risk while the others are "probable."

Scientists estimate that about 100 species disappeared from the Earth between 1600 and 1900, but with the spread of pollution, the press of human populations, and massive destruction of the rain forests, projections are that an average of 100 species per day will be vanishing by the end of the century.

The battle that pitted defenders of the threatened spotted owl against the timber industry in Washington, Oregon and California provided a preview of the coming struggle over the Endangered Species Act.

As Congress pressed for adjournment, lumber-state Sen. Bob Packwood (R-Ore.) tried to get the Senate to adopt an amendment that would have bypassed several steps in the listing process and activated an emergency Endangered Species Committee—informally known as the "God Squad"—that has authority to exempt the spotted owl from the act's protection.

Conservationists, predictably, were outraged. "It was an assault on the integrity of the Endangered Species Act," says the National Wildlife Federation's Robert Irwin. "In the environmental community, the Congress, and the public, this act is viewed as the crown jewel of America's environmental statutes, and you don't mess with the crown jewels."

One of the problems with the 1973 legislation was that although Congress included language requiring development of a national wildlife conservation plan, the lawmakers set no deadline and no plan has ever been produced.

In a sharp critique of the listing program [in 1989], the Interior Department's inspector general reported that in the past 10 years, some 34 species on the waiting list have been designated as extinct yet never have received protection. The report recommended that, considering the urgency of the situation, the Fish and Wildlife Service simply make an en masse listing of all the waiting critters meriting protection.

Fish and Wildlife Service Director John Turner took issue with much of the Interior report. Some of the species cited as having become extinct while they were on the waiting list had actually disappeared before the act came into existence. And he argued that the idea of listing waiting species en masse was politically unrealistic.

The chief problem has been a chronic shortage of money, the inspector general concluded. On the average, a listing costs about $60,000, once officials get through the research, hearings, and requisite publications. That means it would take $38 million to list the 600 waiting species that are already known to be threatened or endangered. Listing the remaining "probables" would cost $78 million more. By comparison, Congress allocates only about $3.5 million a year for the listing program itself.

From the conservationists' viewpoint, the chief failing of the act is that there are not enough resources to implement it effectively, says Michael Bean of the Environmental Defense Fund. The $30 million to $40 million that the Fish and Wildlife Service has for the entire endangered species program compares to about $250 million in tax revenues turned over to the states each year for fish and game activities. "We have to spend more than the pittance we are spending now if we are going to do an effective job of species protection," Bean says.

"The [red-cockaded] woodpecker is a good example of why the act doesn't need to be weakened," says Bean. "We have too many cases like it, where a species is listed for years, but the population continues to go straight down the tubes in spite of this allegedly stringent and restrictive law."

That species of woodpecker, which roosts and nests in old growth pine trees from Texas around the southern crescent and up the East

Coast to Virginia, is a charter member of the list. But after 17 years its numbers are still declining.

Many of the species listed are still without a plan to provide for their recovery, while others are thriving.

Take the red wolf. After the last survivors were captured from their native habitat in the Great Smoky Mountains for a captive breeding program, more than 100 of them are living in the Alligator River wildlife refuge in North Carolina, and plans are being laid to return the species to the Great Smokies.

Similarly, black-footed ferrets are expected to be released later this year in the first attempt to start a wild population. The ranks of the great California condor, missing from the wild since 1987 when the last breeding pair were captured, have swelled to more than two dozen in captive breeding. Ralph Morganwick, an assistant director of the Fish and Wildlife Service, says he expects the first of them to be released "in a couple of years."

The bald eagle is doing so well that ornithologists are reviewing 1990 nesting and hatching data in preparation for a decision on taking the national symbol *off* the endangered list.

In four of its five areas in the lower 48 states, it is listed as endangered, while it is officially cited as "threatened" in the Great Lakes area.

If the recovery target of reaching a total of 2,600 breeding pairs is met, the Forest Service will propose to take the Great Lakes eagle population off the list, and to downgrade the others from endangered to threatened.

But some environmentalists are skeptical about any relaxation just yet. "Having 2,600 pairs is not exactly a secure situation," says John Fitzgerald, counsel for Defenders of Wildlife, another conservation group.

Still, some analysts insist that removing species from the endangered list is as crucial as listing them in the first place, at least as far as the legislation is concerned.

"When we have a success, we ought to delist and get on with it," Morganwick says. "People in the development community are concerned that when we list something, it never comes off, so to maintain faith with everybody, we ought to set reasonable targets for recovery, and when we reach them, we ought to move on."

Conservationists are determined to plug some of these loopholes when Congress begins formally considering the law's extension. "Unless we begin to grasp these problems sooner, we are going to collide again and again in a very painful way," Fitzgerald said. The confrontation over the spotted owl will be followed by similar struggles "until we do what is required in the act and develop a wildlife conservation policy, including threatened and endangered species."

But opponents, too, are preparing for battle. Conservatives, backed by groups ranging from northwestern loggers to Montana ranchers and Louisiana and Mississippi shrimpers, want to make the economic impact of federal protection a consideration in any new version of the law.

The U.S. Chamber of Commerce says one of its goals in the fight will be to make it easier to convene the Endangered Species Committee, a seven-member panel of Cabinet members and civic leaders from around the country, appointed by President Bush and chaired by Lujan, which has authority to exempt endangered species from protection if it considers the economic impact of saving a creature unacceptable.

Other issues will include whether all threatened and endangered subspecies have to be protected wherever they exist.

If Lujan had a free hand to rewrite the 17-year-old law, the Teddy Bear might never join the distinguished company of protected creatures. During the spotted owl scrap earlier this year, Lujan questioned the wisdom of protecting subspecies in all their habitats, at one point observing off-the-cuff that he didn't know the difference between red, brown, and black squirrels and that he considered the Endangered Species Act "too tough."

Environmentalists consider the Interior secretary's question of saving individual subspecies naive—even if politically compelling. "When we lose a subspecies, we lose a component of a species," said David Wilcove, a senior ecologist with the Wilderness Society, "a component which could be critical in the survival of the species itself. Subspecies are in a sense a future species, isolated populations which over time could evolve into species themselves. To ask, 'why save only some subspecies?' is like asking why we save all of Van Gogh's paintings. Why not save two or three of them?"

Although the secretary has not spoken out specifically on the Teddy Bear, it clearly is a case in point, because the animal is a subspecies of the common black bear found in all the major forests of the United States and legally hunted throughout the East. It looks enough like its cousins as to be nearly indistinguishable to the untrained eye.

The secretary clearly is uncomfortable trying to balance what he sometimes finds conflicting responsibilities to administer the act and to oversee the use of public lands. And he yearns for clear-cut answers to questions where politics, science, economics and philosophy collide.

"We ought to look at genetic testing," he said in an interview. "Is the spotted owl in Washington, Oregon, and Northern California the same as the spotted owl in the Southwest? Maybe it's not as endangered as it would appear . . . if these are the same creature, maybe they will adapt to another habitat."

The secretary says he is "very interested in the idea of putting an overall plan together." An important element in his vision of an "overall plan," however, is broadened authority for the God Squad, which is hardly what environmentalists have in mind.

Ironically, Lujan's argument that the act is too strong sometimes brings him close to agreement with some environmentalists who contend that it is too weak. Both believe that it would be effective to designate endangered habitats or even endangered ecosystems.

When the government finally extends its protection to the Louisiana black bear, the Teddy Bear will join other glamorous symbols of the vanishing wilderness such as the bald eagle and the timber wolf.

The conventional wisdom is that the next great collision between environmental and economic interests will be over the Pacific salmon.

For the Teddy Bear, designation as a threatened species would come more than 15 years after Ronald Nowak, a U.S. Fish and Wildlife Service zoologist, first realized that the species was at risk.

Nowak took an interest in the precarious existence of the Louisiana black bear in the mid-1970s, realizing that it was about to be exterminated by the conversion of its habitat in the bottomland hardwood forests into soybean fields.

On top of that, the state still was sanctioning a yearly bear hunt. To make sure there was something to shoot, it imported 165 Minnesota bears, which had made nuisances of themselves at garbage dumps.

The number of Louisiana black bears isn't known, but there is little doubt that they have dwindled well past the danger point.

70. Doctoring, Dollars and Sense

Edwin Chen

Runaway health care costs are a contemporary phenomenon that worries governmental leaders and medical specialists. Patients want the best medical care possible, and doctors want to provide it. The dilemma is who will pay for these ever-increasing costs and how might they be reduced? In his 1990 article in the *Los Angeles Times*, journalist Edwin Chen explores one facet of the rising-cost conundrum—sophisticated medical technology. He reports that a consensus is emerging in the health-care community that "medical technology is a major driving force behind runaway health-care costs, now approaching 12% of the gross national product."

When the federal government in 1984 approved a futuristic shock wave machine that could pulverize kidney stones, doctors nationwide saw new hope that hundreds of thousands of Americans could be helped without surgery.

What Darrell Lewis saw was a gold mine—enormous profits for his employer, Humana Inc., which owns 81 hospitals from California to Florida. "The demographics were great," said Lewis, who is in charge of assessing new technologies for Humana.

As a preemptive strike against competitors, the hospital chain immediately bought six of the big machines, called lithotripters, at $1.6 million each.

Humana's rush was understandable. America was in the middle of what one health economist calls "a medical technology arms race" in which few questions were asked about a new technology's effectiveness or cost.

But no more.

A consensus is emerging that medical technology is a major driving force behind runaway health-care costs, now approaching 12% of the gross national product.

And government regulators, employers, insurers and health care providers are proclaiming an unprecedented resolve to assess emerging medical technologies more closely and to encourage more appropriate use of existing ones—all with an eye on constraining costs.

"Things in the past developed without a whole lot of questions being asked about their efficacy and effect on patient health," said Wayne I. Roe, a Washington-based health-care consultant. "But the squeeze is on."

"The issue with medical technology is not necessarily whether it is good or bad," added Sanford Schwarz, a University of Pennsylvania internist and health economist. "Most technologies are good—under selected circumstances. The challenge is to define the clinical conditions under which a technology is appropriate."

Yet with few guidelines and little agreement on usage, experts see no sign that doctors or patients are ready to abandon the spare-nothing approach to treatment.

"Even now, I think the old philosophy still prevails, by and large," Roe said. "If you can make something that works, it's still very difficult for it not to be developed and used."

"That's the basic problem," Schwarz agreed. "Nobody is willing to control costs when it's them or their relatives involved. The major component missing right now is a lack of consensus or political will to face what is appropriate medical care."

Experts say there could be no better time than now to begin performing more rigorous technology assessment. A veritable flood of products is poised to enter the marketplace in the next decade.

"Ideally, technology should lower costs, but it doesn't," said Dr. Ralph W. Schaffarzick, retired vice president and medical director of California Blue Shield. "Technologies themselves are usually expensive, and utilization of them is often very great because doctors and the public want access to all the newest things."

Schaffarzick said a new product seldom replaces an older one. Instead, doctors often use both the new and the old.

For instance, the CT scanner or the magnetic resonance imager may be much more accurate than X-ray at detecting blood clots in the skull, but Schaffarzick said the physicians "more often than not" use all three. The expenses mount quickly—up to $500 for each use of a CT scanner, $900 for a magnetic resonance image and $60 for an X-ray.

"Some doctors still are not confident with the newer technologies," he said. "And there's always the lurking fear of malpractice—or at least, the excuse of it."

Unquestionably, technology has done much to prolong lives and improve the quality of life.

Yet as Americans live longer, their changing medical needs are dictating more and newer types of treatments, especially for the afflictions of aging. For instance, a person today with heart disease might live long enough, thanks to new medications, to develop Alzheimer's Disease or other ailments.

"It's going to cost more per capita. No question," said William McGiveny, director of the American Medical Assn.'s division of health-care technology.

In addition to brain scans and magnetic resonance imaging, the 20-year boom in medical technology has ushered in devices such as the heart pacemaker, dialysis and a machine that could temporarily take over the functions of the heart during bypass surgery. Those decades also saw a whole generation of new heart drugs and countless biotechnology-based diagnostic and monitoring devices.

"We had a major explosion in innovations," recalled Roe, president of Health Technology Associates.

"But these things were being turned loose without adequate assessment," Schaffarzick said.

During much of that time, the health-care financing system was "rich and overwhelmingly passive," Roe added. "And physicians got used to having lots of new tools. Their income went up every time they got a new tool, so all the financial barriers either broke down or weren't there in the first place."

"What the '90s portend," he said, "are questions, like: Is this surgical procedure of any value versus some medical alternative? Is this new way of monitoring the heart or the blood gases with an invasive, continuous sensor any better than the old way of doing it? Everybody should be asking these questions."

Among those developing standards and guidelines on efficacy and appropriate use of technology are the influential Blue Cross-Blue Shield Assn. and the federal government's Health Care Financing Administration.

"It's everyone's responsibility to look closely at what we are spending money on," said Susan Gleeson, executive director of technology management for Blue Cross-Blue Shield.

The precise extent to which technology is responsible for the rise in medical care costs is unknown. Some estimates put it as high as 50% if "hidden" costs are taken into account.

"There is a general consensus that it's a significant contributor," said Schwarz, who was the first director of the American College of Physicians' Clinical Efficacy Assessment Project and now heads Penn's Leonard Davis Institute of Health Economics.

One dissenter is Dale A. Rublee, a senior AMA policy analyst. "I think technology gets a bad rap in being the scapegoat," he said. "We don't know why health-care costs are rising. Technology is far and away for the good of society."

One way to ensure more appropriate use of technology, experts say, is to adopt a policy of "selective coverage." That was the approach of California Blue Shield when it said it would cover a heart transplant only if it was performed at Stanford University or some other institution with a record of success in such surgery.

"More and more, this will happen," predicted John R. Ball, medical director of the American College of Physicians, which has been a pioneering proponent of rigorous technology assessment.

Schaffarzick called selective coverage a form of health-care rationing that made sense. He said that the current situation—37 million Americans without insurance and 50 million more who are under-insured—is an "unspoken rationing that puts so many people at risk."

"What people need to understand is what kind of rationing is best," Ball said. "We already do it now. We can't hide that fact."

The new-found resolve to manage the proliferation of new medical technologies comes at a propitious time, experts say. The 1990s will witness another explosion of advances, such as the use of lasers to sculpt the corneas of near-sighted people or the ability to identify defective genes in an unfertilized human egg.

"The big issue will be how to pay for these new technologies," said Mark Brand of Amgen Inc., a Thousand Oaks, Calif., biotechnology firm.

Roe cited the example of miniature sensors that will soon be available to monitor the bloodstream.

"But before these devices, which can be pretty expensive, get to the marketplace," Roe said, "somebody's got to ask: What good is it going to be to have a $2,000 sensor living inside someone? I think there will be more delays of new things getting to the marketplace."

Beyond attempting to weed out emerging technologies that may be superfluous or exorbitantly expensive, health planners say, many technologies in current use also need to be assessed.

That also goes for the seemingly endless new uses being found for existing technologies. A classic example of that is the kidney lithotripter, which became the rage in the mid-1980s at Humana and elsewhere.

U.S. hospitals and physician partnerships bought about 250 lithotripters. As the number of patients making use of the machines leveled off to about 125,000 annually, lithotripter owners began looking for other uses for their expensive machines.

Soon they focused on the 1 million Americans who each year experience painful attacks from lumps of cholesterol that form in the gallbladder and block the bile ducts that connect the liver to the digestive tract.

The prospect of using shock waves to break up gallstones was indeed appealing. About 600,000 Americans each year have their gallbladders removed, at a cost of more than $6 billion a year. If the shock wave technique worked, it would be cheaper, faster and less painful than surgery.

But studies from clinical trials now suggest that lithotripters worked for only 10% to 25% of gallstone patients. The treatments also caused disturbing side effects, including blood in the urine and high blood pressure. [In 1989], a Food and Drug Administration advisory panel refused to approve the technology for gallstone treatment.

Since then, physicians have developed an experimental way of removing the gallbladder by using a combination of existing technologies—the laparoscopy and the laser.

Laparoscopy, used widely by gynecologists and knee surgeons, involves the use of a miniature camera attached at the end of a tube that is inserted through a small incision into the body, where it sends images back to a video screen. It enables physicians to use a laser to detach the gallbladder from the liver and remove it.

If the technique pans out, it would allow for a speedier recovery than conventional surgery, according to its leading proponent, Dr. Christopher J. Daly of Pittsburgh. Such an operation would cost about $1,350—roughly half that of a conventional gallbladder removal. He predicted in the January [1990] issue of the newsletter "Health Technology Trends" that perhaps 85% of gallstone patients can be treated with the new procedure.

And as more physicians become trained in laparoscopy, Daly predicted, hospital administrators and technology assessors can expect a rush of new demands from the medical staff for lasers and laparoscopes.

But such requests would have to pass a new test, said Louis B. Hays, recent acting administrator of the Health Care Financing Administration, which sets Medicare payment policies.

"The question will be whether a procedure should be used at all," he said. "We're getting more and more into the question of effectiveness. That's an idea whose time has really come."

No one thinks it will be easy to gain public support for containing the march of medical technology.

"What we need is for the whole society, not just doctors, to be re-educated in terms of expectations," said Ball, who is also executive vice president of the American College of Physicians. "Technology is often not necessary or even medically appropriate, but it's very difficult, because there is a cultural expectation of the application of technology. That's the American Way."

"Americans want more medical innovation," Roe said. "We're a rich society, but we're growing older. Health care and health-care technology are the kinds of good that you want to spend more on rather than less. The issue is, let's spend it well."

71. A Changing American Population: With What Effect?

Nathan Glazer

The racial and ethnic diversity of the American population undergoes constant change. In this article published in *CRS Review* in 1990, Nathan Glazer, professor of education and social structure at Harvard University, reflects on the impact of immigration, particularly as it affects states such as California and New York. Although few wish to reinstate the restrictive immigration policies of the past, according to Glazer, the time may come when we will need to consider actions to deal with the problems created by immigration and the changing composition of the country.

In 1963, completing a study of the ethnic groups of New York City, Senator [Daniel Patrick] Moynihan and I wrote [in *Beyond the Melting Pot*] that "the American nationality is still forming: its processes are mysterious, and the final form, if there is ever to be a final form, is as yet unknown." What we did not expect—what no one could expect—was that the bases of immigration policy would be transformed in 1965, in the course of that remarkable burst of legislation in 1964 and 1965 which proscribed racial discrimination, but also proscribed national and racial preferences in the immigration reform of 1965. Even if we had the foresight to see that the regulation of American foreign immigration by quotas sharply favoring northwestern Europe and banning most of Asia, which had survived the victory over Hitler and the subsequent liberalizing of American attitudes on race, would come to an end, we would never have dreamed that it would have any great consequences for the population of the United States. That immigration would rise under the provision of the 1965 reform to 600,000 a year, the figure of the 1980s, was not foreseen, or expected.

And so the American population changes again. We are far from the figures of the huge migration of the late nineteenth and early twentieth centuries: 600,000 a year for a population of 250 million has a different impact from 1 million a year (at the peak) for a population of 90 million.

Some adjustments to take account of differences between the early and the late 1900s narrow that difference somewhat. Then, we had few illegal immigrants, aside from some Asians. Indeed, how could there be illegal immigrants when there were hardly any restrictions? Today we may have 100,000 to 200,000 or more undocumented entrants who become permanent residents annually.

One important factor that makes the impact of our more modest immigration flow today more equivalent to the greater flows of the earlier part of the century is that immigrants today are more sharply concentrated geographically, so that in some areas the demographic impact is equivalent to what it was the first 25 years of the century. The impact on the main cities that receive immigrants—New York, Los Angeles, San Francisco, Miami—is as great as in the mass immigration of the early years of the century. Perhaps the most substantial difference between then and now, a difference that also serves in some respects to increase the visibility of immigration in American society, is the change in ethnic and racial composition. Almost half the immigrants today are from Asia: most of the rest are from Latin America and the Caribbean. Immigrants of European origin are a small minority.

The effects on the racial and ethnic composition of the United States, or rather some specified parts of the United States, are as great as at the time of the great European immigration. Consider California and New York, the two major immigrant states.

A recent study of population growth in California describes the awesome impact of immigration on the state that takes the largest proportion of immigrants. Of 600,000 legal immigrants a year, about 27 percent indicate they will settle in California; it is generally assumed that a higher percentage of illegal immigrants than that also settles in California. Making certain reasonable and conservative assumptions,

Bouvier and Martin project that California's population, about 24 million in 1980, will be [nearly 30] million in 1990 (a fair assumption—we are already there), and that this decade's increase of [21] percent, followed by lesser increases, will bring California's population to 43 million by 2030.

We may well regard these or any projections 40 years in the future with skepticism (how well would we have done in 1950 projecting the population of the United States in 1990?), but the assumptions seem sound. The demographers quote Lord Bryce, writing in 1909 about a California of 2 million, who asked, "What will happen when California is filled by 50 millions of people . . . the real question will not be about making more wealth for having more people, but whether the people will then be happier or better [off] than they have been hitherto or are at this moment."

The figures for 1990 may be relied on—they show California to be 59 percent non-Hispanic white, 7.5 percent black, 19 percent Hispanic, and 6 percent Asian. One may with only slightly lesser confidence guess that the year 2000 projection will also hold—52 percent non-Hispanic white, 7.5 percent black, 24 percent Hispanic, 8 percent Asian. The large Los Angeles Standard Consolidated Statistical Area, with 11.5 million people in the 1980s, is projected to show the most rapid growth. In 1980 it was already only 61 percent non-Hispanic white (9 percent black, 5 percent Asian, 24 percent Hispanic). That non-Hispanic whites will drop to a minority within a few years seems a certainty. They already are in the "Primary Metropolitan Statistical Area," which has a population larger than New York City. A few years ago the percentage of children of Spanish language background in the Los Angeles public schools passed 50 percent.

Similar projections can be made for our next most populous state, New York, which is expected to be 67 percent non-Hispanic white in 1990, 60 percent non-Hispanic white in 2000, the rest divided between Hispanics and blacks, with a rising Asian proportion. New York City already has a minority of non-Hispanic whites. This city, with 3 percent of the American population, takes in 15 percent of all legal immigrants.

In the United States immigrant groups *become* ethnic groups, not simply assimilated and undifferentiated Americans. So when we have immigration, it is not only the proportion of foreign-born that rises: but the proportions of given ethnic-racial groups rise too. Our history makes these groups distinctive, even unto the second, third, and later generations; and these groups become and remain actors, in their aspect as ethnic groups, on the American scene, more significantly in our great cities than in the country as a whole.

So what? No one is arguing for any restriction of immigration, or for any great change in the numbers upward, or in the composition of immigration. We have happily overcome the ethnocentrism, chauvinism, and prejudice that governed immigration policy between 1924 and 1965. We are dealing with the one major problem that has properly concerned us, illegal immigration; we will see on the basis of experience how the Immigration Reform and Control Act of 1986 is working; and we will try to improve it.

Immigrants otherwise are no great problem for American society. They are probably a lesser burden on our social services than some sections of the native population. Julian Simon, in his current book, *The Economic Consequences of Immigration,* carefully works out these burdens. It is true that in some cities the impact on the schools is severe: Miami can scarcely keep up with the growth of the school population, and similar strains develop in Los Angeles, New York, and other major cities (and many smaller cities) with large immigrant inflows. On the other hand, Simon tells us, the immigrants, predominantly young and of working ages, draw little Social Security. This puts the total public outlay in balance, but is no help to the cities, which pay for schools and do not pay Social Security or receive Social Security taxes. Barry Chiswick demonstrates that in a dozen or so years immigrants may do as well as natives in income. Thomas Muller argues that they are reviving dying sections of our cities, opening retail businesses, occupying under-used housing, buying and improving houses. Ben Wattenberg tells us of the cost of a population that does not grow. With a "birth death" as the result of the end of the baby boom reducing the population entering the labor force, immigration becomes a positive boon. The immigrants bring diversity to our cities and their neighborhoods, and promise that ethnic restaurants and neighborhood festivals will increase in quantity, quality, and variety.

But I think back to Lord Bryce, contemplating a California of 50 million people and asking whether the people will be happier or better off. There may come a time when, with no hint of xenophobia, many Americans may want to say, enough. The frontier closed a century ago. With the increase of population and wealth, land prices and house prices rise, congestion becomes greater and, one may ask a question that is simply not asked, how many Americans are enough? At the margin this would lead us to actions that we would all abhor—limitations on births, closing our borders to those persecuted for their political or religious beliefs—but long before that margin is reached, there are other modifications in immigration policy we might want to consider. Indeed, when we visit countries where the growth of population is more moderate, we often find virtues in stability that it is difficult for us to approximate. I would hope that the discussion of immigration and the growth of the American population and its changing composition would permit these considerations to be raised.

72. Point-Counterpoint: Should Some Illegal Drugs Be Legalized?

Ethan A. Nadelmann
Mark A. R. Kleiman

The nation's drug problem has taken a huge toll in terms of human misery and the costs to our society in economic as well as social and cultural areas. Many Americans believe that illegal drug use is among this nation's most serious problems. The federal government has announced "drug wars" and appointed "drug czars" to combat gang violence and murders and to stop the supply and demand for mind-altering substances. Despite these efforts and "just say no" campaigns, only limited success has been achieved in curtailing illegal drug use. The profit incentive is too high and new types of drugs are regularly available for sale.

As a result, some public officials and commentators argue for a new approach—the legalization of some drugs. Both sides of this issue are explored in articles published in 1990 in *Issues in Science and Technology,* a journal of the National Academy of Sciences. Ethan A. Nadelmann, a professor of politics at Princeton University, argues that legalization should be considered in light of the failure of past criminal justice approaches. Just as Prohibition in the 1920s did not prevent people from drinking alcohol, drug prohibition has also failed as a national policy. Among the many opponents of legalization is Mark A.R. Kleiman of Harvard University's John F. Kennedy School of Government, "We will have simply substituted the government for the local crack dealer as the ultimate recipient of the proceeds of theft," he argues.

Ethan Nadelmann: Legalization Is the Answer

Legalization—I much prefer the term "decriminalization" or "normalization"—means different things to different people. To some it simply means taking the crime, and the profit, out of the drug business.

For some, it's a rallying cry, in much the same way that "repeal prohibition" was used, 60 years ago, for bringing people together from across the political spectrum. . . .

Legalization also refers to a framework of analysis—in particular, cost-benefit analysis. If we look at the current drug prohibition policies and determine, as best we can, their costs and benefits, and then compare them with the costs and benefits of alternative options, it seems to many of us that the best mix ends up looking a lot more like legalization than it does like the current situation.

Finally, legalization implies degrees of emphasis rather than absolutes. For example, alcohol is legal, but it is not legal to drive under the influence of alcohol or to sell it to children. Conversely, we speak about cocaine and the opiates as *il*legal, but in fact doctors can prescribe these drugs.

Baltimore Mayor Kurt Schmoke has suggested that if we are going to have a "War Against Drugs," it is a war that should be headed not by the Attorney General or even by a Drug Czar, but by the Surgeon General. In other words, drug policy should not rely first and foremost on criminal justice sanctions but on public health approaches, combined with some degree of respect for the rights of adult American citizens to make their own choices—even bad ones.

Personally, when I talk about legalization, I mean three things: The first is to make drugs such as marijuana, cocaine, and heroin legal—under fairly restricted conditions, but not as restricted as today. Second is a convergence in our substance abuse policy. We need a policy that is tougher on alcohol and especially tougher on tobacco—not with criminal laws so much as with other measures that would make them less available and less attractive. And at the same time be tough on marijuana, cocaine, and heroin as well, but while relying far less on criminal sanctions.

And third is to more intelligently manage our resources—to stop pouring the billions of dollars that we are now spending on law enforcement approaches down the drain and put them into drug treatment and drug abuse prevention instead.

Drug treatment is certainly no panacea. Most people who go into it end up backsliding. But it does help some people: It makes them less likely to die from overdose and less likely to steal or commit other crimes. The evidence shows that it is worth doing, both for society and for drug abusers themselves. Even without coercing people into treatment, there are already waiting lines for the available treatment facilities.

More important, though, than drug treatment is drug abuse prevention. And here I am talking not so much about K-12 drug education but about "non-specific" services such as prenatal and postnatal care, Head Start programs, inner-city education, and job training. These approaches are not just things in which the United States lags behind most other advanced industrial democracies in providing, they also seem to be the best drug prevention approaches ever developed—if you evaluate them in terms of producing non-drug-abusing, productive, tax-paying citizens down the road.

These are not just the decent and humane things to do. They also turn out to be, dollar for dollar, a lot more cost-effective than building more jails.

Fundamentally, we need to consider legalization because the criminal justice approaches of the past have failed, and those of the present and future are likewise largely doomed to failure. This has nothing to do with squabbles between law enforcement agencies, or corruption in Third World countries, or whether or not we have a Drug Czar, or whether or not his name is William Bennett. Rather, it reflects the nature of the commodity, the nature of the market, and the lucrativeness of it all.

Criminal justice approaches have not only failed to solve the problem, they have made matters far worse. Most of what people identify as part and parcel of the drug problem are in fact the results of drug prohibition, just as when people talked about the alcohol problem 60 years ago, most of what they identified were the results of alcohol prohibition.

Let's look very quickly at some of these approaches: international enforcement, interdiction, and domestic enforcement (of high-level traffickers as well as their street-level sellers).

Can we keep drugs from being exported to the United States. No, we can't. These drugs can be grown virtually everywhere, and to try preventing export from any one place results in "push down, pop up." Push down heroin coming out of Turkey, and it pops up in Mexico. Push it down in Mexico, and it pops up in Southeast Asia. Push down there and it comes from South*west* Asia. We have pushed down in so many places that it pops up virtually everywhere now. The United States is a multi-source heroin-importing country. The same is true with regard to marijuana and cocaine.

Another reason is that international law enforcement has but a tiny effect on the ultimate domestic price of drugs. Even if you double, triple, or quadruple the foreign price, it has almost no impact on the streets.

And finally, this is a business from which hundreds of thousands, if not millions, of people in Latin America are earning a very good living. The drugs are usually indigenous to their areas—opium in parts of Asia, for example, cannabis in Jamaica and parts of Africa, and coca that goes back thousands of years in Latin America—and cause few local problems. Moreover, they appear to bring in much more money than any alternative would provide.

Thus if you spray Latin American peasants' drug crops and try to persuade them to grow macadamia nuts instead, they respond by hiding their crops. And if you go down there, as William Bennett's people have done, and say, "Don't you understand how immoral you are being? You are poisoning the youth of America," the peasants are unimpressed. "Don't lecture us about morality," they say. "Our moral obligation is to do the best we can for ourselves, our families, and our communities. If that means selling this drug, which is native to our country anyway, then so be it." And they might well add another point: "While you *Nortamericanos* are talking to us about morality, your trade representatives are going around the world shoving down tariff barriers so that your farmers can export more tobacco. Are you so much on a moral high ground?"

What about interdiction? I don't know anybody who believes anymore that it makes a difference. Drugs can come into the country in any which way, and in small amounts—arriving by boat, plane, and car, hidden in flowers, chocolates, and statues. Looking for drugs is like looking for a needle in a haystack.

Interdiction *has* worked somewhat with respect to marijuana. But the success has proven counterproductive. The Coast Guard found that as it realized a few successes in interdicting marijuana, the drug lords seemed to be switching to cocaine. And why not? It is less bulky, less smelly, more compact, and more lucrative. This pretty much parallels the responses of bootleggers during prohibition, who switched from beer to hard liquor.

The other consequence of the marijuana interdiction "success" was to transform the country into perhaps the number-one producer of marijuana in the world. Some people think that the United States now produces the world's best marijuana, in fact, and that if the dollar were to drop lower, we would become a major exporter of marijuana.

What about domestic enforcement? If you go after the big drug traffickers—the people who most profitably and egregiously violate the drug laws—it makes little difference. Every time you arrest Mr. Number One, there is Mr. Number Two to fill his shoes. Indeed, it is often from Number Two that the police get the information to arrest Number One.

Similarly, with street-level enforcement, you can clean up some neighborhoods—at least for a while—but can you, for very long, keep drugs out of the hands of people who really want them? You have the same push-down, pop-up effect on the streets as there is on the global scale. Push down on 102nd Street and guess what pops up on 104th Street?

Now, law enforcement does accomplish some things. It reduces availability a little, increases the price, and deters some people. But the costs and other negative consequences of continuing to focus on criminal justice end up making a lot of things much worse.

Consider the direct costs. In 1987, we spent something like $10 billion just enforcing drug laws. It may be close to $20 billion this year. Drug-law violators—and here I am not talking about drug-*related* crimes but drug-law violations such as possession, dealing, distribution, and manu-facturing—are the number-one cause of imprisonment in New York state prisons, in Florida prisons, and as far as I know, in other state prisons as well. They accounted for about 40 percent of all felony indictments in the New York City counts [in 1989] and for over 52 percent in Washington, D.C.—quadruple what it was four years earlier.

When cops say that the urban criminal-justice system is becoming synonymous with drug enforcement systems, they are increasingly correct. In the federal prisons, 40 percent of the people there are there on drug-law violations; between three-quarters of a million and a million people were arrested [in 1989] on drug charges. We now have one million people behind bars in the United States, practically double what the number was just 10 years ago. And a rapidly rising percentage of them are there for violating drug laws.

But although the direct costs are enormous, the indirect costs are far more severe. Drug prohibition is responsible for all sorts of violence and crime—from street-level theft to high-level corruption—that seemingly have little to do with drugs per se.

Consider this: Tobacco is at least as addictive as heroin and cocaine, but have you ever worried about being mugged by a tobacco addict? Of course not, because it is cheap—too cheap, in my view. Heroin and cocaine cost much more to buy, even though they don't cost much more to produce. They are expensive because they are illegal, and addicts are obliged to raise the income, typically, illegally, to pay for them. That would change under a maintenance system, or other forms of drug legalization, in which the prices were lower.

And the systemic violence of the drug-crime connection would also change. There would be far less need for illicit drug traffickers, and thus far fewer occasions for them to settle disputes among themselves by shooting one another, shooting cops and innocent bystanders (including kids) along the way.

Another cost, not much talked about, is the impact of prohibition on drug quality. Simply stated, drugs are more dangerous because they are illegal. Just as tens of thousands of people died or were blinded or poisoned by bad bootleg liquor 60 years ago, perhaps the majority of overdose deaths today are the result of drug prohibition.

Ordinarily, heroin does not kill. It addicts people and makes them constipated. But people overdose because they don't know what they are getting; they don't know if the heroin is 4 percent or 40 percent, or if it is cut with bad stuff, or if it is heroin at all—it may be a synthetic opiate or an amphetamine-type substance.

Just imagine if every time you picked up a bottle of wine, you didn't know whether it was 8 percent alcohol or 80 percent alcohol, or whether it was ethyl alcohol or methyl alcohol. Imagine if every time you took an aspirin, you didn't know if it was 5 milligrams or 500 milligrams.

Life would be a little more interesting, and also a little more dangerous. Fewer people might take those drugs, but more would get sick and die. That is exactly what is happening today with the illicit drug market. Nothing resembling an underground Food and Drug Administration has emerged to regulate the quality of illicit drugs on the streets, and the results are much more deadly.

My strongest argument for legalization, though, is a moral one. Enforcement of drug laws makes a mockery of an essential principle of a free society—that those who do no harm to others should not be harmed by others, and particularly not by the state. The vast majority of the 60 to 70 million Americans who have violated the drug laws in recent years have done no harm to anybody else. In most cases, they have done little or no harm even to themselves. Saying to those people, "You lose your driver's license, you lose your job, you lose your freedom," is, to me, the greatest societal cost of our current drug prohibition system.

Mark Kleiman:
Legalization Is a Simplistic
Solution to a Complex Problem

Debating the abstract question "Should some illegal drugs be legalized?" may not be the most fruitful use of always-scarce intellectual energy. There is serious work to be done in trying to figure out practical ways to reduce the costs of drug abuse, drug dealing, and drug-law enforcement, and I doubt that arguing about legalization helps us do it.

For example, we could discuss how to control alcohol-induced family violence. Or we could discuss what kinds of domestic law-enforcement techniques can reduce the rate of initiation to crack use among adolescents in poor neighborhoods. Or we could discuss how to persuade teenage, first-time expectant mothers to give up alcohol, tobacco, and cocaine. Or we could discuss under what circumstances employers should be allowed to inquire into their employee's drug-use patterns.

What we should *not* do is discuss solutions too simple for the problems they are meant to address. The "War on Drugs" is one such solution. Legalization is another. William Bennett and Ethan Nadelmann seem to agree that there is one simple solution to the drug problem; all they really disagree on is which one of them gets to ride the white horse in the drug-policy melodrama and which one has to wear the black hat.

As an economist, I prefer to think of drugs as products, and of the general drug-policy problem as the need to regulate supply and the conditions of consumption. Psychoactive chemicals confer measurable benefits in medical use, and some of them also confer measurable benefits in nonmedical use—a fact well known to anyone who ever used coffee or amphetamines to write a paper or a nightcap to get to sleep. And new performance-enhancing drugs are being invented at an increasing pace—for memory, for empathy, for cognitive performance.

Many of these drugs are fun to use—certainly a benefit, though not so easily measurable—but all of them are also more or less dangerous to their users. Just as other consumer products such as lawn mowers are dangerous if used incorrectly, drugs may produce physical or psychological damage. And they may produce irresponsible behavior that the user will later regret.

In addition, some drugs, for some users, are also dangerous to other people. Users commit crimes under their influence; users operate heavy machinery and have accidents; users neglect their duties as parents, neighbors, citizens, and employees; users even pass on their habits to their own unborn children, as the drugs are involuntarily consumed by fetuses in utero.

I am not saying that this is true of all drugs or of all users, but merely that some of these psychoactives have costs. The policy challenge is to limit the cost of drug use—to users and to others—and to limit the cost of control. In effect, we are trying to minimize a complicated sum of costs, using laws as instruments.

Possible categories of laws include taxation and regulation. Taxation attempts to reduce consumption by assessing drug users for some of the hidden costs—both to themselves and to other people—of their drug use. But although it is an extremely powerful weapon, the problem with taxation is that it is unspecific, both with respect to users and to circumstances of use. If you can imagine a use tax on alcohol, for example, consider that the optimal tax on a glass of wine at dinner and the optimal tax on somebody's seventh scotch this evening are not the same.

Regulation attempts to be more specific—to reduce potential *problem* use rather than all use. First, we can regulate providers; the time and place of providing drugs, and the type and frequency of promotional activities, can be rigorously defined. We can impose liability on them for the misbehavior of, or injury to, their customers; and we can give them substantial amounts of control with respect to distribution. The extreme example, of course, is prescription medication. We rely on physicians, and to a lesser extent on pharmacists, to regulate access to prescription drugs, whether psychoactive or not.

We can also regulate users. In particular, we can regulate who can use. Age is the most frequent criterion, but not, obviously, the most successful. We can also license drug use based both on knowledge— demonstrated by passing some test—and on continued good behavior. (It has always struck me as odd that if somebody drinks and drives, we take away his driving license and don't figure out some way to take away his drinking license.)

We could think about limiting quantity, particularly if we had a licensing system, since we know that many drugs are dangerous only in excess. The dose, it is said, makes the poison. We could also regulate user behavior by holding users strictly liable for the consequences of their drug behavior.

Against this background of possible tax and regulatory schemes, let me reframe the legalization question. For the drugs now forbidden for nonmedical use—chiefly but not exclusively heroin, cocaine, and marijuana—is there another set of laws, allowing some licit non-medical use, that would be better than the regime we now have?

Legalization is a strictly negative concept: It means that we will not use the prohibition option, but it does not by itself define a new regime. For that we need to undertake a serious task of policy design—what used to be called "social engineering." And this is a task, it seems to me, that the advocates of legalization have been routinely ducking while they go around the country making fun of government officials (who, to be sure, are fairly easy to make fun of).

Let's imagine that we decided to make cocaine licitly available for some "recreational"—that is, non-medical—use. We would, of course, simultaneously try to regulate it with respect to the age of its users. But anyone who glibly says, "Of course, we won't let it be available to kids," then has to explain, given the very large fraction of current cocaine use that goes on among people under the age of 21, how this new post-legalization regime would differ from our current regime.

Another problem: Will it be possible to get enforcement folks to work hard at enforcing a mere age restriction? I invite you to examine the enforcement of the law against adolescent drinking as a possible example of what the enforcement of a law against adolescent cocaine use, post-prohibition, would look like. According to a recent study, something like 40 percent of all high-school-age males have had more than five drinks at a time in the past two weeks. Clearly, regulations can fail just as prohibitions can.

Consider, as well, the effects of legalization on price. Based on the pharmaceutical price of cocaine, a rock of legal, untaxed crack would cost about 25 cents, as opposed to its current 5 dollars. There may be some commodity known to man whose demand is inelastic over a 20-fold change in its price, but I'm not aware of it. My guess is that if a rock of crack cost 25 cents, a very large number of people would try it, and the fraction of people progressing to a period of self-destructive, compulsive use would be substantially higher than it is today.

It is almost impossible to make numerical estimates in the absence of an experiment, but this is not an experiment we can do and then reverse. If the legalization of crack raised the number of users from several million (of whom perhaps a quarter are in bad trouble) to 20 or 25 million (of whom half were in trouble), it would not then be possible to go back and re-prohibit without having to spend some serious money on enforcement.

If, on the other hand, we decided to legalize crack and maintain its current black-market price through taxation, all the users who are now bopping people over the head to get money to buy crack would continue to bop people over the head to get money to buy crack. We will have simply substituted the government for the local crack dealer as the ultimate recipient of the proceeds of theft. In addition, all those who are now supporting their crack habits peacefully, by selling crack to other users, will have been cut off from their source of illicit income. Some of them will give up crack. Others won't, with consequences that are not hard to imagine.

I conclude that my attempt to design a nonprohibitive cocaine-regulation strategy that does better than our current laws has failed. That's not to say that someone else won't succeed. But succeeding in that policy design problem means doing the design work and then making serious predictions about the likely consequences of the new policy.

Too many of today's legalization advocates offer arguments of the form, "legalization won't increase consumption because anyone who really wants [name of drug] can get it right now." That isn't what I would call a serious prediction—nobody in his right mind would bet 10 dollars of real money on an argument that flimsy. We need an analysis that considers how consumption varies as a function of price, ease of access, and social attitudes.

In the absence of well-worked-out policies, why does legalization have a growing constituency? The main reason, I think, is sheer frustration with the status quo. Could anything be worse than the crack problem we have now? But frustration is a bad counselor. As bad as things are now, they could be worse. In policy design, as in medicine, the first maxim is to do no harm.

Chapter 14

Foreign and Defense Policies

Foreign and defense policies should be easy to identify. They are, after all, policies designed to manage U.S. relations with other countries and protect the United States from foreign intrusions. The writers of the Constitution had no difficulty defining these policies, for they were the historic "royal prerogatives" exercised by the crowned heads of every sovereign nation: leading troops into battle and negotiating with foreign powers. Today these functions reside almost exclusively in the hands of the federal government. Even ardent conservatives, who deplore much of the government's involvement in domestic affairs, tend to advocate vigorous (and expensive) foreign and military policies.

It is, however, far more difficult to isolate foreign and military policies today than it was in George Washington's or James Madison's era. One reason is that "peacetime" and "wartime" are no longer clearly delineated. Even when the United States is spared full-scale military involvement, it still must maintain military readiness that would have seemed excessive before World War II; and it must expect to be the target of repeated low-level engagements, including terrorist attacks. Moreover, as noted in Chapter 13, the boundaries between domestic and foreign affairs are not as clear as they once were. In an interdependent world economy, a poor coffee bean harvest in Colombia or a debt crisis in Brazil, for example, can show up in price changes in the neighborhood supermarket. Aided by instantaneous communications, U.S. citizens participate vicariously in events halfway around the world. Even when U.S. economic or political interests are only remotely touched, we still may become enmeshed in circumstances that appeal to our sense of compassion or justice: famine in Ethiopia, elections in Eastern Europe, and racial policy in South Africa are but three examples. In short, numerous domestic issues are buffeted by international developments, just as more and more foreign policies have consequences at home.

In addition, foreign and defense policies traditionally have been perceived and communicated differently from domestic policies in four respects. First, the general public is less informed, less interested, and less predictable in its attitudes about foreign affairs. Domestic news may pack a local punch: if there's a recession, the family's breadwinner may be out of work or the community's businesses may suffer. Foreign developments less often have such a direct, visible impact. Thus, many people's attitudes toward foreign and defense questions are changeable, easily swayed, and dependent on cues from government leaders and news reports.

Second, the communications media tend to cover foreign news in less depth than domestic news. In comparison with domestic news, stories from foreign countries are often hard to report and expensive to transmit. Massacres in Afghanistan, elections in Brazil, demonstrations in China—all these news events depend on the presence of reporters and camera people if they are to be transmitted to western mass publics. As a result, the media often rely on official government statements and reports and resort to stereotypes, personality profiles, and dramatic coverage of crisis events.

Third, fewer interest groups deal with foreign and military policies than with domestic policies and programs. (Military policies fall into two categories: strategy and procurement. Military strategy, like foreign policy, attracts relatively few interest groups; but military procurement, like other domestic matters, is fiercely contested by a myriad of groups.)

Fourth, unlike most domestic issues, foreign and defense issues tend to be resolved by a relatively small circle of decision-makers. These persons work in the White House, the State and Defense departments, and the relevant committees of the House and Senate. Elite decision-makers—diplomats, military strategists, intelligence officials, and international bankers and business people—play especially forceful roles in shaping the nation's policies.

These differences in perception and communication are fading, just as are the subject-matter distinctions between foreign and domestic policies. As communication becomes easier and cheaper, the media are more willing to devote time and space to foreign news. The public, in turn, seems more informed and involved. As the effects of world events reverberate throughout the domestic economy, more interest groups and lobbies insist on being heard in policy decisions. This change in turn is breaking down the monopolies of experts and professionals who deal with these questions.

The Defense Establishment

Defense policymaking straddles the worlds of foreign and domestic affairs. Major strategic decisions—for example, the level of naval strength or the mix of missiles and ground forces in strategic locales—usually involve only specialists in the military bureaucracy. But debates over the economic aspects of defense—such as personnel, procurement, weapons systems, and arms sales—draw participants as numerous and diverse as any conflict over funding of domestic programs.

The Defense Department is the 500-pound gorilla of the federal establishment. A third of a trillion dollars goes to Defense each year, and its staff comprises one million civilian and more than two million military employees. Such resources attract interest groups eager to capture some of the funds. The combination of federal funds and private interests is so potent that President Dwight Eisenhower, in his 1961 farewell address, warned the nation about the "unwarranted influence" of the "military-industrial complex."

More than 30 years have passed since Eisenhower's warning, and his prediction seems to have come to pass. Most military spending decisions—including procurement and personnel support—follow the familiar contours of domestic "distributive" policymaking, in which the government distributes benefits to various contractors, suppliers, and local communities. In Selection 73 ("The Stubborn Osprey Flies On"), Melissa Healy recounts the story of a tilt-rotor aircraft that became a popular spending project.

The Defense Department has struggled to coordinate the nation's military efforts. A relatively young agency, dating only from 1947, it has to contend with fierce, longstanding rivalries among the services—Army, Navy, Marines, and Air Force. Each of them cherishes its own mission and jostles the others for funds, weapons systems, and operational autonomy. Shocking breakdowns of communication were revealed in such engagements as the 1983 Grenada invasion and the 1989 Panama invasion.

By 1986, Congress stepped in and passed a wide-ranging Pentagon reorganization measure designed in part to reduce interservice rivalries and strengthen the position of the head of the Joint Chiefs of Staff. The impressive coordination achieved in the Persian Gulf War was due partly to the reorganization plan, partly to adjustments made in response to earlier mistakes.

Invitation to Struggle

As with domestic affairs, foreign policymaking is constitutionally divided between the executive and legislative branches. Presidents have the burden of leadership in foreign affairs. They appoint ambassadors and other emissaries, receive representatives of other nations, and negotiate treaties. "The president," declared John Marshall in 1799, "is the sole organ of the nation in its external relations, and its sole representative with foreign nations." [1]

The broader tasks of making foreign policy are shared, however, with the legislative branch. The Senate confirms ambassadors and ratifies treaties. Although the president is commander-in-chief of the armed forces, it is Congress that declares war, raises and equips armies and navies, and finances the pursuit of foreign-policy objectives. Major commitments must result from a consensus between the executive and legislative branches. As constitutional scholar Edward S. Corwin observed, these powers constitute "an invitation to struggle" between the president and Congress for the privilege of directing foreign policy. [2]

Because Americans are accustomed to this division of powers, we do not realize how singular it is. Foreign diplomats complain that in every other country of the world, they know where to obtain the views of the "government of the day." But where does one find the views of the U.S. government? One must look not only to the State Department but to the Defense Department and other agencies, as well as strategically placed lawmakers on Capitol Hill. In Selection 74, "Congress and the Presidency in American Foreign Policy," Representative Lee H. Hamilton (D.-Ind.) explains the need for give-and-take between the branches in foreign policymaking.

The War Powers

Sharing the so-called war powers—that is, duties of deploying military forces—has proved to be at best an awkward arrangement. Modern presidents have seen their duty as protecting the lives and property of U.S. citizens abroad and to that end have been willing to involve the nation in military or paramilitary actions. Congress has been more inclined to drag its feet and to stress the costs of military engagement— including loss of life and the danger of a wider war.

Backlash over the lingering Vietnam War (1965-1973) led Congress in 1973 to pass the War Powers Resolution (P.L. 93-148) over President Richard Nixon's veto. Under the resolution, the president must consult with Congress before committing U.S. troops abroad, report any such troop commitment within forty-eight hours, and terminate the use of forces within sixty or ninety days if Congress does not declare war, extend the period by law, or is unable to convene.

The War Powers Resolution has been less effective than Congress had hoped. It may have deterred some military actions, but it has not kept presidents from intervening when they have seen fit to do so. Presidents have submitted reports to Congress under the War Powers Resolution twenty-three times, thirteen times in the Reagan administration alone. Since 1981 the resolution has been an issue in U.S. policy in Central America, Lebanon, Libya, and the Persian Gulf.[3]

Congress has invoked the War Powers Resolution only twice—for actions in Lebanon (1983) and the Persian Gulf (1991). Most of the time members of Congress have preferred to sit on the sidelines, questioning or applauding the president's decisions long after they were made and once the outcome is clear. Presidents as well as members of Congress question whether the resolution could survive a real or prolonged crisis between the two branches. In Selection 75, "The Constitution and the War Making Power," Senator Max Baucus (D-Mont.) offers a thoughtful revisionist appraisal of the situation.

The circumstances surrounding the Persian Gulf War dramatically illustrate the dilemma of the so-called war powers. On the one hand, President Bush led the nation into war through a series of steps including deployment of troops, orchestration of an international coalition, lobbying for a deadline for Iraqi withdrawal from Kuwait, then launching the counterattack when the deadline was spurned. At each presidentially initiated stage of the engagement, the policy options narrowed until the president's chosen course of action was almost the only one remaining. The events of 1990-1991 left little doubt about a president's ability to lead the nation to war, and to leave Congress with little choice but to follow him.

Congress, for its part, debated the president's actions at some length. The allied military buildup triggered an extensive discussion of war powers during the fall of 1990. In January 1991 the new Congress debated, and passed, a resolution (Public Law 102-1) authorizing the use of force in the Persian Gulf. The War Powers Resolution was invoked in the 1991 resolution and in President Bush's subsequent reports to Congress. Advocates of congressional war-making prerogatives were thus left with at least the hope for future consultation in the deadly serious business of going to war.

Notes

1. Quoted by Edward S. Corwin in *The President: Office and Powers, 1787-1957*, 4th rev. ed. (New York: New York University Press, 1957), 177.
2. *Ibid.*, 171.
3. Ellen C. Collier, *War Powers Resolution: Presidential Compliance*, Washington, D.C.: CRS Issue Brief (October 5, 1990), 1.

73. The Stubborn Osprey Flies On

Melissa Healy

Military hardware constitutes one of the most popular government spending programs. The products presumably help ensure the nation's security, and their manufacture benefits the local economies where they are produced. Even when a weapon is of questionable utility, its symbolic and economic value may keep it alive. Such a weapon is the V-22 Osprey, a tilt-rotor aircraft that can fly like a conventional plane but takes off and lands like a helicopter. The plane's contractors and subcontractors, in such locales as Pennsylvania, Texas, and New York, kept the project alive by enlisting the support of legislators representing those areas. The unfolding story, as told by Melissa Healy in the *Los Angeles Times,* in 1990, reveals much about the pork-barrel politics of defense procurement.

On a clear Washington day last spring, a flashy red-white-and-blue warplane glided smoothly toward the U.S. Capitol, hovered helicopter-style over the neatly tended lawn and landed—to hearty applause—beside a throng of well-wishers assembled on the steps. It was a spectacle of the sort that only the military can produce—a heart-pounding mixture of impressive new weaponry and patriotic spirit, designed to win a place in the budget for yet another piece of military hardware.

But the audience—composed mainly of lawmakers and lobbyists—was entirely civilian. Nary a uniform was in sight.

The reception was typical of what has greeted the plane, a V-22 Osprey, since its inception. The Osprey—a tilt-rotor aircraft that can fly like a conventional plane and take off and land like a helicopter—has passed initial muster at the Defense Department, but Pentagon planners since have concluded that the $30-billion price tag simply is too expensive. In 1989, Defense Secretary Dick Cheney announced the Osprey would be the first major U.S. weapons system to be eliminated by the Bush Administration in the face of increasing pressures for defense cutbacks. And he has been trying to kill it ever since.

But the Osprey, named after a particularly stubborn fish hawk, has held on tenaciously, and has become the most intrepid survivor yet of the sweeping post-Cold War defense cutback which, [since 1988], has slashed $244 billion from the Pentagon's five-year spending program, a plan that initially totaled $1.75 trillion over six years. For two years in a row, the House and Senate Armed Services committees have overturned the Pentagon's kill recommendation for the Osprey, and the aircraft is conspicuously in the budget that Congress passed Oct. 27 [1990].

How can such a program survive those odds?

The story of how the Osprey has remained alive is a fascinating tale that involves a bitter cat fight between Pentagon budget-cutters and pork-barrel politicians, an unlikely crusade initiated by a junior congressman, the threat of unwanted competition from the Japanese, and an intriguing new defense-spending strategy for the 1990s that calls for selling a weapons system to Congress on the notion that it can be adapted for civilian use as well.

"This program has become a competitiveness issue, and this is a new wrinkle," says Gordon Adams, director of the Washington-based Defense Budget Project, which is critical of military spending patterns. "That's a sure sign of a declining defense budget—that you're going to have to make a broader case for a new defense program," Adams says. "And to the extent that defense contractors feel they have to do that, it's probably a good thing."

The Osprey's saga began in 1986, during the Ronald Reagan Administration's $3-trillion defense buildup, when the aircraft—then known by the designation JVX—had quietly won initial acceptance in the Pentagon's tortuous weapons-acquisition process. In the weapons-buying frenzy of the day, the JVX—built jointly by Bell Helicopter of Ft. Worth and Boeing Helicopter of Philadelphia—drew little attention from critics.

By the time Cheney came to office in March, 1989, the Osprey appeared destined for a bright future. The Pentagon had spent $1.3 billion to develop the plane. Four test models had been built or approved for construction, and the Marine Corps had promised to buy 552 Ospreys once production began.

But in early 1989, the Osprey began encountering some ominous crosswinds: Auditors in the Pentagon's Office of Program Analysis and Evaluation, an internal watchdog agency whose staffers were known as the Whiz Kids, issued a report arguing that the military could perform the same jobs tens of billions of dollars more cheaply by using standard helicopters that already were on hand. The Osprey, in short, was proving too expensive—and unnecessary.

With anti-defense-spending sentiment burgeoning—and orders from the White House to slash billions from the Pentagon budget—it was an argument that Cheney, himself a former congressman could not resist. On April 21, 1989, pleading that "painful cuts" had to be made, Cheney announced he was eliminating the Osprey program. "I had to cut somewhere, and rather than stretch out all the programs and run everything at an inefficient rate, I opted for knocking specific programs out of the budget," he said.

While the Osprey was designed to carry 24 combat-ready troops and would be able to land where no fixed-wing aircraft would dare to tread, Cheney agreed with the argument that already available helicopters could do that too, and for a lot less cost.

Cheney's decision caused some mild expressions of surprise on Capitol Hill, where lawmakers had cynically come to expect that the Pentagon would never recommend killing a program on its own. But to Rep. Curt Weldon (R-Pa.), this was nothing short of stunning. With 2,000 jobs in his largely suburban Philadelphia-area district dependent on the program—and the promise of many more if the Osprey program ever really took off, Weldon down-played his earlier speeches on community firefighting programs and began what eventually would become an almost one-man crusade to keep the Osprey aloft.

As a junior member of the House Armed Services Committee, Weldon at least had some entree to Congress' deliberations on the Osprey. But the outlook was hardly promising. As the House panel moved later in the summer of 1989 to draft the 1990 defense bill, its chairman, Rep. Les Aspin (D-Wis.), was against opposing Cheney on the V-22.

But Weldon secured backing for the Osprey by joining his forces with another group of lawmakers whose own pet project, the F-14 fighter, had also been on Cheney's hit list. The alliance threw V-22 supporters together with lawmakers who had home-district ties to the Grumman Corp. of Bethpage, N.Y., the F-14's manufacturer, and its subcontractors in New York, California and elsewhere.

The coalition included a sizable group of congressional aircraft-carrier enthusiasts, who feared that the Pentagon was buying too few planes for the Navy's 15-carrier fleet. The Osprey program alone guaranteed support of the Pennsylvania and Texas delegations in whose districts the plane would be manufactured.

To Weldon's delight, the effort succeeded. The panel's final bill earmarked $1 billion for additional F-14s and $351 million for the development and early production of the Osprey. The Senate—indifferently—went along.

But Cheney refused to give up. The following January, he threw down the gauntlet, serving notice that the Pentagon would not use the money earmarked for early production for the V-22, but would shift the funds instead to meet the Defense Department's other priorities. In early February, when the Administration sent Congress its budget for fiscal 1991, the Osprey program was missing—again. Round 2 had begun.

Weldon knew he would have a tougher fight on his hands this time, and moved quickly to make sure his troops would be on board. In January, he called executives of the Osprey's two major manufacturers, Bell Helicopter President L. M. (Jack) Horner and Boeing

Helicopter President Edward Renouard, into his office and gave them an ultimatum. Weldon was prepared to "go the the wall" for the V-22, but the manufacturers had to be ready to pull out the stops as well.

The decision wasn't an easy one for the two firms. If they continued to oppose Cheney's kill order it might well strain their relations with the Defense Department, which is their single biggest customer. And to make matters worse, Boeing—a principal contractor on the B-2 Stealth bomber as well—was already tied up in a much bigger lobbying fight for that program, which was under attack on Capitol Hill and also about to be scaled back by Cheney. But eventually, the two executives told Weldon they would go along.

The young Pennsylvania lawmaker then delicately approached military brass for a similar commitment. The Marines said they'd go along—"verrry carefully," Weldon, 43, recalls. "Believe me, I would never have fought this battle if the military leaders had told me, 'Curt, you're wasting your time, we don't want this,'" the congressman insists.

With that backing in hand, the Osprey supporters came up with a novel—and soon-to-be successful—strategy: They would seek to broaden congressional support for the V-22 by selling lawmakers on its potential as a short-hop commuter plane. The Osprey's tilt-rotor technology not only would open routes to cities that currently had no major airport, but it also could save older airports millions of dollars in runway improvements necessary to accommodate bigger planes, the Osprey lobby would argue. Some analysts predicted the civilian market for the Osprey ultimately could approach more than 2,000 aircraft—almost four times the Pentagon's projected buy.

To some, the Osprey aircraft sets a standard for future Pentagon programs in lean budgetary times. Like the V-22, they say, those weapons most worthy of support will be multitalented workhorses that will benefit the civilian sector as well.

"You can't sell a B-2 bomber to Trans World Airlines, and you can't sell a nuclear-powered submarine to Carnival Cruise Lines, but the V-22, everybody's champing at the bit to get," Weldon asserts.

Meanwhile, the campaign continued—and does even today. The red-white-and-blue Osprey that landed on the east front of the Capitol [in 1990] also made appearances at the Dayton Airshow, in New York's Battery Park and at other spectacles across the country. Bell Helicopter's Horner criss-crossed the country speaking to the editorial boards of newspapers. Weldon and several other lawmakers took to the steps of the Smithsonian Institution's Air and Space Museum—a warehouse of aerospace technologies pioneered by the Pentagon—to announce the creation of the "Tilt-Rotor Technology Coalition." And the Osprey Lobby, as it is disparagingly known, has published dozens of ads hailing the airplane's attributes.

Bell Helicopter and Boeing both have compiled lists of Osprey subcontractors in each congressional district and circulated them to Weldon's Tilt-Rotor Technology Coalition, which has been hard at work spreading the message. And the manufacturers used their own nationwide reach—"the network of our subcontractors and their employees," Bell Helicopter's Horner says. "Our Textron family, and all 33 divisions of Textron [Bell's parent firm] and their chairmen talked to their employees and chambers of commerce."

Their contentions found receptive ears. In California alone, preliminary surveys by the state Transportation Department concluded that tilt-rotor planes could relieve airport congestion significantly for as many as 13 million passengers a year on shuttle service connecting Los Angeles, San Diego and San Francisco. If the lawmakers voted to support the Osprey program, the local communities could have the aircraft, and the Pentagon would be forced to pay the cost of developing it, both lawmakers and local officials reasoned. The peace dividend—of sorts— finally had arrived.

The tactic worked—instantly. Within weeks, the Osprey program counted among its supporters everyone from shuttle-magnate Donald Trump and hostage-rescuer H. Ross Perot Jr. to Rep. James L. Oberstar (D-Minn.), chairman of the aviation subcommittee of the powerful Public Works and Transportation Committee. More important, the civilian potential openly beckoned the support of virtually every lawmaker whose constituency traveled by air.

The blossoming campaign also got an unexpected boost from the threat of competition from Japan. [In the spring of 1990] visiting Japanese Trade Minister Hikaru Matsunaga told the Osprey's U.S. manufacturers: "If you produce this aircraft, I guarantee you we will buy it. If you do not, I guarantee we will build it ourselves."

For congressional backers of the plane, Matsunaga's challenge amounted to fighting words—and added a whole new "international competitiveness" dimension to the Osprey. Suddenly, a plane that was sold initially as a military weapon—critical to future Marine landings, to Third World commando raids and to search-and-rescue missions—had become a test of America's will to defend its historic lead in aerospace against a burgeoning Japanese threat.

Lobbyists for the Osprey seized on the new opening in grand style. In July [1990], just days before the House and Senate Armed Services committees moved to draft their versions of the 1991 defense spending bill, the manufacturers of the Osprey underscored the new trade stake by placing a Korean-made toy model of the plane on the desk of every lawmaker.

In an accompanying letter, three House members in whose districts the Osprey would be built warned colleagues that "our fiercest economic competitors have already duplicated the model, and they are avidly pursuing development of their own tilt-rotor aircaft. ... Our technological leadership can quickly erode."

Perhaps unsurprisingly, Congress, more preoccupied than ever about jobs, unfair trade practices and the future of U.S. industry, this year demanded to continue the Osprey, and insisted that the Pentagon—traditionally the incubator for new aerospace technology—must pay to build it. If the Defense Department refused to pioneer and adopt the revolutionary tilt-rotor technology, Osprey proponents argued, the United States would cede to Japan its long-held dominance in the civilian aircraft of the future.

But supporters insist as well that while politics and pork barrel might have won the Osprey a stay of execution, only the plane's multifaceted potential can explain Congress' continued defiance of the Pentagon's termination order.

And in the end, fate—in the person of Iraqi President Saddam Hussein—may have intervened to make a final pitch for the Osprey. Iraq's invasion of Kuwait—and the massive deployment of military forces to Saudi Arabia—appear[ed] to ... harden ... Congress' growing resistance to financing bombers and nuclear missiles.

Humiliated in his defeat when his recommendation to kill the Osprey was overturned in 1989, the House Armed Services Committee's Aspin [later] backed the Osprey lobby's bid to restore $603 million for the program—including $438 million for early production of the first full-scale aircraft. Operation Desert Shield "proves the wisdom" of such committee actions, Aspin said in a speech following the panel's drafting session.

74. Congress and the Presidency in American Foreign Policy

Rep. Lee H. Hamilton

The president, it is widely though erroneously thought, monopolizes the making of U.S. foreign policy. True, the president and his emissaries take charge of day-to-day diplomacy, but that does not mean they are free to shape foreign policy as they wish. Congress is increasingly an equal partner in foreign as well as domestic affairs; presidents ignore

Congress's input at their peril. Consultation and mutual trust are essential if the interbranch relationship is to succeed. Lee H. Hamilton, a Democrat from Indiana who has served in the House of Representatives since 1964, is a senior member of the House Foreign Affairs Committee and in 1986-1987 chaired the House Iran-contra investigating panel. This essay, published in the *Presidential Studies Quarterly* in 1988, is based on his address to an annual student symposium of the Center for the Study of the Presidency.

Some years ago a news reporter asked President Truman, "Who makes American foreign policy?" And President Truman's response was, "I make American foreign policy." A few years later a similar question was put to then Secretary of State, Dean Rusk, and Secretary Rusk said, "The President of the United States makes foreign policy."

Today most members of the Congress would not agree with President Truman and Secretary Rusk, although they may very well have been right in their day. Rather, they would hear the words of the distinguished Constitutional scholar, Edwin Corwin, who said ... that the United States Constitution is an invitation to the president and to the Congress to struggle for the privilege of conducting American foreign policy. Members of Congress today would acknowledge that the President should play the principal role in foreign policy making. However, they also believe that the Congress of the United States should play a strong and independent role.

Now there are several aspects of the current debate about the role of the President and the role of the Congress in American foreign policy that both the President and the Congress could agree upon. First, the power of the President, despite the role played by the Congress, is formidable. Under the Constitution, the President is the Commander in Chief of the armed forces. This constitutional charge; the unity of the executive branch; its control of information and other factors give the President an unassailable preeminence in foreign policy. Second, understanding the key role of the President, the Constitution of the United States enumerates most of the foreign policy powers in Article I on the Congress. In general, Congress is instructed to "provide for the common defence" and to declare war. Congress has great power, although not exclusive power over the purse.

The important role of the Congress in the foreign policy process is recognized here and abroad. Lobbyists for foreign policy issues stream to Capitol Hill. In public meetings across America constituents come to the meetings of their representatives to plead with their Congressman or Congresswoman about foreign policy issues. Visiting heads of government a few years ago used to come to Washington and visit the President; the Chairman of the World Bank; the Secretary of Defense; the Secretary of State, and go home. Now they insist on coming to Capitol

Hill to meet with members of the Congress. Ambassadors who are assigned to Washington parade the halls of the Congress on a daily basis.

It is worth remembering that despite the intense foreign policy debates that occur in this country, there remains a very broad consensus on most issues. For example, support for NATO and the Western security system; support for Middle East policy in broad terms; and economic and security assistance to the areas of the Middle East, Africa, and Central America. There is general support for tough policies against international terrorism and drug trafficking; so also there is general support for the opening to China. Today the areas of broad consensus of agreement in foreign policy are far greater than the areas of contention which get so much attention in the press. . . .

Members of Congress today know that every tough decision that is hammered out within the executive branch and hotly debated there, will also face a similar debate in the United States Congress. Periods of Congressional assertiveness in foreign policy have been frequent in this nation's history, and we are in such a period today. The Vietnam experience has been the most potent, but not the only experience that has served as a catalyst to congressional activism in congressional foreign policy.

Competition between the President and the Congress need not, and in my view, should not be viewed as having a winner and a loser. Debate, tension, and review can lead to decisions and actions which stand a better chance in serving the American national interest, and reflecting the values of the American people. Total cooperation between the two branches of government should not be regarded as the essential condition of sound foreign policy. The concern of the Congress should be to strike a reasonable balance between responsible criticism on the one hand, based on measured oversight of the executive branch, and responsible cooperation on the other hand, stimulated by good and sound procedures of consultation between the President and the members of Congress.

Permit me to give you a quick assessment of Congress' role in foreign policy. In doing so, I begin with some of the weaknesses in Congress in conducting or helping to conduct American foreign policy, and there are several. Diplomacy requires speed, but the Congress moves very slowly. Diplomacy requires flexibility and tact and nuance, but this does not describe Congressional action. We say yes or no to legislation. We approve or we reject aid to a given country. We grant aid or we take it away. Diplomacy requires secrecy; the Congress often leaks sensitive matters. Diplomacy requires a long view of the national interest; Congress is influenced by short term interest and often has its eye too much on the coming election. Diplomacy requires expertise, but Congress is often ignorant of foreign affairs; it changes its membership frequently and is overburdened with a very heavy schedule. Diplomacy requires sustained interest; the Congress' approach to foreign policy is sporadic and eclectic; it tends to focus on the immediate hot spots in the world. Diplomacy requires attention to a lot of interrelated problems; Congress tends to focus on narrow problems and often sees broad problems from the perspective of narrow interest. Diplomacy requires strong leadership, but power in the United States Congress is diffused. Congress cannot organize itself quickly and effectively on many issues.

Now these weaknesses must be balanced against a number of strengths. Congress is a deliberative body and deliberation often prevents error. Congress can act quickly upon occasion. Congress can often bring flexibility to diplomacy. A contact by a foreign official with a member of Congress is not an official contact, but it is a contact that can often be useful. Many, if not most leaks, come from the executive branch not from the Congress. Congress can play a valuable educational role, and individual members of Congress develop considerable skill in foreign policy. But Congress' strengths are principally its accessibility and its representativeness. If a constituent of mine wants to make his or her views known with respect to foreign policy, he or she cannot call up the President of the United States; cannot call up the Secretary of State; cannot even call up an assistant secretary of state, but he or she can certainly contact their congressman and make views known to them. That accessibility is a source of strength to the United States Congress in foreign policy making. *Representativeness,* which is the key characteristic of the United States Congress, is especially important because the executive branch cannot effectively pursue any foreign policy for an extended period of time without the support of the American people; and congressional support is a primary expression of the people's approval. The President is not likely to gain the support of the American people if he cannot gain the support of the United States Congress.

We hear frequent calls for bipartisanship. Presidents often make calls for bipartisanship. We all want to see bipartisanship in American foreign policy. We are feeling better if this nation stands united, speaking with one unambiguous firm voice. Often, however, these calls for bipartisanship are little more than appeals to the United States Congress to go along with the President's policy; to be more supportive of stated administration policy. Frankly such calls for bipartisanship usually seek to have Congress follow the President, never the opposite. . . .

The basis for bipartisanship and informed consent is trust and consultation. Now I understand that consultation with the Congress today is an extremely difficult task. There was a day, as for example in the Eisenhower Administration, when the President or the Secretary of State could call up Speaker [Sam] Rayburn and Senate Majority Leader [Lyndon] Johnson, talk with them and consult with the Congress. No longer can that be done. Members of Congress are younger; more sophisticated; more diverse, more independent; less respectful of seniority and traditional patterns of authority. There isn't any single person; there isn't any single committee, that the President can consult with and consider the process of consultation complete. Consultation by the executive, to be successful, has to be broad, detailed, and continuous.

The appropriate role for the Congress in foreign policy is to help reconcile conflicting pressures and responsibilities. It can help formulate policies but the President ought to implement those policies, not the Congress. The Congress can check excessive use of power by the presidency; the Congress can lend great support to the President when necessary and desirable in the conduct of foreign policy. The Congress can convey its views to the people of the President's policy and it can help inform and educate the people on foreign policy. The Congress constantly must juggle its representation of the people on the one hand and its own judgment as to where the national interest lies on the other. The two are not always the same. The Congress must balance its role as adversary against its role as a partner; its role as a critic against its role as a supporter; its inside private game, if you will, against the outside public game; its eagerness to assist in formulation of policy against its uneasiness in standing back and watching policy execution, especially when it does not agree with the matter of execution.

The following then are my conclusions about foreign policy making in our government. The power of the presidency is such that the President will continue to be and should continue to be, the dominant force in making American foreign policy. There are definite problems with the wrong sort of congressional involvement in foreign policy, stemming from some of the weaknesses that I referred to, just a moment ago. The Congress should investigate and provide oversight over foreign policy and help formulate general policy and principle. But Congress should not attempt to run foreign policy on a day to day basis. The power of the purse, and until recently, the legislative veto, have provided checks against unrestricted presidential power. Unrestricted presidential power is neither necessary nor tolerable in a free society. Those checks are needed. And whatever may be said about the constitutionality of the legislative veto, Congress obtained more prior consultation and better information from the President in those areas where the veto existed.

The key is *prior consultation*, and if the executive chooses that route, prior consultation, Congress then can be seen as an ally not as a foe of the President in foreign affairs. But such consultation is not easy to come by. At a minimum it means regular bipartisan briefings; ad hoc consultative groups set up for whatever the particular issue may be; a regular parliamentary question and answer session with, if not the President, then the Secretary of State; consultation on policy *before not after* a policy has been formulated. I think there are several ways *not* to conduct that consultation; to come before the Congress after a lengthy interagency debate and perhaps a 55, 45 decision within the executive branch and then to say to the Congress we had no other alternative is not the way to consult. Members of Congress know that these debates take place within the executive branch and they know that in foreign policy there are always other options and alternatives. To come to brief the Congress and to call that briefing a consultation is not the way to consult. In those instances, the executive is *informing* the Congress but *not* consulting. Similarly, to handle the Congress the way presidents often do with respect to arms control, for example, when they talk a lot about procedures but very little about substance; when they talk about atmosphere, but don't tell us really what is going on; that's not the way to consult either.

In the final analysis, I am convinced that in the framework of effective prior consultation the President will and should be given the initiative on foreign policy matters. What is essential is that the two branches of government have mutual respect for one another. So often the executive looks upon the Congress as an obstacle to be overcome, *not* as a partner in the process. We in the Congress must show a greater sensitivity to the difficulty of trying to legislate American foreign policy. For its part, the executive branch should do more than just touch base with legislators to placate them on issues of foreign policy. The purpose, I think, to be sought is *a genuine dialogue*, if you will, between the two branches of government on foreign policy questions. The executive branch is often reluctant to realize that Congress has a genuine place in the formulation of policy. But Congress is often reluctant to realize that the executive branch has a need for flexibility in the execution of the foreign policy of the day. Effective prior consultation, better information on the issues of the day; a deep respect for the shared powers given to each branch by the Constitution, these are the best ways to lubricate, if you will, this foreign policy process. With these assets there will usually emerge a coherent strategy significantly strengthened by congressional participation.

The separation of powers under our Constitution produces a healthy and a creative tension between the executive and the legislative branches. The process of making foreign policy in this country is never going to be tidy and clear-cut and neat. Sometimes it is going to be a bit messy and not always will the steps be clearly delineated. The diversity and the complexity of foreign policy is such that there will never be complete accord. Our expectations should not be extravagant, given the nature of the process, but the alternative to making the foreign policy system work better is confusion in a complicated and dangerous world, and that is not acceptable. The foreign policy process provided in our Constitution works if we understand it and if we use it with prudence and discretion.

75. The Constitution and the War Making Power

Sen. Max Baucus

Few historians or commentators believe the division of responsibility for war powers has worked well. Since passage of the War Powers Resolution in 1973, the nation several times has been involved in combat abroad, not always with the consultation or approval of Congress. In his speech, delivered on the Senate floor, and subsequently printed in the *Congressional Record* in 1983, Sen. Max Baucus reviews the background and evolution of the 1973 resolution, arguing that it helped restore the balance of power between the two branches. Not all observers, however, would agree with this optimistic assessment.

M r. President ... the people of this country have been faced with two international crises that have involved the use of American forces and the loss of American lives outside the borders of the United States. One was the brutal and tragic bombing of the Marine barracks in Beirut. The other was the armed American invasion and occupation of the Caribbean island of Grenada.

Each of these crises has raised basic and immediate questions— questions about why American troops were sent to Lebanon and Grenada in the first place, what their purpose is for staying, and how long it will take them to accomplish their objectives. All these questions are extremely important, and they all deserve prompt and public response.

But recent events have also raised a more fundamental and far-reaching question that we have tended to gloss over in the heat of current crises. In both Lebanon and Grenada, the introduction of American forces was undertaken at the initiative of the President alone, without prior authorization by the Congress. The question raised by such unilateral action is what, if any, role the Congress and the American people are to play in determining whether U.S. troops should be committed to hostilities on foreign soil.

In the context of current events, this question may seem to be an esoteric one. But it is a question that goes to the very foundation of our governmental structure and the delicate system of checks and balances embodied in our Constitution. It is a question that we can no longer afford to answer on a purely pragmatic and piecemeal basis.

Our Founding Fathers gave clear and distinct directions as to who was to hold the warmaking authority in the new Nation they were fashioning. In the Constitution, they designated the President as the Commander-in-Chief of the Armed Forces, or, as Alexander Hamilton described it in the *Federalist Papers,* "the first General and Admiral of the Confederacy." But they specifically left the power to use those Armed Forces—the power to declare war—in the hands of the Congress. The notes of the original Constitutional Convention leave no doubt that the Framers intended to give the President independent warmaking authority only "to repel sudden attacks" upon the United States. All other authority relating to the commitment of the Nation to war was to be vested exclusively in the Congress.

The decision of the Framers to place the warmaking power in the legislative branch was based primarily on their fear that the monarchical tyrannies from which they had just gained freedom would recur in their new Nation. To avoid the known dangers of concentrating the awesome power to make war in any one man, they placed it instead in the governmental body most directly representative of and responsive to popular sentiment. In this way, they sought to give the American people a stronger voice in their own destiny and to eliminate the possibility of future oppressive and unpopular wars. The benefit of congressional control over the use of armed force was succinctly noted by Thomas Jefferson in a letter to James Madison: "We have already given in example one effectual check on the Dog of war by transferring the power of letting him loose from the executive to the legislative body...."

Throughout the first hundred years of this country's history, few questions were raised about the Congress' ultimate responsibility for committing the Nation's Armed Forces to combat. Abraham Lincoln, speaking as a Congressman against an unauthorized use of American troops by President Polk, warned specifically of the dangers inherent in executive usurpation of the congressional warmaking power:

> Allow a President to invade a neighboring nation, whenever he shall deem it necessary to repel an invasion, and you allow him to do so, whenever he may choose to say he deems it necessary for such purpose—and you allow him to make war at pleasure.

It was not until the 20th century that "making war at pleasure" became a consistent, rather than an occasional, practice. Time and again during this century, Presidents sent American troops into foreign hostilities without prior authorization from the Congress. Our forces were sent into armed conflicts around the globe—into Central America and South America, into the Caribbean, into the Far East and the Middle

East, and most notably into Southeast Asia—all in the name of the national interest, all at the individual initiative of the President, and all with only ex post facto approval by the governmental body holding the exclusive power to make such commitments. In 1964, the nadir of congressional control and the height of congressional acquiescence was reached by the passage of the Gulf of Tonkin resolution, which gave the President virtually limitless power to use armed military force in Southeast Asia. The state of affairs existing at the end of the 1960s was aptly described by Senator Jacob Javits:

> We live in an age of undeclared war, which has meant Presidential war. Prolonged engagement in undeclared, Presidential wars has created a most dangerous imbalance in our Constitutional system of checks and balances.

In 1973, Congress began the process of recapturing its constitutional authority over the making of war by the passage of the War Powers Resolution. The resolution recognized that modern times may in some circumstances justify the exercise of immediate military force by the President, but it also sets limits on the President's ability to maintain a military presence in areas of hostile activity without explicit authorization from Congress. Specifically, it states that the President may, in urgent circumstances, inject armed American forces into actual or potential hostilities. However, before doing so, he or she must take every possible step to consult with Congress, and within 48 hours of the troop commitment, must issue a detailed report outlining the purpose and estimated duration of the American involvement. All U.S. troops must be withdrawn from the area of hostilities within 60 days unless Congress specifically authorizes a longer term of activity.

There is no doubt in my mind that the passage of the War Powers Resolution constituted a vital step toward reestablishing the proper balance between the executive and legislative branches in the realm of warmaking authority. More importantly, it constituted a vital step toward amplifying the voice of American people in discussions and decisions on the fundamental issue of whether there should be war or peace.

But the existence of the War Powers Resolution is not enough in itself. Without implementation, it is nothing more than a piece of paper. Those of us who are concerned about maintaining the constitutional system of checks and balances must be vigilant in insuring that the provisions and purpose of the resolution are faithfully fulfilled by the executive branch. We cannot afford to allow the occurrence of immediate crises to distort our constitutional vision. In short, we cannot afford to allow the 1980s to become another era of Presidential war or war at pleasure.

The situation in Lebanon and Grenada has evoked sharply different degrees of vigilance from Congress. When presented with the issue of continuing the American presence in Lebanon, the Congress authorized a full 18-month extension. It did so even in the absence of any solid and substantive explanation by the President as to the scope or purpose of the American mission there. I supported a much shorter, 60-day period of authorization. In my view, a period of 2 months is more than sufficient to allow the President to justify continued American involvement in the region. The Congress and the people of this Nation should demand such a justification before sanctioning lengthy and essentially unfettered executive discretion in the use of the country's Armed Forces.

In the controversy surrounding Grenada, the Congress has been much swifter to act and has given a much clearer indication of its willingness and ability to control the use of American Armed Forces in hostilities abroad. Within days of the initial invasion of the island, both Houses of Congress have specifically invoked the War Powers Resolution, thereby allowing a continuance of our military presence for a maximum of 60 days. That period can, of course, be extended, but only by the exercise of the warmaking power vested in the Congress by the Constitution.

Our Founding Fathers firmly believed that the welfare and future of the United States would be seriously threatened if the power to make war could be exercised by any single individual in the new government. I believe their fear was justified then, and I believe it is justified now. Presidential war—war that is undertaken without the express consent of the representative arm of the Federal Government—is anathema to both our sensibilities and our Constitution. For the sake of our Nation, we must never let it occur again. . . .

Chapter 15

Governing in the Twenty-First Century

The year 1987 marked the bicentennial of the Constitution, the working governmental plan of the United States. The institutions of the U.S. government date from 1789, the year the document was ratified by the states. In 1991 Americans honored the all-important addendum to the Constitution, the Bill of Rights.

As noted in Chapter 1, the Constitution is one of the oldest and most durable government charters in the world. When the founders gathered in Philadelphia in the summer of 1787, no nation had a single written constitution; today, nearly all do, although the hopeful ideals of some countries scarcely have been realized. The U.S. Constitution has undergone relatively few formal changes in its 200-year history—only twenty-six amendments in all. Of these, only a few address the basic structure of the system envisioned by the founders. The Twelfth Amendment revised electoral college balloting for the president and vice president; the Seventeenth instituted direct election of senators; the Twentieth changed the calendar of officeholding; the Twenty-second limited presidents to two terms in office; and the Twenty-fifth established a procedure for dealing with the death or disability of the president.

When the federal government was established, the United States was a nation far different from what it is today. The population was sparse, mostly rural, largely uneducated. The nation's social structure was simple; changes occurred gradually and were communicated slowly; government tasks were few. Several thousand miles of ocean insulated the new nation from the maneuvering of the great powers.

The population today is large, growing, and mainly urban and suburban. Because of longer life spans and moderate birth rates, the median age in the United States is rising: in 1986, for the first time, Americans aged sixty-five and older outnumbered teenagers. Geographic mobility continues to mark our national experience. Throughout most of this century the centers of population have been steadily shifting from the farms and small towns to the cities and their suburbs.

Today the movement is from the Northeast and rural Midwest to the South and Southwest (the so-called sunbelt states).

Racial, ethnic, and cultural diversity mark Americans of the late twentieth century. The early republic was primarily a society of white males, immigrants from the British Isles and northwest continental Europe. Neither women nor blacks participated in the affairs of state (the Constitution even provided that slaves be counted in the census as only three-fifths of a free person). Political upheavals (including a civil war) and waves of immigrants have broadened citizen participation in politics.

Technological miracles—mass production, electrical appliances, the automobile and the airplane, electronic communications, computers, and medical advances—have shrunk distances, made physical life easier, and fostered a more vivid sense of the national community. They have also made us part of a "global village," in which events and developments in any part of the world are apt to affect us.

Social changes have accompanied these demographic, political, and technological changes. More Americans work than used to be the case—including women. (Almost 60 percent of married women with children work outside the home.) In spite of the growing work force, we have more leisure time, and we retire at an earlier age. This means, among other things, that the issues that concern us go beyond jobs and financial well-being to those that affect our values, aesthetics, and ideological preferences.

To open this final chapter, a pair of articles probe the changing nature of America and its ways of coping with problems. In "America's Decadent Puritans" (Selection 76), the editors of The Economist, a British journal, remind us of what can best be described as problematic traits in the American character. As a superpower, the United States has exerted a positive force throughout the world in its commitment to freedom and self-determination. Yet the nation's moral certitude and quickness to seek military solutions to complex problems threatens other nations and breeds suspicion and resentment.

Demographic and technological shifts are the theme of Selection 77, "Where Is America Going?" Television journalist Robert MacNeil reviews the shift from an industrial to a postindustrial society. Like the editors of The Economist, MacNeil worries more about the nation's character than about its physical, economic, or governmental attributes.

The survival of the U.S. government over two centuries is, of course, no small achievement. Its institutions have withstood repeated stress and turbulence—riots, political assassinations, domestic scandals (such as Watergate), dubious foreign involvements (Vietnam, among others), and even a bloody civil war. In Selection 78, "Point-Counterpoint: Constitutional Reform," former representative and World Bank president Barber Conable (R-N.Y.) delivers a sober vote of confidence for the governmental apparatus, arguing that conflict and stalemate are just what the founders intended as a safeguard against tyranny. Political scientist James L. Sundquist, in contrast, calls for constitutional change. Although realistic about the chances for passage of amendments embodying even modest reforms, Sundquist argues that political leaders ought to devote serious attention to the question. Unlike Conable, he believes that stalemate and fragmentation will continue to be the foremost maladies of the system.

In view of the sweeping social and intellectual challenges facing the country, amending the Constitution may seem a trivial exercise. Nonetheless a number of commentators believe that steps must be taken to provide more coherence to the branches of government than the founders envisioned. Many advocate that the president and Congress be bound together more tightly by some elements of parliamentary government. Alternatives include allowing incumbent members of Congress to serve in the president's cabinet; establishing simultaneous four- or six-year terms for presidents and legislators alike; requiring voters to cast a single ballot not only for a party's presidential and vice-presidential ticket but also for a party's House and Senate candidates as a bloc; and authorizing the president or Congress, or both, to call for new elections to replace a "failed government."

Whatever the arguments for or against specific constitutional amendments, the debate is, in all probability, largely academic. Few reform proposals command intense support from the public. For all the Americans who revere the document, few have extensive knowledge of its specific provisions, and few exhibit deep feelings about them. The system for proposing and ratifying amendments is rigorous, challenging reformers to demonstrate not only numerical support but also staying power over time. The much debated Equal Rights Amendment (ERA), whose ratification seemed certain when it was proposed in 1972, eventually fell three states short of the thirty-eight (three-quarters of fifty) needed for passage. ERA was a dramatic lesson in the difficulty of making formal amendments to the Constitution.

There is no guarantee that the nation's successful adaptations in the past will translate into equally successful ones in the future. It is likely that the challenges facing the country will continue to grow in complexity and subtlety and that the margins for error will narrow. One thing is certain: the coming years will not be tranquil. Crisis is the hallmark of great powers, especially those governed by principles of popular government. As the early statesman Fisher Ames once observed, democracy as a form of politics resembles a wooden raft: it is exceedingly difficult to sink, but one's feet are always getting wet.

76. America's Decadent Puritans

Editors of *The Economist*

Emergent trends in the United States often dismay our friends and supporters abroad, just as they confound and enrage those who wish us ill. In 1990 the editors of *The Economist*, a London-based journal with a tradition of free-market ideology and pro-American sentiments, published a sharp critique of current American attitudes. They criticized what they term "decadent puritanism," which they define as "an odd combination of ducking responsibility and telling everyone else what to do." Evasion of responsibility is seen in the tendency to blame others for national failures and to evade candid self-criticism in favor of "politically correct" rationalizations. The result is a society that is becoming more conformist, that is prone to seek legalistic solutions to problems, and that takes itself far too seriously. "Lighten up" is a leading message for twenty-first-century America.

Considering the alternatives, it has been easy to admire the American way these past few decades. It was and is demonstrably better at making its average citizens rich and free than rival systems. Culturally, too, the world has voted for America by seeking everything from jeans to Michael Jackson. Yet if, today you stop the average European, or Japanese, or Latin American, or for full effect, Canadian in the street and ask him what he thinks about America, you are as likely to hear contempt as praise.

The Japanese will probably mention idleness and self-indulgence, the European philistinism and naivety, the Latin American insensitivity and boorishness. Someone will use the word materialist. Drugs, guns and crime will feature; so will a television culture catering to the lower common denominator of public taste, a political system corruptible by money, shocking contrasts of wealth and poverty, and a moralistic and litigious approach to free expression.

America attracts such bile partly because it is more self-critical than other nations. Hypocrisy is often in the eye of the beholder: how dare a European look down his nose at a country to whose universities his brightest fellow-citizens choose to flock? Foreign criticism often attacks American habits that the critics themselves happily adopt a few years later: from refrigerators and Elvis Presley to negative campaigning and aerobics. To criticise America is to criticise what the future holds in store.

This newspaper is unashamedly Americanophile, knowing that the British pot is at least as black as the American kettle. But it has misgivings about the direction in which some of America's "culture" is heading—precisely because the American way today tends to be the way of the world tomorrow. By culture we mean not painting and music, but way of living. The worry is about what might be called a "decadent puritanism" within America: an odd combination of ducking responsibility and telling everyone else what to do.

The decadence lies in too readily blaming others for problems, rather than accepting responsibility oneself. America's litigiousness is virtually banishing the concept of bad luck. The most notorious (and overexposed) examples come from tort law. A hotel refuses to allow an able-bodied guest to swim in its shallow rooftop pool because there is no lifeguard on duty. A drunken driver can sue his host for allowing him to get drunk. But there are other examples. If a prominent citizen becomes an alcoholic or is caught indulging some illegal appetite, he all too often claims he is a victim, not a fool. The habit of pleading insanity as an excuse for a crime is spreading. Increasingly, too, people are blaming their genes and finding sympathetic (and often foolish) scientific support. The exaggerated claims by a few scientists that they have found "genes for" alcoholism, or aggression, are well couched to prevent people taking the rap for their own actions.

To allow legal redress for negligence, or to seek to rehabilitate rather than punish victims—these are worthy aims. But fair redress is not always appropriate; sometimes the buck must simply stop. Just as an over-padded welfare state breeds a habit of blaming and expecting help from government, so America's legalism breeds a habit of shifting burdens on to somebody else. It saps initiative out of an economy quite as effectively as the state-sponsored variety.

Another facet of this phenomenon is the warped idea that the problem with America's underclass is a lack of self-esteem, and that the answer to poor educational performance is to teach more self-esteem. Bunk. The characteristic that in the past drove generations of immigrants from the underclass to prosperity was not self-esteem, it was self-discipline. The reason that Japanese schoolchildren—and the children of Asian immigrants in America—learn so much more than their American counterparts is discipline, not self-esteem.

To see how far such evasiveness has caught on, look at the new abundance of euphemism. Prisons have become "rehabilitative correctional facilities", housewives are "homemakers", deaf people are "hearing-impaired", the Cerebral Palsy society tells journalists never to use the word "suffer" about those with that "disease" (forbidden), "affliction" (forbidden), condition (allowed). Jargon cannot alter reality. How refreshing to hear a politician who favours both abortion and the death penalty described bluntly as "pro-death".

Take race. There are few countries on earth in which people are generally less prejudiced about colour than America, stereotypes of the old South and Bensonhurst notwithstanding. Yet there are few countries where the issue looms so large; where pressure groups are so quick to take offence at a careless remark, or where words are made to carry such a weight of meaning. "Black" is fast following negro into the lexicon of the forbidden, to be replaced by "African-American" in the never-ending search for a label without overtones. Some universities, egged on by their students, have recently imposed disgraceful restrictions on free speech rather than let bigots speak out on campus and be judged for what they are.

As for puritanism, America's search for fairness has begun to conflict with its famous tolerance for new peoples, new ideas and new technologies. A conformist tyranny of the majority, an intolerance of any eccentricity, is creeping into America, the west coast in particular. An increasingly puritanical approach to art, married to a paranoid suspicion of child-abuse, has made a photographer who takes pictures of parents with their children naked on the beach into a target for the FBI. Add to that sort of thing the ruthless prudishness of the television networks about anything except gratuitous violence, and the gradual assertion of "correct" ways of thinking about such things as smoking and affirmative action. It all adds up to a culture of conformity that would rather bore than shock.

A television script-writer recently admitted that he puts cigarettes into the hands only of baddies. A whole industry of pressure groups has arisen to try to persuade television producers to push "correct" ideas on their (fictional) programmes: smoking is bad for you, concern for the homeless is right, plastic bags are bad for the environment. All true, all admirable. But fiction is fiction, not a set of cautionary tales. (Perhaps the success of the surreal serial "Twin Peaks" will reverse this trend.)

As Americans get ever richer, they seem to grow more risk-averse, so that they become paranoid about hazardous waste in their district, obsessed with their cholesterol levels, and ready to spend large premiums for organic vegetables. It being a free world, they are welcome to do so, even if the risks from hazardous waste are exaggerated, or the risks from natural carcinogens in organic vegetables greater than from pesticides. But must they become killjoys in the process? Being bossed by faddish doctors is something people have come to expect. But neighbours and friends (and advertisers) have no need to be ruthlessly disapproving of the fellow who prefers cream and an early coronary to self-absorption in a costly gym building muscles he will never need.

None of these things is confined to America, but—like everything else—they breed faster and more lushly in America. And now the infection has spread to politicians, who have discovered that a quick way to television prominence is to take outraged offense at every imagined slight. Careers can collapse because of a single "gaffe" that does not pass some ideological litmus test. Television seems to have done its best to drive humour out of politics. Can you imagine Lyndon Johnson getting away with half of his witticisms today? If we are all to enjoy the twenty-first century, America must lighten up a bit.

77. Where Is America Going?

Robert MacNeil

The technological, social, and political innovations that have occurred in our lifetime promise even more fundamental changes in the future. We have already witnessed "revolutions" associated with civil rights, feminism, environmentalism, consumerism, and—most important of all—the shift from an industrial to a postindustrial economy. Demographic changes already in place will inevitably alter our nation's political life in the future: for example, the shift toward racial and ethnic minorities and the aging of the population. These changes will be matched by technological innovations. Even more daunting are the psychological challenges facing the nation's citizens; here the trends are less than reassuring. Do we still hold firm to the standards and values associated with our rise as a nation? Are we sufficiently devoted to the discipline of hard work, making goods, and producing services? Robert MacNeil, a Canadian, is a keen observer of the American character as co-host of the "MacNeil-Lehrer News Hour" on public television. His thoughts on this subject were given in a speech to the Economics Club of Detroit in 1990, subsequently published in *Vital Speeches of the Day*.

In 1989 my son graduated from high school and I talked to the graduating class. It made me think about my own high school graduation [in 1949] and how enormously things have changed in that time.

For example, I went to an all boys school in Canada. Girls were thought to be a dangerous distraction for boys. The idea was that if there were no girls around we wouldn't think about them. Girls were not permitted but cigarettes were. Imagine! They thought that cigarettes were less harmful to us than girls. That is how certainties can change in just four decades. . . .

On the day I graduated most of the girls who were our friends knew that their careers would be marriage. Period. Any woman here knows that's quite a change. The birth control pill had not been invented. Think how that has changed life. Panty hose had not been invented and ladies did not think themselves properly dressed in public without stockings, gloves and a hat.

The environment, if anybody used the word, was the area around you physically or psychologically, the urban environment. Until 1962 when Rachael Carson wrote "A Silent Spring," we did not think very much about the environment in terms of ecosystems. We put lead in gasoline and asbestos in schools, PCBs in transformers and everything in our rivers. . . .

Forty years ago America was a racially segregated country. In many states black Americans had to use separate restrooms and could not stay in the same hotels as whites or eat in the same restaurants; and they could scarcely vote. Forty years ago: like South Africa today. . . .

Tennis was a tiny, elite sport. Football was played on real grass and football players' mothers got very upset because they got grass stains on their nice uniforms. But never mind, Ronald Reagan was on television in the soap commercials to tell them what to use to get them clean again. And the women of those days were very grateful for his advice.

This was a country of more solutions than problems. Oh yes, there was life without a superbowl.

In short, many of the things we journalists like to call "revolutions" had not happened, the black revolution, women's revolution, the gay liberation movement, the environmental movement, the diet-exercise revolution, many medical revolutions, and the computer revolution, which created the biggest revolution of all, the third industrial revolution.

So in only 40 years, things have changed in some pretty drastic ways. The revolutions I have mentioned have made profound changes in how Americans work, dress, eat, travel, deal with illness, amuse themselves, think, pray, get educated, get married or don't, have children or don't—and so on. And, such is the pace of change now that we can confidently expect that things will change even more quickly in the next 40 years. . . .

Let us try to peer into the future to try to see what are the revolutions waiting to happen. What will be the forces shaping the next phase of this democratic experiment?

Let's start with the one force we can do almost nothing about, demographics: the way the population is changing.

America is a country that is getting older and less white. The most dramatic change is the aging of the U.S. population. There is no historical precedent for it. Life expectancy has been increasing steadily since 1950 due principally to the rapid decline in deaths from heart disease and stroke. The use of cholesterol-lowering drugs and clot dissolving agents could drive the rates even lower. That is one factor. So is improved nutrition and ideas about more exercise and less smoking and drinking.

Another factor will be a "senior boom" when the postwar baby boom reaches retirement age starting about 2010. A third factor is that younger Americans are having fewer babies and there are relatively fewer young Americans to have them. As a result a growing proportion of the U.S. population will be elderly. Through the first half of the 21st century, one American in five will be 65 or older. The population over 85 is growing most rapidly. By the year 2010 their numbers will double to nearly 5 million. Whoever the Willard Scott of that day is, he won't have enough time (it would take the entire Today Show) to say Happy Birthday to all the Americans 100 years old on any day.

Let's think of some of the consequences of this senior boom.

Today some 12 million elderly Americans need assistance with daily activities. By the year 2020, the number will be 23 million. Most such care is still provided by family members—meaning women. It is estimated already that the average household couple has more parents to look after than children. The average woman is likely to devote more years to an elderly relative than to caring for a dependent child—17 years for child care, 18 years for elder care. . . .

So will the growing number of elderly Americans needing health care. Since their medical needs are more complicated, they will drive the cost of health care up even faster than it has been going, with an impact on the costs all younger Americans pay in taxes or insurance. The impact on medicare and medicaid will reach crisis proportions. The political battles over benefits for the elderly and the taxes the young will have to pay to finance them have only begun.

Only the battle will be different from the past. Older Americans are not only more numerous: they vote. They will increasingly have the political clout to decide these issues. There will be real grounds for generational warfare on the political scene. Self-interest could even drive alienated younger Americans back to the voting booth. . . .

Another effect. If more Americans are older as a share of the population, fewer must be younger. With fewer entry age people joining the work force, there will be a scarcity of workers. Older Americans will have to stay longer at work and will need incentives to do so. Retirement patterns will change with an impact on the retirement industry and social security. One way of balancing the staggering cost of paying so much social security might be to delay it. Make the average retirement age 68 or 70. . . .

Before we leave the elderly, one more prediction: the reality will grow. We are on the verge over the next 20 years or so, of phenomenal medical discoveries, chiefly through genetic research. We will not only break open the genetic secrets of one disease after another: it is quite likely that we will uncover the secrets of the aging process itself. Why do skin cells break down at a certain age, why does menopause in women arrive in the fourth to fifth decade? It is quite possible that knowing such answers we will be able to control the effects, thus increasing life expectancy even further. And that would mean even larger numbers of older Americans as well as much healthier middle aged and younger Americans.

And that brings us to the second factor that will shape our future: technology.

It is dangerous to make predictions about new technology beyond a few years. They always fall short or childishly exaggerate. If you look at what the most advanced thinkers thought the future would look like when they designed the 1939 World's Fair, you will smile at the quaintness of their vision. They were prisoners of their time and its attitudes as we are of ours. We can never see far enough.

With that caution, let us take a look. . . .

In our lifetimes two things have happened that would leave the philosophers of other ages gasping with astonishment. In the first place we have developed the capacity to end human life, to make ourselves extinct: not just to kill a few thousands on a battlefield here and there. But to snuff out the entire human species: perhaps even to render our planet incapable of sustaining life for thousands of years. Fortunately we seem to be drawing back from such madness.

In the second place, we have reached a point in technology where man's genius has given him the tools, or the way to design the tools, to solve almost any physical problem the human mind can imagine.

We can travel into space and will go much further in the next fifty years, perhaps establishing colonies in the near solar system. We can explore the farthest depths of the sea and reveal secrets lost for thousands of years. We cannot, it is true, tame the seas, or calm the hurricanes, volcanoes or earthquakes. But we understand them better every day. . . .

Computers plus biological knowledge are beginning to give us bio-technology which could revolutionise the production of food. In theory desirable genetic characteristics in a steak or an egg, or a stalk of wheat can be discovered and replicated endlessly in factories. That holds the hope of solving man's oldest problem, feeding the human race. The population of the world, now about 5 billion, is expected to double to 10 billion by the year 2035. Most of that growth will occur in the Third World which cannot reliably feed itself now. Experts say that in the interim we will have to produce as much food as mankind did in its entire history. . . . It is unlikely that it will be done by planting more land out into crops. . . . The food will have to come from some techno-logical innovation like genetic engineering. . . .

The same may be true of energy. It may be possible a few decades from now to create a clean and renewable kind of energy; like a genetically-engineered tree that spits something like gasoline. That may be necessary because the comfortable supplies of oil we now enjoy—after two big scares in the 70s—are temporary. Sometime early in the next century, perhaps only 20 years from now, the crunch will come again. With the population growing, and more countries industrializing, the need for petroleum will soar. They will need oil and raw materials from oil to drive their development, to raise their living standards, to become more like us. But the world supply of oil is finite and as it becomes scarcer, the price will rise dramatically. Everything that uses oil—cars, trucks, electricity generating plants, home heating, chemical and plastics industries—will be transformed by the shortage. Things made from petroleum could become too expensive to use. . . .

I keep mentioning computers. We have only begun to realise the potential of the information processing revolution. Some experts believe within just 20 years these machines will be one to ten thousand times better and faster than they are now.

Early in the century, it was a great novelty for an American household to have one electric motor in the house. Now it is routine to have scores of such motors, in vacuum cleaners, tooth brushes, razors, pencil sharpeners, knife grinders, can openers and hair dryers. The computer will become as ubiquitous.

Technology leads us to the third factor that is going to shape America's future profoundly—and that is competition. Competition is a concept that is only beginning to creep into the American psyche, or should we say *creep back* because it used to be there.

In 1945, the United States bestrode the world like a colossus and commanded 75 percent of the GNP for the globe. Today it is close to 20 percent. That decline is not all due to American failure. America helped other countries, particularly its former enemies, to prosper and world gross product has grown. But it means that the world is a very different place from that at the end of World War II. By 1992, the United States will no longer possess the largest unified market in the world. That will be the European Community. For all real purposes it already exists.

We're all familiar with the figures for the decline in the American share of the market in electronics, machine tools, and automobiles.

Since the Vietnam War, America's relative position in the world has changed radically. But public attitudes change much more slowly, because to accept a change in status undermines a nation's myths about itself. The greater the power, the harder the myths may be to change. First you must recognize change, admit change, then apply that recognition inwardly, to the spiritual and political part of the national psyche.

Just as big a change in the future as razzle dazzle high technology and a different age distribution, America is going to undergo a change of psychology, a change of thinking about the world. I think we are just beginning that process, just beginning to discover interdependence.

This is complicated by the biggest psychological change of all and the most sudden, the conversion of the Soviet Union from Evil Empire to almost the status of normal state. Our political system has only begun to digest that reality. It will take years to dismantle the psychological and material distortions of American life (positive and negative) produced by the Cold War. It is an interesting question: was the Cold War so good for some parts of the American economy (however it bent other American values out of shape) that ending it will be very painful? . . .

So the biggest changes facing us may well be *psychological*. If you look back, that was true over the last 40 years and it probably will be in the next.

These are some of the realities that will shape our modes of living and thinking:

Being American, a person or a product, will no longer automatically mean being the best. Being best will have to be competed for.

In the future there will be major mutual surrenders of national sovereignty (each nation will give up a little of its independence) on such matters as the environment.

And there will be surrenders of individual rights. For example, it would not surprise me at all if smoking were made much more widely illegal. It may simply be too expensive for the national health system (which is inevitable long before then) to pay the costs of the illness and death that smoking create. Some kind of coordinated national health system is inevitable because the nation cannot indefinitely tolerate the rising costs of health care (much higher as a percentage than other countries) which may offer the best treatment in the world for some, but which still leaves millions of Americans out. You know that move is getting serious when General Motors and Chrysler are leading the charge because their health care costs are out of control.

I think it is probable that we and our children will live with higher taxes. We are in a dream world at present. We do not pay our way and we neglect many needs. How can you be the world's leading democracy, the shining light to the world, lecturing the Chinese and Russians about the virtues of a free society, when something like a fifth of your own population, 40 million people, have no real share in the dream you parade to the world—in housing, medical care, employment, education, opportunity? You do not solve that by appeals to voluntaryism. It will catch up and it will have to be paid for and that is going to be hard with the debt that has been accumulated for the next generation.

One thing that will have to be paid for is education. If we don't solve the education problem there will be no hope of remaining competitive in the world, or retaining America's dwindling lead in high technology.

America led the second industrial revolution because it had the best educated work force in the world. It is now, as we know, in serious danger of trailing in the third industrial revolution because this nation has one of the worst educated work forces in the leading industrial countries. But what to do about it, once we have recognised the problem? . . .

Despite all the talk of an education crisis, at the federal level you do not feel the sense of urgency that was apparent in this country in 1958, when the Sputnik scare galvanised a rush to science and math education, with federal backing. It does not sound like a national emergency—not like drugs. But by all accounts it *is* a national emergency. Education plus investment translates into productivity. Productivity translates into standard of living.

The American standard of living has marked time for a decade and a half while that of competitor countries has risen. And that's not counting things like health care and social security systems that are superior in some of those other countries and add to the quality of life. If the trends of the 70s and 80s continued, those countries would surpass the U.S. in productivity and standard of living.

That doesn't sound as dramatic as Communists at the gates (you can't build a sexy weapons system to fight it) but it is probably now a greater threat than communism to the American Way of Life.

In the series Learning in America, our business correspondent, Paul Solman, went to a high school near Chicago. Half of the seniors were headed for college. He asked how many intended to work in a factory. Not one. One said: "A factory gets cold in the winter. It's hot in the summer, you know, you sweat a lot, you're dirty all the time. If you'd like a better job, you might have to sit in an office, maybe sign a couple of papers a day and get the same amount of money."

Another said: "Oh, I don't really see myself working eight hours a day, you know, five days a week or four days a week. That's not what I want to do for the rest of my life." In their own language, where are these kids coming from? They are coming from a society that has taught them such attitudes.

This has become a hedonist, a pleasure-seeking society. I have just published a book about my childhood and my parents and the exercise made me think a lot about them. They were married one month before Wall Street crashed in 1929 and my father was out of work for three years. That colored their thinking and my upbringing. . . .

Such attitudes are no longer the governing attitudes in this culture. The attitude is "I want it all and I want it now." This is a society that lives to gratify itself. Thank God, you say, that's what keeps us prosperous, the consumer drives the economy. Americans want things like asparagus, tomatoes and strawberries that grow naturally in certain seasons—all year around. So by a combination of imports, genetic manipulation, cold storage and sophisticated shipping and marketing, we can have them all year around. Wonderfully efficient. The Soviets can't get tomatoes reliably to market even in high season. We have created and satisfied enormous demand and the wheels of commerce turn with wondrous ease, a model to the world.

The *New Yorker* did a long study of the tomato developed for all season growing and shipping, called the Square Tomato. It revealed that tomatoes had been bred so tough that, proportionate to their weight . . . they had impact resistance greater than [that] required on car bumpers!

We have become brilliant at breaking down the natural conservatism, or caution in grown up people and converting ourselves into children. I want it now. I don't want to wait five minutes.

Now how are you going to turn that around, start converting to a society that will postpone some gratification, build up savings, borrow less? Not until the lightning of some terrible swift sword cuts through this dream of all wishes always fulfilled.

I think the politics of this country—at least at the national level—show there is no appetite for such lightning, for such a sharp dose of reality. . . .

78. Point-Counterpoint: Constitutional Reform

Barber Conable
James L. Sundquist

The Bicentennial era is an appropriate time to think seriously about the Constitution's strong and weak features and about possible reform. Barber Conable, among many others, believes that the Constitution has functioned well since 1787, allowing conflicting views to be voiced in an institutional arrangement that promotes free expression and protects minority rights. James L. Sundquist counters that structural reform is needed. He devoted several years to studying the history of constitutional reform and to considering the desirability and likelihood of change. The results of his research are well worth reading in *Effective Government and Constitutional Reform* (1986). Conable represented a congressional district in Rochester, N.Y., for twenty years and later served as president of the World Bank. Sundquist is emeritus senior fellow at the Brookings Institution in Washington, D.C. Conable's article was published in *Roll Call* in 1984, Sundquist's in *This Constitution* also in 1984.

Barber Conable:
Government Is Working

My terminal legislative condition has caused me recently to muse more than usual about the interesting job that has claimed my energies over the past 20 years. To oversimplify my conclusions, I believe that representative government is alive and well here in Washington, that the governmental system conceived by the Founding Fathers was wise and a continuing part of our heritage, that a realistic expectancy of government and an understanding of how it functions are probably more important than any of the specific things government does, and that I am blessed in this skeptical age to have had the experience which brings these conclusions forth.

This optimistic assessment seems to fly in the face of the well-known mess which at any given time clutters up the Washington landscape. Why, you may well ask, are not our problems solved if government is functioning as it should? Why aren't we more secure, happier, and more satisfied that our prospects are brighter than those of our ancestors? Maybe messes result from governments trying to do too much, not too little.

I didn't say representative government was efficient or that the government was dealing well with our problems, only that it is working out the way it was intended and that we are the better for it. Those who want a government that solves everybody's problems efficiently should turn to some other system than representative democracy. When decision rests on the consent of the governed, it comes slowly, only after consensus has built or crisis has focused public attention in some unusual way, the representatives in the meantime hanging back until the signs are unmistakable. Government decision, then, is not the cutting edge of change but a belated reaction to change.

Fortunately, our society has many decision makers outside Washington, in the churches and non-profits, in the other levels of government, in the private sector, in the schools and the community organizations. In short, the involved citizens of America do their own thing, bring about change, and then drag government kicking and screaming into recognizing that change has occurred and that it should be reflected in the way the government does business.

The irony is that the traditional American liberal believes that this conservative, lagging force should be the major instrumentality of change in our society. Liberal thinkers describe the way government ought to be, not the way it is, far behind the curve because accountability makes it so. In effect, they are yearning for philosopher-kings with the power and the will to do for the people what the people are not yet ready for, rather than for representatives.

One of the lessons of history is that people with the power to be philosopher-kings quickly become more kings than philosophers, and not comfortable purveyors of liberalism. It's safer to let the people decide first, even though it's not very inspiring to have a laggard government. Don't expect too much: realism about the way governments function is better in the long run than the disillusionment that follows wishful thinking.

The Founding Fathers didn't want efficient, adventurous governments, fearing they would intrude on our individual liberties. I think they were right, and I offer our freedom, stability and prosperity as evidence. I'm not indicting our government when I describe it in these terms, but I'm saying that its role was properly designed not to damage the dynamics of a free society.

James L. Sundquist:
. . . But Not as Well as It Should

Representative Conable has a high tolerance level. He acknowledges the "well-known mess" in Washington, admits that inefficiency and delay characterize the government's response to national needs, but then counsels his readers to lower their expectations, stop asking the government to "deal . . . well with our problems," and just accept this best-of-all-possible governmental systems.

He reasons that if we keep our government inefficient enough, it will be incapable of embarking on "adventurous" efforts to change society. True enough. But that is the wrong issue. In these days of neo-conservatism and neo-liberalism, nobody is going to try to remake anything much, whichever party is in power—as anyone following the 1984 campaign must know. The issue is a more fundamental one: whether the government has the institutional capacity to fulfill its *inescapable* responsibilities.

Take the deficit. Running in the $150-200 billion range as far ahead as anyone can see, it is scarcely a matter that can be left to those "decision makers outside Washington"—churches and non-profits, states and cities, the private sector, schools and community organizations—who Mr. Conable tells us should lead the government. The responsibility for coping with the deficit falls squarely on Washington's decision-makers, including the Ways and Means Committee on which the Congressman has served so long with such great distinction.

And on this matter, virtually everyone warns that the "laggard" tendency of our government, which Mr. Conable finds so praiseworthy, is in fact a peril. President Reagan calls the size of the deficit outrageous and demands a balanced budget. Leaders of both parties in both houses of the Congress warn that the country is headed for disaster. Wall Street agrees. So, save for a few ideologues, do economists both in and out of government. Yet no action anywhere near commensurate with the scale of the problem is in sight.

One could go on to list other issues that only the government can deal with: the unchecked flow of illegal aliens, the financial crisis of Medicare, revolutions in Central America, and so on. But the point is clear: A government deliberately stripped of the capacity to be adventurous and to "do too much" also lacks capacity to do that bare minimum of things that it cannot escape doing and that are crucial to the country's security and well-being.

So, even as we praise the genuine merits of the constitutional system the Framers gave us, it is surely timely during these Bicentennial years to ask whether some greater degree of efficiency, dispatch, responsibility, and accountability might be achieved without jeopardizing the conservative ideal of limited government that Mr. Conable ably espouses.

I suggest, among other questions to be asked as we approach the Bicentennial celebration, these:

Would an electoral system that encouraged, rather than discouraged, unified party control of the three centers of decision-making—Presidency, Senate, and House—make for more effective and responsible government?

Would longer terms for the President and for House members enable them to rise to a higher level of statesmanship in confronting crucial issues?

Would a span longer than two years between national elections, and a life of more than two years for a Congress, enable decision-makers to come to grips with issues now left unresolved each two years for lack of time?

Whenever deadlock and quarrelling between the President and the Congress reduce the government to immobility, could a better solution be devised than simply waiting helplessly until the next presidential election comes around?

Such questions do not challenge the fundamental structure of the government. They simply suggest that, perhaps, the constitutional structure is not beyond improvement. The Founding Fathers who, after all, scrapped the Articles of Confederation and wrote a wholly new instrument of government, were among the most "adventurous" of all our forebears. They would be the last to understand how, two hundred years later, anyone could regard complacency as the highest civic virtue.

Appendix

Further Study of
Government and Politics

Those who have read the articles in this collection may want to delve further into American government and politics. Whether studying a specific issue or examining the background and record of an elected official or political figure, researchers face a wealth of materials from which to draw. To find such information is no great feat; it abounds in written and electronic form. What is difficult is to sift the reliable from the unreliable, the significant from the trivial. This brief essay outlines some of the best sources of information and suggests strategies for further research.

Newspapers and Journals

To remain informed about public affairs, one must regularly read a major daily newspaper. The *New York Times* and the *Washington Post* are good choices because they cover government and politics extensively and because they are indexed. A few other papers customarily run original stories of high quality; these include the *Boston Globe*, the *Baltimore Sun*, and the *Los Angeles Times*. Two special papers with national circulation—the *Christian Science Monitor* and the *Wall Street Journal*—contain excellent interpretive articles in nearly every issue.

Beyond these few publications, coverage of politics and government in the average daily newspaper is quite variable. Most papers are owned by large chains, and all subscribe to news services such as those provided by the Associated Press, the *New York Times*, and the *Washington Post-Los Angeles Times* syndicate. When local editors choose knowledgeably from available syndicated material, readers may benefit from sharp reporting; otherwise, the stories may be perfunctory and drastically cut. It is well to remember that the average daily paper wins its readers by local coverage, features, and advertising, not by in-depth analysis of public affairs.

In reading the editorial and opinion pages of the paper, one should be even more cautious. Editorials express the views, sometimes informed and sometimes not, of the editors who run the paper or the company that owns it. Syndicated columnists (whose work usually appears opposite the editorial page—hence the "op-ed" page) tend to woo readers more by forceful opinions or clever writing than by careful reporting or analytical precision. Several exceptions are David S. Broder, an authoritative student of party politics; Mark Shields, a former campaign consultant who writes insightfully about campaign strategies and tactics; and William Safire, who provides thoughtful observations about language and politics.

The three major news magazines—*Time, Newsweek,* and *U.S. News & World Report*—cover leading national and international stories, although in recent years they have cut back somewhat in favor of "lifestyle" items that sell newsstand copies. Their reporters are as good as any, but their stories are so heavily edited and styled that the content sometimes suffers.

Specialized publications offer more to the serious student. These include journals such as *Campaigns and Elections, Foreign Affairs, Foreign Policy,* and *The American Enterprise.* Some scholarly journals are of interest to the general reader: among them, *Congress and the Presidency, Legislative Studies Quarterly,* and *Presidential Studies Quarterly.* Journals of opinion include the conservative *National Review,* the neoconservative *Public Interest,* and the liberal *Nation* and *New Republic.*

Congressional Quarterly Weekly Report and *National Journal* are weekly magazines indispensable for keeping track of Washington events; most serious researchers regularly read one or both of them. These two publications (and their periodic indexes) are normally the first stop for anyone initiating research on public policy. They follow virtually all major institutional and policy developments involving Congress, executive agencies, and the courts. They examine political trends and print analyses by experts on their staff. Congressional Quarterly also publishes an annual *Almanac* that condenses material from its *Weekly Report* along with detailed records of congressional votes.

Reference Books

To find out more about elected officials—members of Congress and governors—two similar publications are highly recommended: *Almanac of American Politics,* compiled by Michael Barone (and associates) and published by National Journal, Inc., and *Politics in America,* edited by Alan Ehrenhalt and published by Congressional Quarterly, Inc. Both feature brief biographies of officials, including committee assignments, interest group ratings, and voting records; profiles of states and congressional districts also are presented.

Congressional Quarterly publishes several other important reference works in this field. *America Votes,* compiled by Richard Scammon and Alice McGillivray and issued biennially, contains primary and general election returns for presidential, gubernatorial, and congressional races for the post-World War II period. *Guide to U.S. Elections* lists historical election results: popular vote returns for gubernatorial elections since 1789, for presidential and House races since 1824, and for Senate elections since 1913.

Deliberations and decisions of the Supreme Court and federal district and appellate courts—scantily covered in conventional media—can be followed in *United States Law Week,* published every Tuesday by the Bureau of National Affairs, Inc. The full texts of Supreme Court decisions are reprinted in two semimonthly publications, *Supreme Court Reporter* (West Publishing Company) and *United States Supreme Court Reports, Lawyers' Edition* (Lawyers Cooperative Publishing Company). Two weekly newspapers catering to the legal profession, *National Law Journal* and *Legal Times of Washington,* contain stories on appointments to federal agencies, personnel changes, departments, politics, executive-legislative relations, regulatory policy, administrative law, and reviews of scholarly literature.

To delve into the details of policies, even more specific publications may be called upon. Thousands of magazines and newsletters cater to every conceivable occupational or recreational interest. Trade, professional, and labor groups rely on periodicals to inform and mobilize their members. Although few of these publications focus primarily on government and politics, all of them run political stories from time to time.

Radio and Television

Ironically, the media with the widest audiences are the least reliable purveyors of information about government and politics. Radio and television are significant, however, in two ways: they convey fast-breaking events with a speed and immediacy that the print media cannot match, and they are the average citizen's primary source of information about the political world. It is useful to be exposed to radio and television if only because they shape public perceptions.

For reflection and analysis, one rarely relies on the electronic media. From their beginnings, radio and television have been primarily entertainment vehicles, assigning news and analysis a distinctly subordinate role. In 1961, Newton Minow, when head of the Federal Communications Commission, described television as "a vast wasteland"; that judgment remains accurate today for much of the reporting of government and political news. Newscasts of the major networks usually present condensed, superficial versions of events.

Notable exceptions to this rule are the "MacNeil-Lehrer News Hour," with Robert MacNeil and Jim Lehrer, on public television; and "All Things Considered," with Washington reporters such as Cokie Roberts and Linda Wertheimer, on public radio. Occasionally, special reports are aired on radio and television that provide in-depth analysis of current issues. Newsmakers in the nation's capital pay close attention to the Sunday morning news shows—"Meet the Press" (NBC), "Face the Nation" (CBS), and "This Week with David Brinkley" (ABC).

More specialized programming is a boon for serious students of government and politics. The Cable News Network (CNN) has built a loyal audience with its all-news format. Equally important, the Cable-Satellite Public Affairs Network (C-SPAN) broadcasts House and Senate sessions, committee hearings, speeches, and public affairs discussions. C-SPAN's programming provides valuable on-site coverage for millions of viewers who otherwise would not have access to these events.

Government Documents

There is a myth that politicians never say what is "really" on their minds, but careful review of the public record will dispel that notion. The Congressional Record is a transcript of House and Senate floor proceedings, which includes the recorded statements of legislators as well as formal votes and other actions of the two houses.

Well-stocked research libraries will have the whole range of congressional documents: bills and resolutions, committee prints, hearings, reports, and other House and Senate documents. From these materials one can trace legislation from inception to passage. Bound volumes of laws passed by Congress and signed by the president are called the United States Statutes at Large; the codified form of these laws, arranged according to fifty topical "titles," is called the United States Code.

Executive branch actions are documented, although not as extensively as those of the legislative branch. The Weekly Compilation of Presidential Documents contains the text of all speeches, press conferences, and public letters of the president. These are bound in an annual publication, Public Papers of the President. The president's budget recommendations, usually issued each January, are published in several volumes. In addition to the budget itself (a document hundreds of pages long), several supplements are quite useful for students of government. These include the *Appendix,* which provides details for thousands of appropriations accounts; *Special Analyses,* which contain in-depth studies and trend data; and *Historical Tables,* which supply data on budget receipts, outlays, surpluses, deficits, and debt from 1940 to (projections for) the current year.

Current federal regulations are printed in the *Federal Register,* a daily publication. The official handbook of the federal government is the annual *United States Government Manual,* which briefly describes the purpose, functions, organization, and key personnel of government agencies in the three branches. Statistical information on economic, social, and political subjects is listed in the annual *Statistical Abstract of the United States.*

Most of these reference materials are available in libraries of all sizes. All of them are readily available in university and research libraries. In conjunction with the basic interpretive books listed in the next section, these sources will provide ample information for the student of government and politics.

Suggested Readings

Chapter 1:
The Constitutional Framework

Farrand, Max, ed. *The Records of the Federal Convention of 1787.* New Haven, Conn.: Yale University Press, 1937.

Hamilton, Alexander, John Jay, and James Madison. *The Federalist.* Edited by Benjamin Fletcher Wright. Cambridge, Mass.: Harvard University Press, 1966.

Wills, Garry. *Inventing America.* Garden City, N.Y.: Doubleday, 1978.

Wood, Gordon S. *The Creation of the American Republic, 1776-1787.* New York: W. W. Norton, 1969.

Chapter 2:
Federalism: National, State, and Local Government

Dye, Thomas. *American Federalism.* Lexington, Mass.: Lexington Books, 1989.

Elazar, Daniel J. *American Federalism: A View from the States.* 3d ed. New York: Harper & Row, 1984.

Sundquist, James L. *Making Federalism Work.* Washington, D.C.: Brookings Institution, 1969.

Walker, David B. *Toward a Functioning Federalism.* Cambridge, Mass.: Winthrop, 1981.

Welborn, David, and Jesse Burkhead. *Intergovernmental Relations in the American Administrative State: The Johnson Presidency.* Austin, Tex.: University of Texas Press, 1989.

Chapter 3:
Public Opinion and Participation

Berger, Arthur, ed. *Political Culture and Public Opinion.* New Brunswick, N.J.: Transaction, 1989.

Cantril, Albert H. *The Opinion Connection: Polling, Politics, and the Press.* Washington, D.C.: CQ Press, 1991.

Conway, M. Margaret *Political Participation in the United States.* Washington, D.C.: CQ Press, 1991.

Cronin, Thomas E. *Direct Democracy: The Politics of Initiative, Referendum, and Recall.* Cambridge, Mass.: Harvard University Press, 1989.

Natchez, Peter B. *Images of Voting/Visions of Democracy: Voting Behavior and Democratic Theory.* New York: Basic Books, 1985.

Chapter 4:
Political Parties

Epstein, Leon D. *Political Parties in the American Mold.* Madison, Wis.: University of Wisconsin Press, 1986.

Sabato, Larry J. *The Party's Just Begun.* Glenview, Ill.: Scott, Foresman, 1988.

Sorauf, Frank J. *Party Politics in America.* 5th ed. Boston: Little, Brown, 1984.

Sundquist, James L. *Dynamics of the Party System.* Washington, D.C.: Brookings Institution, 1983.

Chapter 5:
Political Interest Groups

Berry, Jeffrey M. *The Interest Group Society.* Boston: Little, Brown, 1984.

Cigler, Allen J., and Burdett A. Loomis, eds. *Interest Group Politics.* 3d ed. Washington, D.C.: CQ Press, 1991.

Lowi, Theodore J. *The End of Liberalism.* New York: W. W. Norton, 1969.

Schlozman, Kay Lehman, and John T. Tierney. *Organized Interests and American Democracy.* New York: Harper & Row, 1986.

Truman, David B. *The Governmental Process.* 2d ed. New York: Alfred A. Knopf, 1971.

Chapter 6:
Communications Media and Politics

Broder, David S. *Behind the Front Page*. New York: Simon & Schuster, 1987.

Cook, Timothy. *Making Laws and Making News*. Washington, D.C.: Brookings Institution, 1989.

Entman, Robert. *Democracy without Citizens: Media and the Decay of American Politics*. New York: Oxford University Press, 1989.

Graber, Doris. *Mass Media and American Politics*. 3d ed. Washington, D.C.: CQ Press, 1989.

Halberstam, David. *The Powers That Be*. New York: Alfred A. Knopf, 1981.

Chapter 7:
Campaigns and Elections

Ehrenhalt, Alan. *The United States of Ambition: Politicians, Power, and the Pursuit of Office*. New York: Times Books, 1991.

Herrnson, Paul S. *Party Campaigning in the 1980s*. Cambridge, Mass.: Harvard University Press, 1988.

Jackson, Brooks. *Honest Graft: Big Money and the American Political Process*. Washington, D.C.: Farragut Publishing Co., 1990.

Magleby, David, and Candice Nelson. *The Money Chase: Congressional Campaign Finance Reform*. Washington, D.C.: Brookings Institution, 1990.

Reichley, James A., ed. *Elections American Style*. Washington, D.C.: Brookings Institution, 1987

Chapter 8:
Congress

Davidson, Roger H., and Walter J. Oleszek. *Congress and Its Members*. 3d ed. Washington, D.C.: CQ Press, 1990.

Fenno, Richard F., Jr. *Home Style: House Members in Their Districts*. Boston: Little, Brown, 1978.

Krehbiel, Keith. *Information and Legislative Organization*. Ann Arbor, Mich.: University of Michigan Press, 1991.

Oleszek, Walter J. *Congressional Procedures and the Policy Process*. 3d ed. Washington, D.C.: CQ Press, 1989.

Smith, Stephen S., and Christopher Deering. *Committees in Congress*. 2d ed. Washington, D.C.: CQ Press, 1990.

Chapter 9:
The Presidency

Corwin, Edward S. *The President: Office and Powers, 1787-1957*. 4th rev. ed. New York: New York University Press, 1957.

Cronin, Thomas, ed. *Inventing the American Presidency*. Lawrence: University Press of Kansas, 1989.

Fisher, Louis. *Constitutional Conflicts between Congress and the President*, 3d rev. ed. Lawrence: University Press of Kansas, 1991.

Neustadt, Richard E. *Presidential Power and the Modern Presidents*. New York: The Free Press, 1990.

Pfiffner, James. *The Strategic Presidency*. Chicago: The Dorsey Press, 1988.

Chapter 10: The Bureaucracy

Aberbach, Joel D. *Keeping a Watchful Eye: The Politics of Congressional Oversight*. Washington, D.C.: Brookings Institution, 1990.

Fesler, James, and Donald Kettl. *The Politics of the Administrative Process*. Chatham, N.J.: Chatham House, 1991.

Heclo, Hugh. *A Government of Strangers*. Washington, D.C.: Brookings Institution, 1977.

Seidman, Harold, and Robert Gilmour. *Politics, Position, and Power: The Dynamics of Federal Organization*. 4th ed. New York: Oxford University Press, 1986.

Wilson, James Q. *Bureaucracy: What Government Agencies Do and Why They Do It*. New York: Basic Books, 1989.

Chapter 11:
The Federal Courts

Fisher, Louis. *Constitutional Dialogues*. Princeton, N.J.: Princeton University Press, 1988.

Levy, Leonard W. *Original Intent and the Framers' Constitution*. New York: Macmillan, 1988.

Levy, Leonard W., Kenneth Karst, and Dennis Mahony, eds. *Judicial Power and the Constitution*. New York: Macmillan, 1990.

O'Brien, David. *Storm Center: The Supreme Court in American Politics*. New York: Simon & Schuster, 1987.

Rehnquist, William. *The Supreme Court*. New York: William Morrow, 1987.

Chapter 12:
Civil Rights and Individual Liberties

Kluger, Richard. *Simple Justice: The History of Brown v. Board of Education and Black America's Struggle for Equality.* New York: Alfred A. Knopf, 1976.

Levy, Leonard, Kenneth Karst, and Dennis Mahoney, eds. *The First Amendment.* New York: Macmillan, 1990.

Lewis, Anthony. *Gideon's Trumpet.* New York: Random House, 1964.

Chapter 13:
Domestic Policy

Anderson, James. *Public Policymaking.* Boston: Houghton Mifflin, 1990.

Donahue, John A. *The Privatization Decision: Public Ends, Private Means.* New York: Basic Books, 1989.

Ippolito, Dennis S. *Uncertain Legacies: Federal Budget Policy from Roosevelt through Reagan.* Charlottesville, Va.: University Press of Virginia, 1990.

Kelman, Steven. *Making Public Policy: A Hopeful View of American Government.* New York: Basic Books, 1987.

Smith, Hedrick. *The Power Game: How Washington Works.* New York: Random House, 1988.

Chapter 14:
Foreign and Defense Policies

Edwards, George III, and Wallace Earl Walker, eds. *National Security and the U.S. Constitution.* Baltimore: Johns Hopkins University Press, 1988.

Glennon, Michael J. *Constitutional Diplomacy.* Princeton, N.J.: Princeton University Press, 1990.

Henkin, Louis. *Constitutionalism, Democracy, and Foreign Affairs.* New York: Columbia University Press, 1990.

Keynes, Edward. *Undeclared War: Twilight Zone of Constitutional Power.* University Park, Pa.: Pennsylvania State University Press, 1991.

Koh, Harold. *The National Security Constitution.* New Haven, Conn.: Yale University Press, 1990.

Chapter 15:
Governing in the Twenty-First Century

Barber, Benjamin R. *Strong Democracy: Participatory Politics for a New Age.* Berkeley, Calif.: University of California Press, 1984.

Chubb, John E., and Paul E. Peterson, eds. *Can the Government Govern?* Washington, D.C.: Brookings Institution, 1989.

Nye, Joseph. *Bound to Lead: The Changing Nature of American Power.* New York: Basic Books, 1990.

Sundquist, James L. *Constitutional Reform and Effective Government.* Washington, D.C.: Brookings Institution, 1986.

Credits for the Readings

Chapter 1:
The Constitutional Framework

1 From *The American Enterprise*, May/June 1990, pp. 70-75. Reprinted with permission from the New York Times Syndication Sales Corporation.

2 *Federalist* No. 10

3 From *The Political Science Teacher* (Spring 1990): 10-12. Reprinted with permission.

4 Remarks of Supreme Court Justice Thurgood Marshall at the Annual Seminar of the San Francisco Patent and Trademark Law Association in Maui, Hawaii. Reprinted in the *Congressional Record*, May 7, 1987, pp. E1808-E1809.

5 From *this Constitution: A Bicentennial Chronicle*, September 1983, published by Project '87 of the American Historical Association and the American Political Science Association. Reprinted with permission.

Chapter 2:
Federalism: National, State, and Local Government

6 *McCulloch v. Maryland* (4 Wheat. 316, 1819).

7 From *The Brookings Review* (Summer 1989): 34-38. Reprinted with permission.

8 From *State Legislatures*, April 1987, pp. 16-20. Copyright © 1987 by the National Conference of State Legislatures. Reprinted with permission.

9 From *State Government News*, December 1990, pp. 10-11. Copyright ©

1990 by the Council of State Governments. Reprinted with permission.

10 From *Governing* magazine, December 1988, pp. 17-21. Copyright © 1988. Reprinted with permission.

11 From the *Washington Post*, June 14, 1987, p. A1. Copyright © 1987. Reprinted with permission.

Chapter 3:
Public Opinion and Participation

12 From *American Demographics* (June 1989): 25-27, 62-63. Copyright © June 1989. Reprinted with permission.

13 From *What's Next*, Vol. 10, No. 1 (Fall 1987): 1-3. Reprinted with permission.

14 From *U.S. News and World Report*, December 25, 1989/January 1, 1990. Copyright © 1989, 1990. Reprinted with permission.

15 From *The Kettering Review* (Fall 1988): 32-38. Reprinted with permission.

Chapter 4:
Political Parties

16 From *Encounter* magazine, January 1983, pp. 17-22. 44 Great Windmill Street, London, England. All rights reserved. Reprinted with permission.

17 (1) From the *New York Times*, April 10, 1988, p. 31. Copyright © by the New York Times Company. Reprinted with permission. (2) From the *Washington Post*, April 10, 1988, p. B5. Copyright © 1988. Reprinted with permission.

18 From *The Brookings Review* (Summer 1989): 21-25. Reprinted with permission.

19 From the *Washington Post*, December 2, 1990, pp. C1-C2. Copyright © 1990 by the Washington Post Writers Group. Reprinted with permission.

20 From *Campaigns & Elections, The Journal of Political Action* (Summer 1985): 58-60. Washington, D.C. Reprinted with permission.

21 From *Political Science Quarterly* (Winter 1988-1989): 613-635. Reprinted with permission.

Chapter 5:
Political Interest Groups

22 From *The Kettering Review* (Winter 1983): 8-13. Reprinted with permission.

23 From *The American Enterprise* (January/February 1990): 47-51. Reprinted with permission from the New York Times Syndication Sales Corporation.

24 From "Congress and Pressure Groups: Lobbying in a Modern Democracy," Senate Committee on Governmental Affairs, Committee print no. 99-161, 1986.

25 From the *Washington Post Magazine*, November 13, 1988, pp. 27-29. Reprinted with permission.

Chapter 6:
Communications Media and Politics

26 From the *New York Times*, May 24, 1990, op ed. Copyright © 1990 by the New York Times Company. Reprinted with permission.

27 From *Public Opinion*, Vol. 11, No.5 (January/February 1989): 18 ff. Reprinted with permission.

28 From the *Washington Post*, January 14, 1990, pp. B1, B4. Copyright © 1990 by the Washington Post Writers Group. Reprinted with permission.

29 From Stephen Hess, *The Government/Press Connection* (Washington, D.C.: Brookings Institution, 1984), chap. 7. Reprinted with permission.

Chapter 7:
Campaigns and Elections

30 (1) From the *Washington Post*, November 6, 1988, p. C2. Copyright © 1988. Reprinted with permission. (2) From the *New York Times*, November 10, 1988, op ed. Copyright © 1990 by the New York Times Company. Reprinted with permission.

31 From *Public Opinion*, Vol. 11, No. 1 (May/June 1988): 2 ff. Reprinted with permission of the American Enterprise Institute for Public Policy Research, Washington, D.C.

32 From the *Washington Post*, January 17, 1989, p. A1. Copyright © 1989. Reprinted with permission.

33 From *Congressional Quarterly Weekly Report*, May 22, 1990, pp. 1621-1626. Reprinted with permission.

Chapter 8:
Congress

34 *Federalist* No. 51.

35 From the *Washington Post*, March 6, 1990, p. A3. Copyright © 1990. Reprinted with permission.

36 From the *Congressional Record*, October 8, 1983, 2059-2063.

37 From Otis Pike's testimony before the Special House Task Force on Ethics, May 3, 1989. Reprinted in the *Congressional Record*, May 10, 1989, pp. H1814-H1817.

38 From *Washingtonian* magazine, September 1982, pp. 180-189. Reprinted with permission.

39 From the *National Journal*, August 4, 1990, pp. 1876-1881. Copyright © 1990 by National Journal Inc. All rights reserved. Reprinted with permission.

40 From *The Public Interest*, No. 100 (Summer 1990): 15-24. Copyright © 1990 by National Affairs Inc. Reprinted with permission of the author.

41 From the Institute of Governmental Studies at Berkeley, *Public Affairs Report* (November 1990): 8-9. Reprinted with permission.

Chapter 9:
The Presidency

42 *Federalist* No. 70.

43 From Woodrow Wilson, *Constitutional Government in the United States* (New York: Columbia University Press, 1908), 54-61.

44 From the Institute of Governmental Studies at Berkeley, *Public Affairs Report*, Vol. 30, No. 2 (March 1989): 1-3. Reprinted with permission.

45 From *Political Science and Politics* (March 1990): 7-13. Reprinted with permission.

46 From American Agenda, "White House Organization," *Report to the*

Forty-First President (November 8, 1988), II, 1-9.

47 From *The Brookings Review*, Vol. 7 (Fall 1989): 11-15. Reprinted with permission.

Chapter 10:
The Bureaucracy

48 From *Political Science Quarterly*, Vol. 102, No. 2 (Summer 1987): 217-232. Reprinted with permission.

49 An original article prepared exclusively for this book.

50 From *USA Today Magazine*, September 1990, Vol. 119, No. 2544. Copyright © 1990 by the Society for the Advancement of Education. Reprinted with permission.

51 From *The CRS Review*, June 1989, pp. 25-27.

52 From the *Los Angeles Times*, October 1, 1985. Copyright © 1985. Reprinted with permission.

53 Remarks of Paul A. Volcker before the Council for Excellence in Government, "The Report of the National Commission on the Public Service One Year Later." Reprinted in the *Congressional Record*, June 5, 1990, pp. S7403-S75405.

Chapter 11:
The Federal Courts

54 From *National Forum*, Vol. LXIV, No. 4 (Fall 1984): 26-28, 33. Reprinted with permission of *National Forum: The Phi Kappa Phi Journal*.

55 *Federalist* No. 78.

56 *Marbury v. Madison* (1 Cranch 137, 1803).

57 From Robert A. Carp and Ronald Stidham, *Judicial Process in America* (Washington, D.C.: CQ Press, 1990), pp. 210-213. Reprinted with permission.

58 From the *Congressional Record*, March 10, 1986, S2331-S2335.

59 From "Nomination of David H. Souter To Be an Associate Justice of the United States Supreme Court," Senate Judiciary Exec. Rept. 101-32, 101st Congress, 2d Session (1990), pp. 80-82, 83-84, 90-91.

60 From Byron R. White, "The Work of the Supreme Court: A Nuts and

Bolts Description," in *New York State Bar Journal*, October 1982, 346-349, 383-386. Reprinted with permission.

Chapter 12:
Civil Rights and Individual Liberties

61 From "Citizen's Guide to Individual Rights Under the Constitution of the United States of America," Senate Committee on the Judiciary, 94th Cong., 2d sess. (October 1976).

62 From the *Congressional Record*, September 24, 1986, S13619-S13621.

63 (1) From the *Los Angeles Times*, July 10, 1990, p. B7. Reprinted with permission from the NAACP. (2) From Shelby Steele, *The Content of Our Character* (New York: St. Martin's Press, 1990). Copyright © 1990 by Shelby Steele. Reprinted with permission of St. Martin's Press, Inc.

64 *Texas V. Johnson* (109 S. Ct. 2533, 1989).

65 From the *Congressional Record*, 1990, pp. H4003-H4004, H4048-H4050, H4085-H4086.

Chapter 13:
Domestic Policy

66 From *Columbia Journalism Review* (July/August 1990): 40-45. Copyright © 1990. Reprinted with permission.

67 From *Public Administration Review* (November/December 1990): 693-700. Copyright © 1990 by the American Society for Public Administration, 1120 G St., NW, Suite 500, Washington, D.C. 20005. Reprinted with permission.

68 From the *Washington Post*, July 29, 1990, p. A1. Copyright © 1990. Reprinted with permission.

69 From the *Los Angeles Times*, December 19, 1990, p. A1. Copyright © 1990. Reprinted with permission.

70 From the *Los Angeles Times*, February 28, 1990, p. A1. Copyright © 1990. Reprinted with permission.

71 From *The CRS Review* (January/Febuary 1990): 9-10.

72 From *Issues in Science and Technology*, Vol. 6, No. 4 (Summer 1990). Copyright © 1990 by the National Academy of Sciences, Washington, D.C. Reprinted with permission from Ethan Nadelmann and Mark A. R. Kleiman.

Chapter 14:
Foreign and Defense Policies

73 From the *Los Angeles Times*, November 29, 1990, p. A1 ff. Copyright ©
1990. Reprinted with permission.

74 From *Presidential Studies Quarterly* (Summer 1988): 507-513. Reprinted
with permission.

75 Reprinted from the *Congressional Record*, November 3, 1983, S15403-
S15404.

Chapter 15:
Governing in the Twenty-First Century

76 From *The Economist*, July 28, 1990. Copyright © The Economist
Newspaper Limited. Reprinted with permission.

77 From *Vital Speeches of the Day*, June 15, 1990, pp. 539-544. Reprinted
with permission.

78 (1) From *Roll Call*, April 19, 1984. (2) From *this Constitution* (Winter
1984): 42-43. Reprinted by permission.